江苏统计年鉴

STATISTICAL YEARBOOK OF JIANGSU

1 9 9 7

（总第 14 期）

江苏省统计局　编

中国统计出版社

(京)新登字 041 号

图书在版编目(CIP)数据

江苏统计年鉴 1997/江苏省统计局编.—北京:中国统计出版社,1997.7
ISBN 7—5037—2483—8

Ⅰ.江…
Ⅱ.江…
Ⅲ.统计资料—江苏—1997—年鉴
Ⅳ.**C**832.53—54

中国版本图书馆 **CIP** 数据核字(97)第 12565 号

中国统计出版社出版
(北京市西城区三里河月坛南街 75 号 100826)
南京人民印刷厂印刷
*
889×1194 毫米 16 开本 30 印张 4 彩页 120 万字
1997 年 7 月第 1 版 1997 年 7 月第 1 次印刷
印数:1—3000 册
*
定价:115 元

南京禄口机场是江苏省、南京市、国家民航总局联合投资、联合建设的国家重点工程。该工程于1995年2月28日开工，1997年7月1日建成通航，为国内一流水平的现代化机场。

省委、省政府举行南京禄口机场首航典礼大会

架起蓝天银桥　通向五洲四海

设计新颖、造型独特、功能齐全的机场航站楼

沪宁高速公路江苏段建设里程258公里，全封闭、全立交、双向四车道，主线设计行车速度120公里／小时。于1992年6月14日开工建设，1996年9月15日建成通车。江泽民总书记亲自题写“沪宁高速公路江苏段”路名。沪宁高速公路江苏段工程气势恢宏，技术标准高，施工难度大，是我国第一条水网地区修建的长里程高速公路。

沪宁高速公路贯穿于江苏经济最发达的苏南地区，连接南京、镇江、常州、无锡、苏州、上海六市，对于构筑江苏现代化交通骨架，改善投资环境，扩大对外开放，确保江苏经济快速健康发展，具有十分重要的意义。

沪宁高速公路

宁连一级公路

南京邮政大厦

苏州工业园区努力建设与国际经济接轨的一流投资环境，图为首期开发区南部工业区的一角。这里正在形成一个以电子和生物化学产业为主要特色的高新技术产业群。美国的HARRIS、AMD、LILLY，日本的HITACHI，韩国的SAMSUNG，法国的L'OREAL等高新技术产业的跨国公司都在这里建立了自己的发展基地。

让各国投资商宾至如归，是苏州工业园区从新加坡经验中获得的重要启迪之一。图为园区建成的第一所外籍人员子女学校。这所学校由中新苏州工业园区开发有限公司投资兴建，目前已经成了来自12个国家和地区的77个外籍孩子的“家”。

泰州

泰州城市新貌

新建地级泰州市，位于江苏中部，长江北岸，淮河下游，下辖兴化、靖江、泰兴、姜堰和海陵区共四市一区，总面积5793平方公里，总人口495万。

泰州素有“汉唐古郡，淮海名区”之称，水陆交通便捷。盛产农副产品稻麦、棉花、银杏、荷藕等。工业发展迅速，拥有春兰、林海、扬子江药业等55家规模企业集团，空调、摩托车、汽车配件、日用化妆品，减速机等50多个产品的生产规模、市场占有率名列全国前茅。

宿迁

新建地级宿迁市，位于江苏省北部徐、淮、连的中心地带，下辖宿豫、沭阳、泗阳、泗洪四县和宿城区，总面积8660平方公里，总人口478万。

宿迁物产丰饶，是优质农副产品产区，盛产粮食、棉花、油料和木材。境内洪泽湖、骆马湖拥有303万亩的优质水面。矿产资源丰富，石英砂、蓝晶石、破瓷砂、钾矿、金红石等多种矿藏均有较高的开采价值。以洋河、双沟为代表的大曲酒在国内外享有盛誉。

宿迁市万亩连片吨粮田

至诚 凝聚发展

南京金丝利房地产开发有限公司系92年兴办的中外合资企业，经过四年多的艰难创业，至今已发展成为拥有5亿元资产的大型房地产企业。公司在激烈的市场竞争中，凭可靠的资信，一流的人才，诚实的作风，雄厚的实力，树立了良好的企业形象。公司在连续获得96年南京市房地产开发企业双十强，省特AAA资信企业的同时，又获南京市外商投资先进企业及南京市外商投资"精英企业"及外资企业五十强等荣誉。

公司首建开发项目金丝利国际大厦(原名为金丝利国际娱乐城)，建筑高度158m，建筑面积72,000m^2，地上42层，地下3层。集国际五星级酒店、餐饮、娱乐、购物、办公为一体，并引进国外最先进的信息和自动化管理系统，成为南京市功能最齐全的现代化高级涉外综合楼，堪称金陵第一。大厦已于96年9月完成主楼结构封顶，预计明年初大厦全面竣工并交付使用。

金丝利国际大厦是公司重点项目，在大厦建设中公司充实项目管理班子，加大现场指挥力量。标准层施工连续创造五天一层、四天半一层以至四天一层的高层施工新纪录，实现大厦提前封顶。为了大厦的独特弧形幕墙设计需要，我公司经十余次谈判与韩国最大生产企业 HANKUK 玻璃公司签约，标志着金丝利国际大厦将成为华东地区采用磁控溅射膜弧形玻璃第一家。此外大厦建设过程中，大厦利用知名度通过激烈的竞争招标，成功地引进了一批世界名牌产品设备。如美国爱德华 IRC－3火灾自动报警系统和西门子程控交换机，约克锅炉、开利冷水机组和瑞士迅达电梯等，使大厦成为南京乃至江苏省硬件档次最高、管理软件最好的酒店。公司与美国ITT 喜来登国际酒店管理集团签定了技术服务合同，使大厦在功能分布、服务流程等方面为五星级酒店标准提供可靠的技术保障。

公司在注重建一流项目、创一流效益的同时，积极着手开发中、短期项目。为与大厦开业配套，拓宽大厦东侧的牌楼巷道路和停车场工程将与主楼同时开业。公司在南京城郊结合部九龙小区、莫愁新区及市中心上海路、王府路段有多项住宅开发项目，形成了规模较大的综合开发能力，进一步扩充了公司实力。

金丝利房地产开发有限公司为努力适应市场竞争形势，不断加强企业内部建设，逐步形成了具有现代企业特点的、高效率的内部管理机制，并形成了一支充满活力的具有较高思想素质和专业水平，具有事业心和责任感的专业队伍。

在市场经济迅速发展的大潮中，金丝利房地产开发有限公司将迈着坚实的步伐，创出更新的佳绩。

总经理：黄永久

黄永久总经理陪同国家烟草局倪益瑾局长视察工地

公司法定地址：南京市汉中路156号
法人代表：何泽华
总经理：黄永久
电话：(025) 6521699
传真：(025) 6521698
邮编：210029

总经理：陈兴汉　女士

中国 南京市龙蟠路222号
ADD: NO.222LONGPAN ROAD
NANJING CHINA.
TEL: 025-5501604 5502480
FAX: 025-5502482
POS: 210037

南京栖霞建设集团（原名：南京市栖霞城镇建设综合开发集团；简称：南京栖霞开发集团），成立于1993年5月28日。

集团核心层南京栖霞建设（集团）公司是国营独资企业；紧密层有：海南南都经济建设开发总公司；南京栖霞建设集团物业有限公司、南京栖霞建设集团物资有限公司、南京栖霞建设集团营销咨询有限公司、南京栖霞建设集团建筑设计有限公司、中外合资南京东方房地产开发有限公司、中外合资南京金港房地产开发有限公司和中外合资南京兴隆房地产开发有限公司等企业。

南京栖霞建设（集团）公司是国家一级房地产开发企业，是国家建设部现代企业制度试点单位，省、市建行、工商行、农行连续三年特级“AAA”资信企业。自1984年成立以来，历经十余年艰苦创业，总开工面150万m^2，总竣工面98万m^2，工程一次验收合格率100%，优良品率保持在80%以上，32个项目被评为省、市优质样板工程。93年、94年分别被评为“江苏省房地产开发企业50强”第五名、第一名；95年被评为“江苏省第三产业200强”企业；96年被评为江苏省人民政府先进集体、江苏省“住宅商品房质量信得过单位”。总经理陈兴汉女士先后被市委、市政府评为“95-96年度南京市劳动模范”、“有功共产党员”、“建设新南京有功个人”。

集团目前拥有位于南京东郊风景区的正在建设和将要开发的土地千余亩。集团现有在册员工中具有高、中级职称的科技人员占40%以上。经过大学教育者超过90%。

集团将以“立广厦于天地，奉爱心于人间”作为自己的经营理念，把“诚信、敬业、完美”作为自己的企业宗旨，发扬“携手向上”的“砖石精神”，高呼“员工随企业成长，建筑与时代同步”的口号，通过导入CIS和ISO9000国际质量认证，再创企业一个成长的高峰，成为国内房地产业的典范和名牌企业。

总经理：徐孝先　先生

南通市建筑安装工程总公司

南通市建筑安装工程总公司企业主要负责人：徐孝先，男，1945年9月出生，他以南通县驻拉萨工程指挥部总指挥的身份指挥施工的拉萨饭店及其配套工程，以惊人的速度和过硬的质量获得好评，荣膺全国建筑质量最高荣誉奖“鲁班金像奖”，他本人荣立二等功。1989年底至今，他一直担任南通市建筑安装工程总公司总经理一职。1995-1996年公司连续两次获得全国建筑工程质量最高荣誉奖“鲁班金像奖”。

企业概况：该公司成立于1952年，1959年被建设部评为“勤俭办企业红旗单位”，公司领导受到朱德、陈毅等领导人接见。1989年底以来，企业进行了一系列改革，走出了一条具有自身特色的项目管理之路，既增强了企业活力，又提高了企业的整体战斗力和经济效益。公司连续六年保持了“重合同、守信用企业”和“省特级（AAA）资信企业”荣誉称号；连续四年入选全国500家最大经营规模和最佳经济效益建筑企业。一九九六年，该公司承建的南通醋酸纤维二期工程再次荣获“鲁班奖”，打破了南通建筑队伍在南通本地没有“鲁班奖”工程的纪录。

合作意向：第三产业和建筑相关产业的发展
公司前景：使企业发展成为具有较强综合实力的名牌企业
地址：南通市青年中路76号
邮编：226006
电话：0513-5516356
传真：0513-5517207

江苏省 统计局

竭诚为社会各界提供统计信息查询服务

省委常委、常务副省长季允石由省局领导陪同在统计信息查询服务系统上查询资料。

江苏省统计局成功研制了信息查询系统，该系统内容丰富，涵盖了历年来全省重要统计数据，为党政领导科学决策提供了重要依据。

江苏省统计局统计信息查询服务系统

省人大、省政协代表阅读和查询统计资料。

编 者 说 明

一、《江苏统计年鉴——1997》(以下简称《年鉴》)是一部全面、系统反映江苏省1996年及历史重要年份国民经济和社会发展情况的资料性年刊。本书收录了江苏省及各市、县大量的社会、经济、科技统计信息。

二、全书内容分为十七个部分,即:1. 行政区划和自然资源;2. 综合;3. 人口、劳动力;4. 人民生活;5. 固定资产投资;6. 能源、原材料生产和消费;7. 物价;8. 城市建设、环境保护;9. 农业;10. 工业;11. 建筑业;12. 交通运输、邮电业;13. 国内贸易;14. 对外经济贸易和旅游业;15. 财政、金融、保险;16. 科技、教育;17. 文化、体育、卫生、其他。为反映江苏区域发展特色,特增加苏南、苏中、苏北区域经济和分市、县国民经济总量、均量和序列指标。书末还附有主要统计指标解释。

三、资料中所使用的度量衡单位均采用国际统一标准计量单位。

四、《年鉴》表中"…"表示数据不足本表最小单位数;"空格"表示该项统计指标数据不详或无该项数据;"#"表示其中项。

五、《年鉴》公开发行以来,深受国内外读者的好评。为进一步适应扩大开放的需要,《年鉴》自今年起改为中英文对照版。由于我们编辑水平有限,书中难免有不足之处,欢迎广大读者提出宝贵意见,以便我们进一步改进《年鉴》的编辑工作,更好地为广大读者服务。

Complier's Notes

Jiangsu Statistical Yearbook 1997 called hereafter Yearbook for short is an annual statistic publication, which covers comprehensively and systemtically the data of national economy and social development in Jiangsu Province in 1997 and some other historically important years, and collects a great deal of statistical information of social, economic, scientific and technological development.

The Yearbook is organized into seventeen parts, i. e., 1. Divisions of Administrative Areas and Natural Resources; 2. General Survey; 3. Population and Employment; 4. Poeple's Livelihood; 5. Fixed Assets Investment; 6. Energy, Raw Materials Production and Consumption; 7. Prices; 8. Urban Construction, Environment and Protection; 9. Agriculture; 10. Industry; 11. Construction; 12. Transportation, Postal and Telecommunication Services; 13. Domestic Trade; 14. Foreign Economy, Trade and Tourism; 15. Finance, Banking and Insurance; 16. Science and Technology, Education; 17. Culture, Sports, Public Health and Others. In order to reflect the regional characteristic development, the Yearbook specially includes the indicators of the total, average, and alignment of regional economy as well as some other cities and countries numbers of the national economic development in southern Jiangsu, middle Jiangsu, northern Jiangsu. Explanatory notes for major indicators are provided at the end of the book.

The units of measurement used in the Yearbook are internationally standard measurement units.

In the Yearbook:

"…"refers to data not large enough to be rounded into the unit. "empty" refers to data of a given item not available. "#" refers to the major component item.

Since openly issued, the Yearbook has received favourable comments from the readers both at home and abroad. In order to meet the demands of enlargeing opening, the Yearbook is transferred into a billingual edition of Chinese and English from this year on. Due to the limitation of the editors' ability, weaknesses and shortcomings are unavoiable. Welcome valuable suggestions from the general readers, so that the editorial work for the Yearbook can be further improved, and better services be made for the mass of readers.

目　　录

CONTENTS

3 人口、劳动力
POPULATION & EMPLOYMENT

4 人民生活
PEOPLE'S LIVELIHOOD

5 固定资产投资
FIXED ASSETS INVESTMENT

6 能源、原材料生产和消费
ENERGY, RAW MATERIAL PRODUCTION AND CONSUMPTION

7 物价
PRICE

8 城市建设、环境保护
URBAN CONSTRUCTION, EMVIRONMENT AND PROTECTION

9 农业
AGRICULTURE

10 工业
INDUSTRY

11 建筑业
CONSTRUCTION

12 交通运输、邮电业
TRANSPORTATION, POSTAL AND TELECOMMUNICATION SERVICES

13 国内贸易
DOMESTIC TRADE

14 对外经济贸易和旅游
FOREIGN ECONOMY, TRADE AND TOURISM

16 科技 教育
SCIENCE AND TECHNOLOGY, EDUCATION

17 文化、体育、卫生、其他
CULTURE, SPORTS, PUBLIC HEALTH AND OTHERS

二 市县篇
SECTIONS OF THE CITIES AND COUNTIES

1 区域经济主要指标
MAJOR INDICATORS OF REGIONAL ECONOMY

2 市县社会经济主要指标
MAJOR SOCIAL ECONOMIC INDICATORS OF COUNTY

3 县(市)社会经济序列指标
SOCIAL ECONOMIC INDICATORS OF COUNTY (CITY) BY RANK

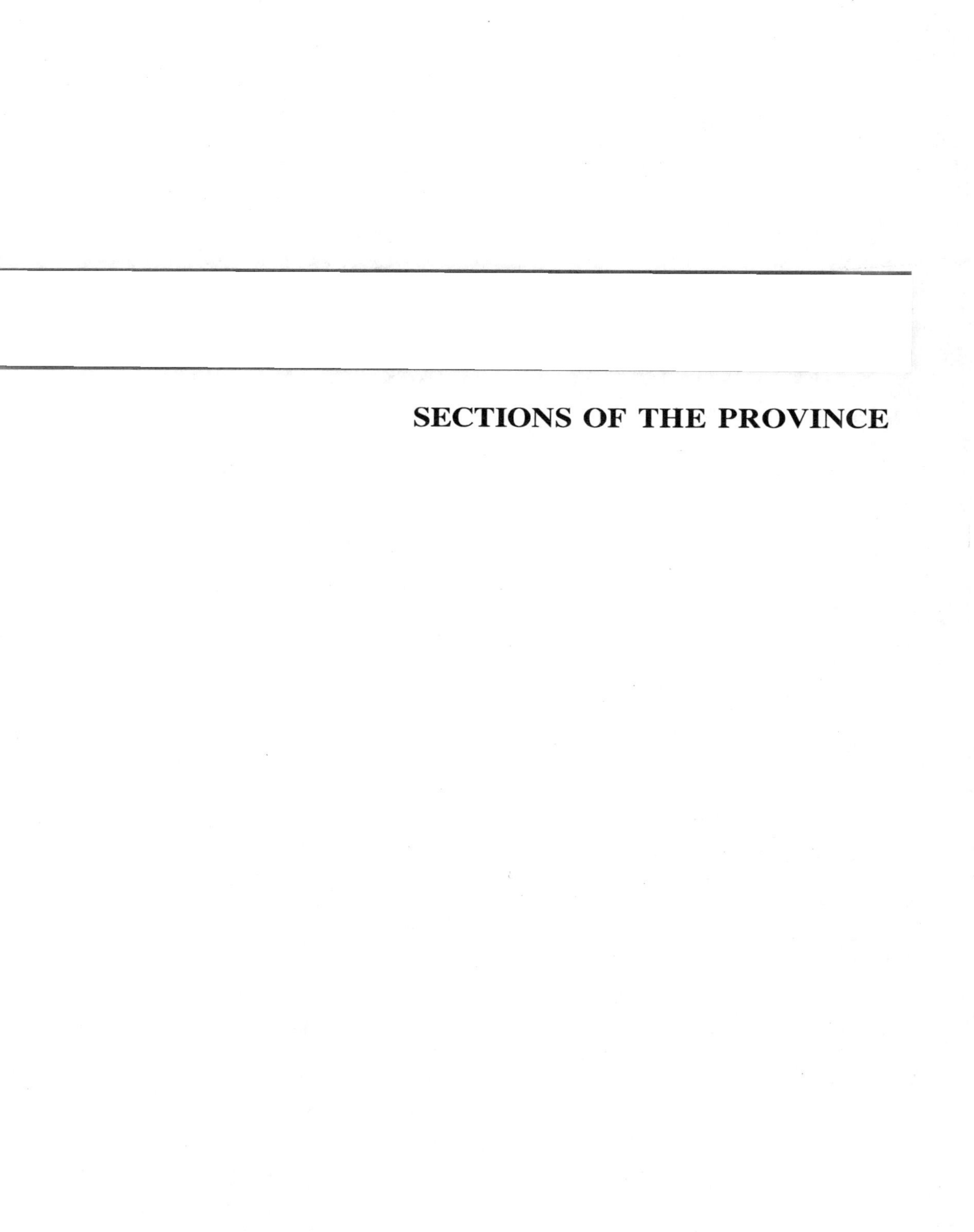

SECTIONS OF THE PROVINCE

江苏省统计局关于
1996年国民经济和社会发展的统计公报

1996年是实施"九五"计划和2010年远景目标的第一年。全省人民在省委、省政府领导下,认真贯彻党的十四届五中、六中全会精神,正确处理改革、发展与稳定的关系,积极推进两个根本性转变,加快实施三大战略,国民经济继续保持平稳快速增长格局,物价涨幅明显回落,城乡人民生活进一步改善,各项社会事业取得新的进展,基本实现了为"九五"开好局、起好步的总体要求。全年完成国内生产总值6004.2亿元,比上年增长12.2%。其中,第一产业增加值965.3亿元,增长7.8%;第二产业增加值3074.1亿元,增长12.3%;第三产业增加值1964.8亿元,增长14.3%。三次产业增加值在国内生产总值中的比重为:第一产业16.1%,第二产业51.2%,第三产业32.7%。存在的主要问题是,经济结构性矛盾仍较突出,农业基础地位尚待进一步加强,工业经济效益不够理想,部分企业生产经营和职工生活比较困难。

一、农林牧渔业

种植业生产获得丰收,对稳定经济、保障市场供应起到了积极作用。全年完成种植业增加值656.3亿元,比上年增长5.9%。主要农产品产量中,粮食单产、总产双超历史,棉花在播种面积减少的情况下仍实现计划目标,油料总产为历史上第二个丰收年,其他产品有增有减。

主要农产品产量如下:

	1996年	比上年增长(%)
粮　食	3476.4万吨	5.8
谷　物	3301.1万吨	6.2
豆　类	79.4万吨	−10.0
薯　类	95.9万吨	6.3
棉　花	53.7万吨	−4.3
油　料	147.5万吨	−7.5
其中:油菜籽	106.3万吨	−2.9
甜　菜	2.3万吨	318.2
烤　烟	0.3万吨	14.5
黄红麻	0.3万吨	−27.0
蚕　茧	9.2万吨	−50.5
茶　叶	1.1万吨	3.5
水　果	123.3万吨	21.6

林业生产建设和绿化工作在完善中提高。全年完成造林面积21.6千公顷,重点林业工程建设取得明显成效,主要林产品产量有所增加。

畜牧业稳定发展,肉、禽、蛋、奶等畜产品产量均有不同程度增长。

主要畜产品产量和牲畜存栏头数如下:

	1996年	比上年增长(%)
猪牛羊肉	228.0万吨	4.7
牛　奶	10.5万吨	4.7
肉猪出栏数	2832.6万头	2.8
猪年末存栏数	2063.9万头	−2.6
羊年末存栏数	1370.3万只	7.6
大牲畜年末存栏数	137.3万头	11.4
禽　蛋	190.7万吨	8.8

渔业生产继续增长。全年水产品产量245.7万吨,比上年增长12%。其中,淡水产品产量166.2万吨,增长7.7%;海水产品产量79.5万吨,增长22.1%。

由于国家提高农产品收购价格,科技大面积推广应用,农业产业化步伐加快,农业生产结构得到进一步调整和优化。多种经营较快发展,"菜篮子"工程建设成效显著。全年林牧渔业及农民家庭兼营的商品性工业增加值占农业增加值比重为37.2%,比上年提高3.4个百分点。

农业生产条件得到改善，农业资源综合开发进展顺利。全省财政用于支农支出及农林水事业费为22.7亿元，比上年增长13.5%。年末全省农业机械总动力2297.4万千瓦，比上年末增长3.2%；大中型拖拉机3万台，增长31.4%；小型和手扶拖拉机76.5万台，增长2%；农用载重汽车2.6万辆，增长6.9%；化肥施用量306.7万吨(折纯)，增长4.7%；农村用电量252.2亿千瓦小时，增长5.9%。水利建设进一步加强，治淮、治太等重点工程加快实施，农田有效灌溉面积达3837.8千公顷。全年建设吨粮田89.3千公顷，改造中低产田216.7千公顷，均超额完成了年度计划。

以乡镇企业为主体的农村非农产业继续较快增长，农村经济综合实力进一步增强。全省农村工业、建筑业、运输业和批发、零售贸易业、餐饮业等非农业产值比上年增长15.2%。

二、工业和建筑业

工业生产克服市场、资金等多种制约，保持平稳运行。全年完成工业增加值2754.8亿元，比上年增长11%。

轻重工业增长基本同步。全年轻工业完成产值3765.5亿元，比上年增长15.6%；重工业完成产值4153.8亿元，增长17.2%。产品结构有所调整，能源、原材料等主要产品产量有较大增长，产品质量和档次明显提高。新产品生产增势较猛，全年完成新产品产值比上年增长29.9%。

主要工业产品产量如下：

	1996年	比上年增长(%)
纱	83.3万吨	−3.4
布	34.6亿米	−29.3
呢绒	19134.0万米	−32.2
机制纸及纸板	163.4万吨	−2.5
原　盐	359.5万吨	4.1
家用洗衣机	117.8万台	30.5
家用电冰箱	20.7万台	80.9
电风扇	1939.6万台	−6.9
电视机	410.5万部	−10.3
其中：彩电	258.3万部	3.0
原　煤	2606.5万吨	−1.7
原　油	122.0万吨	20.3
原油加工量	1021.4万吨	4.6
发电量	756.9亿千瓦小时	8.1
钢	446.6万吨	23.9
成品钢材	795.6万吨	1.0
水　泥	4040.3万吨	1.9
平板玻璃	1131.6万重量箱	30.3
硫　酸	175.4万吨	2.2
纯　碱	74.8万吨	28.7
烧　碱	57.6万吨	11.1
汽　车	11.0万辆	−12.0
拖拉机(大中型)	0.4万台	102.2
化肥(折100%)	184.3万吨	−3.9
化学纤维	105.9万吨	3.7

企业改革继续深化。现代企业制度试点工作取得新进展，国家级试点企业4家、省级试点企业127家中的120家按省政府12个试点配套文件组织实施，在企业改制、增资减债、强化管理等方面取得初步成效。第二批试点企业开始启动。企业组织结构调整步伐加快，在巩固和完善1995年组建的10家省级重点企业集团的基础上，1996年又新组建了南钢、海外、沙钢、阳光等11家省级重点企业集团；全省还新组建冠以省名的企业集团271家，其中乡镇企业集团186家。继续推进兼并、破产、租赁、托管以及股份合作制等多种形式，进一步搞活中小企业，全省中小企业不同形式的改制面达50%以上。乡镇企业通过深化改革，多项经济指标继续稳定增长。股份制试点逐步规范，全年新组建股份有限公司15家，累计组建股份有限公司362家。积极推进国有资产管理营运体制改革，国有资产流动和重组步伐进一步加快。

工业经济效益仍然不够理想。年末乡及乡以上独立核算工业企业亏损面达22.7%，全年实现利润比上年下降12.7%。影响工业经济效益总体水平提高的主要原因是，增本减利因素继续增加，企业开工不足，产成品库存偏大，产品结构、企业组织结构和产业结构还不适应发展社会主义市场经济的要求。

建筑业稳定发展。全年完成建筑业增加值319.3亿元,比上年增长26.3%。全省建筑企业房屋建筑施工面积8709.8万平方米,比上年增长2.6%;房屋建筑竣工面积8252.1万平方米,增长1.37倍;全员劳动生产率47547元,提高12%。建筑企业全年完成利润总额14.95亿元,比上年增长86.6%。

三、固定资产投资

固定资产投资适度增长。全年全社会完成固定资产投资1949.5亿元,比上年增长16%,增幅回落10.2个百分点。

在全社会固定资产投资中,国有经济投资708.6亿元,比上年增长17.6%;集体经济投资465.2亿元,下降5.3%;城乡居民个人投资275.7亿元,增长28.7%;其他各种经济类型投资500亿元,增长34.3%。按投资种类分,全省基本建设投资481.1亿元,增长32.8%,增幅与上年基本持平;更新改造投资238.2亿元,增长8.9%,比上年回落19.4个百分点;房地产开发投资232.6亿元,下降3.4%。

全年基建和更改施工项目8132个,施工项目计划总投资2051.8亿元。全部建成投产项目5872个,新增固定资产614.5亿元。

投资结构有所改善。第一产业完成投资57.5亿元,比上年增长40.4%;第二产业完成投资905.4亿元,增长10.5%;第三产业完成投资986.7亿元,增长20.4%。基建和更改中,用于能源工业投资112.6亿元,增长42.1%;用于交通运输邮电通讯业投资168.6亿元,增长33.9%。

重点建设和基础设施建设取得较大进展,重点技术改造得到加强。沪宁高速公路江苏段和宁连、宁通一级公路建成通车,宁盐、宁徐一级公路半幅通车。江阴长江公路大桥和南京禄口机场建设进度加快。一批重点建设工程已经建成,徐州华润电力有限公司彭城发电厂一号机组并网发电,扶贫通电工程提前完成任务,实现村村通电的目标。技术改造一期"双加"工程开工实施率为83.3%,高于全国平均水平10个百分点,二期"双加"工程开始启动。

全省基本建设新增的主要生产能力有:火力发电机组42万千瓦,输电线路78公里,变电设备能力28万千伏安,年产水泥135万吨、塑料树脂及共聚物10000万吨,新改建公路里程1023公里,城市自来水供水能力15万吨/日。

四、交通和邮电

交通运输生产持续增长。全年完成增加值254.7亿元,比上年增长15.4%。运输紧张状况有所改善。

各种运输方式完成的客货运输周转量如下:

	1996年	比上年增长(%)
货物周转量	1440.2亿吨公里	6.1
铁路	380.1亿吨公里	−3.4
公路	317.1亿吨公里	12.8
水运	712.3亿吨公里	6.2
管道	30.7亿吨公里	−2.8
旅客周转量	669.4亿人公里	6.9
铁路	143.9亿人公里	−12.1
公路	523.0亿人公里	13.9
水运	2.5亿人公里	−26.7
港口货物吞吐量	30622万吨	0.3

邮电通信业继续较快发展。全年完成增加值60.3亿元,比上年增长32.9%。完成邮电业务总量96亿元,增长32.9%;业务收入89.7亿元,增长36.8%。公用通信能力进一步提高。年末局用交换机容量达825万门,净增228.2万门,其中市内电话已装容量净增107.2万门,农话已装容量净增121万门。城乡住宅电话用户达336万户,新增80.7万户。全省电话普及率每百人达10.5部,比上年提高3部。

五、国内贸易和市场物价

国内消费品市场繁荣稳定。全年社会消费品零售总额2005.4亿元(含城乡居民生活住房零售额),比上年增长21.5%,扣除价格因素,实际增长13.8%。主要商品货源充裕,生产资料市场销售平稳,食品和新型家电销势较好,餐饮业比较兴旺。

在社会消费品零售总额中,城市(包括县城)实现1361.6亿元,比上年增长25.4%;农村实现643.8亿元,增长14.1%,比城市低11.3个百分点。

各种经济类型的消费品零售额全面增长。非国有经济继续领先。其中,私营经济58亿元,增长69.6%;个体经济394.2亿元,增长30.5%;其他经济(主要是农民对城镇居民零售额)246.1亿元,增长29%。

分行业看,批发零售贸易业零售额1337.2亿元,增长18.8%;餐饮业126亿元,增长39.7%;制造业186.7亿元,增长4.1%;其他行业355.5亿元,增长39.6%。

市场流通体制改革进一步深化。一批改制后的大型国有流通企业集团在竞争中不断壮大,私营、个体及股份制流通企业迅速发展,流通格局呈多元化趋势。市场建设在进一步完善网络的基础上,逐步向高层次、远辐射、大规模发展,现代流通方式积极推广。全省共新批建了各类市场40多个,其中省级市场10个。全省10—20亿元的市场237家,21—50亿元的市场7家,50—100亿元的市场4家,100亿元以上的市场2家。

抑制通货膨胀取得明显成效。全省认真执行国家宏观调控政策,及时出台了一系列以抑制通货膨胀为目标的措施,使物价涨幅降至1993年以来的最低水平,实现了年初确定的物价控制目标。全省商品零售价格比上年上涨6.8%,增幅回落7.5个百分点。

各类价格比上年上涨幅度(%)

1.居民消费价格	9.3
其中:城　市	10.8
农　村	7.1
其中:食　品	9.6
粮　食	8.0
油　脂	—8.4
肉禽及其制品	6.5
蛋　类	15.5
水产品	6.8
鲜　菜	40.5
衣　着	8.7
家庭设备及用品	2.6
交通和通讯工具	—2.1
娱乐教育文化用品	9.7
居　住	17.3
服务项目	12.3
2.商品零售价格	6.8
其中:城　市	6.8
农　村	6.8
3.农业生产资料价格	6.6
4.原材料、燃料、动力购进价格	3.9
5.工业品出厂价格	0.6
6.固定资产投资价格	3.2
7.农产品收购价格	2.0

六、对　外　经　济

在国家对外经贸政策进行较大调整的宏观环境下,全省各地、各部门努力克服困难,坚定不移地扩大对外开放,多渠道、全方位地发展开放型经济,提高对外开放水平,开放型经济继续保持稳定增长。

对外贸易稳中有升。全年自营进出口总额达202.2亿美元,比上年增长20.4%。其中,出口131.2美元,增长11.3%;进口70.9亿美元,增长41.8%。外商投资企业和其他有权生产企业的出口持续大幅度增长,比重上升,全年出口额66.2亿美元,增幅达25.2%,占全省出口总额的份额由上年的44.8%提高到50.4%。市场多元化战略取得新进展,全省出口商品销往177个国家和地区。

实际利用外资规模继续扩大。全省实际利用外资55亿美元,比上年增长4.1%。新批外商投资企业虽比上年减少,但由于世界著名跨国公司扩大投资,使利用外资呈现大项目增多、外商出资比重加大的良好态势。全年新批外商投资企业中,总投资1000万美元以上的项目达352个。全省平均每家新批外资企业的合同外资364万美元,比上年增加45万美元。

对外经济技术合作不断拓展。全省对外承包工程和劳务合作新签合同金额7.3亿美元,完成营业额6.8亿美元,分别比上年增长8.9%和33.9%。全年新批境外非贸易企业19家,总投资4558万美元。经济技术合作的方式开始转变,承包工程、项目总承包、技术服务的比重上升。各类开发区建设步伐加快,苏州工业园区等国家级、省级开发区已成为外引内联的窗口和新的经济增长点。

国际旅游业发展势头良好。全省共接待旅游、参观、访问及从事各项活动的过夜海外游客83.7万人次,旅游外汇收入 3.17 亿美元，分别比上年增长 9%和 22%。

七、财政、金融和保险业

财税体制和金融体制改革进一步深化。健全财政职能，整顿和规范财税、会计工作秩序，以分税制为核心、增值税为主体的财税体制运行正常。人民银行各级分支行积极履行职能，初步实施政策性金融与商业性金融的分离，专业银行向商业银行转化已经起步，新组建招商银行南京分行。社会保障和分配制度改革稳步推进。养老保险和失业保险制度改革取得新突破，社会统筹与个人帐户相结合的新养老保险筹资模式基本确立，建立了城市居民最低生活保障制度。

财政收支基本平衡。全年财政收入 428 亿元，其中地方财政收入 223.2 亿元，分别比上年增长 22.3%和 29.3%；在地方财政收入中，工商税收完成 163.5 亿元，增长 25.8%。全年财政支出 310.9 亿元，比上年增长 22.7%.

金融形势基本平稳。年末全社会各项存款余额 4649 亿元，贷款余额 3575 亿元，分别比年初增加 1100.8 亿元和 629.3 亿元，继续保持存差格局。存款中，企业存款余额 1642 亿元，城乡居民储蓄存款余额 2570 亿元，分别比年初增加 440.6 亿元和 642.6 亿元。贷款中，短期贷款余额 2714 亿元，中长期贷款余额 494 亿元，分别比年初增加 491 亿元和 72.7 亿元。

保险事业进一步发展。全年中保系统承保总额 6874 亿元，比上年增长 25.6%。保费收入 37 亿元，增长 27.4%。其中，财产险保费收入 22.7 亿元，人身险保费收入 14.3 亿元。财产险赔款金额 10.8 亿元，人身险给付金额 7 亿元。

八、科学技术和教育

科技队伍不断壮大。年末全省县级以上国有独立研究与开发机构 431 个，高等院校办科研机构 410 个，大中型工业企业办科研机构 1620 个。全省共有各类专业技术人员 189 万人，比上年增长 2.2%。科研机构、高等院校、独立核算工业企业中，从事科技活动人员 35 万人，其中科学家和工程师 11.5 万人。全省拥有中国科学院院士 42 人，中国工程院院士 16 人。

科技经费增加。全年科研机构、高等院校和工业企业等单位用于科技活动的经费支出为 134 亿元，其中研究与发展经费支出 26.4 亿元，相当于国内生产总值的 0.44%。

科学研究成效显著。全省共获国家级重大科技成果 40 项，其中国家发明奖 6 项，国家科技进步奖 34 项；获得省级重大科技成果 317 项，其中一等奖 4 项、二等奖 36 项、三等奖 105 项、四等奖 172 项。科技成果向现实生产力转化步伐加快，启动实施重大科技攻关项目和重点攻关项目 275 个。科技基础设施建设取得进展。国家南方农药创制中心江苏基地、生化工程技术研究中心等基础设施已启动建设。至 1996 年底，全省已建各类重点实验室、工程技术研究中心等 104 个，其中国家重点实验室 17 个、国家工程技术研究中心 11 个。

技术市场活跃。全年共签订技术合同 3.1 万项，技术贸易成交额 22.3 亿元，比上年增长 22.9%。专利事业稳步发展。全年申请专利 4980 件，授权专利 2578 件，分别比上年增长 22%和 7%。省政府与国家专利局联合举办的'96 中国专利及新产品博览会获得成功。

高新技术产业规模扩大。国家级高新技术产业开发区、沿江火炬高新技术产业开发带和苏北星火密集区建设步伐加快。全年高新技术产品产值 370 亿元；技工贸总收入 400 亿元，比上年增长 50%。全省高新技术企业 537 家，当年认定高技术产品 317 项、国家级新产品 258 项、省级新产品 483 项。

各类教育事业继续发展。全省招收研究生 0.45 万人，在学研究生 1. 22 万人，分别比上年增加 0.08 万人和 0.15 万人。普通高校招收本专科学生 7.43 万人，在校学生 22.06 万人，分别比上年增加 0.68 万人和 1.20 万人。扩招 1.2 万名大学生的任务顺利完成。各类中等专业技术学校在校学生 40.99 万人，比上年增加 9.12 万人。职业中学高中在校学生 25.79 万人。全省普通中学在校学生 323.55 万人，小学在校学生 687.82 万人，分别比上年增加 6.80 万人和 43.05 万人。小学学龄儿童入学率达 99.8%。有普及九年义务教育任务的 4 县 38 个乡镇已通过国家验收，全省普及九年义务教育和扫除青壮年文盲的目标基本实现。幼儿教育和对弱智、残疾儿童的特殊教育也有一定发展。

成人教育和教育现代化建设进一步发展。全年成人高等学校招收本专科学生 6.5 万人，在校学生 16.05 万人，分别比上年增加 1.07 万人和 2.76 万人。成人中等专业学校在校学生 16.54 万人，比上年减少 1.55 万人。成人中学及初等学校在校学生 38.91 万人，减少 4.06 万人。教师住房建设力度加大，全省教师住房建设竣工面积 134 万平方米，相当于"八五"前四年的总和。教学质量和办学条件进一步改善。苏南教育现代化工程和苏北教育促小康工程全面实施。

九、文化、卫生、体育和环境保护

文化事业继续发展。年末全省共有艺术表演团体 131 个，文化馆 108 个，公共图书馆 96 个，博物馆 73 个，文化艺术档案馆 1 个，广播电台 61 座，中、短波广播发射台和转播台 21 座，电视台 54 座，一千瓦以上电视发射台和转播台 73 座。各类电影放映单位 3126 个。全年报纸出版 17.5 亿份，各类杂志出版 7062.4 万册，图书出版 45264.3 万册。坚持以"五个一工程"为龙头，推动整个精神产品生产，一批优秀作品在全国获奖。群众性精神文明建设取得良好成效。

卫生事业进一步发展。年末共有各类卫生机构 14944 个(含个体诊所)；拥有医院病床 15.8 万张，比上年增长 1.9%。

共有专业卫生技术人员25万人，其中医生11.3万人，分别比上年增长1.9%和1.1%；拥有中西医师8.7万人，护师和护士6.7万人，分别增长1.8%和3.9%。医疗制度改革扩大试点工作进展较快，在总结推广镇江市职工医疗制度改革经验的基础上，新增加苏州、无锡、南通、盐城四市作为医疗制度改革扩大试点城市。

体育事业成绩显著。在1996年世界和亚洲重大比赛中，我省有1人创1项世界纪录、1人破1项亚洲纪录、7人获9项世界冠军、6人获5项世界亚军、5人获4项世界第三；有12人获14项亚洲冠军、8人获3项亚洲亚军。在国家体委统计的96年度竞技体育“贡献奖”排名榜上，我省首次以419分排列全国第一位。同时，在全国最高水平比赛中，我省体育健儿共获金牌20枚、银牌26枚、铜牌16枚。

环境保护工作取得积极进展。年末全省环境保护系统人员共有5800人，各级环境监测站101个，企、事业单位环境监测人员4100个。全年共完成环境污染治理项目678个，完成总投资3.1亿元。建成烟尘控制区146个，面积达1179.2平方公里；建成环境噪声达标区149个，面积为657.4平方公里。进行了重污染企业的关停并转工作，118家年产量在5000吨以下的小造 纸厂已全部关闭，淮北高氟和污染严重地区改水工程进展较快。但环保问题仍较突出。

十、人口与人民生活

计划生育工作取得积极成效。全年人口出生率12.11‰，比上年下降0.21个千分点；死亡率6.58‰，上升0.02个千分点。自然增长率由上年的5.76‰下降为5.53‰。年末全省常住人口7110.16万人（户籍人口为6908.13万人），比上年末增加44.14万人。

城乡居民生活水平进一步提高。全年城镇居民人均生活费收入4689元，比上年增长11.4%，扣除价格因素，实际收入与上年基本持平。城镇居民人均消费性支出4057元。但城镇居民收入水平不平衡，减收面扩大，部分地区职工生活比较困难。据抽样调查，全省城镇居民家庭中减收户的由上年的35.5%上升到42.4%。农村居民人均纯收入达3029元，比上年增长23.3%，扣除价格因素，实际增长12.6%。农民人均生活消费支出2414元。农村贫困人口比重缩小。

劳动就业形势比较稳定。年末全省各类职业介绍机构发展到1973家，全年城镇新就业人员20.78万人。年末城镇登记失业人数45.19万人，登记失业率2.2%。年末全省城镇职工904.4万人，比上年减少11.6万人；城镇私营和个体从业人员72.8万人，增加6.9万人。实施再就业工程力度进一步加大，全年安排再就业人员40多万人。全年职工工资总额达591.7亿元，比上年增长9.2%；职工平均工资6564元，增长10.5%，扣除价格因素，与上年基本持平。

城乡居民居住条件进一步改善。全年城镇新建住宅1842万平方米，农村新建住宅7380万平方米。

注：本公报中数据如与后表中数据不同，请以表中数据为准。

STATISTICAL COMMUNIQUE OF JIANGSU PROVINCE STATISTICAL BUREAU ON 1996 NATIONAL ECONOMIC AND SOCIAL DEVELOPMENT

1996 was the first year in which the "Ninth Five-Year Program" and the "Year 2010 Target" were carried out. Under the leadership of the provincial Party committee and the provincial people's government, the people all over the province concientiously implemented the spirit of the Fifth and the Sixth Plenary Sessions of the Fourteenth Central Committee of CPC, correctly handled the relationship between reform, development and stabitily , positively pushed on two basic changes, and speeded up the three great strategies. As a result, moderately fast development was scored in national economy; significant achievement was made in curbing inflation; improvement was seen in people's life, and new progress was registered in social and cultural undertakings.

The gross domestic product (GDP) of the year was 600. 42 billion yuan, up by 12. 2 percent over the previous year. Of this total, the value-added of the primary industry was 96. 53 billion yuan, up by 7. 8 percent; the value-added of the secondary industry was 307. 41 billion yuan, up by 12. 3 percent; and the value-added of the tertiary industry was 196. 48 billion, up by 14. 3 percent. The proportion of the value-added by type of industry in GDP is as follows: 16. 1 percent of primary industry, 51. 2 percent of secondary industry and 32. 7 percent of tertiary industry. However, the problems of irrational economic structures were still prominent and the agricultural foundation needed further strengthening; the economic efficiency of industry was not satisfying; there was difficulty in the management and operation and the life of workers in some enterprises.

I **Agriculture**

Another good harvest was achieved in crop cultivation, which played an active role in stabilizing economy and ensuring market supplies. The value-added crop cultivation in the year was 65. 63 billion yuan, up by 5. 9 percent over the previous year. Among the chief agricultural products, the per mu and total output of grain hit the historical record; the plan for cotton, with the planting areas decreased, was still finished; the total output of oil-bearing crops was the second harvest year in history. There were ups and downs in other crop agricultural products.

The output of major farm products was as follows:

	1996 (10000 tons)	Increase over 1995 (percent)
Grain	3476. 4	5. 8
Cereal	3301. 1	6. 2
Soybeans	79. 4	—10
Tubers	95. 9	6. 3
Cotton	53. 7	—4. 3
Oil-bearing crops	147. 5	—7. 5
rapeseed	106. 3	—2. 9
Beetroots	2. 3	318. 2
Cured tobacco	0. 3	14. 5
Jute and ambary hemp	0. 3	—27
Sikworm cocoons	9. 2	—50. 5
Tea	1. 1	3. 5
Fruits	123. 3	21. 6

Continued improvement was seen in forestry production and afforest in 1996. The new afforested areas were 21. 6 kilohectares. Significant progress was made in the state key forestry projects, and theoutput of major forest projects was increased.

Steady growth was made in animal husbandry with differentgrowths in the output of animal products such as meat, poultry, egg, and milk.

The output of major animal products and livestock headage were as follows:

	1996	Icrease over 1995 (percent)
Meat of pork, beef and mutton	2280000 (tons)	4.7
Cow milk	105000 (tons)	4.7
Pigs out stock	28326000 (head)	2.8
Pigs in stock (year-end)	20639000 (head)	−2.6
Sheep and goats in stock (year-end)	13703000 (head)	7.6
Large animals in stock (year-end)	1373000 (head)	11.4
Poulty eggs	1907000 (tons)	8.8

Continued growth was made in fishery production. The output of aquatic products in 1996 was 2280000 tons, up by 12 percent over the previous year, with the output of fresh water products being 1660000 tons, up by 7.7 percent and that of marine products 795000 tons, up by 12.2 percent.

Due to increasing purchasing prices and of farm products, extensive utilized application of science and technology, progress was made in improving agricultural structure and accelerating diversified economy development. There was remarkable efficiency in the construction of "Project Vegetable Basket". Proportion of value-added by forestry, animal husbandry fishery and commodity industry of rural households in agriculture was 37.2 percent, up by 3.4 percent point over the previous year.

Further improvement was made in the material equipment level for agricultural production, resouces in agriculture were tapped smoothly. Government expenditures on agriculture production and administration were 2.2 billion yuan, up by 13.5 percent over previous year. Total agricultural machinery power was 22974000 Kilowatt in the year-end, up by 3.2 percent; large and medium agricultural tractors were 30000 units, up by 31.4 percen; mini-tractors were 765000 units, pu by 2 percent; trucks for agricultural use were 26000 units, up by 6.9 percent; consumption of chemical fertilizers wrs 3067000 tons, (100 percent effective content equivalent) up by 4.7 percent; electricity consumed in rural area was 25.2 billion kilowatt-hours, up by 5.9 percent. Water conservancy facilities were further strengthened and the construction of the key projects of Huai River and Taihu Lake was speeded up . Effectively irrigated areas were 38378000 hectares. Ton-grain areas were constructed for 893000 hectares, and the middle and low grain areas were transformed by 2167000 hectares, both exceeding the task prescribed in the year plan.

Rapid growth was made in township and village enterprises, the gross output value of township and village enterprises, construction, transportation and wholesale and retail trade kept growth, up by 15.2 percent over the previous year.

Ⅱ Industry and Construction

The industrial production, overcoming various restrainments such as markets and funds, kept steady growth, and the total value-added of the industrial sector was 275.48 billion yuan, up by 11 percent over the previous year.

The growth of the light industry and the heavy industry almost kept the same pace. The gross output values of the light industry and the heavy industry were respectively 376.55 billion yuan, up by 15.6 percent over the previous year, and 415.38 billion yuan, up by 17.2 percent. Production structure was adjusted; the industry output of sources energy, raw material kept rapid growth. Quality and grade of products were improved obviously. New products were increased rapidly, the gross output value of which was up by 29.9 percent over previous year.

The output of major industrial products was as follows:

	1996	Increase over 1995 (percent)
Yarn	833000 (tons)	−3.4
Cloth	3460000000 (meter)	−29.3
Woolen piece goods	191340000 (meter)	−32.2
Machine-made paper and paperhoard	1634000 (tons)	−2.5
Salt	3595000 (tons)	4.1
Household washing machines	1178000 (unit)	30.5
Household refrigerators	207000 (unit)	80.9
Electric fans	19396000 (unit)	−6.9
Television sets	4105000 (unit)	−10.3
#Color TV sets	2583000 (unit)	3
Coal	26065000 (ton)	−1.7
Crude oil	1220000 (tons)	20.3
Crude oil processing	10214000 (tons)	4.6
Electricity	75690000000 kilowatt-hour	8.1
Steel	4466000 (tons)	23.9

Rolled-steel final products	7956000 (tons)	1
Cement	40403000 (tons)	1. 9
Plate glass	11316000 (wt, case)	30. 3
Sulphuric acid	1754000 (tons)	2. 2
Soda ash	748000 (tons)	28. 7
Coustic soda	576000 (tons)	11. 1
Motor vehicles	110000 (unit)	—12
Large and medium tractors	4000 (unit)	102. 2
Chemical fertilizers (100%)	1843000 (tons)	—3. 9
Chemical fibers	1059000 (tons)	3. 7

The reform of the enterprise system was further deepened. There was new development in the experiment work of modern enterprise system. The four state-level experiment enterprises, and the 120 out of province-level experiment enterprises, according to the twelve experiment supporting files of the provincial government, and organized corres ponding implementation and made initial achievements in the system reform, capital increase and debt decrease, and the intensified management.

The work of the second group of experiment enterprises were started. The adjustment of enterprises organization structures was speeded up. On the basis of strengthening and perfecting the 10 key province-level enterprise groups established in 1995, 11 more groups were set up in 1996, such as Nanjing Iron Plant, Overseas, Shazhou Iron Plant and Sunshine. Entitled to use the provincial name were 271 more enterprise groups, 186 of which were township enterprise groups. The various reforms of enterprises such annexation, bankruptcy, lease, trusteeship and share holding systems were promoted. The medium and small size enterprises were further invigorated, and about 50 % of them adopted different forms of the system reform. Through deepening reform, the township enterprises made continued stable growth in many economic indices. The experiments of share holding enterprises were standardized gradually. As a result, the accumulative total of limitedliability companies was 326, with 15 newly established in the year. The system reforms of the state-owned capital management and opertation was actively carried forward, and the circulation and reconstruction of the state-owned capital was accelerated.

The efficiency of the industrial economy was not satisfying enough. The deficit scale of the independently account enterprises at and above the township level reached 22. 7 %, while the yearly profits realized decreased 12. 7 %. The major factors influencing the gross efficiency level of the industrial economy were that the elements of increasing capital and decreasing profits continued to grow; that the enterprise was operating under capacity, that the stock of products was enlarged; and that the structures of products, enterprise organization and industrial sectors were not suitable for the development of the socialist market economy.

The construction industry continued to develop steadily. The value-added of this sector was 31. 93 billion yuan, up by 26. 3 percent over the previous year. Floor space under construction was 87098000 square meters, up by 2. 6 percent. Floor space completed was 82521000 square meters, up by 1. 37 times. The rate of all staff and worker's efficiency was 48547 yuan, up by 12 percent. Profits completed in construction were 1,495 billion yuan, up by 86. 6 percent.

Ⅲ Investment in Fixed Assets

The scale of investment in fixed assets was appropriate. The completed investment in fixed assets of country in 1996 was 194. 95 billion yuan, representing an increase of 16 percent over the previous year, or 10. 2 percentage points lower than the growth in previous year.

Of all the social fixed assets investment, the investment of state-owned units was 70. 86 billion yuan, up by 17. 6 percent; the investment of collective units, 46. 52 billion yuan, an decrease of 5. 3 percent; the investment of urban and rural residents, 27. 57 billion yuan, up by 28. 7 percent; and the investment of other types of ownership, 50 billion yuan, up by 34. 3 percent. The investment in capital construction was 47. 66 billion yuan, up by 32. 8 percent, or the same points as the growth in the previous year; the investment in technical updating and transformation reached 23. 82 billion yuan, an increase of 8. 9 percent, or 19. 4 percentage points lower than the growth in the previous year; the investment in real estate was 23. 26 billion yuan, down by 3. 4 percent.

The year 1996 saw the completion of 8132 projects. Plan investment was 205. 18 billion yuan; fully completed projects turned over for production were 5002, with newly increased fixed assets up to 52. 49 billion yuan.

The investment structures were improved. The completed investment was 5. 75 billion yuan in primary industry, up by 40. 4 percent; 90. 54 billion yuan in secondary industry, up by 10. 5 percent; 98. 67 billion yuan in tertiary industry, up by 20. 4 percent. Among construction and updating, 11. 26 billion yuan were invested in energy industry, up by 42. 1 percent; 16. 86 billion yuan in transport, post and telecommunications, up by 33. 9 percent.

The key projects and infrastructure construction made great progress, and the key technical updating and transformation were strengthened. The expressway from Shanghai to Nanjing and the first class highway from Nanjing to Nanton, Nanjing to Lianyungang were completed. Jiangyin Yangtze River Bridge and Nanjing Lukou Airport were constructed rapidly. A group of key projects of construction were complete. The No. 1 generate unite of Pengcheng Power Plant, Xuzhou Huarun Power Ltd. Co. began its operation and was paralleled into the transmission network to complete the project "help the poor and send the electricity" ahead of schedule and realize the targets "electrify every village". The operation rate of the first phase of technical transformation in the project "double strengthening" was 83. 3, 10 points higher that the national average level. The second phase of the project was also started.

The newly-increased production capacity in capital construction was 420000 kilowatt of power generation, transformation electricity circuits 78 kilometers, cement 1350000 tons, plastic resin and polymer 10 million tons, newly built and rebuilt highway 1023 kms, tap water 150000 tons per day in city.

Ⅳ Transportation, Post and Telecommunications

The overall level of telecommunications and transportation development kept growth. The value-added of the sector in 1996 was 25. 48 billion yuan, an increase of 15. 4 percent over the previous year. The tense situation in transportation was relieved.

Turnover volume of passenger and freight transportation by various means was as follows:

	1996	Increase over 1995 (percent)
Volume of freight traffic	144 billion-km	6. 1
Railway	38 billion-km	−3. 4
Highway	31. 71 billion-km	12. 8
Waterway	71. 2 billion-km	6. 2
Pipelines	3. 07 billion-km	−2. 8
Volume of passenger transport	66. 9 billion-km	6. 9
Railway	14. 39 billion-km	−12. 1
Highway	52. 3 billion-km	13. 9
Waterway	0. 25 billion-km	−26. 7
Volume of cargo handled at ports	306. 22 million tons	0. 3

The business transactions of post and telecommunication services made continued fast development. The gross revenue in the year totaled 9. 6 billion yuan, up by 32. 9 percent over the previous year, and the added-value was 6. 03 billion yuan, up by 8. 97 billion yuan, up by 32. 9 percent. The business service revenue was 8. 97 billion yuan, up by 36. 8 percent. The capacity of switchboards in the end of year reached 8. 25 million gates, or 2. 282 million gates increase over that in the previous year. The telephone subscribers in urban and rural areas topped 3. 36 million, the new subscribers increased 0. 807 million. There were 10. 5 telephones for every 100 households, increasing three telephones over the previous year.

Ⅴ Domestic Trade and Market Prices

Domestic market of consumer goods was prosperous and stable. In 1996, the total retail sales of consumer goods was 200. 54 billion yuan(including living house in urban and rural areas), up by 21. 5 percent over the previous year, with a real growth of 13. 8 percent (price hike deducted). The supply sources of major commodities were rich;the market sale of production materials were stable; the food and the new types of household electric appliances sold well; and the catering business was rather prosperous.

The total retail sales of consumer goods in cities (including countytowns) reached 136. 16 billion yuan, up by 25. 4 percent; and the total retail sales of consumer goods was 64. 38 billion yuan in the rural areas, up by 14. 1 percent, lower than citylevel 11. 3 percentage points.

The retail sales of consumer goods grew in full scale in terms of different ownership. The retail sales of non-state-ownership was in the lead. The private outlets was 5. 8 billion yuan, up by 69. 6 percent; individual outlets was 30. 42 billion yuan, up by 30. 5 percent; outlets of other forms of ownership, 24. 61 billion yuan, up by 29 percent.

In terms of different industries, the retail sales of the wholesale and retail trades were 133. 72 billion yuan, up by 18. 8 percent; the catering industry, 12. 6 billion yuan, up by 39. 7 percent; manufacture trade 18. 67 billion yuan, up by 4. 1 percent; the other industries, 35. 5 billion yuan, up by 39. 6 percent.

The reform of the market circulation system was further deepened. A team of large state-owned circulation enterprise groups were strengthened in competition; private-owned, individual and share-holding circulation enterprises developed quickly; and the format of circulation development tended to be diversified. On the basis of improved networks, the market construction was led gradually to a higher level, further radiation and larger scale, and the modern circulation styles were actively popularized. Newly set up in the province were 40-odd various markets, 10 of which were of the province level. The province enjoyed 237 markets on the 1～2 billion yuan level, 7 markets on the 2. 1～5 billion yuan level, 4 markets on the 5～10 billion yuan level, and 2 markets on the level above 10 billion yuan.

Significant achievement was achieved in curbing inflation, and the increase rate of market prices was not only slowed down continuously, but reached the lowest level since 1993. The retail price index was up 6. 8 percent. The growth rate was down 7. 5 percentage points.

Increase in prices as compared with 1996 was as follows:

	Increase in 1996 over 1995 (%)
1. Consumer price index	9. 3
Of 1. 1: Urban areas	10. 8
Rural areas	7. 1
Of 1. 2: Food	9. 6
Grain	8
Oil or fat	—8. 4
Meat and poultry products	6. 5
Eggs	15. 5
Aquatic products	6. 8
Fresh vegetables	40. 5
Clothing	8. 7
Household appliances and articles	2. 6
Transport and telecommunication goods	—2. 1
Cultural and recreational articales	9. 7
Housing	17. 3
Services	12. 3
2. Retail price index	6. 8
Urban and areas	6. 8
Rural areas	6. 8
3. Retail prices for means of agricultural production	6. 6
4. Purchasing prices for raw materials, energy and power	3. 9
5. Producer's prices of manufactured products	0. 6
6. Price of investment in fixed asstes	3. 2
7. Purchasing prices for farm and sideline products	2

Ⅵ Foreign Economics

Under the general climate that the state made a great policy adjustment on foreign trade, the concerned departments of the whole province tried hard to overcome difficulties and resolutely insisted on enlarging opening to the outside world. The open-type economy was developed in multiple channels and all directions, and a continuous stable growth was achieved.

The scale of foreign trade expanded. In 1996, total volume of export and import reached 20. 22 billion US dollars, up by 20. 4 percent over the previous year, of which the value of export was 13. 12 billion US dollars, up by 11. 3 percent; and the value of import was 7. 09 billion US dollars, up by 41. 8 percent. The export value of direct foreign investment and other interrelating enterprises was further enlarged, of which the value of export was 6. 62 billion US dollars, up by 25. 2 percent, the share in the export rose from 44. 8 percent to 50. 4 percent. The commodities of export were sold to 177 countries and regions.

Steady growth was achieved in the utilization of foreign capitals. In 1996, foreign capitals actually utilized amounted to 5. 5 billion US dollars, up by 4. 1 percent. Though the number of new foreign investment enterprises was decreased, large projects were increased. In 1996, there were 352 new foreign investment enterprises, each over 10 million US dollars. Average value of foreign business contract was 3. 64 million US dollars in every new foreign enterprise, increasing 450000 US dollars in total.

Continuous progress was made in economic and technical cooperation with foreign countries. Construction projects and labor projects contracted by the province with foreign countries in 1996 amounted to 0. 73 billion US dollars, up by 8. 9 percent, and the accomplished operation revenue was 0. 68 billion US dollars, up by 33. 9 percent. New non-trade enterprises were increased, and total investment reached 45. 58 million US dollars. The approaches of economic and technical cooperation were changed, and the proportion of contracted projects, general contract of items and technical services rose up. The construction of various development zones were speeded up, and some state and province level development zones, such as Suzhou Industrial Garden, became the window of domestic combinations and foreign attractions and the new economic growing points.

International tourism achieved new progress. In 1996, the whole province received 837000 foreigner tourists for sightseeing visits and other activities, up by 9 percent. Income of foreign exchanges from tourism reached 0. 317 billion US dollars, up by 22 percent.

Ⅶ Finance, Banking and Insurance

There was a still deeper reform in the systems of finance and banking. Financial functions were improved; orders of financial taxes and accounting work were adjusted and standardized; and the financial tax system, with the tax classification as focus and the value-added tax as main part, was put into normal operation. Branches of the people's bank at various levels actively carried out their responsibilities and brought about a basic separation between the administrative finance and the commerical finance. The transformation of specialized banks into commercial banks was initiated, and the Merchant's Bank Nanjing Branch was newly established. The reform on social insurance and distribution system was pushed forward stable. There was a breakthrough in the reform of the old-age insurance and unemployment insurance system, and the model of raising old-age insurance funds by combining the social planning with personal accounts was generally established. The system of insuring the lowest living standard for urban residents was also set up.

Financial revenue and expenditure kept basically balance. In 1996, financial revenue reached 42. 8 billion yuan, in which, local financial revenue was 22. 32 billion yuan, up by 22. 3 percent and 29. 3 percent. In the local financial revenue, industrial and commercial taxes were completed by 16. 35 billion yuan, up by 25. 8 percent. The yearly financial expenditure was 31. 09 billion yuan, up by 22. 7 percent over the previous year.

The banking situation was basically stable. Savings deposit balance in various forms of the whole society at the end of 1996 totaled 464. 9 billion yuan, an increase of 110. 08 billion yuan. Of this total, savings balance of enterprises accounted for 164. 2 billion yuan, an increase of 44. 06 billion yuan more than at the beginning of 1996. The savings deposits balance by urban and rural residents reached 257 billion yuan, an increase of 64. 26 billion yuan. Loan balance totaled 357. 5 billion yuan, an increase of 62. 93 billion yuan, with short-term loans balance of 27. 14 billion yuan, and middle and long term loans 49. 4 billion yuan, an inccrease of 49. 4 billion yuan and 7. 27 billion yuan more than those at beginning of this year.

Fairly big progress was made in insurance service. In 1996, the total accepted premium of insurance various kinds totaled 687. 4 billion yuan in People's Insurance Company of China in Jiangsu System, up by 25. 6 percent. The insurance premium was 3. 7 billion yuan, up by 27. 4 percent over the previous year. The premium of property insurance of various kinds was 2. 27 billion yuan, and the premium of life insurance was 1. 43 billion yuan. The insurance companies paid an indemnity of 1. 08 billion yuan as reparations in property insurance programmes, and 0. 7 billion yuan as reparations in life insurance programmes.

Ⅷ Science and Technology and Education

Scientific and technical personnel grew in size. By the end of 1996, there were 431 state-owned independent research and development institutions at and above county level, with another 410 research institutions affiliated to universities, 1620 research institutions affiliated to large and medium industrial enterprises. There were 1. 89 milliom scientific and technical persons, up by 2. 2 percent. A total of 0. 35 milliom people were engaged in scientific and technological activities in research institutions, universities and independent industrial enterprises, in which 11. 5 thousand were scientists or engineers. The province held 42 academicians of the Chinese Academy of Sciences and 16 academicians of the Chinese Academy of Engineering in the year.

Financial input into scientific and technological activities increased. The expenditure of research institutions, universities and industrial enterprises on scientific and technological activities in 1996 was 13. 4 billion yuan, 2. 64 billion yuan of which were spent on research and development, accounting for 0. 44 percent of GDP.

In 1996, there were 40 key scienfitic results of the state grade, including 6 national invention prizes and 34 national prizes of progress in science and technology; 317 key scientific and technological results of the province grade, with 4 first-class prizes, 36 second-class prizes, 105 third-class prizes, and 172 fourth-class prizes. 257 key scientific and technological projects began operation. By end of 1996, 104 key laboratories and engineering and technological centers were completed, including 17 national laboratories, 11 national engineering and technological centers.

Markets for the technology transfer became more brist. In 1996, a total of 31000 contracts on the transfer of technology were signed, up by 22. 9 percent. The patent business was basically stable, and 4982 applications for patent were received while 2578 panentts were authorized, up by 22 percent and 7 percent.

The scale of high and new technology expanded, with the gross output value for the whole year amounting to 37 billion yuan; and the revenue of technology, industry and trade were 40 billion yuan, up by 50 percent. There were 537 high and new technological enterprises in the province, and 317 high and new technological products were confirmed, in which 258 were state-grade new products and 483 the province grade new products.

New progress was made in educational undertakings. The enrollment of new graduate students was 4500 persons, an increase of 800 over the previous year. And the total number of students taking graduate course was 12200 persons, an increase of 1500 persons. Institutions of higher learning took in 74300 new undergraduate students, or 6800 more than that in the previous year, and the total number of enrolled undergraduate students was 220600, an increase of 12000 persons. There were 409900 students studying in various types of secondary vocational and technical schools, or 91200 more than those of the previous year, and 257900 senior students in vocational middle schools. There were 3. 2355 million students in regular secondary schools, and 6. 8782 million in primary schools, an increase of 68000 and 430500 students respectively. New progress was achieved in the implementation of 9-year compulsory education programme. The enrollment rate of primary-school-age children was 99. 8 percent. The 38 towns and villages of 4 counties assigned with the task of disseminating the nine year compulsory education program were appraised by the state, and the goal of disseminating the program and eliminating the illiteracy of the young people were generally accomplished. Preschool education and the special education of the disabled and slow children were also developed to a certain extent.

There was further development in the adult education and the construction of educational modernization. 65000 people were enrolled by universities and colleges for adults in the year and there were 160500 students in school, respectively 10700 and 27600 more than the previous year. The number of students in secondary technical schools for adults was 165400, a decrease of 15500 people by the previous year. The number of students in secondary and primary schools for adults was 389100, a decrease of 40600 peole. There was a bigger input in the housing construction for teachers, and 1. 34 million square meters of building space were completed, a total sum of the completed building space in the first four years of the Eighth Year Plan. Teaching qualities and conditions were further improved. The project of realizing modern education in the Southern Jiangsu and the project of promoting moderately well-off education in the Northern Jiangsu were comprehensively implemented.

Ⅸ Culture, Public Health, Sports and Environmental Protection

Culture and art undertakings continued to make progress. By the end of 1996, there were 131 art-performing groups, 108 culture centers, 96 publiclibraries, 73 museums, 1 archives, 61 radio brosdcasting stations, 21 medium and short wave radieo transmitting and relaying stations, 54 television stations and 73 television transmitting and relaying stations, each with a capacity of cover 1000 watts. There were 3126 film-projection units. In 1996, published and issued were 1. 75 billion copies of newspapers; 70. 624 million copies of magzines; and 452. 643 million copies of books. A lot of good works were awarded the national prizes as a result of carrying out "Project Five Ones".

Public health undertakings developed steadily. By the end of 1996, there were 14944 health care institutions, with a total of 0. 158 million beds, up by 1. 9 percent over the previous year. There were 250000 health workers in Jiangsu province, up by 1. 9 percent, with 113000 doctors, up by 1. 1 percent; and the doctors of Chinses medicine with western medicine were 87000 persons, senior and junior nurses were 67000, up by 1. 8 percent and 3. 9 percent. The expenimential scales of medical system reforming were enlarged from Zhenjiang to Suzhou, Wuxi, Nanton and Yiancheng.

Significant headway was made in sports. In 1996, in world and Asian matches, one Jiangsu athlete broke one world record, one broke one Asian record, 7 won 9 world chammpions and 6 won 5 world second place, 5 athletes won 4 world third, 12 athletes won 14 Asian champions, 8 athletes won 3 Asian second. According to the statistics for "The Contributed Prize" by the state commision of sports in 1996, Jiangsu province scored 419 and obtained the national first place for the first time. As to the national matches, athletes won 20 golden medals, 26 silver medals, and 16 bronze medals.

Environment protection was further enchanced. By the end of 1996, there were 5800 people working in the provincial environment protection system, 101 environmental montoring stations 4100 workers;and the number of projects against environment pollution completed within 1996 amounted to 678, absorbing a total investment of 0. 31 billion yuan. There were 146 smoke/dust control zones, covering an area of 1179. 2 square kilometers; and there were the noise pollution was put undeer specified level. By the end of 1996, 118 heavy-pollution producing paper enterprises under 500 tons production capacity were banned, closed or suspened. But the problem of environment protection was still conspicuous.

Ⅹ Population and People's Life

New headway was made in family planning programme. In 1996, the crude birth rate of population was 12. 11 per thousand, a decrease of 0. 21 per thousand points; and the crude death rate was 6. 58 per thousand, an increase of 0. 02 per thousand points, resulting in a natural growth rate of 5. 53 per thousand, a decrease of 0. 23 per thousand points. By the end of 1996, the total population was 71. 1016 million, or an increase of 0. 4414 millon over the figure at the end of 1995.

The household income continued to increase steadily. The annual per capita income for living expense of urban household was 4689 yuan, up 11. 4 percent over the previous year, or a real growth of the same if the increase in prices was excluded. The annual consumption expenditures of urban household per capita were 4057 yuan. However, unbalanced development among different groups of population was till prominent. The life of some of low income households was still difficult. According to the sample examination, the proportion of decreasing income households was increased, from 35. 5 percent to 42. 2 percent. The per capita net income of rural households was 3029 yuan, up by 23. 3 percent, and the real growth was 12. 6 percent if price hike was deducted. The average consumption expenditures of rural household per capita were 2414 yuan.

Labor and employment situation was basically stable. By the end of the year, there were 1973 vocational service institutions. The increase of employed people numbered 0. 2078 million. In the end of 1996, the urban unemployed people were 9. 044 million, a decrease of 0. 116 million. Another 0. 728 million people were employed in private enterprises or were self-employed in urban areas, an increase of 69000 people. There were over 0. 4 million people re-employed in 1996. The total wage bill of staff and workers was 59. 17 billion yuan, up by 9. 2 percent; and the average annual wage of employees was 6564 yuan, up by 10. 5 percent. The level was the same as the previous year if price hike was deducted.

Living conditions were further improved in urban and rural areas. In 1996, the floor space of residential housing completed 18. 42 million square meters in urban area, and 73. 80 million square meters in rural area.

Notes: Refer to the data in the subsequent tables when they are differently mentioned in the present communique.

DIVISIONS OF ADMINISTRATIVE AREAS AND NATURAL RESOURCES

1 行政区划和自然资源
DIVISIONS OF ADMINISTRATIVE AREAS AND NATURAL RESORCES

自 然 概 况

位置

江苏简称苏，位于我国大陆东部沿海中心，介于东经116°18′－121°57′，北纬30°45′－35°20′之间。东濒黄海，西连安徽，北接山东，东南与浙江和上海毗邻。

江苏地处美丽富饶的长江三角洲，平原辽阔，主要有苏南平原、江淮平原、黄淮平原组成，自然条件优越，经济基础较好。

面积

全省面积10.26万平方公里，其中平原面积7.06万平方公里，水面面积1.73万平方公里，海岸线长954公里，耕地面积4435.44万公顷。

河流

全省境内河川交错，水网密布，长江横穿东西400多公里；大运河纵贯南北690公里，西南部有秦淮河，北部有苏北灌溉总渠、沂沭河、通扬运河等。有属全国“五大淡水湖”之列的太湖和洪泽湖，还有阳澄湖、高邮湖等。

资源

江苏以地形地势低平，河湖众多为特点，平原、水面所占比例之大，在全国居首位，成为江苏一大地理优势；水产资源丰富，有广阔的海涂、浅海，东部沿海渔场面积达15.4万平方公里，其中包括著名的吕泗渔场和海州湾渔场，盛产黄鱼、带鱼、昌鱼、虾类、蟹类及贝藻类等。我省也是全国鳗鱼苗的主要产地。矿产资源分布广泛，品种较多。

气候

全省气候具有明显的季风特征，处于亚热带向暖温带过渡地带，大致以淮河－－灌溉总渠一线为界，以南属亚热带湿润季风气候，以北属暖温带湿润季风气候。全省气候温和，雨量适中，四季分明。

DIVISIONS OF ADMINISTRATIVE AREAS AND NATURAL RESOURCES NATURAL SITUATIONS

LOCATION

Jiangsu (Short for Su) lies in the east of the country. It is situated in the center of the costal area, between 116°18′—121°57′E and 30°45′—35°20′, with Yellowsea on the east, Anhui province on the west, Shandong on north, and Zhejiang and Shanghai as its neighbours in the southeast.

Jiangsu seats on the beautiful and abundent Yangtze River Delta, with favorable natural conditions, it is composed of vast plains, such as Northernsu, Jianghui and Huanghui plain etc. There are good economic bases.

AREA

The area of Jiangsu is 102600 square kilometres, among which 70600 square kilometres are plain areas, 17300 square kilometres are water surface. The costline of the province is as long as 954 kilmetres, and the 44354400 hectares of cultivated land.

RIVERS AND LAKES

In Jiangsu, there rivers are crisscross throughout the province, and distributes the network of waterways. The Yangtze River travels whole area of Jiangsu, from west to east, for more than 400 kilometres. The grand canal flows sourh to north for 690 kilometres.

There are Qinhui River in the southeast of Jiangsu, Subei general irrigation canal, Qishu River and Tongyang canal etc. in the north part. The Taihu Lake and Hongze Lake are both listed among the ranks of the national "Five Large Fresh Water Lakes". Besides there are Yangchenghu Lake and Gaoyouhu Lake etc.

RESOURCES

The province is characterstic of topographical features in low and flat terrains, with numerous rivers and lakes. The proportion of plain and watersurface area is so large, that it makes the province the first in China, and become a geographical superiority proportion. There are plentiful aquatic resources, vast shallow sea beaches and epeiric seas. There are 154000 square kilometres of fishing grounds on the eastern coastal area, composed of famous Lushi and Haizhouwan fishing grounds, abound in yellow croaker, hairtail, butterfish, shrimp and crab, and shellfish and algae. Jiangsu is also a main producing area of young eel in the country. Mineral resources are widely dispersed over, with numerous varieties.

CLIMATE

Located in a transition area from subtripical zone to temperature zone, Jiangsu shows a distinct characteristic of monsoon. Taking the Hui river to general irrigation canal as a line of demarcation approximateky, the climate to the south of the line belongs to monsoon of tropical moist zone, while the climate to the north of the line belongs to monsoon of warm moistzone. Jiangsu has a warm climate, with moderate rainfall and distinct seasons.

1—1 主要城市月平均气温(1996)
MONTHLY AVERAGE TEMPERATURE IN MAJOR CITIES

单位:摄氏度 (℃)

市名 City	1月 Jan.	2月 Feb.	3月 Mar.	4月 Apr.	5月 May	6月 June	7月 July	8月 Aug.	9月 Sept.	10月 Oct.	11月 Nov.	12月 Dec.
南京市 Nanjing	2.5	3.4	7.8	14.6	20.3	24.8	26.8	27.9	24.0	17.9	10.5	4.8
无锡市 Wuxi	3.2	3.6	7.7	13.5	19.8	24.7	26.9	27.5	24.3	18.4	11.8	5.9
徐州市 Xuzhou	0.9	1.9	7.3	14.5	20.7	25.6	26.9	26.8	21.9	15.8	7.3	3.6
常州市 Changzhou	3.5	3.9	7.9	14.5	20.4	25.0	27.1	28.1	24.7	18.7	11.5	6.2
苏州市 Suzhou	3.8	4.2	7.9	13.4	20.0	24.7	26.8	27.7	24.6	18.8	12.5	6.5
南通市 Nantong	3.3	3.2	7.3	12.8	18.8	24.1	26.4	27.0	23.8	18.2	11.7	5.6
连云港市 Lianyungang	1.0	2.0	6.7	13.7	20.2	24.7	26.5	26.8	22.5	16.5	8.0	3.4
淮阴市 Huiyin	1.5	2.4	7.0	14.3	19.8	24.8	26.8	26.8	22.6	16.7	8.6	4.4
盐城市 Yancheng	2.0	2.3	6.6	12.9	18.8	24.0	26.2	26.7	22.6	17.2	9.7	4.3
扬州市 Yangzhou	2.6	3.2	7.6	14.6	20.1	24.7	26.8	27.8	23.9	18.0	10.3	5.2
镇江市 Zhenjiang	3.2	3.7	7.8	14.6	20.3	24.9	26.9	28.0	24.4	18.4	10.9	6.1

1—2 主要城市月降水量(1996)
MONTHLY PRECIPITATION IN MAJOR CITIES

单位:毫米 (millimeters)

市名 City	1月 Jan.	2月 Feb.	3月 Mar.	4月 Apr.	5月 May	6月 June	7月 July	8月 Aug.	9月 Sept.	10月 Oct.	11月 Nov.	12月 Dec.
南京市 Nanjing	53.6	18.4	134.4	25.7	85.5	225.6	370.1	82.7	34.3	82.4	94.8	6.0
无锡市 Wuxi	96.5	18.2	134.1	31.2	47.7	228.1	290.1	145.5	13.9	76.3	52.1	18.5
徐州市 Xuzhou	8.4	17.7	31.3	42.1	5.7	260.9	324.9	16.7	125.4	65.1	66.5	1.1
常州市 Changzhou	82.6	20.9	151.8	38.9	66.8	236.0	227.8	129.8	43.2	88.6	84.0	10.6
苏州市 Suzhou	99.6	17.8	145.9	46.4	24.3	264.6	259.3	118.7	23.5	66.0	56.4	22.0
南通市 Nantong	71.0	17.5	119.9	27.0	54.6	214.9	185.4	67.4	72.5	62.2	89.8	14.4
连云港市 Lianyungang	11.3	5.8	46.2	55.6	0.4	259.3	236.6	58.0	145.2	44.3	51.7	2.4
淮阴市 Huiyin	20.4	19.2	71.4	44.5	13.5	286.9	198.9	61.0	82.4	80.4	147.7	6.7
盐城市 Yancheng	34.3	14.8	103.6	53.8	24.9	256.3	339.8	60.8	82.2	92.5	149.1	17.6
扬州市 Yangzhou	57.0	24.8	137.1	27.1	51.8	234.9	312.4	129.9	34.6	69.1	125.0	9.9
镇江市 Zhenjiang	63.4	22.6	157.9	27.8	68.1	213.3	346.0	21.5	58.5	81.8	117.2	9.0

1—3 行 政 区 划 (1996)
ADMINISTRATIVE DIVISIONS

单位:个 (number)

市 名 City		县级单位数 Number of Counties	#县级市 Cities	各级市单位数 Number of Cities	市辖区数 Districts Under City Adiministration
合 计	**Total**	**64**	**31**	**44**	**43**
南 京 市	Nanjing	5		1	10
无 锡 市	Wuxi	3	3	4	5
徐 州 市	Xuzhou	6	2	3	5
常 州 市	Changzhou	3	3	4	4
苏 州 市	Suzhou	6	6	7	4
南 通 市	Nantong	6	4	5	2
连 云 港 市	Lianyungang	4		1	4
淮 阴 市	Huaiyin	6	1	2	2
盐 城 市	Yancheng	8	2	3	1
扬 州 市	Yangzhou	5	3	4	2
镇 江 市	Zhenjiang	4	3	4	2
泰 州 市	Taizhou	4	4	5	1
宿 迁 市	Xuqian	4		1	1

续表 Continued

单位:个 (number)

市 名 City		镇 Town	乡 Township	街道办事处 Subdistrict Office	居民委员会 Neighbourhood Committee	村民委员会 Villagers' Committee
合 计	**Total**	**1016**	**965**	**215**	**6119**	**35649**
南 京 市	Nanjing	67	52	49	1115	1706
无 锡 市	Wuxi	95	22	27	689	2082
徐 州 市	Xuzhou	70	114	36	465	3490
常 州 市	Changzhou	81	56	18	459	1904
苏 州 市	Suzhou	158	4	22	1101	3313
南 通 市	Nantong	104	153	9	379	4662
连 云 港 市	Lianyungang	47	72	8	256	2114
淮 阴 市	Huaiyin	47	115	8	156	2590
盐 城 市	Yancheng	102	94	18	425	4154
扬 州 市	Yangzhou	81	77	4	398	2333
镇 江 市	Zhenjiang	63	27	8	305	1415
泰 州 市	Taizhou	71	84	8	296	3605
宿 迁 市	Xuqian	30	95		75	2281

2

GENERAL SURVEY

2 综　　合
GENERAL SURVEY

从统计看 1996 年的江苏
JIANGSU IN STATISTICS '96

江　苏　的　地　位
POSITION OF JIANGSU IN THE COUNTRY

国内生产总值	Gross Domestic Products	占全国	8.9%	Percentage in the country
#第三产业	Tertiary Industry	占全国	9.3%	Percentage in the country
全社会固定资产投资总额	Gross Value of Total Investment by Fixed Assets	占全国	8.2%	Percentage in the country
社会商品零售总额	Total Retail Sales of Consumer Goods	占全国	7.9%	Percentage in the country
外贸进出口总值	Total Value of Imports and Exports	占全国	7.1%	Percentage in the country
#出口总值	Total Value of Exports	占全国	7.7%	Percentage in the country
粮食产量	Output of Grain	占全国	7.1%	Percentage in the country
棉花产量	Output of Cotton	占全国	12.8%	Percentage in the country
油料产量	Output of Oil-Bearing Crops	占全国	6.7%	Percentage in the country
大学在校学生数	Students Enrollment in Institution of Higher Education	占全国	7.3%	Percentage in the country

江　苏　的　人　口
POPULATION OF JIANGSU

年末人口	Population (year-end)	7110.16	万人	(10000 persons)
从业人员	Employment	3647.09	万人	(10000 persons)
#职工人数	Staff and Workers	905.52	万人	(10000 persons)
出生人数	Births	85.84	万人	(10000 persons)
死亡人数	Deaths	46.64	万人	(10000 persons)
结婚人数	Marriages	54.71	万对	(10000 pairs)
离婚人数	Divorces	4.72	万对	(10000 pairs)
人口密度	Density of Population	693	人/平方公里	(person/sq·km)
人口平均期望寿命(1995 年)	Life Expectancy (1995)	72.66	岁	(year)

江苏经济的发展
ECONOMIC DEVELOPMENT OF JIANGSU

		1952—1996年平均增长 1952—1996 Average Annual Growth Rate	1978—1996年平均增长 1978—1996 Average Annual Growth Rate
国内生产总值	Gross Domestic Products	8.2	12.7
#第三产业	Tertiary Industry	8.5	15.6
工农业总产值	Gross Output Value of Agriculture	13.1	19.5
农业产值	Gross Output Value of Agriculture	4.8	7.0
工业产值	Gross Output Value of Industry	15.2	20.6
货物运输量	Freight Traffic	9.5	10.2
全社会固定资产投资	Total Investment in Fixed Assets	18.2	28.4
社会商品零售总额	Total Retail Sales of Consumer Goods	11.3	19.0
外贸自营出口总额	Total Value of Exports by Foreign Trade		21.1
财政收入	Financial Revenue	9.9	11.3

江苏的一天
ONE DAY IN JIANGSU

国内生产总值	Gross Domestic Products	16.45	亿元	(100000000 yuan)
#第三产业	Tertiary Industry	5.38	亿元	(100000000 yuan)
工农业总产值	Gross Output Value of Industry and Agriculture	36.66	亿元	(100000000 yuan)
#工业总产值	Gross Output Value of Industry	31.66	亿元	(100000000 yuan)
货物运输量	Freight Traffic	231.96	万吨	(10000 ton)
全社会住宅竣工面积	Total Floor Space of Residence Completed	25.73	万平方米	(10000 sq·m)
社会消费品零售总额	Total Retail Sales of Consumer Goods	5.30	亿元	(100000000 yuan)
财政收入	Financial Revenue	11726	万元	(10000 yuan)
出版报纸	Newspapers Published	479	万份	(10000)
邮寄函件	Letters Delivered	148	万件	(10000)

国内生产总值及发展速度

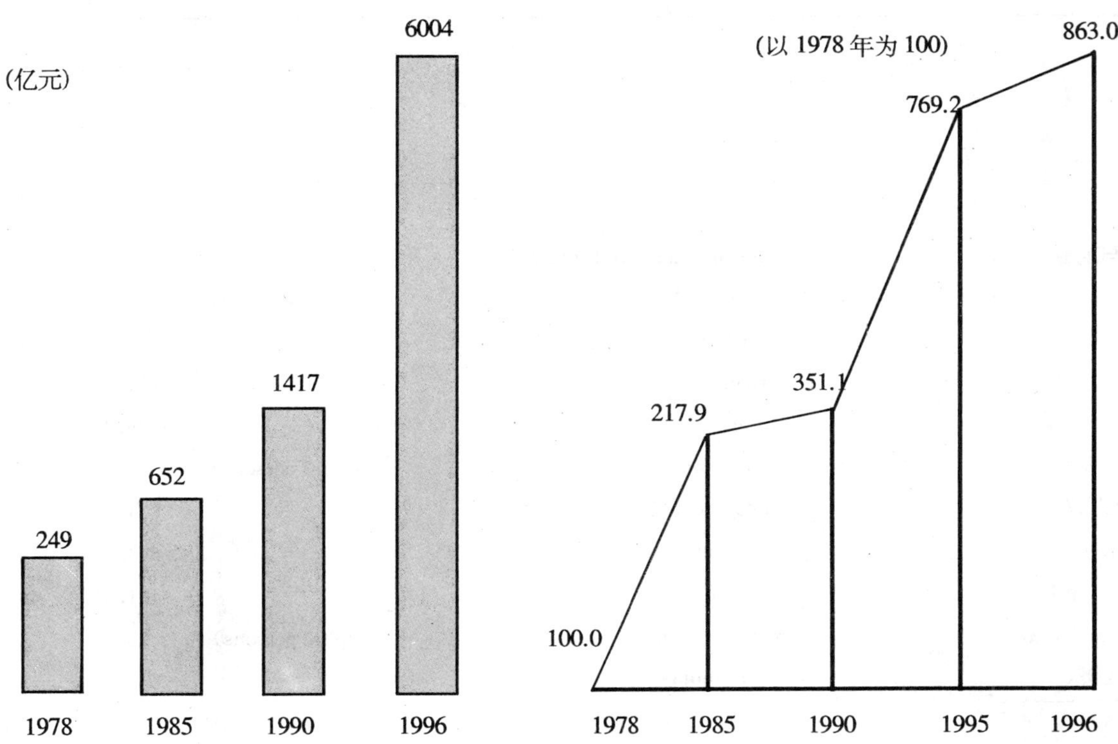

国内生产总值构成（%）

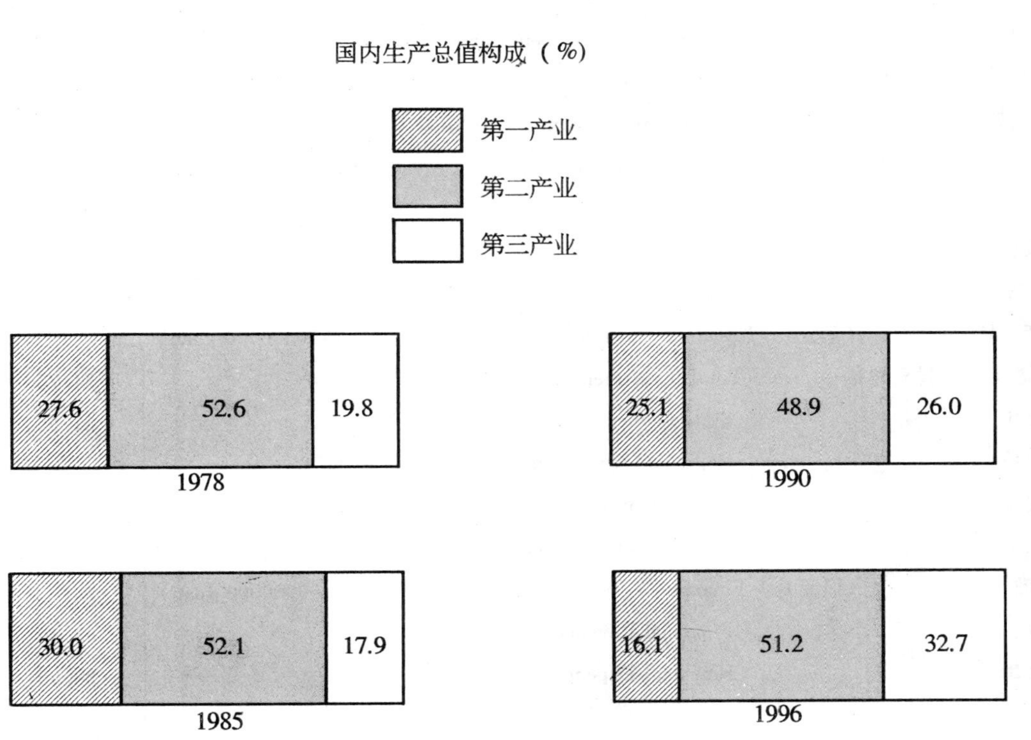

2—1 国民经济和社会发展总量与速度指标
INDICES OF TOTAL NUMBER AND SPEED OF NATIONAL ECONOMY AND SOCIAL DEVELOPMENT

指标		Items		总量指标 1980	总量指标 1985
人口与就业		**Population and Employment**			
人口	(万人)	Population	(10000 persons)		
年末人口		Population (year-end)		5938.19	6213.48
市镇人口		Urban		901.78	1596.15
乡村人口		Rural		5036.41	4617.33
就业	(万人)	Employment	(10000 persons)		
从业人数		Employment		2821.03	3262.97
#职工人数		Staff and Workers		644.15	782.44
#国有经济		State Owned Units		401.98	468.80
城镇失业人数		Unemployment	(10000 persons)	55.47	23.63
宏观经济		**Macroeconomy**			
国民核算	(亿元)	National Accounting	(100000000 yuan)		
国内生产总值		Gross Domestic Products		319.80	651.82
第一产业		Primary Industry		94.24	195.66
第二产业		Secondary Industry		167.41	339.56
第三产业		Tertiary Industry		58.15	116.60
国内支出总额		Gross Domestic Expenditures			
#总消费		Total Consumption		175.47	353.72
居民消费		Resident Consumption		154.72	300.86
社会消费		Public Consumption		20.75	52.86
总投资		Total Investment		97.44	271.42
固定投资		Fixed Assets		58.25	193.25
存货		Stock		39.19	78.17
固定资产投资	(亿元)	Investment in Fixed Assets	(100000000 yuan)		
全社会固定资产投资总额		Total Investment in Fixed Assets		34.73	191.93
#国有单位		State Owned Units		31.65	80.43
集体单位		Colletive Owned Units			59.06
#基本建设		Capital Construction		26.15	47.35
更新改造		Reformation and Replacement		5.50	24.73
财政	(亿元)	Finance	(100000000 yuan)		
财政收入		Financial Revenue		63.36	89.00
财政支出		Financial Expenditure		28.95	20.53

Number			速　度　指　标　Speed						
			指　数（1996年为下列各年%） 1996 As The Percentage Of Following Years				平　均　增　长　% Average Annual Growth Rate		
1990	1995	1996	1980	1985	1990	1995	1980—1990	1985—1995	1980—1996
6766.90	7066.02	7110.16	119.7	114.4	105.1	100.6	1.3	1.3	1.1
1458.94	1929.09	1942.50	215.4	121.7	133.1	100.7	4.9	1.9	4.9
5307.96	5136.93	5167.66	102.6	111.9	97.4	100.6	0.5	1.1	0.2
3569.13	3649.69	3647.09	129.3	111.8	102.2	99.9	2.4	1.1	1.6
879.85	915.98	905.52	140.6	115.7	102.9	98.9	3.2	1.6	2.2
536.88	576.24	575.48	143.2	122.8	107.2	99.9	2.9	2.1	2.3
52.72	42.32	45.19	81.5	191.2	85.7	106.8	—0.5	6.0	—1.3
1416.50	5155.25	6004.21	735.2	396.1	245.8	112.2	11.6	13.4	13.3
355.17	848.35	965.29	239.1	152.2	140.4	107.8	5.5	3.5	5.6
692.59	2715.26	3074.12	901.3	456.4	282.7	112.3	12.3	15.1	14.7
368.74	1591.64	1964.80	1275.5	637.3	274.9	114.3	16.6	18.7	17.2
717.36	2250.66	2721.84	451.2	256.5	198.7	113.1	8.5	8.5	9.9
608.29	1806.43	2218.68	395.6	234.4	186.9	114.5	7.8	7.4	9.0
109.07	444.23	503.16	903.6	394.5	264.0	107.9	13.1	13.8	14.7
588.44	2479.30	2798.62	1328.9	498.7	274.2	110.8	17.1	16.2	17.5
374.12	1756.88	2062.17	1613.9	508.9	298.2	115.4	18.4	16.0	19.0
214.32	722.42	736.45	921.9	482.2	230.2	101.1	14.9	16.9	14.9
356.30	1680.17	1949.53	5613.4	1015.8	547.2	116.0	26.2	24.2	28.6
134.86	602.70	708.60	2238.9	881.0	525.4	117.6	15.6	22.3	21.4
74.87	491.08	465.21		787.7	621.4	94.7		23.6	
74.32	362.15	481.07	1839.7	1016.0	647.3	132.8	11.0	22.6	20.0
41.53	218.78	238.23	4331.5	963.3	573.6	108.9	22.4	24.4	26.6
136.20	350.08	427.99	675.5	480.9	314.2	122.3	8.0	14.7	12.7
100.97	253.49	310.94	1074.1	615.4	308.0	122.7	13.3	17.5	16.0

续表 1

指　　标	Items	总量指标 1980	1985
物　价　（上年＝100）	Price　(preceeding year＝100)		
商品零售价格总指数	Overall Retail Price Index	105.8	109.5
城市居民消费价格总指数	Overall Urban Residents Cost of Living Index	105.7	109.6
农付产品收购价格总指数	Overall Farm and Sideline Products Purchasing Price Index	104.3	106.9
利用外资　（亿美元）	Utilization of Foreign Capital　(100000000 USD)		
签订利用外资协议额	Value of Foreign Capital Through Signed Contracts	0.05	1.96
实际利用外资额	Value of Foreign Capital Actually Used		0.93
产　业	**Industry**		
农　业	Agriculture Production		
耕地面积　（千公顷）	Areas Under Cultivation　(1000 hectares)	4641.38	4604.03
农林牧渔业劳动力　（万人）	Farming, Forestry, Animal Husbandry and Fishery Labor Force　(10000 persons)	1810	1703.20
农林牧渔业总产值　（亿元）	Gross Output Value of FFAF　(100000000 yuan)	138.45	288.55
主要农产品产量　（万吨）	Output of Major Farm Products　(10000 tons)		
粮　食	Grain	2417.95	3126.52
棉　花	Cotton	41.81	47.91
油　料	Oil-Bearing Crops	38.64	108.78
糖　料	Sugar Crops	5.15	26.34
蚕　茧	Silkworm Cocoons	3.82	7.31
猪牛羊肉	Pork, Beef and Mutton	107.24	138.9
水产品	Aquatic Products	42.71	67.54
工　业	Industry		
工业总产值　（亿元）	Gross Output Value of Industry　(100000000 yuan)	467.82	1036.67
# 乡以上工业	Township Level and above	423.86	860.87
农村工业	Rural Industry	109.33	385.54
主要工业产品产量	Output of Major Products		
钢　（万吨）	Steel　(10000 tons)	68.17	98.97
成品钢材	Rolled-Steel	104.87	145.18
发电量　（亿千瓦小时）	Electricity　(100000000 kwh)	156.32	234.48
原　煤　（万吨）	Coal　(10000 tons)	1690.00	2193.85
农用化肥(折100%)　（万吨）	Chemical Furtilizers　(10000 tons)	111.61	121.71
化学农药	Chemical Pesticide	5.75	4.27
水　泥	Cement	629.19	1116.90
化学纤维	Chemical Fiber	3.26	12.52
机制纸及纸板	Machine-Made Paper and Paperboard	28.76	50.00

Continued 1

Number			速　度　指　标　Speed						
			指　数（1996年为下列各年%） 1996 As The Percentage Of Following Years				平　均　增　长　% Average Annual Growth Rate		
1990	1995	1996	1980	1985	1990	1995	1980—1990	1985—1995	1980—1996
102.3	114.3	106.8	378.7	329.5	192.6	106.8	7.0	11.9	8.7
103.4	116.2	110.8	459.5	388.1	224.4	110.8	7.1	14.4	9.9
98.7	114.3	102.0	413.4	344.9	203.5	102.0	6.2	14.5	9.4
3.62	130.23	101.97	203940.0	5202.6	2816.9	78.30	53.5	52.1	61.0
4.39	52.87	55.03		5917.2	1253.5	104.1		49.8	
4557.86	4448.31	4435.44	95.6	96.3	97.3	99.7	—0.2	—0.3	—0.3
1714.49	1541.33	1530.20	84.5	89.8	89.3	99.3	—0.6	—1.0	—1.1
580.53	1686.78	1824.19	322.4	204.4	170.1	107.4	6.6	6.6	7.6
3264.15	3286.30	3476.35	143.8	111.2	106.5	105.8	3.0	0.5	2.3
46.42	56.16	53.75	128.6	112.2	115.8	95.7	1.0	17.2	1.6
112.39	159.46	147.50	381.7	135.6	131.2	92.5	11.3	3.9	8.7
22.26	23.37	22.94	445.4	87.1	103.1	98.2	15.8	—1.2	9.8
12.00	18.62	9.22	241.4	126.1	76.8	49.5	12.1	9.8	5.7
158.38	217.82	227.97	212.6	164.1	143.9	104.7	4.0	4.6	4.8
118.25	219.47	245.72	575.3	363.8	207.8	112.0	10.7	12.5	11.6
2764.10	9807.19	11555.60	2124.2	971.9	464.8	118.1	16.4	23.5	21.0
2147.88	6982.46	7919.25	1575.6	788.1	409.6	116.4	14.4	21.1	18.8
1251.95	5815.30	7182.91	6836.7	1966.4	706.2	121.2	25.5	32.1	30.2
190.18	360.40	446.62	655.2	451.3	234.8	123.9	10.8	13.8	12.5
203.01	787.89	795.58	758.6	548.0	391.9	101.0	6.8	18.4	13.5
404.47	700.41	756.87	484.2	322.8	187.1	108.1	10.0	11.6	10.4
2407.79	2650.72	2606.52	154.2	118.8	108.3	98.3	3.6	1.9	2.8
145.90	191.85	184.30	165.1	151.4	126.3	96.1	2.7	4.7	3.2
4.51	12.18	8.93	155.3	209.1	198.0	73.3	—2.4	11.1	2.8
1532.89	3966.42	4040.28	642.1	361.7	263.6	101.9	9.3	13.5	12.3
40.76	102.20	105.94	3249.7	846.2	259.9	103.7	28.7	23.4	24.3
74.82	167.55	163.38	568.1	326.8	218.4	97.5	10.0	12.9	11.5

续表 2

指标		Items		总量指标 1980	1985
建筑业		Construction			
建筑业企业人数	（万人）	Enployment	（10000 persons）	68.18	124.09
建筑业总产值	（亿元）	Gross Output Value	（100000000 yuan）	27.33	82.63
施工房屋面积	（万平方米）	Floor Space of Building Under Construstion	（10000 sq・m）	3189.80	5570.32
竣工房屋面积	（万平方米）	Floor Space of Building Completed	（10000 sq・m）	2296.09	3527.20
交通运输		Transportation			
货运量	（万吨）	Freight Traffic	（10000 tons）	16527	17893
#铁路		Railways		3420	4037
公路		Highways		4427	4797
水运		Waterways		6482	7626
客运量	（万人）	Passenger Traffic	（10000 persons）	31008	49818
#铁路		Railways		3364	4819
公路		Highways		26463	42342
水运		Waterways		4175	2644
港口货物吞吐量	（万吨）	Cargo Handled at Seaports	（10000 tons）	12053	16022
邮电通信业		Postal and Telecommunication Services			
邮电业务计费总量	（亿元）	Business Revenue of PTS	（100000000 yuan）	1.12	1.97
函件	（亿件）	Letters Delivered	（100000000 pieces）	2.00	2.78
订销报刊累计份数	（亿份）	Newspapers and Magazines Distributed Accumulately		9.63	17.06
电话机	（万部）	Telephone	（10000）		43.27
城市		Urban			28.37
农村		Rural			14.90
国内商业		Domestic Trade			
社会消费品零售总额	（亿元）	Total Value of Retail Sales	（100000000 yuan）	122.56	262.57
对外经济贸易和旅游		Foreign Trade and Tourism			
进出口总额	（亿美元）	Total Value of Imports and Exports	（100000000 USD）	9.46	19.47
进口		Imports		0.92	3.89
出口		Exports		8.54	15.58
旅游人数	（万人）	Number of Tourists	（10000 persons）	26.28	50.71
金融保险		Banking and Insurance			
金融机构存款	（亿元）	Deposits of Banking Organization	（10000 yuan）	95.54	247.13
金融机构贷款	（亿元）	Loans of Banking Organization	（10000 yuan）	159.10	387.05
国内保险承保额	（亿元）	Domestic Insurance Value	（10000 yuan）		962.95

Continued 2

Number			速　度　指　标　Speed						
			指　数（1996年为下列各年%）1996 As The Percentage Of Following Years				平　均　增　长　% Average Annual Growth Rate		
1990	1995	1996	1980	1985	1990	1995	1980—1990	1985—1995	1980—1996
124.31	232.94	220.71	323.7	177.9	177.6	94.8	6.2	6.5	7.6
147.23	998.11	1049.42	3839.8	1270.0	712.8	105.1		28.3	
5240.98	16646.14	15672.95	491.3	281.4	299.0	94.2	5.1	11.6	10.5
3307.93	8739.38	8252.13	359.4	234.0	249.5	94.4	3.7	9.5	8.3
51186	81830	84666	512.3	473.2	165.4	103.5	12.0	16.4	10.8
4235	4143	4361	127.5	108.0	103.0	105.3	2.2	0.3	1.5
27904	49578	50571	1142.3	1054.2	181.23	102.00	20.2	26.3	16.4
17695	27161	28819	444.6	377.9	162.9	106.1	10.6	13.5	9.8
48382	84915	91980	296.6	184.6	190.1	108.3	4.6	5.5	7.0
4788	5185	4502	133.8	93.4	94.0	86.8	3.6	0.7	1.8
41850	78947	86801	328.0	205.0	207.4	110.0	4.7	6.4	7.7
1701	623	499	12.0	18.9	29.3	80.1	—8.6	—13.5	—12.4
17002	20177	30622	254.1	191.1	180.1	151.8	3.5	2.3	6.0
4.95	70.79	94.48	8435.7	4795.9	1908.7	133.5	16.0	43.0	31.9
3.30	5.31	5.41	270.5	194.6	163.9	101.9	5.1	6.7	6.4
10.99	18.16	17.68	183.6	103.6	160.9	97.4	1.3	0.6	3.9
89.94	491.98	681.20		1574.3	757.4	138.5		27.5	
63.30	333.90	431.97		1522.6	682.4	129.4		28.0	
26.64	158.08	249.23		1672.7	935.6	157.7		26.6	
515.43	1650.00	1932.89	1577.1	736.1	375.0	116.6	15.5	20.2	18.8
38.97	167.94	202.16	2137.0	1038.3	518.8	120.4	15.2	24.0	21.1
9.47	50.02	70.94	7710.9	1823.7	749.1	141.8	26.3	29.1	31.2
29.50	117.92	131.22	1536.5	842.2	444.8	111.3	13.2	22.4	18.6
72.48	76.77	83.71	318.5	165.1	115.5	109.0	10.7	4.2	7.5
858.54	3500.49	4649.49	4866.5	1881.4	541.6	132.8	24.6	30.4	27.5
1009.04	2875.39	3574.85	2248.3	923.6	354.3	124.3	20.3	22.2	21.5
2667.04	5472.66	5853.14		607.8	219.5	107.0		19.0	

指 标 Items		总量指标 1980	1985
教育、科技、文化	**Education,Science and Technology and Culture**		
教　育	Education		
高等学校在校学生（万人）	Students Enrollment in Institutions of Higher Education (10000 persons)	8.41	11.96
中等专业学校在校学生（万人）	Students Enrollment in Specialized Secondary Schools (10000 persons)	6.11	9.25
普通中学在校学生（万人）	Students Enrollment in Regular Secondary Schools (10000 persons)	320.49	284.73
小学在校学生（万人）	Students Enrollment in Primary Schools (10000 persons)	836.90	677.92
科　技	Science and Technology		
县以上科研机构数（个）	Number of Scientific & Technological Research Institutions of County Level and Above		274
各类专业技术人员（万人）	Scientific and Technical Personnel (10000 persons)	43.87	83.41
文　化	Culture		
图书出版量（亿册）	Books Published (100000000)	2.12	2.67
杂志出版量（万册）	Magazines Issued (10000)	2373	5091
报纸出版量（亿份）	Newspapers Issued (100000000)	2.68	9.33
家庭、生活、环境	**Family,People's Livelihood and Environment**		
家　庭	Family		
家庭总户数（万户）	Total Households (10000 households)	1471.76	1633.62
城镇居民平均每户家庭人口（人）	Average Persons Per Household in Urban Area (persons)	4.20	3.64
农村居民平均每户家庭人口（人）	Average Persons Per Household in Rural Area (persons)	4.90	4.38
居　住	Housing		
城市居民人均居住面积（平方米）	Urban Residents Per Capita Living Space (sq・m)	6.40	7.20
农村居民人均生活用房面积（平方米）	Rural Residents Per Capita Living Space (sq・m)	12.48	16.37

Continued 3

Number			速　度　指　标　Speed						
			指　数（1996年为下列各年%） 1996 As The Percentage Of Following Years				平　均　增　长　% Average Annual Growth Rate		
1990	1995	1996	1980	1985	1990	1995	1980—1990	1985—1995	1980—1996
14.69	20.86	22.06	262.3	184.5	150.2	105.8	5.7	5.7	6.2
13.99	31.87	40.99	670.9	443.1	293.0	128.6	8.6	13.2	12.6
281.97	316.75	323.55	101.0	113.6	114.8	102.2	—1.3	1.1	0.1
612.29	644.77	687.82	82.2	101.5	112.3	106.7	—3.1	—0.5	—1.2
326	337	338		123.4	103.7	100.3		2.1	
158.86	184.97	189.49	431.9	227.2	119.3	102.4	13.7	8.3	9.6
3.44	4.05	4.51	212.7	168.9	131.1	111.4	5.0	4.3	4.8
4107	7005	7062	297.6	138.7	172.0	100.8	5.6	3.2	7.1
8.27	15.95	17.49	652.6	187.5	211.5	109.7	11.9	5.5	12.4
1806.78	2066.09	2014.21	136.9	123.3	111.5	97.5	2.1	2.4	2.0
3.34	3.19	3.18	75.7	87.4	95.2	99.7	—3.3	—1.3	—1.7
4.1	4.0	4.0	81.6	91.3	97.6	100.0	—1.8	—0.9	—1.3
9.06	10.59	10.61	165.8	147.4	117.1	100.2	3.5	3.9	3.2
22.33	25.71	29.60	237.2	180.8	132.6	115.1	6.0	4.6	5.6

续表 4

指　　　　标　　　　Items		总量指标 1980	1985
生　活	People's Livelihood		
城镇居民人均生活费收入（元）	Urban Household Per Capita Income Available for Living (yuan)	433	766
农村居民人均纯收入（元）	Rural Household Per Capita Net Income (yuan)	218	493
城乡居民储蓄存款余额（亿元）	Deposits Balance in Urban and Rural Areas (100000000 yuan)	23.72	99.35
工资和福利	Wage and Welfare		
工资总额（亿元）	Total Wage (100000000 yuan)	41.63	86.17
职工平均工资（元）	Average Wage for Staff (100000000 yuan)	667	1135
职工保险福利费（亿元）	Labor Insurance and Welfare Funds (100000000 yuan)	4.12	11.02
离退休、退职职工保险福利费（亿元）	Labor Insurance and Welfare for Retiree (100000000 yuan)	2.94	9.16
卫　生	Health Care		
卫生机构数（个）	Number of Health Care Organizations	9943	115.5
#医　院	Hospital	2457	2460
床位数（万张）	Number of Hospital Beds (10000)	12.75	14.29
#医　院	Hospital	11.62	12.65
卫生技术人员数（万人）	Number of Medical Technical Personnels (10000 persons)	15.04	18.28
#医　生	Doctors	6.10	7.65
市政建设	Urban Civil Construction		
自来水供应量（亿吨）	Volume of Tap Water Supply (100000000 tons)	4.52	7.66
排水管道长度（公里）	Length of Sewer Pipelines (km)	1650	2277
年末实有道路长度（公里）	Year-end Length of Paved Road (km)	1881	2437
环　境	Environment		
治理污染资金使用额（亿元）	Funds Used for Pollution Treatment (100000000 yuan)	0.91	1.65
安排治理项目（个）	Treatment Projects Arranged (unit)	1412	1615
工业废水处理量（亿吨）	Volume of Industrial Waste Water Treatment (10000 tons)	1.53	5.00
工业粉尘回收量（万吨）	Volume of Industrial Dust Retrieved (10000 tons)		71

Continued 4

Number			速　度　指　标　Speed						
			指　数（1996年为下列各年%）1996 As The Percentage Of Following Years				平　均　增　长　% Average Annual Growth Rate		
1990	1995	1996	1980	1985	1990	1995	1980－1990	1985－1995	1980－1996
1464	4209	4689	1082.9	612.1	320.3	111.4	13.0	18.6	16.1
884	2457	3029	1389.4	614.4	324.7	123.3	15.0	17.4	17.9
470.86	1922.33	2570.28	10835.9	2587.1	545.9	133.7	34.8	34.5	34.0
184.60	541.62	595.72	1431.0	691.3	322.7	110.0	16.1	20.2	18.1
2129	5943	6603	990.0	581.8	310.2	111.1	12.3	18.0	15.4
31.56	63.87	73.41	1781.8	666.2	232.6	114.9	22.6	19.2	19.7
29.37	103.75	127.85	4348.6	1395.7	435.3	123.2	25.9	27.5	26.6
12366	12039	14944	150.3	129.8	120.9	124.1	2.2	0.5	2.6
2491	2534	2617	106.5	106.4	105.1	103.3	0.1	0.3	0.4
16.45	17.46	17.03	133.6	119.2	103.5	97.5	2.6	2.0	1.8
14.54	15.48	15.78	135.8	124.7	108.5	101.9	2.3	2.0	1.9
21.35	24.55	25.02	166.4	136.9	117.2	101.2	3.6	3.0	3.2
9.94	11.22	11.34	185.9	148.2	114.1	101.1	5.0	3.9	4.0
25.67	38.23	34.94	773.0	456.1	136.1	91.4	19.0	17.4	13.6
4099	8262	8860	537.0	389.1	216.2	107.2	9.5	13.8	11.1
5812	8163	8552	454.7	350.9	147.1	104.8	11.9	12.9	9.9
2.48	5.42	4.69	515.4	284.2	189.1	86.5	10.6	12.6	10.8
1382	919	481	34.1	29.8	34.8	52.3	－0.2	－5.5	－6.5
5.92	11.28	13.94	911.1	278.8	235.5	123.6	14.5	8.5	14.8
81	112	211		297.2	260.5	188.4		4.7	

2—2 国民经济和社会发展结构指标
STRUCTURAL INDICATORS OF NATIONAL ECONOMY AND SOCIAL DEVELOPMENT

单位：% (percent)

指标	Items	1980	1985	1990	1996
人口与就业	**Population and Employment**				
人　口	Population				
城乡结构	Urban and Rural Composition				
城　镇	Urban	15.2	25.7	21.5	27.3
乡　村	Rural	84.8	74.3	78.5	72.7
性别结构	Sex				
男	Male	50.6	51.0	50.9	50.8
女	Female	49.4	49.0	49.1	49.2
就　业	Employment				
产业结构	Industrial Structures				
第一产业	Primary Industry	70.4	53.2	48.9	42.5
第二产业	Secondary Industry	19.4	32.7	33.8	34.2
第三产业	Tertiary Industry	10.2	14.1	17.3	23.3
经济类型结构	Structures by Ownership				
国有单位	State-owned	14.2	14.4	15.0	15.8
城镇集体单位	Collective-owned	8.6	9.4	9.1	7.0
其他经济类型单位	Others		0.3	0.6	2.0
城镇私营企业和个体劳动者	Urban Private Enterprises and Industrial Laborers	0.1	0.4	0.7	2.0
乡村劳动者	Village Laborers	77.1	75.7	74.7	72.9
宏观经济	**Macro Economy**				
国民核算	National Accounting				
国内生产总值产业结构	GDP Structures				
第一产业	Primary Industry	29.5	30.0	25.1	16.1
第二产业	Secondary Industry	52.3	52.1	48.9	51.2
第三产业	Tertiary Industry	18.2	17.9	26.0	32.7
国内支出结构	Domestic Expenditures				
总消费	Total Consumption	54.9	54.3	50.6	45.3
居民消费	Personal Consumption	48.4	46.2	42.9	37.0
农　民	Agricultural Resident	32.9	33.7	28.5	21.9
非农民居民	Nonagricultural Resident	15.5	12.4	14.5	15.1
社会消费	Social Consumption	6.5	8.1	7.7	8.4
总投资	Total Investment	30.5	41.6	41.5	46.6
固定资产	Fixed Assets	18.2	29.6	26.4	34.3
存　货	Goods on Stock	12.3	12.0	15.1	12.3
净出口	Net Export	14.6	4.1	7.8	8.1
投　资	Investment				
经济类型结构	Structures by Ownership				
国有单位	State-owned		41.9	37.9	36.3
集体单位	Collective-owned		30.8	21.0	23.9
#农　村	Rural		20.6	15.2	18.1
其他经济单位	Others				25.6
个　体	Individual		27.3	41.1	14.1
#农　村	Rural		26.5	40.1	13.4

续表 1 Continued 1

单位:% (percent)

指 标	Items	1980	1985	1990	1996
资金来源结构	Structures of Finance Sources				
国家预算资金	State Appropriation		9.0	4.2	1.2
国内贷款	Domestic Loans		19.2	12.8	14.5
利用外资	Foreign Investment		2.1	4.5	17.2
自筹资金	Fundraising		33.6	29.9	51.4
其他投资	Others		36.1	48.7	15.7
财 政	Public Finance				
财政支出结构	Structure of Financial Expendicture				
农业支出	Agriculture	22.1	9.1	9.1	6.0
基本建设	Capital Construction	29.9	14.3	5.6	6.8
教 育	Education	14.9	18.3	18.1	21.4
利用外资	Utilization of Foreign Capital				
实际利用外资结构	Structures of Value of Foreign Capital Actually Used				
对外借款	Loans from Abroad		58.8	63.1	4.6
外商直接投资	Direct Investment by Foreigners		12.8	32.2	92.2
外商其他投资	Other Investment by Foreigners		28.4	4.7	3.2
能源生产与消费	Energy Production and Consumption				
能源生产总量结构	Structures of Total Energy Production				
原 煤	Coal		94.7	93.0	91.3
原 油	Crude Oil		4.8	6.6	8.5
天 然 气	Natural Gas		0.3	0.3	0.1
水 电	Hydropower		0.2	0.1	…
产业经济	**Industrial Economy**				
农 业	Agriculture				
农林牧渔业产值结构	Structures of Gross Output Value of FFAF				
农 业	Farming	76.6	69.9	62.4	58.2
林 业	Forestry	1.4	1.6	1.4	1.3
牧 业	Animal Husbandry	19.2	23.1	27.7	27.4
渔 业	Fishery	2.8	5.4	8.5	13.1
工 业	Industry				
乡及以上工业产值结构	Structures of Gross Output Value of Township Level and Above				
按经济类型分	Grouped by Ownership				
国有工业	State-owned	57.3	49.5	44.2	28.3
集体工业	Colletive-owned	32.8	48.3	50.9	50.2
其他经济类型	Others	0.1	2.2	4.9	21.5
按轻重分	Grouped by Light and Heavy Industry				
轻工业	Light Industry	57.3	53.3	54.6	49.1
重工业	Heavy Industry	42.7	46.7	45.4	50.9
农村工业产值结构	Structures of Gross Output Value of Vallage Level and Below				
乡办工业	Village	59.8	54.9	51.3	50.0
村办工业	Village	40.2	39.1	38.3	38.5
村以下办工业	Village Below		6.0	10.4	11.5

续表 2　Continued 2

单位：%　(percent)

指　　标	Items	1980	1985	1990	1996
建 筑 业	Construction				
建筑企业总产值结构	Structures of Gross Output Value of Construction Enterprises				
国有经济	State-owned	15.7	17.3	21.7	36.0
地　　方	Local-owned	15.7	13.2	14.6	30.4
部　　属	Central-owned		4.1	7.1	5.6
城镇集体经济	Colletive-owned	16.1	13.1	20.2	24.2
乡镇企业及其它经济	Rural and Township Industry and Others	68.2	69.6	58.1	39.8
运 输 业	Transportation				
货运量结构	Structures of Freight Traffic Volume				
按运输方式分	By Type				
铁　　路	Railways	20.7	22.6	8.3	5.2
公　　路	Highways	26.8	26.8	54.5	59.7
水　　运	Waterways	39.2	42.6	34.6	34.0
国内商业	Domestic Trade				
社会消费品零售总额结构	Total Retail Sales of Consumer Goods				
国有经济	State-owned	39.6	33.2	33.5	26.5
集体经济	Collective-owned	56.8	51.5	44.7	31.2
联营经济	Joint-owned	0.1	0.1	0.2	0.5
个体经济	Indivial	0.4	10.1	13.6	20.4
其他经济单位	Others	3.1	5.1	8.0	21.4
对外经济贸易和国际旅游	Foreign Trade and International Tourism				
出口商品结构	Structures of Exports				
农副产品	Agricultural and Sideline Products		13.2	7.4	5.9
轻工产品	Light Industrial Products		69.1	69.4	58.4
重工产品	Heavy Industrial Produsts		17.7	23.2	35.7
来华旅游人数结构	Structures of Tourists				
外 国 人	Foreigners		80.4	30.2	65.8
华　　侨	Overseas Chinese		2.0	2.3	2.7
港澳台同胞	Hongkong, Macao and Taiwan Chinese		18.7	67.5	31.5
教育、科技、文化	**Education, Science and Culture**				
教　　育	Education				
在校学生结构	Structures of Student Enrollment				
大 学 生	College and University Students	0.6	1.1	1.2	1.6
中 学 生	Secondary School Students	43.4	46.3	48.6	50.1
小 学 生	Primary School Students	56.0	52.9	50.2	48.3
专任教师结构	Full-time Teachers by Type				
大　　学	College and University	3.4	5.2	5.6	5.1
中　　学	Secondary School	36.3	36.9	39.8	42.6
小　　学	Primary School	60.3	57.9	54.6	52.2
科　　技	Science and Technology				
各类专业技术人员结构	Structures of Scientific & Technical Personnel				

续表 3 Continued 3

单位:% (percent)

指 标 Items		1980	1985	1990	1996
工程技术人员	Engineering	22.0	24.8	20.0	23.7
农业技术人员	Agriculture	2.6	2.1	1.5	1.9
科学研究人员	Scientific Research	3.4	1.9	1.2	1.0
卫生技术人员	Health Care	20.6	16.0	8.7	11.5
教学人员	Teaching	39.0	43.0	28.0	31.2
家庭、生活、环境	**Family,People's Livelihood and Environment**				
家　庭	Family				
家庭户结构	Structures of Members of Household				
一代户	A Married Couple			7.4	5.3
二代户	Two Generation			12.4	15.9
三代及以上户	Three Generation and Oveer			80.2	78.8
生　活	People's Livelihood				
城镇居民消费结构	Structures of Urban Household Consumption				
食品类	Food	55.1	52.5	55.5	51.0
衣着类	Clothing	17.1	16.1	13.2	12.0
用品及其他	Daily Use Article and Others	16.1	21.3	24.9	29.5
居　住	Residence	11.7	10.1	6.4	7.5
农村居民消费结构	Structures of Rural Household Consumption				
食品类	Food	58.0	52.1	52.3	51.2
衣着类	Clothing	12.5	9.0	7.4	6.9
用品及其他	Daily Use Article and Others	17.1	10.1	15.8	25.0
居　住	Residence	12.4	19.6	24.5	16.9
福　利	Social Welfare				
职工保险福利费结构	Structures of Staff Insurance and Welfare				
国有单位	State-owned	73.7	71.5	72.3	74.1
城镇集体单位	Urban Colletive-owned	26.3	28.5	25.0	17.5
其他单位	Others			2.7	8.4
离退休人员结构	Structures of Retired Staff and workers				
国有单位	State-owned	69.3	62.2	64.9	69.7
城镇集体单位	Urban Colletive-owned	30.7	37.3	33.3	25.4
其他单位	Others		0.5	1.8	4.9
卫　生	Health Care				
医生结构	Doctors by Type				
中　医	Doctors of Traditional Chinese Medicine	23.3	19.3	15.1	13.5
西医师	Doctors of Western Medicine	40.2	46.4	63.3	65.8
西医士	Junior Doctors of Western Medicine	36.5	34.2	21.6	20.7
医院床位结构	Hospital Beds by Structures				
县以上医院	Hospitals at County Level and Above	47.2	53.0	57.2	58.5
环境、灾害	Environment, Disaster				
治理污染资金使用结构	Uses of Funds in Pollution Treatment				
治理废水	Waste Water Treatment			57.7	40.5
治理废气	Waste Gas Treatment			25.7	40.1
治理固体废物	Waste Residue Treatment			9.6	3.8
治理噪声	Noise Abatement			2.1	9.8
其　他	Others			4.9	5.8

2—3 江　苏　的　一　天
ONE DAY IN JIANGSU

指　标	Items	1980	1985	1990	1996
全省每天创造的财富	**Daily Production**				
国内生产总值　(亿元)	Gross Domestic Product (100000000 yuan)	0.88	1.79	3.88	16.45
工农业总产值　(亿元)	Gross Output Value of Industry and Agriculture (100000000 yuan)	1.66	3.63	9.16	36.66
农业总产值	Gross Output Value of Agriculture	0.38	0.79	1.59	5.00
工业总产值	Gross Output Value of Industry	1.28	2.84	7.57	31.66
财政收入　(亿元)	Financial Revenue (100000000 yuan)	1736	2438	3732	11726
钢　(万吨)	Steel (10000 tons)	0.19	0.27	0.52	1.22
成品钢材　(万吨)	Rolled Steel (10000 tons)	0.29	0.40	0.56	2.18
发电量　(亿千瓦小时)	Electricity (100000000 Kwh)	0.43	0.64	1.11	2.07
原煤　(万吨)	Coal (10000 tons)	4.63	6.01	6.60	7.14
水泥　(万吨)	Cement (10000 tons)	1.72	3.06	4.20	11.1
布　(万米)	Cloth (10000 m)	492	577	792	947
机制纸及纸板　(吨)	Machine-Made Paper and Paperboards (tonss)	788	1370	2050	4476
全省每天消费量	**Daily Consumption**				
城乡居民消费额(万元)	Consumption of Urban and Rural Residents (10000 yuan)	4239	8243	16665	60786
平均每人消费额　(元)	Per Capita Consumption (yuan)	0.72	1.33	2.48	8.58
城镇居民每人生活费支出　(元)	Per Capita Living Expenditure of Urban Residents (yuan)	1.19	1.97	3.67	11.12
#食品消费	Food Consumption	0.66	1.04	2.04	5.67
农民每人生活消费支出　(元)	Per Capita Living Expenditure of Rural Residents (yuan)	0.53	1.14	2.16	6.62
#食品消费	Food Consumption	0.31	0.59	1.13	3.39
社会消费品零售总额　(亿元)	Total Retail Sales of Consumption Goods (100000000 yuan)	0.34	0.72	1.41	5.30
每天其他经济活动	**Other Daily Economic Activities**				
货物运输量　(万吨)	Freight Traffic (10000 tons)	45.27	4902	140.24	231.96
旅客运输量　(万人)	Passenger Traffic (10000 persons)	84.95	136.49	132.55	252.00
房屋建筑竣工面积　(万平方米)	Floor Space Completed of Buildings (10000 sq·m)	2.90	25.33	32.14	35.00
#住宅竣工面积	Floor Space Completed of Residential Housing	1.41	19.51	27.97	25.73
出版报纸　(万份)	Newspaper Published (10000 copies)	73	256	227	479
邮寄函件　(万件)	Letters Delivered (10000 pieces)	55	76	90	148
每天人口变动和婚姻	**Daily Population Changes and Marriages**				
出生人数　(人)	Births (persons)	2381	1839	3780	2352
死亡人数　(人)	Deaths (persons)	1065	996	1202	1278
结婚对数　(对)	Marriages (couples)	1085	1178	1432	1499
离婚对数　(对)	Divorces (couples)	33	38	78	129

注：国内生产总值、工业、农业总产值均按当年价格计算(下同)。

Note: Gross domestic produst, output value of industry and agriculture are counted by current price (so does the following).

2—4 江苏国民经济占全国的比重(1996)
PERCENTAGE OF JIANGSU'S NATIONAL ECONOMY IN THE COUNTRY

指标	Items	全国 Country	江苏 Jiangsu	江苏占全国的比重(%) Percentage in the Country of Jiangsu
年末总人口 (万人)	Year-end Total Population (10000 persons)	122389	7110.16	5.8
国内生产总值 (亿元)	Domestic Gross Products (100000000 yuan)	67795	6004.21	8.9
第一产业	Primary Industry	13550	965.29	7.1
第二产业	Secondary Industry	33148	3074.12	9.3
第三产业	Tertiary Industry	21097	1964.80	9.3
全社会固定资产投资 (亿元)	Total Investment in Fixed Assets (100000000 yuan)	23660	1949.53	8.2
#基本建设	Capital Construction	8399	481.07	5.7
更新改造	Technical Updates and Transformation	3745	238.23	6.4
社会消费品零售总额 (亿元)	Total Retail Sales of Consumer Goods (100000000 yuan)	24614	1932.89	7.9
对外贸易进出口总额 (亿美元)	Total Value of Imports and Exports (100000000 USD)	2899	206.88	7.1
#出口总额	Exports	1511	116.01	7.7
实际利用外资 (亿美元)	Value of Foreign Capital Used (100000000 USD)	552.7	55.03	10.0
普通高等学校在校学生数 (万人)	Students Enrollment in Institutions of High Education (10000 persons)	302	22.06	7.3
医院病床数 (万张)	Hospital Beds (10000)	287	15.78	5.5
卫生技术人员 (万人)	Medical Technical Personnel (10000 persons)	431	25.02	5.8
#医生	Doctors	138	11.34	8.2
全部职工平均工资 (元)	Average Wage of Total Staff and Workers (yuan)	6210	6603	
农民人均纯收入 (元)	Per Capita Net Income of Rural Residents (yuan)	1926	3029	
城镇居民年平均生活费收入 (元)	Annual Per Capita Income Available for Living of Urban Residents (yuan)	4377	4689	
城乡居民储蓄存款余额 (亿元)	Savings Deposit Balance of Urban and Rural Residents (100000000 yuan)	38521	2570.28	6.7
工农业主要产品产量 (万吨)	Output of Major Industrial Products and Agricultural Products (10000 tons)			
粮食	Grain	49000	3476.35	7.1
棉花	Cotton	420	53.75	12.8
油料	Oil-Bearing Crops	2200	147.50	6.7
猪、牛、羊肉	Pork, Beaf and Mutton	4760	227.97	4.8
钢	Steel	10110	446.62	4.4
成品钢材	Rolled-steel	8611	795.58	9.2
原煤	Coal	137481	2606.52	1.9
发电量 (亿千瓦小时)	Electricity (Kmh)	10750	756.87	7.0
水泥	Cement	49000	4040.28	8.2
农用化肥(折100%)	Chemical Fertilizers (convert into 100 %)	2660	184.30	6.9
化学纤维	Chemical Fibers	334.39	105.94	31.7
布 (亿米)	Cloth (10000000 m)	221.20	34.55	15.6
机制纸及纸板	Machine-Made Paper and Paperboard	2094.15	163.38	7.8
家用电冰箱 (万台)	Household Refrigerators (10000)	928.22	20.71	2.2
电视机 (万台)	Television Sets (10000)	3077.01	410.54	13.3

注:外贸进出口总额为海关数。
Note: The data of total value of imports and exports by foreign trade are from the Customs.

2—5 全省人均国民经济主要指标
MAJOR PER CAPITA INDICATORS OF JIANGSU NATIONAL ECONOMY

指标	Items	1980	1985	1990	1996
国内生产总值 （元）	Gross Domestic Products (yuan)	541	1053	2109	8471
工农业总产值 （元）	Gross Output Value of Industry and Agriculture (yuan)	1025	2140	4980	18876
农业产值	Output Value of Agriculture	234	466	864	2574
工业产值	Output Value of Industry	791	1674	4115	16303
财政收入 （元）	Financial Revenue (yuan)	107	144	200	604
财政支出 （元）	Financial Expenditures (yuan)	49	82	148	439
全社会固定资产投资额 （元）	Total Value of Investment in Fixed Assets (yuan)	59	310	530	2750
# 基本建设	Capital Construction	44	76	111	679
更新改造	Technical Updates and Tranformation	9	40	62	336
城镇集体	Rural Collective	5	32	31	112
农民人均纯收入 （元）	Per Capita Net Income of Rural Residents (yuan)	218	493	884	3029
城镇居民年均生活费收入 （元）	Annual Per Capita Income Available for Living of Urban Residents (yuan)	433	766	1464	4689
年末城乡居民储蓄存款 （元）	Year-end Savings Deposit of Urban and Rural Residents (yuan)	40	160	696	3615
社会消费品零售额 （元）	Total Retail Sales of Consumer Goods (yuan)	207	424	767	2727
外贸自营出口总额 （美元）	Total Value of Exports of Foreign Trade by Self-management (USD)	14	25	44	185
高等学校在校学生数 （人/万人）	Student Enrollment in Institution of Higher Education (person/10000 persons)	14	19	22	31
年末医院病床数（张/万人）	Year-end Hospital Beds (bed/10000 persons)	20	20	21	22
年末卫生技术人员数 （人/万人）	Year-end Medical Technical Personnel (person/10000 persons)	25	29	32	35
# 医　生	Doctors	10	12	15	16
主要工农业产品产量 （公斤）	Output of Major Industrial and Agricultural Products (kg)				
粮　食	Grain	409	505	486	490
棉　花	Cotton	7	8	7	8
油　料	Oil-Bearing Crops	7	18	17	21
钢	Steel	12	16	28	63
原　煤	Coal	286	354	358	368
发电量 （千瓦小时）	Electricity (Kwh)	264	379	602	1068

2—6 历年总产出
TOTAL OUTPUT OVER THE YEARS

本表按当年价格计算 (At current prices)

年份 Year	总产出(亿元) Total Output (100000000 yuan)	第一产业 Primary Industry	第二产业 Secondary Industry	#工业 Industry	第三产业 Tertiary Industry	#商业 Commerce
1952	81.54	31.87	27.19	25.53	22.48	11.12
1953	92.06	32.31	32.51	29.81	27.24	12.43
1954	94.00	32.45	34.81	31.66	26.74	12.76
1955	100.53	36.22	35.77	32.82	28.54	12.94
1956	107.08	33.60	41.43	38.60	32.05	14.93
1957	114.15	36.81	44.63	41.01	32.71	15.08
1958	158.03	38.74	82.66	75.22	36.63	13.89
1959	182.82	37.35	104.12	96.00	41.35	15.16
1960	188.33	36.76	110.66	100.32	40.91	12.93
1961	140.88	35.73	67.20	62.50	37.95	15.06
1962	133.12	40.15	56.38	53.36	36.59	12.90
1963	141.37	46.77	58.36	54.66	36.24	12.77
1964	166.61	56.62	72.53	68.17	37.46	12.71
1965	192.52	57.27	97.49	88.08	37.76	14.60
1966	224.09	66.08	115.05	104.19	42.96	15.67
1967	196.39	61.19	93.06	84.80	42.14	14.66
1968	202.00	65.38	93.28	85.48	43.34	15.86
1969	228.23	65.60	114.59	102.80	48.04	16.86
1970	273.85	71.33	149.65	135.47	52.87	18.23
1971	320.40	79.90	184.61	167.15	55.89	19.56
1972	342.65	83.24	202.18	183.38	57.23	20.57
1973	377.87	89.71	227.95	208.10	60.21	20.87
1974	377.82	89.88	227.00	205.39	60.94	21.35
1975	412.28	91.66	260.23	235.28	60.39	21.03
1976	438.59	100.71	271.19	247.59	66.69	21.21
1977	487.98	89.16	326.37	297.12	72.45	22.33
1978	566.85	105.87	378.99	337.65	81.99	22.39
1979	661.26	145.25	427.36	386.05	88.65	29.12
1980	750.12	138.45	515.71	467.82	95.96	32.37
1981	816.27	153.62	557.41	504.94	105.24	34.47
1982	897.85	188.11	593.52	534.87	116.22	35.47
1983	1014.55	206.86	679.67	600.70	128.02	43.11
1984	1239.44	253.82	836.02	745.36	149.60	52.99
1985	1642.70	288.55	1157.52	1036.67	196.63	62.44
1986	1960.44	332.66	1380.16	1235.38	247.62	75.83
1987	2472.22	380.25	1771.85	1590.31	320.12	113.59
1988	3409.56	497.95	2370.81	2152.93	540.80	220.49
1989	3839.67	522.25	2713.50	2507.42	603.92	218.49
1990	4208.23	580.53	2978.51	2764.10	649.19	219.68
1991	4820.22	580.93	3416.59	3161.60	822.70	300.50
1992	6862.87	673.82	5089.59	4673.57	1099.46	415.46
1993	10245.27	875.37	7757.28	7096.46	1612.62	634.18
1994	14163.89	1335.23	10601.01	9826.50	2227.65	816.07
1995	17699.96	1686.78	13053.11	11995.30	2960.07	1104.21
1996	20304.53	1907.54	14764.02	13425.15	3632.97	1331.32

2—7 历年总产出指数
INDICES OF TOTAL OUTPUT OVER THE YEARS

按可比价格计算，1952＝100 （At comparable price 1952＝100）

年份 Year	总产出 Total Output	第一产业 Primary Industry	第二产业 Secondary Industry	#工业 Industry	第三产业 Tertiary Industry	#商业 Commerce
1952	100.0	100.0	100.0	100.0	100.0	100.0
1953	109.5	100.9	121.9	117.6	117.5	108.3
1954	111.1	101.6	132.4	126.5	114.7	110.6
1955	120.1	113.0	134.3	129.7	123.6	113.3
1956	124.7	105.5	162.2	162.2	135.4	127.4
1957	127.0	109.1	169.4	165.9	132.1	123.1
1958	144.9	111.0	271.7	264.1	121.8	93.4
1959	162.3	103.6	366.6	367.9	133.2	98.7
1960	165.1	95.3	407.9	403.4	130.1	83.1
1961	132.6	92.4	247.9	251.5	129.6	103.9
1962	121.8	93.4	200.8	208.5	121.4	86.5
1963	134.4	111.6	211.0	215.5	125.0	89.0
1964	156.4	132.2	264.8	272.3	127.6	87.5
1965	181.6	139.7	372.6	365.0	129.2	101.0
1966	214.9	162.8	452.8	445.8	149.4	110.2
1967	192.9	150.4	371.3	368.1	150.1	105.5
1968	198.1	155.5	378.8	379.1	154.2	114.1
1969	221.5	154.3	482.0	472.5	169.1	120.0
1970	263.7	166.3	653.9	651.2	179.4	129.6
1971	307.3	184.5	808.3	806.5	194.4	137.5
1972	326.4	189.5	889.1	890.0	197.7	143.7
1973	358.3	202.2	1006.2	1015.7	207.1	145.1
1974	360.1	202.5	1009.4	1009.0	210.7	149.2
1975	390.0	204.4	1164.8	1165.2	207.2	145.9
1976	420.8	212.3	1267.0	1285.1	232.1	149.2
1977	463.9	191.0	1524.5	1543.0	249.8	157.0
1978	544.0	232.1	1776.6	1755.8	285.4	157.6
1979	598.9	257.4	1983.5	2000.3	291.2	193.4
1980	671.6	243.2	2380.5	2417.9	304.9	213.6
1981	732.4	262.4	2589.9	2618.8	342.2	229.5
1982	802.5	301.5	2796.8	2820.2	376.6	234.2
1983	908.5	319.4	3242.2	3211.5	415.6	284.8
1984	1090.8	371.9	3955.8	3959.1	477.5	342.1
1985	1379.6	383.5	5250.3	5280.7	599.0	384.3
1986	1595.5	407.5	6115.4	6161.6	731.7	446.8
1987	1912.0	420.2	7474.4	7631.1	906.9	650.5
1988	2399.8	448.1	9385.3	9590.3	1288.2	1153.4
1989	2492.6	449.6	9671.7	10036.5	1422.0	1039.8
1990	2697.8	460.9	10591.2	11042.5	1502.8	1033.3
1991	3052.3	455.7	12113.2	12642.6	1807.1	1356.6
1992	4303.5	515.0	18047.4	18865.3	2272.1	1786.3
1993	5829.5	573.2	25275.4	26796.3	2888.1	2362.6
1994	7479.3	642.4	33358.5	35832.0	3354.2	2502.0
1995	8885.4	730.4	39896.8	42819.2	3904.3	2962.4
1996	10211.3	803.0	46066.3	49214.0	4471.7	3325.8

2—8 历年国内生产总值
GROSS DOMESTIC PRODUCTS OVER THE YEARS

本表按当年价格计算　　　　(At current prices)

年份 Year	国内生产总值(亿元) Gross Domestic Products (100000000 yuan)	第一产业 Primary Industry	第二产业 Secondary Industry	#工业 Industry	第三产业 Tertiary Industry	#商业 Commerce	人均国内生产总值(元/人) Per Capita GDP (yuan)
1952	48.41	25.49	8.53	7.63	14.39	7.14	131
1953	53.42	25.86	10.26	9.21	17.30	8.48	141
1954	53.77	25.81	10.98	9.84	16.98	8.10	140
1955	58.96	29.69	11.29	10.06	17.98	8.61	150
1956	61.90	27.76	13.79	12.44	20.35	9.73	153
1957	65.11	29.94	14.40	12.51	20.77	9.72	157
1958	75.30	29.05	23.17	21.29	23.08	9.54	178
1959	79.62	25.79	27.57	25.30	26.26	10.61	186
1960	86.80	25.68	35.96	33.12	25.16	9.61	203
1961	72.20	25.78	22.89	21.20	23.53	10.14	170
1962	69.20	29.10	17.34	15.69	22.76	9.65	161
1963	75.52	35.27	18.14	16.35	22.11	9.28	172
1964	89.55	42.50	24.01	22.18	23.04	9.58	200
1965	95.10	41.20	30.26	26.87	23.64	9.29	208
1966	109.89	47.53	35.51	32.25	26.85	10.58	235
1967	99.20	44.13	29.53	26.64	25.54	10.52	206
1968	102.84	47.04	29.45	26.95	26.35	10.82	209
1969	111.75	47.22	35.42	31.89	29.11	11.86	221
1970	129.23	51.03	46.16	42.33	32.04	12.88	249
1971	148.04	57.24	56.43	51.73	34.37	13.76	279
1972	157.31	60.20	61.74	56.83	35.37	14.00	291
1973	170.93	64.74	69.28	64.02	36.91	14.70	312
1974	171.94	65.50	69.45	63.57	36.99	14.95	311
1975	184.16	67.59	79.61	72.70	36.96	14.15	329
1976	187.97	62.38	85.04	78.48	40.55	15.48	332
1977	202.40	53.22	105.35	97.15	43.83	16.00	353
1978	249.24	68.71	131.09	117.10	49.44	13.63	430
1979	298.55	104.04	141.14	126.25	53.37	17.64	509
1980	319.80	94.24	167.41	151.22	58.15	18.04	541
1981	350.02	109.39	178.01	161.11	62.62	19.24	586
1982	390.17	135.15	185.52	168.09	69.50	20.84	645
1983	437.65	150.41	210.81	191.52	76.43	23.86	716
1984	518.85	179.00	250.39	228.58	89.46	29.66	843
1985	651.82	195.66	339.56	307.89	116.60	32.98	1053
1986	744.94	224.26	376.32	337.77	144.36	40.09	1193
1987	922.33	246.86	493.69	443.23	181.78	61.60	1462
1988	1208.85	319.18	586.82	526.92	302.85	103.63	1891
1989	1321.85	324.18	657.06	599.91	340.61	102.69	2038
1990	1416.50	355.17	692.59	634.13	368.74	103.25	2103
1991	1601.38	345.14	793.92	725.83	462.32	140.27	2347
1992	2136.02	393.82	1119.26	1017.94	622.94	201.91	3097
1993	2998.16	490.59	1598.05	1451.97	909.52	308.21	4308
1994	4057.39	671.94	2186.77	2002.22	1198.68	389.41	5785
1995	5155.25	848.35	2715.26	2467.63	1591.64	516.89	7299
1996	6004.21	965.29	3074.12	2754.80	1964.80	621.01	8447

2—9 历年国内生产总值指数

INDICES OF GROSS DOMESTIC PRODUCTS OVER THE YEARS

按可比价格计算,1952=100 (At comparable price 1952=100)

年份 Year	国内生产总值 Gross Domestic Product	第一产业 Primary Industry	第二产业 Secondary Industry	#工业 Industry	第三产业 Tertiary Industry	#商业 Commerce	人均国内生产总值 Per Capita GDP
1952	100.0	100.0	100.0	100.0	100.0	100.0	100.0
1953	106.9	101.0	121.0	119.0	116.6	115.2	104.4
1954	107.0	101.0	131.2	129.5	113.7	109.4	102.5
1955	118.9	115.9	133.5	132.0	121.6	117.4	111.3
1956	121.4	109.0	173.4	173.8	134.2	129.4	110.8
1957	121.9	111.0	174.3	166.0	131.0	123.6	108.8
1958	120.4	104.0	243.4	237.5	119.8	99.9	105.4
1959	120.6	89.4	316.0	325.3	132.1	107.6	103.9
1960	124.9	83.3	432.6	456.8	125.0	96.3	107.8
1961	111.4	83.4	275.5	291.5	125.5	109.0	97.1
1962	103.8	84.6	202.6	212.1	118.0	100.9	89.2
1963	118.4	105.2	213.8	220.5	119.1	100.8	99.5
1964	137.8	124.0	286.8	307.5	122.5	102.7	113.7
1965	147.6	125.6	375.0	371.4	126.4	100.1	119.1
1966	173.1	146.4	454.2	454.1	145.9	115.9	136.3
1967	158.9	135.7	383.1	377.1	142.0	118.0	122.1
1968	163.4	139.8	390.1	392.2	146.3	121.1	122.5
1969	174.8	138.9	486.1	488.6	159.9	131.3	127.5
1970	200.9	148.7	663.6	671.7	176.0	142.6	143.1
1971	227.6	165.2	814.3	827.8	186.8	150.8	158.3
1972	239.8	171.3	896.2	921.2	190.9	152.3	163.7
1973	259.0	182.4	1011.4	1049.5	198.3	159.3	174.5
1974	261.5	184.5	1020.4	1038.8	199.7	162.8	174.5
1975	277.5	188.4	1179.3	1216.2	198.1	152.9	182.8
1976	280.3	164.4	1320.2	1382.9	220.4	169.8	182.3
1977	297.9	142.6	1636.2	1711.7	236.0	173.8	191.7
1978	371.4	188.3	2038.8	2110.7	268.8	149.5	236.3
1979	415.9	231.3	2183.9	2279.2	284.1	189.5	261.8
1980	436.0	207.0	2580.8	2729.0	288.6	180.6	272.1
1981	483.3	233.6	2767.9	2928.1	340.3	210.8	298.5
1982	530.9	270.9	2928.6	3107.3	375.8	227.2	324.0
1983	595.1	290.3	3376.3	3596.3	426.7	268.7	359.8
1984	689.8	327.9	3890.4	4121.0	489.1	302.2	413.7
1985	809.2	325.1	5097.1	5418.5	577.6	329.5	482.4
1986	893.1	342.5	5587.5	5894.1	689.3	386.1	527.9
1987	1013.2	344.1	6598.9	6914.9	804.3	549.8	592.7
1988	1211.6	359.1	7772.8	8173.8	1126.7	777.6	699.5
1989	1241.7	348.9	7807.8	8344.1	1252.4	761.7	706.4
1990	1303.9	352.5	8228.5	8838.6	1339.1	756.9	714.2
1991	1412.2	338.6	8964.1	9617.3	1592.9	958.6	763.4
1992	1773.5	374.7	11823.6	12584.2	2010.0	1325.6	948.4
1993	2124.5	384.2	14583.3	15501.2	2515.3	1762.7	1126.4
1994	2475.5	404.3	17841.2	19044.8	2801.8	1860.5	1302.4
1995	2856.7	459.3	20713.6	21977.7	3219.3	2143.3	1492.6
1996	3205.3	494.9	23261.9	24389.2	3681.1	2397.1	1664.2

2—10 历年国内生产总值构成
COMPOSITION OF GROSS DOMESTIC PRODUCTS OVER THE YEARS

本表按当年价格计算 (At current prices)

年份 Year	国内生产总值 Gross Domestic Product	第一产业 Primary Industry	第二产业 Secondary Industry	#工业 Industry	第三产业 Tertiary Industry	#商业 Commerce
1952	100.0	52.7	17.6	15.8	29.7	14.7
1953	100.0	48.4	19.2	17.2	32.4	15.9
1954	100.0	48.0	20.4	18.3	31.6	15.1
1955	100.0	50.4	19.1	17.1	30.5	14.6
1956	100.0	44.8	22.3	20.1	32.9	15.7
1957	100.0	46.0	22.1	19.2	31.9	14.9
1958	100.0	38.6	30.7	28.3	30.7	12.7
1959	100.0	32.4	34.6	31.8	33.0	13.3
1960	100.0	29.6	41.4	38.2	29.0	11.1
1961	100.0	35.7	31.7	29.4	32.6	14.0
1962	100.0	42.1	25.0	22.7	32.9	13.9
1963	100.0	46.7	24.0	21.6	29.3	12.3
1964	100.0	47.5	26.8	24.8	25.7	10.7
1965	100.0	43.3	31.8	28.3	24.9	9.8
1966	100.0	43.3	32.3	29.3	24.4	9.6
1967	100.0	44.5	29.8	26.9	25.7	10.6
1968	100.0	45.8	28.6	26.2	25.6	10.5
1969	100.0	42.3	31.7	28.5	26.0	10.6
1970	100.0	39.5	35.7	32.8	24.8	10.0
1971	100.0	38.7	38.1	34.9	23.2	9.3
1972	100.0	38.3	39.2	36.1	22.5	8.9
1973	100.0	37.9	40.5	37.5	21.6	8.6
1974	100.0	38.1	40.4	37.0	21.5	8.7
1975	100.0	36.7	43.2	39.5	20.1	7.7
1976	100.0	33.2	45.2	41.8	21.6	8.2
1977	100.0	26.3	52.0	48.0	21.7	7.9
1978	100.0	27.6	52.6	47.0	19.8	5.5
1979	100.0	34.8	47.3	42.3	17.9	5.9
1980	100.0	29.5	52.3	47.3	18.2	5.6
1981	100.0	31.3	50.8	46.0	17.9	5.5
1982	100.0	34.6	47.6	43.1	17.8	5.3
1983	100.0	34.4	48.2	43.8	17.4	5.5
1984	100.0	34.5	48.3	44.1	17.2	5.7
1985	100.0	30.0	52.1	47.2	17.9	5.1
1986	100.0	30.1	50.5	45.3	19.4	5.4
1987	100.0	26.8	53.5	48.1	19.7	6.7
1988	100.0	26.4	48.5	43.6	25.1	8.6
1989	100.0	24.5	49.7	45.4	25.8	7.8
1990	100.0	25.1	48.9	44.8	26.0	7.3
1991	100.0	21.5	49.6	45.3	28.9	8.8
1992	100.0	18.4	52.4	47.7	29.2	9.5
1993	100.0	16.4	53.3	48.4	30.3	10.3
1994	100.0	16.6	53.9	49.3	29.5	9.6
1995	100.0	16.4	52.7	47.9	30.9	10.0
1996	100.0	16.1	51.2	45.9	32.7	10.3

2—11 分行业国内生产总值
GROSS DOMESTIC PRODUCTS BY SECTOR

本表按当年价格计算 (At current prices)

年份 Year	国内生产总值(亿元) Gross Domestic Product (100000000 yuan)	第一产业 Primary Industry	第二产业 Secondary Industry	工业 Industry	建筑业 Construction	第三产业 Tertiary Industry	运输邮电业 Transportation Postal and Telecommunication Services	商业 Commerce
1978	249.24	68.71	131.09	117.10	13.99	49.44	6.85	13.63
1979	298.55	104.04	141.14	126.25	14.89	53.37	7.19	17.64
1980	319.80	94.24	167.41	151.22	16.19	58.15	8.10	18.04
1981	350.02	109.39	178.01	161.11	16.90	62.62	9.14	19.24
1982	390.17	135.15	185.52	168.09	17.43	69.50	10.48	20.84
1983	437.65	150.41	210.81	191.52	19.29	76.43	12.36	23.86
1984	518.85	179.00	250.39	228.58	21.81	89.46	16.67	29.66
1985	651.82	195.66	339.56	307.89	31.67	116.60	26.07	32.98
1986	744.94	224.26	376.32	337.77	38.55	144.36	33.67	40.09
1987	922.33	246.86	493.69	443.23	50.46	181.78	43.25	61.60
1988	1208.85	319.18	586.82	526.92	59.90	302.85	59.62	103.63
1989	1321.85	324.18	657.06	599.91	57.15	340.61	62.66	102.69
1990	1416.50	355.17	692.59	634.13	58.46	368.74	63.64	103.25
1991	1601.38	345.14	793.92	725.83	68.09	462.32	80.27	140.27
1992	2136.02	393.82	1119.26	1017.94	101.32	622.94	100.55	201.91
1993	2998.16	490.59	1598.05	1451.97	146.08	909.52	144.11	308.21
1994	4057.39	671.94	2186.77	2002.22	184.55	1198.68	187.19	389.41
1995	5155.25	848.35	2715.26	2467.63	247.63	1591.64	253.52	516.89
1996	6004.21	965.29	3074.12	2754.80	319.32	1964.80	314.91	621.01

续表 Continue

年份 Year	金融保险业 Banking and Insurance	房地产业 Real Estate Management	社会服务业 Social Services	卫生体育社会福利业 Health Care, Sports and Social Welfare	教育文艺广播电影电视业 Education, Culture, Art, Radio Film and Television	科学研究综合技术服务业 Scientific Research and Polytechnical Services	国家政党机关社会团体 Government Agencies, Party and Social Organizations	其他 Others
1978	10.43	5.50	2.89	1.44	4.65	1.45	2.60	
1979	10.27	5.42	2.85	1.42	4.59	1.42	2.57	
1980	11.52	6.08	3.20	1.60	5.13	1.60	2.88	
1981	12.32	6.50	3.42	1.71	5.51	1.70	3.08	
1982	13.74	7.25	3.81	1.91	6.14	1.90	3.43	
1983	14.47	7.64	4.02	2.01	6.45	2.00	3.62	
1984	15.52	8.19	4.30	2.15	6.94	2.15	3.88	
1985	18.91	11.93	5.47	2.92	9.73	2.69	5.90	
1986	25.56	13.50	6.73	3.69	11.44	3.30	6.29	
1987	25.14	14.59	7.79	3.98	14.06	5.10	6.27	
1988	47.44	21.25	16.91	8.42	19.17	7.81	18.60	
1989	65.45	24.72	16.69	10.00	21.92	8.97	27.51	
1990	72.53	27.02	19.88	11.66	24.79	11.09	34.88	
1991	77.81	33.51	25.96	13.92	28.89	14.06	40.90	6.73
1992	109.27	43.89	35.79	17.74	35.49	17.92	51.05	9.33
1993	144.81	74.56	59.79	25.43	45.68	24.75	70.26	11.92
1994	200.34	99.26	82.36	33.53	65.37	34.42	97.79	9.01
1995	270.50	143.61	102.98	44.16	88.37	47.50	112.12	11.99
1996	333.51	194.24	131.81	54.99	106.92	58.53	134.25	14.63

2—12 分行业国内总生产总值指数
INDICES OF GROSS DOMESTIC PRODUCTS BY SECTOR

按可比价格计算，1978=100　　(At comparable price 1978=100)

年份 Year	国内生产总值 Gross Domestic Product	第一产业 Primary Industry	第二产业 Secondary Industry	工业 Industry	建筑业 Construction	第三产业 Tertiary Industry	运输邮电业 Transportation Postal and Telecommunication Services	商业 Commerce
1978	100.0	100.0	100.0	100.0	100.0	100.0	100.0	100.0
1979	112.0	122.9	107.1	108.0	100.4	105.7	102.8	126.7
1980	117.4	109.9	126.6	129.3	105.6	107.3	108.0	120.8
1981	130.2	124.1	135.8	138.7	112.8	126.6	133.5	141.0
1982	143.0	143.9	143.6	147.2	116.0	139.8	152.3	151.9
1983	160.5	154.2	165.6	170.4	128.6	158.7	185.5	179.7
1984	185.8	174.1	195.2	195.3	195.1	181.9	226.3	202.1
1985	217.9	172.7	250.0	256.7	198.0	214.8	346.9	220.3
1986	240.5	181.9	274.1	279.3	233.9	256.4	433.1	258.2
1987	272.8	182.8	323.7	327.6	293.1	299.2	514.1	367.6
1988	326.3	190.7	381.2	387.3	334.6	419.1	595.9	520.0
1989	334.4	185.3	383.0	395.3	287.2	465.9	619.2	509.3
1990	351.1	187.2	403.6	418.8	286.2	498.1	619.9	506.1
1991	380.3	179.8	439.7	455.6	316.1	592.5	725.1	641.0
1992	477.6	199.0	579.9	596.2	453.4	747.7	850.6	886.4
1993	572.1	204.1	715.3	734.4	566.5	935.6	1099.5	1178.6
1994	666.6	214.7	875.1	902.3	661.0	1042.2	1355.5	1244.0
1995	769.3	243.9	1016.0	1041.3	826.9	1197.5	1562.9	1433.1
1996	863.2	262.8	1141.0	1155.6	1044.5	1369.3	1855.8	1602.8

续表 Continue

年份 Year	金融保险业 Banking and Insurance	房地产业 Real Estate Management	社会服务业 Social Services	卫生体育社会福利业 Health Care, Sports and Social Welfare	教育文艺广播电影电视业 Education, Culture, Art, Radio Film and Television	科学研究综合技术服务业 Scientific Research and Polytechnical Services	国家政党机关社会团体 Government Agencies, Party and Social Orgnizations
1978	100.0	100.0	100.0	100.0	100.0	100.0	100.0
1979	96.4	96.5	96.2	96.2	96.7	96.2	96.8
1980	100.8	101.0	101.0	101.3	100.8	100.6	101.0
1981	118.0	118.3	118.3	118.3	118.5	117.0	118.3
1982	131.0	131.2	130.9	131.7	131.4	130.2	131.2
1983	142.4	142.7	142.6	143.0	142.6	141.5	142.8
1984	163.3	163.6	163.1	163.3	161.1	159.8	154.4
1985	165.1	197.8	172.2	184.8	190.8	168.6	206.7
1986	215.1	215.8	204.4	224.7	216.3	199.4	212.3
1987	196.1	216.1	218.9	224.7	246.2	286.2	196.1
1988	311.0	264.6	400.0	399.4	282.3	367.9	490.5
1989	424.3	304.1	389.9	468.4	319.1	417.6	714.7
1990	464.7	328.7	459.3	540.5	356.8	511.3	891.9
1991	487.2	388.7	575.3	619.3	399.5	622.0	1020.3
1992	648.5	458.2	644.4	744.0	462.0	747.4	1185.8
1993	734.9	686.3	735.4	891.9	515.4	863.1	1359.4
1994	822.6	741.7	850.0	986.4	597.1	996.7	1587.2
1995	971.5	927.1	874.7	1121.5	705.8	1155.2	1592.0
1996	1121.5	1147.3	997.0	1277.7	760.5	1286.1	1714.7

2—13 1996年国内生产总值构成项目
STRUCTURE OF DOMESTIC PRODUCTS

本表按当年价格计算 (At current prices)

行业	Items	增加值(亿元) Added Value (100000000 yuan)	劳动者报酬 Payment for Laborer	固定资产折旧 Depreciation of Fixed Assets	生产税净额 Net Amount of Production Tax	营业盈余 Business Surplus
国内生产总值	**Gross Domestic Products**	**6004.21**	**3077.55**	**771.27**	**704.40**	**1450.99**
第一产业	Primary Industry	965.29	866.00	34.26	20.89	44.14
第二产业	Secondary Industry	3074.12	1339.86	377.85	506.95	849.46
工业	Industry	2754.80	1140.49	362.40	473.24	778.67
建筑业	Construction	319.32	199.37	15.45	33.71	70.79
第三产业	Tertiary Industry	1964.80	871.69	359.16	176.56	557.39
农林牧渔服务业	Farming,Forestry,Animal Husbandry and Fishery Services	23.89	15.98	2.48	0.94	4.49
地质勘探业、水利管理业	Geological Prospceeting and Water Conservency	15.42	8.45	4.22	0.62	2.13
交通运输、仓储、邮电通讯业	Transportation,Storage,Postal and Telecommunications Services	314.91	173.31	78.01	30.68	32.91
批发和零售贸易、餐饮业	Wholesale, Retail Trade and Food Services	621.01	302.41	59.39	90.78	168.43
金融保险业	Banking and Insurance	333.51	31.30	9.93	24.82	267.46
房地产业	Real Estate Management	194.24	13.44	150.72	9.80	20.28
社会服务业	Social Services	131.81	77.50	14.78	12.33	27.20
卫生体育社会福利事业	Health Care, Sports and Social Welfare	54.99	40.03	6.65	0.87	7.44
教育文艺广播电影电视业	Education,Culture,Art,Radio,Film and Television	106.92	83.99	12.10	1.51	9.32
科学研究和综合技术服务业	Scientific Research and Polytechnical Services	19.22	12.35	2.59	1.40	2.88
国家政党机关、社会团体	Government Agencies,Party Agencies and Social Organizations	134.25	103.42	16.01	2.08	12.74
其他	Others	14.36	9.51	2.28	0.73	2.11

2—14 按支出法计算的国内生产总值
GROSS DOMESTIC PRODUCT BY EXPENDITURES

本表按当年价格计算 (At current prices)

年份 Year	国内生产总值（亿元） Gross Domestic Product (100000000 yuan)	总消费 Total Consumption	居民消费 Resident Consumption	社会消费 Public Consumption	总投资 Total Investment	固定资产形成 Fixed Assets	库存增加 Goods in Stock	货物和服务净出口 Net Export
1952	48.41	31.49	28.99	2.50	8.60	5.13	3.47	8.32
1953	52.42	33.24	30.34	2.90	9.73	7.90	1.83	9.45
1954	53.77	33.99	30.93	3.06	9.18	4.84	4.34	10.60
1955	58.96	35.93	32.58	3.35	11.90	5.93	5.97	11.13
1956	61.90	37.49	33.05	4.44	12.41	7.71	4.70	12.00
1957	65.11	39.87	34.98	4.89	12.62	8.77	3.85	12.62
1958	75.30	41.74	35.82	5.92	18.82	12.46	6.36	14.74
1959	79.62	43.22	36.42	6.80	23.21	15.56	7.65	13.19
1960	86.80	48.55	42.87	5.68	25.15	21.22	3.93	13.10
1961	72.20	46.31	41.41	4.90	12.05	11.24	0.81	13.84
1962	69.20	45.18	40.85	4.33	7.83	9.28	—1.45	16.19
1963	75.52	47.88	43.81	4.07	13.27	10.19	3.08	14.37
1964	89.55	56.17	51.58	4.59	19.40	11.63	7.77	13.98
1965	95.10	54.83	50.03	4.80	20.91	11.86	9.05	19.36
1966	109.89	60.91	55.63	5.28	27.19	12.31	14.88	21.79
1967	99.20	61.43	56.55	4.88	17.27	10.20	7.07	20.50
1968	102.84	65.62	60.63	4.99	18.44	9.86	8.58	18.78
1969	111.75	65.86	60.01	5.85	20.97	11.47	9.50	24.92
1970	129.23	68.59	61.42	7.17	34.32	15.52	18.80	26.32
1971	148.04	77.56	69.52	8.04	41.39	19.22	22.17	29.09
1972	157.31	85.77	76.34	9.43	40.86	22.03	18.83	30.68
1973	170.93	93.57	83.26	10.31	47.26	24.02	23.24	30.10
1974	171.94	94.69	83.41	11.28	46.56	22.17	24.39	30.69
1975	184.16	99.43	87.81	11.62	52.25	25.85	26.40	32.48
1976	187.97	108.07	95.94	12.13	53.60	28.41	25.19	26.30
1977	202.40	111.54	98.14	13.40	56.92	29.68	27.24	33.94
1978	249.24	130.55	115.15	15.40	77.98	40.40	37.58	40.71
1979	298.55	161.08	142.89	18.19	85.56	46.28	39.28	51.91
1980	319.80	175.47	154.72	20.75	97.44	58.25	39.19	46.89
1981	350.02	198.64	174.30	24.34	97.03	56.83	40.20	54.35
1982	390.17	232.12	203.38	28.74	133.09	95.71	37.38	24.96
1983	437.65	251.98	215.96	36.02	142.21	105.49	36.72	43.46
1984	518.85	297.65	257.86	39.79	198.62	131.39	67.23	22.58
1985	651.82	353.72	300.86	52.86	271.42	193.25	78.17	26.68
1986	744.94	393.05	339.37	53.68	341.74	240.37	101.37	10.15
1987	922.33	478.89	406.84	72.05	411.70	303.45	108.25	31.74
1988	1208.85	594.76	501.62	93.14	528.45	390.46	137.99	85.64
1989	1321.85	662.01	557.60	104.41	528.44	336.24	192.20	131.40
1990	1416.50	717.36	608.29	109.07	588.44	374.12	214.32	110.70
1991	1601.38	835.07	656.99	178.08	694.80	461.98	232.82	71.51
1992	2136.02	960.21	735.62	224.59	1069.20	747.29	321.91	106.61
1993	2998.16	1251.08	984.44	266.64	1589.93	1201.41	388.52	157.15
1994	4057.39	1721.45	1350.89	370.56	2018.95	1434.95	584.00	316.99
1995	5155.25	2250.66	1806.43	444.23	2479.30	1756.88	722.42	425.29
1996	6004.21	2721.84	2218.68	503.16	2798.62	2062.17	736.45	483.75

2—15 总消费及其构成
TOTAL CONSUMPTION AND COMPOSITION

本表按当年价格计算 (At current prices)

年份 Year	总消费(亿元) Total Consumption (100000000 yuan)	居民消费 Resident Consumption	农业居民 Agricultural Resident	自给性 Self-Sufficient	商品性 Commodity Consumption	文化生活服务性 Cultural Life Services	住房及水电 Housing, Water and Electric	住房 Housing
1978	130.55	115.15	76.11	28.31	37.48	4.43	5.89	5.54
1979	161.08	142.89	96.16	35.00	46.22	5.24	9.70	9.16
1980	175.47	154.72	105.13	35.06	54.39	5.68	10.00	9.59
1981	198.64	174.30	121.83	44.83	59.96	6.13	10.91	10.91
1982	232.12	203.38	147.65	54.04	74.67	7.94	11.00	11.00
1983	251.98	215.96	158.02	58.20	77.66	9.97	12.19	9.70
1984	297.65	257.86	188.60	70.81	95.15	11.75	10.89	10.07
1985	353.72	300.86	219.98	77.57	117.73	12.20	12.48	11.55
1986	393.05	339.37	241.01	84.65	123.71	19.28	13.37	12.11
1987	478.89	406.84	282.48	91.99	143.66	28.90	17.93	13.53
1988	594.76	501.62	352.23	118.16	180.18	31.07	22.82	14.90
1989	662.01	557.60	386.40	136.33	193.07	33.54	23.46	19.36
1990	717.36	608.29	403.29	144.96	197.79	38.62	21.92	19.34
1991	835.07	656.99	423.60	149.83	208.63	40.72	24.42	21.12
1992	960.21	735.62	459.99	159.07	228.28	43.56	29.08	24.20
1993	1251.08	984.44	569.94	159.47	300.24	45.43	64.80	48.30
1994	1721.45	1350.89	782.19	265.06	344.82	76.75	95.56	75.56
1995	2250.66	1806.43	1029.92	327.11	406.11	125.84	170.86	133.59
1996	2721.84	2218.68	1314.01	327.98	553.94	192.43	239.66	186.79

续表 Continued

年份 Year	非农业居民 Nonagricultural Residents	商品性 Commodity Consumption	文化生活服务性 Cultural Life Services	住房及水电 Housing, Water and Electric	住房 Housing	社会消费 Public Consumption
1978	39.04	33.18	5.11	0.75	0.50	15.40
1979	46.73	39.95	5.88	0.90	0.52	18.19
1980	49.59	42.20	6.43	0.96	0.56	20.75
1981	52.47	45.00	6.44	1.03	0.59	24.34
1982	55.73	48.26	6.39	1.08	0.60	28.74
1983	57.94	50.15	6.41	1.38	0.76	36.02
1984	69.26	58.99	8.69	1.58	0.88	39.79
1985	80.88	69.58	9.63	1.67	0.94	52.86
1986	98.36	83.75	11.65	2.96	1.52	53.68
1987	124.36	103.76	17.21	3.39	1.67	72.05
1988	149.39	125.55	19.71	4.13	1.87	93.14
1989	171.20	142.79	23.48	4.93	2.16	104.41
1990	205.00	163.47	36.09	5.44	2.61	109.07
1991	233.39	188.14	38.41	6.84	3.00	178.08
1992	275.63	225.50	40.42	9.71	4.23	224.59
1993	414.50	305.25	87.15	22.10	6.79	266.64
1994	568.70	403.39	130.72	34.59	11.50	370.56
1995	776.51	534.89	183.64	57.98	30.66	444.23
1996	904.67	588.76	241.14	74.77	39.85	503.16

2—16 按产业分总投资
TOTAL INVESTMENT BY TYPE OF INDUSTRY

本表按当年价格计算 (At current prices)

年份 Year	总投资 (亿元) Total Investment (100000000 yuan)	固定资产形成 Fixed Assets	库存增加 Goods in Stock	第一产业 Primary Industry 总投资 Total Investment	固定资产形成 Fixed Assets	库存增加 Goods in Stock
1978	77.98	40.40	37.58	6.36	2.23	4.13
1979	85.56	46.28	39.28	7.55	3.23	4.32
1980	97.44	58.25	39.19	6.95	2.44	4.51
1981	97.03	56.83	40.20	7.84	3.22	4.62
1982	133.09	95.71	37.38	8.17	3.76	4.41
1983	142.21	105.49	36.72	8.29	3.85	4.44
1984	198.62	131.39	67.23	11.60	3.51	8.09
1985	271.42	193.25	78.17	12.86	4.50	8.36
1986	341.74	240.37	101.37	12.54	6.29	6.25
1987	411.70	303.45	108.25	16.30	8.50	7.80
1988	528.45	390.46	137.99	21.74	12.49	9.25
1989	528.44	336.24	192.20	19.60	10.76	8.84
1990	588.44	374.12	214.32	26.32	11.97	14.35
1991	694.80	461.98	232.82	27.37	12.94	14.43
1992	1069.20	747.29	321.91	36.29	15.69	20.60
1993	1589.93	1201.41	388.52	45.58	21.87	23.71
1994	2018.95	1434.95	584.00	86.38	48.26	38.12
1995	2479.30	1756.88	722.42	113.74	41.94	71.80
1996	2798.62	2062.17	736.45	149.17	45.41	103.76

续表 Continued

年份 Year	第二产业 Scondary Industry 总投资 Total Investment	固定资产形成 Fixed Assets	库存增加 Goods in Stock	第三产业 Tertiary Industry 总投资 Total Investment	固定资产形成 Fixed Assets	库存增加 Goods in Stock
1978	53.94	27.26	26.68	17.68	10.91	6.77
1979	58.02	30.13	27.89	19.99	12.92	7.07
1980	67.72	39.70	28.02	22.77	16.11	6.66
1981	64.95	36.21	28.74	24.24	17.40	6.84
1982	79.99	53.64	26.35	44.93	38.31	6.62
1983	80.46	54.46	26.00	53.46	47.18	6.28
1984	108.91	61.18	47.73	78.11	66.70	11.41
1985	145.25	89.82	55.43	113.31	98.93	14.38
1986	192.05	114.86	77.19	137.15	119.22	17.93
1987	215.64	141.10	74.54	179.76	153.85	25.91
1988	225.51	146.03	79.48	281.20	231.94	49.26
1989	256.83	125.75	131.08	252.01	199.73	52.28
1990	286.30	139.92	146.38	275.82	222.23	53.59
1991	336.72	196.80	139.92	330.71	252.24	78.47
1992	593.59	399.80	193.79	439.32	331.80	107.52
1993	923.38	669.43	253.95	620.97	510.11	110.86
1994	1073.66	736.45	337.21	858.91	650.24	208.67
1995	1262.85	829.54	433.31	1102.71	885.40	217.31
1996	1356.02	931.49	424.53	1293.43	1085.27	208.16

2—17 按经济类型分总投资
TOTAL INVESTMENT GROUPED BY OWNERSHIP

本表按当年价格计算 (At current prices)

年份 Year	总投资(亿元) Total Investment (100000000 yuan)	固定资产形成 Fixed Assets	国有经济 State-owned Units	集体经济 Collective-owned Units	其他经济 Other Ownership Units	城乡居民私人住房 Private Residence of City and Rural Residents
1978	77.8	40.40	29.67	7.03		3.70
1979	85.56	46.28	34.80	7.42		4.06
1980	97.44	58.25	43.35	10.56		4.34
1981	97.03	56.83	38.90	13.00		4.93
1982	133.09	95.71	50.03	25.89		19.79
1983	142.21	105.49	46.79	21.41		37.29
1984	198.62	131.39	53.85	37.44		40.10
1985	271.42	193.25	81.75	59.06		52.44
1986	341.74	240.37	100.11	61.28		78.98
1987	411.70	303.45	120.03	75.07		108.35
1988	528.45	390.46	164.97	101.11	11.50	112.88
1989	528.44	336.24	134.83	72.60	11.87	116.94
1990	588.44	374.12	145.63	81.92	12.79	133.78
1991	694.80	461.98	185.42	118.54	13.88	144.14
1992	1069.20	747.29	306.47	293.28	22.28	125.26
1993	1589.93	1201.41	426.63	521.17	115.18	138.43
1994	2018.95	1434.95	477.86	603.97	188.89	164.23
1995	2529.30	1756.88	622.10	500.25	379.11	255.42
1996	2798.62	2062.17	755.10	580.08	457.16	269.83

续表 Continued

年份 Year	城镇居民 Urban Residents	乡村居民 Rural Residents	库存增加 Goods in Stock	国有经济 State-owned Units	集体经济 Collective-owned Units	其他经济 Other Ownership Units
1978		3.70	37.58	26.04	11.54	
1979	0.06	4.00	39.28	27.21	12.07	
1980	0.07	4.27	39.19	27.15	12.04	
1981	0.08	4.85	40.20	23.32	16.88	
1982	0.76	19.03	37.38	21.31	16.07	
1983	0.83	36.46	36.72	20.57	16.15	
1984	1.66	38.44	67.23	28.47	38.76	
1985	1.55	50.89	78.17	40.49	37.68	
1986	2.07	76.91	101.37	53.40	47.97	
1987	4.95	103.40	108.25	62.78	45.47	
1988	4.32	108.56	137.99	76.65	46.00	15.34
1989	3.92	113.02	192.20	109.32	62.16	20.72
1990	3.25	130.53	214.32	122.08	69.18	23.06
1991	4.11	140.03	232.82	131.44	76.04	25.34
1992	4.98	120.28	321.91	175.01	110.17	36.73
1993	9.41	129.02	388.52	140.24	186.65	61.63
1994	12.26	151.97	584.00	193.34	287.09	103.57
1995	14.42	241.00	722.42	202.77	343.61	176.04
1996	14.19	255.64	736.45	247.04	251.01	238.40

2—18 历年工农业总产值
GROSS OUTPUT VALUE OF INDUSTRY AND AGRICULTURE OVER THE YEARS

本表按当年价格计算 (At current prices)

年份 Year	工农业总产值(亿元) Gross Output Value of Industry and Agriculture (100000000 yuan)	农业 Agriculture	工业 Industry	轻工业 Light Industry	重工业 Heavy Industry
1949	38.48	22.59	15.89	15.01	0.88
1950	43.27	24.27	19.00	17.94	1.06
1951	49.92	27.37	22.55	21.20	1.35
1952	57.40	31.87	25.53	23.97	1.56
1953	62.12	32.31	29.81	27.66	2.15
1954	64.11	32.45	31.66	29.00	2.66
1955	69.04	36.22	32.82	29.57	3.25
1956	72.20	33.60	38.60	33.54	5.06
1957	77.82	36.81	41.01	34.78	6.23
1958	113.96	38.74	75.22	58.07	17.15
1959	133.35	37.35	96.00	71.81	24.19
1960	137.08	36.76	100.32	68.72	31.60
1961	98.23	35.73	62.50	47.37	15.13
1962	93.51	40.15	53.36	42.95	10.41
1963	101.43	46.77	54.66	72.96	11.70
1964	124.79	56.62	68.17	53.65	14.52
1965	145.35	57.27	88.08	66.28	21.80
1966	170.27	66.08	104.19	74.60	29.59
1967	145.99	61.19	84.80	63.26	21.54
1968	150.86	65.38	85.48	59.49	25.99
1969	168.40	65.60	102.80	69.08	33.72
1970	206.80	71.33	135.47	83.14	52.33
1971	247.05	79.90	167.15	93.59	73.56
1972	266.62	83.24	183.38	101.08	82.30
1973	297.81	89.71	208.10	114.89	93.21
1974	295.27	89.88	205.39	117.45	87.94
1975	326.94	91.66	235.28	130.28	105.00
1976	348.30	100.71	247.59	134.12	112.62
1977	386.28	89.16	297.12	158.12	139.00
1978	443.52	105.87	337.65	176.94	160.71
1979	531.30	145.25	386.05	208.11	177.94
1980	606.27	138.45	467.82	267.97	199.85
1981	658.56	153.62	504.94	307.98	196.96
1982	722.98	188.11	534.87	317.54	217.33
1983	807.56	206.86	600.70	348.56	252.14
1984	999.18	253.82	745.36	433.00	312.36
1985	1325.22	288.55	1036.67	552.23	484.44
1986	1568.04	332.66	1235.38	671.24	564.14
1987	1970.56	380.25	1590.31	859.40	730.91
1988	2650.88	497.95	2152.93	1151.00	1001.93
1989	3029.67	522.25	2507.42	1338.53	1168.89
1990	3344.63	580.53	2764.10	1510.57	1253.53
1991	3742.53	580.93	3161.60	1682.76	1478.84
1992	5347.39	673.82	4673.57	2379.00	2294.57
1993	7971.83	875.37	7096.46	3439.50	3656.96
1994	11161.73	1335.23	9826.50	5014.54	4811.96
1995	11493.97	1686.78	9807.19	4785.42	5021.77
1996	13379.79	1824.19	11555.60	5676.47	5879.13

注：从1995年开始，工业总产值按新规定统计。

Note: Total output value of industry are counted by new regulation since 1995.

2—19 历年工农业总产值指数
INDICES OF GROSS OUTPUT VALUE OF INDUSTRY AND AGRICULTURE OVER THE YEARS

1949=100

年份 Year	工农业总产值 Gross Output Value of Industry and Agriculture	农业 Agriculture	工业 Industry	轻工业 Light Industry	重工业 Heavy Industry
1949	100.0	100.0	100.0	100.0	100.0
1950	113.5	109.1	119.5	119.2	123.1
1951	130.9	122.8	141.9	141.0	153.0
1952	149.7	144.2	160.6	159.1	178.6
1953	162.8	145.5	188.9	184.2	244.4
1954	168.9	146.3	203.1	194.5	306.0
1955	181.0	163.0	208.3	194.9	368.4
1956	196.4	152.2	260.6	232.6	595.7
1957	202.3	157.4	266.6	230.2	700.9
1958	270.9	160.0	424.2	325.2	1608.5
1959	334.9	149.3	590.9	434.5	2461.5
1960	352.8	137.5	648.0	427.5	3283.8
1961	247.2	133.2	404.0	302.4	1618.8
1962	218.6	134.7	334.8	270.6	1102.6
1963	238.6	160.8	346.0	277.5	1165.8
1964	294.2	190.6	437.3	345.9	1529.9
1965	355.9	201.4	577.0	448.2	2117.1
1966	431.2	234.3	710.8	488.7	3366.7
1967	368.3	218.0	583.0	417.3	2565.0
1968	379.8	225.0	600.7	403.4	2960.7
1969	441.7	223.6	749.4	477.9	3995.7
1970	573.9	239.7	1040.8	599.4	6318.8
1971	693.0	266.0	1289.0	664.1	8760.7
1972	753.1	273.2	1422.7	719.7	9871.9
1973	848.6	291.5	1623.7	823.1	11240.4
1974	845.8	292.0	1612.4	848.2	10694.4
1975	950.8	294.7	1861.2	944.4	12870.8
1976	1038.0	306.2	2050.5	1021.0	14475.3
1977	1194.7	275.4	2461.8	1189.7	17929.2
1978	1370.9	334.6	2797.8	1330.2	20707.9
1979	1555.3	371.1	3186.6	1561.8	22875.3
1980	1822.3	350.7	3847.3	2021.4	25552.8
1981	1974.4	378.4	4171.8	2360.5	25144.9
1982	2141.0	434.8	4490.8	2474.5	28080.5
1983	2419.4	460.6	5113.9	2790.0	32420.7
1984	2965.2	536.3	6304.5	3378.2	40947.6
1985	3866.0	553.1	8408.9	4425.1	55903.7
1986	4479.3	587.7	9811.6	5264.6	63611.0
1987	5480.6	605.9	12151.6	6336.4	81715.9
1988	6824.3	646.1	15271.4	7975.7	102496.3
1989	7126.5	648.3	15981.9	8303.0	107964.6
1990	7811.7	664.6	17583.9	9246.4	117011.0
1991	8889.1	657.1	20131.3	10304.4	138466.3
1992	13133.5	742.5	30039.9	14934.2	213695.0
1993	18177.3	826.4	42668.4	20680.9	312033.2
1994	23933.2	926.3	57057.8	28386.0	405576.0
1995	28840.2	1052.7	69176.9	34693.4	487583.5
1996	33776.9	1130.6	81725.4	40979.5	576131.6

2—20 个体工商业基本情况(1996)
SELF-EMPLOYMENT BUSINESS

单位:万元 (10000 yuan)

行业 Sector		户数(户) Households	从业人数(人) Personal (person)	注册资金 Registered Capital	总产值 Total Output Value	销售总额 Total Sales Value	社会消费品零售额 Total Retail Sales of Consumer Goods
总计	**Total**	**1287882**	**2142471**	**899088**	**1509019**	**6970804**	**3204219**
按行业分	Grouped by Sector						
#农林牧渔业	Farming, Forestry, Animal Housbandry and Fishery	6047	10495	3527	33091	1269	3779
制造业	Manufacturing	154077	326530	129489	1400691		142305
建筑业	Construction	2366	7091	3074	72253		
交通运输业	Transportation	149827	228213	179291		1103830	
批发零售贸易业、餐饮业	Wholesale, Retail Sales and Catering Trade	809773	1311127	488689		5350670	3486059
#餐饮业	Catering Trade	114017	259510	76986		624710	479580
社会服务业	Services	158835	245367	89898		486722	205997
#日用品修理业	Daily Use Goods Repairing	61123	86330	22163		152315	62446
其他行业	Other	6536	12424	4716		28225	66079

2—21 私营企业情况(1996)
PRIVATE ENTERPRISES

单位:万元 (10000 yuan)

行业 Sector		户数(户) Households	雇工人数(人) Employees (person)	投资者人数(人) Owners (person)	注册资金 Registered Capital	总产值 Total Output Value	销售总额 Total Sales Value	社会消费品零售额 Total Retail Sales of Consumer Goods
总计	**Total**	**51247**	**508611**	**97292**	**1865501**	**1592843**	**1344401**	**817347**
按行业分	Grouped by Sector							
#农林牧渔业	Farming, Forestry, Animal Housbandry and Fishery	297	2955	547	11491	20578	8291	4815
制造业	Manufacturing	26495	291595	42941	760841	1490420		146825
建筑业	Construction	731	10821	1815	59952	80664		
交通运输业	Transportation	313	3340	769	17021		25609	
批发零售贸易业、餐饮业	Wholesale, Retail Sales and Catering Trade	18932	162352	41165	857163		1184983	613204
#餐饮业	Catering Trade	655	6025	1011	21181		36636	29035
社会服务业	Services	3003	24565	6377	97334		94510	42369
#日用品修理业	Daily Use Goods Repairing	194	1757	406	5864		4918	1502
其他行业	Other	1395	11992	3522	60503		30881	9858

3 人口、劳动力

POPULATION & EMPLOYMENT

3 人口、劳动力
POPULATION & EMPLOYMENT

1 9 9 6

年末总人口	Population (Year-end of 1996)	7110.16	万人	10000 persons
# 男性	Male	3610.72	万人	10000 persons
# 农业人口	Agricultural Population	5261.52	万人	10000 persons
年末总户数	Total Households (Year-end of 1996)	2014.21	万户	10000 household
人口密度	Density of Population	693	人/平方公里	person/sq · k
人口自然增长率	Population Natural Grwoth Rate	5.53	‰	
人口平均期望寿命(1995年)	Life Expectancy	72.66	岁	year old
# 男性	Male	70.37	岁	year old
# 女性	Female	74.96	岁	year old
社会从业人员	Employment	3647.09	万人	10000 persons
# 职工人数	Staff and Workers	905.52	万人	10000 persons
年末离休、退休、退职人员数	Number of VCSR and RRSW by Region	205.02	万人	10000 persons
城镇失业人数	Unemployed in Urban Area	22.34	万人	10000 persons
城镇失业率	Unemployment Rate	2.2	%	percent

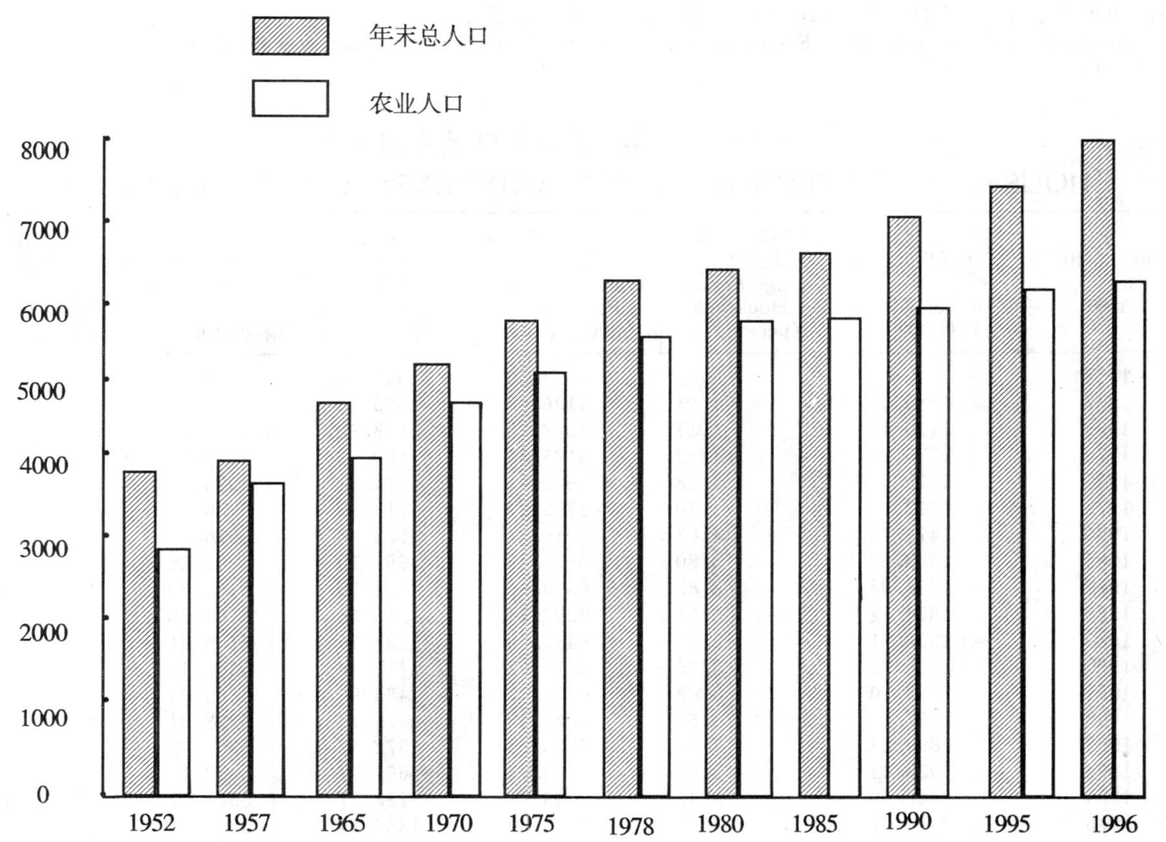

3—1 全省人口数及构成
POPULATION AND COMPOSITION

单位:万人 (10000 persons)

年份 Year	总人口 Total	按性别分 Grouped by Sex				按农业人口、非农业人口分 Grouped by Agriculture and Non-Agriculture			
		男 Male		女 Female		农业人口 Agriculture		非农业人口 Non-Agriculture	
		人口数 Population	比重(%) Proportion	人口数 Population	比重(%) Proportion	人口数 Population	比重(%) Proportion	人口数 Population	比重(%) Proportion
1949	*3512.00	1778.80	50.6	1733.20	49.4	2991.00	85.2	*521.00	14.8
1952	*3739.00	1891.60	50.6	1847.40	49.4	3188.00	85.3	*551.00	14.7
1957	4182.71	2087.06	49.9	2095.65	50.1	3562.05	85.2	620.66	14.8
1965	4623.74	2319.92	50.2	2303.82	49.8	3968.56	85.8	655.18	14.2
1970	5252.09	2635.02	50.2	2617.07	49.8	4651.52	88.6	600.57	11.4
1975	5636.12	2842.86	50.4	2793.26	49.6	4958.86	88.0	677.26	12.0
1978	5834.33	2950.45	50.6	2883.88	49.4	5106.22	87.5	728.11	12.5
1980	5938.19	3003.75	50.6	2934.44	49.4	5085.67	85.6	852.52	14.4
1985	6213.48	3168.25	51.0	3045.23	49.0	5199.87	83.7	1013.61	16.3
1987	6348.00	3241.71	51.1	3106.29	48.9	5172.72	81.5	1175.28	18.5
1988	6438.27	3289.49	51.1	3148.78	48.9	5156.84	80.1	1281.43	19.9
1989	6535.85	3339.10	51.1	3196.75	48.9	5161.79	79.0	1374.06	21.0
1990	6766.90	3443.68	50.9	3323.22	49.1	5345.85	79.0	1421.05	21.0
1991	6843.70	3451.96	50.4	3391.74	49.6	5392.84	78.8	1450.86	21.2
1992	6911.20	3483.24	50.4	3427.96	49.6	5403.18	78.2	1508.02	21.8
1993	6967.27	3513.59	50.4	3453.68	49.6	5331.25	76.5	1636.02	23.5
1994	7020.54	3534.09	50.3	3486.45	49.7	5333.03	76.0	1687.51	24.0
1995	7066.02	3589.56	50.8	3476.46	49.2	5308.39	75.1	1757.63	24.9
1996	7110.16	3610.72	50.8	3499.44	49.2	5261.52	74.0	1848.64	26.0

注:1996年全省常住人口为7110.16万人,户籍人口为6908.13万人。
Resident population was 7110.16 ten thousand people, and household population was 69081.3 ten thousand people in 1996.

3—2 全省户数、平均人口及人口密度
HOUSEHOLD, AVERAGE PERSON AND DENSITY OF POPULATION

年份 Year	户数(万户) Households (10000)	平均每户人数(人/户) Average Person Per Household (person)	年平均人口(万人) Average Person Per Year (10000 persons)	非农业人口 Non-Agriculture	农业人口 Agriculture	人口密度(人/平方公里) Density of Population (person/sq・km)
1952			3697.50	543.00	3154.50	364
1957	985.51	4.24	4136.05	595.43	3540.62	408
1965	1110.13	4.17	4567.75	648.92	3918.83	451
1970	1215.28	4.32	5185.36	609.92	4575.74	512
1975	1315.55	4.28	5600.91	674.71	4926.20	549
1978	1423.11	4.10	5799.80	713.19	5086.61	569
1980	1471.76	4.03	5915.37	838.78	5076.59	579
1985	1633.62	3.80	6192.45	991.19	5201.26	606
1987	1736.98	3.65	6308.96	1158.96	5150.00	619
1988	1834.32	3.51	6393.14	1228.36	5164.78	628
1989	1903.71	3.43	6487.06	1327.75	5159.31	637
1990	1806.78	3.75	6716.62	1411.16	5305.46	660
1991	1859.70	3.68	6805.30	1435.96	5369.34	667
1992	1957.85	3.53	6877.45	1479.44	5398.01	674
1993	1893.28	3.68	6939.24	1572.02	5367.22	679
1994	1923.44	3.65	6993.91	1661.77	5332.14	684
1995	2066.09	3.42	7043.28	1722.57	5320.71	689
1996	2014.21	3.53	7088.09	1803.14	5284.95	693

3—3 全省人口自然变动
POPULATION NATURAL CHANGE

单位:万人 (10000 persons)

年份 Year	出生 Birth		死亡 Death		自然增长 Natural Growth	
	人数 Population	‰	人数 Population	‰	人数 Population	‰
1949	*121.94	34.72	*57.77	16.45	*64.17	18.27
1952	*131.93	35.68	*57.98	15.68	*73.95	20.00
1957	142.19	34.38	42.45	10.26	99.74	24.12
1965	168.59	36.91	43.30	9.48	125.29	27.43
1970	159.06	30.68	35.51	6.85	123.55	23.83
1975	100.01	17.86	36.18	6.46	63.83	11.40
1978	90.62	15.63	35.32	6.09	55.30	9.54
1980	86.90	14.69	38.87	6.57	48.03	8.12
1985	67.11	10.84	36.35	5.87	30.76	4.97
1987	97.27	15.42	36.50	5.79	60.77	9.63
1988	102.46	16.03	37.65	5.89	64.81	10.14
1989	111.27	17.15	36.31	5.60	74.96	11.55
1990	137.96	20.54	43.86	6.53	94.10	14.01
1991	116.03	17.05	44.23	6.50	71.80	10.55
1992	108.04	15.71	46.49	6.76	61.55	8.95
1993	96.94	13.97	45.87	6.61	51.07	7.36
1994	96.38	13.78	47.98	6.86	48.40	6.92
1995	86.77	12.32	46.20	6.56	40.57	5.76
1996	85.84	12.11	46.64	6.58	39.20	5.53

3—4 全省市、镇、县人口数及其构成
CITY, COUNTY POPULATION AND COMPOSITION

单位:万人 (10000 persons)

年份 Year	总人口数 Total Population	市 City		镇 City		县 County	
		人口数 Population	占总人口% Proportion	Population	占总人口% Proportion	Population	占总人口% Proportion
1957	4182.71	471.18	11.3				
1965	4623.74	496.91	10.8	191.23	4.1	3935.60	85.1
1970	5252.09	476.33	9.1	179.91	3.4	4595.85	87.5
1975	5636.12	530.38	9.4	211.09	3.8	4894.65	86.8
1978	5834.32	570.14	9.8	230.63	3.9	5033.55	86.3
1980	5938.19	636.41	10.7	265.37	4.5	5036.41	84.8
1985	6213.48	966.64	15.6	629.51	10.1	4617.33	74.3
1987	6348.00	1803.65	28.4	1077.63	17.0	3466.72	54.6
1988	6438.27	1947.01	30.2	1265.62	19.7	3225.64	50.1
1989	6535.85	2148.50	32.9	1344.96	20.6	3042.39	46.5
1990	6766.90	1043.45	15.4	415.49	6.1	5307.96	78.5
1991	6843.70	1163.43	17.0	424.31	6.2	5255.96	76.8
1992	6911.20	1182.59	17.1	461.13	6.7	5267.48	76.2
1993	6967.27	1199.26	17.2	474.32	6.8	5293.69	76.0
1994	7020.54	1255.58	17.9	477.43	6.8	5287.53	75.3
1995	7066.02	1331.30	18.8	597.79	8.5	5136.93	72.7
1996	7110.16	1328.18	18.7	614.32	8.6	5167.66	72.7

3—5 全省人口年龄构成情况(1996)
POPULATION AGE COMPOSITION

1996年人口变动情况抽样调查资料　　Sampling Survey in 1996

年龄(岁) Age (Year)	人口数(人) Population			占总计的% Proportion		
	合计 Total	男 Male	女 Female	合计 Total	男 Male	女 Female
总计 Total	**40243**	**19944**	**20299**	**100.00**	**49.56**	**50.44**
0—4	2273	1262	1011	5.65	3.14	2.51
5—9	3731	1930	1801	9.27	4.80	4.48
10—14	2987	1567	1420	7.42	3.89	3.53
15—19	2483	1238	1245	6.17	3.08	3.09
20—24	2724	1249	1475	6.77	3.10	3.67
25—29	4190	1962	2228	10.41	4.88	5.54
30—34	4145	2014	2131	10.30	5.00	5.30
35—39	2691	1338	1353	6.69	3.32	3.36
40—44	3497	1783	1714	8.69	4.43	4.26
45—49	2713	1370	1343	6.74	3.40	3.34
50—54	2016	1039	977	5.01	2.58	2.43
55—59	1746	910	836	4.34	2.26	2.08
60—64	1692	829	863	4.20	2.06	2.14
65—69	1323	627	696	3.29	1.56	1.73
70—74	940	442	498	2.34	1.10	1.24
75—79	620	231	389	1.54	0.57	0.97
80—84	332	118	214	0.82	0.29	0.53
85—89	108	29	79	0.27	0.07	0.20
90岁及以上 90 over	32	6	26	0.08	0.01	0.07

3—6 全省15岁及以上人口的婚姻状况(1996)
BASIC STATISTICS ON OF AGE 15 AND ABOVE POPULATION MARRIAGE

1996年人口变动情况抽样调查资料　　Sampling Survey in 1996

婚姻状况 Indication	人口数(人) Population (Person)	占15岁及15岁以上人口的% Proportion of 15 Age and above Population		
		1990	1995	1996
总计 Total	**31252**	**100.00**	**100.00**	**100.00**
未婚 Unmarried	4721	21.65	17.6	15.11
初婚有配偶 First Marriage	23834	71.48	73.91	76.26
再婚有配偶 Remarriage	474		1.58	1.52
离婚 Divorce	164	0.41	0.55	0.52
丧偶 Widowed	2059	6.46	6.36	6.59

3—7 全省家庭户规模(1996)
HOUSEHOLD SCALE

1996年人口变动情况抽样调查资料 Sampling Survey in 1996

规模 Scale		户数(户) Households			占总计的% Proportion		
		1990	1995	1996	1990	1995	1996
总计	**Total**	**17815925**	**157122**	**11337**	**100.00**	**100.00**	**100.00**
一人户	One Person	1313477	10241	605	7.37	6.52	5.34
二人户	Two Person	2213696	26939	1798	12.43	17.15	15.86
三人户	Three Person	5282876	54650	3813	29.65	34.78	33.63
四人户	Four Person	4527948	34694	2626	25.42	22.08	23.16
五人户	Five Person	2662200	19352	1543	14.94	12.32	13.61
六人户	Six Person	1067291	7645	648	5.99	4.86	5.72
七人户	Seven Person	436168	2348	193	2.45	1.49	1.70
八人及以上户	Eight Person and over	312269	1253	111	1.75	0.8	0.98

3—8 全省分年龄育龄妇女生育孩次状况(1996)
LIVE BIRTH AND LIVING CHILDREN FOR WOMEN

1996年人口变动情况抽样调查资料 Sampling Survey in 1996

年龄(岁) Age (Year)	出生人数(人) Birth Persons	孩次状况 Children			生育率(%) Birth Rate
		一孩(%) One Child Proportion	二孩(%) Two Children Proportion	三孩及以上(%) Three and above Children Proportion	
总计 Total	**522**	**87.17**	**11.49**	**1.34**	**45.51**
15—19	11	100.00	0.00	0.00	8.53
20—24	259	97.30	2.70	0.00	166.45
25—29	220	84.09	14.09	1.82	96.92
30—34	23	26.09	69.57	4.35	11.58
35—39	8	12.50	62.50	25.00	0.59
40—44	1	0.00	100.00	0.00	0.00
45—49	0	0.00	0.00	0.00	0.00

3—9 从业人数
EMPLOYMENT

单位：万人 (10000 persons)

年份 Year	从业人数 Total	职工人数 Staff and Workers	国有经济单位 State-Owned Units	城镇集体经济单位 Collective-Owned Units	其他经济类型单位 Other-Ownership Units	城镇私营企业从业人员和个体劳动者 Urban Self-Employment	乡村劳动者 Rural Collective Labors	其他从业人员 Others
1978	2777.72	581.50	366.37	215.13		1.62	2194.60	
1980	2821.03	644.15	401.98	242.17		2.75	2174.13	
1985	3262.97	782.44	468.80	305.39	8.25	11.86	2468.67	
1986	3350.02	816.00	487.91	318.73	9.36	11.69	2522.33	
1987	3429.69	845.26	506.68	326.72	11.86	14.53	2569.90	
1988	3502.65	873.00	527.52	331.40	14.08	16.13	2613.52	
1989	3519.83	867.55	525.24	324.73	17.58	19.09	2633.19	
1990	3569.13	879.85	536.88	323.34	19.63	23.57	2665.71	
1991	3600.27	899.27	551.52	324.91	22.84	21.92	2679.08	
1992	3613.90	904.09	562.69	313.81	27.59	23.63	2686.18	
1993	3639.04	914.73	574.02	293.57	47.14	37.11	2674.39	12.81
1994	3639.90	909.83	571.39	277.77	60.67	52.99	2666.04	11.04
1995	3649.69	915.98	576.24	273.96	65.78	65.89	2657.32	10.50
1996	3647.09	905.52	575.48	256.91	73.13	72.80	2657.98	10.79

注：其他经济类型单位包括联营经济，股份制经济，外商投资经济，港、澳、台投资经济，其他经济单位。

Other economic types include joint ownership, foreign investment, Hongkong, Marco, and Taiwan investment,etc.

3—10 分三次产业的从业人数
THREE INDUSTRY EMPLOYMENT

单位：万人 (10000 persons)

年份 Year	从业人数 Employment	第一产业 Primary Industry		第二产业 Secondary Industry		第三产业 Tertiary Industry	
		人数 Population	比重 (%) Proportion	人数 Population	比重 (%) Proportion	人数 Population	比重 (%) Proportion
1978	2777.72	1937.06	69.7	544.57	19.6	296.09	10.7
1980	2821.03	1987.28	70.4	546.48	19.4	287.27	10.2
1985	3262.97	1738.09	53.2	1065.75	32.7	459.13	14.1
1986	3350.02	1678.71	50.1	1140.36	34.0	530.95	15.9
1987	3429.69	1652.89	48.2	1213.67	35.4	563.13	16.4
1988	3502.65	1654.31	47.2	1251.03	35.7	597.31	17.1
1989	3519.83	1714.69	48.7	1215.40	34.5	589.74	16.8
1990	3569.13	1745.12	48.9	1208.00	33.8	616.01	17.3
1991	3600.27	1770.76	49.2	1200.37	33.3	629.14	17.5
1992	3613.90	1722.00	47.6	1220.76	33.8	671.14	18.6
1993	3639.04	1652.07	45.4	1258.31	34.6	728.66	20.0
1994	3639.90	1616.51	44.4	1250.49	34.4	772.90	21.2
1995	3649.69	1564.70	42.9	1271.74	34.8	813.25	22.3
1996	3647.09	1551.79	42.5	1246.84	34.2	848.46	23.3

3—11 分行业从业人数(1996)
CATEGORY EMPLOYMENT

单位:万人 (10000 persons)

		从业人数 Employment	国有经济单位职工 State-Owned Units	城镇集体单位职工 Collective-Owned Units	其他经济类型单位职工 Others
总计	**Total**	**3647.09**	**575.48**	**256.91**	**73.13**
农、林、牧、渔业	Farming, Forestry, Animal Husbandry and Fishery	1557.35	25.66	1.15	0.09
采掘业	Excavation	27.19	24.04	2.71	0.15
制造业	Manufacturing	930.53	201.36	137.37	61.31
电力、煤气及水的生产和供应业	Power, Gas and Water Production and Supply	13.22	11.39	0.79	0.96
建筑业	Construction	275.90	22.84	16.84	0.72
地质勘查业、水利管理业	Geological Prospecting and Water Conservancy	6.67	6.29	0.26	—
交通运输、仓储及邮电通信业	Transportation, Storge, Postal and Telecommunication Service	149.87	38.11	14.99	1.37
批发和零售贸易、餐饮业	Wholesale, Retail Sales and Gatering Trade	254.53	64.03	55.71	6.00
金融、保险业	Banking and Insurance	16.86	10.68	3.43	0.52
房地产业	Real Estate	5.29	4.20	0.58	0.38
社会服务业	Social Service	48.95	17.97	5.38	1.42
卫生、体育和社会福利业	Health Care, Sports and Social Welfare	38.17	18.68	9.01	0.02
教育、文化艺术和广播电影电视业	Education, Culture, Art, Radio, Film and Television	99.20	76.19	6.65	0.12
科学研究和综合技术服务业	Scientific Research and Polytechnical Service	10.81	8.41	0.18	0.03
国家机关、政党机关和社会团体	Goverment Institution, Party and Social	61.88	42.48	0.75	—
其他行业	Others	150.67	3.15	1.11	0.04

单位:万人 续表 Continued (10000 persons)

		城镇私营企业从业人员和个体劳动者 Urban Self-Employment	乡村劳动者 Rural Labors	其他从业人员 Others
总计	**Total**	**72.80**	**2657.98**	**10.79**
农、林、牧、渔业	Farming, Forestry, Animal Husbandry and Fishery	0.07	1530.20	0.18
采掘业	Excavation	0.02		0.27
制造业	Manufacturing	11.93	515.57	2.99
电力、煤气及水的生产和供应业	Power, Gas and Water Production and Supply			0.08
建筑业	Construction	0.81	233.61	1.08
地质勘查业、水利管理业	Geological Prospecting and Water Conservancy			0.12
交通运输、仓储及邮电通信业	Transportation, Storge, Postal and Telecommunication Service	2.24	92.34	0.82
批发和零售贸易、餐饮业	Wholesale, Retail Sales and Gatering Trade	47.24	79.96	1.59
金融、保险业	Banking and Insurance		2.04	0.19
房地产业	Real Estate			0.13
社会服务业	Social Service	8.85	14.65	0.68
卫生、体育和社会福利业	Health Care, Sports and Social Welfare		10.00	0.46
教育、文化艺术和广播电影电视业	Education, Culture, Art, Radio, Film and Television		14.90	1.34
科学研究和综合技术服务业	Scientific Research and Polytechnical Service		2.06	0.13
国家机关、政党机关和社会团体	Goverment Institution, Party and Social		17.94	0.71
其他行业	Others	1.64	144.71	0.02

3—12 工业、建筑业企业职工人数(1996)
INDUCTRY，CONSTRUCTION EMPLOYEES

单位:万人　　　　(10000 persons)

项目	Items	年末人数 Population	工人和学徒 Workers and Apprentices	工程技术人员 Engineers and Technicians	管理人员 Managers
总计	**Total**	**480.48**	**309.78**	**34.41**	**51.15**
采掘业	Mining and Quarrying	26.90	16.06	0.90	2.02
按经济类型分	Grouped by Style				
国有经济	State-Owned Units	24.04	14.02	0.85	1.82
中央	Central	4.88	2.35	0.32	0.45
地方	Local	19.16	11.67	0.53	1.37
城镇集体经济	Urban Collective-Owned Units	2.71	1.91	0.05	0.20
其他各种经济类型	Other Ownership Units	0.15	0.13	…	…
按轻、重工业分	Grouped by Light & Heavy Industry				
轻工业	Light Industry	3.83	2.63	0.08	0.31
重工业	Heavy Industry	23.07	13.43	0.82	1.71
制造业	Manufacturing	400.04	258.87	27.45	42.84
按经济类型分	Grouped by Style				
国有经济	State-Owned Units	201.36	125.62	15.28	21.22
中央	Central	23.37	13.15	3.31	2.88
地方	Local	177.99	112.47	11.97	18.34
城镇集体经济	Urban Collective-Owned Units	137.37	90.14	7.30	14.56
其他各种经济类型	Other Ownership Units	61.31	43.11	4.87	7.06
按轻、重工业分	Grouped by Light & Heavy Industry				
轻工业	Light Industry	212.40	145.15	11.69	20.64
重工业	Heavy Industry	187.64	113.72	15.76	22.20
电力、煤气及水的生产和供应业	Electric Power, Gas & Water Production & Supply	13.14	9.06	1.33	1.45
按经济类型分	Grouped by Style				
国有经济	State-Owned Units	11.39	7.84	1.15	1.25
中央	Central	4.41	3.07	0.42	0.46
地方	Local	6.98	4.77	0.73	0.79
城镇集体经济	Urban Collective-Owned Units	0.79	0.58	0.05	0.09
其他各种经济类型	Other Ownership Units	0.96	0.64	0.13	0.11
按轻、重工业分	Grouped by Light & Heavy Industry				
轻工业	Light Industry	3.89	2.73	0.34	0.47
重工业	Heavy Industry	9.25	6.33	0.99	0.98
建筑业	Construction	40.40	25.79	4.73	4.84
国有经济	State-Owned Units	22.84	13.90	2.68	2.84
城镇集体经济	Urban Collective-Owned Units	16.84	11.51	1.93	1.87
其他各种经济类型	Other Ownership Units	0.72	0.38	0.12	0.13

3—13 分经济类型女职工人数与比重
FEMALE STAFF AND WORKERS BY OWNERSHIP AND PROPORTION

年份 Year	年末女职工人数(万人) Female Staff and Workers (Year-end) (10000 person)				占全部职工人数的比重(%) Proportion in Total (percent)			
	合计 Total	国有经济单位 State-Owned Units	城镇集体经济单位 Urban Collective-Owned Units	其他经济类型单位 Other Owership Units	合计 Total	国有经济单位 State-Owned Units	城镇集体经济单位 Urban Collective-Owned Units	其他经济类型单位 Other Owership Units
1978	198.19	105.64	92.55		34.1	28.8	43.0	
1980	237.52	128.00	109.52		36.9	31.8	45.2	
1985	295.21	157.13	133.97	4.11	37.7	33.5	43.9	49.8
1986	310.84	165.56	140.65	4.63	38.1	33.9	44.1	49.5
1987	324.33	172.83	145.55	5.95	38.4	34.1	44.5	50.2
1988	337.34	182.03	148.31	7.00	38.6	34.5	44.8	49.7
1989	338.45	182.00	147.66	8.79	39.0	34.7	45.5	50.0
1990	346.63	188.95	147.98	9.70	39.4	35.2	45.8	49.4
1991	355.28	194.27	149.74	11.27	39.5	35.2	46.1	49.3
1992	358.94	200.95	144.38	13.61	39.7	35.7	46.0	49.3
1993	364.71	207.50	134.34	22.87	39.9	36.1	45.8	48.5
1994	362.29	204.80	128.00	29.49	39.8	35.8	46.1	48.6
1995	370.57	211.04	127.47	32.06	40.5	36.6	46.5	48.7
1996	367.41	210.95	120.77	35.69	40.6	36.7	47.0	48.8

3—14 离休、退休、退职人数
NUMBERS OF VCSR, RETIRED AND RESIGNED

单位:万人 (10000 persons)

年份 Year	年末人数 Population (Year-end)	国有经济单位 State-Owned Units	城镇集体经济单位 Urban Collective-Owned Units	其他经济类型单位 Other Owership Units	离、退休人员与在职职工比例 VCSR, Retired Staff and Workers as percentage of Formal Staff and Workers	(以在职职工为100) Formal Staff and Workers=100		
						国有经济单位 State-Owned Units	城镇集体经济单位 Urban Collective-Owned Units	其他经济类型单位 Other Owership Units
1978	21.77	14.19	7.58		3.7	3.9	3.5	
1980	61.52	35.37	26.15		9.6	8.8	10.8	
1985	111.17	61.83	48.35	0.99	14.2	13.2	15.8	12.0
1986	114.50	64.34	48.96	1.20	14.0	13.2	15.4	12.8
1987	125.35	70.07	53.87	1.41	14.8	13.8	16.5	11.9
1988	130.90	74.92	54.15	1.83	15.0	14.2	16.3	13.0
1989	140.42	81.16	57.00	2.26	16.2	15.5	17.6	12.9
1990	153.59	90.68	60.32	2.59	17.5	16.9	18.7	13.2
1991	158.37	93.91	61.50	2.96	17.6	17.0	18.9	13.0
1992	164.68	100.01	61.15	3.52	18.2	17.8	19.5	12.8
1993	173.15	106.09	61.49	5.57	18.9	18.5	20.9	11.8
1994	190.40	110.70	72.43	7.27	20.9	19.4	26.1	12.0
1995	200.39	121.11	71.29	7.99	21.9	21.0	26.0	12.1
1996	205.02	130.85	64.66	9.51	22.6	22.7	25.2	13.0

3—15 城镇失业人数及失业率
UNEMPLOYED POPULATION AND UNEMPLOYED RATE IN URBAN

单位:万人 (10000 persons)

年份 Year	本年失业人数 Total Unemployees	本年失业人员就业人数 Unemployed-Reemployees	年末尚有失业人数 Unemployment	#失业青年 Unemployment Younger	#女失业青年 Unemployment Female Younger	城镇失业率(%) Unemployment Rate
1979	89.00	54.70	34.30			5.4
1980	55.47	32.78	20.29			3.1
1985	23.63	15.25	7.15	5.09	3.17	0.9
1986	26.12	16.23	8.36	6.68	3.95	1.0
1987	27.32	16.93	9.35	7.81	4.39	1.1
1988	31.92	18.94	12.02	9.40	5.20	1.3
1989	51.45	22.03	27.76	18.53	10.93	3.0
1990	52.72	28.06	22.52	17.23	9.21	2.4
1991	43.90	23.33	18.68	13.42	7.81	2.0
1992	42.15	21.43	18.81	14.61	8.44	2.0
1993	41.84	20.64	19.43	15.08	8.36	2.0
1994	43.01	22.19	19.58	14.71	8.20	2.0
1995	42.32	21.49	20.13	14.68	8.02	2.0
1996	45.19	20.78	22.34	13.74	7.37	2.2

3—16 职工人数变动(1996)
NUMBER OF STAFF AND WORKERS CHANGES

单位:万人 (10000 persons)

指标	Items	职工变动人数 Number of Workers and Workers Changes	国有经济单位 State-Owned Units	城镇集体经济单位 Urban Collective-Owned Units	其他经济类型单位 Other Owership Units
职工增加人数	**Number of Workers Increment**	**56.43**	**32.42**	**11.21**	**12.80**
从农村招收	Recruited from Rural	8.75	3.98	2.80	1.97
从城镇招收	Recruited from Urban	8.77	3.92	2.53	2.32
录用的复员转业军人	Demobilized Soldiers	1.49	1.20	0.22	0.07
录用的大、中专、技工学校毕业生	Graduates from University, College, Secondary School and Technical School	12.14	9.34	1.55	1.25
调入人数	Number of the Transferred into	15.41	8.78	3.89	2.74
#省外调入	From Outside City	0.44	0.31	0.10	0.03
其他	Others	9.87	5.20	0.22	4.45
职工减少人数	**Number of Staff and Workers Reduction**	**66.89**	**33.17**	**28.26**	**5.46**
离休、退休、退职	VCSR Retire and Resigned	15.69	10.09	4.56	1.04
开除、除名、辞退	Expet, Name Removed, Discharge	4.83	2.05	2.02	0.76
终止、解除合同	Stop and Terminate the Discharge	9.32	4.08	3.26	1.98
调出人数	Number of the Transferred Out	15.12	8.32	5.14	1.66
#调往省外	To Outside City	0.41	0.35	0.04	0.02
其他	Others	21.93	8.63	13.28	0.02

人民生活 4

PEOPLE'S LIVELIHOOD

4 人 民 生 活
PEOPLE'S LIVELIHOOD

1 9 9 6

职工工资总额	Total Wage Bill of Staff	595.72	亿元	(100000000 yuan)
#国有经济	State-Owned Units	411.30	亿元	(100000000 yuan)
职工平均工资	Average Wage Bill of Staff	6603	元	(yuan)
#国有经济	State-Owned Units	7186	元	(yuan)
保险福利费用总额	Total Value of Insurance and Welfare Funds	201.26	亿元	(100000000 yuan)
#职工保险福利费	Insurance and Welfare Funds of Staff\=Per	73.41	亿元	(100000000 yuan)
城镇居民人均生活费收入	Capita Income Available for Living of Urban Residents	4688.80	元	(yuan)
农民人均纯收入	Per Capita Net Income of Rural Residents	3029.30	元	(yuan)
城乡居民储蓄存款余额	Savings Deposit Balance of Urban and Rural Residents	2570.28	亿元	(100000000 yuan)

职工工资总额（亿元）

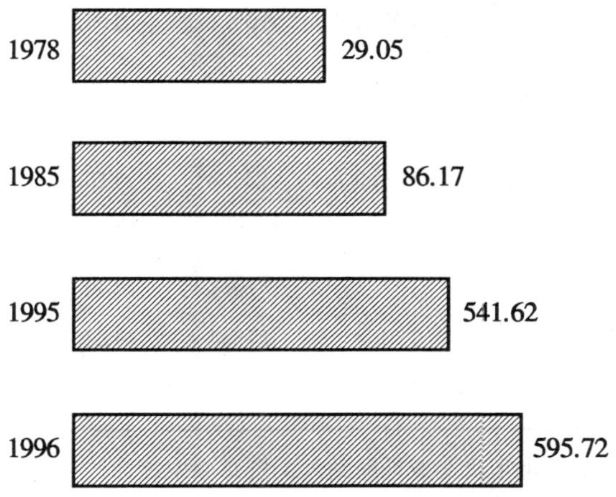

年份	亿元
1978	29.05
1985	86.17
1995	541.62
1996	595.72

职工工资总额构成（%）

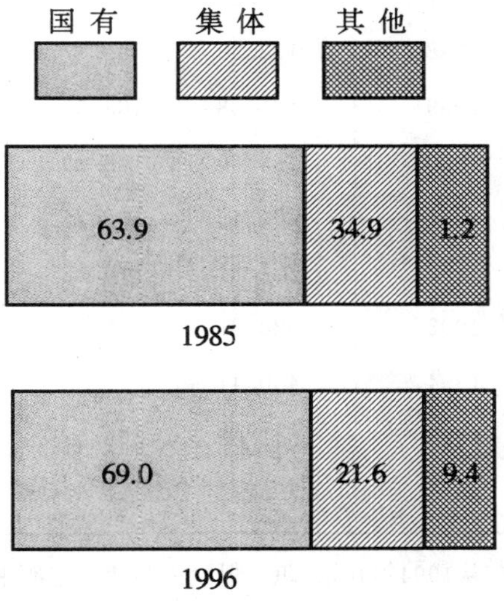

	国有	集体	其他
1985	63.9	34.9	1.2
1996	69.0	21.6	9.4

4—1 职工工资总额及指数

TOTAL WAGE BILL AND INDEX OF FORMAL EMPLOYEES

年份 Year	绝对数（亿元） Value (100 000 000 yuan)				指数（以上年为100） Index(previous year=100)			
	全部职工 Total	国有经济单位 State-Owned Uints	城镇集体经济单位 Collective-Owned Uints	其他经济类型单位 Other-Ownership Units	全部职工 Total Ownership	国有经济单位 State-Owned Units	城镇集体经济单位 Collective-Owned Units	其他经济类型单位 Other-Ownership Units
1971	16.38	11.82	4.56					
1972	18.51	13.04	5.47		113.0	110.3	120.0	
1973	19.38	13.49	5.89		104.7	103.5	107.7	
1974	20.22	13.76	6.46		104.3	102.0	109.7	
1975	21.20	14.03	7.17		104.8	102.0	111.0	
1976	22.50	14.59	7.91		106.1	104.0	110.3	
1977	26.24	17.91	8.33		116.6	122.8	105.3	
1978	29.05	19.84	9.21		110.7	110.8	110.6	
1979	33.10	22.46	10.64		113.9	113.2	115.5	
1980	41.63	27.99	13.64		125.8	124.6	128.2	
1981	44.13	29.60	14.53		106.0	105.8	106.5	
1982	48.14	32.35	15.79		109.1	109.3	108.7	
1983	50.78	34.41	16.37		105.5	106.4	103.7	
1984	67.28	43.34	23.25	0.69	132.5	126.0	142.0	
1985	86.17	55.10	30.09	0.98	128.1	127.1	129.4	142.0
1986	105.56	67.93	36.28	1.35	122.5	123.3	120.6	137.8
1987	121.26	78.09	41.30	1.87	114.9	115.0	113.8	138.5
1988	152.53	99.17	50.60	2.76	125.8	127.0	122.5	147.6
1989	165.38	108.56	53.05	3.77	108.4	109.5	104.8	136.6
1990	184.60	123.25	56.70	4.65	111.6	113.5	106.9	123.3
1991	204.43	136.26	62.05	6.12	110.7	110.6	109.4	131.6
1992	251.51	170.85	71.64	9.02	123.0	125.4	115.4	147.4
1993	328.21	221.91	85.85	20.45	130.5	129.9	119.8	226.7
1994	450.44	312.56	103.32	34.56	137.2	140.8	120.3	169.0
1995	541.62	369.10	126.57	45.95	120.2	118.1	122.5	132.9
1996	595.72	411.30	128.61	55.81	110.0	111.4	101.6	121.5

注：从1994年开始，职工保险福利费用总额中的洗理卫生费及上下班交通补贴纳入工资总额中统计。

Notes: Personal barber and bath fees as well as transportation subsidies for staff in total insurance and welfare funds ha been included in wages since 1994.

4—2 职工工资总额构成（1996）
TOTAL WAGE COMPOSITION OF STAFF

单位:亿元 (100 000 000 yuan)

行业	Sectors	职工工资总额 Total Wages of Staff	#计时和计件标准工作 Hour Rate and Piece Rate Wages	#奖金和计件超额工资 Bcnuses, Piece Rate and Above-quota Aayments	#津贴和补贴 Subsidies and Allowances
总计	**Total**	**595.72**	**344.19**	**94.32**	**136.55**
农、林、牧、渔业	Farming, Foresty, Animal Husbandry and Fishery	13.16	7.88	1.15	3.57
#农业	Farming	7.28	4.33	0.74	1.85
采掘业	Mining and Quarrying	20.94	11.19	3.85	4.73
制造业	Manufacturing	243.03	149.78	42.71	41.87
电力、煤气及水的生产和供应业	Electric Power, Gas and Water Production and Supply	13.89	8.80	2.41	2.25
建筑业	Construction	29.09	16.33	6.06	5.34
#土木工程建筑业	Civil Engineering Construction	21.41	12.36	4.21	3.84
地质勘查业、水利管理业	Geological Prospect and Water Conservency	4.48	2.09	0.39	1.91
交通运输、仓储及邮电通信业	Transportation, Storage, Post and Telecommunication Services	40.33	21.99	7.24	9.72
#仓储业	Storage	1.78	0.99	0.41	0.32
邮电通信业	Post and Telecommunication Services	6.89	3.59	2.09	1.06
批发和零售贸易、餐饮业	Wholesale, Retail Trade and Restaurants	67.64	43.29	10.44	11.78
#零售业	Retail Trade	25.29	16.45	3.63	4.33
餐饮业	Restaurants	2.68	1.62	0.41	0.48
金融、保险业	Banking and Insurance	13.31	5.33	1.72	5.62
#金融业	Banking	12.61	5.04	1.60	5.35
房地产业	Real Estate Management	4.39	2.08	0.85	1.25
社会服务业	Social Services	17.90	9.11	3.17	4.76
#公共服务业	Public Services	7.92	3.80	1.30	2.46
卫生、体育和社会福利业	Health Care, Sports and Social Welfare	21.11	10.32	2.46	7.59
教育、文化艺术和广播电影电视业	Education, Culture and Arts, Radio, Film and Television	59.56	32.58	5.34	20.55
#教育	Education	55.29	30.64	4.67	19.07
科学研究和综合技术服务业	Scientific Research and Polytechnical Services	7.83	3.32	1.14	3.20
国家机关、政党机关和社会团体	Government Agencies, Party Agencies and Social Organizations	35.63	18.13	4.73	11.67
其他行业	Other Sectors	3.43	1.97	0.66	0.74

4—3 分经济类型职工工资总额(1996)
TOTAL WAGE OF STAFF BY OWNERSHIP

单位:亿元 (100 000 000 yuan)

行业	Sectors	合计 Total	国有经济单位 State-Owned Uints	城镇集体经济单位 Collective-Owned Uints	其他经济类型单位 Other-Ownership Uints
总计	**Total**	**595.72**	**411.30**	**128.61**	**55.81**
农、林、牧、渔业	Farming, Foresty, Animal Husbandry and Fishery	13.16	12.56	0.54	0.06
#农业	Farming	7.28	7.21	0.04	0.03
采掘业	Mining and Quarrying	20.94	19.66	1.21	0.07
制造业	Manufacturing	243.03	131.93	66.17	44.93
电力、煤气及水的生产和供应业	Electric Power, Gas and Water Production and Supply	13.89	11.90	0.63	1.36
建筑业	Construction	29.09	18.45	10.04	0.60
#土木工程建筑业	Civil Engineering Construction	21.41	13.37	7.74	0.30
地质勘查业、水利管理业	Geological Prospect and Water Conservency	4.48	4.33	0.15	—
交通运输、仓储及邮电通信业	Transportation, Storage, Post and Telecommunication Services	40.33	32.44	6.83	1.06
#仓储业	Storage	1.78	1.47	0.12	0.19
邮电通信业	Post and Telecommunication Services	6.89	6.24	0.60	0.05
批发和零售贸易、餐饮业	Wholesale, Retail Trade and Restaurants	67.64	36.70	25.68	5.26
#零售业	Retail Trade	25.29	10.63	12.25	2.41
餐饮业	Restaurants	2.68	1.53	0.76	0.39
金融、保险业	Banking and Insurance	13.31	9.99	2.64	0.68
#金融业	Banking	12.61	9.33	2.63	0.65
房地产业	Real Estate Management	4.39	3.54	0.45	0.40
社会服务业	Social Services	17.90	13.59	3.13	1.18
#公共服务业	Public Services	7.92	6.53	1.22	0.17
卫生、体育和社会福利业	Health Care, Sports and Social Welfare	21.11	14.84	6.25	0.02
教育、文化艺术和广播电影电视业	Education, Culture and Arts, Radio, Film and Television	59.56	55.98	3.48	0.10
#教育	Education	55.29	52.16	3.11	0.02
科学研究和综合技术服务业	Scientific Research and Polytechnical Services	7.83	7.65	0.15	0.03
国家机关、政党机关和社会团体	Government Agencies, Party Agencies and Social Organizations	35.63	35.09	0.54	—
其他行业	Other Sectors	3.43	2.65	0.72	0.06

4—4 职工年平均货币工资及指数
ANNUAL AVERAGE MONEY WAGE AND INDEX OF STAFF

年份 year	绝对数(元) Value (yuan)				指数(以上年为100) Index (preceding year=100)			
	全部职工 Total	国有经济单位 State-Owned Units	城镇集体经济单位 Collective-Owned Units	其他经济类型单位 Other-Ownership Units	全部职工 Total	国有经济单位 State-Owned Units	城镇集体经济单位 Collective-Owned Units	其他经济类型单位 Other-Ownership Units
1971	467	502	396					
1972	481	515	415		103.0	102.6	104.8	
1973	476	523	396		99.0	101.6	95.4	
1974	495	543	416		104.0	103.8	105.1	
1975	491	534	423		99.2	98.3	101.7	
1976	483	531	414		98.4	99.4	97.9	
1977	474	517	402		98.1	97.4	97.1	
1978	513	563	432		108.2	108.9	107.5	
1979	565	618	478		110.3	109.8	110.9	
1980	667	721	578		117.8	116.7	120.7	
1981	672	718	594		100.7	99.6	102.8	
1982	703	748	626		104.6	104.2	105.4	
1983	723	768	643		102.8	102.7	102.7	
1984	931	1003	820	1012	128.8	130.6	127.5	
1985	1135	1211	1015	1237	121.9	120.7	123.8	122.2
1986	1327	1430	1166	1468	116.9	118.1	114.9	118.7
1987	1471	1581	1295	1639	110.9	110.6	111.1	111.6
1988	1796	1936	1564	2059	122.1	122.5	120.8	125.6
1989	1918	2082	1639	2185	106.8	107.5	104.8	106.1
1990	2129	2331	1776	2444	111.0	111.9	108.4	111.9
1991	2302	2501	1932	2773	108.1	107.3	108.8	113.5
1992	2800	3057	2292	3370	121.6	122.2	118.6	121.5
1993	3615	3896	2937	4434	129.1	127.4	128.1	131.6
1994	4974	5491	3728	5827	137.6	140.9	126.9	131.4
1995	5943	6441	4621	7137	119.5	117.3	124.0	122.5
1996	6603	7186	4990	7740	111.1	111.6	108.0	108.4

4—5 职工平均货币工资 (1996)
AVERAGE MONEY WAGE OF STAFF

单位:元 (yuan)

行业	Sectors	全部职工 Total	国有经济单位 State-Owned Uints	城镇集体经济单位 Collective-Owned Uints	其他经济类型单位 Other-Ownership Uints
总计	**Total**	**6603**	**7186**	**4990**	**7740**
农、林、牧、渔业	Farming, Foresty, Animal Husbandry and Fishery	4896	4898	4707	6831
#农业	Farming	4880	4869	5702	7128
采掘业	Mining and Quarrying	7738	8132	4427	4600
制造业	Manufacturing	6062	6526	4796	7395
电力、煤气及水的生产和供应业	Electric Power, Gas and Water Production and Supply	10732	10577	8258	14658
建筑业	Construction	7278	8149	6039	8542
#土木工程建筑业	Civil Engineering Construction	6781	7760	5547	7709
地质勘查业、水利管理业	Geological Prospect and Water Conservency	6841	6883	5816	—
交通运输、仓储及邮电通信业	Transportation, Storage, Post and Telecommunication Services	7392	8553	4439	8497
#仓储业	Storage	8161	7995	6468	12316
邮电通信业	Post and Telecommunication Services	10747	10715	11145	10247
批发和零售贸易、餐饮业	Wholesale, Retail Trade and Restaurants	5420	5790	4613	9151
#零售业	Retail Trade	4959	5684	4147	8734
餐饮业	Restaurants	5302	5799	4014	7440
金融、保险业	Banking and Insurance	9219	9463	7812	13528
#金融业	Banking	9204	9462	7813	13704
房地产业	Real Estate Management	8644	8579	7747	10773
社会服务业	Social Services	7325	7662	5878	8595
#公共服务业	Public Services	7563	7847	6237	8788
卫生、体育和社会福利业	Health Care, Sports and Social Welfare	7746	8090	7034	8368
教育、文化艺术和广播电影电视业	Education, Culture and Arts, Radio, Film and Television	7276	7490	4963	8982
#教育	Education	7221	7436	4857	7752
科学研究和综合技术服务业	Scientific Research and Polytechnical Services	9094	9115	8111	9386
国家机关、政党机关和社会团体	Government Agencies, Party Agencies and Social Organizations	8356	8376	7249	—
其他行业	Other Sectors	8100	8557	6762	8719

4—6 职工年平均货币工资构成(1996)
COMPOSITION OF ANNUAL AVERAGE MONEY WAGE OF STAFF

单位:元　　(yuan)

行业	Sectors	职工年平均货币工资 Annual Average Money Wage of Staff	#计时和计件标准工作 Hour Rate and Piece Rate Wage	#奖金和计件超额工资 Bonuses Piece Rate and Above-quota payments	#津贴和补贴 Subsidies and Allowances
总　计	**Total**	**6603**	**3815**	**1045**	**1514**
农、林、牧、渔业	Farming, Foresty, Animal Husbandry and Fishery	4896	2931	426	1328
#农业	Farming	4880	2903	493	1240
采掘业	Mining and Quarrying	7738	4134	1421	1749
制造业	Manufacturing	6062	3737	1066	1045
电力、煤气及水的生产和供应业	Electric Power, Gas and Water Production and Supply	10732	6795	1863	1733
建筑业	Construction	7278	4087	1516	1336
#土木工程建筑业	Civil Engineering Construction	6781	3914	1334	1217
地质勘查业、水利管理业	Geological Prospect and Water Conservency	6841	3193	588	2922
交通运输、仓储及邮电通信业	Transportation, Storage, Post and Telecommunication Services	7392	4031	1327	1782
#仓储业	Storage	8161	4528	1876	1473
邮电通信业	Post and Telecommunication Services	10747	5600	3265	1653
批发和零售贸易、餐饮业	Wholesale, Retail Trade and Restaurants	5420	3469	837	943
#零售业	Retail Trade	4959	3225	711	849
餐饮业	Restaurants	5302	3210	817	941
金融、保险业	Banking and Insurance	9219	3692	1193	3892
#金融业	Banking	9204	3680	1170	3907
房地产业	Real Estate Management	8644	4098	1673	2454
社会服务业	Social Services	7325	3726	1297	1947
#公共服务业	Public Services	7563	3624	1237	2352
卫生、体育和社会福利业	Health Care, Sports and Social Welfare	7746	3786	904	2784
教育、文化艺术和广播电影电视业	Education, Culture and Arts, Radio, Film and Television	7276	3980	652	2510
#教育	Education	7221	4001	610	2490
科学研究和综合技术服务业	Scientific Research and Polytechnical Services	9094	3853	1328	3719
国家机关、政党机关和社会团体	Government Agencies, Party Agencies and Social Organizations	8356	4252	1110	2738
其他行业	Other Sectors	8100	4645	1555	1753

4—7 职工平均工资指数
AVERAGE WAGE IBDEX OF STAFF

(1978=100)

年份 Year	全部职工 Total		国有经济单位 State-Owned Units		城镇集体经济单位 Collective-Owned Units		其他经济类型单位 Other Ownership Units	
	平均货币工资指数 Index of Average Money Wages	平均实际工资指数 Index of Average Real Wages	平均货币工资指数 Index of Average Money Wages	平均实际工资指数 Index of Average Real Wages	平均货币工资指数 Index of Average Real Wages	平均实际工资指数 Index of Average Money Wages	平均货币工资指数 Index of Average Money Wages	平均实际工资指数 Index of Average Real Wages
1978	100.0	100.0	100.0	100.0	100.0	100.0		
1980	130.0	121.7	128.1	119.9	133.8	125.3		
1985	221.2	174.9	215.1	170.0	235.0	185.8	122.2	111.5
1986	258.7	192.2	254.0	188.7	269.9	200.5	145.1	124.4
1987	286.7	192.8	280.8	188.8	299.8	201.6	162.0	125.7
1988	350.1	192.0	343.9	188.6	362.0	198.6	203.5	128.8
1989	373.9	176.8	369.8	174.8	379.4	179.4	215.9	117.8
1990	415.0	189.8	414.0	189.3	411.1	188.0	241.5	127.4
1991	448.7	190.5	444.2	188.6	447.2	189.9	274.0	134.2
1992	545.8	213.2	543.0	212.1	530.6	207.3	333.0	149.9
1993	704.7	231.9	692.0	227.7	679.9	223.7	438.1	166.1
1994	969.6	254.6	975.3	256.1	863.0	226.6	575.8	174.2
1995	1158.5	261.7	1144.0	258.5	1069.7	241.7	705.2	183.6
1996	1287.1	262.5	1276.4	260.3	1155.1	235.5	764.8	179.7

注:其他经济类型单位职工平均工资指数1984年=100。
Note:The Average staff wage index of other ownership units was 100 in 1984.

4—8 保险福利费用总额及指数
TOTAL VALUE INDEX OF INSURANCE AND WELFARE INDEX

年份 Year	绝对数(亿元) Value (100 000 000 yuan)				指数(以上年为100) Index(previous year=100)			
	保险福利费总额 Total Value of Insurance and Welfare Funds	国有经济单位 State-Owned Units	城镇集体经济单位 Collective-Owned Uints	其他经济类型单位 Other-Ownership Uints	保险福利费总额 Total Value of Insurance and Welfare Funds	国有经济单位 State-Owned Units	城镇集体经济单位 Collective-Owned Units	其他经济类型单位 Other-Ownership Units
1978		2.82						
1980	7.06	5.07	1.99			122.5		
1985	20.17	13.57	6.33	0.27	126.5	126.5	125.1	180.0
1986	26.95	18.20	8.40	0.35	133.6	134.1	132.7	129.6
1987	31.86	21.41	9.95	0.50	118.2	117.6	118.5	142.9
1988	42.01	28.39	12.85	0.77	131.9	132.6	129.1	154.0
1989	49.16	33.28	14.82	1.06	117.0	117.2	115.3	137.7
1990	60.94	41.90	17.65	1.39	124.0	125.9	119.1	131.1
1991	68.97	47.87	19.29	1.81	113.2	114.2	109.3	130.2
1992	85.41	60.20	22.83	2.38	123.8	125.8	118.4	131.5
1993	112.04	77.99	29.31	4.74	131.2	129.6	128.4	199.2
1994	136.65	95.74	33.99	6.92	122.0	122.8	116.0	146.0
1995	167.62	118.25	40.44	8.93	122.7	123.5	119.0	129.0
1996	201.26	143.57	45.24	12.45	120.1	121.4	111.9	139.4

注:1. 保险福利费用总额中包括职工及离休、退休、退职人员的保险福利费。
2. 从1990年开始,保险福利费用总额中包括发给离休、退休、退职人员的肉类价格补贴。

Notes:1. Total insurance and welfare funds include insurance and welfare funds for the staff, retired and quited personnel.
2. Total insurance and welfare funds include meat price subsidies for the retired and quited personnel, since 1990.

4—9 职工保险福利费用构成情况(1996)
COMPOSITION OF INSURANCE AND WELFARE FUNDS FOR STAFF

单位:亿元　　(100 000 000 yuan)

指标	Items	合计 Total	国有经济单位 State-Owned Units	城镇集体经济单位 Collective-Owned Uints	其他经济类型单位 Other-Ownership Uints
总计	**Total**	**73.41**	**54.43**	**12.83**	**6.15**
集体保险福利费	Collective Insurance and Welfare Funds	62.46	46.46	10.53	5.47
集体福利事业补贴费及集体福利设施费	Subsidy Funds for Collective Welfare Sercice and Facilities	15.77	11.64	2.47	1.66
文体宣传费	Expences for Culture Activities, Sports and Propaganda	2.15	1.63	0.34	0.18
医疗卫生费	Expences for Medical Care	39.33	29.56	6.79	2.98
其他	Others	5.21	3.63	0.93	0.65
个人保险福利费	Individual Insurance and Welfare Funds	10.95	7.97	2.30	0.68
丧葬抚恤救济费	Funeral Expences and Pensions for Relief	1.24	0.92	0.26	0.06
生活困难补助	Subsidies for Living Expences	1.98	1.40	0.46	0.12
计划生育补贴	Subsidies for Birth Control	1.74	1.21	0.40	0.13
冬季取暖补贴	Subsidies for Winter Warm	0.80	0.65	0.13	0.02
其他	Others	5.19	3.79	1.05	0.35

4—10 离休、退休、退职人员的保险福利费用构成(1996)
COMPOSITION OF INSURANCE AND WELFARE FOR RETIRED AND QUITED PERSONNEL

单位:亿元　　(100 000 000 yuan)

指标	Items	合计 Total	国有经济单位 State-Owned Units	城镇集体经济单位 Collective-Owned Uints	其他经济类型单位 Other-Ownership Uints
保险福利费用总计	**Total Funds for Insurance and Welfare**	**127.85**	**89.14**	**32.41**	**6.30**
离休金	Pension for VCSR	9.90	8.80	0.91	0.19
退休金	Pension for Retirement	86.75	58.67	23.50	4.58
退职生活费	Living Expenses for Resignation	1.87	1.01	0.76	0.10
医疗卫生费	Expences for Medical Care	19.89	15.20	3.72	0.97
交通费补贴	Subsidies for Transportation	0.50	0.41	0.06	0.03
丧葬抚恤救济费	Funeral Expenses and Pensions for Relief	2.25	1.57	0.57	0.11
冬季取暖补贴	Subsidies for Winter Warm	0.20	0.16	0.04	…
其他	Others	6.49	3.32	2.85	0.32

4—11 城镇居民家庭基本情况
BASIC INDICATORS OF URBAN HOUSEHOLD INCOME AND EXPENDITURES

指　　标	Items	1985	1990	1995	1996
调查户数　(户)	Household Surveyed　(household)	1535	2220	2020	2020
平均每户家庭人口　(人)	Average Person Per Household　(person)	3.64	3.34	3.19	3.18
平均每户就业人口　(人)	Average Employment Per Household　(person)	2.18	2.00	1.85	1.83
平均每一就业人口负担人数　(人)	Persons Supported By Each Employee　(person)	1.67	1.67	1.72	1.73
平均每户就业面　(%)	Percentage of Employees Per Household　(%)	59.90	59.88	57.99	57.71
平均每人居住面积　(平方米)	Average Living Floor Space Per Capita　(sq·m)	7.20	9.06	10.59	10.61
平均每人辅助面积　(平方米)	Average Subsidiary Floor Space Per Capita　(sq·m)		3.94	5.72	5.67
平均每人全年可支配收入　(元)	Annual Average Allocatable Income Per Capita　(yuan)	942.73	1599.96	4619.59	5164.08
现金收入　(元)	Cash Income Per Capita　(yuan)	950.90	1852.45	5454.33	6293.40
实际收入	Actual Income	830.78	1613.05	4647.33	5188.01
#生活费收入	Per Capita Income Available for Living	765.76	1463.79	4209.05	4688.80
借贷收入	Debit and Credit	120.12	239.40	807.00	1105.39
#提取储蓄存款	Income Per Capita Draw Money from Bank	86.48	182.39	584.82	832.61
兑售有价证券	Exchange and Sell Valuable Negotiale Securities		2.41	12.34	25.42
在实际收入中　(元)	Among Actual Income　(yuan)				
职工工资性收入	Wages of Staff	593.52	1053.01	3223.10	3471.29
职工从单位得到的其他收入	Other Income of Staff	104.76	146.93	208.24	198.80
个体经营劳动者收入	Income of Individual Laborers	2.69	10.12	36.34	34.50
被聘用和留用离退休人员收入	Reemployment Income of Retirees	5.97	17.64	58.18	62.36
其他就业者收入	Income of Other Employees		2.70	2.21	1.95
其他劳动收入	Part-Time Income	12.92	13.77	56.52	81.52
财产性收入	Interest Dividends and Rent		22.59	65.35	84.40
转移性收入	Pensions, Subside, Donations and Other		276.48	989.41	1149.02
平均每人全年现金支出　(元)	Annual Cash Expenditions Per Capita　(yuan)	927.88	1816.04	5372.69	6117.67
实际支出	Annual Expenditures	768.82	1470.88	4343.08	4961.33
#消费性支出	Living Expenditures	719.59	1338.66	3772.28	4057.50
借贷支出	Debit and Credit Expenditures	159.06	345.16	1029.61	1156.35
#存入储蓄款	Deposit Money in Bank	111.80	278.48	810.72	866.38
购买有价证券	Buy Valuable Nogotiable Securities		6.50	38.72	33.18

4—12 城镇居民家庭年人均现金收入和生活费收入
URBAN HOUSESHOLD ANNUAL PER CAPITA CASH INCOME AND INCOME AVAILABLE FOR LIVING

单位:元 (yuan)

分 组	Grouped	1990	1994	1995	1996
人均现金收入	Cash Income Per Capita	1852.45	4630.54	5454.33	6293.40
最低收入户	Lowest Income	1068.15	2314.76	2997.31	3259.67
低收入户	Low Income	1318.24	3052.39	3704.65	3746.43
中等偏下户	Medium-Low Income	1533.10	3339.26	4096.05	4689.78
中等收入户	Medium Income	1785.93	4338.93	5267.97	5612.64
中等偏上户	Medium-High Income	2093.00	5330.16	6166.18	7596.71
高收入户	High Income	2531.07	6863.42	7383.49	8960.23
最高收入户	Highest Income	3219.55	9408.40	10524.32	12615.85
人均生活费收入	Per Capita Income Available for Living	1463.79	3461.12	4209.05	4688.80
最低收入户	Lowest Income	857.36	1708.92	2149.59	2415.24
低收入户	Low Income	1064.04	2234.23	2733.87	3050.85
中等偏下户	Medium-Low Income	1229.19	2691.81	3335.72	3662.07
中等收入户	Medium Income	1430.24	3227.43	4044.24	4406.72
中等偏上户	Medium-High Income	1661.72	4056.25	4863.93	5432.75
高收入户	High Income	1947.48	5002.08	5860.28	6651.91
最高收入户	Highest Income	2448.00	6658.06	7716.54	8734.02

城乡居民生活消费支出构成(%)

(1996)

城 镇 居 民

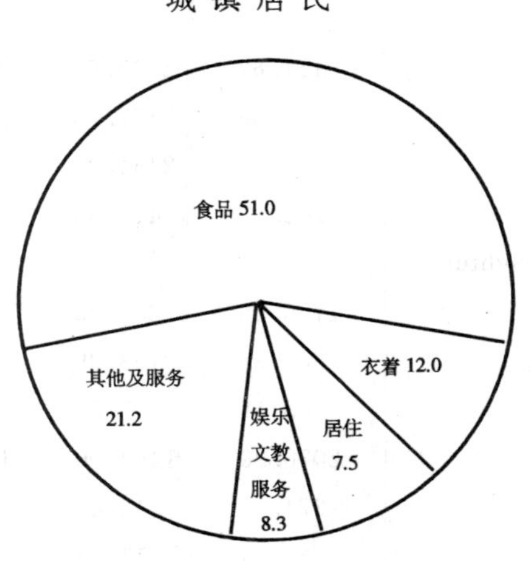

农 村 居 民

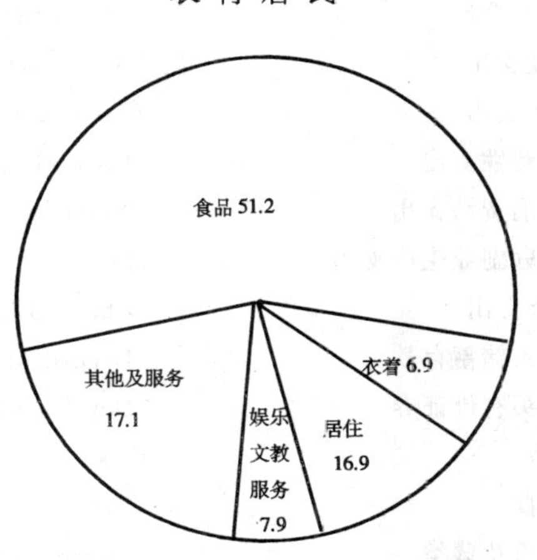

4—13 城镇居民家庭年人均收入支出情况(1996)

单位:元

指标	Items	全省调查户平均水平 Total Average	最低收入户占10% Lowest Income Make up 10%	#更低收入户占5% Lower Income Make up 5%
可支配收入	Annual Allocatable Income Per Capita	5164.08	2746.77	2459.94
现金收入	Cash Income	6293.40	3259.67	2916.54
实际收入	Actual Income	5188.01	2764.06	2476.28
#生活费收入	Per Capita Income Available for Living	4688.80	2415.24	2132.81
全民所有制职工工资	Wages of Staff in State-Owned Units	2659.91	1081.87	831.74
集体所有制职工工资	Wages of Staff in Collective-Owned Units	811.38	887.03	957.86
其它所有制职工全部收入	Total Income of Staff in Other Owned Units	92.97	3.94	
职工从单位得到其他收入	Other Income of Staff	198.80	62.85	43.60
个体经营者的净收益	Net Income of Individual Laborers	34.50	26.41	43.72
个体被雇者收入	Income of Employed Individual Laborers	10.69	4.57	
离退休再就业人员收入	Replacement Income of Retirees	62.36	34.01	7.89
其他就业者收入	Other Employee's Income	1.95	1.45	2.55
其他劳动收入	Part-Time Income	81.52	40.60	55.04
财产性收入	Interest, Dividends and Rent	84.40	23.20	20.94
#利息	Interest	62.46	15.97	13.75
转移性收入	Pensions, Subsidies, Donations and Other	1149.02	598.14	512.93
#离退休金	Pensions for Retirees	930.04	467.58	380.63
家庭副业生产收入	Household Sideline Production Income	0.50		
借贷收入	Debit and Credit Income	1105.39	495.62	440.26
#提取储蓄存款	Draw Money from Bank	832.61	304.53	312.20
兑售有价证券	Exchange and Sell Valuable Negotiable Securities	25.42	7.70	
现金支出	Cash Expenditures	6117.67	3167.63	2838.38
实际支出	Actual Expenditures	4961.33	2877.70	2618.38
消费性支出	Living Expenditures	4057.50	2464.23	2280.81
非消费性支出	Nonliving Expenditures	902.73	412.56	335.96
家庭副业生产支出	Household Sideline Production Expenditures	1.10	0.92	1.61
借贷支出	Debit and Credit Expenditures	1156.35	289.93	220.00
#存入储蓄存款	Deposit Money in Bank	866.38	193.09	149.79
购买有价证券	Buy Valuable Negotiable Securities	33.18	5.30	4.95
食品	Food	2070.29	1494.00	1388.69
#粮食	Grain	274.02	242.40	238.31
淀粉及薯类	Starches and Tubers	21.74	17.24	16.49
干豆类及制品	Beans and Bean Products	47.99	37.43	37.31

AVERAGE PER CAPITA INDICATORS OF URBAN HOUSEHOLD ANNUAL INCOME AND EXPENDITURES

(yuan)

按收入水平分组 Grouped by Level of Income					
低收入户 占 10 % Low Income Make up 10%	中等偏下户 占 20 % Medium-Low Income Make up 20%	中等收入户 占 20 % Medium Income Make up 20%	中等偏上户 占 20 % Medium-High Income Make up 20%	高收入户 占 10 % High Income Make up 10%	最高收入户 占 10 % Highest Income Make up 10%
3374.27	4033.55	4879.37	5973.74	7342.85	9444.46
3746.43	4689.78	5612.64	7596.71	8960.23	12615.85
3392.80	4054.61	4907.24	5998.28	7367.53	9478.66
3050.85	3662.07	4406.72	5432.75	6651.91	8734.02
1362.78	1917.48	2532.85	3339.35	4080.03	5168.46
969.70	900.13	767.60	648.97	981.00	595.91
23.45	38.21	95.69	159.89	159.30	190.92
65.91	103.77	167.22	270.18	326.42	524.02
8.61	52.35	36.51	24.86	17.39	68.18
0.60	13.96	13.49	10.07	13.52	14.82
37.75	37.61	43.24	81.73	89.90	154.81
	0.35	7.96	0.74		
97.81	72.74	64.61	85.43	73.13	168.55
20.77	32.11	48.38	96.50	130.55	359.81
17.08	17.49	39.47	70.39	100.21	270.56
805.39	885.89	1129.69	1277.97	1496.29	2233.18
661.80	727.46	896.05	1050.72	1257.48	1749.06
			2.61		
353.63	635.17	705.40	1598.42	1592.70	3137.19
261.07	465.11	545.18	1194.70	1325.80	2341.47
4.71	15.27	9.89	31.92	68.26	70.75
3667.46	4576.12	5396.72	7411.48	8756.59	12218.49
3230.65	3940.94	4547.62	6037.44	6675.51	8709.98
2838.62	3387.11	3881.99	4847.42	5427.73	6245.65
392.01	553.66	661.79	1188.96	1247.77	2464.32
0.01	0.18	3.83	1.06	0.01	
436.81	635.18	849.11	1374.04	2081.09	3508.51
327.71	474.35	640.68	1058.22	1600.59	2546.45
2.92	24.55	20.45	20.15	41.72	169.85
1692.09	1879.39	2089.78	2308.42	2477.55	2678.92
259.66	266.01	272.32	289.83	287.95	302.97
19.63	21.79	22.18	23.27	23.39	23.60
40.60	43.91	49.87	50.53	55.78	61.22

续表

单位：元

指标	Items	全省调查户平均水平 Total Average	最低收入户占 10 % Lowest Income Make up 10%	#更低收入户占 5 % Lower Income Make up 5%
油脂类	Oil and Fats	65.03	56.40	51.49
肉禽及制品	Meat, Poultry and Related Products	504.11	359.90	325.95
蛋类	Eggs	87.76	64.52	59.65
水产品类	Aquatic Products	198.93	137.26	125.37
菜类	Vegetables	213.34	167.52	155.20
调味品	Flavorings	30.38	22.44	20.37
糖类	Sugar	22.99	15.85	14.93
烟草类	Tobacco	93.53	62.11	60.82
酒和饮料	Liquor	80.93	44.99	37.62
干鲜瓜果类	Dried and Fresh Melons and Fruits	97.50	63.27	50.46
坚果及果仁	Muts and Grains	22.99	13.25	11.09
糕点类	Cake	41.17	29.54	22.75
奶及奶制品	Milk and Dairy Products	35.20	20.78	18.41
其它食品	Other Foods	34.39	21.93	17.55
衣着支出	Clothing	485.29	249.19	219.35
#服装	Garments	280.72	133.75	121.42
衣着材料	Clothing Materials	60.15	29.39	22.31
鞋袜帽及其它	Shoes, Hats, Socks and Other Clothing	124.95	77.61	69.72
设备用品及服务	Facilities, Artical and Service	364.72	112.98	114.09
耐用消费品	Durable Consumer Goods	211.96	35.60	38.26
室内装饰品	Interior Decorations	9.46	1.69	2.13
床上用品	Bed Articals	18.43	9.46	7.95
家庭日用杂品	Daily Use Articals	89.00	56.27	54.22
家具材料	furniture Materials	7.01	0.17	0.28
家庭服务	Household Services	28.86	9.80	11.26
医疗保健	Medicine and Medical Services	94.40	63.26	46.72
交通和通讯	Transportation and Communications	233.48	94.97	112.02
#交通费	Transportation	29.18	16.41	12.81
通讯费	Communications	63.95	32.94	44.99
娱乐文教服务	Recreation, Education and Cultural Services	337.28	180.61	164.39
#耐用消费品	Durable Consumer Goods	57.10	5.71	1.85
教育	Education	184.25	131.04	121.46
文化娱乐	Cultural Recreation	95.92	43.86	41.08
居住	Residence	306.11	193.70	168.56
#房租	Rent	39.86	28.07	16.88
水	Water	16.08	13.13	10.83
电	Electricity	79.74	51.73	48.94
杂项商品和服务	Miscellaneous Commodities and Services	165.94	75.53	66.99
#旅游	Tour	24.93	7.98	10.84

Continued

(yuan)

按收入水平分组 Grouped by Level of Income					
低收入户 占10% Low Income Make up 10%	中等偏下户 占20% Medium-Low Income Make up 20%	中等收入户 占20% Medium Income Make up 20%	中等偏上户 占20% Medium-High Income Make up 20%	高收入户 占10% High Income Make up 10%	最高收入户 占10% Highest Income Make up 10%
61.38	65.50	65.97	68.09	64.56	70.48
423.80	466.49	518.21	564.27	581.10	620.11
72.92	87.15	87.27	96.69	96.66	107.48
157.78	181.98	201.57	228.71	235.25	253.95
175.44	204.39	218.13	232.50	240.76	254.36
26.02	28.01	30.57	34.14	37.28	34.94
18.81	20.22	23.60	24.81	28.75	31.73
66.76	80.97	85.01	116.10	118.49	136.75
53.87	71.77	82.23	101.33	93.05	118.42
74.85	80.30	100.22	111.26	133.40	128.04
16.83	19.49	22.05	25.45	32.69	36.85
32.65	34.56	42.45	43.96	54.12	58.34
20.98	29.33	37.53	37.66	49.97	57.40
24.31	30.03	33.20	41.40	47.98	44.94
311.11	372.98	485.63	569.36	722.92	808.73
170.21	205.05	278.50	337.65	428.39	493.56
37.23	50.38	62.92	66.87	93.01	92.45
91.13	103.67	125.39	141.78	166.75	190.94
154.79	219.78	257.73	627.55	559.35	721.68
60.40	112.09	131.70	400.14	336.23	479.05
1.74	4.86	6.11	12.67	27.38	20.53
11.05	13.46	15.33	25.17	24.01	36.06
66.20	70.85	81.42	106.18	128.76	136.07
4.77	0.40	2.50	20.19	11.18	10.40
10.63	18.12	20.66	63.19	31.80	39.57
59.07	70.84	92.45	111.35	134.54	154.68
112.46	161.89	187.15	292.91	429.38	481.22
14.18	20.96	27.17	32.87	47.91	58.51
34.82	50.51	62.29	90.24	85.17	92.29
212.15	283.34	320.28	361.75	451.14	666.29
25.85	28.81	42.92	49.22	73.28	252.52
135.06	186.76	174.26	203.61	233.18	231.15
51.23	67.77	103.10	108.92	144.68	182.61
211.91	263.81	295.67	378.49	390.69	431.38
32.48	36.83	40.33	44.12	47.83	51.37
13.59	15.30	16.97	17.78	16.28	18.59
59.74	72.70	83.48	94.49	89.86	103.21
85.03	135.08	153.29	197.59	262.16	302.76
6.08	20.88	16.68	36.69	43.86	50.50

4—14 城镇居民家庭平均每人全年购买主要商品数量 URBAN HOUSEHOLD ANNUAL PER CAPITA PURCHASES OF MAJOR COMMODITIES

单位:公斤 (kg)

项目	Items	1978	1980	1985	1990	1995	1996
粮食(贸易粮)	Grain (Processed)	155.00	162.60	128.60	119.00	96.31	93.59
植物油	Edible Vegetable Oil	4.00	4.20	7.30	6.98	7.31	7.14
鲜菜	Fresh Vegetables	115.00	181.20	122.00	117.73	112.30	107.57
猪肉	Pork	11.25	18.00	16.40	18.49	19.86	19.50
牛羊肉	Beef and Mutton	1.00	2.40	1.10	2.38	1.40	1.95
家禽	Poultry	2.40	2.40	6.00	4.35	7.11	6.46
鲜蛋	Fresh Eggs	4.10	4.20	8.50	7.54	10.89	10.85
鱼虾	Fish and Shrimp	5.50	9.00	9.90	10.76	14.31	14.51
食糖	Sugar	2.00	3.00	2.80	2.83	2.04	2.08
卷烟 (盒)	Cigarettes (pack)	25.00	30.00	48.70	33.62	26.10	22.77
白酒	Liquor			2.30	2.78	2.71	2.64
茶叶	Tea		0.18	0.20	0.18	0.13	0.15
鲜瓜果	Fresh Mealon and Fruits		15.00	38.00	45.32	48.87	41.81
糖果	Candy		1.20	1.00	0.62	0.66	0.58
糕点	Cake		3.00	4.40	3.94	3.11	2.94
鲜奶	Fresh Dairy		3.60	5.50	3.72	3.84	4.00
服装 (件)	Clothing (peice)					4.82	4.49
棉布 (米)	Cotton Cloth (m)	4.00	4.48	2.59	1.23	0.47	0.46
化纤布 (米)	Chemical Fiber Cloth (m)	4.60	2.24	2.21	1.52	1.33	1.24
呢绒 (米)	Woolen Fabric (m)	0.10	0.31	0.51	0.30	0.23	0.16
绸缎 (米)	Silk and Stins (m)	0.30	0.44	0.80	0.41	0.22	0.16
布鞋 (双)	Cloth Shoes (pairs)		0.65	0.30	0.28	0.15	0.14
皮鞋 (双)	Leather Shoes (pairs))	0.20	0.58	0.63	0.52	0.64	0.66
肥皂 (块)	Soap (pcs)		9.14	5.80	3.12	1.75	1.60
洗衣粉	Detergent		0.41	0.80	0.73	0.85	0.88

注:家禽、鲜蛋、鱼虾、鲜瓜果,1992年因方法制度改变,均包括其他禽及制品、其他蛋及制品、其他鱼及制品、其他鲜瓜果及制品。

Note: Poultry, fresh eggs, fish and shrimp, fresh mealon and fruits include other poultry, eggs, fish, fresh mealon and fruits, and their relative products, as the change of statistical methood and regulation since 1992.

4—15 城镇居民家庭居住情况
LIVING CONDITIONS OF URBAN HOUSEHOLD

单位:户 (household)

指 标	Items	1990	1994	1995	1996
总 计	**Total**	**2220**	**2020**	**2020**	**2020**
按居住面积分	Grouped by Residential Space				
无房户	No Housing				
4平方米以下	Lower 4 sq·m	40	36	27	28
4—6平方米	4—6 sq·m	287	253	212	205
6—8平方米	6—8 sq·m	496	463	437	423
8—10平方米	8—10 sq·m	1307	469	452	459
10—12平方米	10—12 sq·m		244	272	277
12—14平方米	12—14 sq·m		200	229	236
14平方米以上	Over 14 sq·m		354	391	392
按卫生设备拥有分	Grouped by Possession of Sanitary Equipment				
无卫生设备	No Sanitary Equipment	1204	840	775	737
有浴室厕所	Provided with Bathroom and Toilet	296	755	865	893
有厕所无浴室	Provided with Toilet but No Bathroom	547	335	306	320
公用卫生设备	Public Sanitary Equipment	173	70	74	70
按厨房使用分	Grouped by Usage of Kitchen				
无厨房	No Kitchen	217	114	89	73
独用厨房	Sololy Kitchen	1891	1846	1870	1890
公用厨房	Public Kitchen	112	60	62	56
按房屋产权分	Grouped by Ownership of Housing				
公房	Residence of Public Property	1664	1211	1173	1059
租赁私房	Rent Private Owned Residence	23	22	13	11
自有房	One's Own Residence	532	787	834	950
其他	Others	1			
按燃料使用分	Grouped by Usage of Fuel				
管道煤气	Piping Gas	174	282	313	336
液化石油气	Liquified Petroleum Gas (LPG)	629	1056	1089	1154
煤	Coal	1416	671	606	527
其他	Others	1	12	11	3
按住宅建筑式样分	Grouped by Type of Construction				
家庭单栋配套楼房	Single Household Flat Storied Building		15	21	24
单元式配套住宅	Multi-Entrances Flat Residence		1001	1036	1055
一居室	One Room		139	130	115
二居室	Two Rooms		560	573	598
三居室	Three Rooms		276	313	321
四居室及以上	Four Rooms Over		26	19	20
普通楼房	Ordinary Storied Building		295	287	285
其它住宅	Others		710	676	656

4—16 城镇居民家庭平均每百户年末耐用品拥有量

URBAN HOUSEHOLD YEAR—END POSSESION OF DURABLE CONSUMER GOODS PER 100HOUSEHOLDS

项目		Items	1985	1990	1995	1996
毛皮大衣	(件)	Fur Coats	16.00	23.90	31.31	36.88
呢大衣	(件)	Woolen Coats	148.00	206.90	257.18	274.00
毛毯	(条)	Woolen Blankets	76.00	112.83	130.54	133.00
地毯	(平方米)	Carpets			138.29	128.67
大衣柜	(个)	Wardrobes	97.00	105.92	93.60	93.25
沙发	(个)	Sofas	116.00	149.20	152.55	149.94
写字台	(张)	Writting Desks	83.00	97.87	99.34	99.72
组合家具	(套)	Combined Furniture	2.00	9.41	29.68	30.90
沙发床	(个)	Sofa Beds	2.00	10.73	20.97	23.99
自行车	(辆)	Bicycles	166.00	217.04	237.46	237.96
缝纫机	(架)	Sewing Machines	73.10	71.79	69.48	69.31
电风扇	(台)	Electric Fans	102.00	220.16	259.07	267.11
洗衣机	(台)	Washing Machines	48.00	85.81	95.35	96.59
电冰箱	(台)	Refrigerators	6.00	48.09	69.42	72.28
冰柜	(台)	Freezers			1.93	2.27
摩托车	(辆)	Motorcycles	1.00	1.90	6.77	8.99
电视机	(台)	Television Sets	91.00	118.65	124.85	125.64
#彩电		Color TV Sets	9.00	51.46	85.22	87.97
收录机	(台)	Recorders	41.00	70.71	74.73	76.01
#立体声收录机		Stereo-Recorders	18.00	38.32	27.85	27.82
照相机	(架)	Cameras	7.00	17.11	28.57	30.09
中高档乐器	(件)	Medium and High-Grade Musical Instruments	3.00	7.45	5.37	5.81
钢琴	(架)	Pianos			0.52	0.64
空调器	(台)	Air Conditioners		0.07	10.53	14.79
电炊具	(个)	Electric Cooking Tools	3.00	45.83	111.05	118.33
组合音响	(套)	Hi-Fi Systems		0.62	10.09	10.64
录放像机	(台)	Videorecorders		2.45	20.57	21.35
游戏机	(台)	Computer Games			21.66	22.53
淋浴热水器	(台)	Showers			30.80	33.38
脱排油烟机	(台)	Range Hoods			34.26	37.79
吸尘器	(台)	Vacum Cleaners			13.37	12.74

4—17 农民家庭基本情况
BASIC INDICATORS OF RURAL HOUSEHOLDS

指　　　　标	Items	1990	1995	1996
调查户数　　　（户）	**Households Surveyed　(Household)**	**3400**	**3400**	**3400**
调查户人口　　（人）	**Residents Surveyed　(person)**			
常住人口	Permanent Residents	14071	13644	13449
平均每户常住人口	Average Permanent Residents Per Household	4.1	4.0	4.0
平均每户整、半劳动力	Average Full-Time and Part-Time Laborers Per Household	2.78	2.79	2.71
平均每个劳动力负担人口（包括劳动力本人）	Average Persons Suported by Each Laborer (including the laborer-self)	1.5	1.4	1.5
平均每人全年收入　（元）	Average Per Capita Annual Income (yuan)			
总收入	Total Revenue	1182.0	3290.9	4009.8
纯收入	Net Income	883.8	2456.9	3029.3
现金收入	Cash Income	1119.1	2696.4	3676.0
按人均纯收入水平分组的户数占调查总户数的比重（%）	**Percentage of Households by Per Capita Annual Net Income　(%)**			
300元以下	Below 300 yuan	6.0	0.4	0.3
300—500元	300—500	16.5	0.6	0.4
500—800元	500—800	28.8	2.8	1.3
800—1500元	800—1500	35.0	20.2	12.4
1500—2000元	1500—2000	8.2	18.4	17.7
2000元以上	2000 yuan and Over	5.5	57.6	67.9
平均每人全年支出　（元）	**Average Per Capita Annual Expenditures (yuan)**			
总支出	Total Expenditures	1095.0	2861.6	3511.8
#家庭经营性支出	Household Business Expenditures	234.5	675.2	808.3
生活消费支出	Living Expenditures	787.0	1938.0	2414.4
其他非借贷性支出	Other Non-Credit Expenditures	17.6	79.1	110.1
现金支出	Cash Expenditures	1049.7	2466.1	3295.2
#生产性费用	Productive Costs	208.5	579.9	730.3
缴纳税金、上交集体承包费、集体提留和摊派	Taxes and Payments to Collective	42.8	83.9	83.9
生活消费支出	Consumption Expenditures	569.7	1285.8	1793.8
储蓄借贷支出	Savings and Credit Expenditures	153.8	357.8	443.1

4—18 农民家庭平均每人总收入和纯收入
ANNUAL PER CAPITA REVENUE AND NET INCOME OF RURAL HOUSEHOLDS

单位:元　　(yuan)

<table>
<tr><th>指　标</th><th>Items</th><th>1990</th><th>1995</th><th>1996</th></tr>
<tr><td>总 收 入</td><td>Total Revenue</td><td>1182. 0</td><td>3290. 9</td><td>4009. 8</td></tr>
<tr><td>基本收入</td><td>Basic Income</td><td>1148. 9</td><td>3189. 9</td><td>3841. 7</td></tr>
<tr><td>劳动者的报酬收入</td><td>Reward of Labourers</td><td>300. 6</td><td>821. 9</td><td>1119. 4</td></tr>
<tr><td>#在集体组织中劳动的报酬收入</td><td>Collective Organizes</td><td>30. 0</td><td>81. 8</td><td>126. 0</td></tr>
<tr><td>在企业劳动得到的报酬收入</td><td>Enterprises</td><td>270. 6</td><td>715. 4</td><td>930. 9</td></tr>
<tr><td>家庭经营收入</td><td>House Business Revenue</td><td>848. 3</td><td>2368. 0</td><td>2722. 3</td></tr>
<tr><td>#种植业收入</td><td>Faming</td><td>458. 3</td><td>1452. 5</td><td>1514. 7</td></tr>
<tr><td>林业收入</td><td>Forestry</td><td>8. 7</td><td>12. 7</td><td>13. 3</td></tr>
<tr><td>牧业收入</td><td>Animal Husbandry</td><td>233. 6</td><td>483. 0</td><td>532. 0</td></tr>
<tr><td>渔业收入</td><td>Fishery</td><td>18. 7</td><td>44. 6</td><td>43. 0</td></tr>
<tr><td>手工业收入</td><td>Handicraft</td><td>19. 4</td><td>62. 7</td><td>90. 4</td></tr>
<tr><td>采集捕猎收入</td><td>Gathering and Hunting</td><td>1. 9</td><td>2. 8</td><td>5. 8</td></tr>
<tr><td>工业收入</td><td>Industry</td><td>14. 3</td><td>31. 6</td><td>76. 5</td></tr>
<tr><td>建筑业收入</td><td>Construction</td><td>26. 8</td><td>99. 9</td><td>148. 2</td></tr>
<tr><td>运输业收入</td><td>Transportation</td><td>21. 5</td><td>60. 3</td><td>103. 8</td></tr>
<tr><td>商业收入</td><td>Commerce</td><td>14. 8</td><td>54. 4</td><td>76. 2</td></tr>
<tr><td>饮食业收入</td><td>Food Services</td><td>2. 7</td><td>7. 3</td><td>10. 6</td></tr>
<tr><td>服务业收入</td><td>Services Trade</td><td>12. 4</td><td>26. 4</td><td>53. 6</td></tr>
<tr><td>转移性收入</td><td>Transfer Income</td><td rowspan="2">33. 1</td><td>75. 5</td><td>111. 7</td></tr>
<tr><td>财产性收入</td><td>Property Income</td><td>25. 5</td><td>56. 4</td></tr>
<tr><td>纯 收 入</td><td>Net Income</td><td>883. 8</td><td>2456. 9</td><td>3029. 3</td></tr>
<tr><td>劳动者的报酬收入</td><td>Reward of Labourers</td><td>300. 6</td><td>821. 9</td><td>1119. 4</td></tr>
<tr><td>家庭经营收入</td><td>Household Business</td><td>557. 5</td><td>1544. 4</td><td>1749. 0</td></tr>
<tr><td>转移性收入</td><td>Transfer Income</td><td rowspan="2">25. 7</td><td>65. 0</td><td>104. 5</td></tr>
<tr><td>财产性收入</td><td>Property Income</td><td>25. 6</td><td>56. 4</td></tr>
</table>

4—19 农民家庭平均每人生活消费支出
PER CAPITA RURAL HOUSEHOLD LIVING EXPENDITURES

单位:元 (yuan)

指标	Items	1990	1994	1995	1996
生活消费支出	**Toatl Living Expenditures**	**787.0**	**1500.5**	**1938.0**	**2414.4**
食品	Food	411.6	822.9	1061.4	1235.6
主食	Grain	81.0	298.7	412.3	391.4
副食	Non-Staple Food	231.4	369.1	456.0	573.8
其他	Others	99.2	155.1	193.1	270.4
衣着	Clothing	57.9	99.6	126.8	166.0
居住	Residence	193.2	258.6	344.6	408.3
住房和电费	Housing and Electricity	168.5	200.5	294.3	329.8
燃料	Fuel	24.7	45.9	33.0	48.9
其他	Others		12.2	17.3	29.6
家庭设备、用品及服务	Household Facilities, Articales and Services	53.3	115.1	133.0	178.9
医疗保健	Medicine and Medical Services	22.7	43.7	49.1	76.8
交通和通讯	Traffic and Communications	10.0	37.7	52.3	92.4
文化教育娱乐用品及服务	Cultural, Education and Recreation Artical and Services	34.7	96.5	139.2	191.8
其他商品和服务	Other Commodity and Services	3.6	26.4	31.6	64.6

4—20 农民家庭房屋情况
RURAL HOUSEHOLD HOUSING CONDITIONS

指标	Items	1990	1994	1995	1996
平均每人年末生活用房面积 (平方米)	Living Floor Space Per Capita Space of Houses by the End of Year (sq. m)	22.3	25.5	25.7	29.6
#砖木结构	Brick and Wood Structures	16.5	19.7	19.5	19.6
钢筋混凝土结构	Reinforced Concrete Structures	3.1	4.3	4.8	9.0
平均每户本年新建房屋	Rooms Newly Built Per Household Within the year				
新建房屋间数占使用间数比重 (%)	The Proportion of Rooms Newly Built in the Rooms in Use (%)	5.8	6.2	4.5	5.6
新建房屋每间价值 (元)	Value of Per Room Newly Built (yuan)	3479.0	5856.2	7750.0	7703.8
每平方米价值 (元)	Value of Per Square Metre (yuan)	145.8	235.9	308.5	306.3
平均每人年内新建房屋面积 (平方米)	Per Capita Space of the Rooms Newly Built Within the Year (sq. m)	1.7	1.7	1.3	1.7
#砖木结构	Brick and Wood Structures	1.3	1.0	0.8	0.7
钢筋混凝土结构	Reinforced Concrete Structures	0.4	0.5	0.5	1.0
生活用房	Living Houses	1.6	1.5	1.2	1.4
楼房	Multi-Floor Houses	0.9	0.8	0.6	0.7

4－21 农民家庭平均每人全年主要消费品消费量
RURAL HOUSEHOLD PER CAPITA CONSUMPTION ON MAJOR CONSUMER GOODS

指标		Items		1990	1994	1995	1996
粮食(原粮)	(公斤)	Grain (Unprocessed Grains)	(k.g)	275.9	267.7	264.0	273.6
#稻谷	(公斤)	Paddy	(k.g)	163.8	184.0	184.4	190.8
蔬菜	(公斤)	Fresh Vegetables	(k.g)	129.2	103.4	120.2	117.3
植物油	(公斤)	Edible Vegetable Oil	(k.g)	6.6	6.6	7.6	8.1
动物油	(公斤)	Edible Animal Oil	(k.g)	0.4	0.6	0.6	0.8
肉类	(公斤)	Meat	(k.g)	9.5	9.7	10.5	14.7
#猪肉	(公斤)	Pork	(k.g)	9.0	8.7	10.0	12.9
家禽	(公斤)	Poultry	(k.g)	1.5	2.7	3.2	4.0
蛋类	(公斤)	Eggs	(k.g)	6.0	6.8	7.6	8.7
鱼虾	(公斤)	Fish and Shrimp	(k.g)	4.9	6.3	6.8	9.5
食糖	(公斤)	Sugar	(k.g)	1.9	1.8	1.7	1.8
卷烟	(盒)	Cigarettes	(packs)	36.4	27.9	27.8	39.2
酒	(公斤)	Liquor	(k.g)	7.1	8.3	8.3	9.8
棉布	(米)	Cotton Cloth	(m)	0.9	0.7	0.4	0.5
化纤布	(米)	Chemical Fiber	(m)	2.1	2.1	2.1	2.0
呢绒	(米)	Woolen Fabric	(m)	0.09	0.11	0.09	0.15
绸缎	(米)	Silk and Satin	(m)	0.05	0.03	0.02	0.02
毛线及毛线衣裤	(公斤)	Knitting Wool and Knitwear	(k.g)	0.08	0.13	0.16	0.22
肥皂	(块)	Soaps	(pcs)	0.7	0.3	0.2	0.2

4－22 农民家庭年末平均每百户耐用消费品拥有量
RURAL HOUSEHOLD YEAR－END POSSESSION OF DURABLE CONSUMER GOODS PER 100 HOUSEHOLDS

指标		Items	1990	1991	1995	1996
自行车	(辆)	Bicycles	159.1	179.6	183.4	184.1
缝纫机	(架)	Sewing Machines	49.8	67.5	63.0	64.3
收音机	(台)	Radio Sets	52.2	39.3	42.3	34.7
钟表	(只)	Clocks and Watches	259.0	284.5	293.0	289.2
手表	(只)	Wristwatches	197.6	195.9	202.6	193.1
电视机	(台)	TV Sets	54.4	89.7	96.6	105.5
#彩色电视机	(台)	Color TV Sets	6.2	18.3	21.9	28.2
收录机	(台)	Recorders	19.1	28.8	32.7	34.6
洗衣机	(台)	Washing Machines	15.0	26.1	29.8	37.1
电风扇	(台)	Electric Fans	86.2	152.6	167.6	182.2
电冰箱	(台)	Refrigerators	1.5	6.7	9.1	13.6
摩托车	(辆)	Motorcyles	1.5	6.1	8.6	14.6
照相机	(架)	Cameras	1.1	2.0	2.3	3.9
大型家具		Large Size Furnitures	411.5	731.8	745.1	799.1
(每件价值50元以上的)	(件)	(Each Cost 50 Yuan Over)				
#沙发	(件)	Sofas	49.2	75.3	86.3	97.1
大衣柜	(个)	Wardrobes	93.9	104.7	109.1	97.9
写字台	(张)	Writing Desks	81.4	94.2	96.6	99.1

4－23 主要年份城乡居民储蓄存款年末余额
SAVINGS DEPOSIT BALANCE OF URBAN AND RURAL RESIDENTS BY THE END OF YEAR IN MAJOR YEARS

单位:亿元 (100 000 000 yuan)

年份 Year	城乡居民储蓄存款 Urban and Rural Residents	城镇居民储蓄存款 Urban Residents	农村居民储蓄存款 Rural Residents	城乡居民每人年末平均储蓄存款(元) Per Capita Savings Deposit of Urban and Rural Residents by the End of Year
1952	0.58	0.58		1.55
1957	1.84	1.46	0.38	4.40
1962	2.09	1.56	0.53	4.82
1965	3.64	2.65	0.99	7.87
1970	4.04	2.87	1.17	7.69
1975	7.76	5.30	2.46	13.77
1978	12.40	7.59	4.81	21.25
1980	23.72	13.86	9.86	39.94
1985	99.35	57.81	41.54	159.89
1986	139.59	81.87	57.72	222.64
1987	193.69	118.60	75.09	305.12
1988	231.85	149.27	82.58	360.11
1989	331.85	226.09	105.76	507.74
1990	470.86	330.73	140.13	695.83
1991	617.60	445.67	171.93	902.44
1992	766.11	562.57	203.54	1108.51
1993	964.22	714.67	249.55	1385.52
1994	1352.57	1026.28	326.29	1926.59
1995	1922.33	1487.97	434.36	2720.53
1996	2570.28	2025.20	545.08	3614.94

固定资产投资 5

FIXED ASSETS INVESTMENT

5 固定资产投资
FIXED ASSETS INVESTMENT

1 9 9 6

全社会固定资产投资完成总额	Total Investment in Fixed Assets	1949.53	亿元	(100000000 yuan)
#国有经济	State-Owned	708.60	亿元	(100000000 yuan)
集体经济	Collective-Owned	465.51	亿元	(100000000 yuan)
#基本建设	Capital Construction	481.07	亿元	(100000000 yuan)
更新改造	Technical Updating and Transformation	238.23	亿元	(100000000 yuan)
房地产开发	Real Estate Development	232.62	亿元	(100000000 yuan)
房屋施工面积	Floor Space of Building Under Construction	16236.53	万平方米	(10000 sq·m)
房屋竣工面积	Floor Space of Building Completed	12776.35	万平方米	(10000 sq·m)

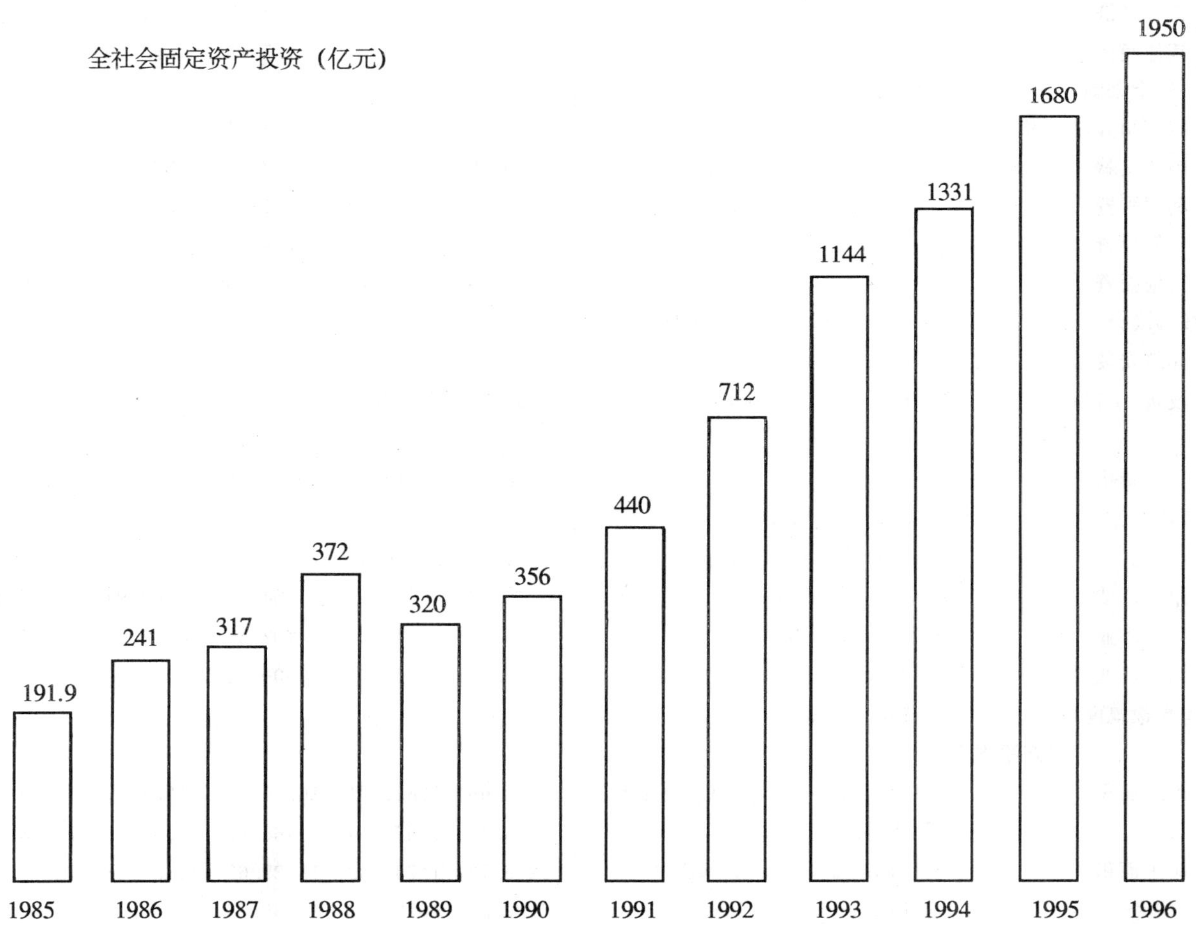

5—1 全社会固定资产投资
TOTAL INVESTMENT IN FIXED ASSETS

指标	Items	1985	1990	1994	1995	1996
投资总额 （亿元）	**Total Value of Investment (100000000 yuan)**	**191.93**	**356.30**	**1331.13**	**1680.17**	**1949.53**
按种类分	Grouped by Type of Construction					
基本建设	Capital Construction	47.35	74.32	274.79	362.15	481.07
更新改造	Technical Updating and Transformation	24.73	41.53	170.53	218.78	238.23
其他投资	Others	27.95	28.09	146.57	192.65	258.19
房地产开发	Real Estate Development		11.71	152.42	240.85	232.62
农村集体	Rural Collective Units	39.46	54.08	411.76	451.52	463.73
城镇个人	City and Town Individuals	1.55	3.83	12.26	14.42	14.19
农村个人	Rural Individuals	50.89	142.74	162.80	199.80	261.50
按经济类型分	Grouped by Ownership					
国有经济	State Owned Units	80.43	134.86	477.86	602.70	708.60
集体经济	Collective Owned Units	59.06	74.87	418.27	491.08	465.21
其他经济	Others	52.44	146.57	435.00	586.39	775.72
按资金来源分	Grouped by Sources of Finance					
国家预算内投资	State Appropriation	17.25	15.02	17.54	25.83	24.01
国内贷款	Domestic Loans	36.79	45.47	242.93	270.16	282.88
利用外资	Foreign Investment	3.98	15.92	151.96	228.89	335.16
自筹投资	Fund Raising	64.45	106.47	744.20	880.02	1001.29
其他投资	Others	69.46	173.42	174.50	275.27	306.19
按构成分	Grouped by Use of Funds					
建筑安装工程	Construction Installation	149.40	284.24	775.84	983.24	1151.16
设备、工器具购置	Purchase of Equipment and Investments	34.41	53.70	437.87	536.48	600.59
其他费用	Others	8.12	18.36	117.42	160.45	197.78
按产业分	Grouped by Industry					
# 住宅	Residential Housing	58.13	156.49	301.23	366.67	403.42
第一产业	Primary Industry	5.46	13.15	24.45	40.94	57.49
第二产业	Secondary Industry	95.06	140.38	702.26	819.54	905.36
第三产业	Tertiary Industry	91.41	202.77	604.42	819.69	986.68
房屋建筑面积 （万平方米）	**Floor Space of Building (10000 sq·m)**					
施工面积	Floor Space Under Construction	10853.65	12821.31	16730.55	16234.74	16236.53
#住宅	Residential Housing	7673.43	10679.54	11466.60	10530.29	10833.81
竣工面积	Floor Space Completed	9246.12	11732.39	13529.62	12452.44	12776.35
#住宅	Residential Housing	7122.23	10209.36	10085.78	9036.00	9392.24

5—2 按经济类型分的全社会固定资产投资(1996)
TOTAL INVESTMENT IN FIXED ASSETS GROUPED BY OWNERSHIP

指 标	Items	总计 Total	国有经济 State-Owned Units	集体经济 Collective Owned Units	#城镇 County	个体经济 Individual Ownership	#农村 Rural	其他经济 Other Ownership	#外商投资经济 Foreign Funded Economic Units
投资总额 (亿元)	**Total Value of Investment (100000000 yuan)**	**1949.53**	**708.60**	**465.21**	**112.40**	**275.69**	**261.50**	**500.03**	**300.23**
按种类分	Grouped by Type of Construction								
基本建设	Capital Construction	481.07	383.61					97.46	73.73
更新改造	Technical Updating and Transformation	238.23	198.44					39.79	25.42
房地产开发	Real Estate Development	232.62	108.42	33.33	33.33			90.87	37.11
其他投资	Others	258.19	18.13	79.07	79.07			160.99	110.46
按资金来源分	Grouped by Sources of Finance								
国家预算内投资	State Appropriation	24.01	19.13	2.28	0.30			2.60	2.09
国内贷款	Domestic Loans	282.88	148.02	79.30	20.98	4.20	4.20	51.36	23.55
利用外资	Foreign Investment	335.16	45.03	16.63	2.79			273.50	193.39
自筹投资	Fund Raising	1001.29	400.41	288.85	63.66	192.49	178.30	119.54	61.66
其他投资	Others	306.19	96.01	78.15	24.67	79.00	79.00	53.03	19.54
按构成分	Grouped by Use of Funds								
建筑安装工程	Construction Installation	1151.16	437.72	226.60	71.20	257.12	242.93	229.72	124.50
设备、工器具购置	Purchase of Equipment and Instruments	600.59	179.08	206.69	31.91	18.57	18.57	196.25	128.43
其他费用	Others	197.78	91.80	31.92	9.29			74.06	47.30
按产业分	Grouped by Industry								
# 住宅	Residential Housing	403.42	100.79	30.18	27.55	233.56	221.48	38.89	10.87
第一产业	Primary Industry	57.49	12.98	12.74	0.36	27.42	27.42	4.35	2.20
第二产业	Secondary Industry	905.36	237.55	340.26	51.03	2.75	2.75	324.80	219.28
第三产业	Tertiary Industry	986.68	458.07	112.21	61.01	245.52	231.33	170.88	78.75
房屋建筑面积 (万平方米)	**Floor Space of Building (10000 sq·m)**								
施工面积	Floor Space Under Construction	16236.53	3892.39	2579.53	1024.03	8003.30	7710.0	1761.31	768.50
#住宅	Residential Housing	10833.81	1858.99	666.41	530.74	7733.14	7485.0	575.27	171.79
竣工面积	Floor Space Completed	12776.35	2095.67	2064.79	717.98	7764.30	7471.0	851.59	367.40
#住宅	Residential Housing	9392.24	1103.77	490.54	376.61	7501.14	7253.0	296.79	92.67

5—3 固定资产投资完成额
FULFILMENT VALUE OF FIXED ASSETS INVESTMENT

单位:亿元 (100 000 000 yuan)

行业	Sector	1985	1990	1995	1996
总计	**Total**	**100.03**	**155.65**	**1014.43**	**1210.11**
农、林、牧、渔业	Farming, Forestry, Animal Husbandry and Fishery	1.11	2.04	2.13	2.90
采掘业	Excavation	5.62	7.71	14.07	17.60
制造业	Manufacturing	48.66	66.69	340.32	383.23
电力、煤气及水的生产和供应业	Electric Power, Gas and Water Producation and Supply	5.66	17.90	77.87	112.49
建筑业	Construction	0.91	0.07	8.82	9.14
地质勘查业、水利管理业	Geological Prospect and Water Conservancy	0.80	1.85	8.41	11.05
交通运输、仓储及邮电通讯业	Transportation, Storage, Postal and Telecommunication Services	10.72	19.02	141.77	201.84
批发和零售贸易、餐饮业	Whole Sale, Retail Trade and Food Services	4.35	5.44	39.19	39.88
金融、保险业	Banking, Insurance	0.42	1.15	6.50	8.51
房地产业	Real estate Management	6.92	17.56	244.90	236.08
社会服务业	Social Services	4.51	1.64	39.36	83.64
卫生、体育和社会福利业	Health Care, Sports and Social Welfare	1.73	1.85	8.62	8.85
教育、文化艺术及广播电影电视业	Education, Culture and Arts, Radio,Film and Television	5.03	7.25	26.16	36.09
科学研究和综合技术服务业	Scientific Research and Polytechnical Services	1.15	0.85	2.63	2.49
国家机关、政党机关和社会团体	Government Agencies, Party Agencies and Social Organizations	2.12	2.75	40.01	44.90
其他行业	Other Sectors	0.32	1.88	13.67	11.42

注:本表不含农村集体及城乡个体投资完成额。
Note: Rural collective units, urban and rural individual investment were not included in this table.

5—4 固定资产投资新增的固定资产
NEWLY INCREASED FIXED ASSETS THROUGH INVESTMENT

单位:亿元 (100 000 000 yuan)

行业	Sector	1985	1990	1995	1996
总计	**Total**	**80.17**	**167.91**	**768.65**	**1010.97**
农、林、牧、渔业	Farming, Forestry, Animal Husbandry and Fishery	1.09	1.80	2.10	2.70
采掘业	Excavation	3.20	3.61	10.87	11.51
制造业	Manufacturing	40.80	89.07	292.16	333.79
电力、煤气及水的生产和供应业	Electric Power, Gas and Water Producation and Supply	4.16	16.48	59.02	80.17
建筑业	Construction	0.69	0.49	8.27	8.84
地质勘查业、水利管理业	Geological Prospect and Water Conservancy	0.56	1.68	5.81	4.95
交通运输、仓储及邮电通讯业	Transportation, Storage, Postal and Telecommunication Services	8.15	17.44	97.64	205.74
批发和零售贸易、餐饮业	Whole Sale, Retail Trade and Food Services	3.31	5.92	34.15	36.35
金融、保险业	Banking, Insurance	0.33	0.91	5.48	5.29
房地产业	Real estate Management	5.71	15.24	147.79	193.65
社会服务业	Social Services	3.91	1.41	30.03	43.71
卫生、体育和社会福利业	Health Care, Sports and Social Welfare	1.07	1.66	7.46	10.67
教育、文化艺术及广播电影电视业	Education, Culture and Arts, Radio,Film and Television	4.40	7.16	22.56	31.22
科学研究和综合技术服务业	Scientific Research and Polytechnical Services	0.75	1.22	2.66	2.18
国家机关、政党机关和社会团体	Government Agencies, Party Agencies and Social Organizations	1.80	2.49	33.46	31.18
其他行业	Other Sectors	0.24	1.33	9.19	9.02

注:本表不含农村集体及城乡个体投资新增的固定资产。
Note: Rural collective units, urban and rural individual investment of newly increased fixed assets were not included in this table.

5—5 国有单位固定资产投资(1996)
FIXED ASSETS INVESTMENT BY STATE OWNED UNITS

单位:亿元 (100 000 000 yuan)

指标	Items	合计 Total	基本建设 Capital Construction	更新改造 Updating and Transformation	其他投资 Others	房地产开发 Real Estate Development
建设项目个数 (个)	Number of Construction Projects (units)					
施工项目	Projects Under Construction	7775	4057	3718		
#大中型项目或限上技改项目	Large and Medium Projects or Projects by Technology Transformation Over Norm	135	48	87		
全部建成投产项目	Total Projects Completed Put Into Operation	5671	2750	2921		
#大中型项目或限上技改项目	Large and Medium Projects or Over-Norm Item	48	8	40		
建成项目投产率 (%)	Rate of Projects Completed Put Into Operation (%)	72.9	67.8	78.6		
建设周期 (年)(按项目个数计算)	Construction Cycle (By Number of Projects)	1.37	1.48	1.27		
财务拨款、贷款合计	Total Financial Allowcation and Loans	782.01	408.20	205.04	18.10	150.67
国家预算内投资	State Appropriation	19.07	17.53	1.15		0.39
国内贷款	Domestic Loans	151.15	69.88	46.75	0.98	33.54
利用外资	Foreign Investment	44.64	31.31	11.25	1.89	0.19
自筹投资	Fund Raising	400.85	223.52	131.04	12.89	33.40
其他投资	Others	103.46	39.14	4.20	2.34	57.78
投资总额	Total Value of Investment	708.60	383.61	198.44	18.13	108.42
按构成分	Grouped by Use of Funds					
# 建筑工程	Construction Projects	388.20	254.12	40.56	17.31	76.21
安装工程	Installation Projects	49.52	23.56	23.59	0.01	2.36
设备、工具、器具购置	Purchase of Equipment, Tools and Instruments	179.08	56.86	121.58	0.13	0.51
按产业分	Grouped by Industry					
第一产业	Primary Industry	12.98	11.58	1.40		
第二产业	Secondary Industry	237.55	111.27	123.54	2.74	
第三产业	Tertiary Industry	458.07	260.76	73.50	15.39	108.42
#运输邮电通讯业	Transportation, Postal and Telecommunication	178.39	99.14	63.86	15.39	
住宅	Residential Housing	100.79	30.27	1.36		69.16
按建设性质分	Grouped by Type of Construction					
#新建	New Construction	164.09	153.96	10.13		
扩建	Expension	385.30	163.54	113.34		108.42
改建	Replacement	145.98	58.74	69.11	18.13	
房屋建筑面积 (万平方米)	Floor Space of Building (10000 sq·m)					
施工面积	Floor Space Under Construction	3892.39	1895.62	272.50	0.56	1723.71
#住宅	Residential Housing	1858.99	567.53	26.57		1264.89
竣工面积	Floor Space Completed	2095.67	1034.21	181.65	0.48	879.33
#住宅	Residential Housing	1103.77	366.36	19.89		717.52

注:财务拨、贷款合计中包括上年末结余资金。

Note: Total financial allowcation and loans includes balance funds by the end of last year.

5—6 基本建设、更新改造和房地产开发投资(1996)
INVESTMENT IN CAPITAL CONSTRUCTION, UPDATING AND TRANSFORMATION, AND REAL ESTATE DEVELOPMENT

单位:亿元 (100 000 000 yuan)

指 标	Items	合 计 Total	基本建设 Capital Construction	更新改造 Updating and Transformation	房地产开发 Real Estate Development
投资总额 (亿元)	**Total Value of Investment**	**951.92**	**481.07**	**238.23**	**232.62**
按资金来源分	Grouped by Sources of Finance				
国家预算内投资	State Appropriation	21.23	19.07	1.29	0.87
国内贷款	Domestic Loans	188.62	78.40	53.45	56.77
利用外资	Foreign Investment	140.65	97.26	28.81	14.58
自筹投资	Fund Raising	453.71	244.69	149.84	59.18
其他投资	Others	147.71	41.65	4.84	101.22
按隶属关系分	Grouped by Administrative Relationship				
中央项目	Central Government Projects	195.92	121.31	70.36	4.25
地方项目	Local Projects	756.00	359.76	167.87	228.37
按构成分	Grouped by Use of Funds				
建筑安装工程	Construction and Installation	570.37	322.89	79.08	168.40
设备、工器具购置	Purchase of Equipment and Instruments	236.37	87.97	143.35	5.05
其他费用	Others	145.18	70.21	15.80	59.17
按建设性质分	Grouped by Type of Construction				
#新建	New Construction	225.63	206.92	18.71	
扩建	Expension	569.37	198.51	138.24	232.62
改建	Replacement	143.09	68.25	74.84	
按用途分	Grouped by Industry				
# 住宅	Residential Housing	161.14	30.63	1.32	129.19
第一产业	Primary Industry	13.30	11.90	1.40	
第二产业	Secondary Industry	339.90	176.93	162.97	
第三产业	Tertiary Industry	598.72	292.24	73.86	232.62
新增固定资产	**Newly Incraesed Fixed Assets**	**805.72**	**391.12**	**223.38**	**191.22**
建设项目个数 (个)	**Construction Projects**				
施工项目	Projects Under Construction	8132	4192	3940	
#大中型项目或限上技改项目	Large and Medium Projects or Over-Norm Item	135	48	87	
全部建成投产项目	Total Projects Completed Put Into Use	5872	2812	3060	
#大中型项目或限上技改项目	Large and Medium Projects or Over-Norm Item	48	8	40	
房屋建筑面积 (万平方米)	Floor Space of Building (10000 sq·m)				
施工面积	Floor Space Under Construction	5655.37	2027.22	332.85	3295.30
竣工面积	Floor Space Completed	2944.27	1097.57	213.38	1633.32
#住宅	Residential Housing	1684.07	372.03	21.16	1290.88

5－7　基本建设、更新改造投资完成额
FULFILMENT VALUE OF CAPITAL CONSTRUCTION, UPDATING AND TRANSFORMATION INVESTMENT

单位:亿元　　(100 000 000 yuan)

年份 Year	农业 Agriculture	轻工业 Light Industry	重工业 Heavey Industry	#能源工业 Sources of Energy	运输邮电业 Transportation, Postal and Telecommunication
1980	1.91	6.00	13.63	6.28	1.92
1985	1.16	13.29	30.47	11.44	7.40
1986	1.01	18.27	15.43	14.67	9.44
1987	1.78	23.50	58.45	22.65	12.51
1988	1.94	29.87	70.94	24.07	11.16
1989	1.64	21.40	54.34	18.61	12.48
1990	2.58	19.31	54.55	22.52	15.92
1991	3.49	26.63	72.63	30.52	20.14
1992	4.40	43.78	103.45	40.22	37.48
1993	6.77	63.89	126.10	45.15	55.31
1994	8.35	83.56	146.34	47.66	82.24
1995	9.94	86.57	205.97	79.22	125.87
1996	13.30	69.14	263.58	112.60	168.55

5－8　基本建设、更新改造投资完成额
FULFILMENT VALUE OF CAPITAL CONSTRUCTION, UPDATING AND TRANSFORMATION INVESTMENT

单位:亿元　　(100 000 000 yuan)

年份 Year	基本建设 Capital Construction				更新改造 Updating and Transformation			
	投资额 Investment Value	#新建 New Construction	#扩建 Expension	#改建 Replacement	投资额 Investment Value	#新建 New Construction	#扩建 Expension	#改建 Replacement
1980	26.15	7.63	11.07	7.38	5.50	0.29	2.30	2.75
1985	47.35	19.01	22.76	4.87	24.73	0.48	9.83	11.84
1986	60.42	26.62	26.46	6.46	34.04	1.57	17.24	13.92
1987	78.89	40.15	29.27	7.30	43.04	1.66	21.98	8.10
1988	90.85	45.40	33.67	9.12	54.15	3.44	30.02	19.22
1989	75.12	34.34	29.83	8.49	41.12	2.04	22.54	15.12
1990	74.32	31.80	43.12	10.18	41.53	1.44	22.75	16.07
1991	92.09	38.61	40.35	12.02	58.92	1.98	32.31	22.70
1992	155.84	81.09	57.10	15.45	93.72	4.24	49.73	38.08
1993	212.11	106.53	76.18	26.55	145.13	8.94	78.60	55.40
1994	274.79	124.75	113.06	33.31	170.53	12.42	91.62	62.49
1995	362.15	159.88	148.14	47.76	218.78	32.91	108.02	72.19
1996	481.07	206.92	198.51	68.25	238.23	18.71	138.24	74.85

5—9 基本建设施工项目计划总投资及完成情况

FULFILMENT OF GENERAL INVESTMENT PLAN BY CAPITAL CONSTRUCTION PROJECTS UNDER CONSTRUCTION

单位:亿元 (100 000 000 yuan)

指标	Items	1985	1990	1995	1996
施工项目 (个)	Projects Under Construction	3729	3171	3878	4192
全部建成投产项目 (个)	Projects Fully Completed Put Into Operation	1754	1739	2523	2812
计划总投资	Plan of General Investments	277.70	449.42	1138.60	1549.99
自开始建设至本年底累计完成投资	Total Investment value Completed Since the Beginning of Construction to the End of This Year	128.89	305.81	725.44	916.75
本年完成投资	Investments Completed In This Year	47.35	74.32	362.15	481.07
累计新增固定资产	Newly Increased Fixed Assets Accumulately	70.54	209.68	423.06	527.54
不增加固定资产的投资	Investment which did not Increase Fixed Assets	6.61	7.99	3.31	10.67
未完工程累计完成投资	Projects Incompleted Fulfil Investment Accumulately	51.74	88.14	299.07	378.54
全部建成尚需投资	Investment will be Needed As the Projects Fully Complete	148.81	143.61	413.16	633.24
项目建成投产率 (%)	Rate of Investment of Projects Completed (%)	47.0	54.8	65.1	67.1
未完工程占用率 (%)	Occupied Rate of Projects Incompleted (%)	109.3	118.6	82.6	78.7
建设周期 (年)	Construction Cycle (year)	5.86	6.05	3.14	3.22

5—10 基本建设施工大中型项目计划总投资及完成情况

FULFILMENT OF GENERAL INVESTMENT PLAN BY LARGE AND MEDIUM CAPITAL CONSTRUCTION PROJECTS UNDER CONSTRUCTION

单位:亿元 (100 000 000 yuan)

指标	Items	1985	1990	1995	1996
施工项目 (个)	Projects Under Construction	47	50	49	48
全部建成投产项目 (个)	Projects Fully Completed Put Into Operation	7	7	7	8
计划总投资	Plan of General Investments	195.14	316.64	602.07	747.37
自开始建设至本年底累计完成投资	Total Investment value Completed Since the Beginning of Construction to the End of This Year	79.38	221.78	332.22	371.76
本年完成投资	Investments Completed In This Year	21.17	38.70	115.62	154.48
累计新增固定资产	Newly Increased Fixed Assets Accumulately	39.92	157.62	190.76	198.72
不增加固定资产的投资	Investment which did not Increase Fixed Assets	4.81	9.37	1.96	0.38
未完工程累计完成投资	Projects Incompleted Fulfil Investment Accumulately	34.65	54.79	139.50	172.66
全部建成尚需投资	Investment will be Needed As the Projects Fully Complete	115.76	94.86	269.85	375.61
项目建成投产率 (%)	Rate of Investment of Projects Completed (%)	14.9	14.0	14.3	16.7
未完工程占用率 (%)	Occupied Rate of Projects Incompleted (%)	163.7	141.6	120.7	111.8
建设周期 (年)	Construction Cycle (year)	9.22	8.18	5.21	4.84

5—11 基本建设投资完成额
FULFILMENT VALUE OF CAPITAL CONSTRUCTION INVESTMENT

单位:亿元 (100 000 000 yuan)

年份 Year	农业 Agriculture	轻工业 Light Industry	重工业 Heavey Industry	#能源工业 Sources of Energy	运输邮电业 Transportation, Postal and Telecommunication
1980	1.83	4.23	10.59	4.91	1.67
1981	0.49	2.11	7.55	2.93	1.05
1982	0.44	3.92	6.67	2.57	2.04
1983	0.80	4.77	8.22	3.19	3.15
1984	0.86	3.60	13.29	6.05	4.40
1985	0.88	3.46	19.23	7.15	6.30
1986	0.76	5.62	25.05	10.66	8.47
1987	1.11	7.08	39.11	18.24	10.33
1988	0.29	9.51	46.24	18.76	9.23
1989	0.17	7.21	35.55	14.99	9.79
1990	1.92	6.70	34.79	17.64	12.19
1991	2.77	7.38	44.33	23.94	13.93
1992	3.49	12.46	57.14	34.24	30.27
1993	5.48	17.50	58.86	35.71	36.39
1994	7.34	34.94	65.48	37.58	52.94
1995	8.65	28.73	94.94	59.22	88.08
1996	11.90	21.55	149.46	90.20	104.52

5—12 基本建设投资施工和竣工的房屋建筑面积
CAPITAL CONSTRUCTION INVESTMENT UNDER CONSTRUCTION AND FLOOR SPACE COMPLETED OF BUILDING

单位:万平方米 (10000 sq·m)

年份 Year	施工的房屋建筑面积 Floor Space of Building Under Construction	#住宅 Residential Housing	竣工的房屋建筑面积 Floor Space of Building Completed	#住宅 Residential Housing	房屋建筑面积竣工率(%) Rate of Floor Space of Building Completed
1978	880.00	359.91	466.00	213.67	53.0
1980	1631.61	854.76	834.19	461.86	51.1
1985	1753.88	855.80	821.30	451.61	46.8
1986	1737.06	830.80	949.44	520.87	54.7
1987	1526.00	561.40	808.23	380.89	53.0
1988	1518.05	595.00	766.81	345.94	50.5
1989	1272.83	504.40	689.11	295.63	54.1
1990	1112.59	400.68	567.96	218.37	51.0
1991	1190.25	433.99	586.45	225.52	49.3
1992	1602.51	568.41	779.75	322.07	48.7
1993	1645.87	449.19	858.13	277.20	52.1
1994	1731.45	517.24	921.61	334.04	53.2
1995	1895.78	541.01	1031.75	353.06	54.4
1996	2027.22	574.07	1097.57	372.03	54.1

5—13 国民经济各行业按建设性质分的基本建设投资(1996)
CAPITAL CONSTRUCTION INVESTMENT OF STATE-OWNED UNITS BY TYPE OF CONSTRUCTION AND SECTOR

单位:亿元 (100 000 000 yuan)

行业	Sector	投资额 Invest-ment	#新建 New Construc-tion	#扩建 Expen-sion	#改建 Replace-ment
全省总计	**Provincial**	**481.07**	**206.92**	**198.51**	**68.25**
农、林、牧、渔业	**Farming, Forestry, Animal Husbandry and Fishery**	**1.32**	**0.50**	**0.49**	**0.33**
农业	Farming	0.53	0.20	0.23	0.10
林业	Forestry	0.06	0.03	0.03	
畜牧业	Animal Husbandry	0.12		0.10	0.02
渔业	Fishery	0.25	0.20	0.05	
农林牧渔服务业	Services	0.36	0.07	0.08	0.21
采掘业	**Excavation**	**8.03**	**0.86**	**7.11**	**0.06**
煤炭采选业	Coal Mining and Processing	5.54	0.82	4.67	0.05
石油和天然气开采业	Petroleum and Natural Gas Extraction	2.22		2.22	
黑色金属矿采选业	Ferrous Merals Mining and Processing				
有色金属矿采选业	Nonferrous Metals Mining and Processing				
非金属矿采选业	Nonmetal Minerals Mining and Processing	0.27	0.04	0.22	0.01
其他矿采选业	Other Minerals Mining and Processing				
木材及竹材采运业	Logging and Transport of Timber and Bamboo				
制造业	**Manufacturing**	**78.81**	**19.78**	**44.01**	**13.53**
食品加工业	Food Processing	1.18	0.69	0.35	0.12
食品制造业	Food Production	0.38	0.15	0.18	0.03
饮料制造业	Beverage Production	0.76		0.14	0.62
烟草加工业	Tobacco Processing	0.28		0.28	
纺织业	Textile Industry	0.81	0.05	0.10	0.65
服装及纤维制品制造业	Garments and Other Fiber Products	0.09	0.02	0.03	0.04
皮革毛皮羽绒及制品业	Leather, Furs, Down and Related Products				
木材加工及竹藤棕草制品业	Timber Processing, Bamboo, Cane, Palm Fiber and Straw Products	0.26	0.26		
家具制造业	Furniture Manufacturing	0.10	0.04		0.06
造纸及纸制品业	Papermaking and Paper Products	0.83	0.81		0.02
印刷业记录媒介的复制	Printing and Record Pressing	0.05	0.04		0.01
文教体育用品制造业	Stationery, Education and Sports Goods				
石油加工及炼焦业	Petroleum Processing and Coking Products	5.43		5.43	
化学原料及制品制造业	Raw Chemical Materials and Chemical Products	17.25	0.61	16.28	0.35
医药制造业	Medical and Pharmaceutical Products	1.28	0.12	1.03	0.13
化学纤维制造业	Chemical Fibers	7.60	1.53	6.05	0.02
橡胶制品业	Rubber Products	8.96			8.96
塑料制品业	Plastic Products	0.44	0.07	0.34	0.01
非金属矿物制品业	Nonmetal Mineral Products	10.66	9.32	0.87	0.35
黑色金属冶炼及压延加工业	Smelting and Pressing of Ferrous Meltas	0.23	0.03	0.19	0.01

续表1 Continued 1

单位:亿元 (100 000 000 yuan)

行业	Sector	投资额 Investment	#新建 New Construction	#扩建 Expension	#改建 Replacement
有色金属冶炼及压延加工业	Smelting and Pressing of Nonferrous Metals	0.07	0.07		
金属制品业	Metal Products	0.11	0.05	0.01	0.03
普通机械制造业	Ordinary Machinery Manufacturing	2.26	1.18	0.37	0.71
专用设备制造业	Special Purposes Equipment Manufacturing	6.22	0.10	5.96	0.11
交通运输设备制造业	Transportation Equipment Manufacturing	2.56	0.66	0.33	0.90
电气机械及器材制造业	Electric Equipment and Machinery	1.66	0.88	0.14	0.09
电子及通信设备制造业	Electronic and Telecommunications	8.81	2.83	5.90	0.08
仪器仪表及文化办公用机械制造业	Instruments, Meters, Cultural and Official Machinery	0.29	0.03	0.03	0.23
其他制造业	Other Manufacturing	0.24	0.24		
电力、煤气及水的生产和供应业	**Electric Power, Gas and Water Production and Supply**	**84.17**	**46.05**	**34.30**	**3.81**
电力、蒸气、热水生产和供应业	Electric Power, Steam and Hot Water Production and Supply	74.66	39.52	31.41	3.73
煤气的生产和供应业	Gas Production and Supply	2.34	1.57	0.74	0.02
自来水的生产和供应业	Tap Water Production and Supply	7.17	4.96	2.15	0.06
建筑业	**Construction**	**5.91**	**2.70**	**1.65**	**1.56**
土木工程建筑业	Civil Engineering Construction	5.61	2.67	1.65	1.29
线路、管道和设备安装业	Circuit, Pipelines and Equipment Installation	0.27			0.27
建筑物的装修装饰业	Building Fitting up and Decorations	0.03	0.03		
地质勘查、水利管理业	**Geological Prospecting and Water Conservancy**	**10.71**	**1.26**	**6.62**	**2.81**
地质勘查业	Geological Prospecting	0.13		0.06	0.06
水利管理业	Water Conservancy	10.58	1.26	6.56	2.75
交通运输、仓储及邮电通信业	**Transportation, Storage, Postal and Telecommunications Services**	**105.46**	**60.02**	**22.79**	**22.53**
铁路运输业	Railways	4.52		1.50	3.02
公路运输业	Highways	44.32	33.79	3.82	6.68
管道运输业	Pipelines				
水上运输业	Waterways	1.37	0.12	0.22	0.98
航空运输业	Airways	4.02	3.40	0.62	
交通运输辅助业	Subsidiary Transportation	28.03	16.17	3.62	8.22
其他交通运输业	Other Transportation	7.93	5.46		2.47
仓储业	Storage	0.94	0.57	0.35	0.01
邮电通信业	Postal and Telecommunications Services	14.33	0.51	12.66	1.15
批发和零售贸易餐饮业	**Wholesale, Retail Trade and Food Services**	**23.49**	**5.54**	**16.09**	**1.68**
食品饮料烟草和家庭用品批发业	Wholesale Food, Drink, Tobacco and Household Articles	4.27	0.81	2.67	0.65
能源材料和机械电子设备批发业	Wholesale Energy, Material and Electronic Equipment	2.37	0.98	1.05	0.30

续表2　Continued 2

单位:亿元　　(100 000 000 yuan)

行　业	Sector	投资额 Investment	#新建 New Construction	#扩建 Expension	#改建 Replacement
其他批发业	Other Wholesale	0.31	0.17	0.08	0.06
零售业	Retail	15.29	3.02	11.94	0.33
商业经纪与代理业	Commercial Management and Agencies	0.03			0.03
餐饮业	Food Services	1.22	0.56	0.35	0.31
金融、保险业	**Banking and Insurance**	**7.39**	**2.27**	**4.64**	**0.43**
金融业	Banking	7.06	2.05	4.56	0.42
保险业	Insurance	0.33	0.22	0.08	0.01
房地产业	**Real Estate Management**	**2.88**	**1.12**	**0.39**	**1.37**
房地产开发与经营业	Real Estate Development and Management	1.04	0.85	0.19	
房地产管理业	Manage Real Estate Management	1.84	0.27	0.20	1.37
房地产代理与经纪业	Real Estate Management and Agencies				
社会服务业	**Social Services**	**58.45**	**38.34**	**17.40**	**2.32**
公共服务业	Public Services	42.38	25.74	14.48	2.13
居民服务业	Residential Services	0.34	0.05	0.10	…
旅馆业	Hotels	12.91	11.88	0.86	0.17
租赁服务业	Rentals				
旅游业	Touism	0.96	0.01	0.94	0.01
娱乐服务业	Recreational Services	1.67	0.65	0.98	
信息、咨询服务业	Information and Consultancy Services	…			…
计算机应用服务业	Computer Supply Services				
其他社会服务业	Other Social Services	0.19	0.01	0.04	0.01
卫生体育和社会福利业	**Health Care, Sports and Social Welfare**	**6.73**	**1.36**	**3.74**	**1.20**
卫生	Health Care	5.45	0.77	3.24	1.11
体育	Sports	0.74	0.24	0.42	0.08
社会福利保障业	Social Welfare	0.54	0.35	0.08	0.01
教育、文化艺术和广播电影电视业	**Education, Culture and Arts, Radio, Film and Television**	**33.87**	**5.81**	**20.95**	**5.73**
教育	Education	29.00	4.82	17.31	5.51
文化艺术业	Culture and Arts	2.42	0.41	1.87	0.12
广播、电影、电视业	Radio, Film and Television	2.45	0.58	1.77	0.10
科学研究和综合技术服务业	**Scientific Research and Polytechnical Services**	**2.27**	**0.59**	**0.62**	**1.03**
科学研究业	Scientific Research	1.53	0.48	0.54	0.49
综合技术服务业	Polytechnical Services	0.74	0.11	0.08	0.54
国家机关、政党机关和社会团体	**Government Agencies, Party Agencies and Social Organizations**	**42.53**	**14.23**	**16.34**	**8.68**
#国家机关	Government Agencies and Party	41.49	14.01	15.83	8.59
政党机关	Agencies	0.41	0.10	0.12	
其他行业	**Other Sectors**	**9.05**	**6.49**	**1.37**	**1.18**

注:改建不含单纯建造生活设施投资。

Note: Replacement excludes construction for human services only, such as schools, medical facilities, housing and etc.

5—14 国民经济各行业基本建设施工、投产项目个数(1996)
CAPITAL CONSTRUCTION PROJECTS UNDER CONSTRUCTION AND PUT INTO USE BY SECTOR

单位:个 (units)

行业	Sector	施工项目(个) Project under Construction (units)	#新开工 Starting This Year	全部建成投产项目(个) Fully Completed Projest Turn Over for Production (unit)	项目建成投产率(%) Rate of Projests Completed & Put into Use (%)
全省总计	**Provincial**	**4192**	**2686**	**2812**	**67.1**
农、林、牧、渔业	**Farming, Forestry, Animal Husbandry and Fishery**	**64**	**54**	**54**	**84.4**
农业	Farming	26	23	24	92.3
林业	Forestry	7	5	6	85.7
畜牧业	Animal Husbandry	2	2	1	50.0
渔业	Fishery	4	4	2	50.0
农林牧渔服务业	Services	25	20	21	84.0
采掘业	**Excavation**	**18**	**9**	**7**	**38.9**
煤炭采选业	Coal Mining and Processing	8	3	4	50.0
石油和天然气开采业	Petroleum and Natural Gas Extraction	1			
黑色金属矿采选业	Ferrous Merals Mining and Processing				
有色金属矿采选业	Nonfferrous Metals Mining and Processing				
非金属矿采选业	Nonmetal Minerals Mining and Processing	9	6	3	33.3
其他矿采选业	Other Minerals Mining and Processing				
木材及竹材采运业	Logging and Transport of Timber and Bamboo				
制造业	**Manufacturing**	**357**	**210**	**210**	**58.8**
食品加工业	Food Processing	34	26	23	67.6
食品制造业	Food Production	11	6	9	81.8
饮料制造业	Beverage Production	14	10	12	85.7
烟草加工业	Tobacco Processing	2		2	100.0
纺织业	Textile Industry	26	16	17	65.4
服装及纤维制品制造业	Garments and Other Fiber Products	5	3	4	80.0
皮革毛皮羽绒及制品业	Leather, Furs, Down and Related Products				
木材加工及竹藤棕草制品业	Timber Processing, Bamboo, Cane, Palm Fiber and Straw Products	3	1	3	100.0
家具制造业	Furniture Manufacturing	2	1	1	50.0
造纸及纸制品业	Papermaking and Paper Products	4	2	2	50.0
印刷业记录媒介的复制	Printing and Record Pressing	5	2	3	60.0
文教体育用品制造业	Stationery, Education and Sports Goods				
石油加工及炼焦业	Petroleum Processing and Coking Products	1			
化学原料及制品制造业	Raw Chemical Materials and Chemical Products	40	27	21	52.5
医药制造业	Medical and Pharmaceutical Products	10	5	7	70.0
化学纤维制造业	Chemical Fibers	6	2	2	33.3
橡胶制品业	Rubber Products	1		1	100.0
塑料制品业	Plastic Products	6	5	4	66.7
非金属矿物制品业	Nonmetal Mineral Products	42	27	23	54.8
黑色金属冶炼及压延加工业	Smelting and Pressing of Ferrous Meltas	6	2	5	83.3

续表1 Continued 1

单位:个 (units)

行 业 Sector		施工项目(个) Project under Construction (units)	#新开工 Starting This Year	全部建成投产项目(个) Fully Completed Projest Turn Over for Production (unit)	项目建成投产率(%) Rate of Projests Completed & Put into Use (%)
有色金属冶炼及压延加工业	Smelting and Pressing of Nonferrous Metals	2	1	1	50.0
金属制品业	Metal Products	8	7	4	50.0
普通机械制造业	Ordinary Machinery Manufacturing	35	20	22	62.9
专用设备制造业	Special Purposes Equipment Manufacturing	29	19	14	48.3
交通运输设备制造业	Transportation Equipment Manufacturing	30	14	12	40.0
电气机械及器材制造业	Electric Equipment and Machinery	15	7	10	66.7
电子及通信设备制造业	Electronic and Telecommunications	11	4	3	27.3
仪器仪表及文化办公用机械制造业	Instruments, Meters, Cultural and Official Machinery	7	2	4	57.1
其他制造业	Other Manufacturing	2	1	1	50.0
电力、煤气及水的生产和供应业	**Electric Power, Gas and Water Production and Supply**	**167**	**90**	**88**	**52.7**
电力、蒸气、热水生产和供应业	Electric Power, Steam and Hot Water Production and Supply	110	55	62	56.4
煤气的生产和供应业	Gas Production and Supply	20	12	10	50.0
自来水的生产和供应业	Tap Water Production and Supply	37	23	16	43.2
建筑业	**Construction**	**45**	**23**	**27**	**60.0**
土木工程建筑业	Civil Engineering Construction	39	21	24	61.5
线路、管道和设备安装业	Circuit, Pipelines and Equipment Installation	4	1	2	50.0
建筑物的装修装饰业	Building Fitting up and Decorations	2	1	1	50.0
地质勘查、水利管理业	**Geological Prospecting and Water Conservancy**	**61**	**37**	**38**	**62.3**
地质勘查业	Geological Prospecting	5	1	3	60.0
水利管理业	Water Conservancy	56	36	35	62.5
交通运输、仓储及邮电通信业	**Transportation, Storage, Postal and Telecommunications Servoces**	**331**	**199**	**221**	**66.8**
铁路运输业	Railways	3		1	33.3
公路运输业	Highways	97	59	69	71.1
管道运输业	Pipelines				
水上运输业	Waterways	14	4	8	57.1
航空运输业	Airways	2	1	1	50.0
交通运输辅助业	Subsidiary Transportation	68	42	45	66.2
其他交通运输业	Other Transportation	6	1	5	83.3
仓储业	Storage	15	3	8	53.3
邮电通信业	Postal and Telecommunications Services	126	89	84	66.7
批发和零售贸易餐饮业	**Wholesale, Retail Trade and Food Services**	**388**	**232**	**271**	**69.8**
食品饮料烟草和家庭用品批发业	Wholesale Food, Drink, Tobacco and Household Articles	128	88	90	70.0
能源材料和机械电子设备批发业	Wholesale Energy, Material and Electronic Equipment	68	36	45	66.2

续表2 Continued 2

单位:个 (units)

行 业	Sector	施工项目(个) Project under Construction (units)	#新开工 Starting This Year	全部建成投产项目(个) Fully Completed Projest Turn Over for Production (unit)	项目建成投产率(%) Rate of Projects Completed & Put into Use (%)
其他批发业	Other Wholesale	18	13	15	83.3
零售业	Retail	152	84	109	71.7
商业经纪与代理业	Commercial Management and Agencies	1			
餐饮业	Food Services	21	11	12	57.1
金融、保险业	**Banking and Insurance**	**131**	**64**	**70**	**53.4**
金融业	Banking	125	62	66	52.8
保险业	Insurance	6	2	4	66.7
房地产业	**Real Estate Management**	**39**	**20**	**22**	**56.4**
房地产开发与经营业	Real Estate Development and Management	13	6	6	46.2
房地产管理业	Manage Real Estate Management	26	14	16	61.5
房地产代理与经纪业	Real Estate Management and Agencies				
社会服务业	**Social Services**	**202**	**137**	**129**	**63.9**
公共服务业	Public Services	137	103	103	75.2
居民服务业	Residential Services	10	4	5	50.0
旅馆业	Hotels	32	18	11	34.3
租赁服务业	Rentals				
旅游业	Touism	6	1	2	33.3
娱乐服务业	Recreational Services	11	7	4	36.4
信息、咨询服务业	Information and Consultancy Services	1	1	1	100.0
计算机应用服务业	Computer Supply Services				
其他社会服务业	Other Social Services	5	3	3	60.0
卫生体育和社会福利业	**Health Care, Sports and Social Welfare**	**224**	**133**	**157**	**70.1**
卫生	Health Care	190	112	138	72.6
体育	Sports	16	8	9	56.3
社会福利保障业	Social Welfare	18	13	10	55.6
教育、文化艺术和广播电影电视业	**Education, Culture and Arts, Radio, FIlm and Television**	**1226**	**871**	**902**	**73.6**
教育	Education	1128	828	853	75.6
文化艺术业	Culture and Arts	48	20	21	43.8
广播、电影、电视业	Radio, Film and Television	50	23	28	56.0
科学研究和综合技术服务业	**Scientific Research and Polytechnical Services**	**59**	**35**	**32**	**54.2**
科学研究业	Scientific Research	29	11	15	51.7
综合技术服务业	Polytechnical Services	30	24	17	56.7
国家机关、政党机关和社会团体	**Government Agencies, Party Agencies and Social Organizations**	**828**	**542**	**558**	**67.4**
#国家机关	Government Agencies and Party	785	522	528	67.3
政党机关	Agencies	18	5	13	72.2
其他行业	**Other Sectors**	**52**	**30**	**26**	**50.0**

5—15 大中型基本建设项目全部建成投产情况(1996)
LARGE AND MEDIUM PROJECTS OF CAPITAL CONSTRUCTION FULLY COMPLETED AND PUT INTO OPERATION

项目名称 Items	建设性质 Type of Construction	自开始建设累计完成投资(万元) Investment Completed Accumulatety since the Beginning of Construction (10000 yuan)	自开始建设累计新增固定资产(万元) Newly Increased Fixed Assets Accumulately since the Beginning of Construction (10000 yuan)	累计新增生产能力(或效益) Newly Increased Capacities (or Results) by Accumulation		
				名称 Items	单位 Unit	累计新增 Newly Increased
中央项目 Central Projects						
交通: 南通港务局狼山港二期后二个泊位 Transportation: Nantong Port Office Lang Shan Last Two Berths Second Stage	扩建 Expansion	26040	25990	新(扩)建沿海港口码头 New Construction (Expansion) Dock of Seaside Port	年吞吐量:万吨 Annual Handled: (10000 tons)	90
					泊位:个 Berth: (Unit)	2
地方项目 Local Projects						
橡胶制品: 南京锦湖轮胎有限公司 Rubber Projects: Nanjing KumHo Tyre Co. Ltd.	改建 Replacement	99045	95000	轮船外胎 Cover Tyre	万条/年 10000 tons/year	300
建材: 江南小野田水泥有限公司 Building Materials: Jiang Nan Xiao Yian Tan Co., Ltd.	新建 New Construction	205744	205744	水泥 Cement	万吨/年 10000 tons/year	134.8
机械: 无锡叶片厂八五基建项目 Machinery: Wuxi Lamina Plant "Eight Five Year" Period Capital Construction Project	扩建 Expansion	16468	16468			

续表 Continued

项目名称 Items	建设性质 Type of Construction	自开始建设累计完成投资（万元） Investment Completed Accumulatety since the Beginning of Construction (10000 yuan)	自开始建设累计新增固定资产（万元） Newly Increased Fixed Assets Accumulately since the Beginning of Construction (10000 yuan)	累计新增生产能力（或效益）Newly Increased Capacities (or Results) by Accumulation		
				名称 Items	单位 Unit	累计新增 Newly Increased
电力： Electric Power：						
盐城射阳港发电厂 Yancheng She Yang Port Power Plant	新建 New Construction	132201	132201	火力发电 Thermal Power	万千瓦 10000 kw	25
				输电线路长度 Length of Transmission Line	公里 km	307
				变电设备 Transformation Equipment	万千伏安 10000 KVA	30.3
自来水： Tap Water：						
南京自来水总公司北河口水厂 Nanjing General Tap Water Co. Bei He Kou Waterworks	扩建 Expension	31685	31150	城市自来水供水能力 Capacity of Urban Tap Water Supply	万吨/日 10000 tons/day	60
无锡水厂30万吨扩建 Wuxi Tap Waterworks 300000 tons Expensions	扩建 Expension	10283	10283	城市自来水供水能力 Capacitycf Urban Tap Water Supply	万吨/日 10000 tons/day	30
				管道长度 Length of Urban Tap Water Pipeline	公里 km	6.6
交通： Transportation：						
宁沪高速路江苏段 The Jiangsu Section of Huning Expressway	新建 New Construction	550200	55000	新建公路 New Construction Highway	公里 km	259
				其中：高速公路 of which：High Speed Highway	公里 km	248

5—16 更新改造投资主要指标
MAJOR ITEMS OF UPDATING AND TRANSFORMATION INVESTMENT

指 标	Items	1985	1990	1995	1996
投资总额 （亿元）	**Total Value of Investment (100000000 yuan)**	**24.73**	**41.53**	**218.78**	**238.23**
按资金来源分	Grouped by Sources of Finance				
国家预算内投资	State Appropriation	1.35	0.50	1.98	1.29
国内贷款	Domestic Loans	11.83	13.02	60.21	53.45
利用外资	Foreign Investment	0.34	3.06	35.28	28.81
自筹投资	Fund Raising	10.83	22.33	113.07	149.84
其他投资	Others	0.38	2.62	8.24	4.84
按构成分	Grouped by Use of Funds				
建筑安装工程	Construction and Installation	9.57	16.04	70.40	79.08
设备工器具购置	Purchase of Equipment and Investments	13.95	21.61	130.99	143.35
其他费用	Others	1.21	3.88	17.39	15.80
按建设性质分	Grouped by Type of Construction				
# 新建	New Construction	0.48	1.44	32.91	18.71
扩建	Expension	9.83	22.75	108.02	138.24
改建	Replacement	11.84	16.07	72.19	74.84
按用途分	Grouped by Applying				
增产	Increasing Output	9.50	15.04	103.57	92.86
节约能源	Economize on Energy	1.07	1.80	4.88	5.04
其他节约	Other Economizations	0.05	0.09	0.64	0.32
增加品种	Increasing Varieties	3.04	6.98	33.40	34.56
提高产品质量	Improve the Quality of Products	2.06	2.98	14.12	13.91
三废治理	Waste Water, Waste Gas and Waste Residue Treatment	0.43	0.52	4.18	4.84
其他	Others	8.58	14.12	57.99	86.70
新增固定资产	**Newly Incraesed Fixed Assets**	**20.21**	**36.96**	**174.91**	**223.38**
建设项目个数 （个）	**Number of Projections Under Construction**	**4397**	**3244**	**3926**	**3940**
全部建成投产项目	Total Projects Completed In Use	2555	1871	2963	3060
房屋建筑面积 （万平方米）	**Floor Space of Building (10000 sq·m)**				
施工面积	Floor Space Under Construction	530.55	353.62	359.69	332.85
#住宅	Residential Housing	114.52	72.44	29.34	28.64
竣工面积	Floor Space Completed	297.56	200.84	225.11	213.38
#住宅	Residential Housing	73.03	45.88	20.67	21.16

5—17 国民经济各行业按建设性质分的更新改造投资(1996)
TECHNICAL UPDATES AND TRANSFORMATION OF INVESTMENT OF STATE-OWNED UNITS BY TYPE OF CONSTRUCTION AND SECTOR

单位:亿元 (100 000 000 yuan)

行业	Sector	投资额 Investment	#新建 New Construction	#扩建 Expension	#改建 Replacement
全省总计	**Provincial**	**238.23**	**18.71**	**138.24**	**74.85**
农、林、牧、渔业	**Farming, Forestry, Animal Husbandry and Fishery**	**1.09**	**0.12**	**0.71**	**0.20**
农业	Farming	0.55		0.43	0.11
林业	Forestry	0.05		0.01	0.03
畜牧业	Animal Husbandry	0.08	0.08		
渔业	Fishery	0.14	0.04	0.10	
农林牧渔服务业	Services	0.27		0.17	0.06
采掘业	**Excavation**	**6.61**	**0.66**	**0.78**	**5.12**
煤炭采选业	Coal Mining and Processing	3.16		0.34	2.80
石油和天然气开采业	Petroleum and Natural Gas Extraction	1.25			1.25
黑色金属矿采选业	Ferrous Metals Mining and Processing	0.17		0.15	0.02
有色金属矿采选业	Nonferrous Metals Mining and Processing	0.07		0.04	0.03
非金属矿采选业	Nonmetal Minerals Mining and Processing	1.96	0.66	0.25	1.02
其他矿采选业	Other Minerals Mining and Processing				
木材及竹材采运业	Logging and Transport of Timber and Bamboo				
制造业	**Manufacturing**	**137.63**	**12.86**	**69.57**	**52.94**
食品加工业	Food Processing	4.42	0.46	3.04	0.78
食品制造业	Food Production	4.15	1.41	2.03	0.67
饮料制造业	Beverage Production	2.21	0.27	1.32	0.43
烟草加工业	Tobacco Processing	1.18			1.18
纺织业	Textile Industry	15.29	0.48	5.23	8.89
服装及纤维制品制造业	Garments and Other Fiber Products	0.21	0.01	0.15	0.05
皮革毛皮羽绒及制品业	Leather, Furs, Down and Related Products	0.21	0.01	0.11	0.09
木材加工及竹藤棕草制品业	Timber Processing, Bamboo, Cane, Palm Fiber and Straw Products	0.67	0.19	0.38	
家具制造业	Furniture Manufacturing				
造纸及纸制品业	Papermaking and Paper Products	4.72	3.55	0.62	0.55
印刷业记录媒介的复制	Printing and Record Pressing	0.97	0.06	0.29	0.35
文教体育用品制造业	Stationery, Education and Sports Goods	0.09		0.03	0.06
石油加工及炼焦业	Petroleum Processing and Coking Products	2.88	0.01	0.86	2.01
化学原料及制品制造业	Raw Chemical Materials and Chemical Products	29.36	1.35	11.85	15.90
医药制造业	Medical and Pharmaceutical Products	1.88	0.62	0.99	0.27
化学纤维制造业	Chemical Fibers	2.01	0.22	1.56	0.07
橡胶制品业	Rubber Products	0.92		0.87	0.05
塑料制品业	Plastic Products	0.73	0.05	0.39	0.29
非金属矿物制品业	Nonmetal Mineral Products	10.33	0.56	5.80	3.92
黑色金属冶炼及压延加工业	Smelting and Pressing of Ferrous Meltas	11.46		8.04	3.42

续表1 Continued 1

单位:亿元 (100 000 000 yuan)

行业	Sector	投资额 Investment	#新建 New Construction	#扩建 Expension	#改建 Replacement
有色金属冶炼及压延加工业	Smelting and Pressing of Nonferrous Metals	4.30	0.35	1.07	2.88
金属制品业	Metal Products	1.26	0.52	0.12	0.61
普通机械制造业	Ordinary Machinery Manufacturing	11.89	0.86	5.89	5.08
专用设备制造业	Special Purposes Equipment Manufacturing	6.71		5.23	1.35
交通运输设备制造业	Transportation Equipment Manufacturing	6.42	0.11	4.37	1.90
电气机械及器材制造业	Electric Equipment and Machinery	5.31		4.52	0.70
电子及通信设备制造业	Electronic and Telecommunications	6.85	1.77	4.01	1.04
仪器仪表及文化办公用机械制造业	Instruments, Meters, Cultural and Official Machinery	0.85		0.47	0.38
其他制造业	Other Manufacturing	0.35		0.33	0.02
电力、煤气及水的生产和供应业	**Electric Power, Gas and Water Production and Supply**	**17.47**	**2.06**	**9.93**	**5.24**
电力、蒸气、热水生产和供应业	Electric Power, Steam and Hot Water Production and Supply	14.91	1.75	8.21	4.71
煤气的生产和供应业	Gas Production and Supply	0.21	0.14		0.07
自来水的生产和供应业	Tap Water Production and Supply	2.35	0.17	1.72	0.46
建筑业	**Construction**	**1.26**		**0.13**	**0.38**
土木工程建筑业	Civil Engineering Construction	1.09			0.37
线路、管道和设备安装业	Circuit, Pipelines and Equipment Installation	0.15			0.01
建筑物的装修装饰业	Building Fitting up and Decorations	0.02			
地质勘查、水利管理业	**Geological Prospecting and Water Conservancy**	**0.33**		**0.07**	**0.25**
地质勘查业	Geological Prospecting	0.02		0.02	
水利管理业	Water Conservancy	0.31		0.05	0.25
交通运输、仓储及邮电通信业	**Transportation, Storage, Postal and Telecommunications Servoces**	**64.21**	**2.51**	**53.24**	**6.28**
铁路运输业	Railways	0.11			0.11
公路运输业	Highways	2.64		0.70	0.30
管道运输业	Pipelines				
水上运输业	Waterways	0.40	0.05	0.16	0.02
航空运输业	Airways	0.01			0.01
交通运输辅助业	Subsidiary Transportation	2.77	0.06	0.36	2.34
其他交通运输业	Other Transportation				
仓储业	Storage	0.18	0.02	0.02	0.14
邮电通信业	Postal and Telecommunications Services	58.10	2.38	52.0	3.36
批发和零售贸易餐饮业	**Wholesale, Retail Trade and Food Services**	**1.30**	**0.27**	**0.58**	**0.41**
食品饮料烟草和家庭用品批发业	Wholesale Food, Drink, Tobacco and Household Articles	0.50	0.21	0.18	0.11
能源材料和机械电子设备批发业	Wholesale Energy, Material and Electronic Equipment	0.24	0.03	0.11	0.08

续表2 Continued 2

单位:亿元 (100 000 000 yuan)

行业	Sector	投资额 Investment	#新建 New Construction	#扩建 Expension	#改建 Replacement
其他批发业	Other Wholesale	0.04		0.02	0.02
零售业	Retail	0.49	0.03	0.27	0.18
商业经纪与代理业	Commercial Management and Agencies				
餐饮业	Food Services	0.03			0.02
金融、保险业	**Banking and Insurance**	**0.04**			**0.04**
金融业	Banking	0.01			0.01
保险业	Insurance	0.03			0.03
房地产业	**Real Estate Management**	**0.03**			**0.02**
房地产开发与经营业	Real Estate Development and Management	0.01			
房地产管理业	Manage Real Estate Management	0.02			0.02
房地产代理与经纪业	Real Estate Management and Agencies				
社会服务业	**Social Services**	**5.17**	**0.04**	**1.49**	**3.32**
公共服务业	Public Services	3.95	0.04	1.49	2.11
居民服务业	Residential Services	0.01			
旅馆业	Hotels	1.21			1.21
租赁服务业	Rentals				
旅游业	Touism				
娱乐服务业	Recreational Services				
信息、咨询服务业	Information and Consultancy Services				
计算机应用服务业	Computer Supply Services				
其他社会服务业	Other Social Services				
卫生体育和社会福利业	**Health Care, Sports and Social Welfare**	**0.88**	**0.04**	**0.39**	**0.24**
卫生	Health Care	0.88	0.04	0.39	0.24
体育	Sports				
社会福利保障业	Social Welfare				
教育、文化艺术和广播电影电视业	**Education, Culture and Arts, Radio, Film and Television**	**0.19**	**0.01**	**0.05**	**0.04**
教育	Education	0.05		0.02	0.02
文化艺术业	Culture and Arts	0.01		0.01	
广播、电影、电视业	Radio, Film and Television	0.13	0.01	0.02	0.02
科学研究和综合技术服务业	**Scientific Research and Polytechnical Services**	**0.23**		**0.20**	**0.01**
科学研究业	Scientific Research				
综合技术服务业	Polytechnical Services	0.23		0.20	0.01
国家机关、政党机关和社会团体	**Government Agencies, Party Agencies and Social Organizations**	**1.33**	**0.11**	**0.83**	**0.28**
#国家机关	Government Agencies and Party	1.30	0.11	0.83	0.25
政党机关	Agencies	0.03			0.03
其他行业	**Other Sectors**	**0.46**	**0.03**	**0.27**	**0.08**

5-18 国民经济各行业更新改造施工、投产项目个数(1996)
TECHNICAL UPDATES AND TRANSFORMATION PROJECTS UNDER CONSTRUCTION AND PUT INTO USE BY SECTOR

单位:个 (units)

行业	Sector	施工项目(个) Project under Construction (units)	#新开工 Starting This Year	全部建成投产项目(个) Fully Completed Projest Turn Over for Production (unit)	项目建成投产率(%) Rate of Projests Completed & Put into Use (%)
全省总计	**Provincial**	**3940**	**3073**	**3060**	**77.7**
农、林、牧、渔业	**Farming, Forestry, Animal Husbandry and Fishery**	**69**	**60**	**55**	**79.7**
农业	Farming	36	29	26	72.2
林业	Forestry	6	6	5	83.3
畜牧业	Animal Husbandry	2	1	2	100.0
渔业	Fishery	9	8	7	77.8
农林牧渔服务业	Services	16	16	15	93.8
采掘业	**Excavation**	**61**	**37**	**31**	**50.8**
煤炭采选业	Coal Mining and Processing	26	13	11	42.3
石油和天然气开采业	Petroleum and Natural Gas Extraction	1			
黑色金属矿采选业	Ferrous Metals Mining and Processing	3	2	1	33.3
有色金属矿采选业	Nonferrous Metals Mining and Processing	4	2		
非金属矿采选业	Nonmetal Minerals Mining and Processing	27	20	19	70.4
其他矿采选业	Other Minerals Mining and Processing				
木材及竹材采运业	Logging and Transport of Timber and Bamboo				
制造业	**Manufacturing**	**2234**	**1617**	**1608**	**72.0**
食品加工业	Food Processing	225	201	195	86.7
食品制造业	Food Production	80	63	61	76.3
饮料制造业	Beverage Production	63	56	56	88.9
烟草加工业	Tobacco Processing	6	5	2	33.3
纺织业	Textile Industry	188	128	149	79.3
服装及纤维制品制造业	Garments and Other Fiber Products	9	8	9	100.0
皮革毛皮羽绒及制品业	Leather, Furs, Down and Related Products	7	5	6	85.7
木材加工及竹藤棕草制品业	Timber Processing, Bamboo, Cane, Palm Fiber and Straw Products	11	10	9	81.8
家具制造业	Furniture Manufacturing				
造纸及纸制品业	Papermaking and Paper Products	43	31	36	83.7
印刷业记录媒介的复制	Printing and Record Pressing	29	19	25	86.2
文教体育用品制造业	Stationery, Education and Sports Goods	7	6	5	71.4
石油加工及炼焦业	Petroleum Processing and Coking Products	37	27	28	75.7
化学原料及制品制造业	Raw Chemical Materials and Chemical Products	493	393	381	77.3
医药制造业	Medical and Pharmaceutical Products	68	47	48	70.6
化学纤维制造业	Chemical Fibers	36	25	24	66.7
橡胶制品业	Rubber Products	15	6	8	53.3
塑料制品业	Plastic Products	20	17	17	85.0
非金属矿物制品业	Nonmetal Mineral Products	161	116	122	75.8
黑色金属冶炼及压延加工业	Smelting and Pressing of Ferrous Meltas	65	31	43	66.2

续表1　Continued 1

单位:个　　(units)

行　　业	Sector	施工项目(个) Project under Construction (units)	#新开工 Starting This Year	全部建成投产项目(个) Fully Completed Projest Turn Over for Production (unit)	项目建成投产率(%) Rate of Projests Completed & Put into Use (%)
有色金属冶炼及压延加工业	Smelting and Pressing of Nonferrous Metals	15	5	8	53.3
金属制品业	Metal Products	40	31	29	72.5
普通机械制造业	Ordinary Machinery Manufacturing	187	105	94	50.3
专用设备制造业	Special Purposes Equipment Manufacturing	114	80	74	64.9
交通运输设备制造业	Transportation Equipment Manufacturing	134	81	56	41.8
电气机械及器材制造业	Electric Equipment and Machinery	68	47	45	66.2
电子及通信设备制造业	Electronic and Telecommunications	65	33	43	66.2
仪器仪表及文化办公用机械制造业	Instruments, Meters, Cultural and Official Machinery	41	35	31	75.6
其他制造业	Other Manufacturing	7	6	4	57.1
电力、煤气及水的生产和供应业	**Electric Power, Gas and Water Production and Supply**	**243**	**192**	**179**	**73.7**
电力、蒸气、热水生产和供应业	Electric Power, Steam and Hot Water Production and Supply	202	163	146	72.3
煤气的生产和供应业	Gas Production and Supply	2	2	2	100.0
自来水的生产和供应业	Tap Water Production and Supply	39	27	31	79.5
建筑业	**Construction**	**19**	**17**	**17**	**89.5**
土木工程建筑业	Civil Engineering Construction	17	15	15	88.2
线路、管道和设备安装业	Circuit, Pipelines and Equipment Installation	1	1	1	100.0
建筑物的装修装饰业	Building Fitting up and Decorations	1	1	1	100.0
地质勘查、水利管理业	**Geological Prospecting and Water Conservancy**	**11**	**10**	**8**	**72.7**
地质勘查业	Geological Prospecting	1	1	1	100.0
水利管理业	Water Conservancy	10	9	7	70.0
交通运输、仓储及邮电通信业	**Transportation, Storage, Postal and Telecommunications Servoces**	**917**	**845**	**815**	**88.9**
铁路运输业	Railways	2	1	2	100.0
公路运输业	Highways	16	12	12	75.0
管道运输业	Pipelines				
水上运输业	Waterways	11	7	9	81.8
航空运输业	Airways	1	1	1	100.0
交通运输辅助业	Subsidiary Transportation	45	41	33	73.3
其他交通运输业	Other Transportation				
仓储业	Storage	11	9	7	63.6
邮电通信业	Postal and Telecommunications Services	831	774	751	90.4
批发和零售贸易餐饮业	**Wholesale, Retail Trade and Food Services**	**132**	**81**	**121**	**91.7**
食品饮料烟草和家庭用品批发业	Wholesale Food, Drink, Tobacco and Household Articles	64	24	59	92.2
能源材料和机械电子设备批发业	Wholesale Energy, Material and Electronic Equipment	24	17	22	91.7

续表2　Continued 2

单位:个　(units)

行　业　Sector		施工项目（个） Project under Construction (units)	#新开工 Starting This Year	全部建成投产项目（个） Fully Completed Projest Turn Over for Production (unit)	项目建成投产率（%） Rate of Projests Completed & Put into Use (%)
其他批发业	Other Wholesale	5	5	5	100.0
零售业	Retail	33	30	30	90.9
商业经纪与代理业	Commercial Management and Agencies				
餐饮业	Food Services	6	5	5	83.3
金融、保险业	**Banking and Insurance**	**3**	**2**	**2**	**66.7**
金融业	Banking	2	1	1	50.0
保险业	Insurance	1	1	1	100.0
房地产业	**Real Estate Management**	**2**	**2**	**2**	**100.0**
房地产开发与经营业	Real Estate Development and Management				
房地产管理业	Manage Real Estate Management	2	2	2	100.0
房地产代理与经纪业	Real Estate Management and Agencies				
社会服务业	**Social Services**	**180**	**158**	**168**	**93.3**
公共服务业	Public Services	172	153	161	93.6
居民服务业	Residential Services	1	1	1	100.0
旅馆业	Hotels	7	4	6	85.7
租赁服务业	Rentals				
旅游业	Touism				
娱乐服务业	Recreational Services				
信息、咨询服务业	Information and Consultancy Services				
计算机应用服务业	Computer Supply Services				
其他社会服务业	Other Social Services				
卫生体育和社会福利业	**Health Care, Sports and Social Welfare**	**15**	**11**	**12**	**80.0**
卫生	Health Care	15	11	12	80.0
体育	Sports				
社会福利保障业	Social Welfare				
教育、文化艺术和广播电影电视业	**Education, Culture and Arts, Radio, FIlm and Television**	**10**	**6**	**9**	**90.0**
教育	Education	5	3	4	80.0
文化艺术业	Culture and Arts	1		1	100.0
广播、电影、电视业	Radio, Film and Television	4	3	4	100.0
科学研究和综合技术服务业	**Scientific Research and Polytechnical Services**	**2**		**1**	**50.0**
科学研究业	Scientific Research				
综合技术服务业	Polytechnical Services	2		1	50.0
国家机关、政党机关和社会团体	**Government Agencies, Party Agencies and Social Organizations**	**31**	**26**	**23**	**74.2**
#国家机关	Government Agencies and Party	30	25	22	73.3
政党机关	Agencies	1	1	1	100.0
其他行业	**Other Sectors**	**11**	**9**	**9**	**81.8**

5—19 限额以上更新改造项目全部建成投产情况(1996)
INDICATIORS OF TECHNICAL UPDATING AND TRANSFORMATION PROJECTS (OVER NORM) FULLY COMPLETED AND PUT INTO OPERATION

项目名称 Items	建设性质 Type of Construction	自开始建设累计完成投资(万元) Investment Completed Accumulatety since the Beginning of Construction (10000 yuan)	自开始建设累计新增固定资产(万元) Newly Increased Fixed Assets Accumulately since the Beginning of Construction (10000 yuan)	累计新增生产能力(或效益) Newly Increased Capacities (or Results) by Accumulation		
				名称 Items	单位 Unit	累计新增 Newly Increased
中央项目 **Central Projects**						
机械: 中国第一汽车集团公司无锡柴油机厂 Machinery: China First Motor Vehical Group Co. Wuxi Diesel Engine Plant	改建 Replacement	9910	9910			
电子: 南京乐金熊电器有限公司 Electronic: Nanjing Le Jing Panda Electric Appliance Co. Ltd.	新建 New Construction	11247	11247	家用洗衣机 Household Washing Machine	万台/年 10000/year	25
中国华晶电子集团公司录像机专用生产线 China Hua Jing Electronic Group Co. Videorecorder Circuit Productoin for a Special Purpose	扩建 Expansion	9560	9560	大中规模半导体集成电路 Large and Medium Scale Semiconductor Integrated Circuit	万块/年 10000/year	1900
中国华晶电子集团公司1—1.5 Umic大生产技术研究 China Huajing Electronic Group Co. 1—1.5 Umic Large Production Technology Research	改建 Replacement	6443	6443			
邮电通信: 南京电信局移动通信网三期扩容 Postal Telecommunication: Office of Nanjing Telecommunications Mobile Communication Network Third Stage Capacities Expansion	扩建 Expansion	7878	7878			

续表1　Continued 1

项目名称 Items	建设性质 Type of Construction	自开始建设累计完成投资（万元） Investment Completed Accumulatety since the Beginning of Construction (10000 yuan)	自开始建设累计新增固定资产（万元） Newly Increased Fixed Assets Accumulately since the Beginning of Construction (10000 yuan)	累计新增生产能力(或效益) Newly Increased Capacities (or Results) by Accumulation		
				名称 Items	单位 Unit	累计新增 Newly Increased
南京电信局能仁里长途2.1万路 Office of Nanjing Telecommunications Neng Ren li Long Distance 2. 1 Ten Thousand Wire	扩建 Expansion	8172	8172	长途自动电话交换机设备 Equipment of Automatic Distance Telephone Switch	路端 Line	21000
南京电信局移动通信网四期扩容 Office of Nanjing Telecommunications Mobile Communication Network Fourth Stage Capacities Expansion	扩建 Expansion	6855	6855			
无锡邮电局移动B网扩容 Office of Wuxi Postal and Telecommunications Mobile Network B Capacities Expansion	扩建 Expansion	5851	5851			
无锡邮电局移动G网扩容 Office of Wuxi Postal and Telecommunication s Mobile Network G Capacities Expansion	扩建 Expansion	9592	9592			
扬州邮电局市话程控 Office of Yangzhou Postal and Telecommunications Urban Telephones Program Controll	扩建 Expansion	6486	6486	市内电话交换机 Urban Telephone Switchborad	门 Unit	54000
扬州邮电局网路扩容 Office of Yangzhou Postal and Telecommunications Network Capacities Expansion	扩建 Expansion	10050	10050			

续表2 Continued 2

项目名称 Items	建设性质 Type of Construction	自开始建设累计完成投资（万元） Investment Completed Accumulatety since the Beginning of Construction (10000 yuan)	自开始建设累计新增固定资产（万元） Newly Increased Fixed Assets Accumulately since the Beginning of Construction (10000 yuan)	累计新增生产能力（或效益）Newly Increased Capacities (or Results) by Accumulation		
				名称 Items	单位 Unit	累计新增 Newly Increased
扬州邮电局移动交换机 Office of Yangzhou Postal and Telecommunications Mobile Switchborads	扩建 Expansion	7928	7928			
科研： Scientific Resaerch： 南京七二四研究所〇五二专项 Nanjing No. 724 Research Institute 052 Special Project	扩建 Expansion	4400	4400			
地方项目 **Local Projects**						
食品：徐州维维集团 Food：Xuzhou Wei Wei Group	扩建 Expansion	11982	7258	乳制品 Milk and Daily Products	吨/年 ton/year	24000
纺织： 常州黑牡丹（集团）股份有限公司引进设备 Textile： Changzhou Black Peony Group Share Holding Co. Ltd. Import Equipments	改建 Replacement	4000	4000			
常熟市印染总厂仿真丝印染后整线 Changshu Municipality General Mill of Printing and Dyeing Motellized Silk Finishing Line	改建 Replacement	4560	4560			
国营涟水色织厂引进无梭织机及配套设备 State Run Lian Shiu Color Weaving Mill Imported Shuttless Loom and Complete Set Equipment	改建 Replacement	4751	4751	棉布织机 Cotton Cloth Loom	台 Unit	56

续表3　Continued 3

项目名称 Items	建设性质 Type of Construction	自开始建设累计完成投资（万元） Investment Completed Accumulatety since the Beginning of Construction (10000 yuan)	自开始建设累计新增固定资产（万元） Newly Increased Fixed Assets Accumulately since the Beginning of Construction (10000 yuan)	累计新增生产能力（或效益） Newly Increased Capacities (or Results) by Accumulation		
				名称 Items	单位 Unit	累计新增 Newly Increased
化工： 阜宁化肥厂四改六工程 Chemical: Funing Chemical Fertilizer Plant Technical Transformation of No. 6 Project	扩建 Expansion	3348	3348	氮肥 Nitrogen Fertilizer	吨/年 ton/year	9200
苏州化工农药集团公司治理石棉碱污染 Suzhou Chemical Pesticide Group Co. Treatment of Asbestos Soda Pullution	扩建 Expansion	8669	8669	烧碱 Caustic Soda	吨/年 ton/year	20000
苏州精细化工集团公司 Suzhou Meticulous Chemical Group Co.	扩建 Expansion	4805	4805	钾肥 Potassium Fertilizer	吨/年 ton/year	20000
南京化纤股份有限公司1000吨/年粘胶长丝 Nanjing Chemical Fiber Share Holding Co. Ltd. 1000 tons/year Viscose Filament Yarn	扩建 Expansion	4980	4980	化学纤维 Chemical Fiber	吨/年 ton/year	1000
玻璃制品： 南通玻璃一厂技改 Glass Finished Products: Nantong Glass Factory Technical Transformation	扩建 Expansion	3797	3797			
黑色金属： 盐城市八菱集团公司 Ferrous Metal: Yancheng Municipality Ba Ling Group Co.	新建 New Construction	13380	13380			

续表4　Continued 4

项目名称 Items	建设性质 Type of Construction	自开始建设累计完成投资（万元） Investment Completed Accumulatety since the Beginning of Construction (10000 yuan)	自开始建设累计新增固定资产（万元） Newly Increased Fixed Assets Accumulately since the Beginning of Construction (10000 yuan)	累计新增生产能力（或效益）Newly Increased Capacities (or Results) by Accumulation		
				名称 Items	单位 Unit	累计新增 Newly Increased
南京第二钢铁厂金来钢铁公司 Nanjing No. 2 Iron and Steel Plant Jing Lai Iron and Steel Co.	改建 Replacement	7363	7363	炼钢 Steel-Making	万吨/年 10000 tons/year	10
南京钢铁厂2号焦炉工程 Nanjing Iron and Steel Plant No. 2 Coke Furnace Project	改建 Replacement	13347	13347	焦炭 Coke-Making	万吨/年 10000 tons/year	28
南京钢铁厂二轧带钢工程 Nanjing Iron and Steel Plant Second Rolling of Strip Steel Project	改建 Replacement	6445	6445	热轧薄钢板 Thin Steel Plate by Hot Rolling	万吨/年 10000 tons/year	20
南京钢铁厂转炉扩容及连铸改造 Nanjing Iron and Steel Plant Converter Capacity Expansion and Transformation of Connecting Cast	改建 Replacement	5318	5318			
南通宝钢新日制铁有限公司增建2号电炉及配套设施 Nantong Bao Shan Iron and Steel Plant Xin Ri Iron-Smelting Co. Ltd. Added Construction of No. 2 Electric Stove and Complete Set Equipment	扩建 Expansion	14000	12584	炼钢 Steel-Making	万吨/年 10000 tons/year	11
南通宝钢新日制铁有限公司棒材轧钢车间 Nantong Bao Shan Iron and Steel Plant Xin Ri Iron-Smelting Co. Ltd. Cudgel-Meterial Steel Rolling Work Shop	扩建 Expansion	13600	12261	炼钢 Steel-Making	万吨/年 10000 tons/year	24

续表5　Continued 5

项目名称 Items	建设性质 Type of Construction	自开始建设累计完成投资（万元）Investment Completed Accumulatety since the Beginning of Construction (10000 yuan)	自开始建设累计新增固定资产（万元）Newly Increased Fixed Assets Accumulately since the Beginning of Construction (10000 yuan)	累计新增生产能力（或效益）Newly Increased Capacities (or Results) by Accumulation		
				名称 Items	单位 Unit	累计新增 Newly Increased
有色金属：南京白云石矿镁厂 Non-Ferrous Metal: Nanjing Dolomite Mine Magnesium Plant	改建 Replacement	8262	8262			
南京铜加工厂 Nanjing Copper Feocessing Plant	改建 Replacement	16270	15802			
苏州钻石金属粉有限公司铜金粉生产线 Suzhou Diamond Metal Powder Co. Ltd. Copper Metal Powder Production Line	扩建 Expansion	4557	4557			
金属制品：南京工业搪瓷厂东陶有限公司 Metal Finished Products: Nanjing Industrial Enamel Factory Dong Tao Co. Ltd.	新建 New Construction	24074	24074	日用搪瓷制品 Daily Enamel Products	万吨/年 10000 tons/year	0.35
机械：扬州柴油机厂4142柴油机 Machinery: Yangzhou Disel Engine Plant 4142 Disel Engine	扩建 Expansion	5900	5900	柴油机制造 Disel Engine-Making	台/年 Unit/year 万千瓦 10000 kw	40000 60
汽车制造：扬州客车制造厂八五技改 Motor Vehical Manufacturing: Yangzhou Coach-Making Plant "Eight Five" Period Technical Transformation	扩建 Expansion	15228	15228	汽车制造 Motor Vehicals Manufacturing	辆/年 Unit/year	1000

续表6 Continued 6

项目名称 Items	建设性质 Type of Construction	自开始建设累计完成投资（万元） Investment Completed Accumulatety since the Beginning of Construction (10000 yuan)	自开始建设累计新增固定资产（万元） Newly Increased Fixed Assets Accumulately since the Beginning of Construction (10000 yuan)	累计新增生产能力（或效益） Newly Increased Capacities (or Results) by Accumulation		
				名称 Items	单位 Unit	累计新增 Newly Increased
南京微型汽车厂微型汽车 Nanjing Miniature Motor Vehical Manufacturing Plant Miniature Motor Vehical	扩建 Expansion	4193	4193	汽车制造 Motor Vehicals Manufacturing	辆/年 Unit/year	20000
洗衣机制造： 无锡博西威家用电器有限公司滚动洗衣机 Washing Machine Manufacturing: Wuxi Bo Xi Wei Household Electric Appliance Co. Ltd. Rolling Washing Machines	扩建 Expansion	17600	17600	家用洗衣机 Household Washing Machine Manufacturing	万台/年 10000/year	50
家用电冰箱： 南京新联机械厂技改 Household Refrigerator: Nanjing Xin Lian Machinery Plant Technical Transformation	扩建 Expansion	16697	16697	家用电冰箱 Household Refrigerator Manufacturing	万台/年 10000/year	50
电子： 镇江市接插件总厂录像机接插件 Electronic: Zhenjiang Jiont and Insert Pieces General Factory Joint and Insert Pieces of Vediocorder	扩建 Expansion	6058	6058			
电力： 南通天生港发电有限公司125工程 Power: Nantong Tian Sheng Gang Power Generating Co. Ltd. 125 Project	扩建 Expansion	90385	90385	火力发电 Thermal Power	万千瓦 10000 kw	25

5—20 房地产开发投资主要指标
MAJOR ITEMS OF REAL ESTATE DEVELOPMENT INVESTMENT

指　　标	Items	1990	1994	1995	1996
投资总额　（亿元）	**Total Value of Investment (100000000 yuan)**	**11.71**	**152.42**	**240.85**	**232.62**
按资金来源分	Grouped by Sources of Finance				
国家预算内投资	State Appropriation	0.02	0.89	0.90	0.87
国内贷款	Domestic Loans	1.73	30.24	48.05	56.77
利用外资	Foreign Investment		13.31	24.51	14.58
自筹投资	Fund Raising	5.44	61.69	71.09	59.18
其他投资	Other	4.52	46.29	96.30	101.22
按构成分	Grouped by Use of Funds				
建筑安装工程	Construction and Installation	9.97	115.09	172.76	168.40
设备工器具购置	Purchase of Equipment and Investments	0.01	1.60	5.96	5.05
其他费用	Others	1.73	35.73	62.13	59.17
按工程用途分	Grouped by Use of Project				
# 住宅	Residential Housing	9.76	102.95	139.24	129.19
第三产业	Tertiary Industry	11.71	152.42	240.85	232.62
新增固定资产　（亿元）	**Newly Incraese Fixed Assets (100000000 yuan)**	**9.74**	**93.39**	**145.24**	**191.22**
房屋建筑面积（万平方米）	**Floor Space of Building (10000 sq・m)**				
施工面积	Floor Space Under Construction	555.45	2711.93	3510.13	3295.30
#住宅	Residential Housing	481.80	1927.88	2502.75	2246.48
竣工面积	Floor Space Completed	293.94	1254.60	1630.06	1633.32
#住宅	Residential Housing	257.12	1039.72	1339.47	1290.88
土地开发投资额　（亿元）	**Value of Investment of Land Development (100000000 yuan)**		**19.43**	**26.70**	**26.93**
土地开发面积（万平方米）	Areas of Land Development (10000 sq・m)		1561.55	1329.00	796.65
商品房销售额　（亿元）	**Sales Value of Commodity House (100000000 yuan)**	**14.55**	**72.81**	**107.38**	**123.59**
商品房销售建筑面积（万平方米）	Sales Space Construction of Commodity House (10000 sq・m)	250.02	616.97	798.31	856.13

注：土地开发投资与开发面积从1993年起开始统计。
Notes: Investment of land development and space development are counted since 1993.

5—21 城镇集体固定资产投资主要指标
MAIN ITEMS OF FIXED ASSETS BY CITIES AND TOWNS COLLECTIVE UNITS

指　　标	Items	1985	1990	1995	1996
投资总额　（亿元）	**Total Value of Investment (100000000 yuan)**	**19.60**	**20.79**	**89.30**	**79.07**
按资金来源分	Grouped by Sources of Finance				
国家预算内投资	State Appropriation	1.28	0.18	0.27	0.23
国内贷款	Domestic Loans	8.49	7.33	20.06	15.05
利用外资	Foreign Investment	0.30	0.49	3.43	2.77
自筹投资	Fund Raising	8.21	10.87	56.62	52.39
其他投资	Others	1.32	1.92	8.92	8.63
按构成分	Grouped by Use of Funds				
建筑安装工程	Construction and Installation	10.30	10.04	47.45	43.54
设备工器具购置	Purchase of Equipment and Investments	8.53	9.56	37.38	31.63
其他投资	Others	0.77	1.19	4.47	3.90
按建设性质分	Grouped by Type of Construction				
#新建	New Construction	2.75	2.92	9.40	10.66
扩建	Expension	10.57	11.16	56.88	42.90
改建	Replacement	4.84	5.41	17.85	21.16
按产业分	Grouped by Industry				
#住宅	Residential Housing	2.85	2.17	4.80	4.52
第一产业	Primary Industry	0.34	0.27	0.34	0.36
第二产业	Secondary Industry	13.14	15.62	57.16	51.03
第三产业	Tertiary Industry	6.12	4.90	31.80	27.68
新增固定资产	**Newly Incraesed Fixed Assets**	**16.44**	**20.13**	**82.69**	**70.13**
施工项目个数　（个）	**Number of Projections Under Construction**	**3339**	**2859**	**3417**	**3031**
全部建成投产项目	Fully Completed Project Turn Over for Production	1879	1821	2750	2432
房屋建筑面积（万平方米）	**Floor Space of Building (10000 sq·m)**				
施工面积	Floor Space Under Construction	770.70	362.37	494.37	472.99
#住宅	Residential Housing	281.16	116.55	96.07	92.58
竣工面积	Floor Space Completed	434.86	232.42	354.02	356.11
#住宅	Residential Housing	159.62	79.67	68.10	73.87

5－22 农村集体固定资产投资主要指标
MAIN ITEMS OF FIXED ASSETS BY RURAL COLLECTIVE UNITS

指标	Items	1993	1994	1995	1996
投资总额 （亿元）	**Total Value of Investment** (100000000 **yuan**)	**388.96**	**411.76**	**451.52**	**463.73**
按资金来源分	Grouped by Sources of Finance				
国家预算内投资	State Appropriation	4.30	3.67	3.47	2.37
国内贷款	Domestic Loans	89.73	72.85	71.09	68.16
利用外资	Foreign Investment	44.55	59.84	61.87	69.84
自筹投资	Fund Raising	205.35	213.02	253.20	258.22
其他投资	Others	45.03	62.38	61.89	65.14
按构成分	Grouped by Use of Funds				
建筑安装工程	Construction and Installation	173.68	172.18	183.17	202.06
设备工器具购置	Purchase of Equipment and Investments	195.06	218.11	246.01	231.40
其他投资	Others	20.22	21.47	22.34	30.27
按建设性质分	Grouped by Type of Construction				
#新建	New Construction	163.66	171.28	164.79	169.86
扩建	Expension	155.86	166.08	196.13	219.87
改建	Replacement	53.63	55.53	72.64	57.20
按产业分	Grouped by Industry				
#住宅	Residential Housing	6.63	7.03	7.71	3.45
第一产业	Primary Industry	4.69	6.82	12.01	16.27
第二产业	Secondary Industry	337.71	349.10	376.56	380.16
第三产业	Tertiary Industry	46.56	55.84	62.95	67.30
新增固定资产	**Newly Increased Fixed Assets**	**319.54**	**337.85**	**380.96**	**389.81**
施工项目个数 （个）	**Number of Projections Under Construction**	**28893**	**29109**	**31910**	**26564**
全部建成投产项目	Fully Completed Project Turn Over for Production	24763	26017	28540	23824
房屋建筑面积 （万平方米）	**Floor Space of Building** (10000 **sq·m**)				
施工面积	Floor Space Under Construction	2700.69	2116.07	2073.83	1875.69
#住宅	Residential Housing	242.70	184.57	206.73	152.99
竣工面积	Floor Space Completed	2217.56	1850.81	1759.28	1598.97
#住宅	Residential Housing	188.27	156.78	168.30	129.37

5—23 城镇工矿区私人建房
BUILDING CONSTRUCTION BY PRIVATES INDUSTRIAL AND MINING IN REGIONS OF CITIES AND TOWNS

年份 Year	建房户数（户） Building Construction (Household)	竣工房屋建筑面积（万平方米） Floor Space of Building Completed (10000 sq·m)	#住宅 Residential Housing	竣工房屋价值（万元） Value of Building Completed (10000 yuan)	#住宅 Residential Housing
1985	29111	161.84	142.00	15549	13383
1986	26830	176.95	161.35	20718	18179
1987	35688	261.13	278.09	49474	39976
1988	28549	265.05	223.65	50833	42421
1989	29183	219.48	203.96	46062	39437
1990	23686	191.70	163.50	38276	32502
1991	21374	178.29	155.17	46535	41118
1992	20624	293.79	176.68	58648	49778
1993	27690	265.65	225.27	94147	76902
1994	34906	280.74	220.48	122582	94863
1995	24716	310.72	273.10	144205	122940
1996	25654	293.30	248.14	141910	120729

注：本表不包括农业户在城镇地域内的建房投资及面积。

Notes: Building construction and space investment by rural household in arear of cities and towns did not include in this table.

5—24 农村个人固定资产投资
FIXED ASSETS INVESTMENT BY RURAL INDIVIDUALS

年份 Year	投资总额（亿元） Total Investment (100000000 yuan)	竣工房屋投资 Investment In Buildings Completed	#住宅 Residential Housing	生产性固定资产投资 Investment In Productive Fixed Asseets	竣工房屋建筑面积（万平方米） Floor Space of Building Completed (10000 sq·m)	#住宅 Residential Housing
1985	50.89	46.21	42.75	4.68	6783.57	6104.02
1986	76.91	69.83	64.61	7.08	10252.00	9225.00
1987	103.40	93.34	90.78	10.06	10879.93	10619.65
1988	119.30	105.53	100.64	13.77	10323.35	9432.41
1989	124.20	117.30	103.63	6.90	13771.40	8758.82
1990	142.74	134.87	130.53	7.87	9490.74	9276.26
1991	153.37	141.88	140.03	11.49	9225.00	8902.00
1992	141.68	120.28	120.28	21.40	7220.00	6681.00
1993	151.98	129.02	129.02	22.96	7745.00	7167.00
1994	162.80	149.16	149.16	13.64	8549.00	8237.00
1995	199.80	171.76	171.76	28.04	7032.00	6805.00
1996	261.50	221.48	221.48	40.02	7471.00	7253.00

能源、原材料生产和消费 6

ENERGY, RAW MATERIAL PRODUCTION AND CONSUMPTION

6 能源、原材料生产和消费
ENERGY, RAW MATERIAL PRODUCTION AND CONSUMPTION

1 9 9 6

能源消费总值	Total Energy Consumption	808.81	亿元	(100000000 yuan)
能源库存总值	Total Energy Stock	31.20	亿元	(100000000 yuan)
原材料消费总值	Total Raw Material Consumption	4023.39	亿元	(100000000 yuan)
煤炭消费量	Total Coal Consumption	6041.12	万吨	(10000 tons)
焦炭消费量	Coke Consumption	252.52	万吨	(10000 tons)
生铁消费量	Pig Iron Consumption	251.55	万吨	(10000 tons)
钢材消费量	Steel Consumption	493.64	万吨	(10000 tons)

能源生产消费总量

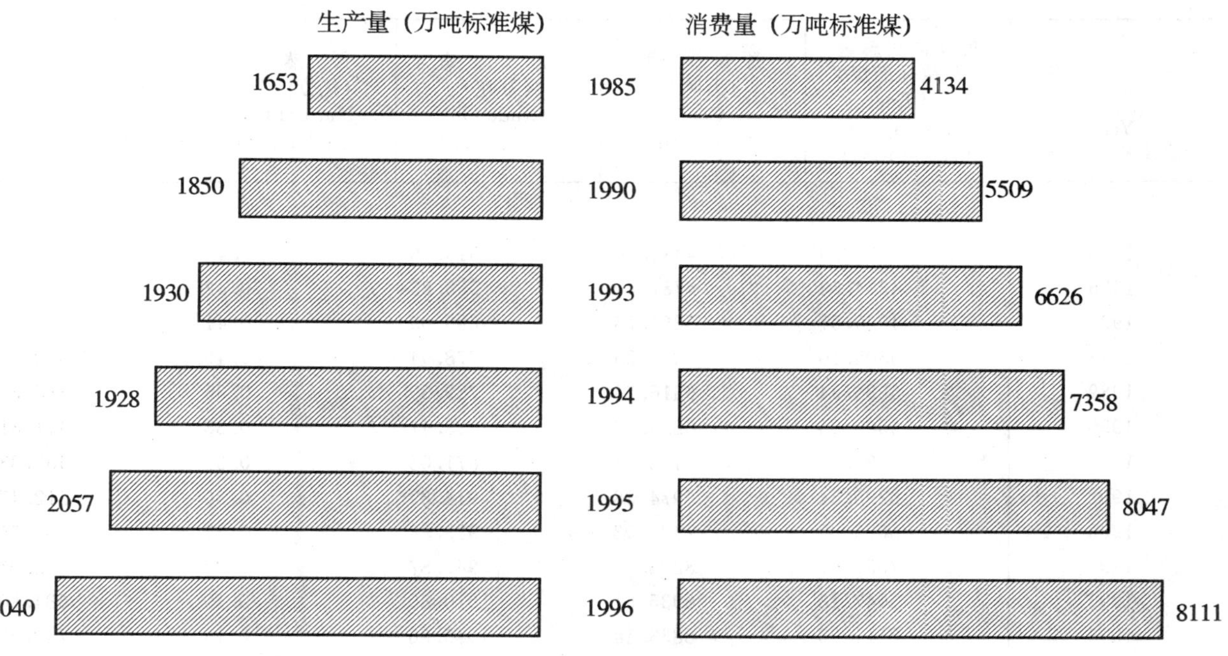

6—1 能 源 生 产 总 量
TOTAL PRODUCTION OF ENERGY

年 份 Year	能源生产总量（万吨标准煤）Total Energy Production (10000 tons)	原 煤 Coal	原 油 Crude Oil	天 然 气 Natural Gas	水 电 Hydro-Power
1985	1652.94	1566.00	79.73	5.00	2.21
1986	1686.48	1593.55	85.87	5.59	1.47
1987	1730.93	1628.90	94.00	5.45	2.58
1988	1776.04	1665.58	102.86	5.32	2.28
1989	1868.74	1747.21	114.69	4.66	2.18
1990	1849.85	1719.88	122.86	5.05	2.06
1991	1903.87	1764.71	132.86	4.39	1.91
1992	1891.50	1755.58	130.86	3.99	1.07
1993	1929.64	1789.70	135.15	3.59	1.20
1994	1927.55	1788.21	135.76	3.06	0.52
1995	2056.57	1888.52	144.87	2.31	2.46
1996	2039.64	1861.84	174.29	1.70	0.59

6—2 能 源 消 费 总 量
TOTAL CONSUMPTION OF ENERGY

年 份 Year	能源消费总量（万吨标准煤）Total Energy Consumption (10000 tons)	原 煤（万吨）Coal (10000 tons)	原 油（万吨）Crude Oil (1000 tons)	天 然 气（亿立方米）Natural Gas (0.1 billion cum.)	电 力（亿千瓦小时）Power (0.1 billion kw/h)
1985	4133.58	4481.40	515.56	0.41	277.38
1986	4384.53	4787.00	553.88	0.42	306.40
1987	4920.61	5363.75	686.65	0.41	341.44
1988	5508.10	6071.85	778.94	0.40	372.66
1989	5586.54	6316.78	789.39	0.35	388.51
1990	5509.06	6223.36	823.47	0.38	411.81
1991	5780.82	6413.24	871.08	0.33	453.33
1992	6296.54	6974.38	914.89	0.30	512.47
1993	6625.80	7420.03	938.88	0.27	567.75
1994	7357.67	8294.64	947.87	0.23	642.01
1995	8047.18	8935.51	1010.80	0.19	684.80
1996	8111.23	8833.14	1045.96	0.14	748.57

6—3 原材料能源消费与库存总值(1996)
TOTAL RAW MATERIAL ENERGY CONSUMPTION AND STOCK

单位:亿元 (100 000 000 yuan)

行业	Sectors	本年消费总值 Consumption	工业生产 Industry
总计	**Total**	**4832.20**	**4505.93**
能源总值	Total Energy	808.81	761.27
原材料总值	Total Raw Materials	4023.39	3744.67
黑色金属材料类	Ferrous Metal Materials	560.27	481.11
有色金属材料类	Nonferrous Metal Materials	178.91	170.76
化工类	Chemical Industry	549.24	543.15
建材类	Building Materials	167.57	55.74
木材类	Timber	54.00	38.73
金属制品类	Metal Products	50.49	46.09
一次转移价值的机电产品类	Machinery and Electric Products of Transfer Value	606.57	585.78
其他类	Others	1856.35	1823.31
按国民经济行业大类分	Grouped by Sectors		
工业小计	**Industry**	**4530.77**	**4497.06**
采掘业	Mining and Quarrying	35.49	33.29
煤炭采选业	Coal Mining and Processing	24.45	23.05
石油和天然气开采业	Petroleum and Natural Gas Extraction	4.38	3.75
黑色金属矿采选业	Ferrous Metal Mining and Processing	0.32	0.32
有色金属矿采选业	Nonferrous Metal Mining and Processing	0.97	0.97
非金属矿采选业	Nonmetal Mineral Mining and Processing	5.36	5.21
制造业	Manufacturing	4334.34	430.42
#食品加工业	Food Processing	317.27	316.70
食品制造业	Food Production	73.72	73.45
饮料制造业	Beverage Production	52.22	51.95
烟草加工业	Tobacco Processing	7.86	7.66
纺织业	Textile Industry	862.52	855.70
服装及其他纤维制品制造业	Garments and Other Fiber Products	100.13	99.36
皮革、毛皮、羽绒及其制品业	Leather, Furs, Down and Related Products	36.53	36.25
木材加工及竹、藤、棕、草制品业	Timber Processing, Bamboo, Cane, Palm Fiber and Straw Products	22.49	22.48
家具制造业	Furniture Manufacturing	5.62	5.61
造纸及纸制品业	Papermaking and Paper Products	38.05	37.73
印刷业、记录媒介的复制	Printing and Record Medium Reproduced	16.91	16.86
文教体育用品制造业	Stationery, Educational and Sports Goods	21.93	21.78
石油加工及炼焦业	Petroleum Processing and Coking Products	108.34	106.97
化学原料及化学制品制造业	Raw Chemical Materials and Chemical Products	518.71	512.28

续表 1　Continued 1

单位:亿元　　(100 000 000 yuan)

行　业	Sectors	建筑施工 Construction	运输邮电 Transportation Post and Telecommunication Service	年末库存总值 Stock (Year-end)
总　计	**Total**	**240.77**	**73.71**	**414.65**
能源总值	Total Energy	10.26	31.78	31.20
原材料总值	Total Raw Materials	230.50	41.93	383.46
黑色金属材料类	Ferrous Metal Materials	75.48	2.45	67.61
有色金属材料类	Nonferrous Metal Materials	7.77	0.21	18.50
化工类	Chemical Industry	3.00	2.39	36.86
建材类	Building Materials	106.91	4.09	7.27
木材类	Timber	14.93	0.28	6.26
金属制品类	Metal Products	2.55	1.80	5.15
一次转移价值的机电产品类	Machinery and Electric Products of Transfer Value	6.91	13.44	90.67
其他类	Others	12.94	17.27	151.15
按国民经济行业大类分	Grouped by Sectors			
工业小计	**Industry**	17.01	6.73	400.81
采掘业	Mining and Quarrying	1.77	0.06	517
煤炭采选业	Coal Mining and Processing	1.36	0.04	3.72
石油和天然气开采业	Petroleum and Natural Gas Extraction	0.38		0.67
黑色金属矿采选业	Ferrous Metal Mining and Processing			0.03
有色金属矿采选业	Nonferrous Metal Mining and Processing			0.16
非金属矿采选业	Nonmetal Mineral Mining and Processing	0.03	0.02	0.58
制造业	Manufacturing	14.12	6.63	381.14
#食品加工业	Food Processing	0.11	0.05	19.44
食品制造业	Food Production	0.03	0.10	5.31
饮料制造业	Beverage Production	0.15		4.77
烟草加工业	Tobacco Processing		0.20	2.57
纺织业	Textile Industry	3.68	0.38	62.74
服装及其他纤维制品制造业	Garments and Other Fiber Products	0.02	0.15	7.52
皮革、毛皮、羽绒及其制品业	Leather, Furs, Down and Related Products		0.01	3.33
木材加工及竹、藤、棕、草制品业	Timber Processing, Bamboo, Cane, Palm Fiber and Straw Products			4.00
家具制造业	Furniture Manufacturing			0.68
造纸及纸制品业	Papermaking and Paper Products	0.03	0.01	3.48
印刷业、记录媒介的复制	Printing and Record Medium Reproduced		0.03	2.86
文教体育用品制造业	Stationery, Educational and Sports Goods	0.02	0.03	2.11
石油加工及炼焦业	Petroleum Processing and Coking Products	0.91	0.39	4.52
化学原料及化学制品制造业	Raw Chemical Materials and Chemical Products	5.14	0.47	32.43

续表 2 Continued 2

单位:亿元 (100 000 000 yuan)

行业	Sectors	本年消费总值 Consumption	工业生产 Industry
医药制造业	Medical and Pharmaceutical Products	107.92	107.57
化学纤维制造业	Chemical Fibers	146.99	146.48
橡胶制品业	Rubber Products	34.42	34.36
塑料制品业	Plastic Products	68.40	67.94
非金属矿物制品业	Nonmetal Mineral Products	128.73	127.05
黑色金属冶炼及压延加工业	Smelting and Pressing of Ferrous Metals	187.45	187.33
有色金属冶炼及压延加工业	Smelting and Pressing of Nonferrous Metals	52.07	52.03
金属制品业	Metal Products	81.92	81.44
普通机械制造业	Ordinary Machinery Manufacturing	365.21	363.34
专用设备制造业	Special Purpose Equipment Manufacturing	192.21	190.99
交通运输设备制造业	Transportation Equipment Manufacturing	236.22	232.41
武器弹药制造业	Weapon and Ammunition Manufacturing	0.04	0.04
电气机械及器材制造业	Electric Equipment and Machinery	278.39	277.63
电子及通信设备制造业	Electronic and Telecommunications Manufaturing	186.20	185.22
仪器仪表及文化、办公用机械制造业	Instruments, Meters, Cultural and Official Machinery	31.08	30.96
其他制造业	Other Manufacturing	54.80	54.64
电力、煤气及水的生产和供应业	Electric Power, Gas and Water Production and Supply	160.94	159.58
电力、蒸汽、热水的生产和供应业	Electric Power, Gas and Water Production and Supply	146.93	145.95
煤气生产和供应业	Gas Production and Supply	5.10	5.04
自来水的生产和供应业	Tap Water Production and Supply	8.92	8.59
建筑业小计	**Construction**	**227.48**	**4.62**
土木工程建筑业	Construction of civil Engineering	211.54	3.58
线路管道和设备安装	Line and Equipments Installation	11.87	0.08
装修装饰业	Buildings Decoration	4.06	0.96
交通运输、仓储及邮电通信业	**Transportation, Storage, Postal and Telecommunications Services**	**73.95**	**4.26**
铁路运输业	Railway	8.67	0.26
公路运输业	Highway	12.57	1.59
管道运输业	Pipeline	2.08	
水上运输业	Waterway	11.67	1.61
航空运输业	Airway	2.43	
交通运输辅助业中港口业	Transportation Subsidiary	5.14	0.74
其他交通运输业	Other Transportation	0.01	
邮电通信业	Communications	31.37	0.05

续表 3 Continued 3

单位:亿元 (100 000 000 yuan)

行业	Sectors	建筑施工 Construction	运输邮电 Transportation Post and Telecommunication Service	年末库存总值 Stock (Year-end)
医药制造业	Medical and Pharmaceutical Products	0.08	0.11	7.35
化学纤维制造业	Chemical Fibers	0.10	0.01	6.30
橡胶制品业	Rubber Products	0.03	0.02	1.79
塑料制品业	Plastic Products	0.02	0.34	7.65
非金属矿物制品业	Nonmetal Mineral Products	0.82	0.15	13.52
黑色金属冶炼及压延加工业	Smelting and Pressing of Ferrous Metals	0.06	0.02	19.68
有色金属冶炼及压延加工业	Smelting and Pressing of Nonferrous Metals			4.18
金属制品业	Metal Products	0.35	0.04	7.24
普通机械制造业	Ordinary Machinery Manufacturing	1.17	0.15	42.48
专用设备制造业	Special Purpose Equipment Manufacturing	0.17	0.50	20.49
交通运输设备制造业	Transportation Equipment Manufacturing	0.45	3.01	31.14
武器弹药制造业	Weapon and Ammunition Manufacturing			0.03
电气机械及器材制造业	Electric Equipment and Machinery	0.35	0.17	25.60
电子及通信设备制造业	Electronic and Telecommunications Manufacturing	0.39	0.14	24.72
仪器仪表及文化、办公用机械制造业	Instruments, Meters, Cultural and Official Machinery	0.04	0.07	6.07
其他制造业	Other Manufacturing	0.02	0.07	7.15
电力、煤气及水的生产和供应业	Electric Power, Gas and Water Production and Supply	1.11	0.04	14.50
电力、蒸汽、热水的生产和供应业	Electric Power, Gas and Water Production and Supply	0.82	0.01	12.72
煤气生产和供应业	Gas Production and Supply	0.04	0.02	0.58
自来水的生产和供应业	Tap Water Production and Supply	0.26	0.01	1.20
建筑业小计	**Construction**	**221.77**	**0.54**	**8.90**
土木工程建筑业	Construction of civil Engineering	206.94	0.53	7.62
线路管道和设备安装	Line and Equipments Installation	11.78		1.08
装修装饰业	Buildings Decoration	3.05	0.01	0.20
交通运输、仓储及邮电通信业	**Transportation, Storage, Postal and Telecommunications Services**	**1.99**	**66.44**	**4.95**
铁路运输业	Railway	0.60	7.80	0.68
公路运输业	Highway	0.06	10.88	0.56
管道运输业	Pipeline		2.08	0.14
水上运输业	Waterway	0.02	9.56	0.68
航空运输业	Airway		2.43	0.07
交通运输辅助业中港口业	Transportation Subsidiary	0.21	3.48	0.62
其他交通运输业	Other Transportation		0.01	0.62
邮电通信业	Communications	1.10	30.20	2.19

6—4 主要原材料消费量(1996)
RAW MATERIALS CONSUMPTION

单位:吨 (tons)

名称	Sectors	本年消费量 Consumption	工业生产 Industry	建筑施工 Construction	运输邮电 Transportation Post and Telecommunication Service
生铁	Pig Iron	2515519	2511170	2968	1050
钢材	Steel	4936406	3467400	1399334	42447
#铁道用钢材	Railway Steel	68696	21332	24783	22117
普通大型钢材	Large Common Steel	62585	41017	21018	163
普通中型钢材	Middle Common Steel	394407	247910	142896	1400
普通小型钢材	Small Commom Steel	862132	283745	567297	5330
钢带	Steel Tape	148879	143130	4952	83
线材	Wire Rod	833597	400023	427286	3294
特厚钢板	Thickest Steel Plate	10373	8582	1686	7
中厚钢板	Thickest Steel Plate	721400	637759	75399	3904
薄钢板	Thin Steel Plate	783418	759550	18938	1868
硅钢片	Silicon Steel	82555	82083	126	2
优质钢型材	High Uality Steel	304606	300289	1179	474
无缝钢管	Seamless Steel Tube	144188	115376	25290	1161
焊接钢管	Welded Steel Pipe	153617	106269	43902	2051
铜	Copper	110348	110291	21	19
铝	Aluminium	94315	94204	69	1
铅	Lead	20706	20700	2	3
锌	Zine	23187	23186	1	
锡	Tin	1045	1043	1	1
铜材	Copper Material	108277	107664	318	192
铝材	Aluminium Material	66901	58510	8318	22
硫酸	Sulphuric Acid	1299146	1298825	220	68
烧碱	Caustic Soda	380801	377180	3559	15
纯碱	Soda Ash	234705	234291	293	53
天然橡胶	Natural Rubber	34118	34118		
合成橡胶	Synthetic Rubber	29104	28873	134	97
水泥	Cement	6347033	1191665	5027678	90519
平板玻璃 (重量箱)	Plate Glass (Weight Box)	635256	418652	207766	6950
原木 (立方米)	Log (Cubic Meter)	856923	611324	235499	4788
#原木直接消费	Log Immediate Consumption Log	679698	513058	160056	2500
锯材 (立方米)	Sawed (Cubic Meter)	307180	138801	161723	6186
润滑油	Lubricating Oil	92116	82685	1125	7942

6—5 主要能源消费和库存量(1996)
ENERGY CONSUMPTION AND STOCK

名称 Sectors	本年消费量 Consumption	工业生产 Industry	建筑施工 Construction	运输邮电 Transportation Post and Telecommunication Service	年末库存量 Stock (Year-End)	工业生产 Industry	运输邮电 Transportation Post and Telecommunication Service
煤炭 (吨) Coal (tons)	60411244	59804528	38719	211750	6659977	3728882	16300
焦炭 (吨) Coke (tons)	2525197	2522716	273	652	247369	144104	2
焦炉煤气 (万 m³) Coking (10000 cu. m)	61681	61041	639				
其他煤气 (万 m³) Other Gas (tons)	241726	241722			3	3	
原油 (吨) Crude Oil (tons)	10368105	10275177	27	88543	259837	240222	
汽油 (吨) Gasoline (tons)	458496	179321	24003	252595	200964	7458	3520
煤油 (吨) Kerosene (tons)	46014	12694	364	32915	18264	1519	3235
柴油 (吨) Diesel Oil (tons)	762761	299686	29166	428806	211368	20880	12590
燃料油 (吨) Fuel Oil (tons)	1307156	1222671	93	83976	139094	90358	35
液化石油气 (吨) LPG (tons)	294198	292555	755	9	7889	4614	
炼厂干气 (吨) Refirery Dry Gas (tons)	282129	282129			6	6	
天然气 (万 m³) Natural Gas (10000 cu. m)	788	654		44			
热力 (百万千焦) Heat (million Kilo-joule)	62602290	62138053	33250	659			

6—6　1996年主要能源平衡表(全社会)
ENERGY BALANCE

单位:万吨　　　　(10000 tons)

项　　　目	Items	煤　炭 Coal	焦　炭 Coke	原　油 Crude Oil	燃料油 Fuel	汽　油 Gaso-line	柴　油 Diesel	电　力(亿千瓦小时) Electr-ing (100000000) Kw/h
可供消费的能源总量	Total Energy Available for Consumption	8833.14	388.38	1045.96	168.86	176.54	253.84	748.57
能源生产量	Energy Output	2606.52	220.75	122.00	108.08	117.64	230.73	756.87
进口量	Imports	7338.25	182.59	923.97	68.27	125.90	97.28	41.51
出口量	Exports	886.17	0.05	9.94	6.38	74.69	83.84	49.81
年初年末库存差额	Stocks Changes	—225.46	—14.91	9.93	—1.11	7.69	9.67	
能源消费总量	Total Energy Consumption	8833.14	388.38	1045.96	168.86	176.54	253.84	748.57
加工转换投入量	Input in Processing and Transformational	4938.05	2.37	1021.39	15.39		22.89	
火力发电	Hydro-power	3920.93			8.15		22.52	
供热	Heating	428.82			5.90		0.37	
炼焦	Coking	291.78						
炼油	Petroleum Refineries			1021.39				
损失量	Losses			6.82		1.21	1.12	53.08
运输和输配损失	Transportation and Com-plete Form			4.47				53.08
终端消费量	Final Consumption	3895.09	386.01	17.75	153.47	175.33	229.83	695.49
第一产业	Primary Industry	116.19	0.20			10.64	79	70.04
第二产业	Secondary Industry	3519.11	385.67	8.90	145.07	63.00	62.24	497.43
工业	Industry	3515.24	385.63	8.90	144.90	59.82	59.31	490.70
建筑业	Construction	3.87	0.04		0.17	3.18	2.93	6.73
第三产业	Tertiary Industry	65.58	0.14	8.35	8.40	101.68	88.59	44.41
交通运输仓储及邮电通信业	Transportation, Storge and Communications	24.49	0.08	8.35	8.40	74.69	81.89	7.29
批发和零售贸易业、餐饮业	Wholesale and Retail Trade Restaurants	21.09	0.03			2.00	0.70	12.97
其他	Others	20.00	0.03			25.00	6.00	24.15
生活消费	Residential Consumption	194.21						83.61
城镇	Uuban	142.11						36.79
乡村	Rural	52.10						46.82
平衡差额	Balance							

物　价 7

PRICE

7 物　　价
PRICE

1　9　9　6

居民消费价格指数	Resident Consumer Price Index	109. 3
＃ 食品	Foods	109. 6
商品零售价格指数	Retail Price Index	106. 8
工业品出厂价格指数	Industrial Products Producer Price Index	100. 6
轻工业	Light Industry	100. 4
重工业	Heavy Industry	100. 9
原材料、燃料、动力购进价格指数	Raw Material, Fuel, Motive Power and Purchasing Price Index	103. 9
农产品收购价格总指数	Farm Products Purthasing Price Index	102. 0

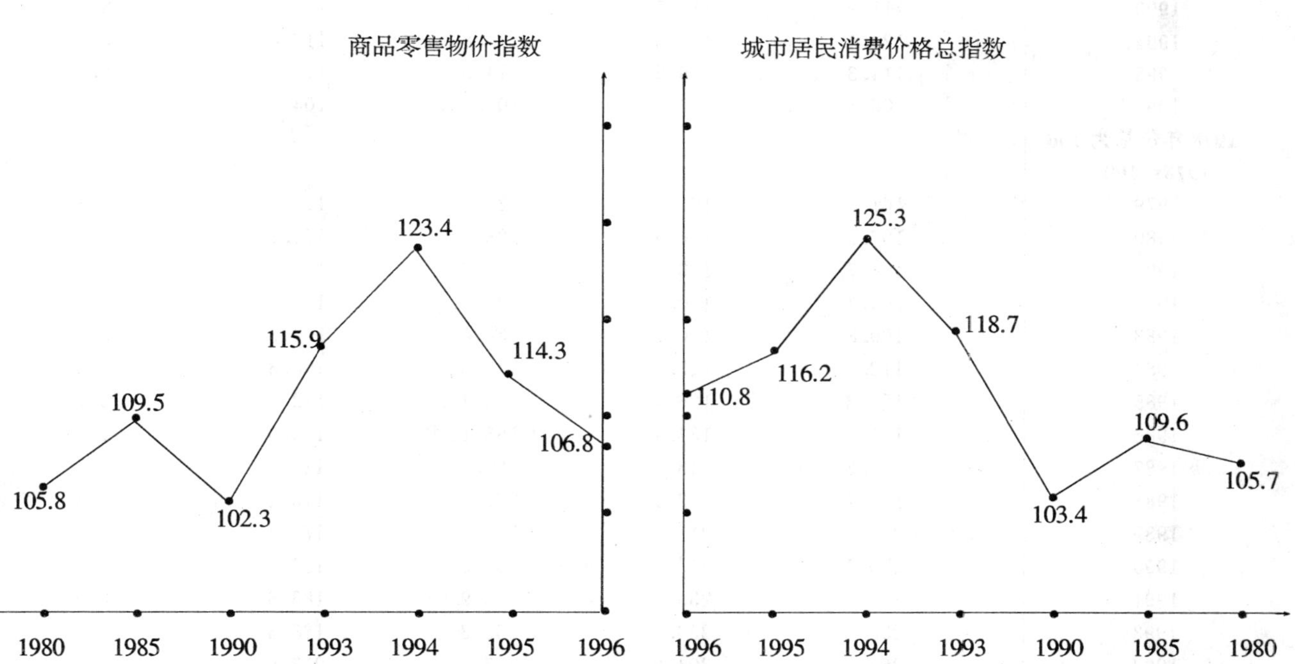

7—1 各种物价总指数
OVERALL PRICE INDICES

年份 Year	全省商品零售价格指数 Retail Price Index	城市居民消费价格总指数 Urban Consumer Price Index	农产品收购价格总指数 Farm Products Purchasing Price Index	农村工业品零售价格总指数 Industrial Products Rural Retail Price Index	工农业商品综合比价指数(以农产品收购价格总指数为100) Industrial and Agricultural Products Price Parity Index
以上年价格为100 Preceding Year=**100**					
1979	101.3	101.0	123.1	100.6	81.7
1980	105.8	105.7	104.3	100.5	96.4
1981	101.4	102.3	102.6	100.9	98.3
1982	100.9	100.9	102.6	101.7	99.1
1983	100.1	100.5	102.1	100.7	98.6
1984	102.5	104.1	104.2	103.8	99.6
1985	109.5	109.6	106.9	103.7	97.0
1986	107.1	106.4	106.1	104.1	98.1
1987	109.3	110.5	110.9	105.7	95.3
1988	122.3	122.6	126.0	117.6	93.3
1989	116.8	116.0	115.8	120.7	104.2
1990	102.3	103.4	98.7	102.8	104.2
1991	104.8	107.7	99.4	101.8	102.4
1992	105.1	108.8	102.8	102.6	99.8
1993	115.9	118.7	114.8	113.6	98.9
1994	123.4	125.3	148.8	117.4	78.9
1995	114.3	116.2	114.3	117.8	103.1
1996	106.8	110.8	102.0	104.6	102.5
以1978年价格为100 **1978=100**					
1979	101.3	101.0	123.1	100.6	81.7
1980	107.3	106.8	128.4	101.1	78.7
1981	108.7	109.2	131.7	102.0	77.4
1982	109.7	110.2	135.2	103.7	76.7
1983	109.8	110.7	138.0	104.5	75.7
1984	112.5	115.2	143.8	108.3	75.3
1985	123.2	126.4	153.7	112.3	73.1
1986	131.9	134.4	163.1	116.9	71.7
1987	144.2	148.6	180.9	123.6	68.3
1988	176.4	182.1	227.9	145.4	63.8
1989	206.0	211.3	263.9	175.4	66.5
1990	210.7	218.5	260.5	180.3	69.2
1991	220.8	235.4	258.9	183.6	70.9
1992	232.1	256.1	266.2	188.3	70.7
1993	269.0	304.0	305.5	213.9	70.0
1994	331.9	380.9	454.6	251.2	55.3
1995	379.4	442.6	519.7	295.9	56.9
1996	405.2	490.4	530.1	309.5	58.4

7—2 各种物价总指数(1996)
OVERALL PRICE INDICES

基期 Base Period	全社会零售物价指数 Retail Price Index			城市居民消费价格总指数 Urban Consumer Price Index	农产品收购价格总指数 Farm Products Purchasing Price Index	农村工业品零售价格总指数 Industrial Products Rural Retail Price Index
	全省 Province	城市 Urban	农村 Rural			
以 1950 年价格为 100 1950=100	502.1	583.1	480.0	664.5	912.3	321.7
以 1952 年价格为 100 1952=100	452.7	525.1	432.8	598.3	877.8	317.7
以 1957 年价格为 100 1957=100	424.7	489.6	408.6	545.1	749.3	318.6
以 1965 年价格为 100 1965=100	399.5	442.5	373.8	497.5	601.5	297.0
以 1970 年价格为 100 1970=100	406.4	449.2	380.2	506.8	576.5	308.6
以 1978 年价格为 100 1978=100	405.2	432.5	380.2	490.4	530.1	309.5
以 1980 年价格为 100 1980=100	378.1	403.0	354.7	459.5	412.9	306.6
以 1981 年价格为 100 1981=100	372.9	393.2	351.6	450.4	402.4	303.8
以 1982 年价格为 100 1982=100	369.6	390.1	348.1	446.5	392.2	298.7
以 1983 年价格为 100 1983=100	369.2	388.6	348.4	443.0	384.1	296.8
以 1984 年价格为 100 1984=100	360.2	374.8	343.3	425.5	368.6	285.9
以 1985 年价格为 100 1985=100	329.0	340.9	314.7	388.1	344.9	275.7
以 1986 年价格为 100 1986=100	307.1	320.1	292.2	364.6	325.0	265.0
以 1987 年价格为 100 1987=100	281.0	288.9	271.5	329.9	293.1	250.4
以 1988 年价格为 100 1988=100	229.8	233.9	223.8	267.9	232.6	213.0
以 1989 年价格为 100 1989=100	196.7	202.2	189.4	232.1	200.9	176.5
以 1990 年价格为 100 1990=100	192.3	197.2	185.7	224.4	203.5	171.5
以 1991 年价格为 100 1991=100	183.5	182.8	182.6	208.3	204.7	168.7
以 1992 年价格为 100 1992=100	174.6	170.5	176.7	191.5	199.1	164.4
以 1993 年价格为 100 1993=100	150.6	146.2	154.1	161.3	173.5	144.7
以 1994 年价格为 100 1994=100	122.1	120.2	123.5	128.7	116.6	123.2
以 1995 年价格为 100 1995=100	106.8	106.8	106.8	110.8	102.0	104.6

7—3 全省商品零售价格分类指数(1996)
RETAIL PRICE INDICES BY CATEGORY

上年＝100　　　　(preceding year＝100)

类别	Category	全省 Province	城市 Urban	农村 Rural
商品零售价格指数	**Retail Price Index**	**106.8**	**106.8**	**106.8**
食品类	Food	110.8	110.6	111.0
饮料、烟酒类	Beverages, Tobacco and Liquor	104.1	105.5	102.5
服装、鞋帽类	Garments, Shoes, Hats	109.7	110.4	108.6
纺织品类	Textiles	106.5	106.9	106.1
中、西药品类	Traditional Chinese and Western Medicines	107.8	107.9	107.5
化妆品类	Cosmetics	104.0	104.2	103.7
书报、杂志	Newspaper and Magazines	145.3	148.7	140.8
文化体育用品类	Stationery and Sports Goods	104.0	103.9	104.2
日用品类	Daily-Use Articles	105.4	105.6	104.9
家用电器类	Household Appliances	97.4	97.0	98.2
首饰类	Jewelery	98.9	99.1	98.4
燃料类	Fuels	108.0	110.0	104.0
建筑装璜材料类	Building Decoration Materials	100.4	99.5	101.6
机电产品类	Mechanical and Electric Products	95.1	94.2	96.5
农业生产资料类	**Means of Agricultural Products**	**106.6**		**106.6**
小农具	Small Farm Tools	111.4		111.4
饲料	Forage Grass	107.3		107.3
幼禽家畜	Young Livestock and Fowls	100.6		100.6
大牲畜	Livestock	111.3		111.3
半机械化农具	Semi-mechanized Farm Equipment	105.8		105.8
机械化农具	Mechanized Farm Equipment	101.3		101.3
化学肥料	Chemical Fertilizer	108.1		108.1
农药及农药械	Medicine and Equipment	108.2		108.2
化学农药	Chemical Medicine	108.3		108.3
农药械	Application Equipment	106.8		106.8
农机用油	Oil for Farm Machinies	102.7		102.7
其他	Others	109.9		109.9

7—4 全省居民消费价格分类指数(1996)
RESIDENTS CONSUMER PRICE INDICES BY CATEGORY

上年=100 (preceding year=100)

类别	Category	全省 Province	城市 Urban	农村 Rural
居民消费价格总指数	**Resident Consumer Price Index**	**109.3**	**110.8**	**107.1**
食品	Foods	109.6	110.6	108.5
粮食	Grain	107.9	107.9	107.3
淀粉及薯类	Starch and Potato	114.3	110.3	117.8
干豆类及豆制品	Beans and Bean Products	117.1	116.9	117.2
油脂类	Oil or Fat	91.6	90.9	92.3
肉禽及其制品	Meat and Poultry	106.5	107.5	105.4
蛋类	Eggs	115.5	115.5	115.5
水产品类	Aquatic Products	106.8	106.4	107.5
菜类	Vegetable Crops	136.6	135.3	139.3
#鲜菜	Fresh Vegetable	140.5	137.6	144.9
调味品	Flavoring	111.4	112.6	110.7
糖类	Sugar	102.1	101.4	102.4
烟草类	Tobacco	101.3	103.5	100.1
酒和饮料	Liquor	105.2	106.4	104.4
干鲜瓜果类	Dried and Fresh Fruits and Melons	105.7	106.0	105.1
#鲜果	Freshes	103.4	103.5	103.4
糕点类	Cake	110.0	110.9	108.9
奶及奶制品	Milk and Its Products	113.3	115.7	111.3
其他食品	Other	108.7	110.2	105.3
饮食业	Catering Trade	110.8	111.4	109.7
衣着类	Clothing	108.7	109.8	107.8
服装	Carments	109.6	110.3	108.7
衣着材料	Material in Clothing	106.5	107.2	106.2
棉布	Cotton Cloth	107.9	106.9	108.1
棉花化纤混纺布	Blend Cloth	104.8	106.2	104.5
化纤布	Chemical Fiber Cloth	105.8	107.5	105.1
呢绒	Woolen Fabric	109.1	113.2	106.8
绸缎	Silk	103.6	102.6	104.4
毛线	Knitting Wool	106.8	105.1	107.8
鞋袜帽及其他衣着	Shoes, Socks, Hats and Other Clothing	109.3	110.2	108.5
家庭设备及用品	Household Appliance	102.6	101.7	103.2

续表 1 Continued 1

上年=100 (preceding year=100)

类别	Category	全省 Province	城市 Urban	农村 Rural
耐用消费品	Durable Consumer Goods	99.8	98.5	100.9
家具	Furniture	102.5	102.5	102.6
家庭设备	Household Equipment	99.0	97.6	100.3
室内装饰品	Room Decoration	103.7	102.5	104.3
床上用品	Bed Articles	105.0	104.3	105.5
家庭日用杂品	Daily-Use Sundries	109.0	109.5	108.4
其他日用品	Others	103.2	102.9	103.5
医疗保健	Medicine and Health Care	107.9	108.7	107.7
医疗器具及保健用品	Medicine and Health Care Articles	103.1	106.3	102.0
中药	Traditional Chinese Medicines	110.4	114.5	109.1
西药	Western Medicines	106.4	104.4	107.3
交通和通讯工具	Traffic and Post	97.9	96.0	99.6
交通工具	Traffic	98.3	96.1	100.0
通讯工具	Post	96.1	95.8	96.4
娱乐教育文化用品	Recreation, Education and Culture Goods	109.7	114.7	105.6
文娱用耐用消费品	Durable Recreation Goods	97.0	96.4	97.4
教材及参考书	Teaching Material and Reference Books	135.5	138.8	132.5
文化娱乐用品	Recreation and Culture Goods	122.9	126.9	117.6
居住	Residence	117.3	131.8	104.9
住房	Housing	116.8	149.3	102.7
建筑材料	Constructure Material	100.8	99.3	101.5
房租	Rent	162.6	215.9	113.9
水、电、燃料	Water, Electricity and Fuel	118.0	121.2	114.3
服务项目	Services	112.3	112.0	112.3
电讯费	Telecommunication	100.6	100.8	100.1
邮费	Postage	109.7	109.3	110.0
交通费	Traffic	112.4	114.7	110.3
洗理美容费	Washing, Haircut	119.4	115.0	122.1
文娱费	Recreation	123.1	118.6	128.0
学杂保育费	Tuition and Children Care	115.5	114.8	116.0
修理及其他服务费	Repair and Other Services	109.6	109.8	109.3
医疗保健服务	Health Care	104.2	106.2	103.6

7—5 农产品收购价格分类指数(1996)
FARM PRODUCTS PURCHASING PRICE INDICES BY CATEGORY

类别	Category	以1975年价格为100 1975=100	以1978年价格为100 1978=100	以1980年价格为100 1980=100	以1985年价格为100 1985=100	以1995年价格为100 1995=100
总指数	**Overall Index**	**564.7**	**536.5**	**413.4**	**344.9**	**102.0**
粮食类	Grain	602.0	592.4	460.0	368.7	101.2
经济作物类	Industrial Corps	571.5	520.3	392.0	361.5	98.7
食用油	Edible Vegetable Oil	386.8	363.3	268.4	228.1	93.6
棉花	Cotton	652.1	589.6	442.0	414.3	100.0
麻类	Jute and Ambary Hemp	700.5	698.7	676.7	686.5	100.0
烟叶	Tobacco	341.0	316.6	310.2	261.0	100.0
茶叶	Tea	666.2	595.5	551.5	489.6	133.8
竹木材类	Bamboo and Timber	571.6	571.6	348.3	289.3	101.1
工业用油料、油漆类	Oil and Lacqure For Industrial Use	649.4	631.7	627.0	655.1	196.6
禽畜产品类	Liverstock Products, Poultry and Eggs	627.0	624.2	492.8	368.8	106.5
肉畜	Livestock For Slaughtering	640.7	640.7	502.6	404.7	103.3
禽蛋	Poultry Eggs	680.8	658.5	515.5	400.5	115.0
皮张	Hides and Shins	846.4	845.9	664.2	449.3	106.1
鬃毛	Bristles	591.1	571.1	473.7	158.2	99.6
其他畜产品	Other Liverstock Products	1216.3	1196.3	992.9	389.3	120.7
蚕茧蚕丝类	Silkworn Cocoons and Silk	368.7	362.1	463.1	276.4	100.7
干鲜果类	Dried and Fresh Fruits	721.4	701.6	628.9	322.1	90.7
瓜果	Melon and Fruits	425.4	411.7	411.7	223.2	89.1
干果	Dried Fruits	3053.3	2706.4	1648.9	624.1	101.8
干鲜菜及调味品类	Dried and Fresh Vegetables, Condiments	515.6	449.5	425.6	382.7	102.0
鲜菜	Fresh Vegetables	655.6	639.5	578.4	409.8	101.8
干菜及调味品	Dried Vegetable and Condiments	311.4	242.3	242.6	245.2	108.1
药材类	Raw Drugs	385.8	372.4	444.8	303.3	109.1
土副产品类	Native Products	295.7	265.8	255.4	238.3	117.1
水产品类	Aquatic Products	1082.5	1078.6	833.4	365.9	107.7

7—6 工业品出厂价格指数
INDUSTRIAL PRODUCTS PRODUCER PRICE INDICES

上年=100 (preceding year=100)

分组名称	Group Name	1993	1994	1995	1996
工业品出厂价格总指数	**Industrial Products Producer Price Indices**	**118.5**	**121.4**	**114.2**	**100.6**
轻工业	Light Industry	108.7	124.9	117.4	100.4
以农产品为原料	Using Farm Products as Raw Materials	108.5	130.2	118.5	102.9
以非农产品为原料	Using Non-Farm Products as Raw Materials	109.1	116.3	115.6	94.7
重工业	Heavy Industry	129.7	117.5	110.7	100.9
采掘	Excavation	137.2	106.8	109.8	105.3
原料	Raw Matericals	140.4	128.2	113.2	100.4
加工	Manufacturing	122.0	110.6	108.9	100.2
生产资料	Means of Productions	126.4	118.3	113.1	100.1
采掘	Excavation	137.2	106.8	109.7	105.3
原料	Raw Matericals	131.2	126.7	116.3	99.3
加工	Manufacturing	121.9	111.8	110.6	99.6
生活资料	Consumer Goods	108.6	125.3	115.4	101.5
食品	Food	110.5	128.5	126.2	105.9
衣着	Clothing	108.3	132.9	115.7	99.6
一般日用品	Daily—Use Articles	109.1	111.0	112.4	101.4
耐用消费品	Durable Consumer Goods	105.9	110.8	100.6	93.5

7—7 分行业主要工业品出厂价格指数
INDUSTRIAL PRODUCTS PRODUCER PRICE INDICES

上年=100 (preceding year=100)

部门名称	Deparment	1993	1994	1995	1996
冶金工业	Metallurgical Industry	166.5	99.8	100.3	96.2
电力工业	Power	137.4	187.0	111.6	106.2
煤炭及炼焦工业	Coal	129.4	105.6	111.2	116.9
石油工业	Petroleum	128.5	117.5	119.1	101.9
化学工业	Chemical	108.8	116.1	124.0	100.6
机械工业	Machine Building	119.6	109.9	104.9	97.5
建筑材料工业	Building Materials	141.2	109.2	107.2	97.2
森林工业	Forestry	142.1	98.8	99.6	91.5
食品工业	Food Manufacturing	110.5	128.5	126.2	105.7
纺织工业	Textile	105.0	135.3	119.2	93.7
缝纫工业	Trailoring	124.0	116.6	103.4	118.3
皮革工业	Leather	124.0	123.2	120.0	114.5
造纸工业	Paper	101.4	103.0	137.7	113.3
文教艺术用品工业	Cultural, Educational Handicrafts Articles	111.4	104.3	111.0	100.0
其它工业	Other Industries	118.4	128.2	140.1	101.3

7—8 原材料、燃料、动力购进价格指数
RAW MATERIAL, FUEL, POWER PURCHASING PRICE INDICES

上年=100 (preceding year=100)

分组名称	Group Name	1993	1994	1995	1996
总指数	**Overall Index**	**125.7**	**120.1**	**117.3**	**103.9**
燃料、动力类	Fuels, Power	126.9	119.9	107.7	112.2
黑色金属材料类	Ferrous Metal	170.1	100.2	96.0	100.1
有色金属材料和电线类	Non-Ferrous Metal and Wire	112.1	106.8	124.5	91.2
化工原料类	Chemical Materials	111.6	107.7	131.7	97.1
木材及纸浆类	Timber and Pulp	136.0	110.4	124.8	94.5
建筑材料类	Construction Materials	151.4	96.0	110.8	97.0
非金属矿类	Non-Metal Mining Industry	134.2	110.9	103.2	97.4
农副产品类	Form and Sideline Products	117.5	130.6	131.9	103.1
纺织原料类	Textile Raw Materials	100.7	140.0	125.7	99.1

城市建设、环境保护 8

URBAN CONSTRUCTION, EMVIRONMENT AND PROTECTION

8 城市建设、环境保护
URBAN CONSTRUCTION, EMVIRONMENT AND PROTECTION

1 9 9 6

城市基础设施投资总额	Total Investment Value of Urban Infrastructure	102.3	亿元	100000000 yuan
全年供水总量	Total Annual Supply of Tap Water	349423	万吨	10000 tons
城市气化率	Population With Access to Urban Gas	86.6	%	%
城市实有道路长度	Length of Urban Roads	8552	公里	Km
人均居住面积	Per Capita Living Space	9.0	平方米/人	sq. m/person
公交营运车辆	Operating Transt Vehicals	7962	辆	
工业废水排放总量	Total Volum of Industrial Waste Water Discharged	219677	万吨	10000 tons
工业废气排放总量	Total Volum of Industrial Waste Gas Emission	7450	亿标立方米	100000000 m^3
污染治理资金额	Total Funds for Polution Treatment	46915	万元	10000 yuan

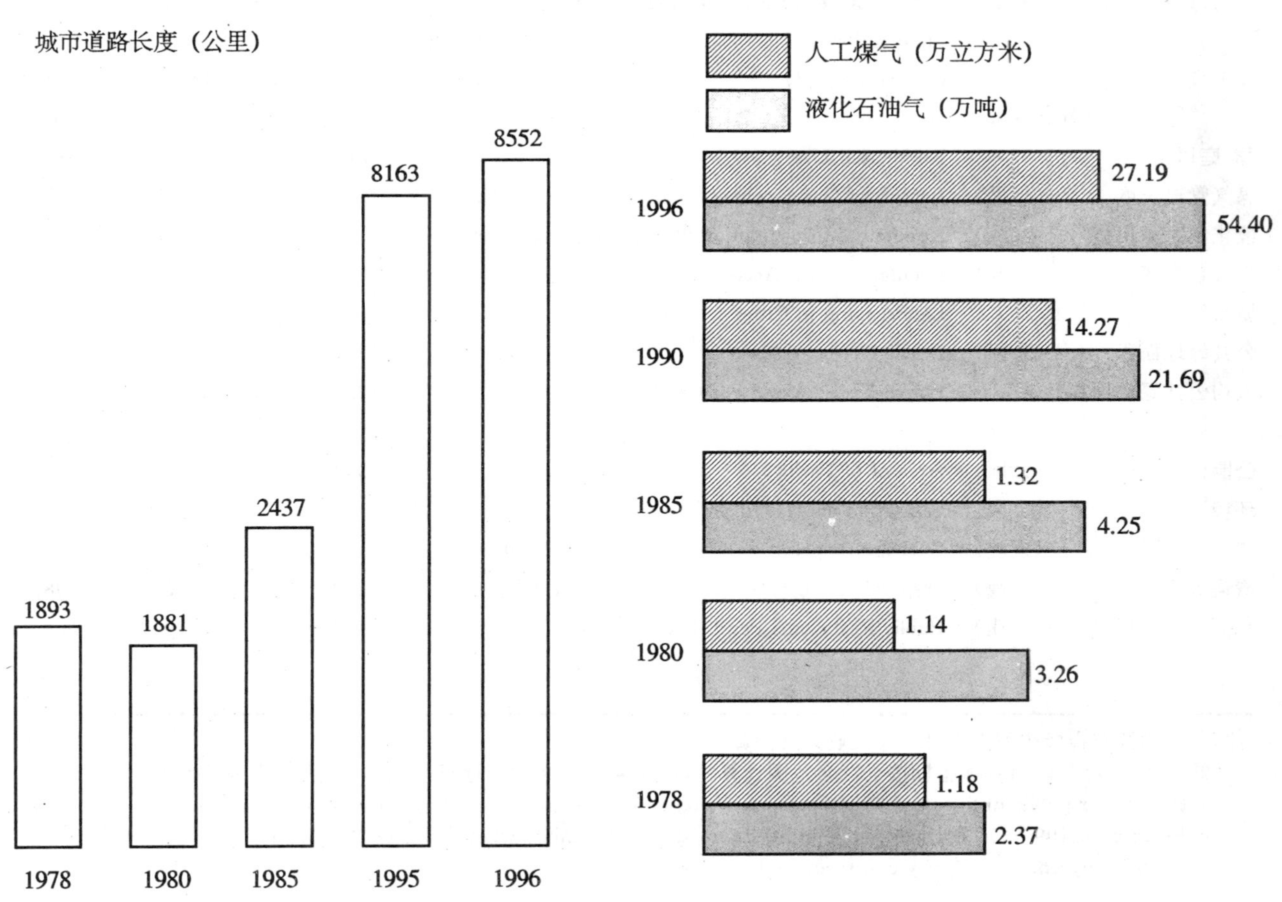

8—1 城市公用事业基本情况
BASIC STATISICS ON URBAN PUBLIC UTILITIES

项目	Items	1980	1985	1990	1996
自来水年供水量（万吨）	Annual Supply of Tap Water (10000 tons)	45221	76609	256664	349423
#生活用水量	Residential Consumption	16323	29280	62369	135429
平均每人生活用水（吨）	Per Capita (tons)	89.0	137.0	176.4	285.3
用水普及率（%）	Population with Access to Tap Water (%)	92.2	89.0	91.3	99.0
公共汽(电)车营运车辆（辆）	Operating Public Transportation Vehicles (Buses and Trolley Buses)	1605	2237	2827	7962
平均每万人拥有公共交通车辆（标台）	Vehicles per 10000 Population (standard unit)			3.6	6.6
年末实有道路长度（公里）	Length of Road (year end) (km)	1881	2437	5812	8552
平均每万人拥有（公里）	Length of Road per 10000 Population (km)	3.7	3.7	6.5	7.8
年末实有道路面积（万平方米）	Area of Road (year end) (10000 sq. m)	1160	1623	5672	9711
每万人拥有（万平方米）	Area of Paved Road Per 10000 Population (10000 sq. m)	2.3	2.5	6.3	8.9
下水道长度（公里）	Length of Sewer Pipelines (km)	1650	2277	4099	8860
平均每万人拥有（公里）	Length of Sewer Pipelines Per 10000 Population (km)	3.3	3.5	4.6	8.1
人工煤气供气量（万立方米）	Coal Gas Supply (10000 cu. m)	11401	13155	142681	271852
#家庭用量	Residential Use	2215	3851	15902	35837
煤气管道长度（公里）	Length of Gas Pipelines (km)	174	446	1118	2758
液化气家庭用量（吨）	Residential Consumption of Liquefied Gas (tons)	31350	38834	122691	468838
用气普及率（%）	Population with Access to Gas (%)	17.8	17.9	36.8	86.6
城市绿化	Landscaping in Cities				
公共绿地面积（公顷）	Public Green Areas (hectare)	1341	1450	3447	7528
人均公共绿地面积（平方米）	Public Green Areas Per Capita (sq. m)	2.7	2.3	3.8	6.9
公园面积（公顷）	Area of Parks (Hectare)	944	1030	2991	5263
环境卫生	Sanitation and Hygiene				
清运垃圾（万吨）	Garbage Disposal (10000 tons)	158	159	288	426
清运粪便（万吨）	Disposal of Night Soil (10000 tons)	232	147	221	198
每万人有公厕（座）	Public Restrooms Per 10000 Population	7.4	7.1	9.0	6.4

注：①人均拥有指标按城市人口中非农业人口计算。
②本表 1990 年以后各项指标按全社会范围计算的，1985 年以前各项指标只按城建部门管理的范围计算。
a)Figrues for public utilities per 10000 persons are based on nonagricultural population in urban areas.
b)Figures for 1990—1995 cover public utilities provided by all units, whereas figrues for other years only cover those provided by units under city construction department.

8—2 城市房屋面积情况
FLOOR SPACE OF URBAN BUILDINGS

单位:万平方米 (10000 sq. m)

年份 市名 Year Cities	年末实有房屋建筑面积 Floor Space of Building (Year End)	#住宅 Rseidential Housing	本年房屋竣工面积 Floor Space of Building Completed Within the Year	#住宅 Rseidential Housing	年末实有房屋减少面积 Decreased Floor Space of Buiding (Year End)	#住宅 Rseidential Housing
1978	7655	3397	451	195		
1979	8554	3791	569	307	117	65
1980	9224	4127	663	386	59	31
1981	10032	4588	782	493	76	41
1982	10772	5043	778	469	71	37
1983	12002	5791	926	575	66	38
1984	12808	6249	894	507	84	53
1985	13811	6722	1039	557	131	87
1986	18000	8592	1203	632	132	85
1987	19139	9139	1189	589	160	109
1988	22552	10565	1433	691	187	125
1989	27898	14735	1457	774	173	131
1990	27179	13460	1169	651	160	119
1991	31523	15785	1317	702	203	144
1992	34899	17632	1635	850	363	260
1993	36890	19378	2261	1331	458	379
1994	34556	17362	2058	1207	361	272
1995	38320	19878	2415	1469	427	288
1996	40865	21386	2495	1443	447	263
市区 Urban District						
南京市区 Nanjing	7595	3772	454	291	85	51
无锡市区 Wuxi	3429	1541	187	95	38	30
徐州市区 Xuzhou	2870	1381	143	78	24	22
常州市区 Changzhou	2520	1246	110	56	17	15
苏州市区 Suzhou	3298	1649	223	127	35	31
南通市区 Nantong	1543	667	140	92	30	28
连云港市区 Lianyungang	1557	720	145	76	2	2
淮阴市区 Huaiyin	978	508	15	12	4	2
盐城市区 Yancheng	877	486	62	34	4	3
扬州市区 Yangzhou	1570	780	96	50	15	10
镇江市区 Zhenjiang	1416	681	41	27	9	8
泰州市区 Taizhou	633	311	21	11	1	1
宿迁市区 Suqian	800	723	11	5	3	1

续表 1　Continued 1

年份　市名 Year　Cities	年末实有住宅使用面积（万平方米） Floor space of Residential Housing in Use (Year-end 10000 sq. m)	年末实有住宅居住面积（万平方米） Floor space of Residential Housing for Living (Year-end 10000 sq. m)	人均使用面积（平方米/人） Per Capita Floorspace in Use (sq. m/person)	人均居住面积（平方米/人） Per Capita Floorspace Living (sq. m/person)	解决缺房户（户） Number of Homeless Households Acquiring Housing Within the Year (Household)
1978		1746		4.3	
1979		1917		4.0	
1980		2097		4.2	
1981		2330		4.5	
1982		2595		4.9	
1983		2950		5.2	
1984		3207		5.4	
1985		3460		5.6	
1986	6263	4064	9.9	6.4	17589
1987	6710	4380	9.9	6.5	29885
1988	7870	5009	10.4	6.6	10789
1989	11053	7113	12.0	7.7	12614
1990	9936	6564	10.8	7.2	14497
1991	11783	7802	11.7	7.7	13587
1992	12998	8714	11.9	8.0	13340
1993	14123	9550	12.3	8.3	7424
1994	12681	8470	12.0	8.0	17189
1995	14670	10118	12.3	8.5	14021
1996	15491	10391	13.5	9.0	20963
市区 Urban District					
南京市区 Nanjing	2697	1955	11.7	8.5	4264
无锡市区 Wuxi	1125	771	12.4	8.5	
徐州市区 Xuzhou	993	632	11.7	7.5	478
常州市区 Changzhou	872	494	15.4	8.7	975
苏州市区 Xuzhou	1090	709	13.6	8.8	1544
南通市区 Nantong	499	302	11.3	6.8	1209
连云港市区 Lianyungang	540	360	12.6	8.4	626
淮阴市区 Huaiyin	399	231	14.2	8.2	2005
盐城市区 Yancheng	353	226	12.6	8.1	610
扬州市区 Yangzhou	590	375	15.6	9.9	1207
镇江市区 Zhenjiang	486	354	11.1	8.1	1364
泰州市区 Taizhou	222	147	12.8	8.4	1668
宿迁市区 Suqian	542	298	15.0	8.2	

8—3 城市自来水情况
INDICATOR OF URBAN TAP WATER SUPPLY

年份 市名 Year Cities	综合生产能力（万吨/日） General Production Capacity 100000 tons/Day	全年供水总量（万吨） Total Aunual Supply of Tap Water (10000 tons)	#生产用水量 Productive Use	#生活用水量 Residential Use	用水人口（万人） Residents With Access to Tap Water (10000 persons)	人均日生活用水量（升） Daily Per Capita Residential Tap Water Comsuption (liter)	城市人口用水普及率（%） Population With Access to Tap Water (%)
1978	112.3	35056	20073	12013	347.2	94.8	83.6
1979	125.1	39163	22408	14271	433.2	102.8	89.5
1980	142.6	45221	26005	16323	463.0	89.0	92.2
1981	157.7	49822	28768	16965	471.8	90.0	91.4
1982	165.0	56319	31149	20627	496.5	112.9	94.4
1983	175.1	62552	34831	22303	532.0	114.9	94.0
1984	212.6	68627	37380	24650	550.1	122.8	92.3
1985	218.9	76609	40908	29280	585.4	137.0	89.0
1986	602.9	177764	128259	39666	691.4	158.0	95.4
1987	706.6	204727	148378	42299	706.1	172.1	90.2
1988	734.9	220433	156689	51146	829.0	169.0	87.2
1989	856.3	233848	167472	54326	896.6	166.0	88.3
1990	941.7	256664	181543	62369	968.0	176.4	91.3
1991	1056.1	282691	201088	68287	1049.2	178.3	93.8
1992	1191.4	317812	224575	77010	1158.6	182.1	96.0
1993	1299.5	342780	239520	83041	1238.6	183.7	97.1
1994	1368.9	358696	243332	93030	1212.3	210.2	98.7
1995	1388.7	382325	190471	105192	1277.5	225.6	98.9
1996	1424.4	349423	192948	135429	1300.7	285.3	99.0
市区 Urban District							
南京市区 Nanjing	497.0	141057	86183	54874	269.40	558.1	100.0
无锡市区 Wuxi	109.6	26041	13447	10401	108.8	262.0	100.0
徐州市区 Xuzhou	74.6	14067	5187	7653	99.1	211.6	100.0
常州市区 Changzhou	54.0	11491	4423	6989	81.5	235.0	100.0
苏州市区 Xuzhou	66.4	21182	7157	9794	89.0	301.4	100.0
南通市区 Nantong	48.0	9583	4055	2844	50.0	155.8	100.0
连云港市区 Lianyungang	39.2	9134	4371	3739	46.7	219.5	97.7
淮阴市区 Huaiyin	15.0	6466	3933	2533	35.6	194.9	99.3
盐城市区 Yancheng	32.0	7043	3387	2227	28.2	216.1	100.0
扬州市区 Yangzhou	35.5	7525	2943	2322	38.0	167.4	100.0
镇江市区 Zhenjiang	52.2	16462	9757	5465	53.1	282.0	100.0
泰州市区 Taizhou	23.7	7624	5517	1651	21.5	210.4	98.9
宿迁市区 Suqian	5.9	1320	840	476	14.3	91.2	92.6

8—4　城市煤气、液化石油气情况
URBAN COAL GAS AND LIQUEFIED PETROLEUM

年份　市名 Year　Cityes	全年供气总量 Total Gas Supply		家庭用气量 Residential Use		用气人口(万人) Population with Access to Gas(10000 Person)		城市气化率(%) Percentage of Population Using Gas for Househhold Use(%)
	人工煤气(万立方米) Coal Gas (10000 Cu. m)	液化石油气(吨) Liquefied Petroleum (tons)	人工煤气(万立方米) Coal Gas (10000 Cu. m)	液化石油气(吨) Liquefied Petroleum (tons)	人工煤气 Coal Gas	液化石油气 Liquefied Petroleum	
1978	11756	23666	1592	22043	15.7	48.4	15.7
1979	11631	29381	1837	27656	17.5	61.0	16.2
1980	11401	32591	2215	31350	20.0	69.6	17.8
1981	10808	36387	2571	35439	21.8	74.0	18.6
1982	11358	37974	2740	37067	21.2	68.6	17.1
1983	11588	39725	2830	38841	23.4	68.5	16.2
1984	12468	40011	3122	38389	28.5	71.1	16.7
1985	13155	42495	3851	38834	39.9	76.2	17.9
1986	15951	118160	5394	60917	51.3	121.4	27.2
1987	109401	129880	7346	73511	73.8	141.1	31.6
1988	108438	178855	10704	92662	81.7	166.9	32.9
1989	140497	190471	13429	105671	93.0	186.1	32.5
1990	142681	216936	15902	122691	101.2	219.3	36.8
1991	142665	252342	17750	137780	116.3	261.2	41.9
1992	147625	337456	20943	190861	131.0	373.1	53.3
1993	153994	442089	23774	258003	150.6	498.0	63.5
1994	184552	574191	26281	337126	180.3	558.8	74.1
1995	282227	436131	30877	361990	213.4	637.3	81.8
1996	271852	543989	35837	468838	243.3	701.2	86.6
市区 Urban District							
南京市区 Nanjing	240021	97284	13409	79491	67.6	146.9	93.3
无锡市区 Wuxi	4159	29201	3435	25605	25.6	49.0	82.0
徐州市区 Xuzhou	3967	18886	2138	17577	22.0	50.0	85.1
常州市区 Changzhou	2624	28995	2235	27085	17.8	44.8	85.0
苏州市区 Xuzhou	5428	39480	4433	38915	30.5	37.8	85.2
南通市区 Nantong	2489	23961	2260	16412	18.0	25.9	99.3
连云港市区 Lianyungang	487	13173	426	13173	3.3	30.7	79.8
淮阴市区 Huaiyin	360	12246	351	9983	3.7	19.1	78.5
盐城市区 Yancheng	—	35998	—	32548	—	23.7	93.2
扬州市区 Yangzhou	1660	10083	1391	8933	14.0	17.4	83.0
镇江市区 Zhenjiang	2481	8247	2158	7621	18.6	18.0	83.8
泰州市区 Taizhou	—	14240	—	14240	—	15.5	89.1
宿迁市区 Suqian	—	960	—	960	—	3.4	35.8

注:1980年～1985年缺液化石油气供气量,表列数为销售总量。

Notes: The figure of liquid petroleum supply is not available, so the data in this table are total sales volume.

8—5 城市市政工程情况
URBAN CIVIL FACILITIES

年份 市名 Year Cities	年末实有道路长度(公里) Length of Roads (Year-end) (Km)	年末实有道路面积(万平方米) Area of Roads (10000 sq. m)	排水管道长度(公里) Length of Drainage Pipelines (Km)	城市污水日处理能力(万吨) Day Capacity of Sewerage Disposal (10000 tons)	城市路灯盏数(盏) Street Lights (Unit)	人均拥有道路面积(平方米/人) Per Capita of Road Areas (sq. m/person)	排水管道密度(公里)(平方米/人) Density of Drainage Pipelines (Km/sq. Km)	污水处理率(%) Rate of Sewerage Disposal (%)
1978	1893	1154	1503					
1979	1837	1118	1513		10455	2.3		
1980	1881	1160	1650	0.1	48338	2.3		0.2
1981	1960	1225	1735	0.6	57669	2.4	4.8	0.2
1982	2174	1324	1852	0.8	54851	2.5	4.9	0.3
1983	2302	1458	2025	1.3	61983	2.6	5.1	0.4
1984	2368	1534	2161	1.7	67320	2.6	5.3	0.5
1985	2437	1623	2277	1.8	71362	2.5	5.3	0.6
1986	4144	3867	2676	83.2	84991	6.2	5.9	1.2
1987	4526	4224	3005	78.0	101472	6.2	6.2	1.0
1988	3998	3878	3522	89.7	110072	5.1	5.9	1.3
1989	6872	6607	3782	91.3	122170	7.7	5.3	23.0
1990	5812	5672	4099	103.5	128647	6.3	5.7	16.4
1991	5658	5216	4872	133.2	143658	5.8	5.4	13.4
1992	6781	6587	5721	155.5	164828	7.0	5.6	16.7
1993	7090	7581	6653	160.7	194088	7.4	4.7	22.9
1994	6150	7094	7019	236.7	193930	7.1	6.0	31.8
1995	8163	8669	8262	273.5	215234	8.3	7.5	38.7
1996	8552	9711	8860	286.0	255695	8.9	7.5	42.7
市区 Urban District								
南京市区 Nanjing	1366	1465	1062	123.5	27534	6.7	6.4	50.4
无锡市区 Wuxi	746	711	1288	20.0	23401	7.8	15.6	12.8
徐州市区 Xuzhou	590	830	395	14.1	16140	9.8	6.6	54.9
常州市区 Changzhou	559	606	714	13.4	16294	8.2	11.0	25.6
苏州市区 Xuzhou	567	655	856	13.0	24128	8.2	11.6	50.7
南通市区 Nantong	278	352	489		9584	8.0	8.5	13.9
连云港市区 Lianyungang	463	424	336	18.0	8239	9.9	6.8	18.6
淮阴市区 Huaiyin	111	185	166	5.9	5302	6.4	5.2	58.8
盐城市区 Yancheng	125	131	105	10.0	5001	5.2	4.4	52.5
扬州市区 Yangzhou	187	242	315	14.9	12906	6.4	7.0	85.0
镇江市区 Zhenjiang	429	399	269	20.7	13900	9.1	5.0	50.1
泰州市区 Taizhou	114	117	139		5230	6.7	6.2	—
宿迁市区 Suqian	192	308	94		1206	32.4	7.8	—

注:1978—1988年污水处理率中只包括城建系统内资料。
Note: Sewerage disposal includes the figure of urban construction department only in 1978—1988.

8－6 城市园林绿化情况

URBAN PARKS, GARDENS AND GREEN AREAS

年份市名 Year Cities	园林绿地面积（公顷） Total Area of Parks, Gardens and Green Areas in Cities (Hectares)	#公共绿地 Public Green Areas	建成区绿化覆盖面积（公顷） Coverage Space of Green Areas Developed (Hectares)	公园 Park 个数（个） Number (Unit)	公园 Park 面积（公顷） Area (Hectares)	游人量（万人次） Vistors to Park and Zoos (10000 person-times)	人均公共绿地面积（平方米） Per Capita Public Green Areas (sq. m)	建成区绿化覆盖率（%） Coverage Rate of Green Area Developed (%)
1978	7303			59	786			
1979	6434			65	842			
1980	6582	1341		72	944		2.7	19.3
1981	7187	1122		73	931	4614	2.3	19.5
1982	7379	1150		73	959	5042	2.2	19.8
1983	8709	1287		75	966	6192	2.3	21.8
1984	7837	1263		78	946	6533	2.1	22.1
1985	7998	1450		83	1030	7003	2.3	20.6
1986	15650	2395	8379	122	1940	7725	3.7	18.3
1987	19424	3530	12074	134	2096	8667	5.1	25.0
1988	18100	3058	11717	158	2540	8727	4.0	19.7
1989	21654	3214	12804	172	2725	8034	3.7	19.2
1990	20337	3447	14112	184	2991	8556	3.8	19.5
1991	19096	3841	16423	201	3071	8247	4.3	18.4
1992	20898	4283	21726	217	2958	8028	4.5	21.4
1993	30174	5882	31133	242	5179	8816	5.8	22.1
1994	33089	6124	34728	241	5396	6610	6.1	29.6
1995	48564	7226	34093	264	5648	7746	6.9	30.8
1996	50558	7528	35964	283	5263	6154	6.9	30.3
市区 Urban District								
南京市区 Nanjing	9620	1832	6682	40	1700	1425	8.0	40.0
无锡市区 Wuxi	2861	620	2731	16	483	1050	6.8	33.1
徐州市区 Xuzhou	2881	671	2003	15	224	327	7.9	33.2
常州市区 Changzhou	1105	301	1909	11	100	339	4.1	29.4
苏州市区 Xuzhou	1852	363	1887	37	315	987	4.5	25.5
南通市区 Nantong	758	207	1430	7	41	230	4.7	24.8
连云港市区 Lianyungang	15021	203	1438	6	52	95	4.8	29.3
淮阴市区 Huaiyin	849	115	984	5	62	72	4.0	30.8
盐城市区 Yancheng	518	147	597	5	73	90	5.8	24.8
扬州市区 Yangzhou	1406	279	1507	16	205	376	7.4	33.5
镇江市区 Zhenjiang	2190	209	1705	14	193	233	4.8	31.8
泰州市区 Taizhou	504	102	588	5	34	51	5.9	26.3
宿迁市区 Suqian	112	26	723	5	25	27	2.7	60.3

注：1980－1985年缺建成区绿化覆盖率，表列数为市区绿化覆盖率。

Note: The figures of coverage of green areas developed are lacking in 1980－1985, so the data in this table are coverage rate of urban green areas.

8—7 城市清洁卫生情况
URBAN ENVIRONMENT SANITATION

年份 市名 Year Cities	清扫面积 (万平方米) Sweeping Areas (10000 sq. m)	生活垃圾清运量 (万吨) Residential Garbages Disposal Cleared (10000 tons)	粪便清运量 (万吨) Night Soil Disposal Cleared (10000 tons)	无害化处理厂日处理能力 (吨) Day Disposal Capacities of No Harmful Disposal Factory (tons)	垃圾粪便年处理量 (万吨) Annual Garbages and Night Soil Disposal Cleared (10000 tons)	环卫机械 (辆) Machines of Environment Sanitation (Set)	公共厕所 (座) Public Toilet
1979	503	79	229			223	3545
1980	601	158	232			296	3712
1981	687	88	229			408	4032
1982	777	99	221			539	4036
1983	793	116	197			605	4497
1984	985	125	180			665	4593
1985	1078	159	147	20		734	4700
1986	1372	190	202	20		920	5448
1987	1676	198	196	120		1067	5556
1988	2056	231	260	120		1181	6912
1989	2136	262	260	162		1735	7910
1990	2445	288	221	385		1322	8072
1991	3068	341	271	1588	357.3	1604	9974
1992	3432	409	419	7622	531.7	1785	9265
1993	4095	408	441	14014	654.1	1998	9162
1994	4240	360	388	16442	658.8	1736	7095
1995	5429	398	209	13810	532.5	2072	7263
1996	6252	426	198	13125	523.9	2144	6932
市区 Urban District							
南京市区 Nanjing	750	79	25	2239	84.1	462	948
无锡市区 Wuxi	456	31	30	100	61.3	193	500
徐州市区 Xuzhou	374	37	2	1050	38.4	159	328
常州市区 Changzhou	321	23	9	610	27.4	143	650
苏州市区 Xuzhou	686	28	29	1260	47.3	164	360
南通市区 Nantong	73	9	3	4	0.1	51	132
连云港市区 Lianyungang	190	17	2	343	11.3	70	716
淮阴市区 Huaiyin	142	13	1	460	13.9	52	112
盐城市区 Yancheng	87	9	4	322	12.3	52	175
扬州市区 Yangzhou	185	13	20	522	32.8	46	260
镇江市区 Zhenjiang	249	18	4	600	21.7	49	159
泰州市区 Taizhou	97	5	8	230	13.0	33	151
宿迁市区 Suqian							

注:垃圾粪便年处理量1996年为无害化处理量。
Notes: Garbags and night soil annual disposal cleared in 1996 was no harmful disposal cleared.

8—8 城市公共汽(电)车、出租汽车情况
URBAN PUBLIC TRANST AND TAXI

年份 市名 Year Cities	年末实有公共汽(电)车营运车数(辆) Operating Public Transt Vehicles (Year-end)	实有公共汽(电)车营运标准车台(标台) Operating Standard Public Transt Vehicles (Standardized)	公共汽(电)车营运线路长度(公里) Length of Public Transt Route (Km)	公共汽(电)车客运总量(万人次) Passengers Carried by Transt (10000 Person Times)	每万人拥有公共交通车辆(标台) Vehicale Per 10000 Population (Standardiged)	出租汽车营运车数(辆) Operating Taxis
1978	1407		1772			
1979	1503		1860	98880		90
1980	1605		1920	100671		150
1981	1771		1876	120794		175
1982	1962		1963	126384		208
1983	2010		2212	131313		215
1984	2128		2739	137097		324
1985	2237		2904	143146		605
1986	2642	2937	3385	145399	4.5	2927
1987	2711	3089	3963	151393	4.3	2980
1988	2844	3186	3780	145027	3.9	3869
1989	2826	3167	4603	135947	3.7	4555
1990	2827	3210	3991	130641	3.6	5775
1991	2968	3727	4229	124409	4.1	5005
1992	4578	4855	6939	120282	5.1	8133
1993	6384	5954	7570	109248	5.8	9838
1994	7367	6808	10127	110921	6.8	12307
1995	3937	7354	8095	11918	7.1	18073
1996	7962	7144	5747	104583	6.6	25403
市区 Urban District						
南京市区 Nanjing	2378	2263	870	39012	9.9	6645
无锡市区 Wuxi	800	779	374	12406	8.6	2306
徐州市区 Xuzhou	854	547	337	11341	6.5	2215
常州市区 Changzhou	348	375	335	8768	5.1	1029
苏州市区 Xuzhou	714	793	256	11626	9.9	2220
南通市区 Nantong	149	185	183	4701	4.2	1654
连云港市区 Lianyungang	74	77	73	972	1.8	1216
淮阴市区 Huaiyin	68	78	38	963	2.7	757
盐城市区 Yancheng	206	165	460	1967	6.5	430
扬州市区 Yangzhou	486	337	383	2836	8.9	1204
镇江市区 Zhenjiang	251	235	261	4156	5.4	997
泰州市区 Taizhou	34	34	35	222	2.0	386
宿迁市区 Suqian						

8—9 主要年份环境保护情况
ENVIRONMENTAL PROTECITION IN MAIN YEARS

项目	Items	1994	1995	1996
工业废水量	**Industrial Waste Water**			
工业废水排放量（万吨）	Industrial Waste Water Discharged (10000 tons)	211577	220184	219677
# 符合排放标准的	According to Standard	145504	144090	151859
工业废水排放的污染物	**Pollution of Industrial Waste Water Discharged**			
汞及其无机化合物（公斤）	Mercury and Inorganic Compound (kg)	42	75	80
镉及其无机化合物（公斤）	Cadmium and Inorganic Compound (kg)	253	656	480
六价铬化合物（公斤）	6-valence Chromium Compound (kg)	26469	58805	12660
砷及其无机化合物（公斤）	Arsenic and Inorganic Compound (kg)	72900	166274	164540
铅及其无机化合物（公斤）	Aluminium and Inorganic Compound (kg)	6518	9021	10930
酚（公斤）	Phenol (kg)	499136	462699	414620
氰化物（公斤）	Cyanide (kg)	111861	97199	96700
石油类（吨）	Petroleum Type (tons)	4482	4697	4356
工业废气排放总量（万标立米）	Industrial Waste Gas Emission (10000 cu. m)	57721446	78721059	74508126
#生产工艺排放的	Waste Gas in the Process of Production	15097038	18880021	16441471
#净化处理的	Gas Purified	10530623	15478687	12372942
二氧化硫排放量（万吨）	Sulphur Dioxide (10000 tons)	98.30	104.47	104.07
烟尘排放量（万吨）	Soot (10000 tons)	52	54	48
工业粉尘产生量（万吨）	Industrial Dust Produced (10000 tons)	142	139	234
排放量（万吨）	Volume Discharged (10000 tons)	29	27	23
回收量（万吨）	Volume Retrieved (10000 tons)	113	112	211
工业粉尘回收率（%）	Rate of Industrial Dust Discharged	79.6	80.6	90.2
固体废渣产生量（万吨）	Solid Waste Residue Produced (10000 tons)	2725	2883	2891
蒸汽锅炉（台/万蒸吨）	Steam Boiler (10000 Steam tons)	5921/6.4	6012/5.9	5392/9.1
工业炉窑（座）	Industrial Stove	4663	3202	3543
其他	**Others**			
"三废"综合利用产品产值（万元）	Output Value of Products Made from Waste Gas, Waste Water and Waste Residue (10000 yuan)	124926	93208	410789
"三废"综合利用产品利润（万元）	Profits Obtained from Waste Gas, Waste Water and Waste Residue (10000 yuan)	39143	32159	37218

8—10 工业"三废"排放及处理情况(1996)

行业名称	Items	工业企业数(个) Number of Enterprises (unit)	工业废水排放总量(万吨) Industrial Waste Water Discharged (10000 tons)	#直接排入海的 Discharged Directly to Sea	#直接排入江河湖的 Discharged Directly to Rivers, Lakes and Reservoirs
总计	**Total**	**5141**	**219677**	**3478**	**201960**
#重点调查企业	Key Sunvey Enterprises	3236	213661	3371	196897
采掘业	Mining and Quarrying	51	1069		910
食品、烟草加工及食品、饮料制造业	Food, Tobacco and Beverage Processing	404	6734	59	5931
纺织业	Textile Industry	432	11833	241	9840
皮革、毛皮、羽绒及其制品业	Leather, Furs, Feather and Related Producets	46	453	4	357
造纸及纸制品业	Papermaking and Paper Products	58	10037	444	8791
印刷业、记录媒介的复制	Printing and Record Pressing	29	62		52
石油加工及炼焦业	Petroleum Processing and Coking	21	2365		2189
化工原料及化学制品制造业	Raw Chemical Materials and Chemical Products	376	80029	1358	75487
医药制造业	Medical and Pharmaceutical Products	110	4536	83	4235
化学纤维制造业	Chemical Fiber	26	4436	186	3055
橡胶制品业	Rubber Products	37	574		441
塑料制品业	Plastic Products	60	473	19	339
非金属矿物制造业	Nonmetal Mineral Industry	218	3288	546	2494
#水泥制造业	Cement Manufacturing	52	855		812
黑色金属冶炼及压延工业	Smelting and Pressing of Ferrous Metals	64	31206		31205
有色金属冶炼及压延工业	Smelting and Pressing of Nonferrous Metals	40	672	4	606
金属制品业	Metal Products	124	1382		1265
机械、电气、电子设备制造业	Machine, Electric and Electronic Equipment Manufacturing	755	10280	96	8293
电力、煤气及水的生产和供应业	Production and Supply of Power, Coal Gas and Tap Water	79	40494	262	38393
其它行业	Other Industries	306	3738	69	3014

DISCHARGE AND TREATMENT OF INDUSTRIAL WASTE WATER, WASTE GAS AND RESIDUE

工业废水排放达标量（万吨） Industrial Waste Water Reaching Discharged Standards (10000 tons)	工业废气排放总量（亿标立方米） Industrial Waste Gas Discharged Standards (100000000 cu. m)	燃料燃烧过程废气排放总量（亿标立方米） Waste Gas Dischanged From Fuel Standards (100000000 cu. m)	#经过消烟除尘的 Soot and Dust Removed	生产工艺过程废气排放总量（亿标立方米） Waste Gas Discharged in the Process of Production Standards (100000000 cu. m)	#经过净化处理的 Gas Purified	工业二氧化硫排放量（吨） Industrial Saplhut Dioxide Discharged (tons)	#生产工艺过程中排放的 Suplhur Dioxide Discharged in the Process of Production
151859	**7450**	**5807**	**5475**	**1644**	**1237**	**1040750**	**62019**
148820	7241	5650	5348	1591	1195	1013039	59459
828	77	34	27	43	42	3785	512
3314	168	101	97	67	66	18233	
8021	168	152	148	16	13	35105	216
269	4	4	3			884	
940	70	58	52	12		8691	
32	1		1			88	
1958	62	43	37	20	14	3761	930
47886	951	686	663	265	207	123200	11261
2694	71	67	42	4	4	23915	66
3107	226	117	106	109	17	35321	
533	19	10	8	9	9	2447	
329	25	13	8	13	12	2246	
2440	881	372	303	509	377	53091	21029
699	531	181	173	350	235	28146	17391
27942	599	315	253	284	276	56528	24006
572	9	7	3	2	1	941	71
972	45	11	9	34	33	2016	117
7754	501	337	307	163	85	22715	350
36989	3274	3258	3222	16	15	611202	875
2240	90	65	59	25	23	8870	26

续表 1

行业名称	Items	工业二氧化硫去除总量（吨） Industrial Sulpur Dioxide Removed (tons)	#生产工艺过程去除的 Removed in the Process of Production	工业烟尘排放量（吨） Industrial Soot Discharged (tons)	工业烟尘去除量（吨） Industrial Soot Removed (tons)
总计	**Total**	**289226**	**87183**	**485346**	**8263680**
#重点调查企业	Key Sunvey Enterprises	284993	83456	468721	8234664
采掘业	Mining and Quarrying	1244	873	9659	10056
食品、烟草加工及食品、饮料制造业	Food, Tobacco and Beverage Processing	1566		7628	32276
纺织业	Textile Industry	5850		18185	53773
皮革、毛皮、羽绒及其制品业	Leather, Furs, Feather and Related Producets	21		313	1270
造纸及纸制品业	Papermaking and Paper Products	1428		2989	14004
印刷业、记录媒介的复制	Printing and Record Pressing			46	134
石油加工及炼焦业	Petroleum Processing and Coking	18604	18590	580	842
化工原料及化学制品制造业	Raw Chemical Materials and Chemical Products	57895	42583	38528	138554
医药制造业	Medical and Pharmaceutical Products	138250	44	1797	10842
化学纤维制造业	Chemical Fiber	1621		5089	48463
橡胶制品业	Rubber Products	388		708	1743
塑料制品业	Plastic Products	149		712	2995
非金属矿物制造业	Nonmetal Mineral Industry	8099	5769	22960	131545
水泥制造业	Cement Manufacturing	3506	2528	5673	35057
黑色金属冶炼及压延工业	Smelting and Pressing of Ferrous Metals	17585	14022	13046	67440
有色金属冶炼及压延工业	Smelting and Pressing of Nonferrous Metals	8		728	944
金属制品业	Metal Products	92		1011	1897
机械、电气、电子设备制造业	Machine, Electric and Electronic Equipment Manufacturing	2470	424	11617	30373
电力、煤气及水的生产和供应业	Production and Supply of Power, Coal Gas and Tap Water	28167	1145	329845	7673345
其它行业	Other Industries	1555	6	3280	14168

Continued 1

工业粉尘排放量（吨） Industrial Dust Discharged (tons)	工业粉尘回收量（吨） Industrial Dust Retrieved (tons)	工业固体废物产生量（万吨） Industrial Waste Residue Produced (10000 tons)	工业固体废物综合利用量（万吨） Industrial Waste Residue Used (10000 tons)	工业固体废物贮存量（万吨） Industrial Waste Residue Stored (10000 tons)	工业固体废物处置量（万吨） Industrial Waste Residue Treatment (10000 tons)	工业固体废物排放量（万吨） Industrial Waste Residue Discharged (10000 tons)	历年累计堆存量（万吨） Volume of Waste Residue Accumulated Over the Years (10000 tons)
231342	**2114436**	**2891**	**2231**	**519**	**133**	**18**	**9247**
222691	2091629	2778	2138	501	131	17	9077
409	1296	554	383	133	33	4	5139
377	7926	107	103		2	2	
67	416	51	50		2		
	30	3	2		1	1	
164	3152	23	19		1	4	
	5						
1457		7	7				
2400	24580	431	382	27	17	3	186
31	53	19	18		1		
		39	23	13	2		163
11	84	4	3				
2	6	3	3				
176741	1765842	72	51	7	14		14
134181	1337955	14	14				
29157	235754	358	327	20	10	2	307
256	125	5	5				
513	20069	22	22		1		
2059	4640	59	51		7		1
6327	12439	995	666	300	38		3266
2720	15212	26	23		2		

续表 2

行　业　名　称　Items		三废综合利用产品产值（万元）Output Value of Products Made from Waste Gas Waste Water and Waste Residues (10000 yuan)	三废综合利用产品利润（万元）Profits Obtained From Waste Water, Waste Gas and Waste Residue (10000 yuan)
总　　计	**Total**	**410788**	**37218**
#重点调查企业	Key Sunvey Enterprises	408558	35929
采掘业	Mining and Quarrying	1197	342
食品、烟草加工及食品、饮料制造业	Food, Tobacco and Beverage Processing	13544	3888
纺织业	Textile Industry	720	453
皮革、毛皮、羽绒及其制品业	Leather, Furs, Feather and Related Producets	34	36
造纸及纸制品业	Papermaking and Paper Products	263737	1553
印刷业、记录媒介的复制	Printing and Record Pressing		18
石油加工及炼焦业	Petroleum Processing and Coking	7499	5124
化工原料及化学制品制造业	Raw Chemical Materials and Chemical Products	54717	13186
医药制造业	Medical and Pharmaceutical Products	3586	912
化学纤维制造业	Chemical Fiber	440	47
橡胶制品业	Rubber Products	634	21
塑料制品业	Plastic Products	279	169
非金属矿物制造业	Nonmetal Mineral Industry	16696	2599
水泥制造业	Cement Manufacturing	6616	727
黑色金属冶炼及压延工业	Smelting and Pressing of Ferrous Metals	29843	4647
有色金属冶炼及压延工业	Smelting and Pressing of Nonferrous Metals	333	206
金属制品业	Metal Products	683	112
机械、电气、电子设备制造业	Machine, Electric and Electronic Equipment Manufacturing	9677	1863
电力、煤气及水的生产和供应业	Production and Supply of Power, Coal Gas and Tap Water	4170	378
其它行业	Other Industries	769	375

Continued 2

污染事故赔款总额（万元）Reparations for Pollution Accidents (10000yuan)	工业锅炉 Industrial Boiler		#烟尘排放达标的 Soot Discharge Standards		工业窑炉数（座）Number of Industrial Store (Unit)	#烟尘排放达标的（座）Soot Discharge Standards (Unit)
	（台）(Unit)	（蒸吨）(Steam tons)	（台）(Unit)	（蒸吨）(Steam tons)		
13841	**5392**	**90794**	**4347**	**59442**	**3543**	**2372**
13809	4231	88109	3497	57247	2881	2023
7	219	726	180	606	60	51
7	521	2504	351	1474	13	11
13519	642	24383	557	2458	80	54
	49	125	42	117	2	2
33	100	656	73	523	2	2
	13	23	9	14	3	1
	25	681	25	601	60	57
159	571	7302	472	5971	462	336
	166	745	138	508	6	4
	59	1890	55	1823	9	9
	51	195	40	154	2	2
	78	243	69	209	4	4
44	198	979	162	865	485	281
2	38	65	32	61	154	102
6	118	1221	104	1106	352	247
	26	46	22	33	65	41
	87	261	78	243	137	106
3	758	2887	662	2558	980	712
11	217	42300	173	37222	35	30
18	333	942	285	762	124	73

8—11 企事业污染治理情况
TREATMENT OF WASTE WATER, WASTE GAS AND RESIDUE BY ENTERPRISES AND INSTITUTIONS

指标	Items	1990	1994	1995	1996
汇总单位数 （个）	**Number of Units Converged**	**3796**	**995**	**1117**	**544**
污染治理资金来源合计 （万元）	**Source of Funds for Pollution Treatment (10000 yuan)**	**24784**	**42243**	**54187**	**46915**
基本建设资金 （万元）	Capital Construction (10000 yuan)	5615	10415	2665	855
更新改造资金 （万元）	Technical Updates and Transformation (10000 yuan)	5901	6834	20882	6698
综合利用利润留成资金 （万元）	Retained Profits (10000 yuan)	417	2124	4863	8144
环境保护补助资金 （万元）	Environment Protection Subsidy Funds (10000 yuan)	7003	4443	4935	3526
贷款 （万元）	Loans (10000 yuan)	3859	2466	2694	3225
其它资金 （万元）	Others (10000 yuan)	1989	15961	17578	24467
污染治理资金使用额 （万元）	**Use of Funds (10000 yuan)**	**24781**	**42334**	**54187**	**46915**
治理废水 （万元）	Waste Water (10000 yuan)	14309	16399	33410	28120
治理废气 （万元）	Waste Gas (10000 yuan)	6358	16810	13428	13167
治理固体废物 （万元）	Waste Residue (10000 yuan)	2368	6623	4554	1672
治理噪声 （万元）	Noice Abatement (10000 yuan)	521	1810	1940	621
其它 （万元）	Others (10000 yuan)	1225	692	855	3335
当年安排治理项目 （个）	**Projects Arranged for Treatment in Those Years**	**1382**	**983**	**919**	**481**
治理废水 （个）	Waste Water	567	354	357	195
治理废气 （个）	Waste Gas	597	428	359	193
治理固体废物 （个）	Solid Waste Residue	49	50	38	18
治理噪声 （个）	Noice Abatement	133	132	127	47
其它 （个）	Others	36	19	38	28
当年竣工项目 （个）	**Projects Completed**	**1307**	**970**	**776**	**497**
治理废水 （个）	Waste Water	533	358	278	181
治理废气 （个）	Waste Gas	565	423	310	217
治理固体废物 （个）	Solid Waste Residue	41	48	38	21
治理噪声 （个）	Noice Abatement	130	123	121	53
其它 （个）	Others	38	18	29	25
当年竣工项目设计处理利用“三废”能力	**Capacities of Projects Completed for the Treatment and Utilization of Waste Water, Waste Gas and Residue by Design**				
处理废水量 （万吨/日）	Waste Water (10000 tons/day)	9.77	19.61	22.62	118.06
处理废气量 （万标立米/时）	Waste Gas (10000 standards cu・m/day/hour)	366.99	5865.00	187.00	405.78
处理利用固体废物量 （万吨/年）	Solid Waste Residue (10000 tons/year)	24.00	50.00	44.00	44.10

农　业 9

AGRICULTURE

9 农　　业
AGRICULTURE

1 9 9 6

乡村劳动力	Rural Labor	2758.49	万人	(10000 persons)
年末实有耕地面积	Cultivated Areas (Year-end)	4435.44	万公顷	(10000 ha)
农林牧渔业总产值(现价)	Farming, Forestry, Animal Husbandry	1824.19	亿元	(100000000 yuan)
农作物播种面积	Sown Areas of Farm Crops	791.41	万公顷	(10000 ha)
粮食产量	Grain Output	3476.35	万吨	(10000 tons)
棉花产量	Cotton Output	53.75	万吨	(10000 tons)
油料产量	Oil-bearing Ouptut	147.50	万吨	(10000 tons)
猪牛羊肉产量	Pork, Beef, Mutton Output	227.97	万吨	(10000 tons)
农业机械总动力	Power of Agricultural Machinery	2297.43	万千瓦	(10000 kilowatt)

农、林、牧、渔业总产值
指数和构成(%)

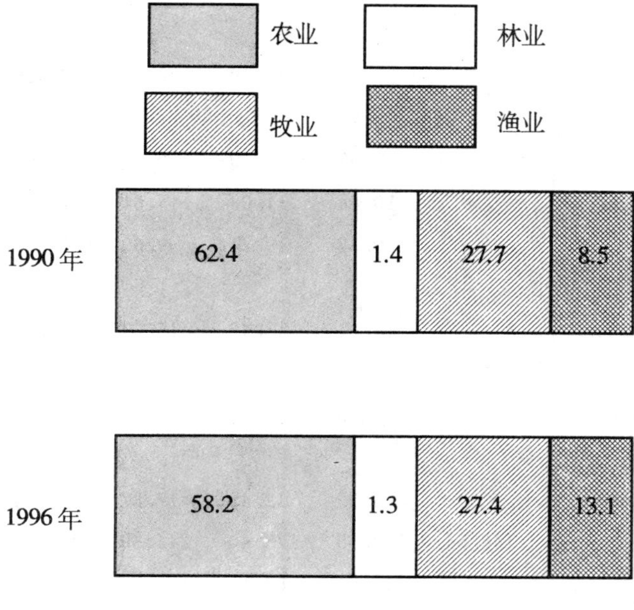

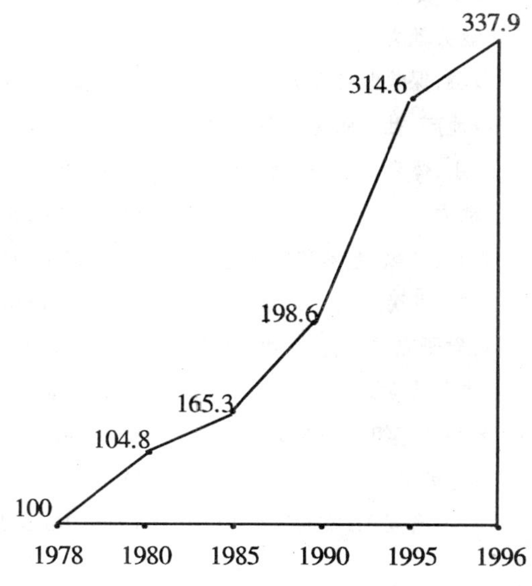

9—1 农村基层组织情况
BASIC RURAL UNITS

单位:万人　　　　(10000 persons)

指　　标	Items	1980	1985	1990	1995	1996
农村组织情况	**Rural Units**					
乡个数	Township	1885	1810	1452	1046	980
镇个数	Town		113	461	799	861
村委会个数	Village Committees	34931	36117	36130	35982	35962
村民小组个数	Villager Group	324969	340075	340198	341984	341870
乡村户数、人口	**Households Rural Population**					
乡村户数　(万户)	Households　(ten thousand)	1251.99	1314.04	1508.15	1516.85	1511.17
乡村人口	Rural Population	5049.30	5150.94	5361.80	5321.01	5305.04
乡村劳动力合计	**Rural Social Labor Force**	**2263.98**	**2598.12**	**2786.86**	**2773.04**	**2758.49**
按性别分	Grouped by Sex					
男劳动力	Male	1115.86	1281.06	1440.65	1424.43	1417.20
女劳动力	Female	1148.12	1317.06	1346.21	1348.61	1341.29
按行业分	Grouped by Sector					
农林牧渔业劳动力	Farming, Forestry, Animal Husbandary, Fishery	1810.00	1703.20	1714.49	1541.33	1530.20
#农业劳动力	Farming		1522.09	1536.12	1326.54	1316.47
工业劳动力	Industry	307.44	481.09	520.73	531.78	515.57
#乡办工业劳动力	Rural Industry	165.29	257.13	276.94	271.05	256.85
建筑业劳动力	Construction		150.18	196.25	227.39	233.61
交通运输、仓储业和邮电通讯业劳动力	Transportation, Storage, Post and Telecommunication		48.08	70.90	92.33	92.34
批发、零售贸易业、餐饮业劳动力	Wholesale, Retail Sales, Food Service		33.64	50.49	73.04	79.96
金融、保险业劳动力	Bank and Insurance		0.97	1.69	2.11	2.04
房地产、社会服务业劳动力	Real Estate, Social Services		10.84	11.08	15.61	14.65
卫生、体育、社会福利业劳动力	Health Care, Sporting, Social Welfare		10.32	10.21	9.69	10.00
教育、文化、艺术和广播电视事业劳动力	Education, Culture, Arts and Radio, Film, Television		19.51	18.40	15.50	14.90
科学研究和综合技术服务事业劳动力	Scientific Research and Ploy-technical Services		1.25	1.73	2.00	2.06
乡经济组织管理劳动力	Rural Economic Management		6.89	12.49	17.37	17.94
其他劳动力	Others	146.54	132.15	178.40	244.89	245.22
#外出合同工、临时工	Labor Force Leaving		47.61	82.11	125.50	122.55

9—2 历年耕地面积
AREAS UNDER CULTIVATION

单位：千公顷 (1000 ha)

年份 Year	年末实有耕地面积 Cultivated Areas	水田 Paddy Fields	旱地 Dry Fields	年内减少 Decrease in Cultivated Area and Cause	#国家基建占地 Capital Construction	人均占有耕地(平方米) Per Cultivated(sq·m) 按乡村人口计算 By Rural Persons	按农林牧渔业劳动力计算 By Farming, Forestry, Animal Husbandry, Fishery Labors
1949	5523.40	2199.60	3323.80			1846.68	
1950	5600.40	2233.40	3367.00			1833.34	
1951	5715.40	2257.73	3457.67			1833.34	
1952	5808.47	2273.47	3535.00			1820.00	3580.12
1953	5888.73	2200.40	3688.33			1806.68	3553.35
1954	5934.27	2266.53	3667.74			1780.01	3506.68
1955	5934.73	2332.00	3602.73			1733.34	3513.35
1956	5884.53	2438.07	3446.46			1673.34	3466.68
1957	5825.20	2545.13	3280.07			1633.34	3960.02
1958	5222.40	2514.13	2708.27			1466.67	4006.69
1959	5086.93	2472.60	2614.33			1440.01	4480.02
1960	5014.00	2341.67	2672.33			1440.01	4040.02
1961	4997.80	2263.73	2734.07			1406.67	3673.35
1962	5016.20	2161.33	2854.87			1360.01	3473.35
1963	5008.40	2161.60	2846.80			1320.01	3300.02
1964	4985.00	2189.80	2795.20			1286.67	3146.68
1965	4947.47	2225.93	2721.54			1246.67	3073.35
1966	4934.40	2289.45	2644.95			1206.67	2906.68
1967	4908.70	2277.65	2631.05			1166.67	2766.68
1968	4870.90	2272.85	2598.05			1126.67	2613.35
1969	4850.36	2334.31	2516.05			1080.01	2466.28
1970	4820.63	2509.13	2311.50			1033.34	2480.01
1971	4784.55	2831.75	1952.80			1006.67	1700.01
1972	4761.97	2865.59	1896.38	26.91	17.23	993.34	2333.35
1973	4737.99	2797.07	1940.92	33.87	16.88	986.67	2300.01
1974	4720.91	2790.15	1930.76	23.13	16.04	966.61	2326.78
1975	4705.53	2484.83	2220.70	23.00	13.39	946.67	2340.01
1976	4689.37	2831.34	1858.03	24.53	17.53	933.34	2293.34
1977	4672.79	2797.36	1875.43	21.81	15.05	920.00	2313.34
1978	4660.79	2743.14	1917.65	20.20	14.60	913.34	2293.34
1979	4650.40	2781.79	1868.61	18.67	13.20	920.00	2360.01
1980	4641.38	2788.62	1852.76	15.27	10.73	913.34	2380.01
1981	4637.01	2775.35	1861.66	11.67	5.67	900.00	2340.01
1982	4631.21	2755.59	1875.62	14.12	4.80	893.34	2326.68
1983	4630.05	2769.02	1861.03	7.67	5.24	893.34	2306.68
1984	4621.09	2837.99	1783.10	15.80	7.13	886.67	2353.35
1985	4604.03	2804.58	1799.45	21.40	5.87	886.67	2700.01
1986	4590.79	2780.11	1810.68	18.59	7.31	893.34	2793.35
1987	4579.81	2770.17	1809.64	18.19	6.21	886.67	2826.68
1988	4568.84	2767.73	1801.11	12.73	5.91	886.67	2820.01
1989	4562.32	2775.97	1786.35	10.43	4.64	886.67	2713.35
1990	4557.86	2804.13	1753.73	8.78	4.63	853.34	2660.01
1991	4549.97	2840.85	1709.12	11.15	4.80	846.67	2613.35
1992	4521.77	2836.81	1684.96	30.96	13.02	840.00	2673.35
1993	4495.66	2711.40	1784.26	28.83	8.71	840.00	2766.68
1994	4464.00	2658.08	1805.92	33.02	11.98	833.34	2806.68
1995	4448.31	2669.68	1778.63	23.69	11.74	833.34	2886.68
1996	4435.44	2692.51	1742.93	16.21	10.58	836.08	2898.62

注：农林牧渔业劳动力中，1984年前包括村及村以下劳动力。
* Before 1984, farming, forestry, animal husbandry and fishery labors included township and village industry labors.

9—3 农村社会总产值
GROSS OUTPUT VALUE OF RURAL

单位:亿元 (100 000 000 yuan)

年份 Year	农村社会总产值 Gross Output of Rural	农林牧渔业总产值 Farming, Forestry, Animal Husbandry, Firshery	农村工业总产值 Rural Industry	农村建筑业总产值 Rural Construction	农村运输业总产值 Rural Transportation	农村批发、零售贸易业、餐饮业总产值 Rural Wholesale, Retail Sale and Food Service
1978	183.97	105.87	62.43	5.81	2.56	7.30
1980	274.13	138.45	109.33	14.55	3.09	8.71
1985	775.71	288.55	385.54	60.75	19.45	21.42
1986	959.73	332.66	497.28	76.96	25.45	27.38
1987	1245.20	380.25	697.41	99.35	33.06	35.13
1988	1703.28	497.95	980.79	132.06	43.58	48.90
1989	1872.41	522.25	1113.84	136.05	46.82	53.45
1990	2072.69	580.53	1251.95	133.99	48.27	57.95
1991	2312.06	580.93	1467.37	149.99	50.45	63.32
1992	3516.37	673.82	2463.26	203.63	69.42	106.24
1993	5650.77	875.37	4192.94	300.79	103.49	178.18
1994	8277.73	1335.23	6099.06	382.14	160.28	301.02
1995	10567.60	1686.78	7703.25	498.77	229.84	448.96
1996	10413.89	1824.19	7182.91	554.88	280.74	571.17

注:由于1996年农村工业总产值口径调整,故总数小于上年,如按同口径相比则增长23.5%。

Due to the change of gross output value of rural industry in 1996, rural total value is smaller than that of last year, comparable increase rate 23.5 percent.

9—4 农村社会总产值指数
INDICES OF GROSS OUTPUT VALUE OF RURAL

(以1978年为100) (1978=100)

年份 Year	农村社会总产值 Gross Output of Rural	农林牧渔业总产值 Farming, Forestry, Animal Husbandry, Firshery	农村工业总产值 Rural Industry	农村建筑业总产值 Rural Construction	农村运输业总产值 Rural Transportation	农村批发、零售贸易业、餐饮业总产值 Rural Wholesale, Retail Sale and Food Service
1978	100.0	100.0	100.0	100.0	100.0	100.0
1980	127.8	104.8	174.0	214.8	103.5	102.4
1985	317.6	165.3	604.8	787.7	571.7	221.0
1986	385.2	175.6	783.1	978.2	733.4	277.0
1987	471.7	181.1	1035.7	1191.9	899.0	335.3
1988	607.5	193.1	1428.8	1491.6	1115.8	439.5
1989	626.6	193.7	1498.1	1441.8	1124.8	450.8
1990	682.4	198.6	1683.9	1397.4	1141.2	480.9
1991	780.9	196.4	2011.0	1578.4	1205.3	531.0
1992	1212.8	221.9	3476.9	2191.4	1693.6	909.8
1993	1837.3	247.0	5650.0	3051.4	2380.2	1438.4
1994	2537.5	276.8	8065.8	3655.5	3475.8	2291.5
1995	3081.3	314.6	9774.8	4538.2	4740.9	3250.8
1996	3663.7	337.9	11868.0	4884.2	5602.1	4000.9

9—5 历年农林牧渔业总产值(当年价格)
GROSS OUTPUT VALUE OF AGRICULTURE (CURRENT PRICE)

单位:亿元 (100 000 000 yuan)

年份 Year	农林牧渔业总产值 Gross Outprt Value of Agriculture	农业 Planting	林业 Foresty	牧业 Animal Husbandry	渔业 Fishery
1949	22.59	19.41	…	3.02	0.16
1952	31.87	26.14	0.03	5.00	0.70
1953	32.31	27.79	0.03	3.65	0.84
1954	32.45	27.10	0.03	4.25	1.07
1955	36.22	32.25	0.04	2.81	1.12
1956	33.60	28.13	0.07	4.26	1.14
1957	36.81	30.10	0.22	5.25	1.24
1958	38.74	33.33	0.35	3.24	1.82
1959	37.35	30.45	0.52	4.06	2.32
1960	36.76	31.96	0.51	2.12	2.17
1961	35.73	31.17	0.39	2.88	1.29
1962	40.15	34.19	0.32	4.48	1.16
1963	46.77	39.88	0.37	5.16	1.36
1964	56.62	48.43	0.40	6.21	1.58
1965	57.27	47.02	0.63	8.25	1.37
1966	66.08	53.53	0.66	10.50	1.39
1967	61.19	51.83	0.61	7.34	1.41
1968	65.38	55.45	0.65	8.04	1.24
1969	65.60	54.65	0.65	9.05	1.25
1970	71.33	57.08	0.85	11.76	1.64
1971	79.90	64.78	0.94	12.34	1.84
1972	83.24	65.95	1.25	14.46	1.58
1973	89.71	73.77	1.08	13.07	1.79
1974	89.88	73.64	1.08	13.27	1.89
1975	91.66	72.17	1.47	15.55	2.47
1976	100.71	82.53	1.31	14.86	2.01
1977	89.16	73.05	1.25	12.90	1.96
1978	105.87	85.17	1.48	16.78	2.44
1979	145.25	114.26	2.03	25.77	3.19
1980	138.45	105.98	1.94	26.65	3.88
1981	153.62	119.90	2.00	27.11	4.61
1982	188.11	145.69	1.96	35.80	4.66
1983	206.86	160.38	3.30	36.66	6.52
1984	253.82	193.28	4.33	47.17	9.04
1985	288.55	201.85	4.63	66.54	15.53
1986	332.66	235.07	5.15	69.83	22.61
1987	380.25	257.90	6.02	87.95	28.38
1988	497.95	310.20	7.29	140.49	39.97
1989	522.25	325.02	7.02	148.13	42.08
1990	580.53	362.46	7.94	160.78	49.35
1991	580.93	354.42	7.55	168.30	50.66
1992	673.82	411.33	9.93	188.64	63.92
1993	875.37	518.55	14.61	236.81	105.40
1994	1335.23	777.94	18.38	390.70	148.21
1995	1686.78	986.15	21.42	475.67	203.54
1996	1824.19	1062.39	23.48	498.97	239.35

9—6 历年农林牧渔业总产值指数
INDICES OF GROSS OUTPUT VALUE OF AGRICULTURE

(以 1949 年为 100)　　　　(1949=100)

年份 Year	农林牧渔业总产值 Gross Output Value of Agriculturd	农业 Planting	林业 Foresty	牧业 Animal Husbandry	渔业 Fishery
1949	100.0	100.0		100.0	100.0
1950	109.1	110.3		104.8	78.9
1951	122.8	123.4		117.3	200.0
1952	144.2	135.7	100.0	166.5	612.2
1953	145.5	149.3	62.5	105.0	387.8
1954	146.3	146.1	62.5	122.7	487.8
1955	163.0	174.3	87.5	80.5	522.0
1956	152.2	152.6	162.5	123.8	526.8
1957	157.4	151.4	900.0	159.0	563.4
1958	160.0	163.5	1487.5	105.2	551.2
1959	149.3	147.4	2137.5	108.9	629.3
1960	137.5	140.7	1925.0	68.7	641.5
1961	133.2	137.5	1412.5	79.0	429.3
1962	134.7	134.1	1387.5	106.8	407.3
1963	160.8	159.6	1150.0	134.3	490.2
1964	190.6	189.8	1287.5	158.5	558.5
1965	201.4	190.7	2162.5	224.6	534.1
1966	234.3	220.2	2187.5	282.8	519.5
1967	218.0	215.8	2187.5	199.1	541.5
1968	225.0	222.8	2212.5	211.9	458.5
1969	223.6	217.1	2212.5	233.0	463.4
1970	239.7	232.5	1487.5	255.0	575.6
1971	266.0	255.2	2387.5	290.2	624.4
1972	273.2	253.5	3062.5	332.9	646.3
1973	291.5	283.4	2625.0	297.3	746.3
1974	292.0	282.9	2537.5	300.9	787.8
1975	294.7	281.6	2487.5	322.3	819.5
1976	306.2	296.1	3012.5	301.1	773.2
1977	275.4	264.9	2987.0	280.1	787.8
1978	334.6	326.8	2525.0	323.9	778.0
1979	371.1	354.7	2650.0	426.8	858.5
1980	350.7	326.0	2637.5	435.8	1014.6
1981	378.4	357.7	2512.5	432.6	1170.7
1982	434.8	404.2	2662.5	535.6	1231.7
1983	460.6	433.3	2950.0	525.9	1226.8
1984	536.3	460.6	3475.0	621.5	1522.0
1985	553.1	456.1	3750.0	727.9	1922.0
1986	587.7	486.4	3650.0	732.5	2592.7
1987	605.9	502.4	3825.0	741.1	2802.4
1988	646.1	526.3	3587.5	847.5	3051.2
1989	648.3	529.4	3387.5	843.1	3102.4
1990	664.6	535.2	3300.5	899.3	3346.3
1991	657.1	513.3	2971.7	946.3	3385.3
1992	742.5	583.6	3538.2	1045.7	3913.7
1993	826.4	619.6	4391.5	1191.6	5275.3
1994	926.3	668.9	4936.8	1400.2	6278.5
1995	1052.7	755.4	5774.3	1551.0	7785.4
1996	1130.6	821.0	6204.0	1599.2	8707.8

注:由于 1952 年以前林业产值很少,故以 1952 年的林业产值为 100。

* Forestry: 1952=100.

9—7 农林牧渔业分项产值
GROSS OUTPOUT VALUE OF FARMING, FORESTRY, ANIMAL HUSBANDRY AND FISHERY BY BRANCH

单位:亿元 (100 000 000 yuan)

指标	Items	总产值(当年价) Gross Output Value (current price)		总产值(1990年不变价) Gross Output Value (1990 fixed price)	
		1995	1996	1995	1996
农林牧渔业总产值	**Tatal**	**1686.78**	**1824.19**	**929.84**	**998.67**
农业产值	Farming	986.15	1062.39	514.64	559.33
种植业产值	Planting	854.10	897.41	382.99	395.15
主产品产值	Main Product	821.97	864.44	360.75	371.56
#粮食	Grain Grops	506.77	533.62	196.72	207.55
棉花	Cotton Grops	89.20	85.76	40.06	38.34
油料	Oil-Bearing Grops	42.48	39.56	22.71	21.00
糖料	Sugar Crops	1.49	0.25	0.34	0.33
蔬菜、瓜类	Vegetables, Melons, Grops	118.75	137.77	55.51	58.29
茶、桑、水果	Tea, Mulberry, Fruit	28.75	27.89	20.55	19.81
副产品产值	Sideline Product	32.13	32.97	22.24	23.59
#粮食作物	Grain Grops	27.90	29.08	19.31	20.80
其他农业产值	Other Grops	132.05	164.98	131.65	164.18
野生植物采集	Wild Plant Gathering	2.03	2.01	1.73	1.87
农民家庭兼营商品性工业	Household Handicraft lnductry	130.02	162.97	129.92	162.31
林业产值	Forestry	21.42	23.48	13.87	14.90
营林	Afforestation	4.51	5.16	2.76	2.79
林产品	Forest Products	3.66	4.43	1.50	1.99
村及村以下竹木采伐	Lumbering in Village below	13.25	13.89	9.61	10.12
牧业产值	Animal Husbandry	475.67	498.97	279.49	288.17
牲畜	Animal	232.99	243.51	113.21	114.16
大牲畜繁殖、增长、增重	Large Domestic Animals, Livestock Breeding	4.22	4.63	2.20	2.33
猪	Hogs	204.11	212.47	101.69	102.05
羊	Sheep and Goats	24.66	26.41	9.32	9.78
家禽的饲养	Poultry Raising	93.58	94.18	56.24	58.88
活的畜禽产品	Live Animal and Poultry Products	114.19	134.75	79.97	92.99
其他动物饲养	Others	33.78	25.16	29.21	21.08
捕猎	Hunting	1.13	1.37	0.86	1.06
渔业产值	Fishery	203.54	239.35	121.84	136.27
海水产品	Seawater Aquatic Products	57.32	70.70	35.67	44.59
淡水产品	Freshwater Aquatic Products	146.22	168.65	86.17	91.68

9—8 农林牧渔业总产值、商品产值及增加值构成
GROSS OUTPUT VALUE, COMMERCIAL VALUE, ADDED-VALUE AND COMPOSITION OF FARMING, FORESTRY, ANIMAL HUSBANDRY AND FISHERY

单位:亿元 (100 000 000 yuan)

指标	Items	1993	1994	1995	1996
农业牧渔业总产值	**Gross Output Value**	**875.37**	**1335.23**	**1686.78**	**1824.19**
农业产值	Farming	518.55	777.94	986.15	1062.39
林业产值	Forestry	14.61	18.38	21.42	23.48
牧业产值	Animal Husbandry	236.81	390.70	475.67	498.97
渔业产值	Fishery	105.40	148.21	203.54	239.35
农林牧渔业商品产值	**Commercial Value**	**545.99**	**852.77**	**1080.78**	**1247.43**
农业商品产值	Farming	260.05	398.09	520.50	596.76
林业商品产值	Forestry	7.64	11.55	13.70	14.57
牧业商品产值	Animal Husbandry	188.24	316.57	373.82	422.37
渔业商品产值	Firshery	90.06	126.56	172.76	213.73
农林牧渔业中间消耗	**Intermediate Use**	**384.79**	**663.30**	**838.43**	**901.08**
农业中间消耗	Farming	187.57	307.69	389.14	434.77
林业中间消耗	Forestry	4.16	7.01	8.01	8.35
牧业中间消耗	Animal Husbandry	151.24	269.35	331.16	335.79
渔业中间消耗	Firshery	41.82	79.25	110.12	122.17
农林牧渔业增加值	**Added-Value**	**490.58**	**671.93**	**848.35**	**923.11**
农业增加值	Farming	330.98	470.25	597.01	627.62
林业增加值	Forestry	10.45	11.37	13.41	15.13
牧业增加值	Animal Husbandry	85.57	121.35	144.51	163.18
渔业增加值	Fishery	63.58	68.96	93.42	117.18

9—9 农作物播种面积
TOTAL SOWN AREAS OF FARM CROPS

单位:千公顷 (1000 ha)

年份 Year	总播种面积 Total Sown Areas	粮食作物 Grain Grops	#小麦 Wheat	#稻谷 Rice	#薯类 Tubers	#玉米 Corn	#大豆 Soybeans
1952	9413. 60	8223. 93	2003. 20	1970. 27	383. 87	604. 87	908. 87
1957	9440. 87	7982. 27	1957. 33	2177. 27	370. 07	589. 20	789. 60
1962	8589. 47	7172. 07	1384. 00	1795. 47	402. 13	493. 73	665. 87
1965	7831. 45	6211. 31	1531. 96	1902. 15	481. 06	449. 41	523. 96
1970	8102. 59	6244. 56	1513. 54	2372. 12	404. 35	464. 92	428. 89
1975	8758. 89	6377. 93	1325. 27	2971. 09	365. 05	379. 02	281. 58
1978	8582. 74	6310. 93	1412. 82	2661. 18	478. 29	445. 01	345. 36
1980	8248. 93	6090. 25	1519. 47	2676. 15	332. 02	386. 21	236. 47
1985	8557. 84	6432. 44	2170. 39	2431. 11	282. 45	659. 62	317. 93
1990	8259. 18	6363. 02	2399. 19	2454. 44	221. 65	461. 01	244. 67
1991	8091. 70	6202. 77	2364. 93	2351. 40	214. 51	426. 44	177. 81
1992	8234. 63	6180. 77	2366. 23	2447. 27	192. 59	421. 14	192. 28
1993	8032. 29	6029. 66	2281. 66	2278. 44	201. 00	472. 37	270. 67
1994	7861. 76	5748. 78	2114. 26	2168. 36	179. 46	458. 95	255. 41
1995	7909. 01	5755. 15	2150. 35	2250. 31	166. 71	461. 98	201. 32
1996	7914. 10	5877. 42	2216. 26	2335. 91	180. 59	467. 83	179. 49

续表 Continued

单位:千公顷 (1000 ha)

年份 Year	经济作物 Economic Crops	#棉花 Cotton Crops	#油菜籽 Rape-seed	#花生 Peanuts	#芝麻 Sesame	#黄红麻 Hemp Crops	#甘蔗 Sugar-cane	#甜菜 Beet-roots	#烤烟 Flue-Cured Tobacco	其他 Others
1952	751. 66	454. 47	109. 37	119. 10	29. 80	11. 51			0. 10	438. 01
1957	871. 73	564. 23	93. 63	160. 26	10. 00	14. 13				586. 87
1962	618. 07	416. 54	71. 79	84. 21	13. 43	6. 21			2. 04	799. 33
1965	807. 39	563. 81	72. 02	116. 47	9. 26	11. 07	0. 14		6. 41	812. 75
1970	797. 58	585. 10	83. 73	71. 50	8. 80	11. 72	0. 08	4. 12	5. 83	1060. 45
1975	869. 05	586. 97	147. 92	72. 27	5. 03	16. 50	0. 74	5. 69	5. 47	1511. 91
1978	905. 84	589. 99	156. 46	65. 49	10. 60	20. 71	0. 75	6. 91	7. 05	1365. 97
1980	957. 04	631. 00	169. 58	83. 79	4. 61	11. 51	0. 35	5. 78	2. 17	1201. 64
1985	1302. 77	592. 24	442. 64	134. 11	12. 85	24. 78	4. 11	4. 39	3. 47	822. 63
1990	1188. 41	572. 13	440. 81	108. 71	5. 85	5. 16	3. 35	2. 23	5. 63	707. 75
1991	1202. 48	550. 61	482. 80	102. 95	4. 79	4. 57	3. 18	0. 73	5. 16	686. 45
1992	1350. 29	673. 43	483. 78	107. 36	7. 14	3. 99	3. 83	0. 70	7. 39	703. 57
1993	1143. 39	517. 65	458. 30	125. 42	8. 65	5. 20	5. 50	1. 31	2. 02	859. 24
1994	1225. 86	534. 57	516. 59	146. 52	6. 65	2. 15	4. 57	0. 70	0. 87	887. 12
1995	1268. 75	564. 90	530. 66	148. 66	7. 54	1. 31	3. 95	0. 17	1. 17	885. 11
1996	1132. 24	485. 91	498. 00	123. 55	9. 19	0. 89	3. 66	0. 87	1. 44	904. 44

9—10 主要农作物播种面积和产量(1996)
TOTAL SOWN AREAS OF FARM CROPS AND OUTUT

指标	Items	播种面积(千公顷) Sown Areas (1000 ha)	亩产(千克) Per mu Output (kg)	总产量(吨) Total Output (tons)
农作物总播种面积	**TOTAL SOWN AREAS OF FARM CROPS**	**7914.10**		
粮食、大豆总计	**Total Grain Soybeans**	**5877.42**	**5915**	**34763512**
夏粮	Summer Grain	2686.65	4470	12009512
小麦	Wheat	2216.26	4576	10142531
元麦	Hull-less Barley	38.87	3415	132740
大麦	Barley	313.70	4510	1414686
蚕豌豆	Broad and Dea Bean	117.82	2712	319555
秋粮	Autumn Grain	3190.77	7131	22754000
稻谷	Rice	2335.91	8006	18701486
早稻	Early Rice	0.35	5303	1856
中稻	Semilate Rice	1519.42	7830	11896722
单季晚稻	Single late Rice	795.64	8375	6663111
双季后作稻	Late Double-crop Rice	20.50	6819	139797
在稻谷中:杂优稻	Among Rice:Hybrid Fine Rice	829.79	7732	6415982
薯类	Tubers	180.59	5309	958777
玉米	Corn	467.83	5556	2599039
高粱	Sorghum	0.53	3028	1605
谷子	Millet	0.12	3350	402
其他秋粮	Others	26.30	2456	64591
大豆	Soybeans	179.49	2385	428100
经济作物	**Economic Crops**	**1132.24**		
棉花	Cotton	485.91	1106	537478
油料	Oil-Bearing Crops	631.14	2337	1475040
#花生	Peanuts	123.55	3209	396463
油菜籽	Repeseed	498.00	2135	1063396
芝麻	Sesame	9.19	1554	14277
麻类	Hemp Grops	1.48	3318	4911
#黄麻	Jute	0.41	3261	1337
红麻	Ambary	0.48	3071	1474
苎麻	Ramie	0.55	3280	1804
糖类	Sugar Crops	4.53	50650	229443
#甘蔗	Sugarcane	3.66	56340	206206
甜菜	Beetroots	0.87	26709	23237
烟叶	Tobacco Crops	1.59	1843	2931
#烤烟	Flue-Cured Tobacco	1.44	1787	2573
药材	Crude drugs	4.37		
其他经济作物	Others	3.22		
#薄荷	Mint	3.21	202	649
留兰香	Spearmint	0.01	100	1
其他农作物	**Others**	**904.44**		
#蔬菜	Vegetable	612.42		
瓜类	Melon Crops	71.73		
绿肥	Organic Fertilizer	110.22		

9—11 主要农产品产量
OUTPUT OF MAJOR FARM CROPS

单位:万吨 (10000 tons)

年份 Year	粮食 Grain	夏粮 Summer Grain	秋粮 Autumn Grain	棉花 Cotton	油料 Oil-Bearing Grops	#花生 Peanuts	#油菜籽 Rapeseed
1949	748.50	217.00	531.50	2.81	15.94	11.82	3.60
1952	997.55	277.85	719.70	9.28	21.68	14.38	6.00
1957	1063.60	274.85	788.75	15.01	25.07	19.81	4.93
1962	965.35	280.65	684.70	8.21	10.27	6.38	3.52
1965	1442.75	379.85	1062.90	26.44	21.68	13.87	7.41
1970	1705.15	415.50	1289.65	32.82	21.67	10.31	10.87
1975	2056.85	524.40	1532.45	45.48	29.64	11.73	17.63
1978	2400.65	677.30	1723.35	47.54	37.44	13.60	23.06
1980	2417.95	873.60	1544.35	41.81	38.64	14.50	23.93
1985	3126.52	1064.46	2062.06	47.91	108.78	34.13	73.11
1986	3339.56	1176.68	2162.88	40.11	116.77	36.49	78.91
1987	3257.70	1154.22	2103.48	44.38	121.10	33.75	86.28
1988	3243.36	1143.90	2099.46	56.22	98.67	35.26	62.40
1989	3282.80	1033.00	2249.80	48.47	99.91	31.25	67.72
1990	3264.15	1143.46	2120.69	46.42	112.39	30.12	81.41
1991	3035.51	1032.43	2003.08	55.71	114.06	28.12	85.32
1992	3320.55	1251.19	2069.36	52.74	127.33	30.51	95.88
1993	3279.70	1152.60	2127.10	42.90	125.71	37.66	87.04
1994	3124.05	1105.29	2018.76	45.71	133.59	44.80	87.77
1995	3286.30	1073.46	2212.84	56.16	159.46	48.43	109.54
1996	3476.35	1200.95	2275.40	53.75	147.50	39.65	106.34

9—12 人均占有主要农产品产量
OUTPUT OF PER PERSON FARM CROPS

单位:千克/人 (kg/person)

年份 Year	粮食产量 Grain	棉花产量 Cotton	油料产量 Oil-Bearing Grops	生猪饲养量（头/人） Output of Raising Pigs	猪、牛、羊肉产量 Output of Pork, Beef and Mutton	水产品产量 Output of Aquatic Products
1952	270.0	2.5	5.9	0.24		4.6
1957	257.0	3.7	6.1	0.34		6.9
1962	225.0	1.9	2.4	0.22		4.5
1965	316.0	5.8	4.8	0.46		5.5
1970	329.0	6.4	4.2	0.50		5.2
1975	367.0	8.1	5.3	0.60		6.5
1978	414.0	8.2	6.5	0.60		6.9
1980	408.5	7.1	6.6	0.70	18.1	7.2
1985	505.0	7.8	17.6	0.64	22.4	10.9
1986	535.0	6.4	18.7	0.65	22.4	12.9
1987	516.4	7.0	19.2	0.60	21.4	14.6
1988	507.3	8.8	15.4	0.59	23.3	16.1
1989	506.1	7.5	15.4	0.60	23.3	17.0
1990	486.0	6.9	16.7	0.59	23.6	17.6
1991	446.1	8.2	16.8	0.59	24.0	17.3
1992	482.8	7.7	18.5	0.61	25.1	19.6
1993	472.6	6.2	18.1	0.62	25.8	22.7
1994	446.7	6.5	19.1	0.65	28.5	25.8
1995	466.6	8.0	22.6	0.69	30.9	31.2
1996	490.4	7.6	20.8	0.69	32.2	34.7

9—13 蚕、茶、果生产情况
STATISTICS ON SILKWORM COCOONS, TEA, FRUIT

单位:万吨、千公顷 (10000 tons、1000 ha)

指标	Items	1980	1985	1990	1995	1996
蚕茧产量	Silkworm Cocoons	3.82	7.31	12.00	18.62	9.22
茶叶产量	Tea	0.53	0.92	1.41	1.06	1.10
红毛茶	Red Tea	0.29	0.46	0.43	0.13	0.11
绿毛茶	Green Tea	0.23	0.45	0.94	0.91	0.94
其他茶	Others	0.01	0.01	0.04	0.02	0.05
水果产量	Fruits	20.63	34.10	49.33	101.35	123.29
#苹果	Apple	4.84	6.56	10.63	32.16	44.07
柑桔	Citrus Fruit	0.56	2.40	3.13	4.57	4.29
梨	Bear	11.19	14.62	15.01	24.30	28.25
葡萄	Grapes	0.28	0.86	2.42	5.79	6.27
桃子	Peach	2.67	3.69	11.27	17.74	18.21
枇杷	Loquat	0.05	0.11	0.20	0.74	0.68
红枣	Date	0.23	0.23	0.19	0.18	0.13
柿子	Persimmon	0.31	0.96	2.96	0.11	0.67
桑园面积	Mulberry Field Area	50.79	110.01	116.33	228.49	119.01
茶园面积	Tea Field Area	11.91	14.31	13.17	19.29	18.14
#当年采摘面积	Pick Area	6.81	9.66	11.04	10.37	13.21
果园	Orchards Field	32.55	46.73	104.86	157.75	149.21
#苹果园	Apple	12.74	14.19	46.30	84.46	78.85
柑桔园	Citrus	1.39	3.53	3.50	2.01	4.02
梨园	Pear	12.22	12.83	14.98	22.89	19.26
葡萄园	Grapes	0.85	2.31	2.59	3.93	3.89

9—14 林 业 生 产 情 况
STATISTICS ON FORESTRY

单位:千公顷 (1000 ha)

指 标	Items	1980	1985	1990	1995	1996
造林面积	Build Forestry Areas	28.47	28.25	19.63	27.20	21.64
用材林	Material Forest	17.43	19.67	11.42	12.44	10.09
经济林	Economic Forest	2.83	3.85	2.10	11.30	7.98
防护林	Windbreak Forest	6.33	4.01	5.80	3.36	3.36
其他林	Others	1.88	0.72	0.31	0.10	0.21
林产品产量	Output of Forestery Products					
油桐籽	Tung-Oil Seed	115	192	41	12	13
油茶籽	Tea-Oil Seed	99	81	27	18	25
乌桕籽	Oriental Arborviate		4	…	1	
竹笋干	Bamboo Shoots	587	603	856	1254	1040
核桃	Walnuts	219	8	4	1	1
板栗	Chestnut	1594	1939	2733	7156	15535
白果	Ginkgo	1996	2525	4037	5303	6094
迹地更新面积	Slash Updateing Areas	0.24	0.95	0.68	1.13	1.67
当年育苗面积	Raise Seedlings Areas	9.55	11.94	7.31	8.89	8.95
幼林抚育作业面积（千公顷次）	Young Growth Works Areas (1000 ha-T)	72.09	94.74	95.03	125.36	116.99
幼林抚育实际面积	Young Growth Actual Areas	46.77	58.29	51.56	61.92	65.75
成林抚育实际面积	Adult Growth Actual Areas	29.26	45.45	58.44	89.87	82.77
林木种子采集量（吨）	Output of Forestry Seeds Pick (Ton)	649	426	90	203	3973
木材采伐量（万立方米）	Output of Timber cut (10000)	27.33	47.25	85.68	153.02	163.84
竹材采伐量 （万根）	Bamboo Cut (10000)	172.98	257.77	403.07	732.38	782.05
年末实有林地面积	Actual Forestry Areas (Year-end)	408.70	438.15	445.82	518.71	543.85
四旁植树 （万株）	Planting (10000)	28751	17640	14901	14633	13953
林木种子园个数（个）	Forest Seeds Fields	20	16	11	16	16
林木种子园面积（公顷）	Forest Seeds Field Areas (ha)	105	48	101	108	94

9—15 畜牧业生产情况
STATISTICS ON LIVESTOCK

指标	Items	1980	1985	1990	1995	1996
牲畜年末头数 （万头）	**Livestock（Year-end） （10000）**					
大牧畜	Large Animals	112.24	85.34	92.50	123.27	137.30
#役畜	Draught Animals	87.40	67.72	66.01	72.26	71.64
牛	Cattle and Buffalo	98.52	68.06	71.48	99.06	116.45
#良种及改良种乳牛	Fine improved Variety Cows	1.36	3.15	3.49	2.93	3.43
马	Horses	4.79	3.34	2.11	2.48	2.36
驴	Donkeys	7.74	11.88	16.55	18.79	15.70
骡	Mules	1.19	2.06	2.36	2.94	2.79
猪	Hogs	2088.75	1950.96	1851.10	2118.97	2063.88
羊 （万只）	Sheep and Goats （10000）	545.73	400.56	850.80	1273.89	1370.28
山羊	Goats	436.53	351.81	797.45	1211.16	1311.73
绵羊	Sheep	109.20	48.75	53.35	62.73	58.55
畜产品产量	**Livestock Products**					
猪牛羊出栏头数 （万头）	Hogs，Sheep and Goats （10000）					
当年肉猪出栏头数	Hogs	2071.12	2012.55	2116.62	2754.90	2832.63
当年出售和自宰的肉用牛	Ox by Selled and Killed	4.49	5.45	12.85	35.62	48.07
当年出售和自宰的肉用羊 （万只）	Sheep and Goats by Selled and Killed （10000）	351.97	326.13	831.81	1724.38	1936.31
肉类产量 （万吨）	Output of Meat （10000 tons）					
猪肉	Pork	104.04	135.61	149.24	195.82	201.38
牛肉	Beef	0.42	0.65	1.86	5.43	7.49
羊肉	Mutton	2.78	2.64	7.28	16.54	19.10
禽肉	Poulty		20.45	34.90	84.33	88.07
其他畜产品产量 （吨）	Others （tons）					
牛奶产量	Cow Milk	26266	74997	86860	99948	104694
羊奶产量	Sheep and Goats Milk	224	461	2152	4378	4306
绵羊毛产量	Sheep Milk	2536	1179	1853	2305	2354
山羊毛产量	Goats Mik	179	132	74	71	128
羊绒	Cashmere		…	1	2	2
蜂蜜	Honey	3325	7632	12186	7275	7020
禽蛋 （万吨）	Poulty Eggs （10000 tons）		60.69	89.72	175.32	190.67

9—16 水 产 品 产 量
OUTPUT OF AQUATIC PRODUCTS

单位:万吨　　(10000 tons)

指　　标	Items	1980	1985	1990	1995	1996
水产品产量	**Output of Aquatic Products**	**42.71**	**67.54**	**118.25**	**219.47**	**245.72**
海水产品产量	Seawater Aquatic Products	22.15	24.10	33.85	65.08	79.50
按生产性质分	Group by Nature					
天然生产	Naturally Grown	20.55	22.58	30.68	56.70	66.10
人工养殖	Artificially Cultured	1.60	1.52	3.17	8.38	13.40
按类别分	Group by Category					
鱼类	Fish	16.38	18.32	22.38	37.71	44.89
虾蟹类	Shrimp, Prawn and Crab	3.21	4.00	6.02	10.74	10.27
贝类	Shell-fish	1.34	1.76	5.24	16.23	23.83
藻类	Algae	1.22	0.02	0.21	0.40	0.51
淡水产品产量	Freshwater Aquatic Products	20.56	43.44	84.40	154.39	166.22
按生产性质分	Group by Nature					
天然生产	Naturally Grown	10.02	10.72	16.42	25.47	25.24
人工养殖	Artificially Cultured	10.54	32.72	67.98	128.92	140.98
按类别分	Group by Category					
鱼类	Fish	17.95	41.00	79.58	139.34	146.05
虾蟹类	Shirmp, Prawn and Crab	1.71	1.29	2.64	9.73	11.07
贝类	Shell fish	0.90	1.15	2.18	5.32	9.10
在海水产品中	**Among Seawater Aquatic**					
大黄鱼	Big Yelow Croaker	1156	598	225	380	915
小黄鱼	Small Yellow Croaker	2539	2478	5382	40575	45989
带鱼	Hairtail	54879	41729	57135	142971	113105
墨鱼	Cuttlefish	1612	7650	1671	3118	4716
水产养殖面积（千公顷）	**Aquatic Raise Areas** (1000 **ha**)	**274.92**	**393.59**	**448.14**	**555.23**	**573.23**
淡水养殖面积	Freshwiter Raise Areas	256.03	345.04	381.27	467.29	474.19
海水养殖面积	Seawater Raise	18.89	48.55	66.87	87.94	99.04

9—17 农业现代化情况
STATISTICS ON AGRICULTURAL MODERNIZATION

单位:千公顷 (1000 ha)

指标	Items	1980	1985	1990	1995	1996
农业机械化情况	**Statistics on Agricultural Machinery**					
机耕面积	Area Ploughed by Tractors	2901.67	3244.04	3632.49	3639.43	3708.75
机播面积	Seeded Area by Tractors	395.07	333.23	1046.41	1730.23	1793.28
#机播三麦面积	Wheats Area by Tractors		313.61	1010.26	1661.56	1531.72
机械植保面积	Plant Protection Area by Tractors		833.31	1727.52	2730.54	2728.70
机械收获面积	Harvest Area by Tractors	17.00	78.79	531.93	1194.21	1524.43
农村电气化情况	**Electrification of Rural**					
农村用电量（亿千瓦小时）	Electricity Consumed in Rural Area (100000000 kw/h)	33.74	63.57	105.26	238.16	252.18
农用物资使用情况	**Used Agricultural Product Material**					
化肥施用量（折纯量）(万吨)	Consumption of Chemical Fertilizers (pure)(10000 tons)	118.17	157.80	221.79	292.77	306.65
每亩耕地施用化肥（折纯量）(千克)	Consumption of Chemical Fertilizers (pure)(kg)	17.0	22.8	32.4	43.8	46.0
农用塑料薄膜使用量（万吨）	Used Plastic Film (10000 tons)				5.35	5.24
农用柴油使用量（万吨）	Used Diesel Oil (10000 tons)			3.12	59.17	65.32
农药使用量（万吨）	Used Agricultural Chemical (10000 tons)			7.98	8.87	9.37
农田水利情况	**Irrigation and Water Conservancy**					
有效灌溉面积	Effective Irrigation Area	3412.98	3587.93	3970.92	3832.78	3837.78
#机电灌溉面积	Electrical Irrigation Area	3121.20	3305.60	3518.06	3803.50	3784.51
机电灌溉面积占有效灌溉面积的比重%	Rate: $\frac{Electrical\ Irrigation\ Area}{Effective\ Irrigatim\ Area}$	91.5	92.1	88.6	99.2	98.6
机电井数（万眼）	Electrical Well (10000)	4.78	4.08	4.89	4.75	5.05
#已配套（万眼）	Form a Complete Set (10000)	3.08	2.26	3.20	3.11	3.26

9—18 主要年份农业机械拥有量 OWNERSHIP OF AGRICUITURAL MACHINERY

年份 Year	农业机械总动力（万千瓦） Total Power of Agricultural Machinery (10000 kw)	农用大中型拖拉机（混合台） Large and Medium Agricultural Tractors	农用小型及手扶拖拉机（万台） Mini and Walking Agricultural Tractors	农用排灌动力机械（万千瓦） Machinery for Agricultural Drainaqe and Irrigation	农用水泵（万台） Agricultural Water Pump (ten thousand sets)	喷灌机械（套） Machinery for Sprinkling (sets)
1952	5.59	48		5.05		
1957	13.32	549		9.79		
1962	66.12	1557	…	60.66		
1965	82.64	2203	0.06	70.27		
1978	855.16	11836	19.25	363.73	29.20	8305
1980	1113.05	16238	25.61	442.48	36.18	24856
1985	1675.06	18902	49.16	450.27	37.75	20809
1986	1811.31	18669	53.84	468.46	38.26	14613
1987	1974.41	19368	60.46	468.97	38.14	11959
1988	2100.85	19118	65.72	473.48	38.62	14471
1989	2212.37	18771	70.02	475.97	40.29	11182
1990	2004.77	19468	71.65	490.83	39.63	9370
1991	1966.61	19952	72.64	492.88	40.73	10687
1992	2016.07	20654	72.41	494.57	41.55	11571
1993	2081.75	21322	73.52	501.35	41.59	12044
1994	2161.40	21458	74.98	507.66	42.63	13068
1995	2226.95	23198	75.04	508.91	43.36	14991
1996	2297.43	30483	76.53	515.99	44.84	15952

续表 1 Continued

年份 Year	联合收割机（台） Combine Harvesters (units)	机动脱粒机（万台） Motorized Huller (ten thousand)	机动喷雾(粉)器（部） Motorized Duster (units)	饲料粉碎机（万部） Fodder Grinder (ten thousand units)	农用载重汽车（辆） Trucks for Agricultural Use	渔用机动船（艘） Fishery Motorized Ship (units)
1952					35	
1957	18				34	2
1962	152	0.63			119	413
1965	176	3.60		…	227	401
1978	295	32.96	20126	10.18	1656	3914
1980	478	40.99	43314	11.88	3343	5179
1985	687	68.51	55136	7.30	10395	16602
1986	897	74.58	51288	6.96	13102	20344
1987	984	79.45	55350	6.72	15803	25912
1988	1363	82.30	57454	6.98	18830	28485
1989	1821	86.36	70816	6.50	19880	33383
1990	2411	89.42	94900	6.51	16132	40728
1991	3583	92.29	113542	6.55	15915	43367
1992	5964	93.37	123699	6.29	16164	44788
1993	7279	94.80	126331	6.06	18076	48792
1994	8604	98.32	132776	5.92	21910	50067
1995	12063	105.22	170785	5.27	24390	50548
1996	20074	105.01	196395	6.32	26077	54206

9—19 农业主要经济效益指标
MAJOR INDICATIONS OF AGRICULTURE

指　　标	Items	1985	1990	1995	1996
每个农村劳动力创造的农村社会总产值（元）	Gross Output Value of Rural By Per Rural Labor (yuan)	2985.66	7437.37	38108.36	37752.14
每个农林牧渔业劳动力创造的农林牧渔业总产值（元）	Gross Output Value of Agriculture By Per Agricultural Labor (yuan)	1696.16	3386.02	10943.67	11921.25
每个农林牧渔业劳动力创造的农林牧渔业净产值（元）	Net Value of Agriculture By Per Agricultural Labor (yuan)	1108.03	2017.86	5626.96	6170.05
每亩耕地创造的种植业产值（元）	Gross Oufput Value of Farming By Per MU Cultivated Land (yuan)	265.94	469.83	1280.04	1348.85
每亩耕地创造的净产值（元）	Net Value By Per MU Cultivated Land (yuan)	200.82	337.40	857.96	893.57
每个农林牧渔业劳动力生产的粮食产量（公斤）	Output of Grain By Per Agricultural Labor (kg)	1835.68	1903.86	2132.12	2271.83
每个农林牧渔业劳动力生产的棉花产量（公斤）	Output of Cotton By Per Agricultural Labor (kg)	28.13	27.08	36.44	35.13
每个农林牧渔业劳动力生产的油料产量（公斤）	Output of Oil-Bearing By Rer Agricultural Labor (kg)	63.87	65.55	103.46	96.39
每个农林牧渔业劳动力生产的肉类产量（公斤）	Output of Meat By Per Agricultural Labor (kg)	93.82	113.18	198.46	209.28
每个农林牧渔业劳动力生产的水产品产量（公斤）	Output of Water Products By Per Agricultural Labor (kg)	39.65	68.97	142.39	160.58
农林牧渔业商品率（%）	Commodity Rate of Agriculture	52.81	58.92	64.07	68.38
农业商品率（%）	Commodity Rate of Farming	45.17	48.28	52.78	56.17
林业商品率（%）	Commodity Rate of Forestry	46.11	41.44	63.96	62.05
牧业商品率（%）	Commodity Rate of Animal Husbandry	70.80	76.68	78.59	84.65
渔业商品率（%）	Commodity Rate of Fishery	78.31	82.76	84.88	89.30
农民人均纯收入（元）	Net Revenue of Per Peasant (yuan)	492.60	883.77	2456.86	3029.32

注：①产值均为现行价格。

②从1996年开始农村工业总产值口径发生变化，故每个农村劳动力创造的农村社会总产值小于上年，如按同口径相比则增长22.1%。

a) Gross output value at current price.

b) Gross output value of rural industry has changed from 1996. Therefore, rural total value is smaller than last year, comparable increase rate 22.1 percent.

9—20 农村乡村企业基本情况
TOWNSHIP AND VILLAGE ENTERPRISES

指　　标	Items	1985	1990	1995	1996
乡村企业单位数　　（个）	**Enterprises**	**98567**	**113159**	**108821**	**105188**
按隶属关系	Grouped by Administrative Relationship				
乡办企业	Township	33541	35018	35720	34196
村办企业	Village	65026	78141	73101	70992
按国民经济部门分	Grouped By Economic Sector				
农业企业	Agriculture	2365	878	725	751
工业企业	Industry	81560	99883	93476	91138
建筑企业	Construction	3087	2933	2589	2459
交通运输企业	Transportation	3826	2670	1744	1670
商业、饮食、服务业及其他	Commerce and Other Services	7729	6795	10287	9170
乡村企业从业人数　　（万人）	**Persons Employed　　(ten thousand)**	**627.09**	**672.93**	**668.44**	**615.27**
按隶属关系分	Grouped by Administrative Relationship				
乡办企业	Township	363.42	381.69	391.01	363.11
村办企业	Village	263.67	291.24	277.43	252.16
按国民经济部门分	Grouped By Economic Sector				
农业企业	Agriculture	6.62	2.35	3.39	1.68
工业企业	Industry	511.66	588.12	576.14	536.16
建筑企业	Construction	83.00	63.20	68.11	59.96
交通运输企业	Transportation	16.24	11.47	6.60	5.86
商业、饮食、服务业及其他	Commerce and Other Service	9.57	7.79	14.20	11.61
乡村企业总收入　　（亿元）	**Total Revenue　　(0.1 billion)**	**352.12**	**951.36**	**5237.46**	**5512.87**
按隶属关系分	Grouped by Administrative Relationship				
乡办企业	Township	217.26	582.81	3014.55	3201.41
村办企业	Village	134.86	368.55	2222.91	2311.46
按国民经济部门分	Grouped By Economic Sector				
农业企业	Agriculture	2.19	1.88	15.94	23.90
工业企业	Industry	310.34	876.98	5140.36	5291.75
建筑企业	Construction	24.00	42.85	17.20	109.57
交通运输企业	Transportation	5.80	8.67	2.08	1.38
商业、饮食、服务业及其他	Commerce and Other Services	9.79	20.98	61.88	86.27

9－21 乡村企业主要经济指标(1996)
MAIN ECONOMIC INDICATORS OF TOWNSHIP AND VILLAGE ENTERPRISES

单位:亿元 (100 000 000 yuan)

指标	Items	合计 Total	乡办 Town-ship	#工业 Industry	村办 Village	#工业 Indutry
营业收入	Operating Revenue	5512.87	3201.41	3016.84	2311.46	2274.91
#营业成本	Operating Cost	4761.09	2754.49	2594.57	2006.60	1975.42
营业费用	Operating Expenses	150.77	85.34	80.32	65.43	63.70
营业税金及附加	Operating Tax And Added	43.57	25.17	20.98	18.40	17.73
管理费用	Management Cost	269.21	167.87	159.72	101.34	99.93
财务费用	Financial Cost	144.35	100.76	98.16	43.59	43.36
利润总额	Total Profits	169.51	87.20	82.64	82.31	81.03
#应交所得税	Payable Income Taxes	32.74	19.87	19.26	12.87	12.68
实交各种税金	Taxes Paid	131.75	78.34	74.57	53.41	52.82
可供分配的利润	Capable Assign Profits	72.35	11.12	6.08	61.23	60.22
#提取盈余公积	Accumulated Fund	49.68	27.58	27.13	22.10	21.91
应付利润	Payable Profit	72.43	37.58	36.72	34.85	34.34
工资总额	Total Wage Bill	297.98	178.62	154.54	119.36	116.99
固定资产原值年末数	Original Value of Fixed Assets (Year-end)	1655.60	1113.17	1089.70	542.43	537.16
累计提取的折旧	Draw Depreciation Funds	386.78	259.61	253.36	127.17	126.13
固定资产净值	Average Balances of Net Value of Fixed Assets	1268.82	853.56	836.34	415.26	411.03
流动资产年末数	Circulating Funds	2189.35	1389.73	1283.34	799.62	790.74
#货币资金	Money Funds	163.18	96.62	91.87	66.56	65.44
存货	Stock	952.66	604.38	554.79	348.28	345.63
流动资产年平均余额	Average Balances of Circulating Funds	2049.54	1286.96	1221.53	762.58	754.75
流动负债平均余额	Average Balance of Loan Circulating	1927.20	1282.67	1219.99	644.53	637.45
本年长短期借款余额	Balance of Long Period and Short Period Lend Money	1094.90	800.71	783.29	294.19	292.66
长期负债合计	Total Long Term Loan	318.76	244.23	242.22	74.53	74.20
亏损企业(个)	Deficit Enterprises	16848	6750	5921	10098	6806
亏损余额	Balance of Deficit	46.07	33.72	33.33	12.35	12.29

10

INDUSTRY

10 工　业
INDUSTRY

1 9 9 6

工业企业单位数	Number of Industrial Enterprises	583051	个	
全部工业总产值(当年价)	Gross output Value of Total Industry	11555.6	亿元	(100000000 yuan)
#乡以上工业	Township Level Above Industry	7919.25	亿元	(100000000 yuan)
乡村工业	Township and Village Industry	6360.41	亿元	(100000000 yuan)
全部独立核算工业	Total Industrial Enterprises with Independent Accounts			
职工人数	Number of Staff and Workers	735.73	万人	(100000000 persons)
资本金合计	Total Capital Assets	2012.25	亿元	(100000000 yuan)
资产总计	Total Property	7713.83	亿元	(100000000 yuan)
负债合计	Total Liability	4992.33	亿元	(100000000 yuan)
产品销售收入	Revenue of Products Sales	6873.68	亿元	(100000000 yuan)
利税总额	Total Pre－Tax Profit	450.20	亿元	(100000000 yuan)

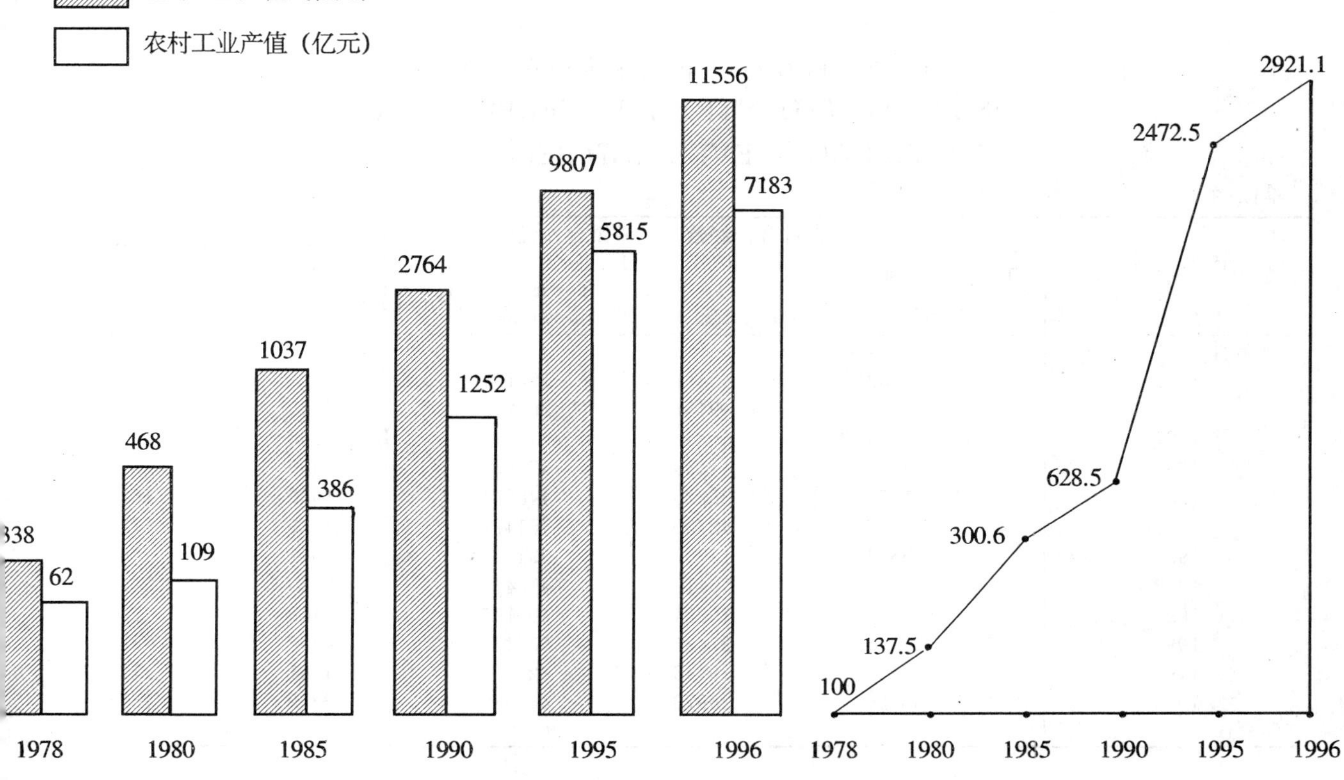

10—1 乡以上工业企业单位数 NUMBER OF INDUSTRIAL ENTERPRISES AT TOWNSHIP LEVEL AND ABOVE

单位:个

年份 Year	企业单位数 Number of Enterprises	#大中型企业 Large and Medium Enterprises	国有经济工业企业 State-Owned Industrial Enterprises	集体经济工业企业 Collective-Owned Industrial Enterprises	其他经济类型工业企业 Others
1978	27257	186	4720	22537	
1979	28568	215	4752	23816	
1980	32687	241	4740	27917	30
1981	33816	269	4860	28906	50
1982	33867	299	4888	28906	73
1983	33846	325	4907	28857	82
1984	37865	375	4630	33143	92
1985	43269	603	4910	38251	108
1986	47248	665	5018	42085	145
1987	47252	777	5035	41952	265
1988	47846	908	5059	42420	367
1989	47351	1123	5055	41810	486
1990	46827	1237	5085	41190	552
1991	45313	1430	4989	39577	747
1992	45363	1596	4995	39259	1109
1993	45554	1876	5216	37303	3035
1994	45033	2183	4896	36129	4008
1995	47474	2329	5639	36943	4892
1996	42795	2462	4812	33355	4628

10—2 村及村以下工业企业单位数 NUMBER OF INDUSTRIAL ENTERPRISES AT VILLAGE LEVEL AND BELOW

单位:个

年份 Year	农村村办工业企业 Village	农村合作经营工业组织 Rural Co-operation	城镇合作经营工业组织 Town Co-operation	农村个体工业 Rural-Individual	城镇个体工业 Town Individual
1985	55553	42411	155103		8694
1986	58976	49457	263206	2533	9807
1987	72764	46857	410848	2668	13571
1988	73207	41439	471661	1889	15983
1989	71751	36229	448394	1960	16888
1990	70357	42730	451477	1456	17285
1991	65514	15702	391976	1371	13068
1992	65949	18412	410465	2269	14462
1993	71426	19824	460197	2118	17633
1994	68190	23436	532435	1898	18334
1995	57263	19443	321034	1741	11708
1996	60820	26973	434339	2339	15785

10—3 各种经济类型工业总产值
GROSS OUTPUT VALUE OF INDUSTRY BY OWNERSHIP

单位:亿元 (100 000 000 yuan)

指标	Items	当年价格 Current Price		不变价格 Constant Price	
		1995	1996	1995	1996
总计	**Total**	**9807.19**	**11555.60**	**8835.03**	**10437.68**
大中型工业企业	Large and Medium Scale Industrial Enterprises	3189.32	3579.98	2756.90	3220.79
乡以上工业总产值	Gross output Value of Township Industrial Enterprises	6982.46	7919.25	6223.50	7244.46
国有工业	State Owned	2096.69	2244.68	1644.02	1805.45
集体工业	Collective Owned	3559.74	3974.16	3335.96	3783.27
其他工业	Others	1326.03	1700.41	1243.52	1655.74
#乡办工业	Township Owned	3014.09	3590.34	2839.34	3422.23
村及村以下工业	Village Level and Below	2801.21	3592.57	2588.30	3155.57
村办工业	Village	2232.09	2770.07	2026.48	2448.23
农村联营工业	Rural Co-operation	61.96	105.89	61.16	91.06
农村个体工业	Rural Individual	507.16	716.61	500.66	616.28
城镇联营及个体工业	Town Co-operation and Individual	23.52	43.78	23.23	37.65
# 城镇个体工业	Town Individual	14.25	31.69	14.08	27.25
轻工业产值	Gross output Value of Light Industry	4785.42	5676.47	4427.52	5229.74
乡以上工业	Town Level and Above	3332.75	3765.50	3075.38	3555.11
村及村以下工业	Village Level and Below	1435.29	1874.69	1334.97	1643.43
村办工业	Village	1033.08	1310.25	937.92	1158.02
农村联营工业	Rural Co-operation	36.29	65.75	35.83	56.54
农村个体工业	Rural Individual	365.92	498.69	361.22	428.87
城镇联营及个体工业	Town Co-operation and Individual	17.38	36.28	17.17	31.20
# 城镇个体工业	Town Individual	11.08	25.88	10.95	22.25
重工业产值	Gross output Value of Heavy Industry	5021.77	5879.13	4407.51	5207.94
乡以上工业	Town Level and Above	3649.71	4153.75	3148.12	3689.35
村及村以下工业	Village Level and Below	1365.92	1717.88	1253.33	1512.14
村办工业	Village	1199.01	1459.82	1088.56	1290.21
农村联营工业	Rural Co-operation	25.67	40.14	25.33	34.52
农村个体工业	Rural Individual	141.24	217.92	139.44	187.41
城镇联营及个体工业	Town Co-operation and Individual	6.14	7.50	6.06	6.45
城镇个体工业	Town Individual	3.17	5.82	3.13	5.00

注:本表按新规定计算(下同)。

Note:This table is calculated by new regulation (and so do follows).

10—4 分行业乡以上工业单位数和总产值(1996)
NUMBER OF ENTERPRISES AND GROSS OUTPUT VALUE OF INDUSTRY AT TOWNSHIP LEVEL AND ABOVE BY BRANCH

行业	Items	单位数(个) Number of Enter-prises	工业总产值(当年价) Gross Output Value of Industry (Current Price)	工业总产值(不变价) Gross Output Value of Industry (Constant Price)
总计	**National Total**	**42795**	**7919.25**	**7244.46**
按经济类型分	**Grouped by Ownership**			
国有经济企业	State-Owned Enterprises	4812	2244.68	1805.45
集体经济企业	Collective-Owned Enterprises	33355	3974.16	3783.27
其他经济企业	Other Ownedship Enterprises	4628	1700.41	1655.74
按轻重工业分	**Grouped by Light & Heavy Industry**			
轻工业	Light Industry	21325	3765.50	3555.11
重工业	Heavy Industry	21470	4153.74	3689.35
按行业分	**Grouped by Sector**			
采掘业	**Mining and Quarrying**			
煤炭采选业	Coal Mining and Processing	62	51.08	19.15
石油和天然气开采业	Petroleum and Natural Gas Extraction	1	11.48	2.83
黑色金属矿采选业	Ferrous Metals Mining and Processing	9	3.55	2.50
有色金属矿采选业	Nonferrous Metals Mining and Processing	12	2.72	2.61
非金属矿采选业	Nonmetal Minerals Mining and Processing	586	42.17	35.25
其他矿采选业	Other Minerals Mining and Processing			
木材及竹材采运业	Logging and Transport of Timber and Bamboo			
制造业	**Manufacturing**			
食品加工业	Food Processing	2097	354.16	234.10
食品制造业	Food Production	1111	126.28	105.29
饮料制造业	Beverage Production	472	93.77	72.98
烟草加工业	Tobacco Processing	9	25.89	18.99
纺织业	Textile Industry	3662	1144.35	1058.27
服装及其他纤维制品制造业	Garments and Other Fiber Products	1894	330.96	297.76
皮革毛皮羽绒及其制品业	Leather, Furs, Down and Related Products	895	128.19	117.82
木材加工及竹藤棕草制品业	Timber Processing, Bamboo, Cane, Palm Fiber and Straw Products	610	57.79	53.03
家具制造业	Furniture Manufacturing	477	26.72	24.71
造纸及纸制品业	Papermaking and Paper Products	734	83.84	75.29
印刷业记录媒介的复制	Printing and Record Pressing	1196	63.62	58.83
文教体育用品制造业	Stationery, Education and Sports Goods	661	72.20	69.23
石油加工及炼焦业	Petroleum Processing and Coking Products	124	131.45	67.45
化学原料及化学制品制造业	Raw Chemical Materials and Chemical Products	2950	691.84	630.67
医药制造业	Medical and Pharmaceutical Products	379	107.93	142.11
化学纤维制造业	Chemical Fibers	255	192.73	203.39
橡胶制品业	Rubber Products	448	68.52	70.75
塑料制品业	Plastic Products	1796	201.58	205.12
非金属矿物制品业	Nonmetal Mineral Products	5154	428.03	357.44
黑色金属冶炼及压延加工业	Smelting and Pressing of Ferrous Metals	425	302.64	220.00
有色金属冶炼及压延加工业	Smelting and Pressing of Nonferrous Metals	506	171.82	164.63
金属制品业	Metal Products	2896	339.29	329.80
普通机械制造业	Ordinary Machinery Manufacturing	3414	561.11	536.89
专用设备制造业	Special Purposes Equipment Manufacturing	2116	349.77	334.69
交通运输设备制造业	Transportation Equipment Manufacturing	1634	404.02	409.25
电气机械及器材制造业	Electronic Equipment and Machinery	2527	531.14	566.47
电子及通信设备制造业	Electronic and Telecommunications	1061	368.09	478.49
仪器仪表及文化办公用机械制造业	Instruments, Meters, Cultural and Official Machinery	579	72.06	84.07
其他制造业	Other Manufacturing	1327	110.37	105.26
电力、煤气及水的生产供应业	**Electric Power, Gas and Water Production and Supply**			
电力、蒸汽、热水生产供应业	Electric Power, Steam and Hot Water Production and Supply	122	242.41	73.51
煤气的生产和供应业	Gas Production and Supply	17	6.46	3.45
自来水的生产和供应业	Tap Water Production and Supply	574	18.84	12.02

10—5 历年工业总产值

GROSS OUTPUT VALUE OF INDUSTRY OVER THE YEARS

单位:亿元 (100 000 000 yuan)

年份 Year	工业总产值 Total Output Value of Inductry	按轻重工业分 Grouped by Light and Heavy Industry		按经济类型分 Grouped by Ownership				
		轻工业 Light Industry	重工业 Heavy Industry	国有经济 State-Owned	集体经济 Collective-Owned	其他经济 Others	村及村以下办工业 Village Level and Below Run Industry	城镇联营工业及个体工业 City and Town Joint Individual Owned Industry
1950	19.00	17.94	1.06	11.93	7.07			
1951	22.55	21.20	1.35	15.04	7.51			
1952	25.53	23.97	1.56	17.39	8.14			
1953	29.81	27.66	2.15	19.98	9.83			
1954	31.66	29.00	2.66	22.54	9.12			
1955	32.82	29.57	3.25	23.43	9.39			
1956	38.60	33.54	5.06	28.37	10.23			
1957	41.01	34.78	6.23	30.21	10.80			
1958	75.22	58.07	17.15	65.90	9.32			
1959	96.00	71.81	24.19	81.67	14.33			
1960	100.32	68.72	31.60	82.24	18.08			
1961	62.50	47.37	15.13	49.96	12.54			
1962	53.36	42.95	10.41	43.76	9.60			
1963	54.66	42.96	11.70	45.35	9.31			
1964	68.17	53.65	14.52	56.36	11.81			
1965	88.08	66.28	21.80	73.10	12.57		2.41	
1966	104.19	74.60	29.59	84.41	17.25		2.53	
1967	84.80	63.26	21.54	67.09	15.52		2.19	
1968	85.48	59.49	25.99	67.56	15.55		2.37	
1969	102.80	69.08	33.72	82.49	17.94		2.37	
1970	135.47	83.14	52.33	107.68	24.69		3.10	
1971	167.59	93.59	73.56	131.24	32.14		3.77	
1972	183.38	101.08	82.30	141.20	37.74		4.44	
1973	208.10	114.89	93.21	156.63	46.70		4.77	
1974	205.39	117.45	87.94	145.69	53.83		5.87	
1975	235.28	130.28	105.00	161.62	65.22		8.44	
1976	247.59	134.97	112.62	169.03	65.21		13.35	
1977	297.12	158.12	139.00	183.45	92.59		21.08	
1978	337.65	176.94	160.71	207.52	105.28		24.85	
1979	386.05	208.11	177.94	238.58	117.86		29.61	
1980	467.82	267.97	199.85	268.11	153.30	2.45	43.92	0.04
1981	504.94	307.98	196.96	276.70	175.49	3.74	48.91	0.10
1982	534.87	317.54	217.33	297.64	180.79	5.18	50.96	0.30
1983	600.70	348.56	252.14	320.79	209.48	8.00	61.61	0.64
1984	745.36	433.00	312.36	350.35	283.41	12.12	97.93	1.55
1985	1036.67	552.23	484.44	426.24	415.90	18.73	173.76	2.04
1986	1235.38	671.24	564.14	482.50	500.01	22.92	227.92	2.46
1987	1590.31	859.40	730.91	582.51	644.07	34.92	325.34	3.47
1988	2152.93	1151.00	1001.93	747.21	877.54	57.90	465.25	5.03
1989	2507.42	1338.53	1168.89	877.21	1002.62	86.04	535.67	5.88
1990	2764.10	1510.57	1253.53	948.40	1094.82	104.66	609.95	6.27
1991	3161.60	1682.76	1478.84	1045.31	1258.55	160.50	690.17	7.07
1992	4673.57	2379.00	2294.57	1319.21	1934.05	263.36	1146.31	10.64
1993	7096.46	3439.50	3656.96	1651.04	2781.66	626.46	2019.99	17.31
1994	9826.50	5014.54	4811.96	1959.99	3642.09	1206.25	2992.91	25.26
1995	9807.19	4785.42	5021.77	2096.69	3559.74	1326.03	2801.21	23.52
1996	11555.60	5676.47	5879.13	2244.68	3974.16	1700.41	3592.57	43.78

注:1. 本表按当年价格计算。

2. 从1995年起工业产值按新规定计算。

Notes:1)This table is counted by current Prices.

2)Output value of industry is counted by new regulation since 1995.

10—6 历年工业总产值指数

INDICES OF GROSS OUTPUT VALUE OF INDUSTRY OVER THE YEARS

年份 Year	工业总产值 Total Output Value of Inductry	按轻重工业分 Grouped by Light and Heavy Industry		按经济类型分 Grouped by Ownership				
		轻工业 Light Industry	重工业 Heavy Industry	国有经济 State-Owned	集体经济 Collective-Owned	其他经济 Others	村及村以下办工业 Village Level and Below Run Inductry	城镇联营工业及个体工业 City and Town Joint Individual Owned Industry
1949	100.0	100.0	100.0	100.0				
1950	119.5	119.2	123.1	122.8	114.4			
1951	141.9	141.0	153.0	154.8	121.6			
1952	160.6	159.1	178.6	179.0	131.7			
1953	188.9	184.2	244.4	207.0	160.3			
1954	203.1	194.9	368.4	243.3	150.6			
1955	208.3	194.9	306.0	236.5	153.3			
1956	260.6	232.6	595.7	313.2	177.9			
1957	266.6	230.2	700.9	321.0	180.8			
1958	424.2	325.2	1608.5	607.8	135.3			
1959	590.9	434.5	2461.5	822.1	227.0			
1960	648.0	427.5	3283.8	868.6	300.7			
1961	404.0	302.4	1608.5	607.8	135.3			
1962	334.8	270.6	1102.6	449.1	155.0			
1963	346.0	277.5	1165.8	470.9	149.6			
1964	437.3	345.9	1529.9	591.4	194.7			
1965	577.0	448.2	2117.1	760.4	248.0		100.0	
1966	710.8	488.7	3366.7	921.0	229.7		99.6	
1967	583.0	417.3	2565.0	736.8	306.1		86.6	
1968	600.7	403.4	2960.7	757.5	316.1		93.7	
1969	749.4	477.9	3995.7	964.1	373.7		93.7	
1970	1040.8	599.4	6318.8	1358.9	487.9		129.0	
1971	1289.0	664.1	8760.7	1650.1	657.4		156.7	
1972	1422.7	719.7	9871.9	1782.8	776.1		184.5	
1973	1623.7	823.1	11240.4	1991.7	953.7		198.3	
1974	1612.4	484.2	10694.4	1902.7	1053.6		244.1	
1975	1861.2	944.4	12870.8	2120.4	1275.4		350.8	
1976	2050.5	1021.0	14475.3	2218.1	1502.2		554.6	
1977	2461.8	1189.7	17929.2	2527.4	1901.7		891.1	
1978	2797.8	1330.2	20707.9	2886.6	2131.7		1032.4	
1979	3186.6	1561.8	22875.3	3260.6	2443.5		1230.3	
1980	3847.3	2021.4	25552.8	3612.8	3186.4	100.0	1824.8	100.0
1981	4171.8	2360.5	25144.9	3797.7	3553.9	153.3	2062.2	250.0
1982	4490.8	2474.5	28080.5	4075.4	3858.3	209.2	2150.2	750.0
1983	5113.9	2790.0	32420.7	4490.5	4491.5	335.5	2599.6	1600.0
1984	6304.5	3378.2	40947.6	4843.3	6059.9	541.6	4132.1	3875.0
1985	8408.9	4425.1	55903.7	5590.1	8496.0	787.8	7331.6	5100.0
1986	9811.6	5264.6	63611.0	6077.9	10104.0	885.1	9598.7	6150.0
1987	12151.6	6336.4	81715.9	6936.9	12733.9	1419.8	12923.2	8675.0
1988	15271.4	7975.7	102496.3	7915.4	16167.5	2165.6	18007.6	11525.0
1989	15981.9	8303.0	107964.6	8024.5	16846.4	2742.4	19286.5	12525.0
1990	17583.9	9246.4	117011.0	8632.8	18603.2	3404.2	21284.4	12950.0
1991	20131.3	10304.4	138466.3	9227.5	21869.1	5499.4	24083.8	14600.0
1992	30039.9	14934.2	213695.0	11299.1	34050.2	9407.3	41448.2	22815.4
1993	42668.4	20680.9	312033.2	12394.8	46817.3	21069.9	68421.9	34731.5
1994	57057.8	28386.0	405576.0	13109.5	59214.4	38081.7	101818.9	50917.8
1995	69176.9	34693.4	487583.5	14965.8	74870.4	52053.9	115126.6	56406.7
1996	81725.4	40979.5	576131.6	16435.3	84909.6	69309.5	140358.6	91421.1

注:本表按可北价格计算(1949=100)。
Note: This table is counted by constent price (1949=100).

10—7 农村工业、城镇合作经营及个体工业总产值
GROSS OUTPUT VALUE OF INDUSTRY AT RURAL, TOWN CO-OPERATION INDUSTRIAL ENTERPRISES AND INDIVIDUAL INDUSTRY

单位:亿元 (100 000 000 yuan)

年份 Year	农村工业 Rural	乡办工业 Township	村办工业 Village	村以下办工业 Village Level Below	城镇联营工业及个体工业 Town Co-operation and Individual	#城镇个体工业 Town Individual
1965	3.16	0.75	2.41			
1966	4.14	1.61	2.53			
1967	3.57	1.38	2.19			
1968	3.78	1.41	2.37			
1969	4.77	2.40	2.37			
1970	7.19	4.09	3.10			
1971	9.60	5.83	3.77			
1972	11.75	7.31	4.44			
1973	14.02	9.25	4.77			
1974	17.09	11.22	5.87			
1975	23.25	14.81	8.44			
1976	33.31	19.96	13.35			
1977	50.57	29.49	21.08			
1978	62.43	37.58	24.85			
1979	72.29	45.68	29.61			
1980	109.33	65.41	43.92		0.04	0.04
1981	124.79	75.88	48.91		0.10	0.10
1982	132.16	81.20	50.96		0.30	0.30
1983	159.59	97.98	61.61		0.64	0.64
1984	231.02	133.09	87.14	10.79	1.55	1.55
1985	385.54	211.78	150.61	23.15	2.04	2.04
1986	497.28	269.79	190.51	36.98	2.46	1.15
1987	688.52	363.18	268.02	57.32	3.47	1.78
1988	980.79	515.54	376.99	88.26	5.03	2.98
1989	1113.84	578.17	426.66	109.01	5.88	3.52
1990	1251.95	642.00	479.99	129.96	6.27	3.61
1991	1467.37	777.20	565.54	124.63	7.07	4.46
1992	2463.26	1316.95	963.06	183.25	10.64	6.55
1993	4192.94	2172.95	1710.54	309.45	17.31	11.62
1994	6099.06	3106.14	2446.42	546.49	25.26	16.49
1995	5815.30	3014.09	2232.09	569.12	23.52	14.25
1996	7182.91	3590.34	2770.07	822.50	43.78	31.69

注:本表按当年价格计算。
Note: This table is counted by current price.

10—8 农村工业、城镇合作经营及个体工业总产值指数
INDICES OF GROSS OUTPUT VALUE OF INDUSTRY AT RURAL, TOWN CO-OPERATION INDUSTRIAL ENTERPRISES AND INDIVIDUAL INDUSTRY

年份 Year	农村工业 Rural	乡办工业 Township	村办工业 Village	村以下办工业 Village Level Below	城镇联营工业及个体工业 Town Co-operation and Individual	#城镇个体工业 Town Individual
1965	100.0	100.0	100.0			
1966	130.6	211.8	105.0			
1967	112.6	181.6	90.9			
1968	116.7	175.0	98.3			
1969	146.4	298.7	98.3			
1970	219.6	507.9	128.6			
1971	293.1	726.3	156.4			
1972	359.6	915.8	184.2			
1973	430.0	1165.8	197.9			
1974	526.5	1423.7	243.6			
1975	720.5	1894.7	350.2			
1976	1064.0	2681.6	553.9			
1977	1641.0	4071.1	874.7			
1978	1999.4	5069.7	1031.1			
1979	2410.1	6156.6	1228.6			
1980	3477.9	8727.6	1822.4		100.0	100.0
1981	3966.6	10109.2	2029.5		250.0	250.0
1982	4233.1	10951.3	2114.5		750.0	750.0
1983	5113.3	13221.1	2556.4		1600.0	1600.0
1984	7455.2	18210.5	3615.8	100.0	3875.0	3875.0
1985	12092.1	27573.7	6248.1	214.8	5100.0	5100.0
1986	15656.5	35371.1	7905.0	342.7	6150.0	2875.0
1987	20989.6	47248.7	10469.7	500.1	8175.0	4200.0
1988	28566.3	62996.1	14349.0	750.4	11525.0	6825.0
1989	29952.4	64789.5	15106.6	862.1	12550.0	7500.0
1990	33667.8	74057.9	16471.0	996.1	12950.0	7475.0
1991	40207.2	92826.7	19406.9	955.2	14600.0	9222.1
1992	69516.5	161119.3	34243.5	1455.3	22800.9	14045.1
1993	112965.1	258312.3	56977.2	2302.2	34709.4	23348.3
1994	161879.9	357781.2	81844.3	4083.4	50885.4	33261.7
1995	196198.4	461645.1	90577.1	5057.3	56370.8	34209.7
1996	237774.4	556416.5	109427.9	6367.2	140358.6	66208.4

注：本表按可比价格计算(1965=100)。
Note: This table is counted by comparable price (1965=100).

10—9 全部独立核算工业企业财务指标及经济效益
FINANCIAL INDICATORS AND ECONOMIC RESULT OF TOTAL INDUSTRIAL ENTERPRISES WITH INDEPENDENT ACCOUNTING SYSTEMS

指标	Items	1985	1990	1995	1996
企业单位数 (个)	Number of Enterprsises	33486	37480	42676	38506
工业总产值(当年价格) (亿元)	Gross Output Value of Industry(current price) (100000000 yuan)	826.45	2061.29	6819.92	7726.34
固定资产原价 (亿元)	Original Value of Fixed Assets (100000000 yuan)	386.85	992.65	3453.07	4005.75
产品销售收入 (亿元)	Revenue of Product Sales (100000000 yuan)	746.75	1755.80	6272.47	6873.68
利税总额 (亿元)	Total Pre-Tax Profits (100000000 yuan)	135.50	161.30	451.61	450.20
#产品销售税金及附加 (亿元)	Product Sale Pre-Tax and Related Payment (100 000 000 yuan)			61.86	67.38
资金总额 (亿元)	Total Capital Assets (100000000 yuan)	456.32	1265.99	5242.83	6262.59
#全部流动资产年平均余额 (亿元)	Average Balance Circulating Funds (100000000 yuan)			3045.14	3496.72
百元产值实现利税(当年价格) (元)	Pre-Tax Profit per 100 yuan Output Value (current price)(yuan)	16.39	7.83	6.62	5.83
百元销售收入实现利税 (元)	Pre-Tax Profit per 100 yuan Sales Revenue (yuan)	18.15	9.19	7.20	6.55
百元资金实现利税 (元)	Pre-Tax Profit per 100 yuan Assets (yuan)	29.69	12.74	8.61	7.19
百元固定资产原价实现产值 (元)	Output Value per 100 yuan Original Value of Fixd Assets (yuan)	213.64	207.66	197.50	192.88
百元固定资产原价实现利税 (元)	Pre-Tax Profit Value per 100yuan Original Value of Fixed Assets (yuan)	35.03	16.25	13.08	11.24
全部流动资金周转天数 (天)	Turnover of Total Circulating Funds (day/year)			177.20	185.68
本年应交增值税 (亿元)	Added Value Tax (100000000 yuan)			221.25	241.10

10—10 国有经济独立核算工业企业财务指标及经济效益
FINANCIAL INDICATORS AND ECONOMIC RESULT OF STATE-OWNED INDUSTRIALENTERPRISES WITH INDEPENDENT ACCOUNTING SYSTEMS

指标	Items	1985	1990	1995	1996
企业单位数 (个)	Number of Enterprsises	3673	3743	4343	3853
工业总产值(当年价格) (亿元)	Gross Output Value of Industry(current price) (100000000 yuan)	411.45	921.67	2026.64	2175.51
固定资产原价 (亿元)	Original Value of Fixed Assets (100000000 yuan)	255.34	599.47	1647.15	1862.97
产品销售收入 (亿元)	Revenue of Product Sales (100000000 yuan)	390.72	864.49	1948.28	2125.03
利税总额 (亿元)	Total Pre-Tax Profits (100000000 yuan)	77.40	95.66	151.90	144.62
#产品销售税金及附加 (亿元)	Product Sale Pre-Tax and Related Payment (100 000 000 yuan)			30.44	34.01
资金总额 (亿元)	Total Capital Assets (100000000 yuan)	258.57	667.33	1982.39	2425.52
#全部流动资产年平均余额 (亿元)	Average Balance Circulating Funds (100000000 yuan)		233.23	1051.72	1202.92
百元产值实现利税(当年价格) (元)	Pre-Tax Profit per 100 yuan Output Value (current price)(yuan)	18.81	10.38	7.50	6.64
百元销售收入实现利税 (元)	Pre-Tax Profit per 100 yuan Sales Revenue (yuan)	19.81	11.07	7.80	6.81
百元资金实现利税 (元)	Pre-Tax Profit per 100 yuan Assets (yuan)	29.94	14.33	7.66	5.96
百元固定资产原价实现产值 (元)	Output Value per 100 yuan Original Value of Fixd Assets (yuan)	161.14	153.75	123.04	180.85
百元固定资产原价实现利税 (元)	Pre-Tax Profit Value per 100yuan Original Value of Fixed Assets (yuan)	30.31	15.96	9.22	12.02
全部流动资金周转天数 (天)	Turnover of Total Circulating Funds (day/year)		97.12	197.03	206.62
本年应交增值税 (亿元)	Added Value Tax (100000000 yuan)			87.12	91.52

10—11 独立核算工业企业主要指标(1996)

单位:亿元

行　业	Items	企业单位数(个) Number of Enterprises (Unit)	工业总产值 Gross Output Value of Industry	工业增加值 Added-Value of Industry
总　计	**National Total**	**38506**	**7726.34**	**1827.72**
按经济类型分	**Grouped by Ownership**			
国有经济	State-Owned Enterprises	3853	2175.51	562.91
集体经济	Collective-Owned Enterprises	30234	3876.85	872.04
股份制经济	Share Holding Enterpises	299	234.71	51.89
外商投资经济	Foreign Funded Enterprises	1750	735.96	169.44
港澳台投资经济	Overseas Chinese from HongKong, Macao and Taiwan Funded	1786	552.70	138.89
按轻重工业分	**Grouped by Light & Heavy Industry**			
轻工业	Light Industry	18889	3648.95	823.57
以农产品为原料	Using Farm Products as Raw Materials	11834	2393.28	538.00
以非农产品为原料	Using Non-Farm Products as Raw Materials	7055	1255.67	285.57
重工业	Heavy Industry	19617	4077.38	1004.15
采掘工业	Extraction	555	101.07	45.95
原料工业	Raw Materials	3419	1380.31	342.58
加工工业	Manufacturing	15643	2596.00	615.62
按企业规模分	**Grouped by Size of Enterprises**			
大型企业	Large	533	2028.57	547.76
中型企业	Medium	1929	1551.42	344.63
小型企业	Small	36044	4146.35	935.32
按行业分	**Grouped by Size of Enterprises**			
煤炭采选业	Coal Mining and Processing	62	51.08	28.64
石油和天然气开采业	Petroleum and Natural Gas Extraction	1	11.48	5.54
黑色金属矿采选业	Ferrous Metals Mining and Processing	8	3.50	1.25
有色金属矿采选业	Nonferrous Metals Mining and Processing	12	2.72	0.81
非金属矿采选业	Nonmetal Minerals Mining and Processing	524	39.70	14.24
其他矿采选业	Other Minerals Mining and Processing			
木材及竹材采运业	Logging and Transport of Timber and Bamboo			
食品加工业	Food Processing	1728	311.34	46.42
食品制造业	Food Manufacturing	837	118.12	26.85
饮料制造业	Beverage Manufacturing	414	92.24	26.95
烟草加工业	Tobacco Processing	9	25.89	18.17
纺织业	Textile Industry	3488	1135.24	250.46
服装及其他纤维制品制造业	Garments and Other Fiber Products	1703	321.96	73.89
皮革毛皮羽绒及其制品业	Leather, Furs, Down and Related Products	767	125.87	28.48
木材加工及竹藤棕草制品业	Timber Processing, Bamboo, Cane, Palm Fiber and Straw Products	519	54.35	11.35
家具制造业	Furniture Manufacturing	419	25.54	6.40
造纸及纸制品业	Papermaking and Paper Products	663	82.15	19.88
印刷业记录媒介的复制	Printing and Record Pressing	1025	58.18	15.96
文教体育用品制造业	Stationery, Educational and Sports Goods	549	69.36	16.24
石油加工及炼焦业	Petroleum Processing and Coking Produets	120	131.41	23.88
化学原料及制品制造业	Raw Chemical Materials and Chemical Products	2731	681.28	155.63
医药制造业	Medical and Pharmaceutical Products	357	106.94	27.03
化学纤维制造业	Chemical Fibers	243	192.26	38.80
橡胶制品业	Rubber Products	411	67.46	16.02
塑料制品业	Plastic Products	1612	192.67	43.57
非金属矿物制品业	Nonmetal Mineral Products	4689	412.13	107.96
黑色金属冶炼及压延加工业	Smelting and Pressing of Ferrous Metals	406	293.08	53.71
有色金属冶炼及压延加工业	Smelting and Pressing of Noferrous Metals	486	170.60	32.09
金属制品业	Metal Products	2662	329.67	73.53
普通机械制造业	Ordinary Machinery Manufacturing	3116	552.41	138.61
专用设备制造业	Special Purposes Equipment Manufacturing	1969	345.11	82.77
交通运输设备制造业	Transportation Equipment Manufacturing	1367	394.40	89.58
电气机械及器材制造业	Electric Equipment and Machinery	2250	525.51	123.74
电子及通信设备制造业	Electronic and Telecommunications	1001	366.21	83.40
仪器仪表及文化办公用机械	Instruments, Meters, Cultural and Official Machinery	528	69.65	17.30
其他制造业	Other Manufactruing	1140	99.61	23.35
电力蒸气热水生产供应业	Eletricity Power, Steam and Hot Water Production and Supply	114	241.62	98.37
煤气的生产和供应业	Gas Production and Supply	16	6.45	0.35
自来水的生产和供应业	Tap Water Production and Supply	557	18.73	6.37

MAJOR INDICATORS OF INDUSTRIAL ENTERPRISES WITH INDEPENDENT ACCOUNTING SYSTEMS

(100 000 000 yuan)

资本金合计 Total Capital Assets	资产合计 Total Prperty	流动资产合计 Circulating Funds	流动资产年平均余额 Average Balance Circulating Funds	固定资产合计 Fixed Assets	固定资产原价 Original Value of Fixed Assets	固定资产净值年平均余额 Average Balances Net Value of Fixed Asstes
2012.25	**7713.83**	**3723.57**	**3496.72**	**3363.22**	**4005.75**	**2765.87**
676.56	3025.62	1293.80	1202.92	1505.86	1862.97	1222.60
675.76	2761.01	1545.03	1474.52	1029.64	1226.22	838.12
83.56	354.28	171.35	159.21	154.08	169.19	133.17
332.88	855.07	368.29	332.85	383.52	429.77	331.45
203.99	558.82	263.61	247.22	230.24	246.99	192.71
830.53	3163.80	1572.56	1488.60	1353.88	1559.01	1116.29
481.36	1898.58	928.73	878.93	834.01	976.45	689.23
349.17	1265.22	643.83	609.67	519.88	582.56	427.06
1181.72	4550.02	2151.01	2008.12	2009.33	2446.74	1649.58
50.45	146.86	50.53	47.66	85.32	124.64	76.23
492.65	1740.12	631.24	587.42	957.81	1153.64	781.40
638.62	2663.04	1469.25	1373.04	966.20	1168.46	791.95
651.45	2677.15	1134.14	1055.69	1297.40	1594.20	1055.26
382.41	1622.58	789.10	746.23	697.60	829.98	567.39
978.39	3414.10	1800.33	1694.81	1368.22	1581.57	1143.22
30.97	77.36	26.22	24.94	45.52	69.00	41.99
8.41	30.98	9.62	9.04	18.72	27.83	16.66
1.03	4.14	1.92	1.75	2.13	2.84	1.98
1.15	4.98	1.36	1.15	2.80	3.00	2.36
12.55	49.93	21.50	20.69	26.10	33.38	22.23
43.27	200.55	105.77	99.42	79.17	91.15	66.43
30.49	113.74	52.08	47.34	53.28	59.18	43.84
22.58	101.62	50.42	47.65	44.57	50.83	36.55
4.21	25.01	10.53	7.91	12.97	15.86	11.09
230.31	939.27	423.33	409.88	444.54	524.13	362.61
63.30	196.45	110.24	103.30	73.07	85.01	62.30
23.21	81.37	50.24	47.59	25.32	30.91	22.25
12.76	44.75	23.21	20.90	17.63	20.43	15.82
6.74	23.31	14.00	13.07	7.76	9.11	6.57
20.60	84.39	39.91	35.56	40.13	41.78	30.65
14.84	54.20	28.66	26.01	22.46	28.09	19.27
12.96	43.49	26.22	24.64	14.31	16.18	12.11
28.10	97.95	42.02	41.59	50.33	76.67	34.27
185.34	689.89	286.94	273.77	346.77	438.23	289.35
28.47	114.60	58.12	55.12	50.11	50.76	36.26
77.50	285.71	107.68	105.47	156.57	174.48	137.85
17.88	67.10	31.06	29.76	24.69	27.43	19.54
54.08	167.84	81.87	83.54	72.23	85.93	60.83
121.83	458.00	188.66	181.48	227.15	261.76	186.24
101.28	346.89	151.54	143.27	160.65	161.10	112.93
25.10	111.61	61.46	59.32	42.81	47.40	34.75
76.20	282.29	159.13	146.95	104.66	119.84	84.85
123.00	586.21	353.95	330.54	197.84	242.65	157.29
80.55	339.88	197.03	185.65	122.07	150.32	100.04
99.25	415.33	217.47	200.55	154.73	176.00	122.34
117.80	457.04	278.09	258.37	136.11	159.19	112.32
108.63	442.30	256.91	233.81	127.33	161.24	105.34
22.15	81.93	45.13	43.27	31.03	38.55	25.41
20.33	68.86	40.17	38.66	23.07	28.28	20.37
150.12	535.72	147.21	124.73	342.02	427.65	302.51
6.87	20.27	4.56	4.48	14.73	16.38	11.85
27.97	67.85	18.76	15.17	47.23	52.52	36.21

续表 1

单位:亿元

行业	Items	流动负债合计 Circulating Liabilities	长期负债合计 Long-Term Liabilities	所有者权益 Total Owners Rights and Interests
总　计	**National Total**	**3822.98**	**1171.73**	**2721.50**
按经济类型分	**Grouped by Ownership**			
国有经济	State-Owned Enterprises	1333.02	581.93	1110.44
集体经济	Collective-Owned Enterprises	1641.34	315.88	804.40
股份制经济	Share Holding Enterpises	123.37	58.25	172.67
外商投资经济	Foreign Funded Enterprises	380.66	109.43	367.03
港澳台投资经济	Overseas Chinese from HongKong, Macao and Taiwan Funded	258.75	83.79	216.25
按轻重工业分	**Grouped by Light & Heavy Industry**			
轻工业	Light Industry	1689.66	429.14	1045.48
以农产品为原料	Using Farm Products as Raw Materials	1064.96	258.93	575.18
以非农产品为原料	Using Non-Farm Products as Raw Materials	624.71	170.21	470.29
重工业	Heavy Industry	2133.32	742.59	1676.02
采掘工业	Extraction	54.10	27.41	65.35
原料工业	Raw Materials	656.95	365.13	717.73
加工工业	Manufacturing	1422.27	350.06	892.94
按企业规模分	**Grouped by Size of Enterprises**			
大型企业	Large	1018.52	547.48	1111.15
中型企业	Medium	832.83	250.22	540.19
小型企业	Small	1971.63	374.03	1070.16
按行业分	**Grouped by Size of Enterprises**			
煤炭采选业	Coal Mining and Processing	31.70	11.83	33.82
石油和天然气开采业	Petroleum and Natural Gas Extraction	7.63	9.96	13.39
黑色金属矿采选业	Ferrous Metals Mining and Processing	2.26	0.64	1.25
有色金属矿采选业	Nonferrous Metals Mining and Processing	1.98	1.34	1.66
非金属矿采选业	Nonmetal Minerals Mining and Processing	19.92	6.29	23.72
其他矿采选业	Other Minerals Mining and Processing			
木材及竹材采运业	Logging and Transport of Timber and Bamboo			
食品加工业	Food Processing	128.38	18.01	54.15
食品制造业	Food Manufacturing	63.79	11.43	38.52
饮料制造业	Beverage Manufacturing	57.59	10.38	33.66
烟草加工业	Tobacco Processing	14.53	1.75	8.72
纺织业	Textile Industry	504.20	166.36	269.22
服装及其他纤维制品制造业	Garments and Other Fiber Products	112.06	13.15	71.23
皮革毛皮羽绒及其制品业	Leather, Furs, Down and Related Products	52.87	5.95	22.55
木材加工及竹藤棕草制品业	Timber Processing, Bamboo, Cane, Palm Fiber and Straw Products	26.60	4.02	14.13
家具制造业	Furniture Manufacturing	14.47	1.56	7.29
造纸及纸制品业	Papermaking and Paper Products	45.65	15.62	23.13
印刷业记录媒介的复制	Printing and Record Pressing	28.75	6.82	18.63
文教体育用品制造业	Stationery, Educational and Sports Goods	26.35	1.90	15.26
石油加工及炼焦业	Petroleum Processing and Coking Produets	34.43	17.31	46.22
化学原料及制品制造业	Raw Chemical Materials and Chemical Products	311.57	128.97	249.32
医药制造业	Medical and Pharmaceutical Products	58.60	16.81	39.19
化学纤维制造业	Chemical Fibers	91.92	57.88	135.90
橡胶制品业	Rubber Products	34.62	8.99	23.50
塑料制品业	Plastic Products	87.71	21.72	58.41
非金属矿物制品业	Nonmetal Mineral Products	226.03	70.65	161.36
黑色金属冶炼及压延加工业	Smelting and Pressing of Ferrous Metals	162.83	45.48	138.58
有色金属冶炼及压延加工业	Smelting and Pressing of Noferrous Metals	66.50	17.52	27.58
金属制品业	Metal Products	163.73	27.10	91.45
普通机械制造业	Ordinary Machinery Manufacturing	330.12	59.97	196.15
专用设备制造业	Special Purposes Equipment Manufacturing	188.07	35.27	116.54
交通运输设备制造业	Transportation Equipment Manufacturing	200.91	65.63	148.78
电气机械及器材制造业	Electric Equipment and Machinery	258.06	45.32	155.92
电子及通信设备制造业	Electronic and Telecommunications	241.42	69.98	130.83
仪器仪表及文化办公用机械	Instruments, Meters, Cultural and Official Machinery	43.78	8.41	29.72
其他制造业	Other Manufactruing	40.66	5.92	22.28
电力蒸气热水生产供应业	Eletricity Power, Steam and Hot Water Production and Supply	124.47	165.49	245.76
煤气的生产和供应业	Gas Production and Supply	4.48	3.87	11.64
自来水的生产和供应业	Tap Water Production and Supply	13.94	12.40	41.51

Continued 1

(100 000 000 yuan)

产品销售收入 Revnue of Product Sales	产品销售成本 Costs of Product Sales	产品销售税金及附加 Product Sales Pre-Tax and Related Payments	产品销售利润 Product Sales After-Tax Profits	利润总额 Total After-Tax Profits	本年应交增值税 Added Value Tax	利税总额 Total Pre-Tax Profits
6873.68	**5812.63**	**67.37**	**779.40**	**141.73**	**241.10**	**450.20**
2125.03	1774.59	34.01	256.72	19.09	91.52	144.62
3215.04	2744.92	25.64	348.88	65.66	99.86	191.16
229.46	190.28	1.19	31.70	11.99	9.84	23.01
664.00	564.56	3.42	70.27	20.72	20.27	44.41
502.28	418.86	2.38	56.94	23.50	15.38	41.27
3163.01	2703.87	36.47	323.05	59.72	100.57	196.76
2076.87	1805.29	26.19	194.95	32.02	62.24	120.45
1086.14	898.58	10.28	128.10	27.69	38.33	76.30
3710.67	3108.76	30.90	456.35	82.01	140.53	253.44
94.69	71.48	1.15	20.21	1.15	5.95	8.24
1313.39	1137.42	13.52	130.16	26.80	57.42	97.73
2302.58	1899.86	16.23	305.99	54.07	77.17	147.46
2027.73	1684.24	31.18	251.22	75.95	88.82	195.95
1388.80	1175.70	10.61	162.07	15.86	47.53	74.01
3457.15	2952.69	25.57	366.11	49.91	104.75	180.23
52.46	36.77	0.64	14.37	0.20	4.00	4.85
11.39	9.80	0.13	1.45	0.13	0.76	1.02
2.85	2.57	0.02	0.26	0.02	0.11	0.15
2.21	1.49	0.01	0.61	0.10	0.08	0.19
32.41	24.85	0.64	5.18	0.48	1.60	2.72
262.79	238.55	0.69	16.79	2.10	3.39	6.18
109.89	92.12	0.40	10.94	3.75	3.72	7.87
82.55	60.30	7.04	9.94	1.74	4.34	13.12
26.67	11.91	11.18	3.52	2.30	2.91	16.40
995.62	890.22	3.92	87.94	6.66	28.59	39.18
265.44	229.81	1.04	26.69	6.74	6.79	14.56
103.43	90.56	0.40	9.36	1.37	2.89	4.66
48.22	42.35	0.38	4.18	1.06	1.50	2.94
20.66	17.26	0.17	2.51	0.63	0.68	1.48
75.35	63.83	0.41	8.83	0.87	3.04	4.32
50.20	40.47	0.41	7.51	2.36	2.40	5.16
60.74	51.84	0.23	6.62	1.66	1.80	3.69
149.58	130.01	5.83	12.51	1.79	6.75	14.37
599.52	493.19	5.14	85.47	14.17	21.85	41.17
95.68	71.23	0.54	15.99	3.34	4.71	8.59
179.85	153.97	0.78	22.76	9.32	6.98	17.08
57.12	47.45	0.53	7.43	1.03	2.07	3.62
164.86	140.24	0.89	18.75	2.77	5.50	9.16
341.73	285.91	3.70	40.49	3.52	14.16	21.38
272.86	249.83	1.60	19.25	0.67	6.86	8.59
133.11	119.05	0.63	11.21	1.94	3.23	5.80
279.86	236.41	1.88	30.87	5.22	8.19	15.30
490.62	392.84	2.59	76.07	16.11	18.82	37.52
306.50	248.82	1.70	45.24	6.45	10.34	18.48
367.57	316.50	6.36	36.03	6.30	11.51	24.18
456.67	366.04	3.19	59.30	17.43	17.74	38.35
334.18	280.19	1.20	40.82	6.14	9.14	16.49
62.23	49.44	0.26	9.60	1.25	2.24	3.75
81.80	71.17	0.73	7.46	0.66	2.56	3.96
274.31	235.18	2.45	22.68	12.38	18.81	33.63
5.83	7.45	0.02	−1.79	−0.81	0.17	−0.62
16.60	12.76	0.16	2.50	−0.10	0.83	0.89

10—12 国有独立核算工业企业主要指标(1996)

单位:亿元

行业	Items	企业单位数(个) Number of Enterprises (Unit)	工业总产值 Gross Output Value of Industry	工业增加值 Added-Value of Industry
总计	**National Total**	**3853**	**2175.51**	**562.91**
按轻重工业分	**Grouped by Light & Heavy Industry**			
轻工业	Light Industry	2049	744.43	174.42
以农产品为原料	Using Farm Products as Raw Materials	1554	580.20	133.51
以非农产品为原料	Using Non-Farm Products as Raw Materials	495	164.23	40.91
重工业	Heavy Industry	1804	1431.08	388.49
采掘工业	Extraction	64	68.65	36.84
原料工业	Raw Materials	356	637.04	179.31
加工工业	Manufacturing	1384	725.39	172.34
按企业规模分	**Grouped by Size of Enterprises**			
大型企业	Large	314	1198.90	353.41
中型企业	Medium	783	567.59	127.37
小型企业	Small	2756	409.01	82.13
按行业分	**Grouped by Size of Enterprises**			
煤炭采选业	Coal Mining and Processing	26	47.34	27.30
石油和天然气开采业	Petroleum and Natural Gas Extraction	1	11.48	5.54
黑色金属矿采选业	Ferrous Metals Mining and Processing	2	1.79	0.79
有色金属矿采选业	Nonferrous Metals Mining and Processing	5	1.68	0.71
非金属矿采选业	Nonmetal Minerals Mining and Processing	41	12.33	6.41
其他矿采选业	Other Minerals Mining and Processing			
木材及竹材采运业	Logging and Transport of Timber and Bamboo			
食品加工业	Food Processing	620	160.81	21.18
食品制造业	Food Manufacturing	221	47.99	11.48
饮料制造业	Beverage Manufacturing	103	50.14	15.91
烟草加工业	Tobacco Processing	7	25.52	18.10
纺织业	Textile Industry	314	243.49	52.38
服装及其他纤维制品制造业	Garments and Other Fiber Products	35	9.18	1.72
皮革毛皮羽绒及其制品业	Leather, Furs, Down and Related Products	24	5.30	1.59
木材加工及竹藤棕草制品业	Timber Processing, Bamboo, Cane, Palm Fiber and Straw Products	20	1.73	0.39
家具制造业	Furniture Manufacturing	16	1.59	0.53
造纸及纸制品业	Papermaking and Paper Products	46	14.20	3.69
印刷业记录媒介的复制	Printing and Record Pressing	126	9.81	3.29
文教体育用品制造业	Stationery, Educational and Sports Goods	9	1.58	0.45
石油加工及炼焦业	Petroleum Processing and Coking Produets	11	108.96	20.08
化学原料及制品制造业	Raw Chemical Materials and Chemical Products	280	305.47	75.32
医药制造业	Medical and Pharmaceutical Products	106	56.31	13.51
化学纤维制造业	Chemical Fibers	21	19.59	3.20
橡胶制品业	Rubber Products	22	10.45	2.67
塑料制品业	Plastic Products	45	7.68	1.43
非金属矿物制品业	Nonmetal Mineral Products	318	74.97	22.67
黑色金属冶炼及压延加工业	Smelting and Pressing of Ferrous Metals	37	110.58	20.30
有色金属冶炼及压延加工业	Smelting and Pressing of Noferrous Metals	20	16.40	3.16
金属制品业	Metal Products	112	21.01	5.18
普通机械制造业	Ordinary Machinery Manufacturing	289	167.04	44.40
专用设备制造业	Special Purposes Equipment Manufacturing	270	83.02	19.13
交通运输设备制造业	Transportation Equipment Manufacturing	156	178.79	41.78
电气机械及器材制造业	Electric Equipment and Machinery	155	56.63	13.74
电子及通信设备制造业	Electronic and Telecommunications	114	96.94	20.66
仪器仪表及文化办公用机械	Instruments, Meters, Cultural and Official Machinery	68	13.70	4.32
其他制造业	Other Manufactruing	61	3.98	0.94
电力蒸气及水生产供应业	Eletricity Power, Steam and Hot Water Production and Supply	62	180.80	74.31
煤气的生产和供应业	Gas Production and Supply	13	6.04	0.24
自来水的生产和供应业	Tap Water Production and Supply	74	10.79	4.22

MAJOR INDICATORS OF STATE-OWNED INDUSTRIAL ENTERPRISES WITH INDEPENDENT ACCOUNTING SYSTEM

(100 000 000 yuan)

资本金合计 Total Capital Assets	资产合计 Total Prperty	流动资产合计 Circulating Funds	流动资产年平均余额 Average Balance Circulating Funds	固定资产合计 Fixed Assets	固定资产原价 Original Value of Fixed Assets	固定资产净值年平均余额 Average Balances Net Value of Fixed Asstes
676.56	**3025.62**	**1293.80**	**1202.92**	**1505.86**	**1862.97**	**1222.60**
177.46	901.12	394.62	370.17	446.49	508.66	355.97
110.71	614.02	277.27	260.77	297.74	347.26	243.90
66.75	287.11	117.35	109.40	148.75	161.41	112.07
499.09	2124.49	899.18	832.75	1059.37	1354.31	866.63
45.02	130.13	42.71	40.45	77.52	114.81	69.42
279.49	984.51	336.07	311.22	580.70	745.17	469.03
174.58	1009.85	520.40	481.09	401.15	494.33	328.19
419.33	1759.43	716.72	664.67	901.65	1148.97	728.22
158.05	785.58	351.95	327.98	375.41	444.41	304.71
99.18	480.60	225.14	210.27	228.80	269.59	189.67
30.21	74.60	25.19	24.03	44.00	67.20	40.75
8.41	30.98	9.62	9.04	18.72	27.83	16.66
0.81	3.14	1.35	1.21	1.72	2.42	1.64
1.02	3.79	1.16	0.98	1.85	1.98	1.46
7.75	36.39	14.58	14.29	20.42	25.85	17.20
18.33	108.61	57.15	53.29	47.63	56.73	41.55
9.23	51.92	22.44	20.37	24.49	26.79	19.84
10.73	64.01	31.19	29.78	29.40	33.72	24.44
4.16	24.74	10.33	7.73	12.91	15.78	11.04
55.07	295.98	123.80	120.95	151.43	176.05	120.46
2.32	10.83	5.58	4.63	4.67	5.52	4.15
1.24	6.66	3.70	3.14	2.48	3.19	2.30
0.45	2.91	1.26	1.13	1.34	1.45	0.93
0.28	1.97	0.96	0.91	0.88	1.10	0.78
2.87	20.36	8.46	7.13	10.81	11.02	7.68
3.12	14.34	5.72	5.39	7.72	10.22	6.86
0.30	1.79	1.12	0.86	0.50	0.64	0.49
23.93	81.29	34.25	34.41	43.16	69.17	28.70
108.31	397.63	139.22	132.71	224.70	301.33	190.15
16.08	69.68	32.69	31.07	32.96	30.88	21.79
5.72	32.36	8.99	9.29	18.86	19.89	12.76
1.98	12.55	5.51	5.97	5.45	5.61	3.64
1.96	12.22	4.66	4.60	6.45	6.79	4.47
23.96	145.84	49.15	46.60	82.53	95.93	64.58
46.55	178.82	74.37	68.55	89.76	93.72	64.05
2.21	19.69	8.47	7.80	9.13	10.97	7.60
6.11	30.18	15.90	14.24	12.38	14.70	10.32
34.24	233.23	138.17	129.87	82.78	105.41	66.22
21.02	116.21	60.31	57.12	49.36	62.26	42.46
46.38	232.26	115.51	101.70	88.02	99.60	69.41
12.71	70.37	39.25	37.61	26.57	32.29	21.88
25.71	167.43	96.16	87.85	49.20	62.77	37.54
7.20	33.20	17.07	15.88	14.03	18.24	11.69
1.25	4.43	2.07	1.87	1.95	2.45	1.73
104.04	356.47	108.49	94.60	231.19	300.53	201.37
6.83	19.54	4.41	4.32	14.34	16.22	11.71
23.67	58.17	15.12	11.63	41.49	46.06	31.71

续表 1

单位:亿元

行业	Items	流动负债合计 Circulating Liabilities	长期负债合计 Long-Term Liabilities	所有者权益 Total Owner's Rights and Interests
总计	**National Total**	**1333.02**	**581.93**	**1110.44**
按轻重工业分	**Grouped by Light & Heavy Industry**			
轻工业	Light Industry	472.94	164.71	263.46
以农产品为原料	Using Farm Products as Raw Materials	343.80	109.61	160.61
以非农产品为原料	Using Non-Farm Products as Raw Materials	129.14	55.11	102.85
重工业	Heavy Industry	860.08	417.22	846.99
采掘工业	Extraction	45.49	25.70	58.94
原料工业	Raw Materials	315.73	205.12	463.38
加工工业	Manufacturing	498.86	186.40	324.67
按企业规模分	**Grouped by Size of Enterprises**			
大型企业	Large	671.02	367.31	721.10
中型企业	Medium	389.43	141.32	254.83
小型企业	Small	272.57	73.30	134.51
按行业分	**Grouped by Size of Enterprises**			
煤炭采选业	Coal Mining and Processing	30.23	11.38	32.99
石油和天然气开采业	Petroleum and Natural Gas Extraction	7.63	9.96	13.39
黑色金属矿采选业	Ferrous Metals Mining and Processing	1.60	0.61	0.92
有色金属矿采选业	Nonferrous Metals Mining and Processing	1.26	1.07	1.46
非金属矿采选业	Nonmetal Minerals Mining and Processing	13.28	5.17	17.94
其他矿采选业	Other Minerals Mining and Processing			
木材及竹材采运业	Logging and Transport of Timber and Bamboo			
食品加工业	Food Processing	75.59	9.58	23.43
食品制造业	Food Manufacturing	29.23	6.64	16.05
饮料制造业	Beverage Manufacturing	39.23	6.95	17.83
烟草加工业	Tobacco Processing	14.37	1.75	8.62
纺织业	Textile Industry	147.55	73.62	74.81
服装及其他纤维制品制造业	Garments and Other Fiber Products	5.75	1.15	3.93
皮革毛皮羽绒及其制品业	Leather, Furs, Down and Related Products	4.48	0.84	1.34
木材加工及竹藤棕草制品业	Timber Processing, Bamboo, Cane, Palm Fiber and Straw Products	1.78	0.28	0.84
家具制造业	Furniture Manufacturing	0.92	0.49	0.56
造纸及纸制品业	Papermaking and Paper Products	11.03	4.34	4.99
印刷业记录媒介的复制	Printing and Record Pressing	7.51	2.82	4.01
文教体育用品制造业	Stationery, Educational and Sports Goods	1.40	0.11	0.28
石油加工及炼焦业	Petroleum Processing and Coking Produets	24.41	15.86	41.02
化学原料及制品制造业	Raw Chemical Materials and Chemical Products	141.27	94.97	161.39
医药制造业	Medical and Pharmaceutical Products	33.99	10.78	24.91
化学纤维制造业	Chemical Fibers	15.56	8.29	8.51
橡胶制品业	Rubber Products	6.25	3.31	2.99
塑料制品业	Plastic Products	6.40	3.34	2.48
非金属矿物制品业	Nonmetal Mineral Products	58.17	32.49	55.22
黑色金属冶炼及压延加工业	Smelting and Pressing of Ferrous Metals	80.48	19.65	78.69
有色金属冶炼及压延加工业	Smelting and Pressing of Noferrous Metals	8.22	6.28	5.20
金属制品业	Metal Products	15.66	4.11	10.42
普通机械制造业	Ordinary Machinery Manufacturing	129.98	30.15	73.14
专用设备制造业	Special Purposes Equipment Manufacturing	60.47	16.78	38.96
交通运输设备制造业	Transportation Equipment Manufacturing	98.77	46.31	87.18
电气机械及器材制造业	Electric Equipment and Machinery	37.43	9.29	23.65
电子及通信设备制造业	Electronic and Telecommunications	90.24	39.34	37.85
仪器仪表及文化办公用机械	Instruments, Meters, Cultural and Official Machinery	17.08	4.80	11.32
其他制造业	Other Manufactruing	2.45	0.48	1.49
电力蒸气热水生产供应业	Eletricity Power, Steam and Hot Water Production and Supply	98.24	83.74	174.49
煤气的生产和供应业	Gas Production and Supply	4.09	3.56	11.61
自来水的生产和供应业	Tap Water Production and Supply	10.60	11.61	35.96

Continued 1

(100 000 000 yuan)

产品销售收入 Revnue of Product Sales	产品销售成本 Costs of Product Sales	产品销售税金及附加 Product Sales Pre-Tax and Related Payments	产品销售利润 Product Sales After-Tax Profits	利润总额 Total After-Tax Profits	本年应交增值税 Added Value Tax	利税总额 Total Pre-Tax Profits
2125.03	**1774.59**	**34.01**	**256.72**	**19.09**	**91.52**	**144.62**
684.39	574.45	18.85	70.76	−1.97	26.60	43.48
535.77	454.96	17.92	50.19	0.02	19.62	37.55
148.62	119.49	0.93	20.48	−1.99	6.98	5.93
1440.64	1200.14	15.16	186.05	21.06	64.92	101.14
69.74	50.72	0.81	17.42	0.13	5.17	6.11
670.43	577.30	8.48	66.96	14.40	35.21	58.09
700.47	572.12	5.87	101.67	6.54	24.54	36.95
1247.19	1032.78	26.33	153.69	27.26	59.45	113.04
526.58	441.35	5.86	65.25	−3.67	21.12	23.32
351.26	300.47	1.82	37.78	−4.50	10.95	8.27
49.23	34.16	0.61	13.89	0.03	3.87	4.50
11.39	9.80	0.13	1.45	0.13	0.76	1.02
1.51	1.38	0.01	0.12	−0.07	0.09	0.03
1.59	0.98	0.01	0.52	0.07	0.08	0.16
11.41	7.58	0.31	2.85	−0.36	0.89	0.84
130.36	119.98	0.18	7.03	−1.35	1.14	−0.03
48.75	41.31	0.08	4.77	1.99	1.32	3.40
44.91	31.21	5.47	5.70	0.25	2.86	8.58
26.33	11.62	11.18	3.48	2.29	2.90	16.37
235.68	211.17	0.75	21.29	−3.31	9.13	6.56
8.35	7.22	0.02	0.97	−0.06	0.14	0.10
4.61	3.74	0.02	0.58	−0.14	0.20	0.07
1.52	1.35	0.02	0.10	−0.02	0.06	0.05
1.47	1.11	0.01	0.26	0.08	0.07	0.16
13.13	10.20	0.06	2.41	0.18	0.72	0.96
9.03	7.14	0.11	1.55	−0.10	0.57	0.59
1.27	1.06	0.00	0.17	−0.06	0.04	−0.02
129.21	112.01	5.46	11.07	1.62	6.27	13.35
283.49	230.08	1.71	48.02	6.56	11.75	20.02
52.32	39.49	0.22	8.55	1.17	2.82	4.21
19.56	17.11	0.05	2.28	−0.20	0.58	0.44
10.00	8.02	0.17	1.55	−0.14	0.43	0.47
6.83	5.66	0.04	0.97	−0.14	0.28	0.19
67.74	55.04	0.41	9.21	−2.27	4.01	2.15
111.64	103.00	0.40	7.38	−0.51	4.04	3.93
13.51	11.78	0.03	1.53	0.25	0.40	0.69
19.99	16.17	0.12	2.97	0.11	0.83	1.06
164.14	129.27	0.78	28.19	3.85	6.71	11.34
77.04	60.92	0.29	13.48	0.38	2.65	3.33
178.65	152.69	3.68	18.05	2.82	5.91	12.41
52.53	41.76	0.22	8.28	0.92	2.44	3.58
94.88	78.98	0.33	11.79	−1.42	2.89	1.80
13.19	9.55	0.06	3.05	−0.34	0.65	0.37
3.22	2.79	0.03	0.21	−0.16	0.09	−0.04
210.48	184.33	0.93	13.12	8.15	13.07	22.15
5.44	7.10	0.02	−1.83	−0.80	0.16	−0.62
10.29	7.62	0.08	1.62	−0.32	0.67	0.43

10—13 集体经济独立核算工业企业主要指标(1996)

单位:亿元

行　　业	Items	企业单位数(个) Number of Enterprises (Unit)	工业总产值 Gross Output Value of Industry	工业增加值 Added-Value of Industry
总　计	**National Total**	**30234**	**3876.85**	**872.04**
按轻重工业分	**Grouped by Light & Heavy Industry**			
轻工业	Light Industry	14149	1964.12	435.38
以农产品为原料	Using Farm Products as Raw Materials	8567	1303.36	286.64
以非农产品为原料	Using Non-Farm Products as Raw Materials	5582	660.76	148.75
重工业	Heavy Industry	16085	1912.73	436.65
采掘工业	Extraction	479	31.69	8.89
原料工业	Raw Materials	2730	553.75	116.33
加工工业	Manufacturing	12876	1327.28	311.43
按企业规模分	**Grouped by Size of Enterprises**			
大型企业	Large	117	400.55	85.52
中型企业	Medium	913	789.76	173.76
小型企业	Small	29204	2686.54	612.76
按行业分	**Grouped by Size of Enterprises**			
煤炭采选业	Coal Mining and Processing	36	3.74	1.34
石油和天然气开采业	Petroleum and Natural Gas Extraction			
黑色金属矿采选业	Ferrous Metals Mining and Processing	6	1.71	0.46
有色金属矿采选业	Nonferrous Metals Mining and Processing	7	1.04	0.10
非金属矿采选业	Nonmetal Minerals Mining and Processing	471	26.65	7.61
其他矿采选业	Other Minerals Mining and Processing			
木材及竹材采运业	Logging and Transport of Timber and Bamboo			
食品加工业	Food Processing	960	88.20	14.39
食品制造业	Food Manufacturing	509	39.47	8.02
饮料制造业	Beverage Manufacturing	268	20.17	5.25
烟草加工业	Tobacco Processing	2	0.36	0.06
纺织业	Textile Industry	2732	730.65	160.78
服装及其他纤维制品制造业	Garments and Other Fiber Products	1172	201.80	46.30
皮革毛皮羽绒及其制品业	Leather, Furs, Down and Related Products	554	59.84	13.50
木材加工及竹藤棕草制品业	Timber Processing, Bamboo, Cane, Palm Fiber and Straw Products	424	29.63	6.28
家具制造业	Furniture Manufacturing	352	18.41	4.37
造纸及纸制品业	Papermaking and Paper Products	560	47.92	11.76
印刷业记录媒介的复制	Printing and Record Pressing	841	41.00	10.43
文教体育用品制造业	Stationery, Educational and Sports Goods	420	42.90	10.62
石油加工及炼焦业	Petroleum Processing and Coking Produets	95	18.93	3.35
化学原料及制品制造业	Raw Chemical Materials and Chemical Products	2198	307.69	67.07
医药制造业	Medical and Pharmaceutical Products	192	33.95	8.86
化学纤维制造业	Chemical Fibers	173	70.67	13.71
橡胶制品业	Rubber Products	339	32.65	7.68
塑料制品业	Plastic Products	1310	122.13	26.76
非金属矿物制品业	Nonmetal Mineral Products	4156	288.52	73.87
黑色金属冶炼及压延加工业	Smelting and Pressing of Ferrous Metals	333	149.64	28.59
有色金属冶炼及压延加工业	Smelting and Pressing of Noferrous Metals	401	125.43	24.84
金属制品业	Metal Products	2274	223.28	49.48
普通机械制造业	Ordinary Machinery Manufacturing	2581	269.82	65.52
专用设备制造业	Special Purposes Equipment Manufacturing	1536	211.40	49.91
交通运输设备制造业	Transportation Equipment Manufacturing	1070	162.10	35.75
电气机械及器材制造业	Electric Equipment and Machinery	1803	300.33	67.23
电子及通信设备制造业	Electronic and Telecommunications	644	90.23	20.33
仪器仪表及文化办公用机械	Instruments, Meters, Cultural and Official Machinery	374	27.95	7.54
其他制造业	Other Manufactruing	925	73.08	16.48
电力蒸气热水生产供应业	Eletricity Power, Steam and Hot Water Production and Supply	33	7.51	1.62
煤气的生产和供应业	Gas Production and Supply	2	0.08	0.03
自来水的生产和供应业	Tap Water Production and Supply	481	7.94	2.15

MAJOR INDICATORS OF COLLECTIVE-OWNED INDUSTRIAL ENTERPRISES WITH INDEPENDENT ACCOUNTING SYSTEM

(100 000 000 yuan)

资本金合计 Total Capital Assets	资产合计 Total Prperty	流动资产合计 Circulating Funds	流动资产年平均余额 Average Balance Circulating Funds	固定资产合计 Fixed Assets	固定资产原价 Original Value of Fixed Assets	固定资产净值年平均余额 Average Balances Net Value of Fixed Asstes
675.76	**2761.01**	**1545.03**	**1474.52**	**1029.64**	**1226.22**	**838.12**
327.73	1320.24	716.06	684.60	515.86	611.93	422.72
211.28	858.36	448.56	427.61	352.20	418.07	287.24
116.45	461.88	267.50	256.99	163.66	193.86	135.48
348.03	1440.76	828.97	789.92	513.78	614.30	415.40
4.98	16.14	7.64	7.06	7.43	9.40	6.44
96.14	397.01	198.94	192.66	166.14	184.85	129.44
246.91	1027.60	622.39	590.19	340.21	420.04	279.52
74.91	282.76	131.89	120.58	129.53	147.87	100.06
159.34	637.41	332.03	316.77	246.93	295.98	201.84
441.52	1840.83	1081.11	1037.16	653.18	782.37	536.22
0.75	2.75	1.04	0.91	1.52	1.80	1.23
0.21	1.01	0.57	0.54	0.41	0.43	0.34
0.14	1.18	0.20	0.17	0.95	1.02	0.90
4.36	12.95	6.74	6.25	5.30	7.10	4.65
9.81	46.98	27.76	25.93	15.82	17.99	12.36
6.42	26.21	14.95	13.35	10.19	12.07	8.63
4.55	17.14	9.22	8.96	7.10	7.81	5.50
0.05	0.27	0.20	0.18	0.07	0.08	0.05
118.37	492.26	233.42	225.93	222.53	268.05	181.56
35.72	118.25	68.83	64.32	41.12	47.91	34.12
9.44	38.46	24.92	24.12	11.34	13.81	10.11
4.79	17.49	9.94	9.29	6.45	7.53	5.39
3.78	14.24	8.97	8.64	4.42	5.24	3.73
7.65	38.76	20.39	18.27	16.98	16.84	11.50
7.84	31.01	18.79	17.21	10.61	12.83	8.86
7.69	26.27	15.68	14.94	8.62	9.82	7.42
2.87	13.24	6.38	6.16	5.38	5.65	4.44
49.68	201.12	110.26	106.98	77.90	89.66	62.61
6.00	26.01	15.29	14.18	9.40	11.33	7.87
13.52	59.48	21.49	20.77	33.35	38.82	28.82
6.07	25.23	14.66	13.55	9.19	10.70	7.31
22.60	88.50	48.26	46.48	33.06	41.00	28.13
56.32	217.76	115.54	113.62	88.19	108.08	71.37
27.52	120.31	61.16	58.88	47.15	49.35	35.75
14.86	66.77	40.13	38.60	23.22	26.28	18.78
38.64	158.02	94.63	89.81	53.43	62.41	42.31
49.77	219.46	139.34	130.53	70.70	88.72	57.29
40.25	165.89	105.20	99.07	51.59	66.39	41.86
26.86	112.11	65.35	63.17	40.61	47.21	32.78
50.66	217.87	137.13	128.47	63.77	75.86	52.89
21.69	86.18	55.04	53.00	23.51	31.24	20.45
7.33	27.38	16.51	15.98	8.83	10.15	6.64
10.79	49.11	28.92	28.13	14.34	18.26	12.63
4.44	14.61	4.45	4.60	6.79	8.27	5.26
0.01	0.08	0.03	0.02	0.05	0.06	0.05
4.31	9.68	3.65	3.53	5.73	6.45	4.49

续表 1

单位:亿元

行　业	Items	流动负债合计 Circulating Liabilities	长期负债合计 Long-Term Liabilities	所有者权益 Total Owners Rights and Interests
总　计	**National Total**	**1641.34**	**315.88**	**804.40**
按轻重工业分	**Grouped by Light & Heavy Industry**			
轻工业	Light Industry	785.82	164.00	371.00
以农产品为原料	Using Farm Products as Raw Materials	511.08	110.22	237.62
以非农产品为原料	Using Non-Farm Products as Raw Materials	274.74	53.79	133.38
重工业	Heavy Industry	855.52	151.88	433.41
采掘工业	Extraction	8.48	1.69	5.97
原料工业	Raw Materials	228.00	49.81	119.18
加工工业	Manufacturing	619.05	100.38	308.25
按企业规模分	**Grouped by Size of Enterprises**			
大型企业	Large	121.60	43.92	117.24
中型企业	Medium	342.88	87.03	208.23
小型企业	Small	1176.87	184.93	478.93
按行业分	**Grouped by Size of Enterprises**			
煤炭采选业	Coal Mining and Processing	1.47	0.45	0.83
石油和天然气开采业	Petroleum and Natural Gas Extraction			
黑色金属矿采选业	Ferrous Metals Mining and Processing	0.65	0.03	0.33
有色金属矿采选业	Nonferrous Metals Mining and Processing	0.72	0.27	0.20
非金属矿采选业	Nonmetal Minerals Mining and Processing	6.50	1.12	5.34
其他矿采选业	Other Minerals Mining and Processing			
木材及竹材采运业	Logging and Transport of Timber and Bamboo			
食品加工业	Food Processing	31.36	4.20	11.42
食品制造业	Food Manufacturing	16.49	3.00	6.72
饮料制造业	Beverage Manufacturing	8.93	2.53	5.67
烟草加工业	Tobacco Processing	0.16	0.01	0.10
纺织业	Textile Industry	285.21	72.89	134.72
服装及其他纤维制品制造业	Garments and Other Fiber Products	70.53	8.87	38.85
皮革毛皮羽绒及其制品业	Leather, Furs, Down and Related Products	26.05	3.29	9.11
木材加工及竹藤棕草制品业	Timber Processing, Bamboo, Cane, Palm Fiber and Straw Products	11.06	1.72	4.71
家具制造业	Furniture Manufacturing	9.36	0.81	4.06
造纸及纸制品业	Papermaking and Paper Products	22.85	7.67	8.24
印刷业记录媒介的复制	Printing and Record Pressing	17.08	3.45	10.48
文教体育用品制造业	Stationery, Educational and Sports Goods	15.66	1.22	9.41
石油加工及炼焦业	Petroleum Processing and Coking Produets	7.88	0.87	4.50
化学原料及制品制造业	Raw Chemical Materials and Chemical Products	119.62	20.52	60.95
医药制造业	Medical and Pharmaceutical Products	14.83	3.59	7.59
化学纤维制造业	Chemical Fibers	27.24	17.54	14.70
橡胶制品业	Rubber Products	15.26	2.66	7.31
塑料制品业	Plastic Products	51.33	11.47	25.70
非金属矿物制品业	Nonmetal Mineral Products	129.50	22.31	65.95
黑色金属冶炼及压延加工业	Smelting and Pressing of Ferrous Metals	67.29	16.82	36.20
有色金属冶炼及压延加工业	Smelting and Pressing of Noferrous Metals	43.65	7.73	15.39
金属制品业	Metal Products	96.79	14.83	46.41
普通机械制造业	Ordinary Machinery Manufacturing	139.89	18.65	60.92
专用设备制造业	Special Purposes Equipment Manufacturing	101.26	12.01	52.62
交通运输设备制造业	Transportation Equipment Manufacturing	65.64	11.28	35.18
电气机械及器材制造业	Electric Equipment and Machinery	131.43	22.84	63.70
电子及通信设备制造业	Electronic and Telecommunications	49.83	11.01	25.31
仪器仪表及文化办公用机械	Instruments, Meters, Cultural and Official Machinery	16.48	2.36	8.54
其他制造业	Other Manufactruing	29.85	4.22	12.04
电力蒸气热水生产供应业	Eletricity Power, Steam and Hot Water Production and Supply	6.06	2.87	5.68
煤气的生产和供应业	Gas Production and Supply	0.08	0.01	−0.01
自来水的生产和供应业	Tap Water Production and Supply	3.33	0.79	5.55

Continued 1

(100 000 000 yuan)

产品销售收入 Revnue of Product Sales	产品销售成本 Costs of Product Sales	产品销售税金及附加 Product Sales Pre-Tax and Related Payments	产品销售利润 Product Sales After-Tax Profits	利润总额 Total After-Tax Profits	本年应交增值税 Added Value Tax	利税总额 Total Pre-Tax Profits
3215.04	**2744.92**	**25.64**	**348.88**	**65.66**	**99.86**	**191.16**
1620.18	1402.79	13.24	162.11	29.34	46.89	89.47
1085.35	954.24	6.60	101.73	19.02	30.59	56.21
534.83	448.55	6.64	60.38	10.32	16.30	33.26
1594.86	1342.12	12.41	186.77	36.32	52.97	101.70
24.47	20.37	0.33	2.76	1.02	0.76	2.11
465.02	409.11	3.22	42.94	8.84	13.33	25.39
1105.37	912.64	8.85	141.07	26.45	38.89	74.19
349.54	301.86	2.87	37.65	18.16	9.85	30.88
680.40	581.05	3.94	75.81	15.62	20.58	40.15
2185.10	1862.01	18.83	235.42	31.88	69.42	120.13
3.23	2.60	0.03	0.47	0.18	0.13	0.34
1.34	1.18	0.01	0.14	0.09	0.02	0.11
0.61	0.51	0.00	0.09	0.02	0.01	0.03
20.51	16.88	0.33	2.29	0.85	0.69	1.86
76.47	68.67	0.41	5.96	2.26	1.58	4.25
32.85	27.93	0.28	3.12	0.58	1.10	1.96
17.71	13.94	0.92	1.69	0.19	0.65	1.76
0.35	0.29	0.00	0.04	0.01	0.01	0.02
613.59	549.01	2.85	53.44	7.86	15.67	26.38
161.25	138.76	0.84	17.15	4.43	4.83	10.10
47.13	40.43	0.27	4.94	0.65	1.62	2.54
24.06	21.18	0.23	1.88	0.37	0.76	1.36
14.14	11.85	0.15	1.70	0.31	0.47	0.93
42.99	36.48	0.29	4.89	0.80	1.64	2.73
34.98	28.43	0.29	4.84	1.85	1.59	3.73
37.62	31.63	0.18	4.51	1.24	1.16	2.58
17.42	15.45	0.36	1.34	0.25	0.44	1.05
258.00	215.51	2.83	30.02	6.97	8.31	18.10
27.33	20.61	0.28	4.76	0.99	0.97	2.24
60.44	53.05	0.33	5.79	1.16	1.29	2.78
27.14	22.63	0.22	3.36	0.56	1.13	1.92
101.45	86.36	0.68	11.36	1.45	3.41	5.54
233.95	196.53	3.11	27.68	6.06	8.62	17.79
133.00	120.85	0.57	10.07	1.63	2.32	4.52
96.20	85.96	0.54	8.07	1.73	2.26	4.53
181.44	152.99	1.54	20.18	2.71	5.56	9.80
218.38	175.93	1.57	31.58	5.42	8.65	15.64
185.32	152.99	1.12	24.53	3.93	5.91	10.97
134.12	116.95	2.27	12.03	2.91	3.70	8.88
245.29	200.84	1.70	30.69	6.81	9.04	17.55
72.70	58.98	0.51	9.77	0.48	2.88	3.86
21.62	16.57	0.16	3.67	0.39	1.00	1.54
59.52	51.63	0.63	5.73	0.36	1.97	2.95
6.52	6.10	0.06	0.28	−0.03	0.32	0.35
0.07	0.07	0.00				
6.30	5.14	0.08	0.88	0.21	0.16	0.46

10－14 全部独立核算工业企业主要经济效益指标(1996)

单位：%

行业	Items	企业亏损面 Rate of Loss Making Enterprises	产值利税率 Rate Between Pre-Tax Profit and Output Value	销售利税率 Rate Between Pre-Tax Profit and Sales
总计	**National Total**	**26.00**	**5.83**	**6.55**
按经济类型分	**Grouped by Ownership**			
国有经济	State-Owned Enterprises	36.13	6.65	6.81
集体经济	Collective-Owned Enterprises	24.16	4.93	5.95
股份制经济	Share Holding Enterpises	25.42	9.81	10.03
外商投资经济	Foreign Funded Enterprises	29.71	6.03	6.69
港澳台投资经济	Overseas Chinese from HongKong, Macao and Taiwan Funded	32.75	7.47	8.22
按轻重工业分	**Grouped by Light & Heavy Industry**			
轻工业	Light Industry	27.24	5.39	6.22
以农产品为原料	Using Farm Products as Raw Materials	27.82	5.03	5.80
以非农产品为原料	Using Non-Farm Products as Raw Materials	26.28	6.08	7.03
重工业	Heavy Industry	24.80	6.22	6.83
采掘工业	Extraction	14.05	8.16	8.71
原料工业	Raw Materials	27.49	7.08	7.44
加工工业	Manufacturing	24.59	5.68	6.40
按企业规模分	**Grouped by Size of Enterprises**			
大型企业	Large	20.26	9.66	9.66
中型企业	Medium	29.29	4.77	5.33
小型企业	Small	25.91	4.35	5.21
按行业分	**Grouped by Size of Enterprises**			
煤炭采选业	Coal Mining and Processing	24.19	9.49	9.24
石油和天然气开采业	Petroleum and Natural Gas Extraction		8.93	9.00
黑色金属矿采选业	Ferrous Metals Mining and Processing	37.50	4.28	5.25
有色金属矿采选业	Nonferrous Metals Mining and Processing	8.33	6.89	8.49
非金属矿采选业	Nonmetal Minerals Mining and Processing	11.64	6.85	8.39
其他矿采选业	Other Minerals Mining and Processing			
木材及竹材采运业	Logging and Transport of Timber and Bamboo			
食品加工业	Food Processing	20.49	1.98	2.35
食品制造业	Food Manufacturing	30.35	6.66	7.16
饮料制造业	Beverage Manufacturing	23.43	14.22	15.89
烟草加工业	Tobacco Processing	11.11	63.34	61.46
纺织业	Textile Industry	35.06	3.45	3.93
服装及其他纤维制品制造业	Garments and Other Fiber Products	29.42	4.52	5.49
皮革毛皮羽绒及其制品业	Leather, Furs, Down and Related Products	27.77	3.70	4.50
木材加工及竹藤棕草制品业	Timber Processing, Bamboo, Cane, Palm Fiber and Straw Products	15.61	5.41	6.10
家具制造业	Furniture Manufacturing	19.09	5.80	7.17
造纸及纸制品业	Papermaking and Paper Products	22.93	5.26	5.74
印刷业记录媒介的复制	Printing and Record Pressing	23.41	8.88	10.29
文教体育用品制造业	Stationery, Educational and Sports Goods	23.32	5.32	6.07
石油加工及炼焦业	Petroleum Processing and Coking Produets	22.50	10.94	9.61
化学原料及制品制造业	Raw Chemical Materials and Chemical Products	25.56	6.04	6.87
医药制造业	Medical and Pharmaceutical Products	30.25	8.03	8.98
化学纤维制造业	Chemical Fibers	33.74	8.88	9.50
橡胶制品业	Rubber Products	24.82	5.37	6.34
塑料制品业	Plastic Products	28.85	4.76	5.56
非金属矿物制品业	Nonmetal Mineral Products	19.04	5.19	6.26
黑色金属冶炼及压延加工业	Smelting and Pressing of Ferrous Metals	35.22	2.93	3.15
有色金属冶炼及压延加工业	Smelting and Pressing of Noferrous Metals	30.66	3.40	4.36
金属制品业	Metal Products	26.03	4.64	5.47
普通机械制造业	Ordinary Machinery Manufacturing	26.19	6.79	7.65
专用设备制造业	Special Purposes Equipment Manufacturing	29.51	5.35	6.03
交通运输设备制造业	Transportation Equipment Manufacturing	27.43	6.13	6.58
电气机械及器材制造业	Electric Equipment and Machinery	26.93	7.30	8.40
电子及通信设备制造业	Electronic and Telecommunications	33.57	4.50	4.93
仪器仪表及文化办公用机械	Instruments, Meters, Cultural and Official Machinery	32.01	5.39	6.03
其他制造业	Other Manufactruing	25.09	3.97	4.84
电力蒸气热水生产供应业	Eletricity Power, Steam and Hot Water Production and Supply	21.05	13.92	12.26
煤气的生产和供应业	Gas Production and Supply	75.00	－9.54	－10.56
自来水的生产和供应业	Tap Water Production and Supply	7.36	4.75	5.36

MAJOR ECONOMIC RESULT INDITATORS OF TOTAL INDUSTRIAL ENTERPRISES WITH INDEPENDENT ACCOUNTING SYSTEMS

(%)

工业增加值率 Rate Between Value-Added and Total Produsts in Industry	资金利税率 Rate Between Pre-Tax Profit and Assets	百元固定资产原价实现的利税（元） Pre-Tax Profit Per 100 yuan Original Value of Fixed Assets(yuan)	百元销售收入实现的利润（元） Profit Per 100 yuan Sales Revenue (yuan)	成本费用利润率 Rate Between Profit and Cost	流动资产周转次数（次/年） Turnover of Total Circulating Funds (time/year)	全员劳动生产率（元/人） Total Labor Productivity (yuan/person)
20.99	**7.19**	**11.24**	**2.06**	**2.11**	**1.97**	**24842.20**
22.50	5.96	7.76	0.90	0.91	1.77	23416.76
20.17	8.27	15.59	2.04	2.08	2.18	21952.36
19.01	7.87	13.60	5.23	5.52	1.44	33621.42
20.84	6.69	10.33	3.12	3.20	1.99	47163.12
22.33	9.38	16.71	4.68	4.90	2.03	44901.88
20.13	7.55	12.62	1.89	1.93	2.12	23113.20
20.20	7.68	12.34	1.54	1.57	2.36	22313.76
20.01	7.36	13.10	2.55	2.62	1.78	24786.18
21.75	6.93	10.36	2.21	2.26	1.85	26465.96
40.13	6.65	6.61	1.21	1.23	1.99	16139.83
21.66	7.14	8.47	2.04	2.10	2.24	41574.36
21.08	6.81	12.62	2.35	2.40	1.68	22924.78
23.30	9.28	12.29	3.75	3.93	1.92	39546.19
19.57	5.63	8.92	1.14	1.15	1.86	22362.68
20.36	6.35	11.40	1.44	1.46	2.04	21108.21
47.90	7.24	7.02	0.39	0.40	2.10	16141.24
41.89	3.99	3.68	1.13	1.16	1.26	26762.24
32.55	4.02	5.27	0.65	0.64	1.63	14314.34
26.27	5.33	6.25	4.35	4.31	1.92	16086.72
33.10	6.33	8.14	1.48	1.52	1.57	13702.61
13.99	3.73	6.78	0.80	0.80	2.64	24038.49
20.03	8.63	13.30	3.41	3.46	2.32	24561.36
25.70	15.58	25.81	2.11	2.34	1.73	32292.54
60.85	86.31	103.40	8.63	17.06	3.37	335712.12
19.60	5.07	7.48	0.67	0.67	2.43	19799.22
21.00	8.79	17.13	2.54	2.60	2.57	22717.48
20.73	6.67	15.07	1.32	1.33	2.17	25555.91
18.64	8.01	14.39	2.20	2.24	2.31	25004.19
22.70	7.54	16.27	3.03	3.09	1.58	20299.55
21.23	6.53	10.35	1.15	1.16	2.12	19195.99
24.02	11.40	18.38	4.69	4.84	1.93	17831.01
21.22	10.03	22.79	2.73	2.80	2.47	17692.51
15.19	18.94	18.74	1.19	1.25	3.60	57694.89
20.39	7.31	9.39	2.36	2.43	2.19	31531.68
22.27	9.40	16.92	3.49	3.58	1.74	29238.54
17.47	7.02	9.79	5.18	5.44	1.71	41903.17
21.02	7.35	13.21	1.80	1.82	1.92	19516.02
20.19	6.35	10.66	1.68	1.71	1.97	26605.34
23.84	5.82	8.17	1.03	1.04	1.88	15016.91
15.69	3.35	5.33	0.25	0.24	1.90	32035.67
16.63	6.17	12.25	1.46	1.47	2.24	42485.01
20.11	6.60	12.77	1.86	1.90	1.90	24155.66
22.09	7.69	15.46	3.28	3.38	1.48	22623.49
20.98	6.47	12.29	2.10	2.14	1.65	21296.07
19.64	7.49	13.74	1.71	1.75	1.83	28625.63
20.46	10.35	24.09	3.82	3.96	1.77	29266.39
20.18	4.86	10.22	1.84	1.86	1.43	31416.93
22.70	5.46	9.73	2.01	2.03	1.44	17259.45
21.25	6.70	13.98	0.81	0.81	2.12	19522.09
36.31	7.87	7.86	4.51	4.94	2.20	107523.84
4.73	−3.77	−3.76	−13.86	−9.62	1.30	3447.88
31.93	1.73	1.69	−0.62	−0.61	1.09	22233.36

10－15 国有经济独立核算工业企业主要经济效益指标(1996)

单位：%

行业	Items	企业亏损面 Rate of Loss Making Enterprises	产值利税率 Rate Between Pre-Tax Profit and Output Value	销售利税率 Rate Between Pre-Tax Profit and Sales
总计	**National Total**	**36.13**	**6.65**	**6.81**
按轻重工业分	**Grouped by Light & Heavy Industry**			
轻工业	Light Industry	36.51	5.84	6.35
以农产品为原料	Using Farm Products as Raw Materials	36.62	6.47	7.01
以非农产品为原料	Using Non-Farm Products as Raw Materials	36.16	3.61	3.99
重工业	Heavy Industry	35.70	7.07	7.02
采掘工业	Extraction	26.56	8.89	8.76
原料工业	Raw Materials	36.52	9.12	8.66
加工工业	Manufacturing	35.91	5.09	5.27
按企业规模分	**Grouped by Size of Enterprises**			
大型企业	Large	23.89	9.43	9.06
中型企业	Medium	34.23	4.11	4.43
小型企业	Small	38.06	2.02	2.35
按行业分	**Grouped by Size of Enterprises**			
煤炭采选业	Coal Mining and Processing	34.62	9.51	9.15
石油和天然气开采业	Petroleum and Natural Gas Extraction		8.93	9.00
黑色金属矿采选业	Ferrous Metals Mining and Processing	100.00	1.95	2.31
有色金属矿采选业	Nonferrous Metals Mining and Processing		9.29	9.80
非金属矿采选业	Nonmetal Minerals Mining and Processing	19.51	6.78	7.32
其他矿采选业	Other Minerals Mining and Processing			
木材及竹材采运业	Logging and Transport of Timber and Bamboo			
食品加工业	Food Processing	30.48	－0.02	－0.02
食品制造业	Food Manufacturing	46.61	7.08	6.97
饮料制造业	Beverage Manufacturing	39.81	17.12	19.11
烟草加工业	Tobacco Processing	14.29	64.15	62.19
纺织业	Textile Industry	44.59	2.70	2.79
服装及其他纤维制品制造业	Garments and Other Fiber Products	22.86	1.08	1.19
皮革毛皮羽绒及其制品业	Leather, Furs, Down and Related Products	45.83	1.36	1.56
木材加工及竹藤棕草制品业	Timber Processing, Bamboo, Cane, Palm Fiber and Straw Products	30.00	2.89	3.29
家具制造业	Furniture Manufacturing	31.25	10.10	10.88
造纸及纸制品业	Papermaking and Paper Products	32.61	6.77	7.32
印刷业记录媒介的复制	Printing and Record Pressing	34.13	5.97	6.49
文教体育用品制造业	Stationery, Educational and Sports Goods	55.56	－1.07	－1.33
石油加工及炼焦业	Petroleum Processing and Coking Produets	45.45	12.25	10.33
化学原料及制品制造业	Raw Chemical Materials and Chemical Products	32.14	6.55	7.06
医药制造业	Medical and Pharmaceutical Products	28.30	7.48	8.05
化学纤维制造业	Chemical Fibers	47.62	2.22	2.23
橡胶制品业	Rubber Products	36.36	4.46	4.66
塑料制品业	Plastic Products	44.44	2.43	2.74
非金属矿物制品业	Nonmetal Mineral Products	36.48	2.87	3.17
黑色金属冶炼及压延加工业	Smelting and Pressing of Ferrous Metals	51.35	3.55	3.52
有色金属冶炼及压延加工业	Smelting and Pressing of Noferrous Metals	35.00	4.18	5.08
金属制品业	Metal Products	33.04	5.03	5.29
普通机械制造业	Ordinary Machinery Manufacturing	34.95	6.79	6.91
专用设备制造业	Special Purposes Equipment Manufacturing	35.93	4.01	4.32
交通运输设备制造业	Transportation Equipment Manufacturing	42.95	6.94	6.95
电气机械及器材制造业	Electric Equipment and Machinery	31.61	6.32	6.81
电子及通信设备制造业	Electronic and Telecommunications	53.51	1.86	1.90
仪器仪表及文化办公用机械	Instruments, Meters, Cultural and Official Machinery	39.71	2.70	2.81
其他制造业	Other Manufactruing	47.54	－0.92	－1.14
电力蒸气热水生产供应业	Eletricity Power, Steam and Hot Water Production and Supply	19.35	12.25	10.52
煤气的生产和供应业	Gas Production and Supply	84.62	－10.25	－11.38
自来水的生产和供应业	Tap Water Production and Supply	12.16	4.02	4.22

MAJOR ECONOMIC RESULT INDITATORS OF STATE-OWNED INDUSTRIAL ENTERPRISES WITH INDEPENDENT ACCOUNTING SYSTEMS

(%)

工业增加值率 Rate Between Value-Added and Total Produsts in Industry	资金利税率 Rate Between Pre-Tax Profit and Assets	百元固定资产原价实现的利税（元） Pre-Tax Profit Per 100 yuan Original Value of Fixed Assets(yuan)	百元销售收入实现的利润（元） Profit Per 100 yuan Sales Revenue (yuan)	成本费用利润率 Rate Between Profit and Cost	流动资产周转次数（次/年） Turnover of Total Circulating Funds (time/year)	全员劳动生产率（元/人） Total Labor Productivity (yuan/person)
22.50	**5.96**	**7.76**	**0.90**	**0.91**	**1.77**	**23416.76**
20.70	5.99	8.55	−0.29	−0.29	1.85	18235.79
20.37	7.44	10.82			2.06	18875.20
21.83	2.68	3.67	−1.34	−1.30	1.36	16420.21
23.42	5.95	7.47	1.46	1.49	1.73	26840.43
45.92	5.56	5.32	0.18	0.18	1.72	16599.33
24.24	7.44	7.80	2.15	2.24	2.15	45648.68
20.54	4.57	7.47	0.93	0.94	1.46	20697.15
25.30	8.12	9.84	2.19	2.28	1.88	34086.05
19.54	3.69	5.25	−0.70	−0.69	1.61	17091.52
18.14	2.07	3.07	−1.28	−1.25	1.67	13207.71
49.01	6.95	6.70	0.05	0.05	2.05	16127.92
41.89	3.99	3.68	1.13	1.16	1.26	26762.24
38.86	1.23	1.45	−4.44	−4.08	1.25	11853.08
35.93	6.41	7.90	4.61	4.62	1.63	17139.73
45.24	2.65	3.23	−3.17	−3.14	0.80	13057.74
12.39	−0.03	−0.05	−1.03	−1.01	2.45	16793.50
20.71	8.45	12.68	4.08	4.12	2.39	20895.06
27.59	15.83	25.45	0.56	0.64	1.51	29213.06
61.51	87.22	103.75	8.70	17.41	3.41	344588.12
18.57	2.72	3.73	−1.40	−1.37	1.95	14097.48
17.04	1.13	1.80	−0.67	−0.64	1.80	13063.67
25.72	1.33	2.26	−3.06	−2.93	1.47	18520.53
19.27	2.43	3.44	−1.64	−1.54	1.35	7701.96
29.77	9.47	14.54	5.40	5.64	1.61	25855.05
22.59	6.49	8.72	1.37	1.39	1.84	13839.74
29.21	4.79	5.73	−1.07	−1.03	1.68	11501.73
25.51	−1.25	−2.61	−4.75	−4.54	1.47	12441.79
15.25	21.16	19.30	1.26	1.33	3.76	62416.89
21.84	6.20	6.64	2.31	2.38	2.14	29666.46
20.93	7.97	13.64	2.24	2.25	1.68	23983.79
13.97	1.98	2.19	−1.03	−1.01	2.11	18261.83
21.46	4.85	8.31	−1.35	−1.36	1.68	17621.81
16.26	2.06	2.75	−2.00	−1.92	1.48	13339.85
26.40	1.93	2.24	−3.36	−3.18	1.45	13458.07
15.20	2.96	4.19	−0.46	−0.45	1.63	22837.52
16.87	4.45	6.25	1.84	1.83	1.73	25329.65
21.44	4.31	7.20	0.56	0.56	1.40	17334.82
22.86	5.78	10.76	2.35	2.39	1.26	22327.29
20.06	3.34	5.35	0.50	0.49	1.35	15433.96
19.46	7.25	12.46	1.58	1.61	1.76	31542.43
21.07	6.02	11.08	1.74	1.76	1.40	21635.96
18.40	1.44	2.87	−1.50	−1.44	1.08	21148.11
27.84	1.34	2.03	−2.60	−2.48	0.83	11.24.47
21.34	−1.02	−1.50	−4.96	−4.56	1.72	11742.47
36.96	7.48	7.37	3.87	4.26	2.23	99375.16
3.48	−3.86	−3.82	−14.78	−10.04	1.26	2436.91
36.44	1.00	0.94	−3.07	−2.93	0.88	23207.34

10－16 集体经济独立核算工业企业主要经济效益指标(1996)

单位:%

行业	Items	企业亏损面 Rate of Loss Making Enterprises	产值利税率 Rate Between Pre-Tax Profit and Output Value	销售利税率 Rate Between Pre-Tax Profit and Sales
总计	**National Total**	**24.16**	**4.93**	**5.95**
按轻重工业分	**Grouped by Light & Heavy Industry**			
轻工业	Light Industry	25.26	4.56	5.52
以农产品为原料	Using Farm Products as Raw Materials	25.70	4.31	5.18
以非农产品为原料	Using Non-Farm Products as Raw Materials	24.58	5.03	6.22
重工业	Heavy Industry	23.20	5.32	6.38
采掘工业	Extraction	11.90	6.67	8.64
原料工业	Raw Materials	26.12	4.59	5.46
加工工业	Manufacturing	23.00	5.59	6.71
按企业规模分	**Grouped by Size of Enterprises**			
大型企业	Large	11.11	7.71	8.83
中型企业	Medium	26.51	5.08	5.90
小型企业	Small	24.14	4.47	5.50
按行业分	**Grouped by Size of Enterprises**			
煤炭采选业	Coal Mining and Processing	16.67	9.14	10.59
石油和天然气开采业	Petroleum and Natural Gas Extraction			
黑色金属矿采选业	Ferrous Metals Mining and Processing	16.67	6.71	8.57
有色金属矿采选业	Nonferrous Metals Mining and Processing	14.29	3.01	5.07
非金属矿采选业	Nonmetal Minerals Mining and Processing	10.40	6.98	9.07
其他矿采选业	Other Minerals Mining and Processing			
木材及竹材采运业	Logging and Transport of Timber and Bamboo			
食品加工业	Food Processing	13.23	4.82	5.56
食品制造业	Food Manufacturing	22.99	4.97	5.97
饮料制造业	Beverage Manufacturing	16.04	8.75	9.96
烟草加工业	Tobacco Processing		6.55	6.83
纺织业	Textile Industry	34.48	3.61	4.30
服装及其他纤维制品制造业	Garments and Other Fiber Products	28.16	5.00	6.26
皮革毛皮羽绒及其制品业	Leather, Furs, Down and Related Products	26.53	4.25	5.40
木材加工及竹藤棕草制品业	Timber Processing, Bamboo, Cane, Palm Fiber and Straw Products	14.15	4.58	5.65
家具制造业	Furniture Manufacturing	17.90	5.05	6.57
造纸及纸制品业	Papermaking and Paper Products	21.79	5.69	6.34
印刷业记录媒介的复制	Printing and Record Pressing	21.52	9.11	10.67
文教体育用品制造业	Stationery, Educational and Sports Goods	20.95	6.02	6.87
石油加工及炼焦业	Petroleum Processing and Coking Produets	17.89	5.53	6.01
化学原料及制品制造业	Raw Chemical Materials and Chemical Products	24.70	5.88	7.02
医药制造业	Medical and Pharmaceutical Products	31.77	6.58	8.18
化学纤维制造业	Chemical Fibers	32.37	3.94	4.61
橡胶制品业	Rubber Products	23.89	5.87	7.06
塑料制品业	Plastic Products	27.33	4.54	5.46
非金属矿物制品业	Nonmetal Mineral Products	17.30	6.17	7.60
黑色金属冶炼及压延加工业	Smelting and Pressing of Ferrous Metals	33.63	3.02	3.40
有色金属冶炼及压延加工业	Smelting and Pressing of Noferrous Metals	29.43	3.61	4.71
金属制品业	Metal Products	24.98	4.39	5.40
普通机械制造业	Ordinary Machinery Manufacturing	25.38	5.80	7.16
专用设备制造业	Special Purposes Equipment Manufacturing	28.26	5.19	5.92
交通运输设备制造业	Transportation Equipment Manufacturing	25.14	5.48	6.62
电气机械及器材制造业	Electric Equipment and Machinery	25.96	5.84	7.15
电子及通信设备制造业	Electronic and Telecommunications	30.43	4.28	5.31
仪器仪表及文化办公用机械	Instruments, Meters, Cultural and Official Machinery	32.09	5.52	7.14
其他制造业	Other Manufactruing	22.92	4.04	4.96
电力蒸气热水生产供应业	Eletricity Power, Steam and Hot Water Production and Supply	24.24	4.62	5.32
煤气的生产和供应业	Gas Production and Supply	50.00	−4.50	−5.16
自来水的生产和供应业	Tap Water Production and Supply	6.65	5.73	7.22

MAJOR ECONOMIC RESULT INDITATORS OF COLLECTIVE-OWNED INDUSTRIAL ENTERPRISES WITH INDEPENDENT ACCOUNTING SYSTEMS

(%)

工业增加值率 Rate Between Value-Added and Total Produsts in Industry	资金利税率 Rate Between Pre-Tax Profit and Assets	百元固定资产原价实现的利税（元） Pre-Tax Profit Per 100 yuan Original Value of Fixed Assets(yuan)	百元销售收入实现的利润（元） Profit Per 100 yuan Sales Revenue (yuan)	成本费用利润率 Rate Between Profit and Cost	流动资产周转次数（次/年） Turnover of Total Circulating Funds (time/year)	全员劳动生产率（元/人） Total Labor Productivity (yuan/person)
20.17	**8.27**	**15.59**	**2.04**	**2.08**	**2.18**	**21952.36**
19.92	8.08	14.62	1.81	1.84	2.37	21370.54
19.77	7.86	13.44	1.75	1.78	2.54	21233.66
20.22	8.47	17.16	1.93	1.98	2.08	21639.34
20.42	8.44	16.56	2.28	2.33	2.02	22564.91
26.53	15.66	22.49	4.19	4.37	3.46	14445.33
18.60	7.88	13.74	1.90	1.93	2.41	32855.83
21.04	8.53	17.66	2.39	2.45	1.87	20492.86
19.08	14.00	20.88	5.19	5.47	2.90	54029.71
19.49	7.74	13.57	2.30	2.34	2.15	26969.09
20.53	7.64	15.35	1.46	1.48	2.11	19330.99
32.82	15.98	19.02	5.51	5.83	3.55	16417.81
25.45	13.02	26.89	6.41	6.76	2.47	22235.95
9.17	2.89	3.05	3.66	3.55	3.53	11277.47
27.09	17.05	26.19	4.12	4.33	3.28	14194.41
15.19	11.10	23.63	2.95	3.04	2.95	32114.52
18.43	8.93	16.26	1.76	1.78	2.46	21328.25
23.82	12.21	22.60	1.10	1.17	1.98	25592.22
15.10	10.64	31.57	3.61	3.72	1.98	40556.96
19.68	6.47	9.84	1.28	1.29	2.72	20910.52
20.76	10.26	21.08	2.75	2.82	2.51	22222.74
20.35	7.43	18.42	1.37	1.39	1.95	21294.98
19.23	9.25	18.03	1.54	1.56	2.59	21472.00
21.61	7.51	17.72	2.16	2.19	1.64	17906.77
21.59	9.16	16.19	1.86	1.89	2.35	17895.50
22.26	14.32	29.11	5.29	5.52	2.03	18800.39
22.14	11.55	26.31	3.30	3.40	2.52	17326.93
15.43	9.88	18.52	1.42	1.47	2.83	41118.16
19.56	10.68	20.19	2.70	2.79	2.41	32264.98
23.31	10.14	19.73	3.62	3.81	1.93	35325.72
17.07	5.61	7.17	1.93	1.96	2.91	34526.86
20.89	9.18	17.91	2.08	2.11	2.00	16023.78
19.54	7.43	13.51	1.43	1.45	2.18	23000.36
23.55	9.62	16.46	2.59	2.67	2.06	14478.21
16.77	4.77	9.16	1.23	1.23	2.26	43742.47
17.51	7.90	17.25	1.80	1.82	2.49	49023.45
20.00	7.42	15.70	1.49	1.52	2.02	21756.30
21.69	8.33	17.63	2.48	2.53	1.67	19934.31
20.65	7.78	16.51	2.12	2.17	1.87	22656.18
19.92	9.25	18.81	2.17	2.22	2.12	25644.62
19.95	9.68	23.13	2.78	2.85	1.91	23292.83
20.07	5.26	12.37	0.66	0.67	1.37	20405.78
24.28	6.83	15.22	1.81	1.82	1.35	17422.94
20.38	7.25	16.18	0.60	0.60	2.12	17678.00
19.54	3.52	4.20	−0.42	−0.39	1.42	29704.15
36.36	−5.12	−6.40	−7.01	−6.53	3.45	68326.09
25.69	5.67	7.05	3.36	3.42	1.78	20546.83

10—17 乡办独立核算工业企业基本情况
BASIC SITUATION OF TOWNSHIP INDIUSTRIAL ENTERPRISES WITH INDEPENDENT ACCOUNTING SYSTEMS

单位：亿元 (100 000 000 yuan)

指标	Items	1990	1994	1995	1996
企业单位数 （个）	Number of Enterprsises	24828	25324	26130	24116
年末全部职工人数 （万人）	Total Employees (year-end 10000 person)	287.99	320.04	302.10	297.27
工业总产值 （当年价）	Gross Output Value of Industry (current price)	618.91	2984.69	2978.12	3537.80
产品销售收入	Revenue of Product Sales	463.61	2048.86	2639.57	2897.18
#产品销售税金及附加	Product Sales Pre-Tax and Related Payments		21.85	23.72	22.83
利税总额	Total Pre-Tax Profits	30.31	143.06	178.60	187.14
年末固定资产原价	Year End Original Value of Fixed Assets	203.60	687.48	903.74	1063.11
年末固定资产净值	Year End Net Value of Fixed Assets	150.03	486.24	698.31	811.61
全部流动资产年平均余额	Average Balance Circulating Funds		838.16	1067.50	1191.34
本年应交增值税	Added Value Tax Deal with This Year		61.89	75.27	82.85
本年进项税额	Tax Value of Income Items		204.02	295.24	304.13
本年销项税额	Tax Value of Sales Item		262.00	365.64	378.73

10—18 村办工业基本情况
BASIC SITUATION OF INDUSTRIAL ENTERPRISES AT VILLAGE LEVEL AND BELOW

单位：亿元 (100 000 000 yuan)

指标	Items	1990	1994	1995	1996
企业单位数 （个）	Number of Enterprsises	70357	68190	57263	60820
年末全部职工人数 （万人）	Total Employees (year-end 10000 person)	278.04	278.15	264.80	239.00
工业总产值 （当年价）	Gross Output Value of Industry (current price)	479.99	2446.42	2232.09	2770.07
产品销售收入	Revenue of Product Sales	337.85	1595.34	1927.96	2203.28
#产品销售税金及附加	Product Sales Pre-Tax and Related Payments		18.72		19.39
利润总额	Total Pre-Tax Profits	9.78	53.13	68.15	70.28
年末固定资产原价	Year End Original Value of Fixed Assets	104.27	367.37	450.76	512.37
流动资金年末占用数	Year End Circulating Funds	167.63	587.36	694.82	754.06
本年应交增值税	Added Value Tax Deal with This Year		41.98		53.92

10—19 农村联营和个体工业基本情况
BASIC SITUATION OF RURAL CO-OPERATION AND INDIVIDUAL OWNED INDUSTRY

指标		Items	1990	1994	1995	1996
农村联营工业		Rural Co-operation Owned Industry				
户数	（户）	Number of Households (Household)	42730	23436	19443	26973
从业人员	（万人）	Employees (10000 persons)	19.73	17.15	17.82	18.43
总产值(当年价)	（亿元）	Gross Output Value of Industry (current price)	26.54	86.59	61.96	105.89
上交税金	（万元）	Tax Turned Over (10000 yuan)	8291	19072	20792	36145
自有资金	（万元）	Fundraising (10000 yuan)	25697	79222	110702	166266
农村个体工业		Rural Individual Industry				
户数	（万户）	Number of Households (10000 household)	45.15	53.24	30.60	43.43
从业人员	（万人）	Employees (10000 persons)	119.22	155.65	131.05	163.94
总产值(当年价)	（亿元）	Gross Output Value of Industry (current price)(100000000 yuan)	103.43	459.90	439.96	716.61
上交税金	（万元）	Tax Turned Over (10000 yuan)	36811	130625	147503	184761
自有资金	（万元）	Fundraising (10000 yuan)	138643	568711	779437	1043348

10—20 城镇联营和个体工业基本情况
BASIC SITUATION OF TOWN CO-OPERATION AND INDIVIDUAL INDUSTRY

指标		Items	1990	1994	1995	1996
城镇联营工业		Town Co-operation Owned Industry				
户数	（户）	Number of Households (household)	1456	1898	1741	2339
从业人员	（万人）	Employees (10000 persons)	2.34	2.40	4.19	2.28
总产值(当年价)	（亿元）	Gross Output Value of Industry (current price)	2.65	8.78	9.27	12.09
上交税金	（万元）	Tax Turned Over (10000 yuan)	1134	3325	4185	5711
自有资金	（万元）	Fundraising (10000 yuan)	4342	9666	20555	34246
城镇个体工业		Town Individual Industry				
户数(万户)		Number of Households (10000 household)	1.73	1.83	1.17	1.58
从业人员	（万人）	Employees (10000 persons)	3.76	5.22	4.61	5.92
总产值(当年价)	（亿元）	Gross Output Value of Industry (current price)(100000000 yuan)	3.61	16.49	14.25	31.69
上交税金	（万元）	Tax Turned Over (10000 yuan)	1613	5654	6075	12306
自有资金	（万元）	Fundraising (10000 yuan)	6769	18826	32012	51774

10—21 主要工业产品产量
OUTPUT OF MAJOR INDUSTRIAL PRODUCTS

单位:万吨 (10000 tons)

产品名称	Items	1985	1990	1994	1995	1996
钢	Steel	98.97	190.18	330.81	360.40	446.62
生铁	Pig Iron	98.59	154.35	197.26	253.71	253.71
成品钢材	Rolled-steel Final Products	145.18	203.01	674.19	787.89	795.58
#优质钢型材	Quality Rolled	2.85	3.86	20.53	41.52	52.93
线材	Wire Rod Steel	36.97	55.64	141.61	210.77	215.88
薄钢板	Low Gauge Plate	2.84	5.37	11.66	21.97	18.26
无缝钢管	Seamless Steel Pipe	6.22	10.36	25.73	33.69	27.72
铁矿石(原矿)	Iron Mineral (original)	172.27	129.06	191.99	238.16	189.59
发电量 (亿千瓦小时)	Electricity (100000000 Kwh)	234.48	404.47	631.90	700.41	756.87
#火力发电	Fire Power	233.92	403.95	631.48	686.99	756.39
原煤	Coal	2193.85	2407.79	2503.44	2650.72	2606.52
洗精煤	Washing Coal	405.76	434.60	387.49	432.63	367.93
原油	Crude Oil	55.81	86.00	95.03	101.41	122.04
原油加工量	Volume of Crude Oil Processing	499.23	808.66	903.48	976.51	1021.39
汽油	Gosoline	67.98	93.34	120.31	108.07	117.04
煤油	Keroseme	22.13	43.52	41.70	50.64	58.87
燃料油	Fuel Oil	156.08	274.82	263.51	162.04	108.08
硫酸(折100%)	Sulphuric Acid(100%)	97.70	122.47	149.59	171.63	175.43
浓硝酸	Concentrated Nitric Acid	2.14	2.46	3.46	4.64	3.84
盐酸	Hydrochloric Acid	22.70	37.49	44.12	46.71	51.77
烧碱(氢氧化钠)	Caustic Ash(sodium Hydroxide)	24.09	32.87	42.99	51.85	57.56
纯碱(无水碳酸钠)	Soda Ash(Anhydrous Sodium Carbonate)	2.69	17.57	55.61	58.10	74.81
合成氨	Synthetc Ammonic	153.45	164.25	181.02	202.93	224.83
农用化肥(折100%)	Chemical Fertilizers(100%)	121.71	145.90	153.09	191.85	184.30
氮肥	Nitrogen	100.64	110.85	111.24	125.87	136.47
磷肥	Phosphate	20.76	34.83	41.76	63.87	47.02
钾肥	Potassium	0.31	0.22	0.09	2.11	0.80
化学农药(含生物农药)	Chimecal Pesticide	4.27	4.51	6.31	12.18	8.93
乙烯	Ethylene	1.16	27.97	32.25	27.67	41.34
肥皂	Seap	7.12	4.02	4.05	3.92	2.83
合成橡胶 (吨)	Synthetic Rubber (tons)	754	546	439	3592	6850
合成洗涤剂	Synthetic Detergents	8.12	14.39	20.40	38.26	23.98
塑料制品	Plastic Products	32.97	43.35	90.95	246.27	143.93
#农用薄膜	Rural Use Membrane	1.27	1.95	4.04	4.99	4.08
内燃机生产量 (万千瓦)	Output of Internal Combustion Engines (10000 kw)	633.79	931.35	3388.88	4361	4926
#商品量	Commodity Volume	460.79	867.94	3188.37	—	—
金属切削机床 (台)	Metal-cutting Machines	18583	15894	34358	44606	33564
#数控机床	Digital(computer-controled) Machine Tools	8719	871	1935	2785	3120
高精度机床	High Precision Machine Tools	73	181	279	235	245
大型机床	Large Machine Tools	54	89	112	76	48
锻压机械	Forging Press Machines	15167	9590	40326	40487	26970

续表 1 continued

单位:万吨 (10000 tons)

产品名称		Items		1985	1990	1994	1995	1996
化工设备	(吨)	Chemical Industry Equipment	(tons)	16691	24781	77078	102576	55775
汽车	(辆)	Motor Vehicals		24474	46291	129957	125197	110157
#载货汽车		Trucks		15715	32092	64510	59799	44503
客车	(辆)	Passenger Carriage		655	1930	22957	28243	28070
大中型拖拉机	(台)	Large and Medium Tractors		413	1084	752	2138	4323
小型拖拉机	(万台)	Mini-tractors	(10000)	9.16	14.13	21.64	28.92	31.85
缝纫机	(万架)	Sewing Machines	(10000)	97.93	67.24	68.97	67.56	57.40
自行车	(万辆)	Bicycles	(10000)	375.08	400.21	621.02	718.20	442.85
照相机	(万架)	Cameras	(10000)	35.76	18.17	26.37	33.34	28.97
电风扇	(万台)	Electric Fans	(10000)	463.93	969.47	1621.23	2083.24	1939.64
家用电冰箱	(万台)	Household Refrigerators	(10000)	14.87	36.64	23.09	11.45	20.71
家用洗衣机	(万台)	Household Washing Machines	(10000)	75.07	8.77	79.54	90.24	117.79
电视机	(万台)	Television Sets	(10000)	276.45	296.61	502.47	475.89	410.54
#彩色电视机		Color TV Sets	(10000)	25.87	83.18	209.61	250.72	258.34
录放音机	(万台)	Recorders	(10000)	213.91	483.69	530.73	466.70	476.41
收音机	(万台)	Radio	(10000)	559.77	702.29	339.73	315.74	106.39
表	(万只)	Watches	(10000)	447.18	420.31	446.10	481.76	423.06
#手表		Wrist Watches		447.18	386.21	444.29	335.92	321.77
水泥		Cement		1116.90	1532.89	3087.38	3966.42	4040.28
平板玻璃	(万重量箱)	Plate Glass	(10000wt. cases)	301.26	323.96	408.79	868.73	1131.59
卫生陶瓷	(万件)	Health Care Pottery and Porcelains	(10000)	19.41	98.02	137.15	171.49	159.56
日用陶瓷	(万件)	Household Ceramics	(10000)	18124	20510	26439	27638	25990
原盐		Salt		167.10	184.54	289.29	345.47	359.48
罐头		Canned Food		10.16	8.42	8.66	7.04	6.35
饮料酒		Alcoholic Beverages		68.68	94.29	147.20	162.67	154.56
卷烟	(万箱)	Cigaretes	(10000 cases)	87.55	89.45	76.50	78.98	83.35
化学纤维		Chemical Fibers		12.52	40.76	78.09	102.20	105.94
纱		Yarn		46.28	69.46	65.63	86.25	83.33
布	(亿米)	Cloth	(1000000000 m)	21.05	28.91	32.71	48.90	34.55
#纯棉布		Pure Cotton Cloth		10.76	16.06	18.62	25.31	18.84
纯化纤布		Pure Fiber Cloth	(10000 m)	3.55	3.86	5.22	13.67	6.35
毛线	(吨)	Knitting Wool	(tons)	18783	83134	160342	185345	142797
呢绒	(万米)	Woolen Piece Goods	(10000 m)	4574	7316	16157	28212	19134
丝	(吨)	Silk	(tons)	8562	13329	24864	29073	21678
丝织品	(亿米)	Knitting Silk	(100000000 m)	3.25	4.45	8.28	11.21	11.19
机制纸及制板		Machine-made Paper and Paperboard		50	74.82	113.02	167.55	163.38

11 建筑业

CONSTRUCTION

11 建 筑 业
CONSTRUCTION

1 9 9 6

建筑施工企业个数	Construction Enterprises	3528	个	
建筑施工企业职工平均人数	Staff (annual average)	220.71	万人	(10000 persons)
建筑业总产值	Construction Enterprises Output Value	1049.42	亿元	(100000000 yuan)
房屋建筑竣工面积	Floor Space of Building Completed	8252.13	万平方米	(10000 sq·m)
建筑业全员劳动生产率	Overall Labor Produtivity	47547	元/人	(yuan/person)
建筑业技术装备率	Per Capital Machinery Value	3966	元/人	(yuan/person)

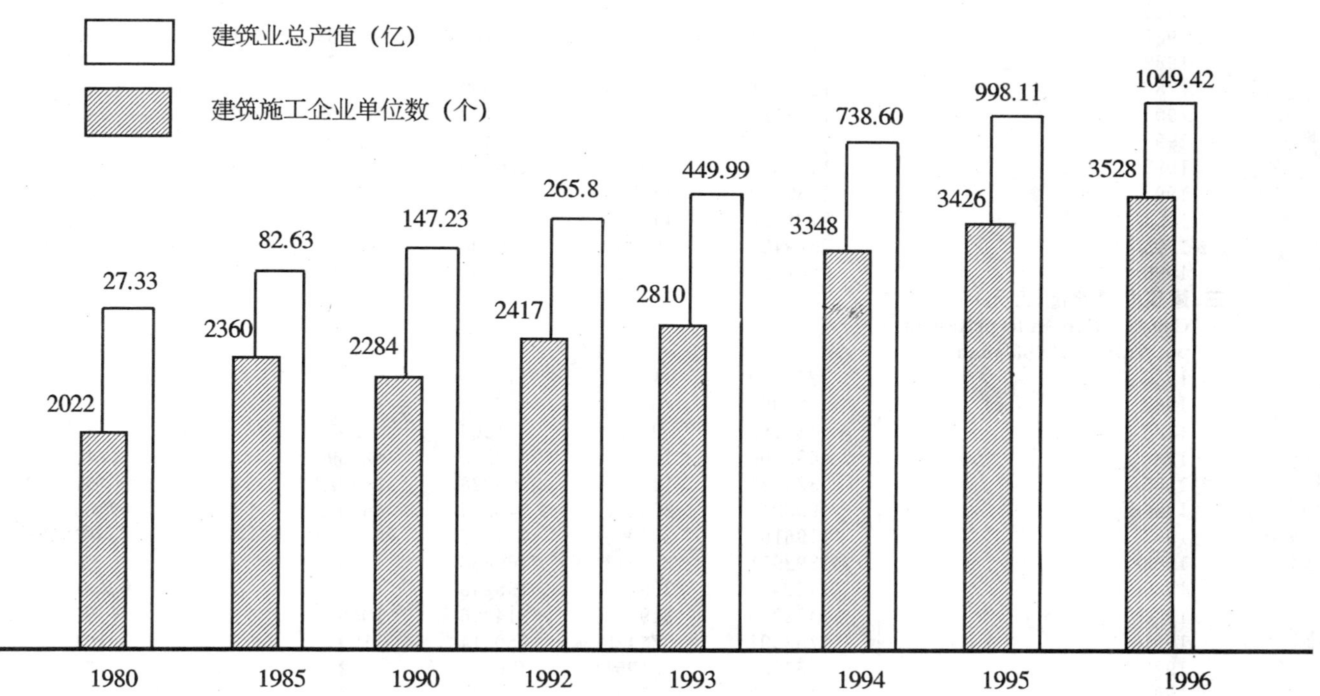

11—1 建筑施工企业概况

MAJOR ECONOMIC INDICATORS OF CONSTRUCTION ENTERPRISE

年份 Year	总计 Total	国有经济 State-Owned	地方 Local Owned	部属 Central Owned	城镇集体经济 Collective Owned	乡镇企业及其它经济 Rural and Township Industry and Others
一、企业单位个数(个) Number of Enterprises						
1980	2022	28	26	2	100	1894
1982	2097	39	34	5	102	1956
1983	2138	50	45	5	107	1981
1984	2282	97	82	15	131	2054
1985	2360	114	86	28	148	2098
1986	2445	147	123	24	149	2149
1987	2532	160	135	25	179	2193
1988	2614	164	136	28	187	2263
1989	2408	175	144	31	204	2029
1990	2284	162	138	24	201	1921
1991	2316	173	147	26	209	1934
1992	2417	203	176	27	251	1963
1993	2810	308	273	35	429	2073
1994	3348	389	353	36	513	2446
1995	3426	406	370	36	505	2515
1996	3528	589	554	35	868	2071
二、全部职工平均人数(人) Staff and Workers (person)						
1980	681831	80158	80158		103539	498134
1982	820043	137732	118056	19676	105337	576974
1983	935749	153085	124960	28125	112239	670425
1984	1064044	159793	127447	32346	124946	779305
1985	1240855	175997	138211	37786	140470	924388
1986	1352039	204519	158109	47410	150957	996563
1987	1442535	214782	150799	63983	169628	1058125
1988	1426444	212518	146239	66279	175373	1038553
1989	1285491	220800	151000	69800	203000	861691
1990	1243129	215285	152430	62855	239425	7884419
1991	1264447	220600	158400	62300	254600	789247
1992	1434373	246700	176600	70100	300700	886973
1993	1750600	345700	275000	70800	340000	1064800
1994	2121720	446000	316000	130000	343700	1332020
1995	2329400	454200	385800	68400	515600	1359600
1996	2207128	595527	521393	74134	552582	1059019
三、建筑业总产值(万元) Construction Enterprise-Output Value (10000 yuan)						
1980	273259	42965	42965		43910	186384
1982	381069	66228	57054	9174	48791	266050
1983	485188	93336	71266	22070	58421	333431
1984	598409	107745	82355	25390	70003	420661
1985	826349	143150	109228	33922	107980	575219
1986	995215	205266	143214	62052	125127	664822
1987	1196168	231925	144477	87448	160969	803274
1988	1392911	271517	169838	101679	192403	928991
1989	1420518	309432	195249	114183	239715	871371
1990	1472266	319993	214906	105087	297614	854659
1991	1762091	378428	260414	118014	343498	1040165
1992	2657999	581951	400712	181239	559896	1516152
1993	4499913	1047257	823986	223271	868656	2584000
1994	7385950	1716036	1310397	405639	1784589	3885325
1995	9981064	2573628	2073888	499740	2597636	4809800
1996	10494202	3779175	3187915	591260	2536252	4178775

续表 1　Continued 1

年　　份 Year	总　计 Total	国有经济 State-Owned	地　方 Local Owned	部　属 Central Owned	城镇集体经　济 Collective Owned	乡镇企业及其它经济 Rural and Township Industry and Others
四、施工房屋面积（万平方米）Floor Space of Building Under Construction （10000 sq・m）						
1980	3189.80	467.30	467.30		588.50	2134.00
1982	3738.48	535.32	488.21	47.11	550.07	2653.09
1983	4115.06	570.95	524.37	46.58	568.32	2975.79
1984	4662.14	558.65	507.99	50.66	594.77	3508.72
1985	5570.32	619.94	536.58	83.36	690.92	4259.46
1986	5934.61	638.72	557.69	81.03	706.20	4589.69
1987	6521.55	687.40	556.80	130.60	807.19	5026.96
1988	6545.10	650.76	535.68	155.08	868.28	5026.06
1989	5447.35	672.60	547.40	125.20	927.70	3847.05
1990	5240.98	699.10	580.30	118.80	1070.40	3471.48
1991	5711.13	778.71	660.44	118.27	1143.12	3789.30
1992	7780.32	1049.90	901.00	148.90	1688.30	5042.12
1993	10229.96	1801.32	1573.13	228.19	2045.54	6383.10
1994	13201.21	2356.00	2062.20	293.90	3269.60	7575.61
1995	16646.14	3470.96	3135.28	335.68	4621.48	8553.70
1996	15672.95	5032.00	4663.09	368.91	3723.69	6917.26
五、竣工房屋面积（万平方米）Floor Space of Building Completed （10000 sq・m）						
1980	2296.09	233.70	233.70		352.83	1709.56
1982	2505.14	259.38	244.21	15.17	335.74	1910.02
1983	2700.39	284.98	263.49	21.49	335.46	2079.95
1984	3033.59	280.56	260.67	19.89	357.71	2395.23
1985	3527.20	272.55	245.03	27.52	382.94	2871.71
1986	3926.24	306.44	281.46	24.98	403.02	3216.78
1987	4083.20	328.32	263.87	64.45	416.08	3338.80
1988	3858.50	265.09	226.77	38.32	429.67	3163.74
1989	3446.47	284.50	246.40	38.10	502.10	2659.87
1990	3307.93	354.40	302.20	52.20	617.00	2336.53
1991	3422.75	361.35	322.27	39.08	618.49	2442.91
1992	4387.99	446.60	395.90	50.70	837.40	3103.99
1993	5767.78	772.59	705.11	67.48	1077.09	3918.10
1994	9336.28	903.20	838.60	64.60	1620.00	6813.08
1995	8739.38	1304.03	1243.04	60.99	2056.55	5378.80
1996	8252.13	1946.38	1872.36	74.02	2141.69	4164.06
六、房屋建筑面积竣工率（%）Rate of Building Completed (percent)	72.0	50.0	50.0		60.0	80.1
1980	67.0	48.5	50.0	32.3	61.0	72.0
1982	73.7	67.4	50.2	46.1	59.0	69.9
1983	63.3	50.2	51.3	39.3	60.1	68.3
1984	66.2	44.0	45.7	33.0	55.4	67.4
1985	62.6	48.0	50.1	30.8	57.1	70.1
1986	62.6	47.8	47.4	49.3	51.5	66.4
1987	59.0	40.7	42.3	33.3	49.5	62.9
1988	63.3	42.3	45.0	30.4	54.1	69.1
1989	63.1	50.7	52.1	43.9	57.6	67.3
1990	59.9	46.4	48.8	33.0	54.1	64.5
1991	56.4	42.5	43.9	34.0	49.6	61.6
1992	56.4	42.9	44.8	29.6	52.7	61.4
1993	70.7	38.3	40.7	22.0	49.5	89.9
1994	52.5	34.9	39.6	18.2	44.5	62.9
1995	52.7	38.7	40.2	20.1	57.5	60.2
1996						

11－2 建筑施工企业主要经济指标(1996)
MAJOR ECONOMIC IINDICATORS OF CONSTRUCTION ENTERPRISES

指标	Items	合计 Total	国有经济 State-Owned	城镇集体经济 Collective Owned	乡镇企业及其它经济 Rural and Township Industry and Others
施工企业个数 (个)	Construction Enterprises	3528	589	868	2071
建筑业总产值 (亿元)	Construction Enterprises Output Value (100000000 yuan)	1049.42	377.92	253.63	417.87
#建筑工程	Construction	930.74	319.80	222.35	388.59
安装工程	Construction and Installation	98.14	43.31	26.92	27.91
建筑业增加值	Construction Added-Value	258.03	100.36	56.94	100.73
#固定资产折旧	Depreciation on Fixed Assers	12.80	5.92	2.77	4.11
应付工资	Wages	142.45	51.81	31.41	59.23
应付福利	Walfare Costs	15.01	5.99	3.58	5.44
工程结算税金及附加	Taxes and Added Taxes of Settle Accounts	25.12	8.94	5.68	10.50
竣工产值 (亿元)	Buildings Completed Output Value (100000000 yuan)	770.06	255.75	187.32	326.99
单位工程施工个数 (个)	Number of Projects Under Construction	71820	19651	21367	30802
#本年新开工	Beginning Projects in this Year	49787	12742	15930	21115
投标承包个数	Projects of Biding System	15124	5436	3990	5698
单位工程竣二个数 (个)	Number of Projects Completed	50944	13174	16600	21170
#优良工程个数	High Quality	14254	4623	4340	5291
房屋建筑施工面积 (万平方米)	Floor Space of Buildings Under Construction (10000 sq・m)	15672.95	5032.00	3723.69	6917.26
#本年新开工	Beginning Projects in this Year	8709.84	2133.12	2111.80	4464.92
投标承包的面积	Floor Space of Biding System	5954.15	2492.21	1339.50	2122.44
房屋建筑竣工面积 (万平方米)	Floor Space of Buildings Completed (10000 sq・m)	8252.13	1946.38	2141.69	4164.06
#优良工程面积	Floor Space of High Quality Projects	3253.47	1015.76	656.29	1581.42
自有机械设备总台数 (万台)	Number of Machines Owned (10000 sets)	51.68	14.70	12.95	24.03
自有机械设备总功率 (万千瓦)	Capacity of Machines Owned	568.50	258.22	118.43	191.85
自有机械设备净值(亿元)	Machinery Owned Net Value (100000000 yuan)	87.55	43.19	15.52	28.84
职工平均人数 (万人)	Staff and Workers (10000) Annual Average (10000 persons)	220.71	59.55	55.26	105.90
全员劳动生产率 (元/人)	Overall Labor Productivity (yuan/person)	47547	63459	45898	39459
技术装备率 (元/人)	Per Capita Machinery Value (yuan/person)	3966	7252	2809	2722
动力装备率 (千瓦/人)	Per Capita Machinery Value (kw/person)	2.58	4.34	2.14	1.81
利润总额 (亿元)	Total Profits (100000000 yuan)	14.95	4.16	3.12	7.67

11—3 建筑施工企业按行业类别分主要经济指标(1996)
MAJOR ECONOMIC INDICATORS BY SPECIALIZE SUBJECT OF CONSTRUCTION ENTERPRISES

指标	Items	土木工程建筑业 Civil Engineering	#房屋建筑业 Building	线路管道设备安装业 Line and Equipment Installation	装修装饰业 Building Decoration
施工企业个数 (个)	Construction Enterprises	2923	2548	270	335
建筑业总产值 (亿元)	Construction Enterprises Output Value (100000000 yuan)	936.93	824.12	81.97	30.52
#建筑工程	Construction	875.53	770.56	28.08	27.13
安装工程	Construction and Installation	43.93	38.18	51.35	2.86
建筑业增加值	Construction Added-Value	225.42	197.52	25.72	6.89
#固定资产折旧	Depreciation on Fixed Assers	11.03	8.69	1.38	0.39
应付工资	Wages	128.67	116.30	10.99	2.79
应付福利	Walfare Costs	13.34	11.93	1.34	0.33
工程结算税金及附加	Taxes and Added Taxes of Settle Accounts	22.29	20.04	2.13	0.70
竣工产值 (亿元)	Buildings Completed Output Value (100000000 yuan)	689.56	610.09	55.85	24.65
单位工程施工个数 (个)	Number of Projects Under Construction	56235	48228	11256	4329
#本年新开工	Beginning Projects in this Year	38353	32488	8078	3356
投标承包个数	Projects of Biding System	13894	12145	823	407
单位工程竣工个数 (个)	Number of Projects Completed	38468	32315	8901	3575
#优良工程个数	High Quality	10669	8526	2778	807
房屋建筑施工面积 (万平方米)	Floor Space of Buildings Under Construction (10000 sq·m)	15345.10	14704.67	168.99	158.86
#本年新开工	Beginning Projects in this Year	8500.46	8114.65	86.05	123.33
投标承包的面积	Floor Space of Biding System	5879.25	5532.92	34.62	40.28
房屋建筑竣工面积 (万平方米)	Floor Space of Buildings Completed (10000 sq·m)	8047.45	7731.24	92.44	112.24
#优良工程面积	Floor Space of High Quality Projects	3190.85	3109.61	22.73	39.89
自有机械设备总台数 (万台)	Number of Machines Owned (10000 sets)	46.05	40.56	3.64	1.99
自有机械设备总功率 (万千瓦)	Capacity of Machines Owned	503.09	365.16	53.43	11.98
自有机械设备净值(亿元)	Machinery Owned Net Value (100000000 yuan)	77.53	51.35	7.90	2.12
职工平均人数 (万人)	Staff and Workers (10000) Annual Average (10000 persons)	205.69	185.61	10.41	4.61
全员劳动生产率 (元/人)	Overall Labor Productivity (yuan/person)	45551	44400	78706	66179
技术装备率 (元/人)	Per Capita Machinery Value (yuan/person)	3769	2767	7583	4602
动力装备率 (千瓦/人)	Per Capita Machinery Value (kw/person)	2.4	2.0	5.1	2.6
利润总额 (亿元)	Total Profits (100000000 yuan)	12.77	11.11	1.59	0.59

11—4 建筑业企业财务状况(1996)
CONSTRUCTION FINIANCEIAL INDICATOERS

单位:万元 (10000 yuan)

指标	Items	合计 Total	#国有经济 State-Owned	#地方企业 Local Owned	#城镇集体经济 Collective Owned
资本金合计	**Total Capital Assets**	**1736758**	**606506**	**509143**	**429591**
年末资产负债	**Total Liability (year-end)**				
流动资产合计	Criculating Funds	7718804	3425424	2942381	2053671
#存货	Stock	3473240	1296210	1203270	1104569
#在建工程	Under Building Project	2696261	1001974	969944	907854
固定资产合计	Total Fixed	1584307	713322	561228	346363
固定资产原价合计	Total Original Value of Fixed Assets	2114562	980223	762622	453164
#生产经营用	Used by Product	1628698	715115	570269	356885
累计折旧	Total Depreciation Drawn	564535	275403	207497	113935
#本年折旧	Draw Depreciation	127958	59185	45385	27725
资产总计	Total Property	9666553	4289966	3615321	2505600
流动负债合计	Total Circulating Liability	7258069	3362227	2861876	1942405
长期负债合计	Total Long-term Liability	182160	107706	76587	41954
所有者权益合计	Right and Interests (year-end)	216812	796796	654854	506724
#股本	Stock	142343	42921	40654	27467
损益与分配	**Loss-profit and Allocation**				
工程结算收入	Project Avenue	7669071	3012850	2401656	1480921
工程结算成本	Project Cost	6797248	2655584	2135884	1286934
工程结算税金及附加	Project Taxes-added	251245	89404	70427	56753
工程结算利润	Project Profit	620578	267862	195346	137234
其他业务利润	Other Profit	49657	20501	16888	14801
管理费用	Management Free	444212	200985	156390	107546
#税金	Taxes	13573	4377	3899	2697
利润总额	Total Profit	149524	41565	33678	31163
应交所得税	Payable Income Taxes	36864	11471	9136	8203
转作奖金的利润	Profit as Present	9049	2339	2314	1722
应付利润	Payable Profit	21203	7427	7324	3031
工资、福利费	**Wages, Walfare**				
本年应付工资总额	Payable Total Wages	1424464	518132	438433	314122
本年应付福利费	Payable Total Walfare	150128	59852	50147	35753
建筑业增加值	**Construction Added-Value**	**2580320**	**1003608**	**800949**	**569427**
亏损企业个数	**Number of Loss-Making Enterprises**	**476**	**101**	**99**	**156**

11－5 建筑业按行业类别分财务状况(1996)
CONSTRUCTION FINIANCEIAL INDICATOERS BY SPECIALIZE SUBJECT

单位:万元　　　　(10000 yuan)

指标	Items	土木工程建筑业 Civil Engineering	#房屋建筑业 Building	线路管道设备安装业 Line and Equipment Installation	装修装饰业 Building Decoration
资本金合计	**Total Capital Assets**	**1493481**	**1194927**	**157711**	**85566**
年末资产负债	**Total Liability (year-end)**				
流动资产合计	Criculating Funds	6772361	5867248	727724	218719
#存货	Stock	3165510	2846026	219368	88362
#在建工程	Under Building Project	2496657	2276721	147293	52311
固定资产合计	Total Fixed	1355940	1045789	174929	53438
固定资产原价合计	Total Original Value of Fixed Assets	1814074	1394511	235142	65346
#生产经营用	Used by Product	1399278	1100600	176690	52730
累计折旧	Total Depreciation Drawn	487205	372450	63941	13389
#本年折旧	Draw Depreciation	110293	86872	13817	3848
资产总计	Total Property	8443874	7155135	936550	286129
流动负债合计	Total Circulating Liability	6380626	5500836	701890	175553
长期负债合计	Total Long-term Liability	157099	108077	18212	6849
所有者权益合计	Right and Interests (year-end)	1849514	1496171	214734	98564
#股本	Stock	121527	94883	8969	11847
损益与分配	**Loss-profit and Allocation**				
工程结算收入	Project Avenue	6781786	5852789	653375	233910
工程结算成本	Project Cost	6056754	5243404	540106	200388
工程结算税金及附加	Project Taxes-added	222855	200369	21255	7135
工程结算利润	Project Profit	502178	409017	92013	26387
其他业务利润	Other Profit	44137	36841	4362	1158
管理费用	Management Free	361574	293768	63648	18990
#税金	Taxes	11819	10947	1125	629
利润总额	Total Profit	127727	111115	15926	5871
应交所得税	Payable Income Taxes	30284	27021	4843	1737
转作奖金的利润	Profit as Present	8281	7296	501	267
应付利润	Payable Profit	18464	16662	1200	1539
工资、福利费	**Wages, Walfare**				
本年应付工资总额	Payable Total Wages	1286733	1163027	109945	27786
本年应付福利费	Payable Total Walfare	133404	119257	13447	3277
建筑业增加值	**Construction Added-Value**	**2254172**	**1975156**	**257240**	**68908**
亏损企业个数	**Number of Loss-Making Enterprises**	**359**	**307**	**43**	**74**

交通运输、邮电业 12

TRANSPORTATION, POSTAL AND TELECOMMUNICATION SERVICES

12 交通运输、邮电业

TRANSPORTATION，POSTAL AND TELECOMMUNICATION SERVICES

1 9 9 6

全社会客运量	Total Passenger Traffic	91980	万人	(10000 persons)
#公　　路	Highway	86801	万人	(10000 persons)
全社会货运量	Total Freight Traffic	84666	万吨	(10000 tons)
#公　　路	Highway	50571	万吨	(10000 tons)
邮电业务总量	Total Postal and Telecommunication	96.03	亿元	(1000000000 yuan)
#函　　件	Letters	54075	万件	(10000)
订销报刊累计份数	Newspaper and Magazines Circulation	17.68	亿份	
年末电话用户	Residencial Telephone (Year-end)	446.73	万户	(10000)
年末移动电话用户	Residentcial Mobile Telephone (Year-end)	45.02	万户	(10000)

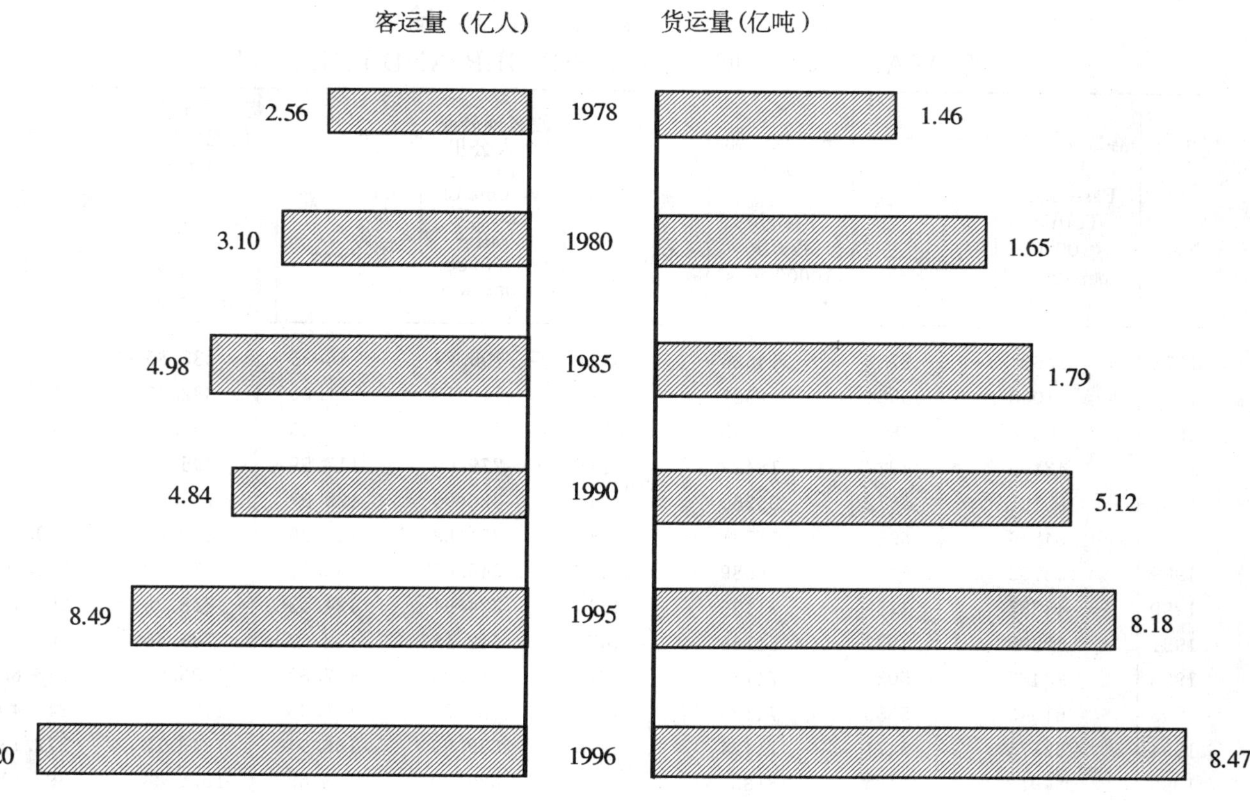

12—1 运输线路长度
LENGTH OF TRANSPORTATION ROUTES

单位:公里 (km)

指标	Items	1990	1994	1995	1996
铁路营业里程	Total Railway in Operation	748	742	472	742
铁路正线延展长度	Mainline Railways Length Completed	1250	1290	1290	1290
公路通车里程	Total Highway in Operation	24772	25891	25970	26659
#晴雨通车里程	Operated by Either Fine or Rain	23582	25198	25352	26080
#有路面里程	Paved	23715	25231	25385	26164
内河航道里程	Navigable Inland Waterways	23665	23787	23803	23832
#水深 1 米以上	Depth Above 1 Meter	20340	22394	22466	22494
公路桥梁 (座)	Highway Bridegs	8886	9753	9793	10297
(米)	(m)	283948	328927	337978	395729
#危险桥 (座)	Dangerous Bridges	144	167	163	168
(米)	(m)	4360	2472	5374	6312
通航河流上永久性水利闸坝 (座)	Permanent Floodgates and Dams Over Navigable Rivers	481	473	436	437
#碍航闸坝 (座)	Floodgates and Dams For Abstruct Navigation	118	134	123	139
输油管道里程	Petroleum Pipelines	334	334	334	334

12—2 全社会客货运输量
TOTAL TRAFFIC OF PASSENGER AND FREIGHT

年份 Year	客运量 (万人) Passenger Traffic (10000 persons)	#铁路 Railway	货运量 (万吨) Freight Traffic (10000 tons)	#铁路 Railway	旅客周转量 (亿人公里) Turnover Volume of Passenger Traffic (100000000 persons/km)	#铁路 Railway	货物周转量 (亿吨公里) Turnover Volume of Freight Traffic (100000000 tons/km)	#铁路 Railway
1978	25624	2752	14626	3224	105.29	46.35	283.85	172.72
1980	31008	3364	16527	3420	140.15	61.60	382.77	186.31
1985	49818	4819	17893	4037	259.96	107.45	460.04	240.48
1986	48105	4927	18429	4143	279.05	117.59	495.94	260.85
1987	55121	5372	55269	4241	326.00	129.37	714.64	271.22
1988	54876	5983	57731	4289	351.89	146.99	830.69	279.31
1989	52102	5421	56989	4489	346.43	138.51	874.12	292.40
1990	48382	4788	51186	4235	324.94	124.13	818.33	297.44
1991	50299	4932	51168	4078	342.12	132.57	789.46	301.73
1992	73462	5035	74171	4343	515.08	147.53	1053.95	333.85
1993	61643	5533	74523	4344	524.05	161.36	1193.87	346.49
1994	62175	5471	71424	4318	539.95	166.94	1246.12	372.13
1995	84915	5185	81830	4143	626.20	163.69	1376.88	393.51
1996	91980	4502	84666	4361	669.36	143.85	1440.15	380.09

12—3 公路运输 HIGHWAY TRANSPORTATION

年份 Year	客运量（万人） Passenger Traffic (10000 persons)	#交通系统 Department of Communication	货运量（万吨） Freight Traffic (10000 tons)	#交通系统 Department of Communication	旅客周转量（亿人公里） Turnover of Passenger Traffic (100000000 person/km)	#交通系统 Department of Communication	货物周转量（亿吨公里） Turnover of Freight Traffic (100000000 ton/km)	#交通系统 Department of Communication
1978	18694	18694	4488	4488	49.93	49.93	11.24	11.24
1980	26463	26463	4427	4427	68.25	68.25	11.45	11.45
1985	42342	42342	4797	4797	143.45	143.45	19.99	19.99
1986	40914	40914	5027	5027	153.40	153.40	21.31	21.31
1987	47067	40902	30525	4938	188.34	166.45	128.50	22.21
1988	46307	38985	29246	4733	196.78	170.90	143.91	24.46
1989	44439	36233	30599	4479	200.90	169.17	174.92	22.70
1990	41850	33822	27904	4238	195.24	157.81	144.46	20.70
1991	43746	34316	27940	4438	204.11	167.32	167.26	21.89
1992	66747	34414	41295	4841	361.28	181.00	179.92	24.60
1993	53331	27573	35060	4535	355.50	166.01	235.07	23.07
1994	54930	21414	36899	4342	367.98	135.62	243.33	21.16
1995	78947	21273	49578	4247	459.08	137.66	281.04	19.63
1996	86801	22168	50571	4077	523.00	143.58	317.03	17.74

12—4 水路运输 WATERWAY TRANSPORTATION

年份 Year	客运量（万人） Passenger Traffic (10000 persons)	货运量（万吨） Freight Traffic (10000 tons)	#内河 Inland Waterways	#海运 Seashipping	旅客周转量（亿人公里） Turnover Volume of Passenger Traffic (100000000 persons/km)	货物周转量（亿吨公里） Turnover Volume of Freight Traffic (100000000 tons/km)	#内河 Inland Waterways	#海运 Seashipping
1978	4175	6557	6557	—	9.01	87.97	87.97	—
1980	4175	6482	6452	30	10.30	93.56	91.51	2.05
1985	2644	7626	7553	73	9.06	151.67	140.60	11.07
1986	2241	7832	7747	85	8.07	166.11	153.61	12.50
1987	2652	19090	19029	61	8.29	267.77	258.87	8.90
1988	2555	22715	22623	92	8.12	358.04	341.85	16.19
1989	2213	20568	20460	108	7.03	362.31	336.34	25.97
1990	1701	17695	17585	110	5.56	331.31	307.19	24.12
1991	1569	17960	17770	190	5.44	280.59	240.23	40.36
1992	1617	27404	27186	218	6.28	605.38	566.47	38.91
1993	2704	34099	33794	305	7.19	578.01	520.51	57.50
1994	1677	29233	28882	351	5.03	598.01	523.20	74.81
1995	623	27161	26729	432	3.43	670.75	585.84	84.91
1996	499	28819	28428	391	2.52	712.33	635.20	77.13

12—5 直属港口货物吞吐量(1996)
CARGO HANDLED AT PORTS DIRECTLY UNDER PROVINCE

单位:万吨 (10000 tons)

指标	Items	连云港 Liangyungang	南京 Nanjing	南通 Nantong	镇江 Zhengjiang	张家港 Zhangjiagang
货物吞吐量合计	**Total Cargo Handled**	**1583**	**5182**	**1711**	**1708**	**900**
外贸吞吐量	Foreight Trade Handled	998	602	320	22	272
进口	Import	352	391	219	14	170
出口	Export	646	211	101	8	102
内贸吞吐量	Domestic Trade Handled	585	4580	1391	1686	628
进口	Import	52	2259	1026	1045	400
出口	Export	533	2321	365	641	228

12—6 直属港口码头泊位和库场能力(1996)
ABILITIES OF BERTH AND STOREGROUND AT PORTS DIRECTLY UNDE PROVINCE

指标	Items	连云港 Liangyungang	南京 Nanjing	南通 Nantong	镇江 Zhengjiang	张家港 Zhangjiagang
码头泊位个数(个)	Berths of Dacks	30	65	39	32	14
码头泊位长度(米)	Lengh of Harbor (m)	5294	5650	3573	3099	2232
#万吨级以上(个)	10000 Tonnage Above	20	14	7	8	10
库场堆存能力	Ability of Storeground Store Up					
总面积(平方米)	Total Area (sq·m)	5147839	537216	247359	355012	304460
总容量(吨)	Total Capacity (tons)	1453230	2220149	735942	624684	1066498
仓库面积(平方米)	Area of Warehouse (sq·m)	67689	59338	19234	37850	37288
容量(吨)	Capacity (tons)	49716	65325	15285	56689	74379
堆场面积(平方米)	Space of Storeground (sq·m)	5080150	477878	228125	317432	267172
容量(吨)	Capacity (tons)	1403514	2154824	720657	567995	992119

12—7 全省民用车辆拥有量
CIVIL VEHICLES BY WHOLE PROVINCE

单位:辆

指标	Items	1990	1994	1995	1996
民用汽车	Civil Vehicles	276813	464548	511903	470927
载货汽车	Trucks	169665	257368	278295	226868
#大　型	Large-Scale	130505	185632	198300	152794
载客汽车	Passenger Vehicles	95549	193169	219875	232128
#大　型	Large Scale	17944	22005	22355	19857
特种汽车	Particular Cars	7658	11739	10960	7920
其他专用汽车	Other Vehicles for Special Use	3941	2272	2773	4011
轮胎式拖拉机	Tyre Shapes Tractors	308017	425082	441198	374183
# 手扶拖拉机	Hand Tractors	264452	320481	327553	291024
摩托车	Motor	235898	976131	1295475	1726894
# 两轮摩托车	Motorcycle	228051	961853	1242212	1713574
其他机动车	Other Motor Vehicles	51472	122159	101560	171552
载货挂车	Cargo Trailers	9589	9797	11420	4792

12—8 全省民用运输船舶拥有量
CIVIL TRANSPORT VESSELS BY WHOLE PROVINCE

指标	Items	1990		1995		1996	
		艘	万吨(客)位 千瓦 10000 tons (seat) Kw	艘	万吨(客)位 千瓦 10000 tons (seat) Kw	艘	万吨(客)位 千瓦 10000 tons (seat) Kw
货　船	Cargo Ships	126244	314.41	111898	544.81	80767	439.97
客　船	Passenger Ships	1029	8.04	919	6.73	1031	6.37
拖　船	Tugboats	4421	37.66	3953	36.69	3246	33.14
货运驳船	Cargo Barges	34068	205.58	24191	196.55	22558	210.47

12—9 独立核算交通运输企业财务状况(1996)
FINANCIAL AFFAIRS OF TRANSPOTATION ENTERPRISES WITH INDEPENDENT ACCOUNTING SYSTEMS

单位:万元 (10000 yuan)

指标	Items	总计 Total	国有经济 State-Owned	集体经济 Collective-Owned	其他经济 Other Ownerships
企业个数	Number of Enterprises	573	235	306	32
#亏损企业(个)	Loss Making Enterprises	270	86	166	18
资本金合计	Total Capital Funds	572048	433575	103561	34912
流动资产年末合计	Total Circulation Funds (Year end)	713883	568262	111002	34619
#存货	Inventory	62552	48868	11129	2555
固定资产年末合计	Total Fixed Assets (Year end)	1329727	1120910	159884	48933
固定资产原价合计	Orginal Value of Fixed Assets	1768749	1456041	235209	77499
#生产经营用	For the Use of Production and Business	1297178	1063545	172899	60734
累计折旧	Depreciation Accumulated	571237	435849	99357	36031
#本年提取的	Drawed in this Year	86320	63530	17816	4974
资产总计	Total Assets	2235416	1851436	289007	94973
流动负债年末合计	Total Circulation Liabilities (Year end)	802285	611439	159132	31714
长期负债年末合计	Total Long Term Liabilities Revenue (Year end)	594554	542302	40166	12086
负债合计	Total Liabilities	1398959	1155458	199700	43801
营运业务收入	Revenue	799699	641328	127206	31165
营业成本	Costs	616683	483741	107361	25581
营业税金及附加	Pre-tax and Related Payment	21091	15779	4264	1048
营运费用	Business Expenditures	10720	8313	1987	420
管理费用	Management Expenditures	180141	137252	34636	8253
#税 金	Tax	2929	2045	750	134
营业利润	Product Sales After Tax Profit	−38231	−14004	−20662	−3565
利润总额	Total Profit After-Tax	−21198	−3448	−18128	378
应交所得税	Income Tax Deal With	4619	4040	198	381
转作奖金的利润	Profit Transfered to Bonus	70		70	
应付利润	Profit Deal With	2753	63	69	2621
#已分配股利	Share Hold Profit Distributed	24	18	6	

12—10 独立核算交通运输企业按专业类型分财务状况(1996)
FINANCIAL AFFAIRS OF TRANSPORTATION ENTERPRISES WITH INDEPENDENT ACCOUNTING SYSTEMS (GROUPED OF SECTOR)

单位:万元 (10000 yuan)

指标	Items	总计 Total	公路 Highway	水运 Waterway	港口 Port
企业个数	Number of Enterprises	573	306	173	94
#亏损企业(个)	Loss Making Enterprises	270	117	119	34
资本金合计	Total Capital Funds	572048	147311	201882	222855
流动资产年末合计	Total Circulation Funds (Year end)	713883	191392	310959	21532
#存货	Inventory	62552	23451	13057	26044
固定资产年末合计	Total Fixed Assets (Year end)	1329727	310410	434739	584578
固定资产原价合计	Orginal Value of Fixed Assets	1768749	405811	640721	722217
#生产经营用	For the Use of Production and Business	1297178	262946	453995	580237
累计折旧	Depreciation Accumulated	571237	131930	259863	179444
#本年提取的	Drawed in this Year	86320	22213	35118	28989
资产总计	Total Assets	2235416	541415	852635	841366
流动负债年末合计	Total Circulation Liabilities (Year end)	802285	235422	356514	210349
长期负债年末合计	Total Long Term Liabilities Revenue (Year end)	594554	66125	220198	308231
负债合计	Total Liabilities	1398959	303234	577144	518581
营运业务收入	Revenue	799699	214684	377764	207251
营业成本	Costs	616683	165401	300427	150855
营业税金及附加	Pre-tax and Related Payment	21091	5816	8302	6973
营运费用	Business Expenditures	10720	3553	991	6176
管理费用	Management Expenditures	180141	54528	76441	49172
#税金	Tax	2929	1279	831	819
营业利润	Product Sales After Tax Profit	−38231	−7577	−21450	−9204
利润总额	Total Profit After-Tax	−21198	−868	−13533	−6797
应交所得税	Income Tax Deal With	4619	732	3567	320
转作奖金的利润	Profit Transfered to Bonus	70	68		2
应付利润	Profit Deal With	2753	2696	45	12
#已分配股利	Share Hold Profit Distributed	24	6	18	

12—11 邮电业务基本情况
POSTS AND TELECOMMUNCATIONS SERVICES

指 标 Items		1991	1993	1994	1995	1996
邮电业务总量 （亿元）	Revenue from Posts & Telecommunication Services （100000000 yuan）	13.47	34.51	51.78	72.24	96.03
函件 （亿件）	Letters （100000000）	3.26	4.03	4.60	5.31	5.41
包件 （万件）	Parcels （10000）	757	1375	1638	1619	1569
邮政快件 （万件）	Express Mail （10000）	2859	3043	2950	2809	2646
特快专递 （万件）	Special Express （10000）	38	421	701	870	919
报刊期发数 （万份）	Newspapers and Magazines Circulation （10000）	1621	2115	1829	1655	1567
电报 （万份）	Telegrams （10000）	1957	1502	1009	693	480
传真 （份）	Faxs	57874	187951	234552	277823	319180
长途电话 （万张）	Distance Telephone Calls	14379	45484	64506	85937	92157
年末直拨国际及港澳的用户 （万户）	Direct-Dial Calls Abroad，HK and Macao Telephone （10000 Subscribers）	2.11	21.28	43.09	79.04	99.91
年末市内电话 （万户）	Urban Telephones （10000 Subscribers）	42.06	103.11	165.70	226.54	283.42
#住宅电话 （万户）	Residencial （10000）	15.99	66.35	122.48	176.47	226.22
年末无线寻呼电话用户（万户）	Wireless Telephones （10000）	3.86	29.81	60.67	109.55	200.08
年末移动电话用户 （户）	Mobile Telephones （Subscribers）		23842	98797	231897	450238
年末农村电话 （户）	Rural Telephones （Subscribers）	99943	288480	527551	1036261	1674868
邮电局所 （处）	Post Offices	2991	2981	3017	3218	3297
邮路及农村投递路线总长度 （公里）	Length of Postal Routes and Rural Delivery Routes （km）	291476	295088	296175	302648	309816
汽车邮路	Highway Routes	25467	34190	36942	43766	48657
铁路邮路	Railway Routes	3893	4413	4421	4198	4399
长话电路 （路）	Long Distance Telephone Lines （Line）	16058	47933	71461	64117	88175
电报电路 （路）	Telegraph Lines （Line）	1041	1029	992	940	922
邮电通信工具拥有量（部、门）	Telecommunications Facilites （Unit）					
市话交换机容量 （万门）	City Switchboards Capacity （10000）	71.53	165.87	269.44	382.11	489.35
农话交换机容量 （万部）	Rural Switchboards Capacity （10000）	24.55	88.19	133.74	214.66	335.64
电话机 （万部）	Telephones （10000）	99.34	210.82	340.56	491.98	681.20
城市电话	Urban Telephones	77.46	162.65	245.46	333.90	431.97
农村电话	Rural Telephones	21.88	48.17	95.10	158.08	249.23

国内贸易 13

DOMESTIC TRADE

13 国 内 贸 易
DOMESTIC TRADE

1 9 9 6

社会消费品零售总额	Total Retail Sales of Consumer Goods	1932.89	亿元（100000000 yuan）
批发零售贸易业商品购进总额	Total Purchases of Wholesales and Retail Sales Trade	4790.75	亿元（100000000 yuan）
批发零售贸易业商品销售总额	Total Sales Value of Wholesales and Retail Sales Trade	5215.19	亿元（100000000 yuan）
批发零售贸易业、餐饮业网点数	Number of Outlets in Wholesales, and Catering Retail Sales Trade	967271	个
批发零售贸易业、餐饮业人员数	Numbe of Personnel in Wholesales, and Catering Retail Sales Trade	287.76	万人 （10000 persons）

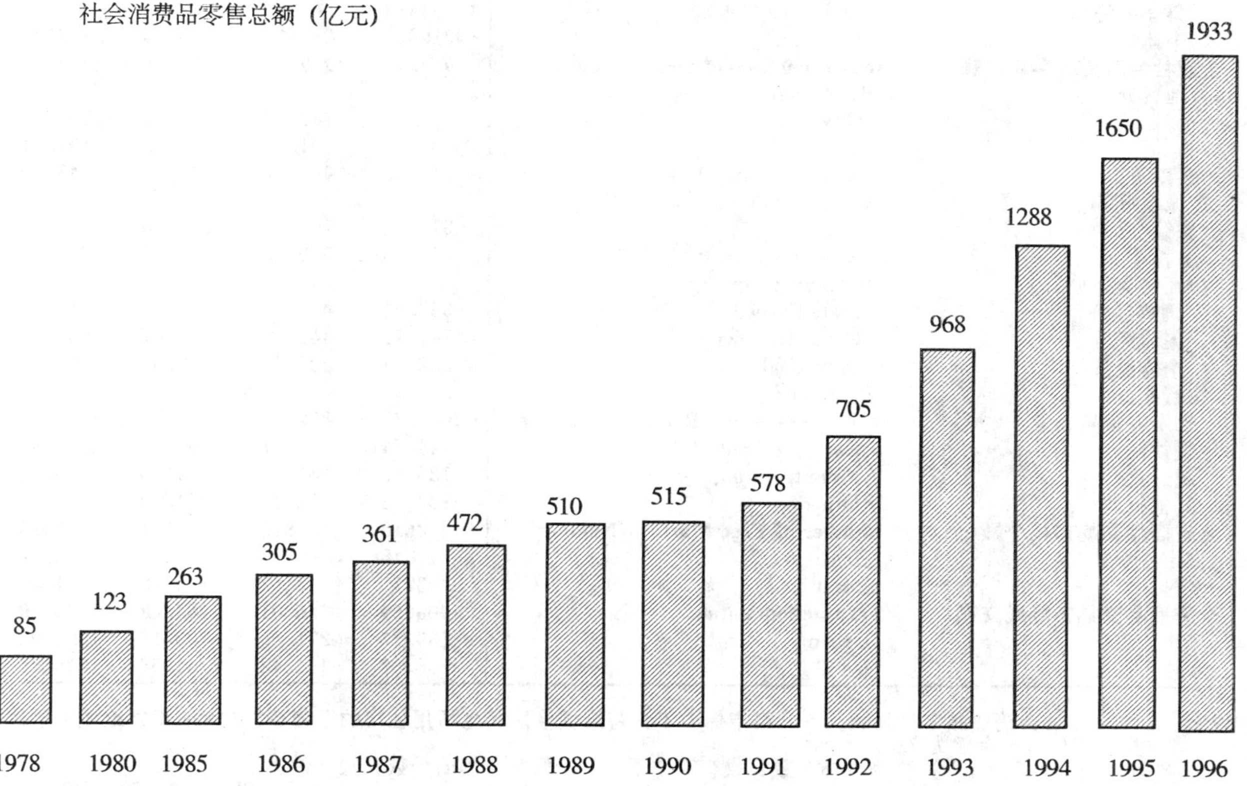

13—1 国内贸易基本情况
DOMESTIC TRADE

单位:亿元 (100 000 000 yuan)

指　　标	Items	1993	1994	1995	1996
全省批发零售贸易业	**Wholesale and Retailsales Trade**				
网点数 (个)	Number of Outlets(Number)	762146	834766	834103	840521
#国有经济	State-Owned	39352	30895	32608	34745
集体经济	Collective-Owned	109349	88455	87094	87641
个体经济	Individual	576997	708250	705793	704131
人员数 (人)	Number of Personnel(Person)	2431014	2311143	2368854	2496000
#国有经济	State-Owned	616321	546955	562625	564313
集体经济	Collective-Owned	798479	636987	619380	653691
个体经济	Individual	820113	1037900	1080122	1120583
商品购进总额	Total Purchases	3440.38	4018.83	4637.20	4790.75
#国有经济	State-Owned	2245.38	2088.73	2357.84	2349.98
集体经济	Collective-Owned	1074.92	1583.55	1900.68	1961.06
商品销售总额	Total Sales Value	3779.58	4339.93	5031.52	5215.19
#国有经济	State-Owned	2424.56	2246.47	2534.35	2554.58
集体经济	Collective-Owned	1218.58	1742.55	2075.33	2156.87
商品库存总额	Total Inventory	470.83	539.12	634.10	684.45
#国有经济	State-Owned	283.40	282.78	335.22	374.16
集体经济	Collective-Owned	168.37	211.26	255.81	254.67
全省餐饮业	Catering Trade				
网点数 (个)	Number of Outlets(Number)	123115	124947	128122	126750
#国有经济	State-Owned	1326	1356	1219	1395
集体经济	Collective-Owned	4971	7363	7101	7229
个体经济	Individual	109494	115873	119140	116095
人员数 (人)	Number of Personnel(Person)	356191	341525	363490	381647
#国有经济	State-Owned	32608	29904	29932	30032
集体经济	Collective-Owned	54483	63929	62662	65535
个体经济	Individual	219809	237870	253713	263726
全省社会消费品零售总额	**Total Retail Sales of Consumer Goods**	**967.77**	**1287.86**	**1650.00**	**1932.89**
按地区分	By Region				
市	City	540.19	748.97	961.71	1157.95
县	Country	86.09	91.13	124.21	131.14
县以下	Below Country Level	341.49	447.76	564.08	643.80
按城乡分	By Urban and Rural				
城镇	Urban	514.24	708.07	936.56	1120.05
乡村	Rural	453.53	579.79	713.44	812.84
按经济类型分	By Ownership				
#国有经济	State Owned	332.51	403.36	496.79	512.08
集体经济	Collcetive Owned	341.72	441.91	531.81	602.83
个体经济	Individual	158.04	220.41	302.03	394.21
按行业分	By Sector				
批发零售贸易业	Wholesales and Retail Sales Trade	665.72	877.67	1125.77	1337.15
餐饮业	Catering Trade	44.74	67.67	90.19	126.02
制造业	Manufacturing	129.88	161.08	179.35	186.71
其他行业	Others	127.43	181.44	254.69	283.01
全省商品交易市场个数(个)	**Number of Free Markets(Number)**	**4618**	**4812**	**5111**	**5353**
城市	Urban	848	950	1293	1314
乡村	Rural	3770	3862	3818	4039
全省商品交易市场成交额	**Transaction Value**	**408.59**	**766.01**	**1464.68**	**2120.50**
城市	Urban	139.77	271.59	703.12	1024.92
乡村	Rural	268.82	494.42	761.56	1095.58

说明:1. 1996年社会消费品零售总额及各分组指标中不含售给城乡居民生活用住房的零售额。(1996年售给城乡居民生活用住房的金额为72.53亿元)。

2. 1993、1994年全省商品交易市场个数和成交额中不含生产资料市场的个数和成交额。

a)In 1996, the resident house was not included in the total retail sales of consumer goods and all the tagets by trips. (the amount of money of the residential house in 1996 was 7.253 billion yuan).

b)In 1993 and 1994, the number and transaction of the means of production were not included in the number of free markets and transaction value.

13－2 全省批发贸易业网点(1996)
NUMBER OF OUTLETS IN WHOLESALE TRADE

单位:个 (number)

项　目	Items	合　计 Total	市 City	县 Country	县以下 Below Country Leverl
合　计	**Total**	**92766**	**46840**	**9948**	**35978**
按经济类型分	By Type of Ownership				
国有经济	State-Owned	24595	14355	4440	5800
集体经济	Colletive-Owned	34712	17420	1908	15384
私营经济	Private	6370	2200	1395	2775
个体经济	Individual	25656	11544	2187	11925
联营经济	Joint Owned	361	332	0	29
股份制经济	Share Holding	966	924	17	25
外商投资经济	Foreign Funded	19	16	0	3
港澳台投资经济	Overseas Chinese from HongKong, Macao and Taiwan Funded	18	17	1	0
其他经济	Others	69	32	0	37
按行业分	By Sector				
食品、饮料、烟草和家庭日用品批发业	Food, Beverage, Tabacco and Daily Use Household Goods in Wholesale Trade	55837	27312	5949	22576
食品、饮料、烟草	Fook, Beverage, Tabacco	27812	11726	2908	13178
棉、麻、土畜产品	Cotton, Jute, Native and Livestock Products	2114	634	349	1131
纺织品、服装和鞋帽	Textile Products, Garments and Shoes, Hats	6266	4914	271	1081
日用百货	Daily Use Goods	9543	4220	1117	4206
日用杂品	Daily Use Articles	3663	1162	619	1882
五金、交电、化工	Hardware, Electrical Appliance and Chemical	4974	3592	368	1014
药品及医疗器械	Medicine and Medical Appliance	1465	1064	317	84
能源、材料和机械电子设备批发业	Energy, Material and Machine Electric Equipment in Wholesale Trade	21193	14129	1926	5138
能源	Energy	3448	2174	559	715
化工材料	Chemical Materials	1564	1145	108	311
木材	Timber	1309	812	144	353
建筑材料	Building Materials	5078	3269	255	1554
矿产品	Ore Products	105	62	31	12
金属材料	Metals	5157	3289	437	1431
机械、电子设备	Machine and Electric Equipment	2210	1721	183	306
汽车、摩托车及零配件	Spare and Component Parts for Automoiled, Motorcycles	1119	895	60	164
再生物资回收	Recycled Materials Collection	1203	762	149	292
其它批发业	Other in Wholesale Trade	15736	5399	2073	8264
工艺美术品	Handicraft Article	120	107	3	10
图书报刊	Books and Newspapers	268	179	72	17
农业生产资料	Agricultural Producer Goods	6105	1311	690	4104
其它类未包括的	Others	9243	3802	1308	4133

13—3 全省批发贸易业人员(1996)
NUMBER OF PERSONNEL IN WHOLESALE TRADE

单位:人 (person)

项目	Items	合计 Total	市 City	县 Country	县以下 Below Country Leverl
合计	**Total**	**818503**	**489236**	**108415**	**220852**
按经济类型分	By Type of Owmership				
国有经济	State-Owned	398870	263399	69131	66340
集体经济	Collective-Owned	307409	164496	28492	114421
私营经济	Private	43229	20350	4622	18257
个体经济	Individual	43851	16997	5513	21341
联营经济	Joint Owned	3796	3620	0	176
股份制经济	Share Holding	20735	19903	635	197
外商投资经济	Foreign Funded	95	78	0	17
港澳台投资经济	Overseas Chinese from HongKong,Macao and Taiwan Funded	253	231	22	0
其他经济	Others	265	162	0	103
按行业分	By Sector				
食品、饮料、烟草和家庭日用品批发业	Food,Beverage,Tabacco and Daily Use Household Goods in Wholesale Trade	482476	278366	65451	138659
食品、饮料、烟草	Food,Beverage,Tabacco	218923	107876	30530	80517
棉、麻、土畜产品	Cotton,Jute,Native and Livestock Products	28279	11425	8258	8596
纺织品、服装和鞋帽	Textile Products,Garments and Shoes,Hats	42990	35281	2203	5506
日用百货	Daily Use Goods	89530	47035	10289	32206
日用杂品	Daily Use Articles	17967	10167	3579	4221
五金、交电、化工	Hardware,Electrical Appliance and Chemical	63258	49100	7178	6980
药品及医疗器械	Medicine and Medical Appliance	21529	17482	3414	633
能源、材料和机械电子设备批发业	Energy,Material and Machine Electric Equipment in Wholesale Trade	235287	166846	29042	39399
能源	Energy	52194	36315	9639	6240
化工材料	Chemical Materials	18790	14909	1309	2572
木材	Timber	15497	10879	2366	2252
建筑材料	Building Materials	37161	23869	2579	10713
矿产品	Ore Products	1354	918	372	64
金属材料	Metals	61503	41587	6971	12945
机械、电子设备	Machine and Electric Equipment	22425	17868	2863	1694
汽车、摩托车及零配件	Spare and Component Parts for Automoiled,Motorcycles	12358	10106	816	1436
再生物资回收	Recycled Materials Collection	14005	10395	2127	1483
其它批发业	Other in Wholesale Trade	100740	44024	13922	42794
工艺美术品	Handicraft Article	1404	1294	17	93
图书报刊	Books and Newpapers	2585	1812	692	81
农业生产资料	Agricultural Producer Goods	49609	17776	8273	23560
其它类未包括的	Others	47142	23142	4940	19060

13—4 全省零售贸易业网点(1996)
NUMBER OF OUTLETS IN RETATL SALES TRADE

单位:个　　　　(number)

项　　目	Items	合　计 Total	市 City	县 Country	县以下 Below Country Leverl
合　　计	**Total**	**747755**	**175502**	**40358**	**531895**
按经济类型分	By Type of Ownership				
国有经济	State-Owned	10150	5963	1545	2642
集体经济	Collective-Owned	52929	18340	2387	32202
私营经济	Private	5118	2633	459	2026
个体经济	Individual	678475	147602	35954	494919
联营经济	Joint Owned	208	121	3	84
股份制经济	Share Holding	348	328	8	12
外商投资经济	Foreign Funded	27	24	0	3
港澳台投资经济	Overseas Chinese from HongKong,Macao and Taiwan Funded	35	35	0	0
其他经济	Others	465	456	2	7
按零售行业分	By Sector of Retail Sale				
食品、饮料、烟草	Food,Beverage and Tabacco	224147	47313	12319	164515
日用百货	Daily Use Goods	140518	25120	8114	107284
纺织品、服装和鞋帽	Textile Products,Garments and Shoes,Hats	55752	10424	5202	40126
日用杂品	Daily Use Articles	36562	5940	1226	29396
五金、交电、化工	Hardwares,Electrical Appliance and Chemical	22204	6193	1069	14942
药品及医疗器械	Medicine and Medical Appliance	2143	1044	152	947
图书报刊	Books and Newpapers	3400	1755	408	1237
其　　它	Others	263029	77713	11868	173448

13—5 全省零售贸易业人员(1996)
NUMBER OF PERSONNEL IN RETAIL SALES TRADE

单位:人　　　　(person)

项　　目	Items	合　计 Total	市 City	县 Country	县以下 Below Country Leverl
合　　计	**Total**	**1677497**	**560061**	**126069**	**991367**
按经济类型分	By Type of Ownership				
国有经济	State-Owned	165443	104860	33047	27536
集体经济	Collective-Owned	346282	149730	20583	175969
私营经济	Private	45789	25313	3475	17001
个体经济	Individual	1076732	238278	68596	769858
联营经济	Joint Owned	4407	3525	31	851
股份制经济	Share Holding	29423	29009	331	83
外商投资经济	Foreign Funded	5234	5215	0	19
港澳台投资经济	Overseas Chinese from HongKong,Macao and Taiwan Funded	3149	3149	0	0
其他经济	Others	1038	982	6	50
按零售行业分	By Sector of Retail Sale				
食品、饮料、烟草	Food,Beverage and Tabacco	451372	121420	37334	292618
日用百货	Daily Use Goods	459135	174082	35071	249982
纺织品、服装和鞋帽	Textile Products,Garments and Shoes,Hats	137074	48553	13117	75404
日用杂品	Daily Use Articles	71461	17354	3054	51053
五金、交电、化工	Hardwares,Electrical Appliance and Chemical	63984	30143	6516	27325
药品及医疗器械	Medicine and Medical Appliance	9113	4328	1528	3257
图书报刊	Books and Newpapers	10076	6227	1555	2294
其　　它	Others	475282	157954	27894	289434

13－6 全 省 餐 饮 业 网 点(1996)
NUMBER OF OUTLETS IN CATERING TRADE

单位:个 (number)

项　　目	Items	合　计 Total	市 City	县 Country	县以下 Below Country Leverl
合　计	**Total**	**126750**	**46644**	**9227**	**70879**
按经济类型分	By Type of Ownership				
国有经济	State-Owned	1395	1087	167	141
集体经济	Collective-Owned	7229	3521	477	3231
私营经济	Private	833	336	45	452
个体经济	Individual	116905	41340	8534	67031
联营经济	Joint Owned	55	50	1	4
股份制经济	Share Holding	58	50	0	8
外商投资经济	Foreign Funded	164	160	0	4
港澳台投资经济	Overseas Chinese from HongKong,Macao and Taiwan Funded	107	97	3	7
其他经济	Others	4	3	0	1
按餐饮行业分	By Sector				
正餐	Dinner	47563	17025	2250	28288
快餐	Fast Food	14213	2627	1815	9771
其他餐饮	Other Catering	64974	26992	5162	32820

13－7 全省餐饮业人员(1996)
NUMBER OF PERSONNEL IN CATERING TRADE

单位:人 (person)

项　　目	Items	合　计 Total	市 City	县 Country	县以下 Below Country Leverl
合　计	**Total**	**381647**	**183078**	**27432**	**171137**
按经济类型分	By Type of Ownership				
国有经济	State-Owned	30032	26236	2501	1295
集体经济	Collcetive-Owned	65535	37166	4790	23579
私营经济	Private	10843	3971	474	6398
个体经济	Individual	263726	105378	19606	138742
联营经济	Joint Owned	771	568	6	197
股份制经济	Share Holding	1677	1617	0	60
外商投资经济	Foreign Funded	5200	4814	0	386
港澳台投资经济	Overseas Chinese from hongKong,Macao and Taiwan Funded	3822	3291	55	476
其他经济	Others	41	37	0	4
按餐饮行业分	By Sector				
正餐	Dinner	194424	97378	12574	84472
快餐	Fast Food	35446	11110	4956	19380
其他餐饮	Other Catering	151777	74590	9902	67285

13—8 批发零售贸易业商品购销存总额(1996)
TOTAL PURCHASE,SALES AND INVENTORY OF WHOLESALE AND RETAIL SALES TRADE

单位:亿元 (100 000 000 yuan)

项　目	Items	商品购进总额 Total Goods Purchase	#农副产品 Farm and SideLine Products	商品销售总额 Total Sales	#批发 Wholesale	商品库存总额 Total Inventory
总　计	**Total**	**4790.75**	**291.95**	**5125.19**	**4218.36**	**684.45**
按经济类型分	By Type of Ownership					
#国有经济	State-Owned	2349.98	146.52	2554.58	2090.09	374.16
集体经济	Collective-Owned	1961.06	138.01	2156.87	1759.59	254.67
私营经济	Private	34.92	0.85	38.80	20.79	6.95
按企业规模分	By Scale of Business					
大型	Large	1409.43	26.28	1538.16	1309.07	166.14
中型	Medium	1833.49	82.79	2038.11	1674.66	260.93
小型	Small	1547.83	182.88	1638.92	1234.63	257.38
按商品类别分	By Type of Goods					
食品、饮料、烟酒类	Food,Beverage,Tabacco and Alcohol			1042.98	800.87	176.74
纺织品类	Textile Products			267.26	210.63	34.02
服装、鞋帽类	Garments,Shoes and Hats			316.09	193.45	53.51
日用品类	Daily Use Goods			286.92	182.55	42.84
家用电器类	Electrical Equipment of Household			375.54	255.27	54.96
文化体育用品类	Use Goods of Cultrue and Sports			55.07	33.55	9.83
化妆品类	Cosmetic			39.96	23.69	7.93
首饰类	Jewelry			22.45	2.66	8.07
中西药品类	Chinese and Western Madecine			122.25	67.62	18.23
书报、杂志类	Books,Newspapers and Magazines			36.78	18.80	7.12
石油及制品类	Oil and Products			258.76	235.23	11.48
煤炭及制品类	Coal and Products			195.35	183.17	10.90
化工材料及制品类	Chemical Materials and Products			407.67	397.35	34.50
木材类	Timber			47.70	40.00	5.21
建筑材料类	Building Materials			131.96	105.22	13.87
黑色金属材料类	Black Metals			412.35	398.63	39.64
有色金属材料类	Color Metals			100.29	96.21	6.20
机电设备类	Machine and Electric Equipment			326.96	294.04	37.66
其他类	Others			768.85	679.42	111.74
#生活消费品	Consumer Goods of Life			32.95	15.46	5.82

13—9 分行业批发零售贸易业商品购销存总额(1996)
TOTAL PURCHASES,SALES AND INVENTORY OF WHOLESALE AND RETAIL SALES TRADE BY SECTOR

单位:亿元 (100 000 000 yuan)

项目	Items	商品购进总额 Total Goods Purchase	#农副产品 Farm and SideLine Products	商品销售总额 Total Sales	#批发 Wholesale	商品库存总额 Total Inventory
总计	**Total**	**4790.75**	**291.95**	**5215.19**	**4218.36**	**684.45**
食品、饮料、烟草和家庭用品批发业	Food,Beverage,Tabacco and Daily Use Household Goods in Wholesale Trade	2025.25	196.43	2204.44	1842.22	327.86
食品、饮料、烟草	Food,Beverage,Tabacco	640.96	133.56	693.67	572.19	121.76
棉、麻、土畜产品	Cotton,Jute,Native and Livesstocks Product	205.20	42.74	223.66	213.92	57.21
纺织品、服装和鞋帽	Textile Products,Garments and Shoes,Hats	405.43	8.45	394.02	366.97	29.13
日用百货	Daily Use goods	289.76	10.47	317.04	233.32	54.96
日用杂品	Daily Use Articles	45.75	0.28	44.78	36.28	5.83
五金、交电、化工	Hardware,Electrical Appliance and Chemical	359.98	0.53	441.64	373.62	44.50
药品及医疗器械	Medicine and Medical Appliance	78.17	0.40	89.63	45.92	14.47
能源、材料和机械电子设备批发业	Energy,Material and Machine Electric Equipment in Wholesale Trade	1447.70	2.80	1564.51	1454.95	128.17
能源	Energy	361.41	0.65	399.83	380.98	24.31
化工材料	Chemical Materials	137.47	0.23	155.87	147.63	12.01
木材	Timber	29.44	0.21	36.39	31.50	3.97
建筑材料	Building Materials	181.30	1.01	176.64	148.98	17.08
矿产品	Ore Products	7.32	0.00	16.76	16.68	0.20
金属材料	Metals	417.88	0.21	444.10	424.25	43.65
机械、电子设备	Machine and Electric Equipment	157.76	0.05	173.45	160.32	14.28
汽车、摩托车及零配件	Spare and Component Parts for Automoiled,Motorcycles	92.52	0.00	93.34	78.11	8.94
再生物资回收	Recycled Materials Collection	62.60	0.44	68.13	66.50	3.73
其他批发业	Other in Wholesale Trade	385.16	13.56	409.21	378.68	45.79
工艺美术品	Handicraft Article	15.26	0.00	15.70	14.67	0.94
图书报刊	Books and Newspapers	23.51	0.00	21.67	17.69	3.33
农业生产资料	Agricultural Producer Goods	251.03	12.26	273.26	253.04	26.64
其他类未包括的	Others	95.36	1.30	98.58	93.28	14.88
零售业	Retail Sales Trade	932.64	79.16	1037.03	542.51	182.63
食品、饮料和烟草	Food,Beverage and Tabacco	144.21	33.31	163.87	74.32	50.07
日用百货	Daily Use Goods	566.96	44.65	634.44	347.78	97.53
纺织品、服装和鞋帽	Textile Products,Garments and Shoes,hats	47.88	0.05	55.42	24.94	9.45
日用杂品	Daily Use Articles	13.99	0.04	12.58	5.70	2.17
五金、交电、化工	Hardware,Electrical Appliance and Chemical	53.61	0.16	62.76	35.73	9.41
药品及医疗器械	Medicine and Medical Appliance	6.14	0.07	8.14	3.91	1.43
图书报刊	Books and Newpapers	17.51	0.00	17.60	2.72	3.32
其他	Others	82.34	0.88	82.22	47.41	9.25

13－10　社会消费品零售总额(按地区和城乡分)
TOTAL RETAIL SALES OF CONSUMER GOODS BY REGION AND URBAN-RURAL

单位:亿元　　(100 000 000 yuan)

年份 Year	社会消费品零售总额 Total Retail Sales of Consumer Goods	按地区分 By Region			按城乡 By Urban and Rural	
		市 City	县 Country	县以下 Below Country Level	城镇 Urban	乡村 Rural
1978	84.79	22.23	16.68	45.88	42.29	42.50
1980	122.56	41.21	23.28	58.07	58.10	64.46
1985	262.57	99.96	45.32	117.29	109.28	153.26
1986	304.58	111.92	51.13	141.53	130.18	174.40
1987	360.74	134.65	60.23	165.86	155.06	205.68
1988	471.83	198.46	66.28	207.09	203.21	268.62
1989	509.56	221.01	68.33	220.22	226.61	282.95
1990	515.43	231.26	67.05	217.12	243.36	272.07
1991	578.12	281.69	67.37	229.06	286.62	291.50
1992	704.52	364.47	74.59	265.46	354.16	350.36
1993	967.77	540.19	86.09	341.49	514.24	453.53
1994	1287.86	748.97	91.13	447.76	708.07	579.79
1995	1650.00	961.71	124.21	564.08	936.56	713.44
1996	1932.89	1157.95	131.14	643.80	1120.05	812.84

13－11　社会消费品零售总额(按经济类型分)
TOTAL RETAIL SALES OF CONSUMER GOODS BY OWNERSHIP

单位:亿元　　(100 000 000 yuan)

年份 Year	按经济类型分 By Ownershop					农民对非农业居民的零售额 Agricultural to Non-agricultural
	国有经济 State-Owned	集体经济 Collective Owned	联营经济 Joint Owned	个体经济 Individual	其他经济 Others	
1978	44.98	59.50	0.00	0.18	1.83	1.83
1980	61.17	87.83	0.08	0.58	4.82	4.82
1985	102.11	158.54	0.31	31.06	15.66	15.66
1986	118.17	182.66	0.42	34.73	19.78	19.78
1987	136.79	214.64	0.69	44.13	25.76	25.76
1988	179.78	271.15	1.19	62.38	34.06	34.06
1989	197.82	280.13	1.19	75.61	42.57	42.57
1990	200.66	267.89	1.16	81.51	47.84	47.84
1991	234.36	286.04	1.95	89.20	54.09	54.09
1992	292.80	325.96	3.12	113.49	67.17	67.17
1993	332.51	341.72	2.11	158.04	133.39	92.64
1994	403.36	441.91	4.73	220.41	217.45	134.20
1995	496.79	531.81	7.97	302.03	311.40	184.88
1996	512.08	602.83	9.40	394.21	414.37	242.75

注:1. 按经济类型分组各项指标1992年及以前为社会商品零售总额,1993年及以后为社会消费品零售总额。
2. 联营经济中1992年及以前含中外、港澳台与大陆合作、合资经济,1993年及以后不含中外、港澳台与大陆合作、合资经济。
3. 个体经济中1992年以前含私营经济,1993年及以后不含私营经济。
4. 1996年社会消费品零售总额及各分组指标中不含售给城乡居民生活用住房的零售额。(1996年售给城乡居民生活用住房的零售额为72.53亿元)。

a)Before 1992,the total values refer to those of retail sales;since 1993,they refer to those of consumer goods.
b)Before 1992,include foreign funded and overseas chinese from Hongkong,Macao and Taiwan in joint-owned; Since 1993, foreign funded and overseas Chinese from Hongkong,Macao and Taiwan were not included in joint-owned.
c)Before 1992,include provide in individual;Since 1993,provide was not included in individual.
d)In 1996,the residential house was not included in the total retail sales of consumer goods and all the tagets by trips.(the amount of money of residential house in 1996 was 7 253 000 yuan).

13—12 社会消费品零售总额(按行业分)
TOTAL RETAIL SALES OF CONSUMER GOODS BY SECTOR

单位:亿元 (100 000 000 yuan)

年份 Year	批发零售贸易业 Wholesales and Retail Sales Trade	餐饮业 Catering Trade	制造业 Manufacturing	其他行业 Others
1978	68.19	3.24	9.16	4.20
1980	93.07	4.72	16.46	8.31
1985	187.25	10.45	37.78	27.09
1986	214.56	12.53	44.91	32.58
1987	249.43	15.84	54.12	41.35
1988	326.26	20.33	71.74	53.50
1989	352.78	22.47	71.76	62.55
1990	358.12	24.17	66.76	66.38
1991	402.89	27.86	72.96	74.41
1992	486.10	33.64	91.34	93.44
1993	665.72	44.74	129.88	127.43
1994	877.67	67.67	161.08	181.44
1995	1125.77	90.19	179.35	254.69
1996	1337.15	126.02	186.71	283.01

13—13 社会消费品零售总额分类
TOTAL RETAIL SALES OF CONSUMER GOODS BY SECTOR

单位:亿元 (100 000 000 yuan)

年份 Year	社会消费品零售总额 Total Retail Sales of Consumer Goods	食品类 Foods	衣着类 Clothing	日用品类 Daily Use Goods	文化娱乐用品类 Goods of Culture and Entertainment	书报杂志类 Books, Newspapers and Magazines	药和医疗用品类 Medicine and Medical Goods	房屋及建筑材料类 Houses and Building Material	燃料类 Fuel
1978	84.79	43.25	20.00	7.60	3.25	0.71	3.89	2.99	3.10
1980	122.56	62.04	28.76	10.14	5.66	1.49	4.30	6.00	4.17
1985	262.57	135.03	56.52	21.55	16.39	3.28	6.91	16.13	6.76
1986	304.58	156.87	59.45	25.52	20.62	3.78	8.67	20.97	8.70
1987	360.74	189.35	71.46	29.20	23.46	3.86	10.17	24.31	8.93
1988	471.83	246.23	89.09	45.81	34.64	4.28	12.75	27.09	11.94
1989	509.56	266.71	99.87	42.19	36.42	5.94	15.04	30.54	12.85
1990	515.43	285.13	91.53	38.12	34.47	6.68	18.55	26.88	14.07
1991	578.12	315.11	102.33	47.41	35.26	8.24	22.73	32.95	14.09
1992	704.52	360.71	126.11	76.09	42.98	11.41	30.51	39.45	17.26
1993	967.77	492.59	167.43	105.58	64.84	15.26	45.49	55.16	21.42
1994	1287.86	655.52	217.65	156.96	78.56	20.61	55.38	79.85	23.33
1995	1650.00	841.50	277.20	199.65	99.00	26.40	69.30	108.90	28.05
1996	1932.89	1005.10	324.35	245.48	117.90	35.20	90.84	78.84	35.18

注:1996年不含售给城乡居民生活用住房的零售额。

Note: The residental houses were not included in total retail sales.

13—14 大中型批发零售贸易餐饮企业财务状况(1996)
WHOLESALE RETAIL SALES AND CATERING ENTERPRISES FINANCIAL SITUATION OF LARGE AND MEDIUM

单位:亿元 (100 000 000 yuan)

项目	Items	资本金合计 Total Capital Funds	资产总计 Total Assets	#流动资产 Circulating Funds	#固定资产 Fixed Asset	负债合计 Total Liabilities	#流动负债 Circulating Funds	#长期负债 Long-Term
批发、零售贸易企业总计	**Total of Wholesale and Retaile Sales Trade**	**194.87**	**1478.54**	**998.72**	**364.85**	**1165.69**	**1049.51**	**116.18**
按经济类型分	By Ownership							
国有经济	State-Owned	97.96	836.70	561.70	214.61	672.49	609.19	63.30
集体经济	Collective-Owned	62.48	435.85	311.26	94.36	338.70	304.69	34.01
股份制经济	Share Holding	26.31	176.05	110.49	47.87	132.00	117.93	14.07
按行业分	By Sector							
食品、饮料、烟草和家庭用品批发业	Food, Beverage, Tabacco and Daily Use Household Goods in Wholesale Trade	68.60	665.74	471.05	147.03	538.52	478.63	59.90
食品、饮料、烟草	Food, Beverage, Tabacco	21.33	184.12	120.33	51.21	131.60	118.53	13.07
棉、麻、土畜产品	Cotton, Jute, Native and Livesstock Products	6.69	129.24	103.92	11.40	118.49	107.30	11.19
纺织品、服装和鞋帽	Textile Products, Garments and Shoes, Hats	11.49	108.09	81.87	16.06	86.73	81.49	5.24
能源、材料和机械电子设备批发业	Energy, Material and Machine Electric Equipment in Wholesale Trade	55.71	432.16	304.17	87.93	355.46	332.76	22.70
能源	Energy	16.34	121.54	77.21	32.24	92.53	86.24	6.29
化工材料	Chemical Materials	4.61	35.86	23.68	6.92	28.25	25.86	2.39
建筑材料	Building Materials	2.50	16.43	9.50	5.41	12.93	11.88	1.05
汽车、摩托车及零配件	Spare and Component Parts for Automoiled, Motorcycles	2.30	18.48	13.77	3.58	15.59	14.87	0.72
其他批发业	Other in Wholesale Trade	13.92	96.56	72.05	18.98	72.62	69.14	3.47
工艺美术品	Handicraft Article	0.67	5.12	3.06	0.76	3.75	2.96	0.79
图书报刊	Books and Newspapers	0.34	4.41	2.75	1.53	2.80	2.61	0.19
农业生产资料	Agricultural Producer Goods	10.19	64.75	49.07	13.39	47.01	45.33	1.68
零售业	Retail Sales Trade	56.63	284.08	151.45	110.91	199.09	168.98	30.11
食品、饮料和烟草	Food, Beverage and Tabacco	4.80	27.02	17.79	8.13	19.41	17.55	1.86
日用百货	Daily Use Goods	42.07	200.94	100.57	82.70	139.29	115.43	23.86
纺织品、服装和鞋帽	Textile Products, Garments and Shoes, Hats	3.86	19.59	9.12	8.98	12.55	10.96	1.59
五金、交电、化工	Hardware, Electrical Appliance and Chemical	1.60	12.48	8.09	4.03	10.93	9.29	1.64
餐饮企业总计	**Total of Catering Trade**	**5.61**	**17.47**	**5.56**	**9.71**	**10.69**	**8.62**	**2.07**
国有经济	State-Owned	1.65	7.97	2.30	4.97	5.82	3.92	1.90
集体经济	Collective-Owned	0.72	1.49	0.32	0.97	0.79	0.71	0.08
股份制经济	Share Holding	0.66	1.75	0.40	1.23	1.06	1.01	0.06

13—15 大中型批发零售贸易餐饮企业财务状况(1996)

WHOLESALE RETAIL SALES AND CATERING ENTERPRISES FINANCIAL SITUATION OF LARGE AND MEDIUM

单位:亿元 (100 000 000 yuan)

项目	Items	所有者权益合计 Ownership Rights and Interests	商品销售收入 Revenue of Product Sales	商品销售成本 Cost of Product Sales	主营业务利润 Profits of Major Vocational Work	其他业务利润 Profits of Other Vocational Work	利润总额 Total Profits
批发、零售贸易企业总计	**Total of Wholesale and Retaile Sales Trade**	**312.85**	**2765.33**	**2509.10**	**124.35**	**9.12**	**13.36**
按经济类型分	By Ownership						
国有经济	State-Owned	164.21	1629.15	1482.62	70.82	5.73	8.18
集体经济	Collective-Owned	97.15	815.90	741.17	34.17	2.37	1.33
股份制经济	Share Holding	44.05	278.85	247.44	17.99	0.94	4.18
按行业分	By Sector						
食品、饮料、烟草和家庭用品批发业	Food,Beverage,Tabacco and Daily Use Household Goods in Wholesale Trade	127.22	1225.23	1111.37	66.10	3.75	16.49
食品、饮料和烟草	Food,Beverage,Tabacco	52.52	358.89	320.48	25.07	2.15	12.60
棉、麻、土畜产品	Cotton,Jute,Native and Livesstock Products	10.75	138.92	128.96	7.43	0.20	−1.09
纺织品、服装和鞋帽	Textile Products,Garments and Shoes,Hats	21.36	228.23	210.96	11.57	0.38	2.50
能源、材料和机械电子设备批发业	Energy,Material and Machine Electric Equipment in Wholesale Trade	76.70	858.95	798.32	22.40	3.48	−4.41
能源	Energy	29.01	266.50	236.85	8.81	0.80	−0.13
化工材料	Chemical Materials	7.61	86.00	81.32	2.43	0.21	−0.29
建筑材料	Building Materials	3.50	24.85	23.18	0.60	0.30	−0.24
汽车、摩托车及零配件	Spare and Component Parts for Automoiled, Motorcycles	2.90	54.46	52.53	0.87	0.18	−0.16
其他批发业	Other in Wholesale Trade	23.94	233.04	210.69	10.14	0.37	1.33
工艺美术品	Handicraft Article	1.37	11.02	9.91	0.81	0.03	0.31
图书报刊	Books and Newspapers	1.60	16.97	11.29	1.03	0.03	0.31
农业生产资料	Agricultural Producer Goods	17.74	158.22	145.76	6.61	0.19	0.27
零售业	Retail Sales Trade	84.99	448.11	388.73	25.71	1.52	−0.04
食品、饮料和烟草	Food,Beverage and Tabacco	7.61	42.79	38.64	1.55	0.33	−0.23
日用百货	Daily Use Goods	61.65	309.29	266.95	18.49	0.83	0.14
纺织品、服装和鞋帽	Textile Products,Garments and Shoes,Hats	7.04	24.54	20.84	1.77	0.16	−0.37
五金、交电、化工	Hardware,Electrical Appliance and Chemical	1.55	20.45	18.11	1.03	0.03	0.01
餐饮企业总计	**Total of Catering Trade**	**6.77**	**13.14**	**5.78**	**2.84**	**0.14**	**0.73**
国有经济	State-Owned	2.15	5.44	2.76	0.58	0.05	−0.02
集体经济	Collective-Owned	0.70	1.25	0.64	0.26	0.08	0.00
股份制经济	Share Holding	0.69	0.85	0.48	0.15	0.00	0.00

对外经济贸易和旅游 14

FOREIGN ECONOMY, TRADE AND TOURISM

14 对外经济贸易和旅游
FOREIGN ECONOMY, TRADE AND TOURISM

1 9 9 6

对外贸易进出口总额	Total Value of Imports and Exports	202.16	亿美元	(USD 100000000)
#出口	Exports	131.22	亿美元	(USD 100000000)
利用外资签订合同金额	Utilization of Foreign Capital Signed Value	101.97	亿美元	(USD 100000000)
#外商直接投资	Direct foreign Investments	98.32	亿美元	(USD 100000000)
实际利用外资	Value of Foreign Capital Actually Used	55.03	亿美元	(USD 100000000)
#外商直接投资	Direct Foreign Investments	50.72	亿美元	(USD 100000000)
旅游人数	Number of Tourists	83.70	万人次	(10000 person-times)
旅游外汇收入	Foreign exchang Income from Tourism	31705	万美元	(USD 10000)

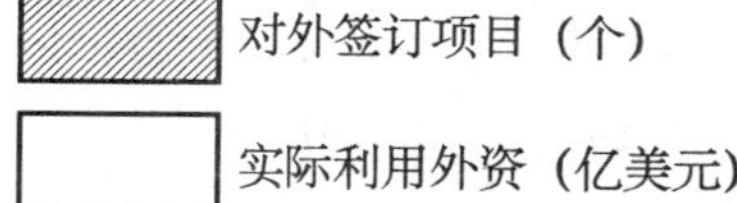

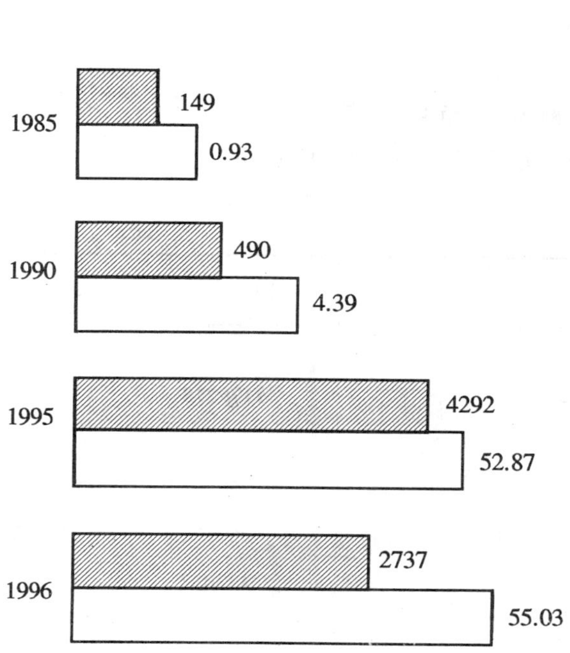

实际利用外资发展速度(%)

(以 1985 年为 100)

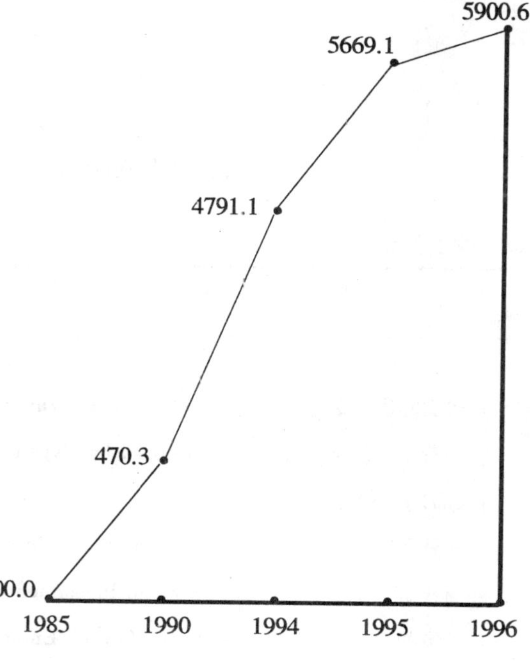

14—1 对外贸易进出口总额
TOTAL VALUE OF IMPORTS AND EXPORTS OF FOREIGN TRADE

单位:万美元 (USD 10 000)

年份 Year	进出口总额 Total Value of Imports and Exports	进口 Imports	#省(部)级公司 Provincial Co. (Ministry) Level	#外商投资企业 Foreign Investment Enterprise	出口 Exports	#省(部)级公司 Provincial Co. (Ministry) Level	#外商投资企业 Foreign Investment Enterprise
1978	42749	903	903		41846	41846	
1979	67675	5777	5777		61898	61898	
1980	94609	9208	9208		85401	85401	
1985	185343	29492	29492		155851	154604	
1986	208165	36175	25024	8008	171991	170844	1072
1987	270245	58380	39211	3010	211865	209396	2231
1988	316498	81511	44762	2749	234987	220816	4503
1989	329714	86563	41161	2509	244111	213227	8862
1990	369452	74457	33210	5541	294995	236864	19314
1991	450431	104377	44453	14248	346053	240179	45415
1992	625145	158050	75413	34420	467095	236976	130639
1993	869951	274090	110158	88974	595861	221480	226850
1994	1290998	388572	138656	145314	902426	267959	368421
1995	1679442	500224	123560	239800	1179218	290257	433012
1996	2021566	709377	134646	392870	1312189	274367	529150

14—2 对外贸易实际出口总额
TOTAL VALUE OF EXPORTS OF FOREIGN TRADE

单位:万美元 (USD 10000)

项目	Items	1995	1996
全省实际出口总额	**Total Export Value of Whole Provice**	**1179218**	**1312189**
按经营单位性质分组:	Grouped by Type of Management		
省(部)级外贸公司	Foreign Trade corporation of Province (Ministry) Level	290257	274367
市县外贸公司	Foreign Trade Corporation of City and County	360171	378213
外商投资企业	Foreign Investment Enterprise	433012	529150
其他有权企业	Other Owned Enterprise	95778	133112

14—3 对外贸易自营进口总额
TOTAL VALUE OF IMPORTS OF FOREIGN TRADE (BY SELF MANAGEMENT)

单位：万美元　　　　(USD 10000)

指　　标	Items	1985	1990	1995	1996
总　　计	**Total**	**29492**	**74457**	**500224**	**709377**
省级部委公司	Provincial Ministries & Commisions Co.	29492	33210	123560	134646
粮　　油	Grain and Edible Oil			766	2229
纺　　织	Textile Products		4332	7366	7031
针　　织	Knitting		1393	1561	751
服　　装	Garments	342	1092	6763	7108
丝　　绸	Silk and Satins		52	3200	2329
土　　产	Local Products	1669	590	4165	787
畜　　产	Animal Products		326	1533	1243
轻　　工	Light Industrial Products		1263	8538	5016
工　　艺	Handicraft	41	1028	2427	2488
陶　　瓷	Pottery and Porcelain			56	288
五　　矿	Hardware and Minerals	100		948	1073
化　　工	Chemicals	182	498	2553	2203
医　　保	Medicine and Medical Products		124	3040	2047
机　　械	Machinery		516	6206	8003
省属生产企业	Province Owned Production Enterprises		25609	32534	42446
各市合计	Cities Total		15638	344130	532285
南　　京	Nanjing		2831	25815	47123
无　　锡	Wuxi		3094	35392	70207
徐　　州	Xuzhou		130	10052	12869
常　　州	Changzhou		1168	22381	35261
苏　　州	Suzhou		3292	180564	261700
南　　通	Nantong		3140	32293	55285
连 云 港	Liangyungang		33	5690	6363
淮　　阴	Huaiyin			190	1418
盐　　城	Yancheng			6220	5963
扬　　州	Yangzhou		1734	19525	13896
镇　　江	Zhenjiang		216	5301	15442
泰　　州	Taizhou			707	6636
宿　　迁	Suqian				122

14—4 本省自营进口商品数量情况
IMPORT COMMODITIES IN VOLUME (BY SELF MANAGEMENT)

单位:万美元 (USD 10000)

商品名称	Items	1985	1990	1995	1996
成套设备及技术引进	Complet Set Equioment and Technology Import	449	2333	20105	81759
机床及工具	Machine tools and Instruments	857	102	2537	4116
#机　床 (台)	Machine Tools (unit)	66	4	63	88
化工机械	Chemical Industrial Machine	1341	367	3900	3735
轻工机械	Light Industrial Machine	7535	1843	11375	—
电子仪器类	Electronic Instruments	3526	2606	10987	2418
#通讯设备	Communicative Equipment	2539	2337	10487	—
钢　材 (吨)	Rolled-Steel (tons)	205489	18933	46768	114356
石油及产品	Petroleum and Related Product	6	903	2910	13909
橡胶及制品	Rubber and Related Product	42	1320	750	5787
化工原料	Industrial Chemical	3179	29961	89976	77316
染料及中间体	Dyestsff and Intermediat	131	610	5239	1059
医疗器械	Medical Appliances	512	933	973	808
家用电器	Household Eelectric Appliances	357	1474	699	9123
纸　浆 (吨)	Paper Pulp (tons)	99		11629	152736
纸　张	Paper	118	884	4802	10400
电视机及音响设备	TV Sets and Sound Equipment	2564	2701	3810	5060
#电视机 (台)	Television Sets (pcs)	56108			
羊　毛 (吨)	Wool (tons)	370	3142	21732	3882
纤维素纤维 (吨)	Artificial Fibers (tons)	1099	17563	5980	3572
合成纤维 (吨)	Synthetic Fibers (tons)	5909	19343	23351	27822
织　物	Fabric	207	646	8033	55610
木　材	Timber	75	4582	2314	10355
畜产类	Animal Products	71	970	1895	21527

注:1996年含外商投资企业进口数。

Note:Imports of foreign investment enterprises were included in 1996.

14—5 对外贸易自营出口总额
TOTAL EXPORTS VALUE OF FOREIGN TRADE (BY SELF-MANAGEMENT)

单位:万美元 (USD 10000)

指标	Items	1985	1990	1995	1996
总计	**Total**	**155851**	**294995**	**1179218**	**1312189**
省级部委公司	Provincial Ministries & Commisions Co.	155851	236864	290257	274367
粮油	Grain and Edible Oil	13890	16219	13230	10108
纺织	Textile Products	44042	26053	24438	21421
针织	Knitting		12770	18618	16738
服装	Garments	14423	25207	26502	25218
丝绸	Silk and Satins	21794	43052	30789	25119
土产	Local Products	17804	10987	10955	11807
畜产	Animal Products		11557	9245	8008
轻工	Light Industrial Products	7815	15206	18837	16530
工艺	Handicraft	3633	14191	12588	12611
陶瓷	Pottery and Porcelain	251	663	2730	2553
五矿	Hardware and Minerals	3207	7784	8148	6539
化工	Chemicals	20775	21399	11634	9850
医保	Medicine and Medical Products	3733	5206	5818	5019
机械	Machinery	2228	10118	13611	12306
省属生产企业	Province Owned Production Enterprises		200	9621	5030
各市合计	Cities Total		57931	879340	1035445
南京	Nanjing		14602	80826	88903
无锡	Wuxi		8635	125286	166328
徐州	Xuzhou		150	14452	21724
常州	Changzhou		3313	76944	95817
苏州	Suzhou		13943	315626	354994
南通	Nantong		13264	137785	152538
连云港	Liangyungang		1383	21999	28451
淮阴	Huaiyin			7736	8827
盐城	Yancheng			15239	24030
扬州	Yangzhou		1247	44493	37499
镇江	Zhenjiang		1394	33813	34748
泰州	Taizhou			5136	20840
宿迁	Suqian			5	746

14—6 对外贸易自营出口商品总额构成
TOTAL EXPORT VALUE OF FOREIGN TRADE AND COMPOSITION (BY SELF-MANAGEMENT)

单位:万美元 (USD 10000)

年份 Year	出口总值 Total Value of Exports	工矿产品 Industrial and Mineral Products		农副产品加工品 Agricultural and Sideline Processing Products	
		金额 Value	占总值(%) of the Total (%)	金额 Value	占总值(%) of the Total (%)
1981	109685	63700	58.1	40200	36.6
1982	119536	52421	43.8	58774	49.2
1983	137242	66580	48.5	58255	42.5
1984	148704	57244	38.5	72117	48.5
1985	155851	68297	43.8	66978	43.0
1986	171991	71030	41.3	80038	46.5
1987	211865	91479	43.2	107022	50.5
1988	234987	99926	42.5	110530	47.1
1989	244111	100759	41.3	123926	50.7
1990	294995	135808	46.0	137472	46.6
1991	346053	166176	48.0	155040	44.8
1992	467095	241637	51.7	198687	42.5
1993	595861	328313	55.1	240249	40.3
1994	902426	485996	53.9	368541	40.8
1995	1179218	685266	58.1	442488	37.5
1996	1312189	817503	62.3	417589	31.8

续表 Continued

单位:万美元 (USD 10000)

年份 Year	农副产品 Agricultural and Sideline Products		轻工产品 Light Industrial Products		重工产品 Heavy Industrial Products	
	金额 Value	占总值(%) of the Total(%)	金额 Value	占总值(%) of the Total(%)	金额 Value	占总值(%) of the Total(%)
1981	5785	5.3	82919	75.6	20981	19.1
1982	8341	7.0	87589	73.3	23606	19.7
1983	12407	9.0	101077	73.7	23758	17.3
1984	19343	13.0	109849	73.9	19512	13.1
1985	20576	13.2	107729	69.1	27546	17.7
1986	20923	12.2	124281	72.2	26787	15.6
1987	13364	6.3	166001	78.4	32500	15.3
1988	24531	10.4	163177	69.5	47279	20.1
1989	19426	8.0	174994	71.7	49691	20.3
1990	21715	7.4	204847	69.4	68433	23.2
1991	24837	7.2	235649	68.1	85567	24.7
1992	26771	5.8	327617	70.1	112707	24.1
1993	27299	4.6	413088	69.3	155474	26.1
1994	47889	5.3	635336	70.4	219201	24.3
1995	51464	4.4	781271	66.2	346483	29.4
1996	77097	5.9	766120	58.4	468972	35.7

14—7 对外贸易主要商品出口数量
EXPORT VOLUME OF MAJOR COMMODITIES (BY FOREIGN TRADE)

商品名称		Items		1985	1990	1995	1996
冻猪肉	(吨)	Frozen Poek	(tons)	25305	26347	1766	1246
冻家禽	(吨)	Frozen Poultry	(tons)	817	1794	3811	4540
猪肉制品	(吨)	pork and Related Products	(tons)	1230	913	3296	
鲜蛋	(吨)	Fresh Eggs	(tons)	3365	360	524	81
再制蛋	(万枚)	Processed Eggs	(10000 pcs)	2161	1020	742	12
水产品	(吨)	Aquatic Products	(tons)	10465	13853	22155	
蔬菜	(吨)	Vegetables	(tons)	22706	29551	61364	98111
猪肉罐头	(吨)	Canned Pork	(tons)	9472	12626	6725	3796
棉花	(吨)	Cotton	(tons)	97734	4652		2000
棉纱	(件)	Cotton Yarn	(pcs))	34487	59696	23680	2877135
棉布	(万米)	Cotton Cloth	(10000 m)	25769	18643	28989	1271468
棉涤沦布	(万米)	Polyester Cotton Cloth	(10000 m)	11065	12312	17732	24645
棉织品	(万美元)	Cotton Textile	(USD 10000)	2763	5421	2744	33573
棉针织品	(万美元)	Cotton Knitted Textile	(USD 10000)	2430	5776	18175	7848
毛针织品	(万美元)	Woolen Knitted Textile	(USD 10000)	1782	2208	10468	16228
呢绒	(万米)	Woolen Piece Goods	(10000 m)	194	111	1613	16257
桑蚕丝	(吨)	Mulberry Silk	(tons)	1661	1189	1255	1232
绸缎	(万米)	Sating	(10000 m)	4957	5479	5838	8489
棉布服装	(万美元)	Cotton Cloth Garments	(USD 10000)	8613	18496	57395	
茶叶	(吨)	Tea	(tons)	1427	1429	1403	1663
猪鬃	(箱)	Bristle	(Chest)	15552	15601	39094	73610
兔毛	(吨)	Rabbit Fur	(tons)	600	444	1321	1076
天鹅绒毯	(万条)	Velvet Blanket	(10000)	150	37	9	70
羽毛	(吨)	Feathers	(tons)	767	318	189	12280
山羊板皮	(吨)	Goat Hides	(tons)	218	105		100000
洗衣粉	(吨)	Detergents	(tons)	3836	1470	1895	1664
皮件	(万美元)	Fur Products	(USD 10000)	990	867	4498	

注:1996年始含外商投资企业出口。

Notes: Exports of foreign investment enterprises were included in 1996.

14—8 海关进口贸易总额(按国别、地区分) TOTAL VALUE OF IMPORTS (CUSTOM STATISICS) (BY COUNTRIES AND REGIONS)

单位:万美元 (USD 10000)

项目	Items	1993	1994	1995	1996
进口总额	**Total Value of Imports**	**447665**	**507280**	**649637**	**908691**
亚洲	Asia	282495	296149	414440	572894
#日本	Japan	119922	136410	194458	246863
非洲	Africa	535	2155	5495	11569
欧洲	Europe	90347	120972	127308	174253
#英国	United Kingdom	5104	7373	7387	9058
意大利	Italy	16637	28559	20332	31740
俄罗斯	Russia	8547	15173	9937	8986
拉丁美洲	Latin America	11665	9269	8635	22149
北美洲	North America	47767	60150	72563	101303
#美国	Unite States	43944	55058	66354	93531
大洋洲	Oceanian	14856	18585	21196	26523
#澳大利亚	Australia	13203	15295	17593	21799

14—9 海关出口贸易总额(按国别、地区分) TOTAL VALUE OF EXPORTS (CUSTOM STATISTICS) (BY COUNTRIES AND REGIONS)

单位:万美元 (USD 10000)

项目	Items	1993	1994	1995	1996
进口总额	**Total Value of Imports**	**465227**	**668627**	**978166**	**1160098**
亚洲	Asia	247538	405486	610220	689767
#日本	Japan	126949	190773	277809	349502
非洲	Africa	6912	7374	12982	15116
欧洲	Europe	89546	111201	159790	200240
#英国	United Kingdom	10153	13074	17913	22473
意大利	Italy	12519	15835	19868	19808
俄罗斯	Russia	3164	2487	3204	4102
拉丁美洲	Latin America	9815	13405	21507	28739
北美洲	North America	103034	120028	159630	208755
#美国	Unite States	93095	109814	142476	188975
大洋洲	Oceanian	8382	11133	14037	17481
#澳大利亚	Australia	7033	9341	11411	14720

14—10 海关进口贸易总值(1996)
TOTAL VALUE OF IMPORTS AND EXPORTS (CUSTOM STATISTICS 1996)

单位:万美元 (USD 10000)

类别	Type	进口 Imports	出口 Exports
总值	**Total Value**	**908691**	**1160098**
活动物、动物产品类	Live Animal, Animal Products	2419	16415
植物产品类	Vegetables, Fruits and Cereals	2418	15263
动植物食用油脂、动植物蜡类	Animal and Vegetable Oil, Fats and Waxes	6121	963
食品、饮料、酒及醋、烟草代用品类	Food, Beverages, Liquor and Vinegar, Tobacco and Tobacco Substitutes	11468	31268
矿产品类	Minerals	17378	7561
化学工业及其相关工业品类	Chemical and Related Products	71011	113957
塑料及制品、橡胶及制品类	Plastics, Rubber and Related Products	36740	23557
生皮、皮革、毛皮及其制品、鞍具等类	Raw Hides, Leather, Furs and Related Products, Saddle etc.	15716	31747
木及制品、稻草、秸秆、篮筐结品类	Wool and Wooden Products, Rices Straw Plaited Products and Basket Wickework	15131	9802
木浆、纸及纸板制品类	Paper Pulp, Paper, Paperboard and Related Products	16940	2908
纺织原料及纺织制品类	Textile Materials and Products	176608	451743
鞋、帽、伞、杖、已加工羽绒制品类	Footwear, Headwear, Umbrellas, Canes and Pressesed Feather Products	3078	43022
石料、水泥、云母及类似材料制品类	Gypsum, Cement, Mica and Related Products	7445	10540
天然或养殖珍珠、包贵金属及制品类	Natural or Cultivated Pearls, Rolled Precious Metal and Related Products	1306	3219
贱金属及其制品类	Base Metals and Related Products	68230	72534
机器、电气设备、录音机及其零件类	Machinery, Electrical Equipment, Recorders and Spare Parts	410458	199381
车辆、航空器、船舶及运输设备类	Locomotives, Aircraft, Ship and Transportation Equipment	7321	36434
光学、照相、电影、乐器零件及附件类	Optical, Photograghic, Film, Instruments Spare Parts and Appendix	31817	32014
			35
杂项制品类	Sundry Goods and Related Products	7059	57572
艺术品、收藏品及古物类	Work of Art, Collection and Antique	26	163
未分类商品	Others		

14—11 利用外资对外签订合同情况
UTILIZATION OF FOREIGN CAPITAL THROUGH SIGNED AGREEMENT

单位：项目：个 金额：万美元　　(USD 10000)

指标	Items	1978—1996		1990		1996	
		项目 Projects	金额 Value	项目 Projects	金额 Value	项目 Projects	金额 Value
总计	**Total**	**34603**	**5394881**	**490**	**36241**	**2737**	**1019742**
对外借款	**Foreign Loans**	**560**	**202156**	**42**	**9759**	**16**	**19198**
外国政府贷款	Government Loans	127	56944	23	7144	11	16022
国际金融组织贷款	Loans from International Monetary Organizations	367	92908	14	1878		
外国银行现汇贷款	Loans of Ready Remittance from Foreign Bank	29	46774	3	326	4	2896
买方信贷	Buyer Credit Loans	12	3994	2	411	1	280
对外发行证券	Issue Negotatiable Securities to Foreign Country	25	1536				
外商直接投资	**Direct Foreign Investment**	**32269**	**5111228**	**395**	**24416**	**2699**	**983169**
合资经营	Joint Venture	27110	3249383	358	14478	1716	509672
合作经营	Cooperative Operation	1593	462756	8	6640	235	98150
独资经营	Sololy Foreign Funded	3566	1399089	29	3298	748	375347
外商其他投资	**Other Foreign Investment**	**1774**	**81497**	**53**	**2066**	**22**	**17375**
对外发行股票	Issue Share Certificate to Foreign Country	3	16417		3	3	16417
补偿贸易中客商作价提供设备	Provide with Equipment in Compensation Trade Priced by Travelling Trader	546	29405	33	454	15	370
加工装配中客商作价提供设备	Provide with Equipment and Assembling Priced by Travelling Trader	929	8154	3	56	4	588
国际租赁	International Loans	296	27521	17	1556		

14—12 实际利用外资情况
ACTUAL UTILIZATION OF FOREIGN CAPITAL

单位：万美元　　(USD 10000)

指标	Items	1985—1996	1990	1995	1996
总计	**Total**	**2231882**	**43861**	**528701**	**550292**
对外借款	**Foreign Loans**	**256867**	**27696**	**41816**	**25258**
外国政府贷款	Government Loans	44666	12660	3067	3643
国际金融组织贷款	Loans from International Monetary Organizations	85198	1360	22371	10572
外国银行现汇贷款	Loans of Ready Remittance from Foreign Bank	95930	11580	4386	10174
买方信贷	Buyer Credit Loans	29162	2096	11992	869
对外发行证券	Issue Negotatiable Securities to Foreign Country	1911			
外商直接投资	**Direct Foreign Investment**	**1908581**	**14110**	**478058**	**507208**
合资经营	Joint Venture	1346069	13787	332166	313368
合作经营	Cooperative Operation	137285	249	27684	32857
独资经营	Sololy Foreign Funded	425227	74	118208	160983
外商其他投资	**Other Foreign Investment**	**66434**	**2055**	**8827**	**17826**
对外发行股票	Issue Share Certificate to Foreign Country	16417			16417
补偿贸易中客商作价提供设备	Provide with Equipment in Compensation TradePriced by Travelling Trader	17779	876	681	821
加工装配中客商作价提供设备	Provide with Equipment and Assembling by Priced Travelling Trader	10521	36	8017	588
国际租赁	International Loans	21717	1143	129	

14—13 对外承包工程和劳务合作(国际公司)
CONTRACTED PROJECTS AND LABOR SERVICES CO-OPERATION WITH FOREIGN COUNTRIES
(INTERNATIONAL CORPORATION)

年份 Year	合同数(份) Number of Contracts	合同金额(万美元) Contracted Value (USD 10000)	实际完成营业额(万美元) Fulfilled Value (USD 10000)	年末在外人数(人) Number of Persons Abroad By the End of Year (persons)
总计 Total				
1978—1980	5	617		
1981	12	921		
1982	18	895		
1983	21	1914		
1984	41	1003		
1985	88	2966		
1986	30	2935		
1987	28	2713		
1988	45	4101		
1989	125	7725		
1990	77	4046	4046	1271
1991	107	7331	6531	3068
1992	97	6854	6323	3094
1993	148	10794	8692	5296
1994	204	24756	13035	7779
1995	309	28113	25928	8206
1996	312	36379	29048	12372
对外承包工程 Contracted Projects				
1978—1980	2	262		
1981				
1982				
1983	2	785		
1984	4	715		
1985	13	262		
1986	11	1776		
1987	11	396		
1988	20	2373		
1989	17	2081		
1990	32	3571	3521	881
1991	40	5843	6157	1677
1992	38	5473	5719	1270
1993	38	6900	5848	2150
1994	70	19868	10694	3786
1995	101	19495	19774	2946
1996	148	24040	22725	3298
对外劳务合作 Labor Services				
1978—1980	3	355		
1981	12	921		
1982	18	895		
1983	19	1129		
1984	37	288		
1985	75	2704		
1986	19	1159		
1987	17	2317		
1988	25	1728		
1989	108	5644		
1990	45	475	525	390
1991	67	1488	373	1391
1992	59	1381	604	1824
1993	110	3895	2844	3146
1994	134	4887	2342	3993
1995	205	8591	6120	5260
1996	163	12253	6287	9068

14—14 旅 游 人 数 和 收 入
NUMBER OF TOURISTS AND FOREIGN EXCHANGE INCOME FROM TOURISM

单位:万人次 (10000 person-times)

指　　标	Items	1985	1990	1994	1995	1996
旅游人数总计	**Total Number of Tourists**	**45.67**	**72.48**	**70.22**	**76.77**	**83.70**
外国人	Foreigners	36.28	21.92	46.06	48.68	55.09
华　侨	Overseas Chinese	0.89	1.65	1.51	1.65	2.24
港澳同胞	Hong Kong, Macao Chinese	8.50	8.25	12.24	14.66	14.06
台　胞	Taiwan Chinese		40.66	10.41	11.78	12.31
#南京市	Nanjing		26.33	21.16	23.17	22.53
无锡市	Wuxi		14.29	13.83	15.06	15.45
常州市	Changzhou		0.66	1.65	1.95	2.05
苏州市	Suzhou		26.16	23.54	24.57	25.11
南通市	Nantong		0.96	2.39	2.96	5.50
扬州市	Yangzhou		1.57	3.42	3.82	5.26
镇江市	Zhenjiang		1.64	3.05	3.76	5.36
旅游外汇收入（亿美元）	**Total Foreign Exchange Income from Tourism** (**USD** 100000000)	**0.46**	**0.71**	**2.22**	**2.60**	**3.17**

14—15 接 待 过 夜 的 外 国 人
FOREIGNERS RECEIEVED OVER NIGHT

单位:人次 (10000 person-times)

国　　别	Country	1990	1993	1994	1995	1996
总　　计	**Total**	**219215**	**455177**	**460620**	**486794**	**550890**
#日　　本	Japan	82559	168804	165758	175849	217946
美　　国	Unite States	17681	51193	43032	40815	46233
新 加 坡	Singapore	9057	35815	30411	37170	34884
德　　国	Germany	9158	20433	24396	27052	25431
英　　国	United Kingdom	6081	26283	23351	19590	22476
法　　国	France	6397	28173	25890	22091	19221
印度尼西亚	Indonesia	1390	8138	8451	8308	7597
加 拿 大	Canada	3726	7874	7389	7402	9026
泰　　国	ThaiLand	5197	6031	5643	6494	7823
意 大 利	Italy	4448	12560	15364	16103	12972
澳大利亚	Australia	3016	5671	6889	6533	7296
菲 律 宾	Philippines	1577	3573	3349	2591	3905

15 财政、金融、保险

FINANCE, BANKING AND INSURANCE

15 财政、金融、保险
FINANCE，BANKING AND INSURANCE

1 9 9 6

财政总收入	Financial Revenue	427.99	亿元	(100000000 yuan)
#地方财政收入	Local Financial Revenue	223.17	亿元	(100000000 yuan)
财政支出	Financial Expenditure	310.94	亿元	(100000000 yuan)
金融机构存款额	Deposits Balance of Banking Institutions	4649.49	亿元	(100000000 yuan)
金融机构贷款额	Loans Balance of Banking Institutions	3574.85	亿元	(100000000 yuan)
银行现金收入	Bank Cash Revenue	7935.11	亿元	(100000000 yuan)
银行现金支出	Bank Cash	8074.89	亿元	(100000000 yuan)
承保额	Insurance Amount	10179.36	亿元	(100000000 yuan)
赔款支出	Settlement	20.07	亿元	(100000000 yuan)

财政总收入和支出

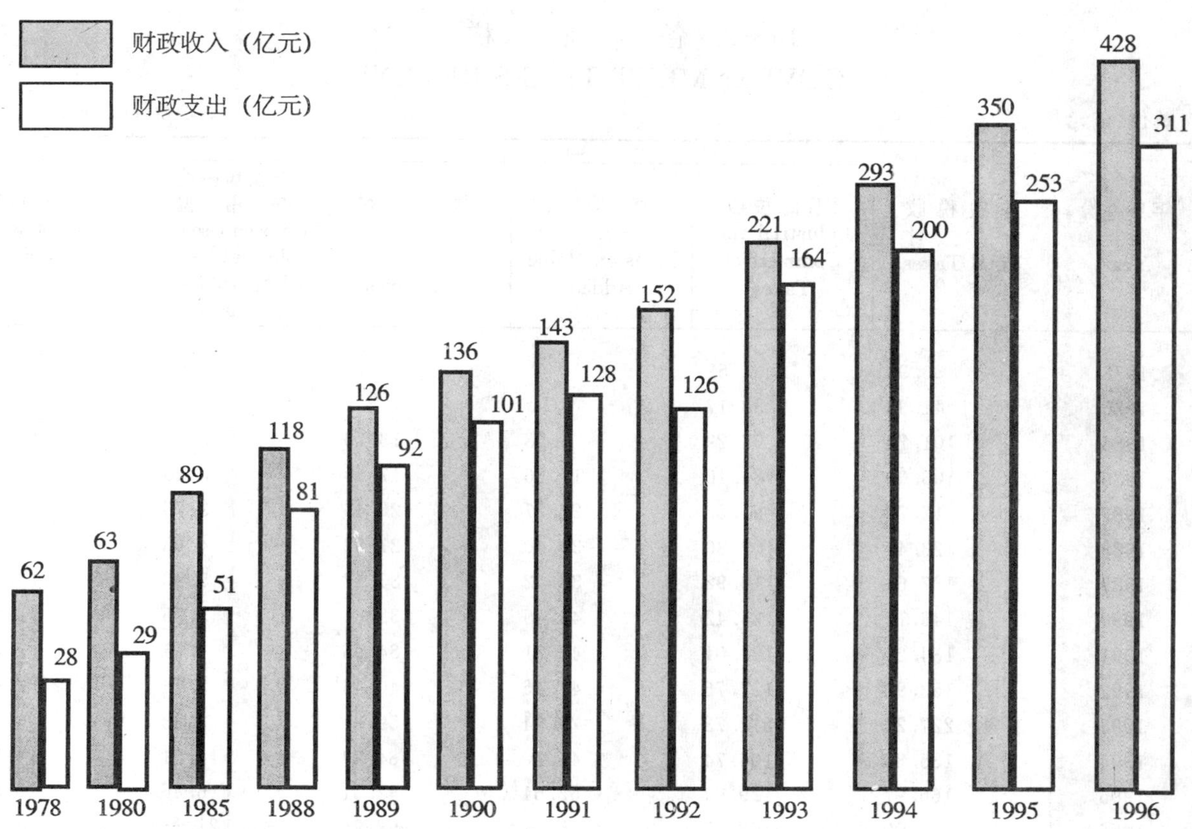

15—1 财 政 收 入
FINANCIAL REVENUE

单位:亿元 (100 000 000 yuan)

年 份 Year	财政总收入 Financial Revenue	#地方财政收入 Local Financial Revenue	#企业收入 Enterprise Revenue	#税收收入 Taxes	#企业亏损补贴 Subsidies to Loss-Making Enterprise	#其他收入 Others
1978	62.29		25.04	35.93	−1.81	0.13
1980	63.36		21.00	41.36	−1.30	0.09
1985	89.00		2.40	101.74	−14.38	0.21
1986	98.73		9.53	103.69	−8.31	0.48
1987	107.17		10.07	112.70	−9.49	0.55
1988	117.96		2.51	123.41	−15.27	1.00
1989	126.39		−6.81	137.64	−22.94	1.92
1990	136.20		−6.19	143.12	−20.14	2.48
1991	143.29		−7.88	134.24	−17.46	1.64
1992	152.31		−2.89	153.92	−12.60	1.70
1993	221.30		−8.40	227.24	−16.70	2.23
1994	293.41	136.62	3.30	135.86	−11.90	4.28
1995	350.08	172.64	9.00	166.97	−11.75	1.01
1996	427.99	223.17	22.22	213.00	−10.46	1.44

15—2 各 项 税 收
GOVERNMENT TAXES REVENUE

单位:亿元 (100 000 000 yuan)

年 份 Year	各项税收合计 Total Taxes	#工商税收 Industrial and Commercial Taxes	#增值税 Taxes on Value-Added	#营业税 Run Taxes	#农牧和耕地占用税 Taxes on Use of Cultivated Land and Agriculture, Animal Husbandry	#企业所得税 Enterprise Income Taxes
1978	35.93	32.52			2.06	
1980	41.36	38.17			1.94	
1985	101.74	77.29	7.58	13.70	3.00	18.00
1986	103.69	84.10	17.26	17.38	3.19	14.96
1987	112.70	91.23	22.27	20.45	3.73	16.21
1988	123.41	102.80	35.40	27.83	4.93	14.53
1989	137.64	116.92	38.62	33.48	5.90	13.75
1990	143.12	125.42	43.45	33.83	5.55	11.13
1991	134.24	121.01	40.71	34.66	4.91	7.74
1992	153.92	137.76	47.46	40.46	7.74	7.89
1993	227.24	212.73	79.74	59.91	7.33	6.87
1994	135.86	106.74	46.10	34.27	14.31	14.81
1995	166.97	129.94	52.61	42.31	16.46	20.57
1996	213.00	163.47	60.89	58.96	21.18	28.35

15—3 地方财政支出 LOCAL FINANCIAL EXPENDITURE

单位:亿元 (100 000 000 yuan)

年份 Year	地方财政支出 Local Expenditure	#基本建设 Capital-Construction	#企业挖潜改造资金 Technical Updates and Tranformation of Enterprise	#科技三项费用 New Products Promotion Funds	#城市维护费 City Maintenance	#科教文卫事业费 Culture, Education Science and Health Care	#行政管理费 Adiministration
1978	28.38	9.26	1.37		0.39	4.98	1.80
1980	28.95	8.67	1.76	0.49	0.67	6.79	2.39
1985	50.53	7.22	1.73	0.71	3.43	14.70	4.88
1986	66.14	6.98	2.19	0.58	4.80	17.61	5.57
1987	68.00	5.91	1.52	0.79	4.27	18.78	5.99
1988	81.45	5.35	2.47	0.67	5.09	22.72	5.94
1989	92.25	5.25	1.80	0.82	5.98	26.16	7.07
1990	100.97	5.70	1.91	1.00	6.12	29.65	8.30
1991	128.18	6.91	2.86	1.31	6.78	32.83	9.39
1992	125.86	7.20	2.59	1.44	6.93	38.28	11.96
1993	163.87	10.18	13.94	2.27	12.70	49.62	16.15
1994	200.17	13.81	12.68	1.59	12.84	72.78	23.45
1995	253.49	18.69	14.62	2.33	17.29	82.69	26.88
1996	310.94	21.00	19.13	3.29	20.31	103.19	33.18

15—4 用于农业的财政支出 SUPPORTING AGRICULTURAL PRODUCTION

单位:亿元 (100 000 000 yuan)

年份 Year	农业支出 Agricultural Expenditure	支援农业生产支出 Expeditures Sopporting Agricultural Production	农林水气象等部门事业费 Agricultural, Forestry, Irrigation Expenditures	农业基础建设支出 Expenditures of Agricultural Capital Construction	#科技三项费用 New Products Promotion Funds	其他 Others
1978	7.11	1.37	2.78	1.97		0.99
1980	6.39	1.31	2.29	1.89	0.04	0.86
1985	4.62	2.04	2.01	0.44	0.07	0.06
1986	5.46	2.46	2.48	0.41	0.08	0.03
1987	5.69	2.58	2.47	0.53	0.08	0.03
1988	6.92	3.59	2.64	0.59	0.06	0.04
1989	8.50	5.11	2.67	0.63	0.07	0.02
1990	9.20	5.47	2.98	0.63	0.10	0.02
1991	11.42	6.19	4.27	0.81	0.11	0.04
1992	11.85	7.15	3.74	0.82	0.12	0.02
1993	19.19	13.83	4.13	1.08	0.11	0.04
1994	17.14	10.52	5.33	1.10	0.13	0.06
1995	14.99	7.17	6.34	1.28	0.19	0.01
1996	18.71	8.26	8.42	1.65	0.35	0.03

15－5 用于文教、卫生、科学部门的财政支出
FINANCIAL EXPENDITURE ON EDUCATION, HEALTH AND SCIENCE

单位：亿元 (100 000 000 yuan)

年份 Year	合计 Total	#教育 Education	#卫生 Health	#公费医疗 Free Medical Services	#科学 Science	#通讯广播 Communication and Broadcast	#计划生育 Birth Control
1978	4.98	3.07	1.35	0.21	0.06	0.11	0.09
1980	6.79	4.31	1.48	0.29	0.07	0.14	0.12
1985	14.70	9.24	2.67	0.81	0.24	0.36	0.24
1986	17.61	10.66	3.31	0.99	0.27	0.47	0.30
1987	18.78	11.25	3.05	1.22	0.68	0.44	0.31
1988	22.72	14.14	3.37	1.68	0.74	0.49	0.34
1989	26.16	15.95	3.75	2.28	0.79	0.56	0.37
1990	29.65	18.24	4.13	2.69	0.94	0.68	0.49
1991	32.83	19.52	4.72	3.37	1.06	0.76	0.58
1992	38.28	23.31	5.17	3.79	1.22	0.85	0.82
1993	49.62	30.33	6.27	5.47	1.43	1.13	1.00
1994	72.78	47.58	8.95	6.61	2.03	1.26	1.17
1995	82.69	52.91	9.62	8.57	2.26	1.41	1.45
1996	103.19	66.68	11.69	10.65	2.86	1.71	1.75

15－6 财政价格补贴
FINANCIAL PRICE SUBSIDIES

单位：亿元 (100 000 000 yuan)

年份 Year	合计 Total	粮棉油价格补贴 Grain, Cotton Price Subsidies	平抑物价等补贴 Subsidies for Price Increases	肉食价格补贴 Subsidies for Increases in Meat Price	其他价格补贴 Others
1978					
1980	4.55	2.21	—	—	2.34
1985	8.17	—	—	1.38	6.79
1986	15.55	10.36	0.89	1.95	2.35
1987	16.94	11.00	2.19	1.51	2.24
1988	18.16	10.80	3.17	1.66	2.53
1989	19.38	11.84	3.36	1.79	2.39
1990	20.37	12.57	3.25	1.74	2.81
1991	18.41	7.32	3.34	2.10	5.65
1992	22.90	12.03	2.00	1.95	6.92
1993	5.48	0.41	0.69	1.61	2.77
1994	6.65	0.41	0.62	1.55	4.07
1995	11.15	0.08	0.16	1.23	9.68
1996	13.00	0.73	0.38	1.21	10.68

15—7 主要年份全社会存贷款年末余额
TOTAL DEPOSIT AND LOANS BALANCE (YEAR—END)

单位:亿元 (100 000 000 yuan)

年份 Year	全社会年末存款余额 Deposit Balance	#银行系统 Bank System	全社会年末贷款余额 Loans Balance	#银行系统 Bank System
1952	3.28	3.28	1.31	1.31
1957	7.38	6.03	12.74	12.53
1962	13.26	13.13	31.10	30.82
1965	20.40	20.47	33.85	33.52
1970	33.15	34.01	56.93	56.39
1975	48.71	48.89	84.98	83.74
1978	60.72	59.87	115.29	112.75
1980	95.54	90.46	159.10	151.97
1982	146.21	140.91	217.87	212.86
1983	171.12	160.71	242.28	228.76
1984	221.68	194.12	333.40	303.02
1985	247.13	218.39	387.05	354.89
1986	353.76	311.49	528.83	482.01
1987	469.10	365.40	675.72	571.68
1988	517.81	395.02	742.10	616.35
1989	640.84	481.43	835.56	688.93
1990	858.54	645.68	1009.04	821.89
1991	1136.51	915.38	1226.82	1043.22
1992	1422.60	1141.82	1470.42	1242.36
1993	1797.33	1456.96	1777.80	1469.35
1994	2481.10	1876.21	2218.15	1775.37
1995	3500.49	2606.45	2875.39	2189.23
1996	4649.49	3509.89	3574.85	2736.45

15—8 银行存贷款年末余额
BANK DEPOSITS AND LOANS BALANCE (YEAR—END)

单位:亿元 (100 000 000 yuan)

指标	Items	1985	1990	1995	1996
各项存款	**Deposits**	**218.39**	**645.68**	**2606.45**	**3509.89**
#企业存款	Enterprises Deposits	80.61	188.21	1021.29	1369.01
财政性存款	Treasury Deposits	6.49	10.37	49.97	58.96
城镇储蓄存款	Urban Savings Deposits	57.81	324.37	1447.10	1961.55
#定期储蓄	Deposits for A Fixed Term		297.57	1236.03	1974.41
农村存款	Rural Deposits	31.50	57.63		
各项贷款余额	**Loans**	**354.89**	**821.89**	**2189.23**	**2736.45**
#短期贷款	Loans for A Short Term	286.17	685.73	1697.69	2089.49
#工业贷款	Industrial Loans	100.31	277.02	606.19	743.56
商业贷款	Commersial Loans	177.06	350.25	736.47	849.59
乡镇企业贷款	Rural and Town Enterprises Loans	15.63	44.78	86.22	101.40
农业贷款	Agricultural Loans	8.47	19.31	45.31	63.06
中长期贷款	Long/Middle Term Loans	31.46	84.49	391.19	475.83

15—9 农村信用合作社存贷款年末余额
RURAL CREDIT ASSOCIATION DEPOSITS AND LOANS BALANCE (YEAR—END)

单位:亿元 (100 000 000 yuan)

指标	Items	1985	1990	1995	1996
各项存款	**Deposits**	**55.86**	**167.14**	**522.30**	**658.11**
#集体农业存款	Collective Agriculture Deposits	6.32	9.51		
乡镇企事业存款	Rural and Towm Enterprises and Adiministration Deposits	6.85	13.65		
农民个人储蓄存款	Individual Deposits	41.54	140.13	434.37	545.08
各项存款	**Loans**	**33.81**	**106.65**	**403.62**	**494.42**
#集体农业贷款	Collective Agriculture Loans	2.35	11.36		
乡镇企事业贷款	Rural and Towm Enterprises and Adiministration Loans	27.65	85.77	281.31	319.24
个体经济户贷款	Individual Loans	0.07	0.07		

15—10 银 行 现 金 收 入
CASH REVENUE OF NATIONAL BANKING SYSTEM

单位:亿元 (100 000 000 yuan)

项 目	Items	1980	1985	1990	1994	1995	1996
收入总计	**Total**	**143.74**	**422.99**	**1240.65**	**5149.10**	**6960.65**	**7935.11**
商品销售收入	Commodity Sales	94.66	220.02	477.31	1366.43	1650.22	1868.83
服务事业收入	Service Trade	8.69	19.62	58.64	196.33	256.82	327.03
税款收入	Taxes	0.20	1.84	7.79	24.18	32.33	38.12
农村信用社收入	Rural Credit Cooperatives		84.96	223.63	720.99	722.87	205.77
乡镇企事业收入	Township Enterprises and Nonprofit Institutions	2.57	16.90	44.16	275.59	389.92	475.09
城乡个体经营收入	Individual Business		0.78	3.72	33.90	90.21	156.38
储蓄存款收入	Saving Deposits	14.63	62.85	343.01	1914.32	2932.99	3827.17
其他金融机构收入	Other Banking Institutions			9.74	133.56	196.50	228.78
汇兑收入	Remittances	1.44	3.55	12.34	52.11	101.94	96.91
债券收入	Debts			9.18	52.05	524.85	43.97
其他收入	Others	3.24	12.47	51.13	379.64	62.70	667.06

15—11 银 行 现 金 支 出
CASH EXPENDITURES OF NATIONAL BANKING SYSTEM

单位:亿元 (100 000 000 yuan)

项 目	Items	1980	1985	1990	1994	1995	1996
支出总计	**Total**	**149.14**	**437.72**	**1251.41**	**5289.50**	**7040.95**	**8074.89**
工资及对个人其他支出	Wages and Other Payments to Individuals	46.85	106.52	262.01	761.21	890.20	977.89
农副产品采购支出	Purchases of Agricultural and Sideline Products	22.76	73.88	132.74	220.43	242.31	232.08
行政企业管理费支出	Government and Enterprises Overhead	7.17	21.05	79.51	395.34	488.54	590.66
农村信用社支出	Rural Credit Cooperatives		131.24	317.33	1002.79	1018.64	440.87
乡镇企事业支出	Township Enterprises and Nonprofit Institutions	5.79	30.20	84.45	429.69	598.29	724.91
个体经营支出	Individual Business		1.40	8.26	59.07	107.18	179.93
储蓄存款支出	Saving Deposists	11.47	51.11	261.61	1738.31	2697.12	3647.85
其他金融机构支出	Other Banking Institutions				103.03	169.18	193.97
汇兑支出	Remittances	3.03	7.80	18.86	66.18	104.82	103.57
工矿产品收购支出	Purchase Industry and Mineral Products		2.15	6.76	31.96	42.07	54.59
债券支出	Debts			7.33	40.99	52.45	57.11
其他支出	Others	4.05	12.36	64.68	440.50	629.66	871.46

15—12 银行现金投放回笼差额
CASH STATISTICS OF NATIONAL BANKING SYSTEM

单位:亿元　　(100 000 000 yuan)

年份 Year	现金收入 Cash Revenue	现金支出 Cash Expenditures	投放 Monetary Issues
1952	30.05	28.49	−1.56
1962	37.20	34.64	−2.56
1965	40.18	40.41	0.23
1970	46.31	44.46	−1.85
1975	68.56	68.93	0.37
1978	85.29	88.98	3.19
1980	143.74	149.14	5.40
1985	422.99	437.72	14.73
1986	531.49	546.12	14.67
1987	696.64	713.69	17.25
1988	966.24	1031.70	65.50
1989	1109.90	1132.10	22.20
1990	1240.65	1251.41	10.76
1991	1533.50	1570.28	36.78
1992	2220.31	2313.48	93.17
1993	3470.96	3586.97	116.01
1994	5149.10	5289.50	140.40
1995	6960.65	7040.95	80.30
1996	7935.11	8074.89	139.78

注:投放栏中的负数表示现金回笼。

Notes: Withdrawal of currency is the negative number in monetary issue.

15—13 信用社现金收支
CASH EXPENDITURES OF RURAL CREDIT COOPERATIVES

单位:亿元　　(100 000 000 yuan)

项目	Items	1990	1994	1995	1996
农村信用社	Rural Credit Cooperatives				
现金收入	Cash Revenue	311.61	1056.64	1421.69	1924.60
#个体存款收入	Individual Savings Deposits	216.37	728.54	952.49	1141.92
现金支出	Cash Expenditures	403.33	1331.61	1709.41	2183.76
#个体存款支出	Individual Savings Deposits	213.35	763.52	969.17	1135.76
城市信用社	Urban Credit Cooperatives				
现金收入	Cash Revenue	26.38	344.32	426.49	459.62
#商品销售收入	Commodity Sales	14.45	152.06	180.17	169.26
服务事业收入	Service Trade	2.48	28.12	33.70	42.35
现金支出	Cash Expenditures	24.77	311.62	390.78	424.91
#集体单位工资支出	Wages to Collective Units	6.01	38.51	43.77	42.16
行政管理费支出	Government and Enterprises Overhead	2.54	48.67	51.86	47.48

15—14 保险业务经济指标
ECONOMIC AND TECHNICAL INDICATORS OF INSURANCE BUSINESS

单位：万元　　　　(10000 yuan)

指标	Items	保额 Insurance Value	保费收入 Premiums	储金收入 Deposit Business	赔款支出 Indemnite Expenditure
总计	**Total**	**101793597**	**526614**	**38209**	**200654**
国内业务合计	Domestic	**87762297**	**482950**	**38209**	**187217**
财产险	Property Insurance	63492561	262056	22394	123484
企财险	Enterprise Property Insurance	40857042	78798		29080
运输工具及责任险	Transportation Equipment and Responsibility Insurance	6225922	145475		76480
货运险	Freight Transport Insurance	8345737	21101		9377
家财险	Family Property Insurance	6279127	9651	20066	4572
农业险	Agricultural Insurance	194084	718	305	376
其他	Others	1590649	6313	2023	3599
人身险	Personal Insurance	24269736	220894	15815	63733
简身险	Simple Personal Insurance	197777	8964		14292
养老金险	Pension Insurance		49864		11451
团体人身险及意外伤害险	Social Organization Personal Insurance Accident Insurance	13087235	27594	5646	11910
子女教育婚嫁金险	Education and Marriage Insurance for Children	28834	29612		331
其他	Others	10955890	104860	10169	25749
涉外业务合计	Overseas Business	14031300	43664		13437
外币　(万美元)	(US$ 10000)	184834	2379		491
中保财产保险公司	**PICC (Property)**				
总计	**Total**	**55549868**	**227161**	**19668**	**108280**
国内财产险	Domestic Property Insurance	45337922	193729	19668	98291
企财险	Enterprise Property Insurance	29287001	56214		23243
运输工具及责任险	Transportation Equipment and Responsibility Insurance	4270946	107768		59986
货运险	Freight Transport Insurance	5430591	15688		7495
家财险	Family Property Insurance	5423535	8435	17340	4008
农业险	Agricultural Insurance	194084	718	305	376
其他	Others	731765	4906	2023	3183
涉外业务	Overseas Business	10211946	33432		9989
中保人寿保险公司	**PICC (Life)**				
总计	**Total**	**13193450**	**142601**	**10169**	**63344**
人身险	Personal Insurance	13193450	142601	10169	63344
简身险	Simple Personal Insurance	197768	7865		14292
养老金险	Pension Insurance		40159		11451
团体人身险及意外伤害险	Social Organization Personal Insurance Accident Insurance	10554731	24854		11521
子女教育婚嫁金险	Education and Marriage Insurance for Children	28834	21033		331
其他	Others	2412117	48690	10169	25749

续表 Continued

单位：万元 (10000 yuan)

		保　额 Insurance Value	保费收入 Premiums	储金收入 Deposit Business	赔款支出 Indemnite Expenditure
中国平安保险(财产)	**PAICC (Property)**				
总　计	**Total**	**7544404**	**22024**	**81**	**5681**
国内财产险	Domestic Property Insurance	7544404	20466	81	5388
企财险	Enterprise Property Insurance	5192111	8739		1979
运输工具及责任险	Transportation Equipment and Responsibility Insurance	694942	9177		2965
货运险	Freight Transport Insurance	1255915	2246		521
家财险	Family Property Insurance	40763	119	81	5
农业险	Agricultural Insurance				
其他	Others	360673	185		100
涉外业务	Overseas Business		1558		293
中国平安保险公司(寿险)	**PAICC (Life)**				
总　计	**Total**	**2297068**	**42321**	**1801**	**389**
人身险	Personal Insurance	2297068	42321	1801	389
简身险	Simple Personal Insurance	9	8		
养老金险	Pension Insurance		3968		
团体人身险及意外伤害险	Social Organization Personal Insurance Accident Insurance	2178226	1470	1801	389
子女教育婚嫁金险	Education and Marriage Insurance for Children		8579		
其他	Others	118833	28296		
中国太平洋保险公司	**CPIC**				
总　计	**Total**	**23208807**	**92507**	**6490**	**22960**
国内财产险	Domestic Property Insurance	10610235	47861	2645	19805
企财险	Enterprise Property Insurance	6377930	13845		4040
运输工具及责任险	Transportation Equipment and Responsibility Insurance	1260034	28530		13529
货运险	Freight Transport Insurance	1659231	3167		1361
家财险	Family Property Insurance	814829	1097	2645	559
农业险	Agricultural Insurance				
其他	Others	498211	1222		316
国内人身险	Personal Insurance	8779218	35972	3845	—
简身险	Simple Personal Insurance		1091		
养老金险	Pension Insurance		5737		
团体人身险及意外伤害险	Social Organization Personal Insurance Accident Insurance	354278	1270	3845	
子女教育婚嫁金险	Education and Marriage Insurance for Children				
其他	Others	8424940	27874		
涉外业务	Abroad Business	3819354	8674		3155

16 科技、教育

SCIENCE AND TECHNOLOGY, EDUCATION

16 科技 教育
SCIENCE AND TECHNOLOGY, EDUCATION

1 9 9 6

科技机构数	Number of Scientific and Technical Research Institutions	2533	个 (unit)
各类专业技术人员	Scientific Technical Personnel in State-Owned Units	189.49	万人 (10000)
高等学校	Institutions of Hige Education	66	所 (10000)
研究生在读人数	Graduate Students Enrollment	1.22	万人 (10000)
普通高校在校学生	Students Enrollment of Regular Institutions of High Education	22.06	万人 (10000)
成人高校在校学生	Students Enrollment of Adult Institutions of High Education	16.05	万人 (10000)
普通中学在校学生	Students Enrollment of Regular Secondary Schools	323.55	万人 (10000)
高校专任教师	Full-time Teachers of Institutions of High Education	2.74	万人 (10000)

各类专业技术人员构成 (%)

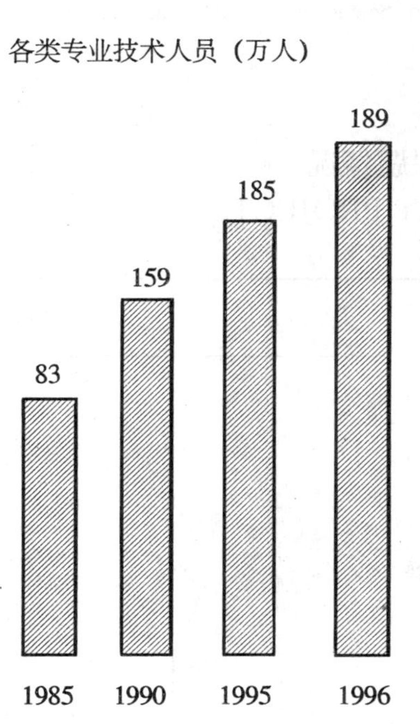

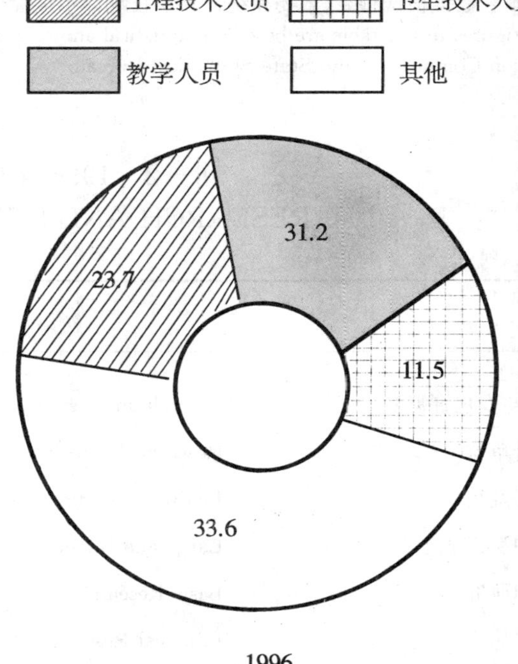

16—1 科技活动基本情况（1996）
BASIC STATISTICS FOR SCIENTIFIC AND TECHNICAL ACTIVITIES

指标	Items	1996
科技机构数（个）	Number of Scientific and Technical Research Institutions	2533
#科研单位	Research Institutions	334
大中型工业企业	Large and Medium Industrial Enterprises	1504
高等院校	Institutions of Higher Education	383
科技活动人员数（万人）	Persons Engaged in Scientific and Technical Activities (10000 Persons)	25.19
#科学家、工程师	Scientists and Engineers	15.11
科技活动经费收入总额（亿元）	Funding for Scientific and Technical Research (100000000 yuan)	95.13
上级拨款	Appropriations	15.55
自筹资金	Private	61.21
银行贷款	Loans	13.46
其他收入	Others	4.91
科技活动经费支出总额（亿元）	Expenditures of Scientific and Technical Research Funds (10^8 yuan)	88.31
#内部支出	Internal Expenses	82.19
#劳务费	Service Fees	13.86
业务费	Professional Fees	25.71
其他	Others	23.76
固定资产购建支出	Purchasing Fixed Assets	18.86
研究与发展经费支出	Research and Development Expenses	25.00
研究与发展经费支出占国内生产总值比重（%）	Proportion of Research and Development Expenses to GDP	0.41

注：本表数据根据科委、教委和统计局科技统计年报综合汇总。

Figures in the table are based on statistical annual report of science from Science and Technology Commission, Education Commission and State Statisitical Bureau.

16—2 1996年研究与发展课题情况
RESEARCH AND DEVELOPMENT PROJECTS

单位：项

指标	Items	1996
研究与发展课题数	Research and Development Projects	14979
#科研单位	Research Institutions	3393
高等院校	Institutes of Higher Education	9786
大中型工业企业	Large and Medium Industrial Enterprises	1717
#基础研究	Basic Research	1978
应用研究	Practical Research	7599
实验发展	Enperiment Development	5402

16—3 县级以上政府部门所属研究与开发机构基本情况
BASIC STATISTICS ON STATE-OWNED RESEARCH AND DEVELOPMENT INSTITUTIONS ABOVE COUNTY LEVEL

项 目	Items	1985	1990	1995	1996
机构数 (个)	Number of Institutions	274	326	337	338
职工总数 (人)	Personnel (person)	40608	55987	53090	51006
#科学家工程师	Scientists and Engineers	12299	24269	24428	21370
其他科技人员	Others	6820	11103	10796	8622
经费收入总额 (万元)	Funds (10000 yuan)	42470.5	107958.1	285637.6	368917.8
#政府拨款	Appropriations from Government	25898.3	33774.7	68776.0	95433.4
经费支出总额 (万元)	Expenditures (10000 yuan)	38841.8	93615.5	285725.4	347514.5
#基本建设支出	Capital Construction	9813.1	7426.3	24379.1	23411.8

注:县级以上政府部门所属研究与开发机构 1991、1992 年不包括国防科工委归口管理的研究机构,以下表同。
Notes:The Institution excluded the National Defence Council's Institutions in 1991,1992,the same as next figures.

16—4 县级以上政府部门所属研究与开发机构(1996)
STATE-OWNED RESEARCH AND DEVELOPMENT INSTITUTIONS ABOVE COUNTY LEVEL

项 目	Items	机构数(个) Institution	职工总数(人) Personnel	#科学家工程师 Scientist and Engineers	经费收入总额(万元) Funds (10000yuan)	#政府拨款 Appropriations	经费支出总额(万元) Expenditures (10000yuan)
总 计	**Total**						
按隶属关系分	By Administrative Relationship						
国务院部门属	Departments of the State Council	57	27044	12883	237267.5	71372.6	221862.4
省 属	Departments of Province	76	13861	5195	75607.7	19193.8	71481.2
省辖市属	Departments of City under Province	205	10101	3292	56042.6	4867.0	54170.9
按国民经济行业分	By Sector						
农、林、牧、渔、水利业	Farming,Forestry,Animal Husbandry,Fishery and Water-Gonservancy	52	5302	1765	24494.7	9266.1	22539.6
制造业	Manufacturing	139	28187	10718	206876.7	63070.1	197590.5
地质普查和勘探业	Geological Prospcting	11	1217	492	5134.7	2513.9	5060.9
建筑业	Construction	17	1356	600	7091.9	410.8	6772.7
交通运输、邮电通讯业	Transportation,Communications	4	349	223	3559.8	615.3	3421.4
房地产管理、公用事业、居民服务和咨询业	Real Estate Managment,Public Facilities Services,Residential Service and Consultancy Services	1	57	4	378.3	0	372.2
卫生、体育和社会福事业	Health Care,Sporting and Social Welfare	22	2201	904	14937.2	3566.9	14276.7
教育、文化艺术和广播电视业	Education,Culture and Arts,Radio,Film and Television	2	33	24	314.3	72.1	280.0
科学研究和综合技术服务事业	Scientific Research and Polytechnical Services	9	8838	4684	45209.3	13638.8	43239.0
其他	Others	18	3466	1956	60920.9	2279.4	53961.5

16—5 县级以上政府部门所属研究与开发成果
STATE-OWNED RESEARCH AND DEVELOPMENT PROJECTS ABOVE COUNTY LEVEL

年份 Year	科学著作(万字) Scientific Works (10000 words)	科学论文(篇) Papers	获奖成果(项) Prized Achievements
1986	2226	2860	
1987	2138	2532	559
1988	1915	2561	511
1989	1717	3265	495
1990	2540	3728	579
1991	2454	3392	525
1992	2086	3962	477
1993	2273	4629	532
1994	2783	4049	494
1995	4196	4662	468
1996	107(部 Book)	4378	490

16—6 县级以上政府部门所属研究与开发机构课题情况(1996)
PROJECTS OF TECHNOLOGY DEVELOPMENT ORGANIZATIONS ABOVE COUNTY LEVEL

项目	Items	课题数(项) Projects (item)	投入人员(人) Labor Force (person)	#科学家工程师 Scientist	投入经费(万元) Funds Input (10000 yuan)	课题平均经费(万元) Per Funds by Project (10000 yuan/item)
总计	**Total**					
按课题来分	By Sources					
国家	National	1096	2535.2	2188.0	7286.21	6.65
地方	Local	1160	2117.1	1620.6	3747.10	3.23
企业委托	Enterprises	830	1865.1	1550.9	35364.3	42.61
自选	Self-selected	611	1445.1	1072.3	4193.73	6.86
国际合作	International coorperate	68	136.0	108.7	406.39	5.98
其他	Others	297	331.6	275.9	1021.74	3.44
按活动类型分	By Type					
基础研究	Basic Research	135	276.8	258.1	536.75	3.98
应用研究	Practical Research	418	836.3	721.4	1839.60	4.40
实验发展	Experiment Development	938	1767.7	1443.8	6024.64	6.42
研究与实验发展成果应用	Used by Research and Experiment Development Projects	1689	3845.3	3032.8	38588.8	33.85
科技服务	Seientific and Technical Service	813	1387.9	1174.4	3335.79	4.10
生产性活动	Product Activities	69	316.3	185.9	1695.62	24.57

16—7 大中型工业企业技术开发情况
BASIC STATISTICS FOR TECHNICAL DEVELOPMENT OF LARGE AND MEIUM INDUSTRIAL ENTERPRISES

单位:亿元 (100 000 000 yuan)

指　　标	Items	1990	1995	1996
企业数	**Number of Enterprise**	**1237**	**2329**	**2462**
#有技术开发机构的企业数	Enterprises Having Technical Development Institutions	715	1068	1017
企业办技术开发机构数(个)	**Development Institutions of Enterprises**	**803**	**1599**	**1504**
从事技术开发的人员数(万人)	**Technical Development Personnel**	**6.35**	**11.48**	**14.61**
#工程技术人员	Technical Personnel	3.62	6.86	8.90
#具有高、中级职称或大学本科及以上学历的人员	Personnel with Senior,Medium, Professional Titles or University and over Education	2.43	3.67	7.26
大专及以下学历具有初级职称的或未评定职称的大、中专人员	Personnel with or without Junior Professional Titles and with Second or university Education	2.14	4.10	
总计中:技术开发机构中的人员	Personnel in Technical Development Institutions	2.93	3.66	3.82
#有高、中级职称或大学本科以上学历人员	Personnel with Senior,Medium,Junior Professional or over University Record	1.25	1.78	2.37
技术开发经费筹集额	**Funds of Technical Development**	**10.96**	**45.80**	**51.38**
#上级拨款	Appropriations from Higher Authorities	0.63	1.76	2.30
专项贷款	Special Loans	3.09	7.49	7.28
本企业自筹	Private Funds	6.50	35.14	36.67
接受外单位委托	Entrusting Funds for Other Unites	0.17	0.89	0.72
技术开发经费支出总额	Expenditures	10.17	42.25	47.16
#技术开发人员经费	Expenses for Technical Development Personnel	1.23	6.81	6.95
原材料费	Expenses of Raw Material	2.67	13.86	14.87
设计、实验、调研费	Design,Experiment,Investigation and Research	1.00	14.70	
固定资产购建费	Purchasing and Fixed Assets	3.02		16.03
总计中:开发新产品用款	Of Total:New Product Development Expenditures	4.96	20.78	27.69
横向技术开发经费	Cross Technical Funds	0.17	2.36	4.11
技术改造支出总额	**Total Technical Updating Expenditures**	**17.9**	**92.21**	**110.04**
技术引进支出总额	Total Technical Introduced	6.31	23.37	39.73
#引进设计、图纸、工艺、专利用款	Design,Blueprint,Technology and Patent Expenditures	0.95	1.85	24.78
用于消化吸收的经费	Digesting and Absorbing Expenditures	0.58	1.17	1.75
购买国内技术用款	Purchasing Domestic Technology	0.13	1.36	2.76
技术开发活动产出	**Technical Development Expenditures**			
新产品销售收入合计	Total New Product Reverue	95.3	329.10	496.06
新产品实现利税	Tax and Profit of New Products	10.43	37.45	47.22
企业开发的科技成果转让收入	Revenue of Scientific and Transfering Technical of the Possession	0.20	0.41	2.64
企业对外技术服务收入	Revenue of Enterprises to Other Unit of Technical Service	0.16	1.16	0.73
企业技术开发成果获奖数	Number for Achievements Prizes in Entriprises		1313	1343
企业专利申请数	Total Patent Application	163	405	542
企业专利获准数	Total Patent Application Certified	98	224	341

16—8 各类专业技术人员数
SCIENTIFC AND TECHNICAL PERSONNEL

单位:万人 (10000 persons)

年份 Year	各类专业技术人员总计 Total	工程技术人员 Engineering	农业技术人员 Agriculture	科学研究人员 Scientific Research	卫生技术人员 Health Care	教学人员 Teaching
1979	22.18	7.83	1.36	1.22	6.77	5.00
1980	43.87	9.63	1.13	1.47	9.02	17.13
1985	83.41	20.70	1.76	1.59	13.35	35.90
1986	89.31	32.33	1.95	1.85	13.80	35.42
1987	102.79	25.68	2.01	1.75	14.29	41.57
1988	125.81	29.06	2.16	1.71	15.74	45.57
1989	150.56	34.08	2.37	1.86	17.42	49.88
1990	158.86	31.84	2.35	1.84	13.87	44.50
1991	166.02	25.86	2.39	0.67	13.54	44.57
1992	174.70	27.36	2.53	0.73	14.17	44.98
1993	172.71	41.72	2.50	2.19	19.90	50.83
1994	179.94	27.88	2.21	0.60	14.99	47.57
1995	184.97	28.38	2.65	0.60	15.48	50.72
1996	189.49	44.82	3.68	1.90	21.75	59.15

注:各类专业技术人员分类指标中,1991年、1992年和1994年、1995年为地方国有单位的各类专业技术人员数。

Note:Of the scientific and technical personnel, numbers in 1991,1992,1994 and 1995 referred to local state-owned personnel.

16—9 地方国有经济单位各类专业技术人员分行业情况
SCIENTIFC AND TECHNICAL PERSONNEL IN LOCAL STATE-OWNED UNITS BY SECTOR

单位:万人 (10000 persons)

行业	Items	1990	1994	1995	1996
总计	**Total**	**112.20**	**127.19**	**130.07**	**136.04**
农、林、牧、渔、水利业	Farming,Forestry,Animal Husbandry, Fishery and Water-Gonservancy	3.63	5.02	5.50	5.70
制造业	Manufacturing	25.60	30.06	30.05	27.42
地质普查和勘探业	Geological Prospcting	0.12	0.11	0.10	1.72
建筑业	Construction	2.51	3.43	3.62	2.66
交通运输、邮电通讯	Transportation, Post and Communications	2.35	3.50	3.45	4.63
商业、公共饮食业、物资供销和仓储业	Commerce,Catering Trade,Material Supply and Storge	9.94	12.73	10.30	8.85
房地产管理、公用事业、居民服务和咨询服务业	Real Estate Managment,Public Facilities Services, Residential Service and Consultancy Services	2.25	4.35	4.85	6.82
卫生、体育和社会福利事业	Health Care,Sporting and Social Welfare	10.98	13.75	14.42	15.10
教育文化艺术和广播电视事业	Education,Culture and Arts,Radio,Film and Television	44.17	50.43	53.93	58.42
科学研究和综合技术服务事业	Scientific Research and Polytechnical Services	2.31	3.21	3.23	4.38
金融保险事业	Financial and Insurance Business	0.02	0.06	0.07	0.24
国家机关、政党机关和社会团体	Govermant Agencies,Party Agencies and Social Organization	8.20			
其他行业	Others	0.12	0.54	0.55	0.10

16—10 地方国有经济单位各类专业技术人员基本情况 SCIENTIFIC AND TECHNICAL PERSONNEL IN LOCAL STATE-OWNED

行　　业	Items	1990	1994	1995	1996
总　计	**Total**	**112.20**	**127.19**	**130.07**	**136.04**
#高级职称	Senior Professional	3.49	4.96	5.77	5.81
中级职称	Medium Titles	25.29	31.21	34.64	37.24
初级职称	Junior Titles	68.46	80.86	78.92	79.84
工程技术人员	Engineering	24.10	27.88	28.38	28.59
农业技术人员	Agriculture	2.32	2.21	2.65	3.24
科学研究人员	Scientific	0.79	0.60	0.60	0.54
卫生技术人员	Health Care	12.74	14.99	15.48	15.79
教学人员	Teaching	41.70	47.57	50.72	54.80
民航飞行技术人员	Civil Aviation				
船舶技术人员	Shipping	0.13	0.18	0.16	0.16
经济人员	Economic	16.40	14.55	13.06	13.03
会计人员	Financial Accounting	8.83	9.27	8.95	9.55
统计人员	Statistical	1.87	1.75	1.57	1.54
翻译人员	Translator	0.21	0.19	0.21	0.21
图书、档案、文博人员	Book, Archive, Curture and Nature	1.62	1.71	1.74	1.75
新闻、出版人员	News Publisher and Announcer	0.54	0.65	0.71	0.80
律师、公证人员	Lowyer	0.19	0.15	0.16	0.17
播音人员	Broadcasting	0.03	0.05	0.05	0.07
工艺美术人员	Crafts Arts	0.20	0.24	0.23	0.23
体育人员	Sporting	0.14	0.15	0.14	0.14
艺术人员	Art	0.39	0.43	0.44	0.42
政工人员	Political Work		4.62	4.82	5.01

16—11 高等学校科技活动情况
BASIC STATISTICS FOR SCIENTIFIC AND TECHNICAL ACTIVITIES IN INSTITUTIONS OF HIGHER

项目	Items	1990	1994	1995	1996
参加科技统计的高校　（所）	**Institutions of Higher Education in Statics**	**51**	**52**	**47**	**47**
从事科技活动人数　（人）	**Personnel in Scientific and Technical Activities**	**54961**	**56755**	**57787**	**57358**
教师	Teachers	28464	27698	28270	27969
其他技术人员	Other Teachnical Persons	23661	26598	27073	26974
辅助人员	Assists	2836	2459	2444	2415
从事研究与发展活动人数（人）	**Perssonnel in Research and Development**	**11163**	**19303**	**20295**	**21052**
#正教授	Professors	798	1640	1908	1935
副教授	Associate Professors	2529	4219	4507	4344
讲　师	Lecturers	2775	4842	4849	4650
助　教	Assistants	1314	1376	1563	1783
研究与发展机构　（个）	**Institution of Research and Development**	**194**	**390**	**408**	383
机构中研究与发展人员	Personnel	3965	5224	5496	5350
当年研究与发展经费收入（万元）	**Revenue of Research and Development** (10000 **yuan**)	**14599**	**41295**	**50695**	**59525**
#科技事业费	Scientific and Technical Funds	1281	1798	4958	8392
主管部门专项费	Speical Funds of Department Resonsible for the Work	2540	6998	7398	7313
国务院各部门专项费	Speical Funds of State Council Department	2600	2679	2728	2892
省专项费	Provincial Special Funds	830	1621	3215	3607
企事业单位委托经费	Entrusting Funds of Enterprises	6071	20135	24705	25145
国家自然科学基金	State Natural Sciences Funds	726	1510	1654	1628
各种收入转入科研经费	Funds from Other Revenues	243	857	1179	5545
研究与发展课题　（项）	**Projects**	**7713**	**8683**	**9810**	**9786**
#基础研究	Basic	1289	1685	1710	1783
应用研究	Practical	4661	5302	6177	6084
实验发展	Experiment Development	1763	1696	1923	1919
研究与发展成果	**Achievements of Research and Development**				
出版科学专著　（部）	Publishing Scientific works	454	463	558	856
发表学术论文　（篇）	Publishing Papers	11018	17331	19153	20564
#国外发表	Abroad	933	1843	2277	2294
全国性学术刊物发表	National Journals	6085	9635	11199	11797
地方性学术刊物发表	Local Journals	4000	5853	5727	6473
鉴定科技成果	Appraisal Scientific Achievenments	761	785	641	718
#国际水平	International	157	205	189	195
国内首创	Domestically First Created	159	191	159	196
国内先进	Domesticially Advanced Level	348	315	261	289
科技成果转让	**Scientific Achievements Transfrred**	**596**	**801**	**660**	**716**
获奖成果数	**Prised Achievements**	**325**	**581**	**743**	**784**
#国家级	National Level	17		35	28
部省级	Provincal Level	308	447	383	484

注：研究与发展机构仅指学校上级主管部门批准的机构。

The institutions of research and development were certified by management department.

16—12 三种专利申请受理量
THREE TYPES OF PATENT APPLICATIONS EXAMINED

		1985	1990	1994	1995	1996
申请受理量合计	Total	688	2706	4007	4078	4980
发　明	Creations and Inventions	240	384	491	538	561
实用新型	Utility Models	436	2085	2879	2708	3209
外观设计	Designs	12	237	637	832	1210
非 职 务	Independent	388	1620	2636	2665	3180
大专院校	Universities and Colleges	164	135	157	164	159
科研单位	Research Institutions	61	112	128	104	112
工矿企业	Industrial and Mineral Enterprises	63	522	642	887	1503
机关团体	Government Agencies and Organizations	12	117	644	258	26

16—13 三种专利授权量
THREE TYPES OF PATENT APPLICATIONS CERTIFIED

		1985	1990	1994	1995	1996
申请受理量合计	Total	7	1455	2436	2413	2578
发　明	Creations and Inventions	1	69	85	72	98
实用新型	Utility Models	6	1236	2068	1884	1781
外观设计	Designs		150	283	457	699
非 职 务	Independent	2	916	1581	1506	1487
大专院校	Universities and Colleges	5	104	122	112	107
科研单位	Research Institutions		78	67	73	71
工矿企业	Industrial and Mineral Enterprises		297	451	447	739
机关团体	Government Agencies and Organizations		60	215	275	175

16－14 各级各类教育事业(1996)

BASIC STATISTICS FOR EDUCATION BY LEVEL AND TYPE

单位:万人 (10000 persons)

指标	Items	学校数(所) School	毕业生数 Graduates	招生数 New Student Enrollment	在校学生数 New Student Enrollment	教职工数 Staff and Teachers	#专任教师 Fulltime Teachers
普通高等学校	Institutions of Higher Education	66	6.39	7.88	23.28	7.08	2.74
研究生	Postgraduates		0.27	0.45	1.22		
本专科学生	Undergraduate and Students of College for Prefessional Training		6.12	7.43	22.06		
中等专业学校	Specialized Secondary Schools	213	8.56	15.38	40.99	2.82	1.39
中等技术学校	Technical Schools	177	7.26	13.81	36.70	2.30	1.13
中等师范学校	Teacher Training Schools	36	1.30	1.57	4.29	0.52	0.26
#幼儿师范	Children Teacher Training Schools	4	0.08	0.10	0.30	0.04	0.02
普通中学	Regular Secondary Schools	4230	92.69	107.75	323.55	26.37	19.28
高中	Senior	936	13.59	20.60	54.08		3.88
初中	Junior	3294	79.10	87.15	269.47		15.40
#小学附设初中班	Vocational Class in Primary Schools		0.02	0.02	0.08		
职业中学	Vocational Schools	441	8.26	9.22	25.85	3.19	2.15
#普中附设职业班	Vocational Class in Regular Secondary Schools		1.48	1.36	4.17		
高中	Senior	440	8.23	9.21	25.79		2.14
初中	Junior	1	0.03	0.01	0.06		0.01
技工学校	Technical Schools	169	2.78	3.93	10.64	1.60	0.78
小学	Primary Schools	25836	90.23	135.31	687.82	31.85	27.96
特殊教育学校	Special Schools	127	0.27	0.51	3.98	0.38	0.28
#盲、聋哑学校	Schools for the Blind, Deaf and Deafmute	72	0.09	0.13	0.82	0.25	0.16
幼儿园	Kindergardens	18763		116.66	206.14	9.90	8.31
工读学校	Missed Children Schools	4			0.02	0.01	0.01
成人高等学校	Adult Education Schools	63	3.24	6.50	16.05	1.17	0.58
#教育学院	Pedagogical College	11	0.15	0.39	0.94	0.24	0.12
成人中等专业学校	Secondary Schools for Adults	246	4.56	6.82	16.54	1.27	0.66
#教师进修学校	Teachers Training Schools	80	1.05	2.25	4.10	0.45	0.23
成人中学	Middle Schools for Adults	851	5.42	6.01	7.66	0.58	0.43
成人技术培训学校	Technical Training Schools for Adults	30554	523.44	439.11	410.93	2.47	1.44
成人初等学校	Primary Schools for Adults	5948	35.86	27.47	31.25	0.58	0.29

附:1996年在研究生中有14个科研机构招收的研究生86人,毕业54人,在读219人,导师318人。

注:1.1995年小学附设初中班24个,普中附设职业班1142个。

2.在成人高校毕业、招生、在读人数中,包括普通高校函授部、夜大学和干部专修科学生数。

Notes: In 1996, fourteen research institutions had 86 new postgraduates persons, 54 persons graduated, 219 persons were in entrollment, teachers 318 persons.

a)There were 24 junior in primary schools, 142 vocational schools in regular secondary schools.

b)Adult education schools include correspondence department or evening universities run by institution of higher education.

16—15 主要年份各级各类学校数
SCHOOLS BY LEVEL AND TYPE

单位:所 (number)

年份 Year	普通高等学校 Institutions of Higher Education	中等学校 Secondary Schools	中等专业学校 Specialized Secondary Schools			普通中学 Regular Secondary Schools
				中等技术学校 Technical Schools	中等师范学校 Teacher Training Schools	
1952	17	466	119	60	59	347
1957	15	1250	80	47	33	1170
1962	35	2196	58	37	21	1859
1965	29	6389	268	248	20	1618
1970	30	4810	47	37	10	4763
1975	25	4938	86	63	23	4852
1978	35	5959	93	70	23	5866
1980	46	5236	116	91	25	4994
1985	70	6881	163	125	38	6255
1990	70	6377	195	161	34	5808
1991	71	6184	194	159	35	5588
1992	72	5934	195	160	35	5349
1993	72	5660	207	172	35	5054
1994	67	5420	213	177	36	4761
1995	67	5093	213	177	36	4439
1996	66	4884	213	177	36	4230

续表 Continued

单位:所 (number)

年份 Year	高中 Senior	初中 Junior	职业中学 Vocational Schools	小学 Primary Schools	幼儿园 Kindergarden	盲、聋哑学校 Schools for the Blind Deaf and Deafmutes
1952	81	266		27070	843	8
1957	159	1011		31757	1415	10
1962	374	1485	279	37712	1994	12
1965	361	1257	4503	41369	1760	10
1970	1198	3565		45504		
1975	2433	2419		44464	6526	14
1978	2942	2924		39703	10240	25
1980	2110	2884	126	38143	14472	25
1985	1078	5177	263	33988	25779	28
1990	1017	4791	374	30557	22799	59
1991	995	4593	402	29770	21329	64
1992	981	4368	390	28753	20699	68
1993	968	4086	399	28183	20283	71
1994	967	3794	446	27636	20287	72
1995	963	3676	441	27062	19716	73
1996	936	3294	441	25836	18763	72

16—16 主要年份各级各类学校招生数
NEW STUDENT ENROLLMENT BY LEVEL AND TYPE OF SCHOOL

单位：万人 (10000 persons)

年份 Year	普通高等学校 Institutions of Higher Education	中等学校 Secondary Schools	中等专业学校 Specialized Secondary Schools			普通中学 Regular Secondary Schools
				中等技术学校 Technical Schools	中等师范学校 Teacher Training Schools	
1952	0.53	12.66	1.59	1.31	0.28	11.07
1957	0.71	21.35	0.78	0.27	0.51	20.57
1962	0.65	23.82	0.16	0.11	0.05	22.53
1965	0.92	47.48	3.36	3.04	0.32	23.39
1970	0.11	69.24	0.67	0.57	0.10	68.57
1975	0.99	140.00	0.88	0.37	0.51	139.12
1978	3.41	174.65	2.03	1.39	0.64	172.62
1980	1.92	121.44	2.17	1.32	0.85	118.25
1985	4.53	103.84	4.36	3.31	1.05	93.37
1990	4.33	109.51	4.28	3.45	0.83	99.08
1991	4.41	112.37	4.61	3.76	0.85	100.50
1992	5.17	117.63	5.12	4.22	0.90	104.14
1993	6.85	118.81	8.42	7.05	1.37	101.53
1994	6.61	129.98	9.97	8.63	1.34	110.45
1995	6.75	136.80	12.27	10.87	1.40	114.03
1996	7.43	132.35	15.38	13.81	1.57	107.75

续表 Continued

单位：万人 (10000 persons)

年份 Year	高中 Senior	初中 Junior	职业中学 Vocational Schools	小学 Primary Scholls	盲、聋哑学校 Schools for the Blind Deaf and Deafmutes
1952	1.09	9.98		76.49	
1957	2.71	17.86		76.58	
1962	3.43	19.10	1.13	89.93	0.01
1965	3.76	19.63	20.73	207.59	
1970	12.60	55.97		149.62	
1975	37.93	101.19		180.33	0.05
1978	49.73	122.89		160.41	0.06
1980	18.80	99.45	1.02	129.91	0.07
1985	14.96	78.41	6.11	105.85	0.08
1990	13.95	85.13	6.15	90.12	0.11
1991	14.20	86.30	7.26	89.51	0.13
1992	14.81	89.33	8.37	98.95	0.11
1993	14.43	87.10	8.86	113.83	0.11
1994	15.83	94.62	9.56	126.03	0.12
1995	18.47	95.56	10.50	130.42	0.15
1996	20.60	87.15	9.22	135.31	0.13

注：普通高校的毕业生数不包括研究生人数。

Notes: The entrollment in regular institutions of higher education did not include that of graduate students. (so does follows)

16－17 主要年份各级各类学校毕业生数
GRADUATES BY LEVEL AND TYPE OF SCHOOLS

单位:万人　　(10000 persons)

年　份 Year	普通高等学校 Institutions of Higher Education	中等学校 Secondary Schools	中等专业学校 Specialized Secondary Schools			普通中学 Regular Secondary Schools
				中等技术学校 Technical Schools	中等师范学校 Teacher Training Schools	
1952	0.17	3.34	0.59	0.43	0.16	2.75
1957	0.29	11.12	1.07	0.73	0.34	10.05
1962	1.58	24.96	2.84	1.59	1.25	21.04
1965	1.17	17.77	0.44	0.38	0.06	16.85
1970	1.60	53.15	0.64	0.57	0.07	52.51
1975	0.79	99.69	0.90	0.40	0.50	98.79
1978	1.51	161.96	0.24	0.18	0.06	161.72
1980	1.07	117.99	1.25	0.60	0.65	116.04
1985	2.19	83.37	2.39	1.65	0.74	78.42
1990	4.34	85.27	3.84	2.85	0.99	76.45
1991	4.42	89.07	4.30	3.40	0.90	79.89
1992	4.26	92.79	4.28	3.40	0.88	83.46
1993	4.02	96.21	4.18	3.36	0.82	86.75
1994	4.47	99.29	4.28	3.43	0.85	88.29
1995	5.95	105.40	5.17	4.24	0.93	92.62
1996	6.12	109.51	8.56	7.26	1.30	92.69

续表　Continued

单位:万人　　(10000 persons)

年　份 Year				小　学 Primary Scholls	盲、聋哑学校 Schools for the Blind, Deaf and Deafmutes
	高　中 Senior	初　中 Junior	职业中学 Vocational Schools		
1952	0.44	2.31		14.29	
1957	1.57	8.48		35.91	
1962	4.05	16.99	1.08	40.88	0.01
1965	3.09	13.76	0.48	40.82	
1970	6.56	45.95		100.66	
1975	29.50	69.29		110.10	0.02
1978	39.23	122.49		136.12	0.01
1980	42.16	73.88	0.70	122.25	0.04
1985	12.82	65.60	2.56	105.68	0.05
1990	13.77	62.68	4.98	103.78	0.04
1991	12.67	67.22	4.88	102.50	0.05
1992	12.71	70.75	5.05	104.03	0.06
1993	13.72	73.03	5.28	99.15	0.06
1994	13.36	74.93	6.72	101.31	0.08
1995	13.65	78.97	7.61	99.03	0.08
1996	13.59	79.10	8.26	90.23	0.09

16—18 主要年份各级各类学校在校学生数
STUDENT ENROLLMENT BY LEVEL AND TYPE OF SCHOOLS

单位:万人 (10000 persons)

年份 Year	普通高等学校 Institutions of Higher Education	中等学校 Secondary Schools	中等专业学校 Specialized Secondary Schools	中等技术学校 Technical Schools	中等师范学校 Teacher Training Schools	普通中学 Regular Secondary Schools
1952	1.13	27.47	4.23	2.38	1.85	23.24
1957	2.91	56.33	5.24	3.49	1.75	51.09
1962	5.25	70.11	2.41	1.73	0.68	65.20
1965	3.90	100.56	6.12	5.60	0.52	67.98
1970	0.11	148.82	0.67	0.57	0.10	148.15
1975	3.00	250.23	2.23	1.21	1.02	248.00
1978	6.05	389.69	3.84	2.22	1.62	385.85
1980	8.41	328.83	6.11	3.99	2.12	320.49
1985	11.96	305.89	9.25	6.88	2.37	284.73
1990	14.69	311.50	13.99	11.42	2.57	281.97
1991	14.47	319.86	14.18	11.66	2.52	288.64
1992	15.27	329.40	14.94	12.41	2.53	294.64
1993	18.02	335.30	19.18	16.08	3.10	293.98
1994	20.15	353.70	24.71	21.23	3.48	304.66
1995	20.86	374.86	31.87	27.91	3.96	316.75
1996	22.06	390.39	40.99	36.70	4.29	323.55

续表 Continued

单位:万人 (10000 persons)

年份 Year	高中 Senior	初中 Junior	职业中学 Vocational Schools	小学 Primary Scholls	幼儿园 Kindergarden	盲、聋哑学校 Schools for the Blind, Deaf and Deafmutes
1952	2.22	21.02		335.20	4.75	0.05
1957	7.32	43.77		412.80	8.88	0.07
1962	11.83	53.37	2.50	448.30	13.73	0.09
1965	10.83	57.15	26.46	698.68	15.49	0.12
1970	21.18	126.97		664.18		
1975	71.59	176.41		925.42	42.98	0.22
1978	101.81	284.04		868.90	67.27	0.32
1980	46.08	274.01	2.23	836.90	123.71	0.36
1985	44.72	240.01	11.91	677.92	165.99	0.43
1990	40.76	241.21	15.54	612.29	165.65	0.63
1991	41.61	247.03	17.04	594.80	187.72	0.68
1992	42.79	251.85	19.82	585.01	201.47	0.67
1993	42.36	251.62	22.14	594.94	206.89	0.68
1994	43.85	260.81	24.33	616.17	208.25	0.80
1995	47.71	269.04	26.24	644.77	214.70	0.86
1996	54.08	269.47	25.85	687.82	206.14	0.82

16—19 主要年份各级各类学校教职工数
SCHOOL STAFF AND WORKERS BY LEVEL AND TYPE OF SCHOOL

单位:万人 (10000 persons)

年份 Year	普通高等学校 Institutions of Higher Education	中等学校 Secondary Schools	中等专业学校 Specialized Secondary Schools		
				中等技术学校 Technical Schools	中等师范学校 Teacher Training Schools
1952	0.46	2.04	0.62	0.30	0.32
1957	0.98	4.01	0.98	0.79	0.19
1962	2.11	6.12	0.81	0.70	0.11
1965	1.96	7.48	1.13	1.03	0.10
1970	2.18	7.69	0.14	0.09	0.05
1975	2.34	14.14	0.68	0.50	0.18
1978	2.99	21.51	1.00	0.76	0.24
1980	3.92	21.83	1.34	1.03	0.31
1985	5.94	24.04	2.03	1.67	0.36
1990	6.96	28.21	2.45	1.98	0.47
1991	7.02	28.88	2.47	2.00	0.47
1992	7.07	29.44	2.48	2.01	0.47
1993	7.10	29.93	2.53	2.05	0.48
1994	7.14	30.59	2.62	2.12	0.50
1995	7.16	31.56	2.67	2.16	0.51
1996	7.08	32.38	2.82	2.30	0.52

续表 Continued

单位:万人 (10000 persons)

年份 Year	普通中学 Senior	职业中学 Vocational Schools	小学 Primary Scholls	幼儿园 Kindergarden	盲、聋哑学校 Schools for the Blind, Deaf and Deafmutes
1952	1.42		9.79	0.16	0.01
1957	3.03		12.15	0.59	0.01
1962	5.11	0.20	16.26	0.98	0.01
1965	5.06	1.29	24.63	0.90	0.02
1970	7.55		22.44		
1975	13.46		29.79	1.79	0.04
1978	20.51		29.23	2.94	0.06
1980	20.35	0.14	31.35	5.10	0.08
1985	21.08	0.93	29.44	7.48	0.10
1990	23.94	1.82	30.57	8.71	0.18
1991	24.53	1.88	30.83	8.90	0.22
1992	24.88	2.08	30.78	8.95	0.23
1993	25.05	2.35	30.75	8.91	0.24
1994	25.40	2.57	31.08	9.58	0.25
1995	25.97	2.92	31.35	9.73	0.26
1996	26.37	3.19	31.85	9.90	0.25

16－20 主要年份各级各类学校专任教师数
FULL-TIME TEACHERS BY LEVEL AND TYPE OF SCHOOL

单位:万人 (10000 persons)

年份 Year	普通高等学校 Institutions of Higher Education	中等学校 Secondary Schools	中等专业学校 Specialized Secondary Schools			普通中学 Regular Secondary Schools
				中等技术学校 Technical Schools	中等师范学校 Teacher Training Schools	
1952	0.17	1.07	0.28	0.12	0.16	0.79
1957	0.46	2.09	0.39	0.30	0.09	0.17
1962	0.98	3.69	0.37	0.31	0.06	3.20
1965	0.87	4.98	0.48	0.43	0.05	3.31
1970	0.98	6.03	0.11	0.08	0.03	5.92
1975	1.01	10.81	0.30	0.20	0.10	10.51
1978	1.34	16.75	0.44	0.31	0.13	16.31
1980	1.59	16.83	0.63	0.47	0.16	15.20
1985	2.30	16.53	0.90	0.72	0.18	14.98
1990	2.76	19.63	1.20	0.97	0.23	17.25
1991	2.76	20.06	1.18	0.95	0.23	17.66
1992	2.70	20.32	1.18	0.95	0.23	17.79
1993	2.70	20.71	1.19	0.96	0.23	18.02
1994	2.73	21.28	1.26	1.01	0.25	18.35
1995	2.73	22.16	1.30	1.04	0.26	18.91
1996	2.74	22.82	1.39	1.13	0.26	19.28

续表 Continued

单位:万人 (10000 persons)

年份 Year			职业中学 Vocational Schools	小学 Primary Scholls	幼儿园 Kindergarden	盲、聋哑学校 Schools for the Blind, Deaf and Deafmutes
	高中 Senior	初中 Junior				
1952				8.84	0.13	0.01
1957	0.28	1.42		11.50	0.40	0.01
1962	0.66	2.54	0.12	15.66	0.45	0.01
1965	0.64	2.67	1.19	24.02	0.52	0.01
1970				20.94		
1975	3.16	7.35		28.01	1.24	0.02
1978	4.58	11.73		27.07	2.32	0.04
1980	2.86	12.34	0.10	27.97	4.41	0.05
1985	2.88	12.10	0.65	25.91	6.06	0.06
1990	3.27	13.98	1.18	26.95	7.21	0.11
1991	3.36	14.30	1.22	27.00	7.48	0.12
1992	3.38	14.41	1.35	26.66	7.47	0.13
1993	3.39	14.63	1.50	25.59	7.40	0.14
1994	3.42	14.93	1.67	26.95	7.99	0.15
1995	3.59	15.32	1.95	27.35	8.14	0.16
1996	3.88	15.40	2.15	27.96	8.31	0.16

16—21 全省研究生数
POSTGRADUATES IN MAIN YEARS

单位:人 (person)

项目	Items	1985	1990	1995	1996
高等学校	**Institutions of Higher Education**				
招生数	New Students Enrollment	2918	2214	3730	4481
在读人数	Students Enrollment	5444	6718	10700	12243
#女性	Female	867	1175	2384	3003
毕业生数	Graduates	1026	2626	2202	2728
研究所(院)	**Research Institutions (Academies)**				
招生数	New Students Enrollment	24	62	65	86
在读人数	Students Enrollment	55	191	191	219
#女性	Female	13	20	27	28
毕业生数	Graduates	29	91	45	54

注:1990年研究所(院)女性研究生在读人数系推算。

Notes: The number of female postgraduates in 1996 was caculated from that in enrollment.

16—22 主要年份各级各类学校女学生和女教师数
FEMALE STUDENTS ENROLLMENT AND TEACHERS BY LEVEL AND TYPE OF SCHOOLS IN MAIN YEARS

单位:人 (person)

项目	Items	1985	1990	1995	1996
女学生数	**Female Students**				
高等学校	Institutions of Higher Education	2.93	4.30	6.79	7.11
中等专业学校	Specialized Secondary Schools	3.36	6.04	16.19	20.81
普通中学	Regular Secondary Schools	110.10	117.64	139.72	143.24
农业、职业中学	Agricultural and Professional Secondary Schools	4.80	6.69	12.30	11.93
小学	Primary Schools	309.30	288.49	306.29	327.47
女学生占学生总数%	**Percentage of Female Students (percent)**				
高等学校	Institutions of Higher Education	24.5	29.3	32.6	32.2
中等专业学校	Specialized Secondary Schools	36.3	43.1	50.8	50.8
普通中学	Regular Secondary Schools	38.7	41.7	44.1	44.3
农业、职业中学	Agricultural and Professional Secondary Schools	40.3	43.1	46.9	46.1
小学	Primary Schools	45.6	47.1	47.5	47.6
女教师数	**Female Teachers**				
高等学校	Institutions of Higher Education	0.57	0.71	0.76	0.81
中等专业学校	Specialized Secondary Schools	0.29	0.42	0.52	0.56
普通中学	Regular Secondary Schools	3.21	4.28	5.58	5.92
农业、职业中学	Agricultural and Professional Secondary Schools	0.14	0.28	0.63	0.73
小学	Primary Schools	9.60	10.34	11.64	12.15
女教师占教师总数%	**Percentage of Female Teachers (percent)**				
高等学校	Institutions of Higher Education	24.8	25.8	27.8	29.6
中等专业学校	Specialized Secondary Schools	32.2	35.2	39.9	40.1
普通中学	Regular Secondary Schools	21.4	24.8	29.5	30.7
农业、职业中学	Agricultural and Professional Secondary Schools	21.8	24.7	32.4	34.1
小学	Primary Schools	37.0	38.4	42.5	43.4

16－23 每一专任教师平均负担在校学生数
STUDENT-TEACHER RATIO BY LEVEL AND TYPE SCHOOL

单位：人 (person)

年份 Year	普通高等学校 Institutions of Higher Education	中等专业学校 Specialized Secondary Schools	普通中学 Regular Secondary Schools	小学 Primary Schools
1949	5.4	13.9	19.5	32.9
1952	6.7	15.1	29.6	37.9
1957	6.4	13.4	30.0	35.9
1962	5.4	6.5	20.4	28.6
1965	4.5	12.8	20.5	29.1
1970	0.1	6.1	25.0	31.7
1971	0.1	8.5	28.9	32.4
1972	1.1	6.4	24.9	32.4
1973	2.0	7.0	22.7	31.6
1974	2.8	8.6	21.7	32.7
1975	3.0	7.4	23.6	33.0
1976	3.6	6.9	25.7	32.8
1977	3.5	5.9	24.9	32.5
1978	4.6	8.7	23.7	32.1
1979	5.0	9.6	22.5	31.1
1980	5.3	9.7	21.1	29.9
1981	5.4	7.3	18.9	27.6
1982	3.8	6.5	18.9	25.8
1983	4.0	7.8	19.5	27.0
1984	4.7	9.3	19.8	26.7
1985	5.2	10.3	19.0	26.2
1986	5.2	10.3	18.6	25.7
1987	5.1	10.6	17.8	25.1
1988	5.3	10.7	16.8	24.4
1989	5.3	11.4	16.4	23.6
1990	5.3	11.7	16.3	22.7
1991	5.2	12.0	16.3	22.0
1992	5.7	12.7	16.6	21.9
1993	6.7	16.1	16.3	22.4
1994	7.4	19.6	16.6	22.9
1995	7.6	24.5	16.8	23.6
1996	8.1	29.5	16.8	24.6

文化、体育、卫生、其他 17

CULTURE, SPORTS, PUBLIC HEALTH AND OTHERS

17 文化、体育、卫生、其他
CULTURE，SPORTS，PUBLIC HEALTH AND OTHERS

1 9 9 6

文化产业机构数	Cultural Institutions	15128	个	
艺术表演团体	Art Performance Troups	131	个	
图书出版量	Books Published	4.51	亿册	(100000000)
杂志出版量	Magazines Published	0.71	亿册	(100000000)
报纸出版量	Newspaper Published	17.49	亿份	(100000000)
等级运动员发展人数	Certified Atheltes	3505	人	
等级裁判员发展人数	Certified Referees	1242	人	
卫生机构数	Health Care Institutions	14944	个	
#医　　院	Hospitals	2617	个	
医院床位数	Hospital Beds	15.78	万张	(10000)
卫生技术人员	Medical Technical Personnel	25.02	万人	(10000)

图书、杂志、报纸出版量

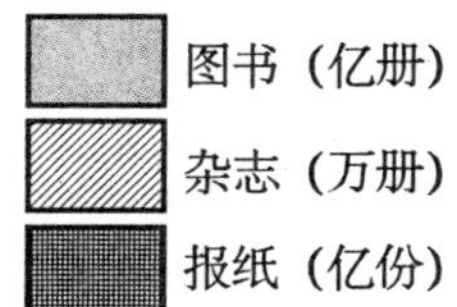

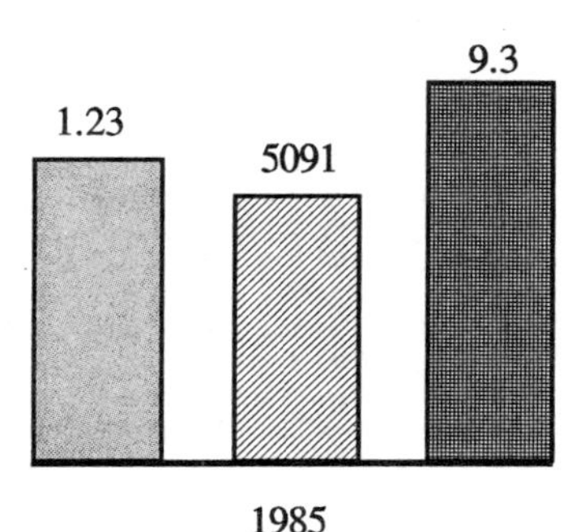

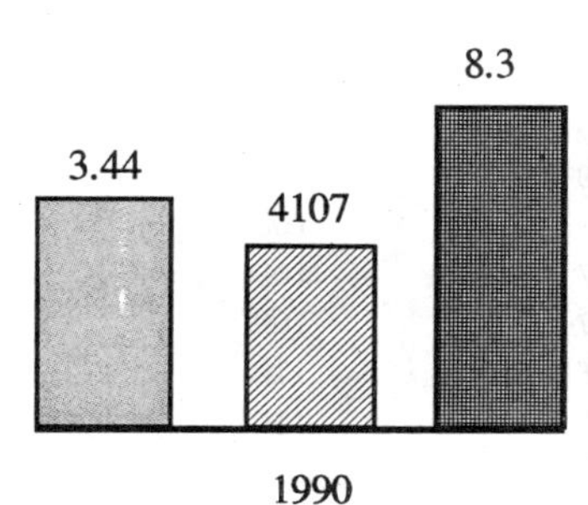

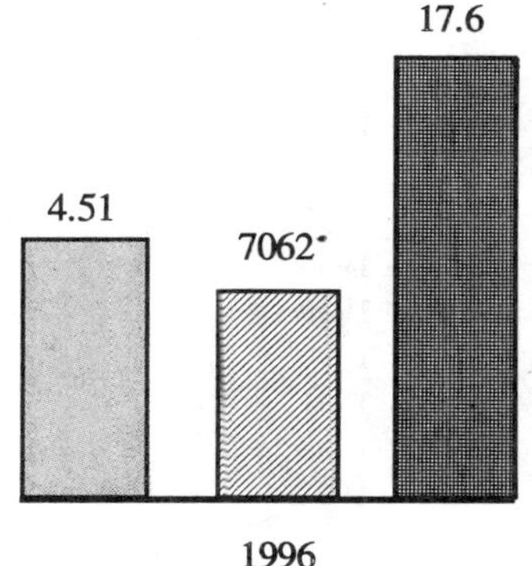

17－1 文化产业机构数、从业人员数(1996)

CULTURAL INSTITUTIONS AND PERSONNEL

单位：机构：个 人员：人 (number、person)

指标	Items	总计 Total		文化部门 Cultural Department		其他部门 Others	
		机构 Institution	人员 Personnel	机构 Institution	人员 Personnel	机构 Institution	人员 Personnel
总计	**Total**	**15128**	**83754**	**6808**	**40451**	**8320**	**43303**
艺术业	Art	351	10660	351	10660		
图书馆业	Libraries	97	2006	97	2006		
群众文化业	Masses Culture	2280	7646	2280	7646		
艺术教育业	Art Education	21	891	21	891		
娱乐业	Entertainment	7833	44665	1553	8517	6280	36148
文艺科研	Art Research Institutions	9	81	9	81		
文物业	Cultural Relics	140	2189	140	2189		
其他文化产业	Others	4397	15616	2357	8461	2040	7155

17－2 主要年份文化艺术、文物事业单位

NUMBER OF INSTITUTIONS FOR CULTURE, ART AND CULTURAL RELICES

单位：个 (number)

年份 Year	艺术表演团体 Art Performance Troups	文化馆 Cultural Centers	文化站 Cultural Stations	公共图书馆 Public Libraries	博物馆 Museums
1952	172	108	651	12	3
1957	218	97	543	25	5
1962	217	99	489	39	12
1965	195	99	889	35	14
1970	113	71	1141	26	15
1975	121	107	1772	62	13
1978	143	110	2093	78	19
1979	155	109	2107	78	19
1980	157	111	2153	82	19
1981	161	110	2173	85	19
1982	157	109	2211	85	19
1983	154	112	2223	89	21
1984	148	109	2285	89	21
1985	147	108	2308	90	31
1986	143	108	2310	91	34
1987	140	109	2300	91	37
1988	140	108	2285	91	45
1989	137	108	2258	91	50
1990	137	109	2166	91	51
1991	137	109	2269	91	58
1992	136	110	2245	91	62
1993	136	110	2256	93	66
1994	137	110	2227	94	68
1995	136	110	2221	94	72
1996	131	108	2160	97	73

17—3 艺术表演事业机构和人员数(1996)
ART PERFORMANCE INSTITUTION AND PERSONNEL

单位：机构：个 人员：人 (number、person)

指标	Items	总计 Total 机构 Institution	总计 Total 人员 Personnel	文化部门 Cultural Department 国有单位 State-Owned 机构 Institution	国有单位 State-Owned 人员 Personnel	集体单位 Collective-Owned 机构 Institution	集体单位 Collective-Owned 人员 Personnel
总计	**Total**	**270**	**9936**	**158**	**6247**	**112**	**3689**
艺术表演团体	Art Performance Troups	131	6273	25	2694	106	3579
#话剧、儿童剧、滑稽剧团	Drama, Children's Play and Comedy Troups	7	396	3	231	4	165
歌舞团、轻音乐团	Song and Dance, Light Music Troups	15	1420	9	1124	6	296
乐队、合唱团	Philharmonic and Chorus Troups	1	18	1	18		
文工团、文宣队	Cultural and Performance Troups	1	26			1	26
戏曲剧团	Local Opera Troups	85	3863	11	1227	74	2636
艺术表演场所	Art Centers	139	3663	133	3553	6	110
#剧场、影剧院	Theaters and Music Halls	128	3450	127	3408	1	42

17—4 艺术教育及其他文化产业机构和人员数(1996)
ART EDUCATION AND OTHER CULTURE INSTITUTION AND PERSONNEL

单位：机构：个 人员：人 (number、person)

指标	Items	总计 Total 机构 Institution	总计 Total 人员 Personnel	文化部门 Cultural Department 国有单位 State-Owned 机构 Institution	国有单位 State-Owned 人员 Personnel	集体单位 Collective-Owned 机构 Institution	集体单位 Collective-Owned 人员 Personnel
教育事业	**Education**	**21**	**891**	**17**	**855**	**4**	**36**
高等艺术学校	Higher Art Education Schools						
中等艺术学校	Secondary Art Schools	9	721	9	721		
文化干部学校	Cultural Cardre Schools	2	8	2	8		
其他艺术教育机构	Others	10	162	6	126	4	36
其他文化产业	**Culture**	**12332**	**61148**	**748**	**5717**	**3175**	**11127**
艺术创作机构	Art Institutions	68	435	66	422	2	13
艺术研究机构	Art Research Institutions	9	81	9	81		
艺术展览机构	Culture, Art and Agency	8	153	8	153		
文化艺术经纪与代理业	Performance Companies	12	62	11	61	1	1
其他	Others	12235	60417	654	5000	3172	11113

17—5 公共图书馆、群众文化事业机构和人员数(1996)
PUBLIC LIBRARIES, MASS CULTURE INSTITUTION AND PERSONNEL

单位：机构：个 人员：人　　(number、person)

指标	Items	总计 Total		文化部门 Cultural Department	
		机构 Institution	人员 Personnel	机构 Institution	人员 Personnel
图书馆事业	Libraries	97	2006	97	2006
#儿童图书馆	Children's Libraries	4	19	4	19
群众文化事业	Mass Culture	2280	7646	2280	7646
群众艺术馆	Mass Art Centers	12	392	12	392
文化馆	Cultural Centers	108	1894	108	1894
文化站	Cultural Stations	2160	5360	2160	5360
#乡镇文化站	Rural Cultural Stations	1994	3745	1994	3745

17—6 文物事业机构和人员数
NUMBER OF INSTITUTIONS AND PERSONNEL IN CULTURAL RELICS

单位：机构：个 人员：人　　(number、person)

指标	Items	机构 Institution		人员 Personnel	
		1995	1996	1995	1996
总计	**Total**	**140**	**140**	**2055**	**2189**
文物单位	Cultural Relics Units	57	56	297	349
文物保护管理单位	Cultural Relics Management	53	54	257	304
其他文物单位	Others	4	2	40	33
博物馆	Museums	72	73	1343	1428
综合性	Synthesized	38	38	857	882
专门性	Special	18	19	261	321
纪念性	Memorial Hall	16	16	225	225
文物商店	Cultural Relics Shops	11	11	415	412

17—7 报纸、杂志出版情况(1996)
BASIC STATISTICS FOR NEWSPAPER AND MAGAZINES PUBLISHED

指标	Items	种数(种) Number of Publications	总印数(万册、万份) Printed Copies (10000)	总印张(万印张) Printed Signatures (10000)
报纸	Newspaper	103	174899	206604
杂志	Magazines	380	7062	19038
综合	Comprehensiveness	17	1259	4245
哲学、社会科学	Philosophy and Social Sciences	74	1496	4933
自然科学、技术	Natural Sciences and Technology	243	1104	3165
文化、教育	Culture and Education	21	2803	5272
文学、艺术	Literature and Art	23	146	1049
少年儿童	Children's Reading Material	2	254	374

17—8 图书出版情况(1996)
BASIC STATISTICS FOR BOOKS PUBLISHED

指标	Items	出版图书种数(种) Number of Publication	#租型图书 Rented Books	总印数(万册、万份) Printed Copies (10000)	总印张(万印张) Printed Signatures (10000)
总计	**Total**	**4953**	**348**	**45066**	**206755**
书籍合计	Books	4437	348	44256	204810
哲学、社会科学	Philosophy and Social Sciences	339	10	274	2732
文化、教育	Culture and Education	2431	337	40876	177216
文学、艺术	Literature and Art	897	1	2360	15477
自然科学、技术	Natural Sciences and Technology	662		552	7589
其他	Others	108		194	1796
图片	Pictures	516		810	1910

注:总印张数中,含不使用《中国标准书号》的活页文选、活页歌篇等35万印张数。

Note: The total printed signatures included 350000 printed signatures of loose-leaf selected works and song, etc.

17—9 电视台及节目制作情况 BASIC STATISTICS ON TELEVISION STATIONS AND SELF PRODUCED PROGRAMS

指标		Items	1985	1990	1995	1996
基本情况		**Basic Statistics**				
电视台	（座）	Television Stations	12	24	52	54
发射台及转播台	（座）	Broadcast Transmitting Stations and Relay Stations	106	131	152	154
节目	（套）	Programs	13	25	56	58
平均每周播出时间	（小时）	Program Hours Per Week (hour)	423	904	2902	3547
电视人口覆盖率	（%）	Population Coverage Rate	76	90	94	95
制作节目时间	**（小时）**	**Produced Programs (hour)**	**3340**	**3330**	**28738**	**41692**
#新闻节目		News Programs	599	1060	4659	5551
文艺节目		Entertainment Programs	826	815	7450	17849
教育节目		Educational Programs	1457	58	544	861

17—10 广播电台及节目制作情况 BASIC STATISTICS ON BROADCASTING AND SELF PRODUCED PROGRAMS

指标		Items	1985	1990	1995	1996
基本情况		**Basic Statistics**				
电台	（座）	Stations	11	22	61	61
发射台及转播台	（座）	Broadcast Transmitting Stations and Relay Stations	13	16	21	21
节目	（套）	Programs	15	31	86	88
平均每日播音时间	（小时）	Program Hours Per Week (hour)	156	280	1075	1143
广播人口覆盖率	（%）	Population Coverage Rate	91	89	87	88
制作节目时间	**（小时）**	**Produced Programs (hour)**	**20670**	**26966**	**197793**	**248814**
#新闻节目		News Programs	3690	4583	24574	34248
文艺节目		Entertainment Programs	8530	11279	90838	108185
教育节目		Educational Programs	1740	899	6168	13241

注：广播发射台及转播台仅指中、短波广播，不含调频广播。
Note: Broadcast transmitting stations and relay stations only referred to MW and SW radio, excluding FM.

17—11 体委系统职工人数 (1996)
PERSONNEL OF PHYSICAL CULTURE AND SPORTS COMMISSIONS

单位:人 (person)

指标 Items		总计 Total	#优秀运动队 Accomplished Athlete Team	#体育运动学校 Physical Cultural and Sports School	#重点业余体校 Key Part-Time Sports School	#普通业余体校 Ordinary Part-TimeSports Shools	#公共体育场(馆) Public Stadiums and Gymnasiums
总计	**Total**	**7585**	**1547**	**674**	**395**	**1057**	**1169**
专职教练员	Full-time coaches	1190	216	189	190	576	—
运动员	Athletes	782	782	—	—	—	—
管理干部	Adiministrative Staff	2162	153	162	74	187	522
专职教师	Full-time Teachers	563	107	217	84	130	—
科技人员	Scientific and Technical Personnel	63	4	13	—	—	8
医务人员	Medical Personnel	81	33	11	4	12	8
其他	Others	2744	252	82	43	152	631

17—12 等级运动员、裁判员发展人数
CERTIFID ATHLETES AND REFEREES BY TYPE OF SPORTS

单位:人 (person)

指标 Items		1985	1990	1995	1996
等级运动员发展人数	Certified Athletes	3009	3199	3359	3505
运动健将	Master Athletes	35	40	54	52
一级	First Grade	61	54	88	112
二级	Second Grade	283	318	441	515
三级	Third Grade	1335	1307	1600	1633
少年级	Juvenile Grade	1295	1480	1176	1193
等级裁判员发展人数	Certified Referees	2019	1428	1471	1242
国家(际)级	National International Referees	25	7	16	17
一级	First Grade	242	86	157	57
二级	Second Grade	503	384	408	394
三级	Third Grade	1249	951	890	774

17—13 群众体育活动情况
MASS SPORTS ACTIVITIES

单位：万人 (10000 persons)

指标	Items	1990	1994	1995	1996
全省各级体委举办运动会情况	**Sports Meeting**				
运动会次数 （次）	Times (time)	1771	976	1008	1173
参加运动会的运动员人数	Persons	68.52	27.92	30.44	38.34
达到国家体育锻炼标准的学生	Students Passed "NPTPS"	656.20	705.23	704.87	729.00
大专院校	Institution of Higher Education		12.90	13.18	13.72
中专、中技	Specialized Secondary and Technical School	3.07	14.82	15.73	18.83
中　学	Secondary School	262.08	284.44	294.11	305.59
小　学	Primary School	391.05	393.07	381.85	390.86

注："NPTPS"指国家体育锻炼标准。
Note: "NPTPS" means National Physical Training Program Standards.

17—14 运动员破全国和省纪录、获国内外奖章情况
BASIC STATISTICS FOR NATIONAL, PROVINCE RECORDS BROKEN AND MEDALS WON AT HOME AND ABROAD

指标	Items	1990	1994	1995	1996
破全国纪录	National Records Broken				
项　数 （项）	Events (time)		4	5	3
人(队)数 （人次）	Persons (person)		5	8	3
次　数 （次）	Times (time)		4	10	
破省纪录	Province Records Broken				
项　数 （项）	Events (time)	4	20	91	75
人(队)数 （人次）	Persons (person)	9	27	37	40
次　数 （次）	Times (time)	9	32	91	
获国内外奖章 （枚）	Medals Won at Home and Abroad				
金质奖章	Gold	58	39	60	43
银质奖章	Silver	30	36	30	34
铜质奖章	Copper	37	41	29	20

17—15 卫生事业基本情况（1996）
BASIC STATISTICS FOR HEALTH CARE

指标	Items	机构数（个）Institutions	床位数（万张）Hospital Beds (10000 bed)	卫生工作人员（万人）Personnel (10000 persons)	#卫生技术人员 Medical Technical Personnel	#医生 Doctors
总计	**Total**	**14944**	**17.03**	**31.90**	**25.02**	**11.34**
医院合计	Total Hospitals	2617	15.78	24.90	19.58	8.15
县及县以上医院小计	Hospitals at County Level and Above	489	9.23	14.29	10.69	4.17
综合医院	Comprehensive Hospitals	296	5.91	9.42	7.08	2.77
中医医院	Hospitals of Chinese Medicines	83	1.14	2.00	1.56	0.66
医学院附属医院	Hospital Attached to Medical Colleges	9	0.41	0.76	0.57	0.23
传染病院	Infectious Diseases Hospitals	13	0.41	0.42	0.30	0.09
精神病院	Mental Hospitals	45	0.69	0.63	0.42	0.15
结核病院	Tuberculosis Hospitals	3	0.04	0.05	0.03	0.01
妇幼保健院	Hospitals for Maternity and Child Care	9	0.15	0.26	0.20	0.06
儿童医院	Children's Hospitals	3	0.08	0.15	0.11	0.04
职业医院	Vocational Hospitals	6	0.06	0.06	0.04	0.01
肿瘤医院	Tumor Hospitals	3	0.10	0.16	0.11	0.04
其他专科医院	Other Specialized Hospitals	19	0.24	0.38	0.27	0.11
区、乡（镇）卫生院	Rural Township Hospitals	2031	6.27	10.13	8.51	3.81
其他医院	Other Hospitals	97	0.28	0.48	0.38	0.17
疗养院、所	Sanatoriums	35	0.69	0.28	0.12	0.04
门诊部、所	Clinics	8410	0.04	3.20	3.16	1.92
专科防治所、站	Specialized Stations	121	0.12	0.31	0.22	0.12
#结核病防治所、站	Tuberculosis Prevention Stations	8		0.01		
职业病防治所、站	Occupational Diseases Control Stations	3	0.02	0.03	0.02	0.01
卫生防疫站	Sanatation and Diseases Control Stations	142	0.03	0.91	0.69	0.51
妇幼保健所、站	Meternity and Child Care Centers	115	0.01	0.24	0.19	0.12
药品检验所、室	Medicines and Chemical Reagent	75		0.10	0.07	
医学科学研究机构	Institutions of Medical Sciences Test Labs	18	0.06	0.16	0.10	0.04
其他卫生机构	Other Health Care Institutions	172	0.30	1.48	0.57	0.28
个体开业	Individual-Run Medical Units	3239		0.32	0.32	0.16

17—16 主要年份卫生机构数
HEALTH CARE INSTITUTIONS

单位:个 (number)

年份 Year	总计 Total	医院 Hospitals	#县级以上医院 Hospitals at County Level Above	疗养院、所 Sanatoriums	门诊部、所 Clinics	专科防治所站 Specialized Stations
1949	259	115	71	3	141	
1952	2896	117	114	16	2688	20
1957	6145	138	135	32	5460	45
1962	11726	490	208	55	10832	50
1965	12253	472	201	39	11418	48
1970	6899	2340	207	5	4231	70
1975	7894	2327	240	5	5212	8
1976	8262	2353	252	6	5521	7
1977	8621	2385	304	6	5738	6
1978	9277	2428	334	7	6301	9
1979	9650	2453	369	9	6639	13
1980	9943	2457	371	11	6910	17
1981	10563	2483	390	16	7495	19
1982	10787	2502	397	20	7689	21
1983	10745	2515	407	22	7628	25
1984	11154	2523	415	24	8004	56
1985	11515	2460	426	32	8405	84
1986	11743	2470	448	32	8609	95
1987	11934	2482	462	35	8777	98
1988	12248	2472	467	36	9105	96
1989	12325	2483	478	34	9159	95
1990	12366	2491	483	35	9178	108
1991	12377	2495	477	36	9187	112
1992	12277	2493	481	36	9082	114
1993	12074	2483	486	36	8867	120
1994	12067	2559	494	36	8785	121
1995	12039	2534	490	35	8784	122
1996	14944	2617	489	35	8410	121

注:1996年卫生机构总数中含个体开业3239个。
Note: The total of health care institutions included individual-run 3239 units in 1996.

续表 Continued

年份 Year	卫生防疫站 Sanatation and Diseases Control Stations	妇幼保健所、站 Meternity and Child Care Centers	药品检验所、站 Medicines and Chemical Reagent	医学科学研究机构 Institutions of Medical Sciences Labs	其他卫生机构 Other Health Care Institutions
1949					
1952	4	31			20
1957	67	174		3	226
1962	97	98	11	4	89
1965	95	85	12		84
1970	70	47	9	2	125
1975	104	71	13	7	147
1976	104	75	22	7	167
1977	106	82	64	9	225
1978	107	84	83	12	246
1979	114	92	82	14	234
1980	119	99	82	11	237
1981	119	98	79	15	239
1982	124	95	79	15	242
1983	123	95	73	15	249
1984	124	100	73	16	234
1985	127	105	72	16	214
1986	129	109	72	16	211
1987	128	112	72	18	212
1988	131	112	72	18	206
1989	135	114	73	16	216
1990	135	114	73	16	216
1991	137	114	74	14	208
1992	135	115	75	14	213
1993	141	117	75	18	217
1994	141	117	75	17	216
1995	141	117	75	17	214
1996	142	115	75	18	172

17—17 主要年份卫生机构人员数
PERSONNEL OF HEALTH CARE INSTITUTIONS

单位:万人 (10000 persons)

年份 Year	总计 Total	卫生技术人员 Medical Technical Personnel	#医生 Doctors	中医 Traditional Chinses Medicine	西医师 Western Medicine Senior	西医士 Western Medicine Junior	#护师、护士 Senior and Junior Nurses	每万人口医生数(人) Doctors of Per 10000 Population
1949	…	…	…	…	…	…	…	…
1952	6.28	5.24	2.62	1.72	0.25	0.64	0.34	7.00
1957	10.32	9.27	3.31	1.98	0.36	0.97	0.61	7.90
1962	9.97	8.47	4.20	1.95	0.65	1.60	1.09	9.60
1965	10.15	8.56	4.52	1.88	0.99	1.65	1.21	9.70
1970	8.50	6.78	3.41	0.97	1.20	1.24	1.59	6.40
1975	13.48	10.79	4.75	1.31	1.63	1.81	1.84	8.40
1976	14.49	11.54	4.96	1.30	1.67	1.99	2.03	8.70
1977	16.45	13.29	5.61	1.49	1.69	2.44	1.83	9.70
1978	17.45	14.00	5.70	1.48	1.90	2.32	1.79	9.70
1979	18.45	14.58	5.71	1.43	2.02	2.26	1.86	9.60
1980	19.03	15.04	6.10	1.42	2.45	2.23	2.08	10.20
1981	20.53	16.23	6.52	1.48	2.84	2.19	2.64	10.80
1982	21.44	16.93	7.16	1.54	3.25	2.37	3.04	11.70
1983	21.92	17.22	7.36	1.49	3.39	2.48	3.27	11.90
1984	22.64	17.68	7.50	1.48	3.48	2.53	3.38	12.10
1985	23.68	18.28	7.65	1.48	3.55	2.62	3.61	12.30
1986	24.53	18.90	7.88	1.47	3.68	2.73	3.78	12.50
1987	25.06	19.18	7.84	1.42	3.65	2.77	3.89	12.30
1988	25.96	20.05	8.60	1.47	4.87	2.26	4.52	13.30
1989	26.82	20.75	9.67	1.50	6.19	1.98	5.06	14.70
1990	27.58	21.35	9.94	1.50	6.29	2.15	5.34	14.60
1991	28.63	22.22	10.20	1.49	6.41	2.30	5.61	14.90
1992	29.39	22.89	10.43	1.49	6.59	2.36	5.76	15.10
1993	30.20	23.44	10.63	1.50	6.80	2.33	5.99	15.30
1994	30.85	24.05	10.94	1.53	7.08	2.33	6.28	15.60
1995	31.57	24.55	11.22	1.52	7.31	2.39	6.44	15.90
1996	31.90	25.02	11.34	1.53	7.46	2.35	6.69	15.95

17—18 主要年份卫生机构床位数
HOSPITAL BEDS

单位:万张 (10000 beds)

年份 Year	总计 Total	医院 Hospitals	#县及县以上医院 County Level and Above	疗养院、所 Sanatoriums	其他卫生机构 Other Health Care Institutions	每万人口医院床位数(张) Hospital Beds of Per 10000 Population
1949	0.46	0.45	0.26	0.01		1.30
1952	1.75	0.83	0.83	0.12	0.80	2.20
1957	2.21	1.32	1.31	0.33	0.56	3.10
1962	5.85	3.71	3.01	0.57	1.57	8.60
1965	6.52	3.98	3.13	0.46	2.08	8.60
1970	7.89	6.88	3.16	0.08	0.93	13.10
1975	10.79	9.57	4.06	0.09	1.13	17.00
1976	11.13	9.88	4.15	0.11	1.14	17.30
1977	11.60	10.43	4.68	0.12	1.05	18.10
1978	12.29	11.07	4.96	0.13	1.09	19.00
1979	12.54	11.40	5.27	0.16	0.98	19.30
1980	12.75	11.62	5.48	0.23	0.90	19.60
1981	13.28	11.96	5.83	0.29	1.03	19.90
1982	13.21	12.01	5.92	0.34	0.86	19.70
1983	13.49	12.25	6.20	0.39	0.85	20.00
1984	13.93	12.50	6.42	0.42	1.01	20.30
1985	14.29	12.65	6.71	0.55	1.09	20.40
1986	14.71	13.07	7.07	0.56	1.08	20.80
1987	15.38	13.59	7.44	0.64	1.15	21.40
1988	15.94	14.06	7.79	0.69	1.19	21.80
1989	16.08	14.22	8.02	0.64	1.22	21.80
1990	16.45	14.54	8.32	0.67	1.24	21.50
1991	16.77	14.85	8.52	0.74	1.18	21.70
1992	17.02	15.07	8.68	0.73	1.22	21.80
1993	17.33	15.29	8.94	0.73	1.31	21.90
1994	17.45	15.42	9.07	0.72	1.31	22.00
1995	17.46	15.48	9.15	0.71	1.27	21.90
1996	17.03	15.78	9.23	0.69	0.56	22.19

17—19 主要年份社会抚恤及社会救济福利费用情况
PERSONS ENJOYING REGULAR SUBSIDY AND COMMISERATE OF COUNTRY

单位：万元 (10000 yuan)

年份 Year	合计 Total	抚恤事业费 Commiserate	社会救济福利事业费 Subsidies of Welfare	自然灾害救济费 Subsidy of Natural Calamity	在合计中：由集体单位供给的 Among Total: Collletive Funds
1979	12548.4	3666.1	5528.3	3354.0	3419.4
1980	15207.9	5137.7	7188.2	2882.0	6175.5
1981	18054.0	6778.2	7229.9	4045.9	7578.1
1982	18551.0	8157.7	8008.7	2384.6	9012.7
1983	22360.3	8900.8	10100.9	3358.6	10181.8
1984	24966.2	9803.5	12547.8	2614.9	11237.4
1985	24095.0	11115.1	10976.1	2003.8	11922.3
1986	29014.8	13513.5	11988.8	3512.5	13174.9
1987	29866.4	12721.7	14205.6	2939.1	14105.5
1988	34902.9	15535.6	16206.7	3160.6	17426.9
1989	40778.0	18265.2	18310.3	4202.5	20082.1
1990	46656.9	20676.1	20333.0	5647.8	21594.7
1991	69567.2	20530.4	27004.6	22032.2	27730.0
1992	60807.8	22548.4	23266.8	14992.6	23433.2
1993	60972.3	25919.9	27447.7	7604.7	27021.9
1994	72275.7	31932.7	34078.1	6264.9	32392.2
1995	87469.8	38965.5	39543.7	8960.6	38558.0
1996	104278.1	48873.6	46469.5	8935.0	47955.2

17—20 享受补助救济人员情况
PERSONS RECEIVING SUBSIDIES OR RELIEF FUNDS

指标	Items	1990	1995	1996
散居孤老残幼人数 （万人）	Persons in Children, Elderly and Disabled Staff Receiving Relief Funds (10000 person)	17.75	15.35	15.30
得到国家定期定量救济人数 （人）	Persons Receiving Periodical and Fixed Government Relief Funds (person)	9325	8449	9063
得到集体给予补助人数 （万人）	Persons Recieving Collective Subsidies (10000 person)	15.56	12.98	12.85
农村困难户得到救济人数 （万人次）	Rural Poor Households Receiving Relif Funds and Subsidies (10000 persons)	184.14	192.77	193.13
城镇困难户得到救济补助人数 （万人次）	Persons in Urban Poor Households Recieving Relief Funds and Subsidies (10000 person)	38.08	21.69	31.96
城镇困难户得到国家定期定量救济人数 （人）	Persons in Urban Poor Households Recieving Periodical and Fixed Government Relief Funds (person)	12354	10234	10103
精减退职老职工得到救济人数 （万人）	Laid-Off, Retired, Elderly Staff Recieving Relief Funds (10000 person)	4.03	3.72	3.67
本年新增扶贫户数 （万户）	Icrease Poor Households (10000 household)	10.26	10.99	11.62
本年脱贫户数 （万户）	Households Leaving the Poor Household Support Program (10000 household)	8.44	9.91	10.39

17—21 社会福利事业单位和工作人员数 SOCIAL WELFARE INSTITUTIONS AND ENTERPRISES AND STAFF WORKERS

指标 Items		1995		1996	
		机构（个） Institu-tions	工作人员（人） Staff	机构（个） Institu-tions	工作人员（人） Staff
总计	**Total**	**11093**	**481890**	**10908**	**467634**
社会福利事业单位	Social Welfare Institutions	3206	15443	3141	15546
民政部门办	Run by Civil Adiministration Departments	88	4810	88	4858
社会办	Run by Communities	3118	10633	3053	10688
社会福利企业单位	Social Welfare Enterprises	7749	463723	7626	449200
民政部门办	Run by Civil Adiministration Departments	431	30730	410	28380
#假肢厂(站)	Artificial Limb Factories	2	127	2	125
#安置农场	Settle Down Farm	1	206	1	195
社会办	Run by Communities	7318	432993	7216	420820
收容遣送站	Collecting and Repatriation Units	25	406	25	404
殡葬事业单位	Funeral and Interment Institution	113	2318	116	2484

17—22 社会福利事业基本情况(1996) BASIC STATISTICS ON SOCIAL WELFARE INSTITUTIONS

指标 Items		院数（个） Homes	工作人员（人） Staff	床位（张） Beds	年末收养人员（人） Persons Housed (year-end)
总计	**Total**	**3141**	**15546**	**75428**	**64914**
民政部门办社会福利事业单位	Run by Civil Administration Departments	88	4858	10797	8579
优抚休、疗养院	Convalescent Homes	18	769	1198	1008
城市福利院	Urban Social Welfare Homes	70	4089	9599	7571
城镇集体办光荣院、敬老院	Run by Urban Collective Units	1372	5274	31267	26410
光荣院	Homes for Disabled Veterans	2	5	25	15
敬老院	Rural Homes for the Elderly	1370	5269	31242	26395
农村集体办光荣院、敬老院	Run by Rural Collective	1681	5414	33364	29925
光荣院	Homes for Disabled Veterans	3	6	23	22
敬老院	Rural Homes for the Elderly	1678	5408	33341	29903

二　市县篇

SECTIONS OF THE CITIES AND COUNTIES

区域经济主要指标 1

MAJOR INDICATORS OF REGIONAL ECONOMY

苏南苏中苏北经济主要指标
MAJOR ECONOMIC INDICATORS OF SOUTH JIANGSU MIDDLE JIANGSU AND NORTH JIANGSU

单位：万元 (10000yuan)

分市名称 Municipality	国内生产总值(当年价) Gross Domestic Product (current price)	第一产业 Primary Industry	第二产业 Secondery Industry	第三产业 Tertiary Industry	工农业总产值(当年价) Total Ontput Value of Industry and Agriculture	工业总产值 Total Output Value of Industry	农业总产值 Total Output Value of Agriculture
苏南合计 Southern Jiangsu Total	**23032990**	**1785433**	**13285967**	**7961590**	**58227917**	**54804174**	**3423743**
苏州市 Suzhou Municipality	10021368	881817	5679552	3459999	24371162	22745223	1625939
无锡市 Wuxi Municipality	8700081	448120	5141358	3110603	22786170	21861116	925054
常州市 Changzhou Municipality	4311541	455496	2465057	1390988	11070585	10197835	872750
苏中合计 Mid Jiangsu Total	**21852259**	**3253015**	**10934872**	**7664372**	**46837718**	**40423324**	**6414394**
南京市 Nanjing Municipality	6748997	488506	3434111	2826380	13210079	12247400	962679
镇江市 Zhenjiang Municipality	3351073	364250	1874332	1112491	7816560	7127727	688833
扬州市 Yangzhou Municipality	3511492	550948	1853811	1106733	7940241	6792184	1148057
泰州市 Taizhou Municipality	2936454	615424	1320089	1000941	6695763	5502413	1193350
南通市 Nantong Municipality	5304243	1233887	2452529	1617827	11175075	8753600	2421475
苏北合计 Northern Jiangsu Total	**13895547**	**4614513**	**5393617**	**3887417**	**32086399**	**22728633**	**9357766**
徐州市 Xuzhou Municipality	5000445	1156698	2263735	1580012	10600593	8329604	2270989
淮阴市 Huaiying Municipality	1732288	689571	584596	458121	3876739	2481136	1395603
盐城市 Yancheng Municipality	3812003	1402253	1412402	997348	9507339	6436742	3070597
连云港市 Lianyungang Municipality	2102004	769689	747780	584535	5329105	3876333	1452772
宿迁市 Suqion Municipality	1248807	596302	385104	267401	2772623	1604818	1167805

续表 1 Continued 1

分市名称 Municipality	土地面积(平方公里) Land Area (sq·km)	年末总人口(万人) Year-end Population (10000 persons)	年末从业人员(万人) Year-end Employment (10000 persons)	#职工人数 Staff and Workers (10000 persons)	#国有经济 State-Owned Units	乡村劳动力(万人) Rural Labor Force (10000 persons)	#农林牧渔业 Farming, Forestry, Animal, Husbandry and Fishery
苏南合计 Southern Jiangsu Total	**17513**	**1342.48**	**763.92**	**222.49**	**127.73**	**521.05**	**156.91**
苏州市 Suzhou Municipality	8488	574.12	323.84	94.51	53.72	228.45	64.07
无锡市 Wuxi Municipality	4650	430.82	235.49	74.28	43.23	158.60	39.90
常州市 Changzhou Municipality	4375	337.54	204.59	53.70	30.78	134.00	52.94
苏中合计 Mid Jiangsu Total	**30788**	**2516.57**	**1461.80**	**389.38**	**238.50**	**1031.88**	**535.85**
南京市 Nanjing Municipality	6516	525.43	297.31	146.43	104.20	138.95	74.93
镇江市 Zhenjiang Municipality	3843	264.80	161.25	44.61	28.23	106.06	46.26
扬州市 Yangzhou Municipality	6638	444.82	245.58	61.67	36.17	182.22	92.48
泰州市 Taizhou Municipality	5790	496.28	280.86	53.20	26.39	225.68	114.37
南通市 Nantong Municipality	8001	785.24	476.80	83.47	43.51	378.97	207.81
苏北合计 Northern Jiangsu Total	**52116**	**3048.97**	**1476.20**	**292.07**	**207.61**	**1205.55**	**837.44**
徐州市 Xuzhou Municipality	11258	859.43	428.26	94.16	73.94	331.03	237.14
淮阴市 Huaiying Municipality	10645	489.63	256.49	48.99	35.26	207.47	146.77
盐城市 Yancheng Municipality	14983	786.12	348.72	73.99	44.80	285.43	181.46
连云港市 Lianyungang Municipality	7368	432.96	218.88	45.06	32.42	167.81	120.68
宿迁市 Suqion Municipality	7862	480.83	223.85	29.87	21.19	213.81	151.39

续表 2　　Continued 2

分市名称 Municipality	粮食产量（万吨） Outpat of Grain (10000tons)	油料产量（吨） Output of Oil-Bearing Crop (tons)	棉花产量（吨） Output of Cotton (tons)	猪牛羊肉产量（吨） Output of Pork, Beef and Mutton (tons)	水产品产量（吨） Output of Aquatic (tons)	农业机械总动力（万千瓦） Total Motive Power of Machinery for Agriculture (10000kwh)	农村用电量（万千瓦小时） Electricity Consumed in Rural Rear (10000kwh)
苏南合计 Southern Jiangsu Total	**603.38**	**257821**	**37533**	**294280**	**469520**	**588.09**	**1328405**
苏州市 Suzhou Municipality	279.10	146606	36594	111165	290532	275.15	558380
无锡市 Wuxi Municipality	157.91	40689		90016	80554	170.00	490041
常州市 Changzhou Municipality	166.37	70526	939	93099	98434	142.94	279984
苏中合计 Mid Jiangsu Total	**1194.99**	**615799**	**182687**	**717313**	**963452**	**742.25**	**697200**
南京市 Nanjing Municipality	179.46	140836	3725	118317	86247	162.53	117795
镇江市 Zhenjiang Municipality	134.45	61337	2493	94706	57419	98.21	113754
扬州市 Yangzhou Municipality	245.45	85088	26188	138511	147663	159.76	113008
泰州市 Taizhou Municipality	286.15	72800	35151	173306	135894	150.79	130812
南通市 Nantong Municipality	349.48	255738	115130	192473	536229	170.96	221831
苏北合计 Northern Jiangsu Total	**1816.56**	**601416**	**317258**	**1381252**	**1161269**	**966.61**	**496185**
徐州市 Xuzhou Municipality	423.01	63771	49432	361674	97988	212.22	198358
淮阴市 Huaiying Municipality	338.11	141409	9774	242486	179561	184.62	52485
盐城市 Yancheng Municipality	485.70	186524	185928	394841	496250	219.72	155638
连云港市 Lianyungang Municipality	269.72	125581	51365	189451	265921	177.87	53265
宿迁市 Suqion Municipality	300.02	84131	20759	192800	121549	172.18	36439

单位:万元　　　　续表 3　Continued 3　　　　(10000yuan)

分市名称 Municipality	乡以上工业产值(现价) Outputvalue of Industry of Township Level and Above (current prisc)	#国有经济 State-Owned Units	集体经济 Collective-Owned Units	全部独立核算工业企业 Total Industrial Enterprises with Independent Accounting			
				资本金合计 Total Capital Assets	流动资产年平均余额 Average Annual Balance Circulating Funds	产品销售收入 Revenue of Product Sales	利税总额 Total Pre-tax Profits
苏南合计 Southern Jiangsu Total	**35971526**	**6570799**	**20692836**	**9629270**	**15341873**	**31211132**	**1943128**
苏州市 Suzhou Municipality	15340805	2795011	8168556	4690799	6157163	13166753	768254
无锡市 Wuxi Municipality	14073601	2260959	8902121	3434826	6085060	12414761	852059
常州市 Changzhou Municipality	6557120	1514829	3622159	1503645	3099650	5629618	322815
苏中合计 Mid Jiangsu Total	**29599194**	**10149489**	**12743994**	**7811241**	**14186140**	**24986481**	**1684955**
南京市 Nanjing Municipality	10069637	5551053	2620753	3171766	5007843	9197414	693750
镇江市 Zhenjiang Municipality	4348592	1142264	2530721	962557	1701250	3062748	192894
扬州市 Yangzhou Municipality	4998437	1382612	2205978	1455844	2652148	4343435	287167
泰州市 Taizhou Municipality	4159723	898848	2208803	943124	2124251	3517842	254061
南通市 Nantong Municipality	6022805	1174712	3177739	1277950	2700648	4865042	257083
苏北合计 Northern Jiangsu Total	**13647800**	**5857505**	**6312540**	**2682663**	**5440698**	**10893798**	**803915**
徐州市 Xuzhou Municipality	4435642	2456577	1682213	1022177	1928048	3554972	299866
淮阴市 Huaiying Municipality	1897487	893681	729098	361823	786184	1518134	133589
盐城市 Yancheng Municipality	4260198	1290116	2443434	661856	1545285	3449751	204476
连云港市 Lianyungang Municipality	2011029	762758	904351	476299	831391	1568280	88230
宿迁市 Suqion Municipality	1043444	454373	553444	160508	349790	802661	77754

续表 4 Continued 4

分市名称 Municipality	社会消费品零售总额（万元）Total Retail Sales of Consumer Goods (10000yuan)	自营出口总额（万美元）Total Value of Exports by Self-manage-Ment (10000USD)	#外商投资企业 Foreign Investment Enterprises	利用外资新签协议合同数（个）Number of Agreements for Foreign Capital Utilization Through Newly Signed Contracts	协议合同外资金额（万美元）Total Value of Roreign Capital Utilization Through Newly Signed Contracts (10000USD)	实际利用外资金额（万美元）Foreign Capital Actually Used (10000USD)	#客商直接投资 Direct Foreign Investment
苏南合计 Southern Jiangsu Total	**6785492**	**659486**	**386793**	**1390**	**719115**	**398134**	**344352**
苏州市 Suzhou Municipality	2660057	385600	240026	747	459904	225685	225685
无锡市 Wuxi Municipality	2549533	173654	96655	402	159305	120685	91475
常州市 Changzhou Municipality	1575902	100232	50112	241	99906	51764	27192
苏中合计 Mid Jiangsu Total	**7999778**	**384827**	**217868**	**937**	**261161**	**151166**	**124999**
南京市 Nanjing Municipality	2985713	94431	37599	438	97708	50716	47166
镇江市 Zhenjiang Municipality	902438	58973	37798	122	50351	24000	18983
扬州市 Yangzhou Municipality	1159684	40514	23932	71	10414	16985	9985
泰州市 Taizhou Municipality	1006765	21980	11401	74	19241	9141	8408
南通市 Nantong Municipality	1945178	168929	107138	232	83447	50324	40457
苏北合计 Northern Jiangsu Total	**4615590**	**89284**	**32211**	**498**	**70823**	**44043**	**30353**
徐州市 Xuzhou Municipality	1451706	22904	8360	122	20791	17284	14052
淮阴市 Huaiying Municipality	674351	9044	865	29	4490	4002	934
盐城市 Yancheng Municipality	1301226	25146	10605	124	7152	10060	6646
连云港市 Lianyungang Municipality	743986	30163	11813	219	34847	11817	8314
宿迁市 Suqion Municipality	444321	2027	568	4	3543	880	407

单位：万元　　　　续表 5　Continued 5　　　　(10000yuan)

分市名称 Municipality	财政收入 Finaneial Revenue	#地方财政收入 Local Financial Revenue	财政支出 Financial Expendi-ture	金融机构存款余额 Deposits Balance of Banking Institutions	金融机构贷款余额 Loans Balance of Banking Institutions	银行现金收入 Cash Revenue of National Banking System	银行现金支出 Cash Expenditure of National Banking System
苏南合计 Southern Jiangsu Total	**1546403**	**746643**	**709585**	**16204216**	**12025970**	**31742039**	**31629584**
苏州市 Suzhou Municipality	640757	324917	315448	7447982	5370165	15144173	15054680
无锡市 Wuxi Municipality	562614	255878	240317	5532623	4015055	10318881	10275382
常州市 Changzhou Municipality	343032	165848	153820	3223611	2640750	6278985	6299522
苏中合计 Mid Jiangsu Total	**1685674**	**818820**	**1000045**	**19360798**	**14059102**	**28789584**	**29871291**
南京市 Nanjing Municipality	787883	361643	401743	8328407	5676672	10608032	10433323
镇江市 Zhenjiang Municipality	178287	87458	107296	1834727	1552813	3732106	4037939
扬州市 Yangzhou Municipality	204067	99717	142919	2420954	2012994	3839746	4202856
泰州市 Taizhou Municipality	207598	109894	146216	2213975	1799569	3795629	4116518
南通市 Nantong Municipality	307839	160108	201871	4562735	3017054	6814071	7080655
苏北合计 Northern Jiangsu Total	**825917**	**447064**	**708334**	**8311316**	**7665590**	**18229174**	**18347797**
徐州市 Xuzhou Municipality	302406	153395	213530	2950050	2388715	5656864	5705958
淮阴市 Huaiying Municipality	128718	59690	108094	1117811	1260536	3003181	2896399
盐城市 Yancheng Municipality	188510	115199	185729	2440212	2215659	4912449	5127139
连云港市 Lianyungang Municipality	129515	84556	120244	1280764	1270659	2963301	2936375
宿迁市 Suqion Municipality	76768	34224	80737	522479	530021	1693379	1681926

续表 6　　Continued 6

分市名称 Municipality	固定资产投资完成额（万元） Total Value of Fixed Assets Fulfilled (10000yuan)	#国有经济 Stale-Owned Units	城镇集体 Rural Collective Owmed Units	房地产投资 Real Estate Investment	公路客运量（万人） Highway Passenger Traffic (10000 person)	公路货运量（万吨） Highway Freight Traffic (10000tons)	邮电业务总量(万元) Revenue From Postal and Tele-commumca-tion Services (10000yuan)
苏南合计 Southern Jiangsu Total	**7022099**	**1428046**	**277117**	**1011753**	**31749**	**15071**	**403980**
苏州市 Suzhou Municipality	3534562	583697	152228	501411	11234	4810	190757
无锡市 Wuxi Municipality	2338901	457872	80343	356756	14004	6418	136054
常州市 Changzhou Municipality	1148636	386477	44546	153586	6512	3843	77169
苏中合计 Mid Jiangsu Total	**6546185**	**2837657**	**303442**	**1107685**	**28377**	**18666**	**393400**
南京市 Nanjing Municipality	3058685	1468805	71117	697029	9926	7094	155441
镇江市 Zhenjiang Municipality	692802	265721	33771	62814	4638	3109	51500
扬州市 Yangzhou Municipality	991856	585640	43942	98329	4415	2437	60330
泰州市 Taizhou Municipality	471577	155895	66091	48265	3017	1714	45653
南通市 Nantong Municipality	1331265	361596	88521	201248	6381	4312	80476
苏北合计 Northern Jiangsu Total	**3057048**	**1330697**	**207428**	**206764**	**20489**	**12423**	**162918**
徐州市 Xuzhou Municipality	1275020	562238	55386	80642	7691	5184	53673
淮阴市 Huaiying Municipality	356355	206045	29018	15231	2150	1082	23265
盐城市 Yancheng Municipality	781872	292623	69273	64633	4813	2722	47845
连云港市 Lianyungang Municipality	517163	217823	43471	43544	4265	2719	27177
宿迁市 Suqion Municipality	126638	51968	10280	2714	1571	716	10958

续表 7　　Continued 7

分市名称 Municipality	全部职工工资总额（万元）Gross Wage Bill of the Staff and Workers (10000yuan)	#国有经济 State-Owned Units	居民人均可支配收入（元）Annual Allocatable Income Per Capita Residents (yuan)	居民人均消费支出（元）Annual Living Expenditure Per Capita of Residents (yuan)	农民人均纯收入(元) Annual Net Income of Peasants (yuan)	保险福利费用总额（万元）Total Funds of Insurance and Welfare (10000yuan)	城乡居民储蓄存款余额（万元）Deposit Saving Balance of Urban and Rural Residents (10000yuan)
苏南合计 Southern Jiangsu Total	**1764980**	**1077222**				**239771**	**8735277**
苏州市 Suzhou Municipality	735361	450781	6591	5264	5088	96504	4082648
无锡市 Wuxi Municipality	599231	365760	6500	5356	4610	83861	2926110
常州市 Changzhou Municipality	430388	260681	6761	4946	4172	59406	1726519
苏中合计 Mid Jiangsu Total	**2654989**	**1807123**				**345291**	**11042590**
南京市 Nanjing Municipality	1172621	901127	5210	4921	3128	162246	3589993
镇江市 Zhenjiang Municipality	296904	203480	5608	4530	3523	31457	1151723
扬州市 Yangzhou Municipality	396691	256223	5535	4352	2937	52646	1563311
泰州市 Taizhou Municipality	266849	151334	5477	4303	2951	34386	1519494
南通市 Nantong Municipality	521924	294959	5915	4640	3168	64556	3218069
苏北合计 Northern Jiangsu Total	**1527238**	**1218370**				**150458**	**5447953**
徐州市 Xuzhou Municipality	584442	506673	5405	4196	2390	58598	1828200
淮阴市 Huaiying Municipality	224669	178408	4234	3768	2276	20271	698254
盐城市 Yancheng Municipality	359964	248603	4736	3725	2546	38671	1753668
连云港市 Lianyungang Municipality	231570	182891	4993	3649	2396	24865	773392
宿迁市 Suqion Municipality	126593	101795	2946	2401	1993	8052	394439

续表 8　　Continued 8

分市名称 Municipality	高等学校在校学生数（人） Student Enrollment of Institutions of High Education (person)	普通中学学生数（万人） Regular Secondary Schools (10000 persons)	各类专业技术人员数（万人） Scientific and Technical Personnel (10000 persons)	#中级技术职称以上人员 Techmical Personnels With Middle Title Level and Over	医院数（个） Hospitals	医院床位数（张） Hospital Beds	医生数（人） Doctors (person)
苏南合计 **Southern Jiangsu Total**	**46739**	**62.65**	**50.48**	**15.03**	**533**	**42274**	**29122**
苏州市 Suzhou Municipality	25749	26.01	20.04	5.63	212	17401	12313
无锡市 Wuxi Municipality	8808	20.93	17.73	5.45	159	14034	9289
常州市 Changzhou Municipality	12182	15.71	12.71	3.95	162	10839	7520
苏中合计 **Mid Jiangsu Total**	**155678**	**104.66**	**83.23**	**27.62**	**1126**	**67300**	**47545**
南京市 Nanjing Municipality	111956	22.90	32.00	13.41	309	20383	15866
镇江市 Zhenjiang Municipality	16433	12.29	8.06	2.62	117	7274	5318
扬州市 Yangzhou Municipality	18930	18.18	14.02	3.88	195	10482	7552
泰州市 Taizhou Municipality		20.03	14.23	3.50	176	10351	6199
南通市 Nantong Municipality	8359	31.26	14.92	4.21	329	18810	12610
苏北合计 **Northern Jiangsu Total**	**38012**	**155.64**	**53.64**	**15.82**	**957**	**41994**	**35306**
徐州市 Xuzhou Municipality	18647	46.32	20.12	6.27	231	15814	11525
淮阴市 Huaiying Municipality	5344	22.23	8.59	3.54	195	7860	5227
盐城市 Yancheng Municipality	7150	39.98	13.45	3.01	252	6951	9845
连云港市 Lianyungang Municipality	6871	24.00	7.45	1.77	147	6603	5130
宿迁市 Suqion Municipality		23.11	4.03	1.23	132	4766	3579

市县社会经济主要指标 2

MAJOR SOCIAL ECONOMIC INDICATORS OF COUNTY

2—1 国民经济综合指标
INDICATORS OF NATIONAL ECONOMIC GENERAL SURVEY (1996)

单位:万元 (10000yuan)

市县名称 Municipality and County		国内生产总值(当年价) Gross Domestic Product (current price)	第一产业 Primary Industry	第二产业 Secondery Industry	第三产业 Tertiary Industry	工农业总产值(当年价) Total Output Value of Industry and Agriculture	#工业总产值 Total Output Value of Industry
南京市	**Nanjing Municipality**	**6748997**	**488506**	**3434111**	**2826380**	**13210079**	**12247400**
市区	Urban District	5110386	67105	2607717	2435564	8497544	8349064
江宁县	Jiangning County	660443	129174	406693	124576	2099400	1844428
江浦县	Jiangpu County	157273	52816	55062	49395	384952	277337
六合县	Liuhe County	297426	95420	124357	77649	750441	565093
溧水县	Lishui County	286322	66402	146212	73708	912299	787849
高淳县	Gaochun County	237147	77589	94070	65488	565443	423629
无锡市	**Wuxi Municipality**	**8700081**	**448120**	**5141358**	**3110603**	**22786170**	**21861116**
市区	Urban District	2656159	32264	1499442	1124453	5072751	5011187
江阴市	Jiangyin City	2220249	133440	1326431	760378	6070665	5809643
宜兴市	Yixing City	1452390	166420	780586	505384	3983007	3607753
锡山市	Xishan City	2317580	115996	1534899	666685	7659747	7432533
徐州市	**Xuzhou Municipality**	**5000445**	**1156698**	**2263735**	**1580012**	**10600593**	**8329604**
市区	Urban District	2102379	73753	1133606	895020	3337694	3199429
丰县	Fengxian County	296472	142541	80256	73675	768056	487613
沛县	Peixian County	429850	162383	137216	130251	1065268	740510
铜山县	Tongshan County	691963	234983	312034	144946	2238049	1783496
睢宁县	Shuining County	325923	148002	100918	77003	933498	615529
新沂市	Xinyi City	365004	148109	115316	101579	915896	622137
邳州市	Pizhou City	551857	228315	188952	134590	1342132	830890
常州市	**Changzhou Municipality**	**4311541**	**455496**	**2465057**	**1390988**	**11070585**	**10197835**
市区	Urban District	1278283	37879	795198	445206	3607096	3535793
溧阳市	Liyang City	720341	132728	356614	230999	1606322	1364998
金坛市	Jintan City	513287	94113	259058	160116	1137087	955460
武进市	Wujin City	1843389	197856	1086541	558992	4720080	4341584
苏州市	**Suzhou Municipality**	**10021368**	**881817**	**5679552**	**3459999**	**24371162**	**22745223**
市区	Urban District	1702766	53316	970537	678913	3568540	3465339
常熟市	Changshu City	1802533	154784	930099	717650	3905243	3627776
张家港市	Zhangjiagang City	2300711	119148	1376526	805037	5195401	4974754
昆山市	Kunshan City	1143808	115407	685578	342823	2481235	2260795

2—1 续表 1 Continued 1

市县名称 Municipality and County	国内生产总值(当年价) Gross Domestic Product (current price)	第一产业 Primary Industry	第二产业 Secondery Industry	第三产业 Tertiary Industry	工农业总产值(当年价) Total Output Value of Industry and Agriculture	#工业总产值 Total Output Value of Industry
吴江市 Wujiang City	1425384	146273	785526	493585	3149098	2883626
太仓市 Taicang City	951201	120012	526188	305001	2039801	1827073
吴县市 Wuxie City	1400295	165124	764703	470468	4031844	3705860
南通市 Nantong Muncipatity	**5304243**	**1233887**	**2452529**	**1617827**	**11175075**	**8753600**
市区 Urban District	1085952	27311	662058	396583	2035623	1983335
海安县 Haian County	501108	170928	158712	171468	992510	677121
如东县 Rudong County	630091	268475	191110	170506	1337026	844775
启东市 Qidong City	851191	237623	364443	249125	1770897	1234178
如皋市 Rugao City	593511	172113	247564	173834	1387135	1058134
通州市 Tongzhou City	905174	225189	389973	290012	2048640	1621508
海门市 Haimen City	800092	147815	370375	281902	1603244	1334549
连云港市 Lianyungang Municipality	**2102004**	**769689**	**747780**	**584535**	**5329105**	**3876333**
市区 Urban District	670630	54785	361297	254548	1388557	1283177
赣榆县 Gaiyu County	473348	213975	155681	103692	1499058	1088802
东海县 Donghai County	440034	220675	127176	92183	1306515	900578
灌云县 Guanyun County	361856	186975	72883	101998	782555	437392
灌南县 Guannan County	156136	93279	30743	32114	352420	166384
淮阴市 Huaiyin Municipality	**1732288**	**689571**	**584596**	**458121**	**3876739**	**2481136**
市区 Urban District	409446	26425	228842	154179	843715	790946
淮阴县 Huaiyin County	217565	101363	72080	44122	528899	326565
涟水县 Lianshui County	200877	122854	35543	42480	429842	163384
洪泽县 Hongze County	133386	64453	41554	27379	383282	239860
盱眙县 Xuyi County	220494	108061	53388	59045	435801	223325
金湖县 Jinhu County	186082	79019	55560	51503	378619	232311
淮安市 Huaian City	364438	187396	97629	79413	876581	504745
盐城市 Yancheng Municipality	**3812003**	**1402253**	**1412402**	**997348**	**9507339**	**6436742**
市区 Urban District	477984	41385	256546	180053	933257	846278
响水县 Xiangshui County	157172	72580	40796	43796	334836	167542
滨海县 Binhai County	281313	144030	65181	72102	573347	288921
阜宁县 Funing County	324106	134173	109069	80864	884397	580112

2—1 续表 2　Continued 2

市县名称 Municipality and County		国内生产总值（当年价）Gross Domestic Product (current price)	第一产业 Primary Industry	第二产业 Secondery Industry	第三产业 Tertiary Industry	工农业总产值（当年价）Total Output Value of Industry and Agriculture	#工业总产值 Tctal Output Value of Industry
射阳县	Sheyang County	512612	230075	178243	104294	1357463	835018
建湖县	Jianhu County	365062	121555	156307	87200	1007900	749293
盐都县	Yandou County	517772	185261	210871	121640	1412250	1038724
东台市	Dongtai City	615000	267000	180000	168000	1578998	992083
大丰市	Dafeng City	560982	206194	215389	139399	1424891	938771
扬州市	**Yangzhou Mucipality**	**3511492**	**550948**	**1853811**	**1106733**	**7940241**	**6792184**
市区	Urban District	1001054	17061	586419	397574	1897417	1850498
宝应县	Baoying County	401001	154589	139413	106999	942972	633433
邗江县	HanJiang County	457513	64320	258167	135026	1237972	1080280
仪征市	Yizheng City	459919	68470	292507	98942	1322810	1198618
高邮市	Gaoyou City	428834	134797	181120	112917	1065182	773218
江都市	Jiangdu City	703614	111711	338301	253602	1473888	1256137
镇江市	**ZhenJiang Municipality**	**3351073**	**364250**	**1874332**	**1112491**	**7816560**	**7127727**
市区	Urban District	966222	16781	540130	409311	1495899	1464197
丹徒县	Dantu County	430767	67067	235928	127772	1175566	1052655
丹阳市	Danyang City	1000029	140012	549049	310968	2426583	2171552
扬中市	Yangzhong City	452658	38766	287464	126428	1089550	1006022
句容市	Jurong City	501397	101624	261761	138012	1628962	1433301
泰州市	**Taizhou Municipality**	**2936454**	**615424**	**1320089**	**1000941**	**6695763**	**5502413**
市区	Urban District	529892	12416	382582	134894	1440491	1418874
兴化市	Xinghua City	564199	235000	160177	169022	1170008	691518
靖江市	JingJiang City	531423	72377	235494	223552	1241990	1108960
泰兴市	Taixing City	771996	177620	307094	287282	1595797	1282372
姜堰市	Jiangyan City	526229	118011	234742	173476	1247477	1000689
宿迁市	**Suqian Municipality**	**1248807**	**596302**	**385104**	**267401**	**2772623**	**1604818**
市区	Urban District	95406	9953	43960	41493	162262	142624
宿豫县	Suyu County	258971	114032	104385	40554	731742	508347
沭阳县	Shuyang County	320020	186170	59799	74051	638868	277119
泗阳县	Siyang County	269223	129505	84815	54903	634386	377963
泗洪县	sihong County	305187	156642	92145	56400	605365	298765

2—2 人　口
POPULATION (1996)

市县名称 Municipality and County	年末总人口（万人）Year-end Total Population (10000 persons)	#非农业人口 Non-Agriculture	平均人口（万人）Average Popalation (10000 persons)	出生人数（人）Birth (person)	死亡人数（人）Death (person)	人口自然增长率（‰）Natural Growth Rate
南京市 Nanjing Municipality	**525.43**	**264.85**	**523.57**	**46575**	**32804**	**2.63**
市区 Urban District	269.38	229.85	267.59	18913	15712	1.20
江宁县 Jiangning County	74.10	10.99	74.05	6777	4458	3.13
江浦县 Jiangpu County	29.71	5.40	29.78	4067	1915	7.23
六合县 Liuhe County	68.32	9.01	68.34	9109	5090	5.88
溧水县 Lishui County	40.82	4.81	40.74	3927	2540	3.40
高淳县 Gaochun County	43.10	4.79	43.07	3782	3089	1.61
无锡市 Wuxi Municipality	**430.82**	**183.88**	**430.01**	**46358**	**28773**	**4.09**
市区 Urban District	108.43	90.95	107.95	13042	6107	6.42
江阴市 Jiangyin City	114.16	31.99	113.94	15545	8392	6.28
宜兴市 Yixing City	109.25	33.74	109.19	8987	7061	1.76
锡山市 Xishan City	98.98	27.20	98.93	8784	7213	1.59
徐州市 Xuzhou Municipality	**859.43**	**176.54**	**855.29**	**81414**	**41982**	**4.61**
市区 Urban District	147.34	100.21	146.24	11831	5939	4.03
丰县 Fengxian County	102.14	8.92	101.82	10837	4906	5.82
沛县 Peixian County	113.32	17.44	112.99	10486	4947	4.90
铜山县 Tongshan County	130.30	14.58	130.10	11556	7707	2.96
睢宁县 Shuining County	122.12	9.82	121.67	13203	6301	5.67
新沂市 Xinyi City	94.10	11.25	92.62	11640	4000	8.25
邳州市 Pizhou City	150.11	14.32	149.85	11861	8182	2.46
常州市 Changzhou Municipality	**337.54**	**124.14**	**335.60**	**33464**	**22239**	**3.34**
市区 Urban District	82.79	73.59	81.72	10127	4496	6.89
溧阳市 Liyang City	77.64	28.62	77.52	8831	5279	4.58
金坛市 Jintan City	54.15	8.47	54.11	4332	3715	1.14
武进市 Wujin City	122.96	13.46	122.25	10174	8749	1.17
苏州市 Suzhou Municipality	**574.12**	**176.00**	**573.51**	**45040**	**40319**	**0.82**
市区 Urban District	106.44	80.14	106.09	7106	7042	0.06
常熟市 Changshu City	104.34	23.42	104.35	8642	8222	0.40
张家港市 Zhangjiagang City	85.20	14.74	85.12	6428	5497	1.09
昆山市 Kunshan City	58.34	15.15	58.19	4470	3777	1.19

2—2 续表1 Continued 1

市县名称 Municipality and County	年末总人口（万人） Year—end Total Population (10000 persons)	#非农业人口 Non—Agricul—ture	平均人口（万人） Average Popalation (10000 persons)	出生人数（人） Birth (person)	死亡人数（人） Death (person)	人口自然增长率（‰） Natural Growth Rate
吴江市 Wujiang City	77.65	15.36	77.68	6326	5443	1.14
太仓市 Taicang City	44.93	10.77	44.91	3635	3894	—0.58
吴县市 Wuxie City	97.22	16.42	97.17	8433	6444	2.05
南通市 Nantong Muncipatity	**785.24**	**240.24**	**784.74**	**70655**	**55610**	**1.92**
市区 Urban District	62.21	44.43	61.60	7005	3168	6.23
海安县 Haian County	99.00	32.70	99.00	8386	6914	1.49
如东县 Rudong County	113.20	43.69	113.33	9291	9134	0.14
启东市 Qidong City	116.66	22.37	116.54	11386	7714	3.15
如皋市 Rugao City	145.14	27.07	145.16	13268	10727	1.75
通州市 Tongzhou City	145.57	35.68	145.67	12211	10418	1.23
海门市 Haimen City	103.46	34.30	103.44	9108	7535	1.52
连云港市 Lianyungang Municipality	**432.96**	**80.50**	**430.37**	**61873**	**20436**	**9.63**
市区 Urban District	58.17	42.69	57.66	6741	2360	7.60
赣榆县 Gaiyu County	100.89	8.18	100.39	15916	5485	10.39
东海县 Donghai County	107.07	9.21	106.25	19662	5455	13.37
灌云县 Guanyun County	98.44	13.42	97.80	13596	3970	9.84
灌南县 Guannan County	68.39	7.00	68.27	5958	3166	4.09
淮阴市 Huaiyin Municipality	**489.63**	**82.30**	**487.42**	**48484**	**23517**	**5.12**
市区 Urban District	48.68	28.93	47.86	5469	1017	9.30
淮阴县 Huaiyin County	80.57	7.83	80.22	9342	4374	6.19
涟水县 Lianshui County	99.10	8.30	98.83	9411	4829	4.64
洪泽县 Hongze County	36.68	7.42	36.71	3959	1859	5.72
盱眙县 Xuyi County	70.95	8.04	70.73	6040	3374	3.77
金湖县 Jinhu County	34.73	6.89	34.68	3009	2076	2.69
淮安市 Huaian City	118.92	14.89	118.39	11254	5988	4.45
盐城市 Yancheng Municipality	**786.12**	**143.93**	**784.83**	**78192**	**45259**	**4.20**
市区 Urban District	56.93	29.31	55.24	7023	2287	8.57
响水县 Xiangshui County	54.63	8.21	54.48	4547	2413	3.92
滨海县 Binhai County	106.68	12.40	106.52	11043	5274	5.42
阜宁县 Funing County	107.70	13.19	107.85	9057	5567	3.24

2—2 续表 2　　Continued 2

市县名称 Municipality and County	年末总人口(万人) Year—end Total Population (10000 persons)	# 非农业人口 Non—Agricul—ture	平均人口(万人) Average Popalation (10000 persons)	出生人数(人) Birth (person)	死亡人数(人) Death (person)	人口自然增长率(‰) Natural Growth Rate
射阳县 Sheyang County	102.31	15.33	102.10	9510	5631	3.80
建湖县 Jianhu County	79.50	14.27	79.50	10034	5894	5.21
盐都县 Yandou County	87.00	14.35	87.69	10829	5025	6.62
东台市 Dongtai City	117.37	22.55	117.48	9410	8454	0.81
大丰市 Dafeng City	74.00	14.32	73.97	6739	4714	2.74
扬州市 Yangzhou Mucipality	**444.82**	**102.28**	**444.34**	**40949**	**30898**	**2.26**
市区 Urban District	49.81	37.75	49.07	5181	2563	5.34
宝应县 Baoying County	90.61	12.75	90.82	7540	6544	1.10
邗江县 HanJiang County	55.19	6.25	55.44	4097	3809	0.52
仪征市 Yizheng City	59.09	15.44	58.92	6216	3990	3.78
高邮市 Gaoyou City	83.18	13.07	83.16	7597	6147	1.74
江都市 Jiangdu City	106.94	17.02	106.93	10318	7845	2.31
镇江市 ZhenJiang Municipality	**264.80**	**87.22**	**264.03**	**26422**	**17328**	**3.44**
市区 Urban District	54.25	43.72	53.36	6794	2773	7.54
丹徒县 Dantu County	41.58	4.85	41.89	3962	3336	1.49
丹阳市 Danyang City	80.96	20.96	80.86	7827	5642	2.70
扬中市 Yangzhong City	27.73	7.57	27.70	2710	2123	2.12
句容市 Jurong City	60.28	10.12	60.22	5129	3454	2.78
泰州市 Taizhou Municipality	**496.28**	**83.96**	**495.61**	**47127**	**30976**	**3.26**
市区 Urban District	27.37	17.44	27.17	2773	1639	4.17
兴化市 Xinghua City	153.54	19.25	153.48	10233	8269	1.28
靖江市 JingJiang City	66.18	12.66	66.10	6187	4063	3.21
泰兴市 Taixing City	142.86	19.24	142.49	18700	9518	6.44
姜堰市 Jiangyan City	106.33	15.37	106.37	9234	7487	1.64
宿迁市 Suqian Municipality	**480.83**	**48.36**	**478.82**	**54637**	**24299**	**6.34**
市区 Urban District	24.71	11.39	24.24	3063	942	8.75
宿豫县 Suyu County	89.51	2.98	89.48	10102	5368	5.29
沭阳县 Shuyang County	158.23	12.11	157.58	19988	7364	8.01
泗阳县 Siyang County	110.85	9.25	110.31	12785	5821	6.31
泗洪县 sihong County	97.53	12.63	97.21	8699	4804	4.01

2—3 劳动力资源
RESOURCE OF LABOR FORCE (1996)

单位：万人 (10000persons)

市县名称 Municipality and County		年末全部从业人员数 Year-end Total Employment	全部职工人数 Total Staff and Workers	#国有经济 State-Owned Units	城镇个体劳动者 Rural Individual Laborer	乡村劳动力 Labor Force in Rural Area	#农林牧渔业 Farming, Forestry, Animal Husbandry and Fishery
南京市	**Nanjing Municipality**	**297.31**	**146.43**	**104.20**	**9.64**	**138.95**	**74.93**
市区	Urban District	159.56	125.64	91.40	7.69	19.37	8.14
江宁县	Jiangning County	42.31	5.71	3.50	1.39	36.21	16.94
江浦县	Jiangpu County	12.92	2.83	1.72	0.11	10.61	5.71
六合县	Liuhe County	34.52	4.74	3.00	0.36	30.89	19.00
溧水县	Lishui County	21.60	4.16	2.40	0.02	18.37	9.70
高淳县	Gaochun County	26.40	3.35	2.18	0.07	23.50	15.44
无锡市	**Wuxi Municipality**	**235.49**	**74.28**	**43.23**	**2.96**	**158.60**	**39.90**
市区	Urban District	61.75	44.44	25.16	1.71	13.43	2.58
江阴市	Jiangyin City	59.59	10.59	5.43	0.96	48.75	10.80
宜兴市	Yixing City	57.32	10.07	6.94	0.27	47.48	17.08
锡山市	Xishan City	56.83	9.18	5.70	0.02	48.94	9.44
徐州市	**Xuzhou Municipality**	**428.26**	**94.16**	**73.94**	**7.23**	**331.03**	**237.14**
市区	Urban District	82.21	56.13	45.78	3.80	20.92	11.36
丰县	Fengxian County	51.22	4.99	3.71	0.33	46.23	38.61
沛县	Peixian County	49.64	6.53	5.00	0.62	42.76	31.36
铜山县	Tongshan County	58.67	7.53	5.78	0.03	51.62	34.36
睢宁县	Shuining County	61.28	5.63	4.40	0.50	57.44	44.08
新沂市	Xinyi City	47.74	5.99	4.12	1.37	41.34	27.10
邳州市	Pizhou City	77.50	7.36	5.15	0.58	70.72	50.27
常州市	**Changzhou Municipality**	**204.59**	**53.70**	**30.78**	**4.21**	**134.00**	**52.94**
市区	Urban District	51.84	32.70	18.60	2.09	14.39	3.01
溧阳市	Liyang City	43.61	6.60	3.95	0.20	34.32	17.76
金坛市	Jintan City	34.92	5.34	3.11	1.81	25.65	12.47
武进市	Wujin City	74.22	9.06	5.12	0.11	59.64	19.70
苏州市	**Suzhou Municipality**	**323.84**	**94.51**	**53.72**	**2.81**	**228.45**	**64.07**
市区	Urban District	59.34	39.36	23.80	1.35	16.70	5.16
常熟市	Changshu City	63.21	12.70	7.02	0.38	50.97	15.12
张家港市	Zhangjiagang City	41.59	10.33	5.65	0.12	32.11	7.49
昆山市	Kunshan City	35.17	8.90	4.14	0.21	26.06	8.52

2—3 续表1 Continued 1

市县名称 Municipality and County		年末全部从业人员数 Year—end Total Employment	全部职工人数 Total Staff and Workers	#国有经济 State—Owned Units	城镇个体劳动者 Rural Individual Laborer	乡村劳动力 Labor Force in Rural Area	#农林牧渔业 Farming, Forestry, Animal Husbandry and Fishery
吴江市	Wujiang City	45.68	8.68	4.54	0.38	37.14	10.31
太仓市	Taicang City	25.76	6.18	3.91	0.15	20.02	6.91
吴县市	Wuxie City	53.09	8.36	4.66	0.22	45.45	10.56
南通市	**Nantong Muncipatity**	**476.80**	**83.47**	**43.51**	**3.40**	**378.97**	**207.81**
市区	Urban District	42.20	26.52	15.09	1.20	12.50	3.14
海安县	Haian County	59.10	9.62	4.04	0.20	45.29	27.33
如东县	Rudong County	67.10	9.33	4.59	0.50	56.26	34.20
启东市	Qidong City	81.30	8.93	4.97	0.20	68.83	36.38
如皋市	Rugao City	79.30	10.14	4.56	0.20	68.47	40.32
通州市	Tongzhou City	83.60	10.92	5.81	0.90	71.44	39.55
海门市	Haimen City	64.20	8.01	4.45	0.20	56.18	26.89
连云港市	**Lianyungang Municipality**	**218.88**	**45.06**	**32.42**	**4.54**	**167.81**	**120.68**
市区	Urban District	35.69	23.36	17.06	1.94	9.37	4.75
赣榆县	Gaiyu County	47.84	5.02	3.60	0.61	42.06	27.03
东海县	Donghai County	54.35	5.72	4.30	0.35	48.12	36.26
灌云县	Guanyun County	45.71	6.93	4.73	1.14	37.55	29.92
灌南县	Guannan County	35.29	4.03	2.73	0.50	30.71	22.72
淮阴市	**Huaiyin Municipality**	**256.49**	**48.99**	**35.26**	**3.55**	**207.47**	**146.77**
市区	Urban District	27.34	16.04	12.26	0.92	11.27	6.69
淮阴县	Huaiyin County	39.60	4.67	3.48	0.49	34.94	24.50
涟水县	Lianshui County	51.05	6.22	4.47	0.50	44.83	34.61
洪泽县	Hongze County	20.19	3.74	2.57	0.25	16.46	11.04
盱眙县	Xuyi County	37.13	5.34	4.21	0.42	31.79	26.47
金湖县	Jinhu County	18.48	4.16	2.88	0.07	14.31	9.71
淮安市	Huaian City	62.70	8.82	5.39	0.90	53.87	33.75
盐城市	**Yancheng Municipality**	**348.72**	**73.99**	**44.80**	**5.26**	**285.43**	**181.46**
市区	Urban District	27.91	16.35	12.26	0.59	12.14	5.91
响水县	Xiangshui County	24.60	4.55	2.77	0.50	19.97	15.38
滨海县	Binhai County	40.99	5.89	3.80	0.51	36.51	26.94
阜宁县	Funing County	44.82	5.84	3.66	0.52	42.29	28.29

2—3 续表 2 Continued 2

市县名称 Municipality and County		年末全部从业人员数 Year—end Total Employment	全部职工人数 Total Staff and Workers	#国有经济 State—Owned Units	城镇个体劳动者 Rural Individual Laborer	乡村劳动力 Labor Force in Rural Area	#农林牧渔业 Farming, Forestry, Animal Husbandry and Fishery
射阳县	Sheyang County	41.42	9.42	5.30	0.54	33.70	23.65
建湖县	Jianhu County	36.80	7.48	3.66	0.60	30.20	17.22
盐都县	Yandou County	38.22	6.35	2.93	0.59	32.76	16.91
东台市	Dongtai City	55.53	10.41	5.73	0.71	46.55	26.72
大丰市	Dafeng City	38.43	7.70	4.69	0.70	31.31	20.44
扬州市	**Yangzhou Mucipality**	**245.58**	**61.67**	**36.17**	**1.44**	**182.22**	**92.48**
市区	Urban District	30.98	23.51	16.71	0.42	6.96	2.17
宝应县	Baoying County	51.10	7.49	4.10	0.34	43.24	28.60
邗江县	HanJiang County	29.39	4.98	2.14	0.04	24.36	7.77
仪征市	Yizheng City	33.15	9.74	5.32	0.17	23.20	11.40
高邮市	Gaoyou City	45.06	7.22	3.69	0.21	37.59	22.78
江都市	Jiangdu City	55.90	8.73	4.21	0.26	46.87	19.76
镇江市	**ZhenJiang Municipality**	**161.25**	**44.61**	**28.23**	**1.73**	**106.06**	**46.26**
市区	Urban District	31.24	23.00	15.92	0.97	5.81	1.82
丹徒县	Dantu County	28.54	4.13	2.32		22.27	9.28
丹阳市	Danyang City	50.67	8.64	5.39	0.35	38.49	16.84
扬中市	Yangzhong City	20.63	4.12	1.86	0.36	13.97	3.98
句容市	Jurong City	30.17	4.72	2.74	0.05	25.52	14.34
泰州市	**Taizhou Municipality**	**280.86**	**53.20**	**26.39**	**1.00**	**225.68**	**114.37**
市区	Urban District	17.25	10.53	5.51	0.28	6.17	2.19
兴化市	Xinghua City	82.26	9.88	5.73	0.18	72.18	46.79
靖江市	JingJiang City	44.52	10.85	4.63	0.16	33.47	12.44
泰兴市	Taixing City	75.35	13.11	6.95	0.19	62.20	28.13
姜堰市	Jiangyan City	61.48	8.83	3.57	0.19	51.66	24.82
宿迁市	**Suqian Municipality**	**223.85**	**29.87**	**21.19**	**2.01**	**213.81**	**151.39**
市区	Urban District		3.72	2.10		5.25	2.49
宿豫县	Suyu County	53.96	4.36	3.11	0.87	44.81	27.51
沭阳县	Shuyang County	70.93	7.83	5.18	0.58	69.80	50.04
泗阳县	Siyang County	48.93	7.35	5.60	0.39	48.44	32.94
泗洪县	sihong County	50.03	6.61	5.20	0.17	45.51	38.41

2—4 农林牧渔业总产值
TOTAL OUTPUT VALUE OF FARMING FORESTRY ANIMAL HUSBANDRY AND FISHERY (1996)

单位:万元 (10000yuan)

市县名称 Municipality and County		农林牧渔业总产值(当年价) Total Output Value of Farming, Forestry, Animal Husbandry and Fishery (current prisc)	#农业产值 Output Value of Farming	#林业产值 Output Value of Forestry	农林牧渔业总产值(1990年不变价格) Total Output Value of Farming, Forestry, Animal Husbamdry and Fishery (1990 con—stant price)	#农业产值 Output Value of Farming	#林业产值 Output Value of Forestry
南京市	**Nanjing Municipality**	**962679**	**540977**	**15238**	**459753**	**233115**	**7602**
市区	Urban District	148480	71322	1273	69704	27662	756
江宁县	Jiangning County	254972	139515	5199	128280	64416	2049
江浦县	Jiangpu County	107615	55473	4530	57163	25512	3978
六合县	Liuhe County	185348	111968	3044	90265	49699	1238
溧水县	Lishui County	124450	77557	860	58986	35402	392
高淳县	Gaochun County	141814	85142	332	64923	36755	153
无锡市	**Wuxi Municipality**	**925054**	**607554**	**13717**	**515989**	**346446**	**5363**
市区	Urban District	61564	28372	757	26473	10464	222
江阴市	Jiangyin City	261022	166037	837	145538	96450	341
宜兴市	Yixing City	375254	266904	11376	228758	168463	4320
锡山市	Xishan City	227214	146241	747	115220	71069	480
徐州市	**Xuzhou Municipality**	**2270989**	**1297733**	**49658**	**1137525**	**605564**	**28439**
市区	Urban District	138265	77845	2211	70557	36198	1371
丰县	Fengxian County	280443	168039	4448	150755	92889	2942
沛县	Peixian County	324758	210326	5991	160114	99525	3641
铜山县	Tongshan County	454553	240937	8575	234698	112219	5477
睢宁县	Shuining County	317969	172428	4780	153712	73722	3143
新沂市	Xinyi City	293759	161555	8239	149976	77543	5457
邳州市	Pizhou City	461242	266603	15414	217713	113468	6408
常州市	**Changzhou Municipality**	**872750**	**530168**	**5085**	**439499**	**254633**	**2597**
市区	Urban District	71303	40473	140	36568	15904	108
溧阳市	Liyang City	241324	149591	3259	108303	66469	1581
金坛市	Jintan City	181627	89479	1002	82058	38379	529
武进市	Wujin City	378496	250625	684	212570	133881	379
苏州市	**Suzhou Municipality**	**1625939**	**1077094**	**6725**	**873938**	**609328**	**3936**
市区	Urban District	103201	59755	138	50708	32083	65
常熟市	Changshu City	277467	200979	993	141485	104764	666
张家港市	Zhangjiagang City	220647	162923	1028	126935	96262	701
昆山市	Kunshan City	220440	133898	1214	112563	70095	988

2—4 续表 1 Continued 1

市县名称 Municipality and County		农林牧渔业总产值(当年价) Total Output Value of Farming, Forestry, Animal Husbandry and Fishery (current prisc)	#农业产值 Output Value of Farming	#林业产值 Output Value of Forestry	农林牧渔业总产值(1990年不变价格) Total Output Value of Farming, Forestry, Animal Husbamdry and Fishery (1990 con—stant price)	#农业产值 Output Value of Farming	#林业产值 Output Value of Forestry
吴江市	Wujiang City	265472	141216	566	132786	68739	261
太仓市	Taicang City	212728	144503	603	113091	85843	381
吴县市	Wuxie City	325984	233820	2183	196370	151542	874
南通市	**Nantong Muncipatity**	**2421475**	**1317283**	**18191**	**1377661**	**765976**	**8222**
市区	Urban District	52288	37296	491	32294	24788	311
海安县	Haian County	315389	147377	853	177703	77670	370
如东县	Rudong County	492251	265498	3370	271561	137911	1471
启东市	Qidong City	536719	237836	1075	307484	143671	600
如皋市	Rugao City	329001	188036	5407	169172	97259	2501
通州市	Tongzhou City	427132	271870	5903	253461	175762	2543
海门市	Haimen City	268695	169370	1092	165986	108915	426
连云港市	**Lianyungang Municipality**	**1452772**	**806859**	**16140**	**789606**	**428035**	**10164**
市区	Urban District	105380	48465	926	59457	25728	648
赣榆县	Gaiyu County	410256	182080	4763	229585	104525	2643
东海县	Donghai County	405937	249924	5392	227822	138258	3393
灌云县	Guanyun County	345163	219973	1393	175332	105936	878
灌南县	Guannan County	186036	106417	3666	97410	53588	2602
淮阴市	**Huaiyin Municipality**	**1395603**	**834479**	**22437**	**813060**	**438387**	**19604**
市区	Urban District	52769	36129	305	28395	17645	251
淮阴县	Huaiyin County	202334	118783	925	111038	58368	754
涟水县	Lianshui County	266458	174796	5317	158027	98787	4693
洪泽县	Hongze County	143422	59075	6786	90873	28259	6085
盱眙县	Xuyi County	212476	140331	1906	113277	67375	1559
金湖县	Jinhu County	146308	72601	4292	90273	33908	3787
淮安市	Huaian City	371836	232764	2906	221177	134045	2475
盐城市	**Yancheng Municipality**	**3070597**	**1470472**	**34604**	**1965248**	**894347**	**26887**
市区	Urban District	86979	38296	831	48617	20317	539
响水县	Xiangshui County	167294	104397	1641	110097	66906	1386
滨海县	Binhai County	284426	154883	3841	165477	86212	2844
阜宁县	Funing County	304285	138757	2849	184045	87311	1843

2—4 续表 2 Continued 2

市县名称 Municipality and County		农林牧渔业总产值(当年价) Total Output Value of Farming, Forestry, Animal Husbandry and Fishery (current prisc)	#农业产值 Output Value of Farming	#林业产值 Output Value of Forestry	农林牧渔业总产值(1990年不变价格) Total Output Value of Farming, Forestry, Animal Husbamdry and Fishery (1990 con—stant price)	#农业产值 Output Value of Farming	#林业产值 Output Value of Forestry
射阳县	Sheyang County	522445	256814	5781	342862	146440	4721
建湖县	Jianhu County	258607	103413	1438	155771	58303	890
盐都县	Yandou County	373526	146802	3326	241511	101767	3480
东台市	Dongtai City	586915	234846	6900	416702	149782	5431
大丰市	Dafeng City	486120	292264	7997	300166	177309	5753
扬州市	**Yangzhou Mucipality**	**1148057**	**643253**	**12430**	**601919**	**322019**	**8838**
市区	Urban District	46919	26928	396	26934	15501	271
宝应县	Bacying County	309539	164857	5121	150068	78595	4051
邗江县	HanJiang County	157692	78169	3082	92134	45111	1975
仪征市	Yizheng City	124192	74464	672	62176	35295	391
高邮市	Gacyou City	291964	166814	1003	157307	80575	703
江都市	Jiangdu City	217751	132021	2156	113300	66942	1447
镇江市	**ZhenJiang Municipality**	**688833**	**431783**	**7807**	**375779**	**229220**	**4505**
市区	Urban District	31702	17482	270	14776	7259	139
丹徒县	Dantu County	122911	77491	1196	62859	37854	663
丹阳市	Danyang City	255031	157231	686	142939	83195	458
扬中市	Yangzhong City	83528	62001	1917	57727	45607	1075
句容市	Jurong City	195661	117578	3738	97478	55305	2170
泰州市	**Taizhou Municipality**	**1193350**	**695925**	**23142**	**660351**	**371311**	**11041**
市区	Urban District	21617	16125	100	11614	8267	63
兴化市	Xinghua City	478490	285223	1549	256727	149260	1002
靖江市	JingJiang City	133030	74813	2944	74008	40838	2244
泰兴市	Taixing City	313425	168533	13742	174577	89009	5679
姜堰市	Jiangyan City	246788	151231	4807	143425	83937	2053
宿迁市	**Suqian Municipality**	**1167805**	**731373**	**21574**	**636654**	**369760**	**18752**
市区	Urban District	19638	12284	252	10527	5837	173
宿豫县	Suyu County	223395	131387	1053	118479	60687	833
沭阳县	Shuyang County	361749	247891	8861	197859	125262	7624
泗阳县	Siyang County	256423	164820	9974	150671	93038	8949
泗洪县	sihong County	306600	174991	1434	159118	84936	1173

2—5 农业机械化和现代化
MECHANIZATION AND MODERNIZATION OF AGRICULTURE (1996)

市县名称 Municipality and County		年末实有耕地面积(千公顷) Tear—end Actyual Areas Under Cultitvation (1000 hectares)	机耕地面积(千公顷) Areas of Mortorized Cultivation (1000 hectares)	有效灌溉面积(千公顷) Available Irrigated Areas (1000 hectares)	农业机械总动力(万千瓦小时) Total Power of Agricltural Machinery (10000kwh)	农用化肥施用量(吨) Comsuption of Chemical Fertilizers (tons)	农村用电量(万千瓦小时) Electricity Comsumed in Rural Areas (10000kwh)
南京市	**Nanjing Municipality**	**211.21**	**153.63**	**199.59**	**162.53**	**158694**	**117795**
市区	Urban District	24.43	16.77	22.73	23.93	20279	41477
江宁县	Jiangning County	52.96	36.19	48.61	41.24	34505	34164
江浦县	Jiangpu County	21.97	12.08	20.52	12.88	12612	4973
六合县	Liuhe County	50.74	34.87	48.89	32.25	38160	14543
溧水县	Lishui County	30.89	24.62	28.37	20.10	14928	14235
高淳县	Gaochun County	30.22	29.10	30.47	32.13	38210	8403
无锡市	**Wuxi Municipality**	**178.00**	**136.00**	**165.92**	**170.00**	**119204**	**490041**
市区	Urban District	8.00	6.00	7.51	10.00	17354	41277
江阴市	Jiangyin City	50.00	39.00	50.07	56.00	23674	163095
宜兴市	Yixing City	72.00	54.00	60.35	50.00	49075	106008
锡山市	Xishan City	48.00	37.00	47.99	54.00	29101	179661
徐州市	**Xuzhou Municipality**	**602.65**	**531.74**	**449.90**	**212.22**	**465274**	**198358**
市区	Urban District	32.38	29.92	23.62	27.62	28626	68402
丰县	Fengxian County	85.68	78.59	69.57	31.80	71247	5180
沛县	Peixian County	77.91	74.99	68.43	35.32	43105	20755
铜山县	Tongshan County	115.15	103.95	91.82	36.37	88658	62230
睢宁县	Shuining County	99.62	85.02	61.01	24.55	59200	10732
新沂市	Xinyi City	80.47	65.27	69.55	25.02	81099	13580
邳州市	Pizhou City	111.44	94.00	65.90	31.54	93339	17479
常州市	**Changzhou Municipality**	**199.36**	**152.40**	**185.62**	**142.94**	**121024**	**279984**
市区	Urban District	10.99	7.97	9.24	10.09	12833	42272
溧阳市	Liyang City	63.20	53.93	55.69	39.12	32989	37751
金坛市	Jintan City	42.59	32.00	40.60	22.78	22884	23334
武进市	Wujin City	82.58	58.50	80.09	70.95	52318	176627
苏州市	**Suzhou Municipality**	**329.86**	**290.29**	**331.11**	**275.15**	**212401**	**558380**
市区	Urban District	17.52	16.52	18.03	12.22	13283	27915
常熟市	Changshu City	65.36	64.50	65.94	40.55	32893	96009
张家港市	Zhangjiagang City	47.58	31.81	47.57	39.50	27170	128661
昆山市	Kunshan City	52.62	41.44	53.40	40.41	39356	58155

2—5 续表1 Continued 1

市县名称 Municipality and County		年末实有耕地面积(千公顷) Tear—end Actyual Areas Under Cultitvation (1000 hectares)	机耕地面积(千公顷) Areas of Mortorized Cultivation (1000 hectares)	有效灌溉面积(千公顷) Available Irrigated Areas (1000 hectares)	农业机械总动力(万千瓦小时) Total Power of Agricltural Machinery (10000kwh)	农用化肥施用量(吨) Comsuption of Chemical Fertilizers (tons)	农村用电量(万千瓦小时) Electricity Comsumed in Rural Areas (10000kwh)
吴江市	Wujiang City	46.67	46.89	46.89	48.91	38650	78615
太仓市	Taicang City	41.37	41.80	40.97	28.20	25358	44401
吴县市	Wuxie City	58.74	47.33	58.31	65.36	35691	124624
南通市	**Nantong Muncipatity**	**466.41**	**291.64**	**364.28**	**170.96**	**257987**	**221831**
市区	Urban District	9.56	8.46	7.52	6.04	7326	20320
海安县	Haian County	62.67	51.60	48.78	32.88	32279	26480
如东县	Rudong County	95.42	68.00	79.98	32.45	59102	27607
启东市	Qidong City	73.54	9.32	38.30	22.64	25872	27304
如皋市	Rugao City	80.90	71.63	56.44	27.88	58420	28500
通州市	Tongzhou City	86.02	67.50	80.21	29.31	39553	47578
海门市	Haimen City	58.30	15.13	53.05	19.76	35435	44042
连云港市	**Lianyungang Municipality**	**315.45**	**280.07**	**255.40**	**177.87**	**253800**	**53265**
市区	Urban District	13.01	12.46	12.97	21.11	13713	4622
赣榆县	Gaiyu County	57.60	56.00	47.05	39.71	43240	15449
东海县	Donghai County	107.98	87.97	87.51	60.12	78144	20829
灌云县	Guanyun County	85.71	74.64	71.31	32.20	73205	7789
灌南县	Guannan County	51.15	49.00	36.56	24.73	45498	4576
淮阴市	**Huaiyin Municipality**	**384.23**	**348.30**	**316.37**	**184.62**	**264345**	**52485**
市区	Urban District	14.44	13.97	12.16	12.58	12334	3941
淮阴县	Huaiyin County	64.36	58.07	48.91	16.95	35931	7797
涟水县	Lianshui County	86.73	76.96	68.94	21.59	42744	8958
洪泽县	Hongze County	28.79	26.00	27.78	29.91	38285	2557
盱眙县	Xuyi County	74.79	66.99	60.03	38.04	38868	4917
金湖县	Jinhu County	34.38	34.26	32.03	31.71	36633	8455
淮安市	Huaian City	80.74	72.05	66.52	33.84	59550	15860
盐城市	**Yancheng Municipality**	**651.00**	**581.86**	**576.64**	**219.72**	**443321**	**155638**
市区	Urban District	20.00	16.92	20.37	5.53	16770	6251
响水县	Xiangshui County	43.10	40.00	40.30	17.27	32714	6010
滨海县	Binhai County	74.36	66.00	52.49	28.54	37732	10070
阜宁县	Funing County	80.14	69.00	68.53	25.13	37032	12591

2—5 续表 2 Continued 2

市县名称 Municipality and County	年末实有耕地面积(千公顷) Tear—end Actyual Areas Under Cultitvation (1000 hectares)	机耕地面积(千公顷) Areas of Mortorized Cultivation (1000 hectares)	有效灌溉面积(千公顷) Available Irrigated Areas (1000 hectares)	农业机械总动力(万千瓦小时) Total Power of Agricltural Machinery (10000kwh)	农用化肥施用量(吨) Comsuption of Chemical Fertilizers (tons)	农村用电量(万千瓦小时) Electricity Comsumed in Rural Areas (10000kwh)
射阳县 Sheyang County	104.41	94.20	98.06	35.88	54347	16336
建湖县 Jianhu County	60.48	48.00	60.58	18.00	28233	17725
盐都县 Yandou County	66.74	62.00	66.98	30.44	56360	22570
东台市 Dongtai City	107.66	96.00	83.86	31.70	75891	32912
大丰市 Dafeng City	94.11	89.74	85.47	27.23	104242	31173
扬州市 Yangzhou Mucipality	**261.82**	**239.29**	**258.50**	**159.76**	**163346**	**113008**
市区 Urban District	5.35	3.07	4.60	4.12	8996	8871
宝应县 Baoying County	56.98	58.33	56.72	27.61	36062	14036
邗江县 HanJiang County	31.85	28.86	30.48	35.30	13169	25772
仪征市 Yizheng City	36.67	33.33	35.23	24.65	27346	12609
高邮市 Gaoyou City	61.97	58.70	62.28	29.19	41890	22970
江都市 Jiangdu City	69.00	57.00	69.19	38.89	35883	28750
镇江市 ZhenJiang Municipality	**158.23**	**109.70**	**131.84**	**98.21**	**102744**	**113754**
市区 Urban District	5.35	3.07	4.21	28.25	3535	16936
丹徒县 Dantu County	34.00	24.23	30.73	2.16	20805	22580
丹阳市 Danyang City	59.88	40.03	48.47	31.27	40314	39090
扬中市 Yangzhong City	10.62	9.10	10.67	11.53	7110	18301
句容市 Jurong City	48.38	33.27	37.76	25.00	30980	16847
泰州市 Taizhou Municipality	**286.87**	**255.02**	**280.76**	**150.79**	**236103**	**130812**
市区 Urban District	5.07	4.02	5.16	4.55	4958	6067
兴化市 Xinghua City	113.35	116.00	115.29	57.58	120000	28007
靖江市 JingJiang City	30.62	20.00	30.75	23.91	25718	30065
泰兴市 Taixing City	73.99	58.70	69.26	31.60	31868	41356
姜堰市 Jiangyan City	63.84	56.30	60.30	33.15	53559	25317
宿迁市 Suqian Municipality	**390.99**	**338.75**	**297.12**	**172.18**	**278693**	**36439**
市区 Urban District	5.40	4.48		3.15	3884	1368
宿豫县 Suyu County	71.93	58.16	66.44	32.39	47764	16058
沭阳县 Shuyang County	134.56	115.94	103.31	49.86	83835	9126
泗阳县 Siyang County	75.40	59.17	54.39	28.91	50295	5745
泗洪县 sihong County	103.70	101.00	72.98	57.87	92915	4142

2—6 农 产 品 产 量
OUTPUT OF AGRICULTURAL PRODUCTS (1996)

市县名称 Municipality and County	粮食产量（万吨） Output of Grain (10000tons)	油料产量（吨） Output of Oil—Bearing Crop (tons)	棉花产量（吨） Output of Cotton (tons)	猪牛羊肉产量（吨） Output of Pork Beef and Mutton (tons)	水产品产量（吨） Output of Aquatic (tons)	猪年末头数（万头） Hogs Year—end (10000head)
南京市 Nanjing Municipality	**179.46**	**140836**	**3725**	**118317**	**86247**	**93.70**
市区 Urban District	12.88	10280	787	17511	10823	14.77
江宁县 Jiangning County	49.40	34639	477	36611	26954	22.17
江浦县 Jiangpu County	17.77	10685	148	11202	11571	9.18
六合县 Liuhe County	44.94	25194	1919	25557	9251	21.72
溧水县 Lishui County	26.69	25822	331	13582	9632	10.18
高淳县 Gaochun County	27.78	34216	63	13854	18016	15.68
无锡市 Wuxi Municipality	**157.91**	**40689**		**90016**	**80554**	**100.35**
市区 Urban District	5.76	2642		8031	13239	9.20
江阴市 Jiangyin City	45.82	3809		25816	17307	34.15
宜兴市 Yixing City	60.83	22990		28273	28000	31.98
锡山市 Xishan City	45.50	11248		27896	22008	25.02
徐州市 Xuzhou Municipality	**423.01**	**63771**	**49432**	**361674**	**97988**	**216.89**
市区 Urban District	26.29	2746	3201	18416	7709	11.85
丰县 Fengxian County	52.24	6766	9000	60499	2010	35.39
沛县 Peixian County	62.25	7000	6120	50331	8000	21.86
铜山县 Tongshan County	79.94	3165	12532	65290	18326	42.00
睢宁县 Shuining County	69.75	9626	6834	65363	16043	37.08
新沂市 Xinyi City	54.29	27459		39870	25000	29.55
邳州市 Pizhou City	78.25	7009	11745	61905	20900	39.16
常州市 Changzhou Municipality	**166.37**	**70526**	**939**	**93099**	**98434**	**88.49**
市区 Urban District	9.82	1202		8299	7110	5.82
溧阳市 Liyang City	46.03	38632	758	25833	24476	11.72
金坛市 Jintan City	36.61	19101	181	14534	25848	32.12
武进市 Wujin City	73.91	11591		44433	41000	38.83
苏州市 Suzhou Municipality	**279.10**	**146606**	**36594**	**111165**	**290532**	**103.64**
市区 Urban District	14.05	6033		13797	22748	6.69
常熟市 Changshu City	52.10	18105	13022	17720	31280	21.40
张家港市 Zhangjiagang City	35.36	12145	13994	15390	14632	10.60
昆山市 Kunshan City	45.49	30375	20	13819	51013	14.50

2—6 续表1 Continued 1

市县名称 Municipality and County		粮食产量（万吨）Output of Grain (10000tons)	油料产量（吨）Output of Oil—Bearing Crop (tons)	棉花产量（吨）Output of Cotton (tons)	猪牛羊肉产量（吨）Output of Pork Beef and Mutton (tons)	水产品产量（吨）Output of Aquatic (tons)	猪年末头数（万头）Hogs Year—end (10000head)
吴江市	Wujiang City	46.33	44059		18075	57037	18.00
太仓市	Taicang City	30.03	15613	9558	13329	51822	11.00
吴县市	Wuxie City	55.74	20276		19035	62000	21.45
南通市	**Nantong Muncipatity**	**349.48**	**255738**	**115130**	**192473**	**536229**	**229.94**
市区	Urban District	9.28	6488	441	5395	5325	3.26
海安县	Haian County	57.97	17707	6248	29496	17855	31.45
如东县	Rudong County	81.41	37220	38869	32258	180533	76.39
启东市	Qidong City	40.75	51931	28196	25427	230209	12.19
如皋市	Rugao City	68.76	26949	9141	53361	15020	65.50
通州市	Tongzhou City	63.14	54459	19221	33195	23109	37.80
海门市	Haimen City	28.17	60984	13014	13341	64178	3.35
连云港市	**Lianyungang Municipality**	**269.72**	**125581**	**51365**	**189451**	**265921**	**171.63**
市区	Urban District	11.32	113	5521	8147	39659	4.15
赣榆县	Gaiyu County	56.91	57814	224	37644	135990	24.77
东海县	Donghai County	90.65	64051	1073	64142	41590	61.78
灌云县	Guanyun County	69.73	480	35766	47575	29516	40.91
灌南县	Guannan County	41.11	3123	8781	31943	19166	40.02
淮阴市	**Huaiyin Municipality**	**338.11**	**141409**	**9774**	**242486**	**179561**	**201.01**
市区	Urban District	12.20	554		8112	3325	7.86
淮阴县	Huaiyin County	44.77	16119	982	43795	10017	37.00
涟水县	Lianshui County	67.63	30479	3529	50675	20679	43.67
洪泽县	Hongze County	30.24	7631		17950	38327	12.80
盱眙县	Xuyi County	65.39	57360	495	29423	28786	30.33
金湖县	Jinhu County	34.53	15637	3606	15264	38312	15.69
淮安市	Huaian City	83.35	13629	1162	77267	40115	53.66
盐城市	**Yancheng Municipality**	**485.70**	**186524**	**185928**	**394841**	**496250**	**345.05**
市区	Urban District	13.34	2655	6082	15039	3665	16.24
响水县	Xiangshui County	33.82	8172	12741	27957	32840	20.50
滨海县	Binhai County	59.62	18147	11506	40572	43459	35.25
阜宁县	Funing County	60.56	17554	9100	92398	24078	87.55

2—6 续表 2 Continued 2

市县名称 Municipality and County		粮食产量(万吨) Output of Grain (10000tons)	油料产量(吨) Output of Oil—Bearing Crop (tons)	棉花产量(吨) Output of Cotton (tons)	猪牛羊肉产量(吨) Output of Pork Beef and Mutton (tons)	水产品产量(吨) Output of Aquatic (tons)	猪年末头数(万头) Hogs Year—end (10000head)
射阳县	Sheyang County	81.65	21267	45666	38883	152897	31.80
建湖县	Jianhu County	46.83	10585	5973	25065	49529	24.76
盐都县	Yandou County	56.42	13389	17450	51636	58671	41.23
东台市	Dongtai City	75.08	63718	30024	57789	66077	57.83
大丰市	Dafeng City	58.38	31037	47386	45502	65034	29.89
扬州市	**Yangzhou Mucipality**	**245.45**	**85088**	**26188**	**138511**	**147663**	**120.05**
市区	Urban District	3.95	1971		8892	2618	4.28
宝应县	Baoying County	57.24	17812	9010	22450	54799	23.80
邗江县	HanJiang County	29.75	13838	61	20481	11495	22.00
仪征市	Yizheng City	33.81	9771	29	19494	4068	19.95
高邮市	Gaoyou City	66.33	25888	13101	41053	53798	28.14
江都市	Jiangdu City	54.37	15808	3987	26141	20885	21.88
镇江市	**ZhenJiang Municipality**	**134.45**	**61337**	**2493**	**94706**	**57419**	**77.04**
市区	Urban District	2.68	2147		4594	4520	3.31
丹徒县	Dantu County	27.94	13047	80	19432	13385	12.23
丹阳市	Danyang City	53.69	15402	622	34212	20781	35.87
扬中市	Yangzhong City	12.77	77		9361	4123	9.96
句容市	Jurong City	37.37	30664	1791	27107	14610	15.67
泰州市	**Taizhou Municipality**	**286.15**	**72800**	**35151**	**173306**	**135894**	**146.87**
市区	Urban District	4.44	2429	22	2080	2163	1.28
兴化市	Xinghua City	119.52	32967	26037	36356	92210	31.00
靖江市	JingJiang City	30.20	4619	4241	22459	7254	28.80
泰兴市	Taixing City	73.66	13417		74152	14069	55.72
姜堰市	Jiangyan City	58.33	19368	4851	38259	20198	30.07
宿迁市	**Suqian Municipality**	**300.02**	**84131**	**20759**	**192800**	**121549**	**170.92**
市区	Urban District	5.08	393	84	2943	1826	2.49
宿豫县	Suyu County	57.43	6218	3518	48759	22594	36.33
沭阳县	Shuyang County	102.81	35875	4641	67690	16120	61.46
泗阳县	Siyang County	51.73	12721	7521	38748	24027	35.42
泗洪县	sihong County	82.97	28924	4995	34660	56982	35.22

2—7 乡以上工业企业单位数
NUMBER OF TOWNSHIP LEVEL AND ABOVE INDUSTRIAL ENTERPRISES (1996)

单位:个

市县名称 Municipality and County		工业企业单位数 Number of Enterprises	#国有经济 State—Owned	#集体经济 Collective—Owned	#私营经济 Privat—Owned	#股份制经济 Share Holding
南京市	**Nanjing Municipality**	**4190**	**549**	**2957**	**22**	**27**
市区	Urban District	2197	300	1470	12	20
江宁县	Jiangning County	683	77	508	8	
江浦县	Jiangpu County	291	33	203	2	3
六合县	Liuhe County	425	49	302		
溧水县	Lishui County	280	47	217		3
高淳县	Gaochun County	314	43	257		1
无锡市	**Wuxi Municipality**	**4190**	**447**	**3217**	**47**	**19**
市区	Urban District	1292	202	828	5	18
江阴市	Jiangyin City	1037	99	855	2	
宜兴市	Yixing City	1024	81	847	13	
锡山市	Xishan City	837	65	687	27	1
徐州市	**Xuzhou Municipality**	**2196**	**314**	**1798**	**4**	**13**
市区	Urban District	496	107	350		10
丰县	Fengxian County	249	24	221	1	
沛县	Peixian County	228	41	178		
铜山县	Tongshan County	268	30	233		
睢宁县	Shuining County	275	32	239		
新沂市	Xinyi City	318	33	277		
邳州市	Pizhou City	362	47	300	3	3
常州市	**Changzhou Municipality**	**3270**	**297**	**2643**	**6**	**17**
市区	Urban District	783	145	449		4
溧阳市	Liyang City	480	48	399	2	4
金坛市	Jintan City	604	41	541		
武进市	Wujin City	1403	63	1254	4	9
苏州市	**Suzhou Municipality**	**5073**	**460**	**3514**	**30**	**21**
市区	Urban District	980	161	596		11
常熟市	Changshu City	932	57	739	9	6
张家港市	Zhangjiagang City	546	42	421		
昆山市	Kunshan City	772	59	396	7	4

2—7 续表1 Continued 1

市县名称 Municipality and County	工业企业单位数 Number of Enterprises	#国有经济 State—Owned	#集体经济 Collective—Owned	#私营经济 Privat—Owned	#股份制经济 Share Holding
吴江市 Wujiang City	489	59	380		
太仓市 Taicang City	612	46	420	5	
吴县市 Wuxie City	742	36	562	9	
南通市 Nantong Muncipatity	**5616**	**425**	**4497**	**37**	**67**
市区 Urban District	782	103	465		18
海安县 Haian County	623	41	531		5
如东县 Rudong County	611	38	488	17	3
启东市 Qidong City	723	61	593		
如皋市 Rugao City	870	56	782		
通州市 Tongzhou City	1069	78	907		1
海门市 Haimen City	938	48	731	20	40
连云港市 Lianyungang Municipality	**2262**	**379**	**1686**	**4**	**9**
市区 Urban District	830	158	545	3	6
赣榆县 Gaiyu County	389	61	300	1	3
东海县 Donghai County	441	75	340		
灌云县 Guanyun County	387	56	323		
灌南县 Guannan County	215	29	178		
淮阴市 Huaiyin Municipality	**2150**	**361**	**1685**	**8**	**18**
市区 Urban District	330	89	217	2	
淮阴县 Huaiyin County	280	31	224	2	3
涟水县 Lianshui County	293	32	256	3	1
洪泽县 Hongze County	226	45	163		6
盱眙县 Xuyi County	298	58	236		
金湖县 Jinhu County	264	46	206		4
淮安市 Huaian City	459	60	383	1	4
盐城市 Yancheng Municipality	**3137**	**412**	**2557**	**12**	**14**
市区 Urban District	217	51	140	2	5
响水县 Xiangshui County	195	35	156	1	1
滨海县 Binhai County	305	36	259	4	
阜宁县 Funing County	382	28	329		4

2—7 续表 2 Continued 2

市县名称 Municipality and County	工业企业单位数 Number of Enterprises	#国有经济 State—Owned	#集体经济 Collective—Owned	#私营经济 Privat—Owned	#股份制经济 Share Holding
射阳县 Sheyang County	397	72	293		
建湖县 Jianhu County	335	40	282		
盐都县 Yandou County	376	33	328	2	2
东台市 Dongtai City	524	66	433	3	2
大丰市 Dafeng City	406	51	337		
扬州市 Yangzhou Mucipality	**3080**	**374**	**2412**	**6**	**67**
市区 Urban District	472	108	265	5	3
宝应县 Baoying County	448	70	326		39
邗江县 HanJiang County	515	43	423	1	8
仪征市 Yizheng City	459	61	379		2
高邮市 Gaoyou City	458	58	384		3
江都市 Jiangdu City	728	34	635		12
镇江市 ZhenJiang Municipality	**3524**	**351**	**2920**	**5**	**16**
市区 Urban District	527	128	302		9
丹徒县 Dantu County	569	44	496		2
丹阳市 Danyang City	1460	95	1303		2
扬中市 Yangzhong City	449	41	381		3
句容市 Jurong City	519	43	438	5	
泰州市 Taizhou Municipality	**2958**	**278**	**2524**	**1**	**14**
市区 Urban District	265	60	164	1	1
兴化市 Xinghua City	643	62	564		3
靖江市 JingJiang City	784	57	678		5
泰兴市 Taixing City	697	60	606		3
姜堰市 Jiangyan City	569	39	512		2
宿迁市 Suqian Municipality	**1148**	**163**	**946**	**3**	**12**
市区 Urban District	93	16	73		
宿豫县 Suyu County	244	31	207		
沭阳县 Shuyang County	299	32	253		7
泗阳县 Siyang County	262	43	204	3	5
泗洪县 sihong County	250	41	209		

2—8 全部工业总产值
GROSS OUTPUT VALUE OF TOTAL INDUSTRY (1996)

单位:万元 (10000yuan)

市县名称 Municipality and County	全部工业总产值(当年价) Gross Output Value of Total Industry (current price)	#乡办工业 Township Enterprises	#村及村以下工业 Village Level and Below Enterprises	全部工业总产值(1990年不变价) Gross Output Value of Total Industry (constant price)	#乡办工业 Township Enterprises	#村及村以下工业 Village Level and Below Enterprises
南京市 Nanjing Municipality	**12247400**	**2330837**	**2167991**	**10855673**	**2209534**	**1921707**
市区 Urban District	8349064	809678	905602	7271050	773732	802726
江宁县 Jiangning County	1844428	753612	758891	1663788	679787	672681
江浦县 Jiangpu County	277337	126533	50719	266811	132264	44957
六合县 Liuhe County	565093	255606	190677	524566	253961	169016
溧水县 Lishui County	787849	232460	143136	735801	231581	126876
高淳县 Gaochun County	423629	152948	118966	393657	138209	105451
无锡市 Wuxi Municipality	**21861116**	**9067847**	**7731766**	**19514860**	**8433488**	**6649319**
市区 Urban District	5011187	499284	1115750	4409129	461759	959545
江阴市 Jiangyin City	5809643	3185172	1948846	5266736	3044064	1676008
宜兴市 Yixing City	3607753	1674120	1588404	3166579	1515128	1366027
锡山市 Xishan City	7432533	3709271	3078766	6672416	3412537	2647739
徐州市 Xuzhou Municipality	**8329604**	**1424235**	**3893962**	**6411318**	**1207374**	**3068478**
市区 Urban District	3199429	302969	945831	2308497	240544	771707
丰县 Fengxian County	487613	104248	282745	383110	94859	215007
沛县 Peixian County	740510	157221	441536	606491	153303	340100
铜山县 Tongshan County	1783496	259855	1063933	1436037	219596	854541
睢宁县 Shuining County	615529	198653	308896	491387	172573	235866
新沂市 Xinyi City	622137	153886	329390	500882	125400	249741
邳州市 Pizhou City	880890	247403	521631	684914	201099	401516
常州市 Changzhou Municipality	**10197835**	**3329785**	**3596530**	**9488912**	**3424884**	**3261230**
市区 Urban District	3535793	635138	608516	3068728	558055	574889
溧阳市 Liyang City	1364998	546632	580384	1234630	518381	502848
金坛市 Jintan City	955460	389613	331771	915466	393764	292641
武进市 Wujin City	4341584	1758402	2075859	4270088	1954684	1890852
苏州市 Suzhou Municipality	**22745223**	**8804791**	**7369173**	**21485389**	**8831985**	**6337489**
市区 Urban District	3465339	415732	725976	3335467	386428	624339
常熟市 Changshu City	3627776	1136775	1570719	3399446	1184665	1350819
张家港市 Zhangjiagang City	4974754	2214471	1638394	4567063	2169442	1409019
昆山市 Kunshan City	2260795	1097078	370729	2185017	1107907	318827

2—8 续表1 Continued 1

市县名称 Municipality and County		全部工业总产值（当年价）Gross Output Value of Total Industry (current price)	#乡办工业 Township Enterprises	#村及村以下工业 Village Level and Below Enterprises	全部工业总产值(1990年不变价) Gross Output Value of Total Industry (constant price)	#乡办工业 Township Enterprises	#村及村以下工业 Village Level and Below Enterprises
吴江市	Wujiang City	2883626	1447800	1072691	2903680	1563516	922514
太仓市	Taicang City	1827073	1017236	491671	1730657	1022048	422837
吴县市	Wuxie City	3705860	1475699	1498993	3364059	1397979	1289134
南通市	**Nantong Muncipatity**	**8753600**	**2517176**	**2609563**	**7969175**	**2425149**	**2279428**
市区	Urban District	1983335	187835	213140	1727949	185774	189904
海安县	Haian County	677121	189644	165380	613542	181300	142259
如东县	Rudong County	844775	250662	263295	754809	249045	226433
启东市	Qidong City	1234178	473962	406780	1176517	449687	378977
如皋市	Rugao City	1058134	231047	433140	965783	207064	371923
通州市	Tongzhou City	1621508	604456	655521	1493214	597438	563748
海门市	Haimen City	1334549	579570	472307	1237361	554841	406184
连云港市	**Lianyungang Municipality**	**3876333**	**660042**	**1783030**	**3171064**	**567964**	**1415424**
市区	Urban District	1283177	152817	234417	1128492	143582	190552
赣榆县	Gaiyu County	1088802	229342	724667	888799	189538	601081
东海县	Donghai County	900578	195688	581185	699078	165397	434019
灌云县	Guanyun County	437392	48921	175478	324838	41500	135118
灌南县	Guannan County	166384	33274	67283	129857	27947	54654
淮阴市	**Huaiyin Municipality**	**2481136**	**470603**	**565950**	**2009516**	**428356**	**476554**
市区	Urban District	790946	34417	56249	627473	35311	48556
淮阴县	Huaiyin County	326565	64845	84626	240370	60067	71279
涟水县	Lianshui County	163384	32118	33075	135126	27877	27967
洪泽县	Hongze County	239860	69848	63856	209150	68376	52966
盱眙县	Xuyi County	223325	67703	41257	163762	53355	33514
金湖县	Jinhu County	232311	64198	72610	205763	61531	62074
淮安市	Huaian City	504745	137474	214277	427872	121839	18098
盐城市	**Yancheng Municipality**	**6436742**	**1910781**	**2175325**	**5424202**	**1659862**	**1860845**
市区	Urban District	846278	37270	132717	658675	27899	115370
响水县	Xiangshui County	167542	31921	28606	140954	29938	24586
滨海县	Binhai County	288921	73584	100380	226135	57769	85932
阜宁县	Funing County	580112	182399	219954	486740	150742	189453

2—8 续表 2 Continued 2

市县名称 Municipality and County		全部工业总产值(当年价) Gross Output Value of Total Industry (current price)	#乡办工业 Township Enterprises	#村及村以下工业 Village Level and Below Enterprises	全部工业总产值(1990年不变价) Gross Output Value of Total Industry (constant price)	#乡办工业 Township Enterprises	#村及村以下工业 Village Level and Below Enterprises
射阳县	Sheyang County	835018	206925	243591	713173	189702	202126
建湖县	Jianhu County	749293	31875	261121	640117	255487	227760
盐都县	Yandou County	1038724	411291	430548	902999	367878	371606
东台市	Dongtai City	992083	330917	448335	843739	282738	381996
大丰市	Dafeng City	938771	317723	310073	811670	297709	262016
扬州市	**Yangzhou Mucipality**	**6792184**	**1724475**	**1757963**	**6212334**	**1588070**	**1564587**
市区	Urban District	1850498	252275	300291	1645711	232618	267258
宝应县	Baoying County	633433	142217	183713	555182	126685	163505
邗江县	HanJiang County	1080280	516147	371079	984673	468821	330261
仪征市	Yizheng City	1198618	109931	124597	1220287	113504	110891
高邮市	Gaoyou City	773218	259874	269509	684507	228215	239863
江都市	Jiangdu City	1256137	444031	508774	1121974	418227	452809
镇江市	**ZhenJiang Municipality**	**7127727**	**2036199**	**2691084**	**6186030**	**1863663**	**2287422**
市区	Urban District	1464197	96452	235305	1180401	85044	200008
丹徒县	Dantu County	1052655	399620	469316	937301	379471	398919
丹阳市	Danyang City	2171552	632592	988929	1958515	593431	840591
扬中市	Yangzhong City	1006022	414099	376327	885846	378207	319878
句容市	Jurong City	1433301	493436	621207	1223967	427510	528026
泰州市	**Taizhou Municipality**	**5502413**	**1525349**	**1309529**	**5627053**	**1528976**	**1126195**
市区	Urban District	1418874	63598	89809	1774273	72376	77236
兴化市	Xinghua City	691518	228616	271907	616496	194758	233840
靖江市	JingJiang City	1108960	499568	197743	1070258	502067	170059
泰兴市	Taixing City	1282372	355916	388392	1243766	385348	334017
姜堰市	Jiangyan City	1000689	377651	361678	922260	374427	311043
宿迁市	**Suqian Municipality**	**1604818**	**333275**	**550484**	**1261935**	**281460**	**417650**
市区	Urban District	142624	10948	30178	129976	8741	22935
宿豫县	Suyu County	508347	98622	284461	413610	93217	214879
沭阳县	Shuyang County	277119	65359	91718	203965	52108	69705
泗阳县	Siyang County	377963	94188	70787	294057	77020	54822
泗洪县	sihong County	298765	64158	73340	220327	50374	55309

2—9 乡以上工业总产值(当年价)
GROSS OUTPUT VALUE OF TOWNSHIP LEVEL AND ABOVE INDUSTRIAL ENTERPRISES (1996)

单位:万元 (10000yuan)

市县名称 Municipality and County		工业总产值 Output Value of Industry	#国有经济 State—Owned	#集体经济 Collective—Owned	#私营经济 Privat—Owned	#股份制经济 Share Holding
南京市	**Nanjing Municipality**	**10069637**	**5551053**	**2620753**	**8058**	**150370**
市区	Urban District	7437349	5115758	885955	3512	143674
江宁县	Jiangning County	1085537	151075	710295	4256	
江浦县	Jiangpu County	224554	34169	109917	290	4550
六合县	Liuhe County	374416	68104	189539		
溧水县	Lishui County	643118	94913	527762		1592
高淳县	Gaochun County	304663	87034	197285		554
无锡市	**Wuxi Municipality**	**14073601**	**2260959**	**8902121**	**149182**	**213593**
市区	Urban District	3858698	1477462	804939	7715	204313
江阴市	Jiangyin City	3841787	237911	3031981	719	
宜兴市	Yixing City	2019349	179750	1570080	13154	
锡山市	Xishan City	4353767	365836	3495121	127594	9280
徐州市	**Xuzhou Municipality**	**4435642**	**2456577**	**1682213**	**1709**	**34919**
市区	Urban District	2253598	1639834	435454		31804
丰县	Fengxian County	204868	79907	122372	533	
沛县	Peixian County	298974	82966	171763		
铜山县	Tongshan County	719563	402462	315275		
睢宁县	Shuining County	306633	76897	210049		
新沂市	Xinyi City	292747	109098	169224		
邳州市	Pizhou City	359259	65413	258076	1176	3115
常州市	**Changzhou Municipality**	**6557120**	**1514829**	**3622159**	**9105**	**355389**
市区	Urban District	2888998	1020346	806845		342941
溧阳市	Liyang City	784614	137355	595888	796	4172
金坛市	Jintan City	617783	129014	437299		
武进市	Wujin City	2265725	228114	1782127	8309	8276
苏州市	**Suzhou Municipality**	**15340805**	**2795011**	**8168556**	**51844**	**95229**
市区	Urban District	2730328	932794	770677		69645
常熟市	Changshu City	2057057	438229	1096455	4048	5861
张家港市	Zhangjiagang City	3336360	656399	2246560		
昆山市	Kunshan City	1888108	154441	581996	2487	19723

2—9 续表 1 Continued 1

市县名称 Municipality and County		工业总产值 Output Value of Industry	#国有经济 State—Owned	#集体经济 Collective—Owned	#私营经济 Privat—Owned	#股份制经济 Share Holding
吴江市	Wujiang City	1804935	233924	1406291		
太仓市	Taicang City	1323875	166774	771811	3406	
吴县市	Wuxie City	2200142	212450	1294766	41903	
南通市	**Nantong Muncipatity**	**6022805**	**1174712**	**3177739**	**10506**	**177187**
市区	Urban District	1779780	591166	324466		58772
海安县	Haian County	459681	70207	335957		7450
如东县	Rudong County	566541	79100	303840	3735	24813
启东市	Qidong City	796002	150017	500825		
如皋市	Rugao City	615948	87267	465345		
通州市	Tongzhou City	947919	116149	674684		18174
海门市	Haimen City	856934	80806	572622	6771	67978
连云港市	**Lianyungang Municipality**	**2011029**	**762758**	**904351**	**4425**	**19580**
市区	Urban District	1004493	469717	321396	3676	11079
赣榆县	Gaiyu County	357389	92247	208690	749	8501
东海县	Donghai County	312510	65179	215393		
灌云县	Guanyun County	238275	97440	102869		
灌南县	Guannan County	98362	38175	56003		
淮阴市	**Huaiyin Municipality**	**1897487**	**893681**	**729098**	**15451**	**83833**
市区	Urban District	733788	460497	147598	14827	
淮阴县	Huaiyin County	235638	48071	97986	258	74482
涟水县	Lianshui County	130021	74162	50324	120	4046
洪泽县	Hongze County	173328	79296	75103		1050
盱眙县	Xuyi County	179909	99610	73650		
金湖县	Jinhu County	157472	43798	102170		2603
淮安市	Huaian City	287331	88247	182267	246	1652
盐城市	**Yancheng Municipality**	**4260198**	**1290116**	**2443434**	**8820**	**201899**
市区	Urban District	713268	421483	98566	6450	168297
响水县	Xiangshui County	138437	48442	87305	159	174
滨海县	Binhai County	188541	86186	95886	1604	3320
阜宁县	Funing County	360158	82913	234122		

2—9 续表 2　　Continued 2

市县名称 Municipality and County		工业总产值 Output Value of Industry	#国有经济 State—Owned	#集体经济 Collective—Owned	#私营经济 Privat—Owned	#股份制经济 Share Holding
射阳县	Sheyang County	591312	182184	325598		
建湖县	Jianhu County	487860	66663	398087		
盐都县	Yandou County	608176	74170	447610	303	28612
东台市	Dongtai City	543748	130779	360030	304	1496
大丰市	Dafeng City	628698	197296	396230		
扬州市	**Yangzhou Mucipality**	**4998437**	**1382612**	**2205978**	**769**	**726133**
市区	Urban District	1541266	851758	307537	264	1873
宝应县	Baoying County	447614	218150	172829		43734
邗江县	HanJiang County	708035	60748	527327	505	18678
仪征市	Yizheng City	1064198	86894	259455		641972
高邮市	Gaoyou City	501311	112137	350381		1871
江都市	Jiangdu City	736013	52925	588449		18005
镇江市	**ZhenJiang Municipality**	**4348592**	**1142264**	**2530721**	**1908**	**89336**
市区	Urban District	1215648	659834	224389		61208
丹徒县	Dantu County	583339	88365	448767		670
丹阳市	Danyang City	1143534	214956	796922		22897
扬中市	Yangzhong City	608522	53175	504412		4561
句容市	Jurong City	797549	125934	556231	1908	
泰州市	**Taizhou Municipality**	**4159723**	**898848**	**2208803**	**79**	**74307**
市区	Urban District	1320342	312880	211039	79	760
兴化市	Xinghua City	418643	127093	269848		11036
靖江市	JingJiang City	906783	188344	631333		7095
泰兴市	Taixing City	876973	194392	614708		363
姜堰市	Jiangyan City	636982	76139	481875		55053
宿迁市	**Suqian Municipality**	**1043444**	**454373**	**553444**	**714**	**6358**
市区	Urban District	112446	18693	91257		
宿豫县	Suyu County	223886	75355	141146		
沭阳县	Shuyang County	182611	86647	85983		3954
泗阳县	Siyang County	299076	136059	147252	714	2404
泗洪县	sihong County	225425	137619	87806		

2—10 全部独立核算工业企业主要财务指标
INDICATORS OF ALL INDUSTRIAL ENTERPRISES WITH INDEPENDENT ACCONTING SYSTEMS (1996)

单位:万元 (10000yuan)

市县名称 Municipality and County		企业单位数(个) Number of Enterprises	#亏损企业 Loss Making Enterprises	全部流动资产年平均余额 Annual Average Balnce Circulating Funds	固定资产原价合计 Original Value of Fixed Assets	产品销售收入 Revenue of Product Sales	利税总额 Total Pre—tax Profits
南京市	**Nanjing Municipality**	**3595**	**845**	**5007843**	**7046790**	**9197414**	**693750**
市区	Urban District	1912	485	4291580	6349464	7184443	600337
江宁县	Jiangning County	561	57	294161	309682	946549	56689
江浦县	Jiangpu County	226	51	94643	79470	163651	7711
六合县	Liuhe County	373	121	97093	100953	241334	5298
溧水县	Lishui County	220	61	151944	118610	464943	13962
高淳县	Gaochun County	303	70	78422	88611	196494	9753
无锡市	**Wuxi Municipality**	**4047**	**1174**	**6085060**	**6187894**	**12414761**	**852059**
市区	Urban District	1244	250	2441942	2638958	3778015	284497
江阴市	Jiangyin City	979	346	1366231	1485648	3452341	291332
宜兴市	Yixing City	987	318	624005	803593	1582577	80533
锡山市	Xishan City	837	260	1652882	1259695	3601828	195697
徐州市	**Xuzhou Municipality**	**2078**	**323**	**1928048**	**2625442**	**3554972**	**299866**
市区	Urban District	475	137	1287436	1917856	1822931	177430
丰县	Fengxian County	242	13	77692	75576	160092	11377
沛县	Peixian County	220	30	92363	103520	216443	13885
铜山县	Tongshan County	251	49	211596	204546	626225	54521
睢宁县	Shuining County	245	13	64974	75649	202132	11171
新沂市	Xinyi City	313	36	100203	136717	236024	11742
邳州市	Pizhou City	332	45	93784	111578	291125	19740
常州市	**Changzhou Municipality**	**3011**	**829**	**3099650**	**2826458**	**5629618**	**322815**
市区	Urban District	743	264	1597964	1671193	2698142	150774
溧阳市	Liyang City	433	76	285087	274289	672396	42963
金坛市	Jintan City	462	127	182655	170733	402401	18977
武进市	Wujin City	1373	362	1033944	710243	1856679	110101
苏州市	**Suzhou Municipality**	**4913**	**1464**	**6157163**	**7464128**	**13166753**	**768254**
市区	Urban District	956	344	1655836	1878518	2488940	115126
常熟市	Changshu City	912	355	943140	1108042	1777584	115793
张家港市	Zhangjiagang City	538	53	1021772	1315532	3002606	211336
昆山市	Kunshan City	734	180	814407	1039938	1749864	103757

2—10 续表 1 Continued 1

市 县 名 称 Municipality and County	企业单位数（个）Number of Enterprises	#亏损企业 Loss Making Enterprises	全部流动资产年平均余额 Annual Average Balnce Circulating Funds	固定资产原价合计 Original Value of Fixed Assets	产品销售收入 Revenue of Product Sales	利税总额 Total Pre-tax Profits
吴江市 Wujiang City	489	141	606701	827063	1552721	85373
太仓市 Taicang City	562	185	489210	523966	969131	49662
吴县市 Wuxie City	722	206	626097	771069	1625907	87207
南通市 Nantong Muncipatity	**5223**	**1755**	**2700648**	**3222093**	**4865042**	**257083**
市区 Urban District	735	361	980921	1587535	1615102	136367
海安县 Haian County	554	286	195410	240402	360274	5255
如东县 Rudong County	593	245	286910	292087	472902	14455
启东市 Qidong City	681	192	286315	260775	640551	32402
如皋市 Rugao City	671	268	256167	248284	440152	4518
通州市 Tongzhou City	1056	243	378875	309462	720122	35821
海门市 Haimen City	933	160	316050	283548	615939	28265
连云港市 Lianyungang Municipality	**1913**	**256**	**831391**	**1063128**	**1568280**	**88230**
市区 Urban District	731	169	512607	766195	765379	46204
赣榆县 Gaiyu County	305	17	78940	79931	268967	14710
东海县 Donghai County	348	32	93035	100970	243687	11296
灌云县 Guanyun County	335	19	100209	70806	205690	9871
灌南县 Guannan County	194	19	46600	45226	84557	6149
淮阴市 Huaiyin Municipality	**1999**	**286**	**786184**	**1085874**	**1518134**	**133589**
市区 Urban District	286	59	359150	573517	628653	80642
淮阴县 Huaiyin County	243	14	73777	152364	134000	12328
涟水县 Lianshui County	274	44	70668	65543	108440	—692
洪泽县 Hongze County	221	13	61981	63430	145325	9820
盱眙县 Xuyi County	281	32	61619	69760	140103	9320
金湖县 Jinhu County	251	60	65640	67696	135604	9496
淮安市 Huaian City	443	64	93351	92964	226009	12674
盐城市 Yancheng Municipality	**2928**	**408**	**1545285**	**1762584**	**3449751**	**204476**
市区 Urban District	213	43	352043	563954	615658	44954
响水县 Xiangshui County	190	31	54846	58363	111112	2675
滨海县 Binhai County	254	33	57145	63369	132053	7630
阜宁县 Funing County	381	11	99012	104678	342173	18112

2—10 续表 2 Continued 2

市县名称 Municipality and County	企业单位数（个） Number of Enterprises	#亏损企业 Loss Making Enterprises	全部流动资产年平均余额 Annual Average Balnce Circulating Funds	固定资产原价合计 Original Value of Fixed Assets	产品销售收入 Revenue of Product Sales	利税总额 Total Pre—tax Profits
射阳县 Sheyang County	347	49	199636	182074	431831	26135
建湖县 Jianhu County	335	41	187354	165493	428615	31909
盐都县 Yandou County	348	37	190788	185393	521243	33369
东台市 Dongtai City	508	87	204182	217262	423748	16720
大丰市 Dafeng City	352	76	200279	216998	443318	22972
扬州市 Yangzhou Mucipality	**2558**	**730**	**2652148**	**3015463**	**4343435**	**287167**
市区 Urban District	364	106	872987	1151553	1375881	75930
宝应县 Baoying County	376	107	174250	155734	360945	16894
邗江县 HanJiang County	451	72	268936	189096	614558	51944
仪征市 Yizheng City	298	95	761273	1072057	966271	95913
高邮市 Gaoyou City	391	105	186443	143366	418280	14845
江都市 Jiangdu City	678	245	388259	303657	607500	31641
镇江市 ZhenJiang Municipality	**2503**	**735**	**1701250**	**1776936**	**3062748**	**192894**
市区 Urban District	462	195	648323	946218	821327	36172
丹徒县 Dantu County	382	98	220089	129792	414337	33652
丹阳市 Danyang City	821	299	409952	395166	848119	42413
扬中市 Yangzhong City	449	92	307791	161551	453113	52173
句容市 Jurong City	389	51	115095	144209	525852	28484
泰州市 Taizhou Municipality	**2723**	**1058**	**2124251**	**1584346**	**3517842**	**254061**
市区 Urban District	240	104	667734	357020	1352040	152053
兴化市 Xinghua City	544	170	217840	213125	319831	5011
靖江市 JingJiang City	768	303	472137	333868	685867	26101
泰兴市 Taixing City	686	275	463737	435108	660526	49780
姜堰市 Jiangyan City	485	206	302803	245225	499578	21116
宿迁市 Suqian Municipality	**1007**	**147**	**349790**	**390560**	**802661**	**77754**
市区 Urban District	89	27	39022	50814	89391	3506
宿豫县 Suyu County	231	46	62779	95737	182401	5227
沭阳县 Shuyang County	231	43	48212	45969	109205	4203
泗阳县 Siyang County	260	15	100574	103147	247467	33089
泗洪县 sihong County	196	16	99203	94893	174197	31729

2—11 国有独立核算工业企业主要财务指标
MAJOR FINANCIAL AFFAIR INDICATORS OF STATE-OWNED INDUSTRIAL ENTERPRISES WITH INDEPENDENT ACCOUNTING SYSTEMS (1996)

单位:万元 (10000yuan)

市县名称 Municipality and County		企业单位数(个) Number of Enterprises	#亏损企业 Loss Making Enterprises	全部流动资产年平均余额 Annual Average Balnce Circulating Funds	固定资产原价合计 Original Value of Fixed Assets	产品销售收入 Revenue of Product Sales	利税总额 Total Pre-tax Profits
南京市	**Nanjing Municipality**	**371**	**126**	**3174829**	**4932893**	**5390430**	**475305**
市区	Urban District	231	78	3034126	4751599	5087144	464434
江宁县	Jiangning County	30	7	50351	68106	113840	4488
江浦县	Jiangpu County	21	9	17557	20591	26242	−238
六合县	Liuhe County	23	17	16761	32046	58723	343
溧水县	Lishui County	29	5	30343	29016	53315	2305
高淳县	Gaochun County	37	10	25691	31535	51166	3973
无锡市	**Wuxi Municipality**	**378**	**118**	**1377476**	**1768481**	**2092359**	**112854**
市区	Urban District	188	47	1024898	1224915	1388759	95108
江阴市	Jiangyin City	60	22	99862	149820	224093	9572
宜兴市	Yixing City	65	26	95887	195897	148905	−1877
锡山市	Xishan City	65	23	156829	197849	330602	10051
徐州市	**Xuzhou Municipality**	**267**	**72**	**1279327**	**2041850**	**1994617**	**201728**
市区	Urban District	96	34	991560	1696023	1305180	145268
丰县	Fengxian County	20	7	32565	36799	60273	4632
沛县	Peixian County	40	5	37117	51494	68294	3934
铜山县	Tongshan County	28	7	106975	94659	383574	37983
睢宁县	Shuining County	23	6	27034	31682	44348	1862
新沂市	Xinyi City	32	7	48873	81108	86977	4035
邳州市	Pizhou City	28	6	35203	50085	45971	4014
常州市	**Changzhou Municipality**	**236**	**86**	**862108**	**1178029**	**1299920**	**79542**
市区	Urban District	129	49	649004	970795	889155	56022
溧阳市	Liyang City	27	6	72313	76501	121856	8669
金坛市	Jintan City	27	16	30588	44495	70236	962
武进市	Wujin City	53	15	110203	86238	218673	13889
苏州市	**Suzhou Municipality**	**417**	**143**	**1362665**	**2511245**	**2489177**	**153919**
市区	Urban District	140	51	578914	1117016	821890	50229
常熟市	Changshu City	54	23	174264	455349	403705	34708
张家港市	Zhangjiagang City	42	8	235722	378503	617120	40526
昆山市	Kunshan City	53	20	80503	140007	155707	4788

2—11 续表 1 Continued 1

市县名称 Municipality and County		企业单位数（个） Number of Enterprises	#亏损企业 Loss Making Enterprises	全部流动资产年平均余额 Annual Average Balnce Circulating Funds	固定资产原价合计 Original Value of Fixed Assets	产品销售收入 Revenue of Product Sales	利税总额 Total Pre—tax Profits
吴江市	Wujiang City	59	23	127150	189968	207124	9623
太仓市	Taicang City	33	10	76597	110490	131256	6671
吴县市	Wuxie City	36	8	89515	119912	152375	7374
南通市	**Nantong Muncipatity**	**348**	**151**	**652567**	**1227288**	**1016272**	**70775**
市区	Urban District	87	39	364602	808917	521483	56964
海安县	Haian County	34	17	24429	43661	56083	—615
如东县	Rudong County	32	17	45038	79034	65918	—2002
启东市	Qidong City	54	26	87643	98356	125042	8658
如皋市	Rugao City	27	12	45232	61590	76143	1415
通州市	Tongzhou City	66	27	58038	81382	99745	4675
海门市	Haimen City	48	13	27585	54348	71858	1680
连云港市	**Lianyungang Municipality**	**294**	**100**	**462774**	**713533**	**587567**	**26838**
市区	Urban District	145	62	329342	580055	355724	18422
赣榆县	Gaiyu County	36	7	33777	37442	63102	2173
东海县	Donghai County	39	18	30234	42153	45126	—2739
灌云县	Guanyun County	50	9	45291	28659	89901	4684
灌南县	Guannan County	24	4	24130	25224	33714	4298
淮阴市	**Huaiyin Municipality**	**305**	**120**	**445622**	**662065**	**769099**	**81766**
市区	Urban District	73	31	245702	423750	432446	72643
淮阴县	Huaiyin County	23	10	28848	33908	38571	—241
涟水县	Lianshui County	28	16	52946	46362	64405	—2368
洪泽县	Hongze County	44	4	23963	39358	57473	4131
盱眙县	Xuyi County	44	17	40697	49300	73705	4404
金湖县	Jinhu County	42	15	19824	34818	42747	3211
淮安市	Huaian City	51	27	33643	34569	59753	—14
盐城市	**Yancheng Municipality**	**362**	**94**	**590338**	**811484**	**1090434**	**61367**
市区	Urban District	48	10	248424	376053	377893	35332
响水县	Xiangshui County	32	14	24442	19413	42022	—686
滨海县	Binhai County	34	12	28388	39945	62994	3166
阜宁县	Funing County	28	3	34079	49212	79472	2881

2—11 续表 2 Continued 2

市县名称 Municipality and County	企业单位数（个）Number of Enterprises	#亏损企业 Loss Making Enterprises	全部流动资产年平均余额 Annual Average Balnce Circulating Funds	固定资产原价合计 Original Value of Fixed Assets	产品销售收入 Revenue of Product Sales	利税总额 Total Pre—tax Profits
射阳县 Sheyang County	60	18	64396	63660	148308	5122
建湖县 Jianhu County	40	10	35071	49687	60635	833
盐都县 Yandou County	33	3	32224	50400	58143	2444
东台市 Dongtai City	59	20	54074	70387	117980	4706
大丰市 Dafeng City	28	4	69240	92727	142987	7569
扬州市 Yangzhou Mucipality	**223**	**105**	**728285**	**1108617**	**1186094**	**62564**
市区 Urban District	79	33	505460	870549	755516	44767
宝应县 Baoying County	35	20	70294	70664	170173	10480
邗江县 HanJiang County	15	9	23898	14891	51405	3486
仪征市 Yizheng City	32	15	53097	67763	78243	1367
高邮市 Gaoyou City	36	19	37937	33390	84377	1533
江都市 Jiangdu City	26	9	37599	51360	46380	931
镇江市 ZhenJiang Municipality	**285**	**122**	**492602**	**843081**	**709069**	**33899**
市区 Urban District	111	70	333732	629387	338195	16845
丹徒县 Dantu County	25	6	17076	23661	54661	1640
丹阳市 Danyang City	87	33	89760	129354	197127	9670
扬中市 Yangzhong City	41	9	26767	19847	44902	3999
句容市 Jurong City	21	4	25267	40832	74184	1745
泰州市 Taizhou Municipality	**219**	**105**	**453884**	**576547**	**825081**	**12213**
市区 Urban District	46	20	173331	178942	360158	11257
兴化市 Xinghua City	43	25	67494	83467	103427	—4291
靖江市 JingJiang City	46	17	93331	119843	170350	1760
泰兴市 Taixing City	59	29	85947	157176	136084	5583
姜堰市 Jiangyan City	25	14	33781	37119	55062	—2096
宿迁市 Suqian Municipality	**142**	**49**	**224416**	**261035**	**363716**	**48106**
市区 Urban District	15	9	13380	25914	19191	—1350
宿豫县 Suyu County	29	10	33442	58422	64641	—287
沭阳县 Shuyang County	29	19	23089	22122	42112	237
泗阳县 Siyang County	43	8	74617	78183	120256	24432
泗洪县 sihong County	26	3	79888	76394	117516	25074

2—12 集体经济独立核算工业企业主要财务指标

MAJOR FINANCIAL AFFAIR INDICATORS OF COLLECTIVE—OWNED INDUSTRIAL ENTERPRISES WITH INDEPENDENT ACCOUNTING SYSTEMS (1996)

单位:万元 (10000yuan)

市县名称 Municipality and County	企业单位数(个) Number of Enterprises	#亏损企业 Loss Making Enterprises	全部流动资产年平均余额 Annual Average Balnce Circulating Funds	固定资产原价合计 Original Value of Fixed Assets	产品销售收入 Revenue of Product Sales	利税总额 Total Pre—tax Profits
南京市 Nanjing Municipality	**2612**	**527**	**922303**	**694107**	**2104598**	**99640**
市区 Urban District	1311	287	487565	332679	760096	32533
江宁县 Jiangning County	435	29	180644	165050	633490	43799
江浦县 Jiangpu County	160	30	47378	33413	75773	3991
六合县 Liuhe County	279	75	47708	39028	107101	2253
溧水县 Lishui County	175	49	113234	80102	397819	11790
高淳县 Gaochun County	252	57	45774	43835	130319	5274
无锡市 Wuxi Municipality	**3148**	**903**	**3138734**	**2597678**	**7616749**	**508686**
市区 Urban District	798	137	439339	312314	867183	51521
江阴市 Jiangyin City	837	298	1001629	972185	2657812	226098
宜兴市 Yixing City	826	258	418343	437847	1216399	71184
锡山市 Xishan City	687	210	1279423	875332	2875355	159883
徐州市 Xuzhou Municipality	**1728**	**234**	**515814**	**485282**	**1299917**	**77699**
市区 Urban District	341	91	193563	156641	361851	19483
丰县 Fengxian County	218	5	44015	38275	97834	6638
沛县 Peixian County	171	24	41577	46701	111311	7150
铜山县 Tongshan County	218	41	102482	108948	240711	16517
睢宁县 Shuining County	218	7	33231	32983	139173	8428
新沂市 Xinyi City	273	28	47300	49361	136053	6343
邳州市 Pizhou City	289	38	53646	52373	212984	13140
常州市 Changzhou Municipality	**2452**	**636**	**1521974**	**1116298**	**2959842**	**162981**
市区 Urban District	426	152	395054	302248	745585	31791
溧阳市 Liyang City	376	60	190452	169571	504388	31424
金坛市 Jintan City	415	106	135292	106522	296301	15138
武进市 Wujin City	1235	318	801176	537957	1413568	84628
苏州市 Suzhou Municipality	**3423**	**1033**	**2984097**	**2833201**	**6844954**	**420118**
市区 Urban District	593	207	456209	312212	680262	26281
常熟市 Changshu City	726	278	576671	467713	921765	59616
张家港市 Zhangjiagang City	414	31	651922	766026	1991356	151057
昆山市 Kunshan City	366	97	273782	212587	563666	36109

2—12 续表 1 Continued 1

市县名称 Municipality and County		企业单位数（个） Number of Enterprises	#亏损企业 Loss Making Enterprises	全部流动资产年平均余额 Annual Average Balnce Circulating Funds	固定资产原价合计 Original Value of Fixed Assets	产品销售收入 Revenue of Product Sales	利税总额 Total Pre—tax Profits
吴江市	Wujiang City	380	106	427973	556205	1220925	70399
太仓市	Taicang City	395	144	233409	212363	564255	25847
吴县市	Wuxie City	549	170	364131	306095	902725	50809
南通市	**Nantong Muncipatity**	**4193**	**1370**	**1303704**	**1112551**	**2389669**	**86197**
市区	Urban District	443	236	178129	174073	279842	7667
海安县	Haian County	469	236	145474	169255	261929	5457
如东县	Rudong County	477	199	168763	133199	237903	7780
启东市	Qidong City	559	147	162599	124719	388159	18123
如皋市	Rugao City	613	244	192437	172665	323899	1903
通州市	Tongzhou City	906	192	254230	185877	487593	25859
海门市	Haimen City	726	116	202072	152763	410344	19408
连云港市	**Lianyungang Municipality**	**1453**	**118**	**234252**	**197785**	**692640**	**40952**
市区	Urban District	485	78	85522	74851	234578	12695
赣榆县	Gaiyu County	243	9	33945	30221	161152	9716
东海县	Donghai County	286	11	47230	41670	168936	12403
灌云县	Guanyun County	277	8	47457	34039	82976	4206
灌南县	Guannan County	162	12	20098	17004	44998	1932
淮阴市	**Huaiyin Municipality**	**1603**	**147**	**248305**	**245735**	**601578**	**36775**
市区	Urban District	190	23	71964	92073	120092	4782
淮阴县	Huaiyin County	206	3	14323	17273	76337	4676
涟水县	Lianshui County	241	28	16196	17920	39010	1488
洪泽县	Hongze County	159	7	32539	19016	69337	4560
盱眙县	Xuyi County	233	14	18739	18406	60389	4239
金湖县	Jinhu County	198	41	40695	28934	84066	5361
淮安市	Huaian City	376	31	53849	52113	152347	11670
盐城市	**Yancheng Municipality**	**2402**	**281**	**768402**	**706681**	**1929035**	**119654**
市区	Urban District	139	26	42426	33203	77992	4522
响水县	Xiangshui County	154	16	29649	38041	66445	3298
滨海县	Binhai County	212	19	26224	25591	64459	4030
阜宁县	Funing County	328	5	55788	47791	224144	13654

2—12 续表 2 Continued 2

市县名称 Municipality and County	企业单位数（个）Number of Enterprises	#亏损企业 Loss Making Enterprises	全部流动资产年平均余额 Annual Average Balnce Circulating Funds	固定资产原价合计 Original Value of Fixed Assets	产品销售收入 Revenue of Product Sales	利税总额 Total Pre-tax Profits
射阳县 Sheyang County	257	25	91682	94094	220166	15388
建湖县 Jianhu County	282	29	141977	109332	348083	29842
盐都县 Yandou County	300	34	128243	112763	385971	24907
东台市 Dongtai City	424	63	134351	131117	267951	10536
大丰市 Dafeng City	306	64	118062	114749	273824	13477
扬州市 Yangzhou Mucipality	**2056**	**541**	**950231**	**787604**	**1826257**	**102713**
市区 Urban District	198	48	164211	147624	270126	13590
宝应县 Baoying County	289	72	78732	66223	141499	4016
邗江县 HanJiang County	389	59	194928	139046	455779	39857
仪征市 Yizheng City	247	73	87328	147685	176468	9139
高邮市 Gaoyou City	339	82	130601	98706	300684	11769
江都市 Jiangdu City	594	207	294431	188320	481701	24342
镇江市 ZhenJiang Municipality	**1981**	**527**	**889030**	**583701**	**1781403**	**125451**
市区 Urban District	264	83	108177	96151	152577	3135
丹徒县 Dantu County	330	83	186174	95158	339512	29829
丹阳市 Danyang City	675	242	274032	195120	575652	27136
扬中市 Yangzhong City	381	76	255089	125495	370949	44545
句容市 Jurong City	331	43	65558	71777	342713	20806
泰州市 Taizhou Municipality	**2351**	**894**	**1150811**	**784369**	**1684483**	**103588**
市区 Urban District	153	72	111294	55597	196724	12972
兴化市 Xinghua City	484	135	135117	117855	200267	9064
靖江市 JingJiang City	673	268	328387	186494	447780	21512
泰兴市 Taixing City	599	233	349565	244602	469170	42828
姜堰市 Jiangyan City	442	186	226448	179821	370542	17212
宿迁市 Suqian Municipality	**829**	**93**	**117349**	**116956**	**419252**	**29213**
市区 Urban District	70	16	23457	23433	68197	4851
宿豫县 Suyu County	198	36	28988	35741	115676	5432
沭阳县 Shuyang County	189	22	21793	17721	59649	3965
泗阳县 Siyang County	202	6	23796	21625	119049	8310
泗洪县 sihong County	170	13	19315	18436	56681	6655

2—13 独立核算工业企业经济效益(一)
ECONOMIC RESULTS OF INDUSTRIAL ENTERPRISES WITH INDEPENDENT ACCOUNTING SYSTEMS (1996)

单位:% (%)

市县名称 Municipality and County	销售利税率 Pre-tax Profits/Product Sales			资金利税率 Pre-tax Profits/Total Assets		
	全部工业企业 Total Industrial Enterprises	国有工业企业 State-Owned	集体工业企业 Collective-Owned	全部工业企业 Total Industrial Enterprises	国有工业企业 State-Owned	集体工业企业 Collective-Owned
南京市 Nanjing Municipality	**7.54**	**8.82**	**4.73**	**7.33**	**7.86**	**7.16**
市区 Urban District	8.36	9.13	4.28	7.27	8.02	4.62
江宁县 Jiangning County	5.99	3.94	6.91	10.78	4.55	14.65
江浦县 Jiangpu County	4.71	−0.91	5.27	5.07	−0.78	5.65
六合县 Liuhe County	2.20	0.58	2.10	3.31	1.07	3.04
溧水县 Lishui County	3.00	4.32	2.96	5.93	4.44	6.96
高淳县 Gaochun County	4.96	7.76	4.05	6.96	8.55	6.99
无锡市 Wuxi Municipality	**6.86**	**5.39**	**6.68**	**8.15**	**4.33**	**10.31**
市区 Urban District	7.53	6.85	5.94	6.70	5.11	8.09
江阴市 Jiangyin City	8.44	4.27	8.51	12.05	4.71	13.65
宜兴市 Yixing City	5.09	−1.26	5.85	6.69	−0.82	9.68
锡山市 Xishan City	5.43	3.04	5.56	7.58	3.23	8.40
徐州市 Xuzhou Municipality	**8.44**	**10.11**	**5.98**	**8.29**	**7.92**	**8.97**
市区 Urban District	9.73	11.13	5.38	7.21	7.20	6.61
丰县 Fengxian County	7.11	7.69	6.78	8.02	7.19	8.76
沛县 Peixian County	6.42	5.76	6.42	8.20	5.26	9.39
铜山县 Tongshan County	8.71	9.90	6.86	15.39	22.35	9.11
睢宁县 Shuining County	5.53	4.20	6.06	9.47	4.03	14.40
新沂市 Xinyi City	4.97	4.64	4.66	5.89	3.88	7.42
邳州市 Pizhou City	6.78	8.73	6.17	11.26	5.86	14.00
常州市 Changzhou Municipality	**5.73**	**6.12**	**5.51**	**6.45**	**4.82**	**7.24**
市区 Urban District	5.59	6.30	4.26	5.53	4.33	5.34
溧阳市 Liyang City	6.39	7.11	6.23	9.24	6.84	10.67
金坛市 Jintan City	4.72	1.37	5.11	6.27	1.53	7.30
武进市 Wujin City	5.93	6.35	5.99	7.28	8.23	7.33
苏州市 Suzhou Municipality	**5.83**	**6.18**	**6.14**	**6.59**	**4.78**	**8.43**
市区 Urban District	4.63	6.11	3.86	3.87	3.69	3.93
常熟市 Changshu City	6.51	8.60	6.47	6.57	6.47	6.66
张家港市 Zhangjiagang City	7.04	6.57	7.59	10.54	7.37	12.69
昆山市 Kunshan City	5.93	3.08	6.41	6.49	2.60	8.45

2—13 续表 1 Continued 1

市县名称 Municipality and County	销售利税率 Pre—tax Profits/Product Sales			资金利税率 Pre—tax Profits/Total Assets		
	全部工业企业 Total Industrial Enterprises	国有工业企业 State—Owned	集体工业企业 Collective—Owned	全部工业企业 Total Industrial Enterprises	国有工业企业 State—Owned	集体工业企业 Collective—Owned
吴江市 Wujiang City	5.50	4.65	5.77	7.08	3.73	8.50
太仓市 Taicang City	5.12	5.08	4.58	5.82	4.37	6.82
吴县市 Wuxie City	5.36	4.84	5.63	6.97	4.11	8.50
南通市 Nantong Muncipatity	**5.28**	**6.96**	**3.61**	**5.26**	**4.71**	**4.27**
市区 Urban District	8.44	10.92	2.74	6.61	6.07	2.82
海安县 Haian County	1.46	—1.10	2.08	1.55	—1.17	2.24
如东县 Rudong County	3.06	—3.04	3.27	2.93	—1.95	3.03
启东市 Qidong City	5.06	6.92	4.67	6.83	5.57	7.17
如皋市 Rugao City	1.03	1.86	0.59	1.08	1.74	0.62
通州市 Tongzhou City	4.97	4.69	5.30	6.10	4.23	6.84
海门市 Haimen City	4.59	2.34	4.73	5.55	2.67	6.36
连云港市 Lianyungang Municipality	**5.63**	**4.57**	**5.91**	**5.50**	**2.74**	**10.92**
市区 Urban District	6.04	5.18	5.41	4.33	2.45	9.32
赣榆县 Gaiyu County	5.47	3.44	6.03	10.85	3.68	17.31
东海县 Donghai County	4.64	—6.07	7.34	6.69	—4.50	16.04
灌云县 Guanyun County	4.80	5.21	5.07	6.48	7.11	5.82
灌南县 Guannan County	7.27	12.75	4.29	7.73	10.33	5.85
淮阴市 Huaiyin Municipality	**8.80**	**10.63**	**6.11**	**8.65**	**9.27**	**8.75**
市区 Urban District	12.83	16.80	3.98	10.87	14.05	3.50
淮阴县 Huaiyin County	9.20	—0.62	6.13	6.18	—0.46	16.95
涟水县 Lianshui County	—0.64	—3.68	3.81	—0.62	—2.90	5.19
洪泽县 Hongze County	6.76	7.19	6.58	9.22	7.96	10.19
盱眙县 Xuyi County	6.65	5.97	7.02	8.40	5.91	13.10
金湖县 Jinhu County	7.00	7.51	6.38	8.49	6.99	9.27
淮安市 Huaian City	5.61	—0.02	7.66	7.85	—0.02	12.63
盐城市 Yancheng Municipality	**5.93**	**5.63**	**6.20**	**7.29**	**5.30**	**9.55**
市区 Urban District	7.30	9.35	5.80	5.82	6.97	6.94
响水县 Xiangshui County	2.41	—1.63	4.96	2.74	—1.73	5.85
滨海县 Binhai County	5.78	5.03	6.25	7.19	5.63	8.97
阜宁县 Funing County	5.29	3.63	6.09	10.17	4.10	14.73

2—13 续表 2 Continued 2

市县名称 Municipality and County	销售利税率 Pre—tax Profits/Product Sales			资金利税率 Pre—tax Profits/Total Assets		
	全部工业企业 Total Industrial Enterprises	国有工业企业 State—Owned	集体工业企业 Collective—Owned	全部工业企业 Total Industrial Enterprises	国有工业企业 State—Owned	集体工业企业 Collective—Owned
射阳县 Sheyang County	6.05	3.45	6.99	8.00	4.75	9.77
建湖县 Jianhu County	7.44	1.37	8.57	10.97	1.26	14.23
盐都县 Yandou County	6.40	4.20	6.45	10.58	3.66	12.27
东台市 Dongtai City	3.95	3.99	3.93	4.67	4.39	4.71
大丰市 Dafeng City	5.18	5.29	4.92	6.42	5.49	6.72
扬州市 Yangzhou Mucipality	**6.61**	**5.27**	**5.62**	**5.85**	**4.21**	**6.88**
市区 Urban District	5.52	5.93	5.03	4.60	4.13	5.27
宝应县 Baoying County	4.68	6.16	2.84	5.98	8.51	3.32
邗江县 HanJiang County	8.45	6.78	8.74	12.91	10.28	13.62
仪征市 Yizheng City	9.93	1.75	5.18	5.72	1.29	4.64
高邮市 Gaoyou City	3.55	1.82	3.91	5.10	2.46	5.81
江都市 Jiangdu City	5.21	2.01	5.05	5.22	1.25	5.76
镇江市 ZhenJiang Municipality	**6.30**	**4.78**	**7.04**	**6.82**	**3.44**	**9.95**
市区 Urban District	4.40	4.98	2.05	3.00	2.48	1.93
丹徒县 Dantu County	8.12	3.00	8.79	11.38	5.09	12.53
丹阳市 Danyang City	5.00	4.91	4.71	6.12	5.37	6.71
扬中市 Yangzhong City	11.51	8.91	12.01	12.36	9.75	12.89
句容市 Jurong City	5.42	2.35	6.07	13.57	3.31	18.98
泰州市 Taizhou Municipality	**7.22**	**1.48**	**6.15**	**7.89**	**1.42**	**6.17**
市区 Urban District	11.25	3.13	6.59	16.57	3.88	8.71
兴化市 Xinghua City	1.57	—4.15	4.53	1.39	—3.30	4.36
靖江市 JingJiang City	3.81	1.03	4.80	3.71	0.98	4.75
泰兴市 Taixing City	7.54	4.10	9.13	6.50	2.83	8.29
姜堰市 Jiangyan City	4.23	—3.81	4.65	4.46	—3.45	4.88
宿迁市 Suqian Municipality	**9.69**	**13.23**	**6.97**	**12.29**	**11.57**	**14.69**
市区 Urban District	3.92	—7.03	7.11	4.77	—4.15	12.88
宿豫县 Suyu County	2.87	—0.44	4.70	3.98	—0.37	10.33
沭阳县 Shuyang County	3.85	0.56	6.65	5.19	0.63	11.15
泗阳县 Siyang County	13.37	20.32	6.98	18.98	18.77	21.31
泗洪县 sihong County	18.21	21.34	11.74	18.41	18.13	19.54

2—14 独立核算工业企业经济效益(二)
ECONOMIC RESULTS OF INDUSTRIAL ENTERPRISES WITH INDEPENDENT ACCOUNTING SYSTEMS (1996)

市县名称 Municipality and County	产值利税率(%) Pre—tax Profits/ Gross Output Value			全员劳动生产率(元/人) Overall Labor Prdductivity (yuan/person)		
	全部工业企业 Total Industrial Enterprises	国有工业企业 State—Owned	集体工业企业 Collective—Owned	全部工业企业 Total Industrial Enterprises	国有工业企业 State—Owned	集体工业企业 Collective—Owned
南京市 Nanjing Municipality	**7.02**	**8.71**	**3.91**	**26978**	**32839**	**16465**
市区 Urban District	8.15	9.16	3.75	28974	34068	12356
江宁县 Jiangning County	5.39	3.32	6.32	27454	29893	27479
江浦县 Jiangpu County	3.64	—0.79	3.85	15114	11545	12819
六合县 Liuhe County	1.49	0.57	1.24	14348	12730	11621
溧水县 Lishui County	2.32	3.19	2.32	23848	15799	27100
高淳县 Gaochun County	3.25	4.66	2.71	18339	23438	16526
无锡市 Wuxi Municipality	**6.11**	**5.08**	**5.76**	**36094**	**25871**	**36676**
市区 Urban District	7.42	6.48	6.49	33761	29018	28985
江阴市 Jiangyin City	7.72	4.20	7.59	40357	20792	38790
宜兴市 Yixing City	4.06	—1.17	4.58	30438	13469	34437
锡山市 Xishan City	4.49	2.75	4.57	38859	28770	39711
徐州市 Xuzhou Municipality	**7.00**	**8.48**	**4.82**	**21088**	**23889**	**15923**
市区 Urban District	7.96	8.94	4.56	22388	24466	14150
丰县 Fengxian County	6.04	6.80	5.63	15801	18387	14439
沛县 Peixian County	4.83	4.74	4.47	17724	11504	21019
铜山县 Tongshan County	7.84	9.85	5.36	26623	43278	16890
睢宁县 Shuining County	4.47	3.46	4.77	14383	10166	15315
新沂市 Xinyi City	4.03	3.71	3.77	16926	19108	15665
邳州市 Pizhou City	5.76	7.38	5.20	18279	15278	17735
常州市 Changzhou Municipality	**5.04**	**5.55**	**4.58**	**23095**	**24576**	**20818**
市区 Urban District	5.25	5.55	3.96	23983	25094	19232
溧阳市 Liyang City	5.71	7.00	5.43	19326	20257	19707
金坛市 Jintan City	3.61	1.25	3.81	19156	19639	18202
武进市 Wujin City	4.88	6.18	4.76	24580	26887	22770
苏州市 Suzhou Municipality	**5.12**	**5.62**	**5.23**	**33741**	**24934**	**32643**
市区 Urban District	4.27	5.55	3.41	24591	22755	17581
常熟市 Changshu City	5.76	8.16	5.53	26862	29780	24888
张家港市 Zhangjiagang City	6.43	6.17	6.85	50463	40113	50010
昆山市 Kunshan City	5.52	3.15	6.27	38082	19457	25373

2—14 续表1 Continued 1

市县名称 Municipality and County		产值利税率(%) Pre—tax Profits/ Gross Output Value			全员劳动生产率(元/人) Overall Labor Prductivity (yuan/person)		
		全部工业企业 Total Industrial Enterprises	国有工业企业 State—Owned	集体工业企业 Collective—Owned	全部工业企业 Total Industrial Enterprises	国有工业企业 State—Owned	集体工业企业 Collective—Owned
吴江市	Wujiang City	4.73	4.11	5.01	34998	21722	39264
太仓市	Taicang City	3.97	4.37	3.40	36788	22255	38311
吴县市	Wuxie City	4.22	3.47	4.13	33174	21028	32125
南通市	**Nantong Muncipatity**	**4.37**	**6.24**	**2.79**	**19787**	**19096**	**16113**
市区	Urban District	7.78	9.85	2.40	26895	24854	12896
海安县	Haian County	1.20	—0.89	1.73	9613	11542	8861
如东县	Rudong County	2.58	—2.68	2.58	14348	12651	12818
启东市	Qidong City	4.20	5.91	3.76	23007	19911	20621
如皋市	Rugao City	0.79	1.82	0.44	14079	10980	14153
通州市	Tongzhou City	3.82	4.39	3.83	18341	12646	19066
海门市	Haimen City	3.32	2.08	3.43	23340	15955	24110
连云港市	**Lianyungang Municipality**	**4.72**	**3.71**	**4.95**	**17767**	**15919**	**16842**
市区	Urban District	4.84	3.94	4.31	19636	17699	17335
赣榆县	Gaiyu County	4.57	2.63	5.24	22967	16962	22665
东海县	Donghai County	4.13	—6.25	6.25	12914	6784	15807
灌云县	Guanyun County	4.39	5.05	4.47	12161	9013	13435
灌南县	Guannan County	6.35	11.41	3.51	12431	16116	10731
淮阴市	**Huaiyin Municipality**	**7.41**	**9.47**	**5.26**	**13333**	**16838**	**8063**
市区	Urban District	11.87	16.07	3.53	11845	21457	3756
淮阴县	Huaiyin County	5.37	—0.54	4.86	27277	8472	16929
涟水县	Lianshui County	—0.55	—3.23	3.14	7368	8766	5920
洪泽县	Hongze County	6.02	5.72	6.33	14740	16644	11864
盱眙县	Xuyi County	5.35	4.65	5.82	16094	16757	14884
金湖县	Jinhu County	6.13	7.41	5.33	15975	11530	18999
淮安市	Huaian City	4.60	—0.02	6.67	10822	14654	9310
盐城市	**Yancheng Municipality**	**4.96**	**4.99**	**5.05**	**17750**	**16258**	**16993**
市区	Urban District	6.33	8.43	4.60	20768	17892	16406
响水县	Xiangshui County	1.95	—1.44	3.81	12063	10956	12354
滨海县	Binhai County	4.84	4.07	5.43	13560	17541	11889
阜宁县	Funing County	5.03	3.47	5.84	17559	14304	17994

2—14 续表 2 Continued 2

市县名称 Municipality and County	产值利税率(%) Pre—tax Profits/Gross Output Value			全员劳动生产率(元/人) Overall Labor Prductivity (yuan/person)		
	全部工业企业 Total Industrial Enterprises	国有工业企业 State—Owned	集体工业企业 Collective—Owned	全部工业企业 Total Industrial Enterprises	国有工业企业 State—Owned	集体工业企业 Collective—Owned
射阳县 Sheyang County	4.70	2.99	5.09	22984	23032	21500
建湖县 Jianhu County	6.54	1.25	7.50	18092	6164	21254
盐都县 Yandou County	5.55	3.30	5.65	23514	18944	22378
东台市 Dongtai City	3.11	3.73	2.94	9230	10180	8605
大丰市 Dafeng City	3.97	4.61	3.56	18349	19399	17837
扬州市 Yangzhou Mucipality	**5.90**	**4.76**	**4.79**	**21548**	**22464**	**17061**
市区 Urban District	5.01	5.32	4.64	24818	26627	16069
宝应县 Baoying County	4.16	5.66	2.44	12226	24262	7731
邗江县 HanJiang County	7.49	6.44	7.66	25037	21145	25618
仪征市 Yizheng City	9.14	1.62	3.70	26074	11368	11112
高邮市 Gaoyou City	3.13	1.53	3.51	16748	15166	16588
江都市 Jiangdu City	4.34	1.83	4.17	18319	9291	18304
镇江市 ZhenJiang Municipality	**4.66**	**3.14**	**5.24**	**29889**	**28767**	**29325**
市区 Urban District	3.02	2.65	1.59	25964	28516	16298
丹徒县 Dantu County	6.24	2.13	7.08	27007	33654	26047
丹阳市 Danyang City	3.94	4.33	3.58	28902	28542	27984
扬中市 Yangzhong City	8.61	7.52	8.87	34796	30920	34817
句容市 Jurong City	3.96	1.96	4.04	41762	25776	44363
泰州市 Taizhou Municipality	**6.18**	**1.40**	**4.74**	**19581**	**14963**	**14898**
市区 Urban District	11.56	3.62	6.23	44831	22485	15533
兴化市 Xinghua City	1.24	—3.51	3.48	9931	10608	9536
靖江市 JingJiang City	2.89	0.95	3.41	13948	11495	14120
泰兴市 Taixing City	5.69	2.88	6.98	16759	14439	17290
姜堰市 Jiangyan City	3.45	—3.49	3.63	16203	9538	16892
宿迁市 Suqian Municipality	**8.03**	**10.97**	**5.85**	**14684**	**14631**	**14788**
市区 Urban District	3.16	—7.24	5.40	15949	2720	22352
宿豫县 Suyu County	2.56	—0.39	4.24	11677	7976	13698
沭阳县 Shuyang County	2.53	0.28	5.65	8834	6769	10016
泗阳县 Siyang County	11.07	17.96	5.65	16252	15179	17402
泗洪县 sihong County	16.90	20.26	10.40	21069	27661	11348

2—15 交 通 邮 电 事 业
TRANSPOTATION, POSTAL AND TELECOMMUNICATION SERVICES (1996)

市县名称 Municipality and County	公路客运量（万人）Highway Passenger Traffic (10000 persons)	公路货运量（万吨）Highway Freight Traffic (10000tons)	水运客运量（万人）Waterway Passenger Traffic (10000 persons)	水运货运量（万吨）Waterway Freight Traffic (10000tons)	邮电业务总量（万元）Revenue from Posts and Telecom—munication (10000yuan)	全年用电量（万千瓦时）Annual Electrieity Consumed (10000kuh)
南京市 Nanjing Municipality	**9926**	**7094**	**110**	**4644**	**155441**	**1041543**
市区 Urban District	7444	4449	110	4484	136447	872298
江宁县 Jiangning County	785	800		8	6415	68424
江浦县 Jiangpu County	761	553		4	2759	17621
六合县 Liuhe County	606	353		49	4099	35882
溧水县 Lishui County	202	615		11	3112	29146
高淳县 Gaochun County	128	324		88	2609	18172
无锡市 Wuxi Municipality	**14004**	**6418**	**59**	**1529**	**136054**	**1033985**
市区 Urban District	6167	2380	59	424	85097	369952
江阴市 Jiangyin City	2701	1746		237	29485	259928
宜兴市 Yixing City	2637	774		603	21472	142880
锡山市 Xishan City	2498	1518		265		261225
徐州市 Xuzhou Municipality	**7691**	**5184**		**633**	**53673**	**743424**
市区 Urban District	4845	1201		43	34886	458224
丰县 Fengxian County	301	288		33	2994	23061
沛县 Peixian County	447	601		113	3779	75502
铜山县 Tongshan County	1002	1346		38		84096
睢宁县 Shuining County	333	344		6	3464	24003
新沂市 Xinyi City	329	565		115	4087	41534
邳州市 Pizhou City	433	839		285	4463	37004
常州市 Changzhou Municipality	**6512**	**3843**	**4**	**1306**	**77169**	**557030**
市区 Urban District	2677	1407		306	61599	240449
溧阳市 Liyang City	1006	1014		191	8520	69585
金坛市 Jintan City	860	310		154	7050	50013
武进市 Wujin City	1969	1112	4	655		196983
苏州市 Suzhou Municipality	**11234**	**4810**	**39**	**3486**	**190757**	**1126972**
市区 Urban District	4683	1220	32	369	80000	243375
常熟市 Changshu City	1595	666		517	28803	153309
张家港市 Zhangjiagang City	979	678		328	25314	240025
昆山市 Kunshan City	1094	380	1	583	21115	104978

2—15 续表 1 Continued 1

市县名称 Municipality and County	公路客运量（万人）Highway Passenger Traffic (10000 persons)	公路货运量（万吨）Highway Freight Traffic (10000tons)	水运客运量（万人）Waterway Passenger Traffic (10000 persons)	水运货运量（万吨）Waterway Freight Traffic (10000tons)	邮电业务总量（万元）Revenue from Posts and Telecom—munication (10000yuan)	全年用电量（万千瓦时）Annual Electrieity Consumed (10000kuh)
吴江市 Wujiang City	630	490		346	21572	138497
太仓市 Taicang City	747	532		117	13953	81893
吴县市 Wuxie City	1506	844	6	1226		164895
南通市 Nantong Muncipatity	**6381**	**4312**	**125**	**1802**	**80476**	**577951**
市区 Urban District	2283	1789	105	270	25670	217103
海安县 Haian County	324	866		314	7902	50134
如东县 Rudong County	678	100		258	7508	70386
启东市 Qidong City	645	300		136	11769	48579
如皋市 Rugao City	649	467	14	333	8537	59280
通州市 Tongzhou City		530		242	10604	70555
海门市 Haimen City	1802	260	6	249	8486	61914
连云港市 Lianyungang Municipality	**4265**	**2719**		**506**	**27177**	**229174**
市区 Urban District	3797	2552		191	15183	126639
赣榆县 Gaiyu County	70	15		120	3943	32458
东海县 Donghai County	284	97		26	3569	35801
灌云县 Guanyun County	24	23		138	2835	20345
灌南县 Guannan County	90	32		31	1647	13931
淮阴市 Huaiyin Municipality	**2150**	**1082**	**35**	**1628**	**23265**	**263923**
市区 Urban District	919	458		1234	9628	126437
淮阴县 Huaiyin County	40	31		18	1563	20544
涟水县 Lianshui County	330	62		37	2016	21669
洪泽县 Hongze County	181	125	14	105	1737	14619
盱眙县 Xuyi County	193	73		82	1899	31183
金湖县 Jinhu County	137	198	21	114	2556	20439
淮安市 Huaian City	351	135		39	3866	29032
盐城市 Yancheng Municipality	**4813**	**2722**	**14**	**6517**	**47845**	**368022**
市区 Urban District	2000	575	14	910	16600	90317
响水县 Xiangshui County	48	136		391	2164	16114
滨海县 Binhai County	96	1061		326	3204	22480
阜宁县 Funing County	215	81		848	3907	31912

2—15 续表 2 Continued 2

市县名称 Municipality and County		公路客运量（万人）Highway Passenger Traffic (10000 persons)	公路货运量（万吨）Highway Freight Traffic (10000tons)	水运客运量（万人）Waterway Passenger Traffic (10000 persons)	水运货运量（万吨）Waterway Freight Traffic (10000tons)	邮电业务总量（万元）Revenue from Posts and Telecom—munication (10000yuan)	全年用电量（万千瓦时）Annual Electrieity Consumed (10000kuh)
射 阳 县	Sheyang County	144	599		1565	5226	42741
建 湖 县	Jianhu County	577	81		782	4668	29057
盐 都 县	Yandou County	722	54		652		30167
东 台 市	Dongtai City	241	81		326	6829	50589
大 丰 市	Dafeng City	770	54		717	5247	54645
扬 州 市	**Yangzhou Mucipality**	**4415**	**2437**	**36**	**1005**	**60330**	**409516**
市 区	Urban District	1810	781	14	290	27540	109189
宝 应 县	Baoying County	227	5		46	5190	35704
邗 江 县	HanJiang County	260	550	3	180		38814
仪 征 市	Yizheng City	897	826	13	71	7005	111783
高 邮 市	Gaoyou City	309	99	6	189	5588	35039
江 都 市	Jiangdu City	912	176		229	15007	78987
镇 江 市	**ZhenJiang Municipality**	**4638**	**3109**	**53**	**1056**	**51500**	**379509**
市 区	Urban District	2698	1024	13	827	25751	202610
丹 徒 县	Dantu County	267	287	40	49		40561
丹 阳 市	Danyang City	590	856		129	12237	81967
扬 中 市	Yangzhong City	253	199		20	8930	24206
句 容 市	Jurong City	829	743		31	4582	30165
泰 州 市	**Taizhou Municipality**	**3017**	**1714**	**125**	**2869**	**45653**	**309321**
市 区	Urban District	95	624	11	96	7486	62573
兴 化 市	Xinghua City	498	163	54	373	6542	54784
靖 江 市	JingJiang City	909	427	4	801	10447	72006
泰 兴 市	Taixing City	920	215	22	141	12817	76513
姜 堰 市	Jiangyan City	596	285	34	1458	8361	43445
宿 迁 市	**Suqian Municipality**	**1571**	**716**		**327**	**10958**	**93982**
市 区	Urban District	178	61		28		
宿 豫 县	Suyu County	18	39		15	3284	23370
沭 阳 县	Shuyang County	500	88		30	2600	24248
泗 阳 县	Siyang County	635	439		155	2678	24050
泗 洪 县	sihong County	240	89		99	2396	22314

2—16 固定资产投资完成额
VALUE OF FIXED ASSETS INVESTMENT FULFILLED (1996)

单位:万元 (10000yuan)

市县名称 Municipality and County	全社会固定资产投资完成额 Value of Total Fixed Assets Investment Fulfilled	#国有经济 State—Owned	#城镇集体经济 Urban Collective—Owned	#其他经济 Others	#房地产开发投资 Investmedt of Real Estate Dovelopment	#农村集体经济 Rural Collective—Owned
南京市 Nanjing Municipality	**3058685**	**1468805**	**71117**	**439570**	**697029**	**343934**
市区 Urban District	2606325	1324476	52811	372108	677246	160129
江宁县 Jiangning County	252434	65650	4116	44362	13761	117733
江浦县 Jiangpu County	55139	18597	1437	22052	923	8764
六合县 Liuhe County	47568	16362	1050	448	2346	24710
溧水县 Lishui County	68825	30102	9025		1898	24240
高淳县 Gaochun County	28394	13618	2678	600	855	8358
无锡市 Wuxi Municipality	**2338901**	**457872**	**80343**	**515609**	**356756**	**915858**
市区 Urban District	1250884	330183	23719	439025	239909	207533
江阴市 Jiangyin City	433550	33773	17323	55041	40444	286101
宜兴市 Yixing City	242118	26651	8665	12772	28478	164472
锡山市 Xishan City	412349	67265	30636	8771	47925	257752
徐州市 Xuzhou Municipality	**1275020**	**562238**	**55386**	**15350**	**80642**	**542778**
市区 Urban District	586498	345685	30376	5909	61909	140599
丰县 Fengxian County	77687	28066	2958		2410	41280
沛县 Peixian County	83157	32154	5788			39831
铜山县 Tongshan County	210799	60320	5152	8000	12012	123693
睢宁县 Shuining County	81103	30325	5126	1260	928	42816
新沂市 Xinyi City	93081	32420	4031		2248	52481
邳州市 Pizhou City	142695	33268	1955	181	1135	102078
常州市 Changzhou Municipality	**1148636**	**386477**	**44546**	**165733**	**153586**	**365560**
市区 Urban District	587450	252340	17285	133635	86653	88265
溧阳市 Liyang City	156586	42105	6507	2907	23868	72092
金坛市 Jintan City	110763	36018	6242	11972	11205	40983
武进市 Wujin City	293837	56014	14512	17219	31860	164220
苏州市 Suzhou Municipality	**3534562**	**583697**	**152228**	**1192242**	**501411**	**1061991**
市区 Urban District	1338211	295353	17615	673791	294709	53633
常熟市 Changshu City	369846	82093	33491	31447	56087	145260
张家港市 Zhangjiagang City	516163	59348	45751	129573	36582	242002
昆山市 Kunshan City	556801	52049	6677	146817	41598	309660

2—16 续表1 Continued 1

市县名称 Municipality and County		全社会固定资产投资完成额 Value of Total Fixed Assets Investment Fulfilled	#国有经济 State—Owned	#城镇集体经济 Urban Collective—Owned	#其他经济 Others	#房地产开发投资 Investmedt of Real Estate Dovelopment	#农村集体经济 Rural Collective—Owned
吴江市	Wujiang City	266070	28768	32269	120000	11356	71703
太仓市	Taicang City	207095	37582	8754	73089	15514	68152
吴县市	Wuxie City	280376	28504	7671	17525	45565	171581
南通市	**Nantong Muncipatity**	**1331265**	**361596**	**88521**	**241401**	**201248**	**367051**
市区	Urban District	519403	151175	9925	204027	119156	34904
海安县	Haian County	105778	32057	24771	800	9107	20598
如东县	Rudong County	96963	27560	4443	10861	5027	38875
启东市	Qidong City	144508	47564	11640	3460	9167	64150
如皋市	Rugao City	133040	32198	18207	4207	21136	41592
通州市	Tongzhou City	186979	41856	10241	7306	30023	84095
海门市	Haimen City	144594	29186	9294	10740	7632	82837
连云港市	**Lianyungang Municipality**	**517163**	**217823**	**43471**	**18449**	**43544**	**175925**
市区	Urban District	258726	140341	29159	17517	39922	26394
赣榆县	Gaiyu County	107904	25576	3644	932	1080	72897
东海县	Donghai County	63389	19855	1572		1440	35034
灌云县	Guanyun County	65839	23923	7320		952	30958
灌南县	Guannan County	21305	8128	1776		150	10642
淮阴市	**Huaiyin Municipality**	**356355**	**206045**	**29018**	**4373**	**15231**	**80502**
市区	Urban District	163270	125162	10607	3160	10313	11074
淮阴县	Huaiyin County	35185	12725	4029	858	1830	11982
涟水县	Lianshui County	27551	12989	2084		1156	4452
洪泽县	Hongze County	26396	12055	2594		20	9436
盱眙县	Xuyi County	33599	18547	886		1300	11058
金湖县	Jinhu County	21939	8320	2799	355	460	9268
淮安市	Huaian City	48415	16247	6019		152	23232
盐城市	**Yancheng Municipality**	**781872**	**292623**	**69273**	**43847**	**64633**	**262268**
市区	Urban District	204655	126403	5505	20629	38365	9517
响水县	Xiangshui County	22123	9044	6042	88	1419	4054
滨海县	Binhai County	26542	10234	1981	520	2084	10951
阜宁县	Funing County	74033	26442	7663		3132	32711

2—16 续表 2 Continued 2

市县名称 Municipality and County	全社会固定资产投资完成额 Value of Total Fixed Assets Investment Fulfilled	#国有经济 State—Owned	#城镇集体经济 Urban Collective—Owned	#其他经济 Others	#房地产开发投资 Investmedt of Real Estate Dovelopment	#农村集体经济 Rural Collective—Owned
射阳县 Sheyang County	92827	32052	10421	8423	4693	30404
建湖县 Jianhu County	86808	17074	16838		2015	46342
盐都县 Yandou County	103321	17556	6666	4946	1820	62342
东台市 Dongtai City	85762	23293	3428	4896	4752	36970
大丰市 Dafeng City	85801	30525	10729	4345	6353	28977
扬州市 Yangzhou Mucipality	**991856**	**585640**	**43942**	**101518**	**98329**	**131107**
市区 Urban District	551694	446512	4239	16839	49841	32165
宝应县 Baoying County	60676	21948	3303	6148	7178	13705
邗江县 HanJiang County	52272	15590	790		7278	22359
仪征市 Yizheng City	164215	62908	12969	67179	16254	3436
高邮市 Gaoyou City	59951	11971	7285	3728	4826	23116
江都市 Jiangdu City	103048	26711	15356	7624	12952	36326
镇江市 ZhenJiang Municipality	**692802**	**265721**	**33771**	**88993**	**62814**	**240602**
市区 Urban District	270644	173647	11922	37804	29083	18015
丹徒县 Dantu County	61906	15358	3638	463	9831	32616
丹阳市 Danyang City	148565	39381	6786	12920	9516	79741
扬中市 Yangzhong City	91662	17049	6850	1000	13016	53453
句容市 Jurong City	120025	20286	4575	36806	1368	56777
泰州市 Taizhou Municipality	**471577**	**155895**	**66091**	**50830**	**48265**	**109233**
市区 Urban District	104932	40999	10472	38625	8002	3125
兴化市 Xinghua City	68758	18304	1653	10231	10939	20917
靖江市 JingJiang City	84777	19723	26943	1050	3765	16303
泰兴市 Taixing City	133130	64994	14480	924	9522	31137
姜堰市 Jiangyan City	79980	11875	12543		16037	37751
宿迁市 Suqian Municipality	**126638**	**51968**	**10280**	**500**	**2714**	**47793**
市区 Urban District	14031	3576	5019		1310	1996
宿豫县 Suyu County	40147	13667	1838			24642
沭阳县 Shuyang County	15686	6609	432	500	584	5765
泗阳县 Siyang County	30829	15666	1471		220	7320
泗洪县 sihong County	25945	12450	1520		600	8070

2—17 国　内　贸　易
DOMESTIC TRADE (1996)

单位:万元　　(10000yuan)

市县名称 Municipality and County	批发零售贸易业商品销售总额 Total Sales in wholesale and Retail Sales trade	社会消费品零售总额 Total Retail Sales of Consumer Goods	批发零售贸易业、餐饮业网点机构(个) Wholesale and Retail Sales Trade Number of Outlets	#个体 Individual	批发零售贸易业、餐饮业人员(人) Whole—Sale and Retail Sales Number of Rersonnel (person)	#个体 Individual
南京市 Nanjing Municipality	**9551855**	**2985713**	**70042**	**59203**	**282190**	**119581**
市区 Urban District	8577714	2420101	43276	35744	204183	74158
江宁县 Jiangning County	247603	166903	6906	5809	20622	11320
江浦县 Jiangpu County	249321	65449	3361	2865	9303	4797
六合县 Liuhe County	206000	133682	7079	6468	20662	12713
溧水县 Lishui County	116709	84434	4613	4116	13539	8493
高淳县 Gaochun County	154508	115144	4807	4201	13881	8100
无锡市 Wuxi Municipality	**10555883**	**2549533**	**69518**	**46638**	**298780**	**72854**
市区 Urban District	3347249	1110781	24967	12871	129472	19470
江阴市 Jiangyin City	2070344	525785	16046	11801	73737	23082
宜兴市 Yixing City	3238392	467831	13860	9250	58206	12266
锡山市 Xishan City	1899898	445136	14645	12716	37365	18036
徐州市 Xuzhou Municipality	**2700579**	**1451706**	**100598**	**91822**	**287649**	**166684**
市区 Urban District	1435388	848926	23520	20531	95881	41927
丰县 Fengxian County	161875	92494	12255	11271	26059	18532
沛县 Peixian County	134243	109634	14001	13143	35049	21685
铜山县 Tongshan County	378758	113006	10493	9783	25401	16530
睢宁县 Shuining County	146976	72674	11238	10088	38214	23399
新沂市 Xinyi City	209428	93889	12407	11341	28578	19270
邳州市 Pizhou City	233911	121083	16684	15665	38467	25341
常州市 Changzhou Municipality	**4251031**	**1575902**	**66803**	**58256**	**190585**	**103714**
市区 Urban District	1545736	629584	18678	15704	64232	25117
溧阳市 Liyang City	684289	330375	13349	11960	31483	17961
金坛市 Jintan City	362131	228973	11920	10499	40890	27164
武进市 Wujin City	1658875	386970	22856	20093	53980	33472
苏州市 Suzhou Municipality	**9201458**	**2660057**	**102707**	**80665**	**327088**	**122771**
市区 Urban District	2475842	714493	15113	10864	88636	17847
常熟市 Changshu City	2222572	604680	26761	21164	73322	35631
张家港市 Zhangjiagang City	1265128	321754	11545	10238	29201	14714
昆山市 Kunshan City	679381	259704	7955	6235	27827	9144

2—17 续表 1 Continued 1

市县名称 Municipality and County		批发零售贸易业商品销售总额 Total Sales in wholesale and Retail Sales trade	社会消费品零售总额 Total Retail Sales of Consumer Goods	批发零售贸易业、餐饮业网点机构（个） Wholesale and Retail Sales Trade Number of Outlets	#个体 Individual	批发零售贸易业、餐饮业人员（人） Whole—Sale and Retail Sales Number of Rersonnel (person)	#个体 Individual
吴江市	Wujiang City	1055944	238811	11950	10707	28713	14942
太仓市	Taicang City	578325	188728	8001	5501	27401	6561
吴县市	Wuxie City	924266	331887	21382	15956	51988	23932
南通市	**Nantong Muncipatity**	**3580348**	**1945178**	**113623**	**97717**	**263889**	**137939**
市区	Urban District	1064193	448495	14090	11193	43420	17476
海安县	Haian County	412802	175189	16102	14019	41251	22820
如东县	Rudong County	410882	227606	16648	14618	32837	17659
启东市	Qidong City	477535	282110	16546	14795	32108	17353
如皋市	Rugao City	322170	240489	18429	16377	34760	18945
通州市	Tongzhou City	534769	295748	15734	12362	42047	20283
海门市	Haimen City	357997	275541	16074	14353	37466	23403
连云港市	**Lianyungang Municipality**	**1471874**	**743986**	**82607**	**75047**	**214265**	**136985**
市区	Urban District	803314	357401	17019	14593	58904	24583
赣榆县	Gaiyu County	184933	122200	15613	14475	29552	21659
东海县	Donghai County	173425	111888	25487	23829	46602	35415
灌云县	Guanyun County	195792	102772	16991	15867	53789	39698
灌南县	Guannan County	114410	49725	7497	6283	25418	15630
淮阴市	**Huaiyin Municipality**	**1296686**	**674351**	**59534**	**52299**	**170877**	**97124**
市区	Urban District	665641	281846	8662	7558	32801	15415
淮阴县	Huaiyin County	93177	49568	7158	5972	21757	11057
涟水县	Lianshui County	81965	65654	13058	12199	30051	21161
洪泽县	Hongze County	97632	50073	5984	4874	18535	7472
盱眙县	Xuyi County	82807	65403	10235	9103	24502	17961
金湖县	Jinhu County	137274	65877	3424	2831	10982	5353
淮安市	Huaian City	138192	95930	11013	9762	32249	18705
盐城市	**Yancheng Municipality**	**2527991**	**1301226**	**112832**	**98711**	**302523**	**184016**
市区	Urban District	814331	381335	9360	7547	39822	14424
响水县	Xiangshui County	101548	46099	6913	6385	16674	10345
滨海县	Binhai County	137469	77635	7950	7012	19524	10407
阜宁县	Funing County	126556	95144	13006	12546	39955	30051

2—17 续表 2 Continued 2

市县名称 Municipality and County	批发零售贸易业商品销售总额 Total Sales in wholesale and Retail Sales trade	社会消费品零售总额 Total Retail Sales of Consumer Goods	批发零售贸易业、餐饮业网点机构（个） Wholesale and Retail Sales Trade Number of Outlets	#个体 Individual	批发零售贸易业、餐饮业人员（人） Whole—Sale and Retail Sales Number of Rersonnel (person)	#个体 Individual
射阳县 Sheyang County	306045	139899	18448	17390	44161	30904
建湖县 Jianhu County	162453	120046	11308	9546	41605	27051
盐都县 Yandou County	238757	111641	13925	9288	31063	19924
东台市 Dongtai City	317858	188468	16266	14662	37655	19343
大丰市 Dafeng City	322974	140959	15656	14335	32064	21567
扬州市 Yangzhou Mucipality	**2046753**	**1159684**	**52496**	**44133**	**155353**	**61822**
市区 Urban District	630811	403093	8815	6568	35004	9393
宝应县 Baoying County	214531	112523	7635	6966	21835	10854
邗江县 HanJiang County	183039	91470	5375	4355	16687	6381
仪征市 Yizheng City	305027	183936	9012	8322	20983	10675
高邮市 Gaoyou City	303797	122873	8911	7450	26691	10863
江都市 Jiangdu City	409548	245789	12748	10472	34153	13656
镇江市 ZhenJiang Municipality	**1721061**	**902438**	**41610**	**34844**	**120109**	**60789**
市区 Urban District	677214	356053	12025	10103	41912	19028
丹徒县 Dantu County	188116	93220	7101	6007	15649	9223
丹阳市 Danyang City	469954	235180	11697	9322	31574	13578
扬中市 Yangzhong City	172501	99378	6757	6354	17701	13013
句容市 Jurong City	213276	118607	4030	3058	13273	5947
泰州市 Taizhou Municipality	**2633387**	**1006765**	**52640**	**44743**	**142636**	**52584**
市区 Urban District	1110222	193549	5591	4388	21257	5817
兴化市 Xinghua City	349590	144297	13784	11324	33426	11518
靖江市 JingJiang City	476570	223601	9905	8546	26899	10203
泰兴市 Taixing City	368560	238804	12011	10173	35358	12882
姜堰市 Jiangyan City	328445	206514	11349	10212	25696	12164
宿迁市 Suqian Municipality	**612996**	**444321**	**43354**	**36959**	**118755**	**67350**
市区 Urban District	38496	52855	2641	2275	11433	5372
宿豫县 Suyu County	148511	86709	9353	8818	18135	13138
沭阳县 Shuyang County	157080	120974	23565	20333	61999	40372
泗阳县 Siyang County	129361	109736	1753	684	9334	1266
泗洪县 sihong County	139548	74047	6042	4849	17854	7202

2—18 利　用　外　资
UTILIZATION OF FOREIGN CAPITAL (1996)

单位:万美元　　　　(USD10000)

市县名称 Municipality and County	利用外资新签协议合同数(个) Utilization of Foreign Capital Thraugh Newly Signed Cotracts (agreement)	#客商直接投资 Direct Foreign Investments	协议合同外资金额 Foreign Funds of Signed Contracts	#客商直接投资 Direct Foreign Investments	实际利用外资 Foreign Capital Actually Used	#客商直接投资 Direct Foreign Investments
南京市 Nanjing Municipality	**438**	**438**	**97708**	**97708**	**50716**	**47166**
市区 Urban District	261	261	74428	74428	38940	35390
江宁县 Jiangning County	138	138	13892	13892	8890	8890
江浦县 Jiangpu County	13	13	249	249	2020	2020
六合县 Liuhe County	15	15	1629	1629	361	361
溧水县 Lishui County	9	9	7496	7496	403	403
高淳县 Gaochun County	2	2	14	14	102	102
无锡市 Wuxi Municipality	**402**	**401**	**159305**	**159300**	**120685**	**91475**
市区 Urban District	183	182	71476	71471	63868	36469
江阴市 Jiangyin City	61	61	28127	28127	24305	22494
宜兴市 Yixing City	53	53	18458	18458	12371	12371
锡山市 Xishan City	105	105	41244	41244	20141	20141
徐州市 Xuzhou Municipality	**122**	**116**	**20791**	**17508**	**17284**	**14052**
市区 Urban District	53	50	11867	10025	11560	9078
丰县 Fengxian County	16	15	374	244	650	520
沛县 Peixian County	8	8	1637	1637	878	878
铜山县 Tongshan County	19	19	2723	2723	1544	1544
睢宁县 Shuining County	2	2	63	63	604	604
新沂市 Xinyi City	14	12	2728	1417	1228	608
邳州市 Pizhou City	10	10	1399	1399	820	820
常州市 Changzhou Municipality	**241**	**148**	**99906**	**65867**	**51764**	**27192**
市区 Urban District	117	57	64573	36430	37670	16857
溧阳市 Liyang City	27	24	6282	6205	1003	874
金坛市 Jintan City	32	14	7568	5326	3252	1909
武进市 Wujin City	66	53	21483	17906	9839	7552
苏州市 Suzhou Municipality	**747**	**746**	**459904**	**459813**	**225685**	**225685**
市区 Urban District	146	146	181072	181072	51579	51579
常熟市 Changshu City	57	57	24567	24567	18058	18058
张家港市 Zhangjiagang City	155	155	100298	100298	56761	56761
昆山市 Kunshan City	148	148	66821	66821	45490	45490

单位:万美元 2—18 续表1 Continued 1 (USD10000)

市县名称 Municipality and County		利用外资新签协议合同数(个) Utilization of Foreign Capital Thraugh Newly Signed Cotracts (agreement)	#客商直接投资 Direct Foreign Investments	协议合同外资金额 Foreign Funds of Signed Contracts	#客商直接投资 Direct Foreign Investments	实际利用外资 Foreign Capital Actually Used	#客商直接投资 Direct Foreign Investments
吴江市	Wujiang City	42	42	15650	15650	15736	15736
太仓市	Taicang City	84	83	23911	23820	15269	15269
吴县市	Wuxie City	115	115	47585	47585	22792	22792
南通市	**Nantong Muncipatity**	**232**	**208**	**83447**	**50308**	**50324**	**40457**
市区	Urban District	78	67	59213	29195	29097	24598
海安县	Haian County	17	14	1680	1140	3069	1861
如东县	Rudong County	15	11	6170	4972	6267	3772
启东市	Qidong City	33	29	5196	4387	4246	3140
如皋市	Rugao City	20	19	2338	1816	1344	822
通州市	Tongzhou City	37	37	5100	5100	4035	4035
海门市	Haimen City	32	31	3750	3698	2266	2229
连云港市	**Lianyungang Municipality**	**219**	**206**	**34847**	**32511**	**11817**	**8314**
市区	Urban District	115	102	24389	22053	9826	6323
赣榆县	Gaiyu County	51	51	1132	1132	493	493
东海县	Donghai County	18	18	7749	7749	891	891
灌云县	Guanyun County	35	35	1577	1577	607	607
灌南县	Guannan County						
淮阴市	**Huaiyin Municipality**	**29**	**29**	**4490**	**4490**	**4002**	**934**
市区	Urban District	9	9	3874	3874	2890	335
淮阴县	Huaiyin County	1	1	14	14	133	
涟水县	Lianshui County	2	2	60	60	35	25
洪泽县	Hongze County	6	6	187	187	318	156
盱眙县	Xuyi County	2	2	88	88	107	
金湖县	Jinhu County	3	3	79	79	163	88
淮安市	Huaian City	6	6	188	188	356	330
盐城市	**Yancheng Municipality**	**124**	**124**	**7152**	**7152**	**10060**	**6646**
市区	Urban District	20	20	1652	1652	3888	2368
响水县	Xiangshui County	2	2	961	961	67	51
滨海县	Binhai County	3	3	106	106	115	32
阜宁县	Funing County	20	20	956	956	410	342

市县名称 Municipality and County	利用外资新签协议合同数(个) Utilization of Foreign Capital Thraugh Newly Signed Cotracts (agreement)	#客商直接投资 Direct Foreign Investments	协议合同外资金额 Foreign Funds of Signed Contracts	#客商直接投资 Direct Foreign Investments	实际利用外资 Foreign Capital Actually Used	#客商直接投资 Direct Foreign Investments
射阳县 Sheyang County	23	23	926	926	1425	1211
建湖县 Jianhu County	9	9	349	349	1028	949
盐都县 Yandou County	24	24	745	745	1310	670
东台市 Dongtai City	10	10	326	326	760	336
大丰市 Dafeng City	13	13	1131	1131	1057	687
扬州市 Yangzhou Mucipality	**71**	**71**	**10414**	**10414**	**16985**	**9985**
市区 Urban District	33	33	6356	6356	12611	5611
宝应县 Baoying County	1	1	14	14	420	420
邗江县 HanJiang County	17	17	2040	2040	1244	1244
仪征市 Yizheng City	3	3	755	755	1490	1490
高邮市 Gaoyou City	6	6	237	237	359	359
江都市 Jiangdu City	11	11	1012	1012	861	861
镇江市 ZhenJiang Municipality	**122**	**121**	**50351**	**48856**	**24000**	**18983**
市区 Urban District	37	36	31382	29887	5734	4239
丹徒县 Dantu County	7	7	2053	2053	1810	1484
丹阳市 Danyang City	27	27	2862	2862	6252	3056
扬中市 Yangzhong City	25	25	2330	2330	3030	3030
句容市 Jurong City	26	26	11724	11724	7174	7174
泰州市 Taizhou Municipality	**74**	**71**	**19241**	**18508**	**9141**	**8408**
市区 Urban District	4	4	1083	1083	2094	2094
兴化市 Xinghua City	6	6	600	600	658	658
靖江市 JingJiang City	13	10	4658	3925	2559	1826
泰兴市 Taixing City	30	30	9794	9794	2467	2467
姜堰市 Jiangyan City	21	21	3106	3106	1363	1363
宿迁市 Suqian Municipality	**4**		**3543**		**880**	**407**
市区 Urban District					6	6
宿豫县 Suyu County	4		3170		356	262
沭阳县 Shuyang County			68		322	43
泗阳县 Siyang County			305		196	96
泗洪县 sihong County						

2—19 财 政 主 要 指 标
MAJOR INDICATORS OF FINANCE (1996)

单位:万元 (10000yuan)

市县名称 Municipality and County	财政收入 Total Financial Revenue	#地方财政收入 Local Revenue	地方财政支出 Local Financial Expenditure	#基本建设支出 Capital Construction	#支农支出及农村水利费支出 Farming and Rural Water Conservang Funds	#教育事业费支出 Educational Services Funds
南京市 Nanjing Municipality	**787883**	**361643**	**401743**	**21710**	**22479**	**56979**
市区 Urban District	699229	311400	330369	20398	13707	38688
江宁县 Jiangning County	34058	19424	24272	388	3065	6363
江浦县 Jiangpu County	12717	6043	8782	105	898	2234
六合县 Liuhe County	13651	7943	12088	193	1632	3012
溧水县 Lishui County	16010	9248	14634	54	1882	3546
高淳县 Gaochun County	12218	7585	11598	572	1295	3136
无锡市 Wuxi Municipality	**562614**	**255878**	**240317**	**9953**	**13852**	**50813**
市区 Urban District	271548	133166	123349	5021	6310	20256
江阴市 Jiangyin City	104430	45037	42983	3896	2241	10172
宜兴市 Yixing City	65355	29744	29597	1000	1719	8442
锡山市 Xishan City	121281	47931	44388	36	3582	11943
徐州市 Xuzhou Municipality	**302406**	**153395**	**213530**	**1977**	**20881**	**69077**
市区 Urban District	188189	78159	85349	1209	7483	15783
丰县 Fengxian County	14308	9790	20248	92	2617	7763
沛县 Peixian County	21534	13461	21725	150	1965	8759
铜山县 Tongshan County	30026	19292	27532	100	2795	12582
睢宁县 Shuining County	14002	10246	19392	153	2207	8076
新沂市 Xinyi City	15125	9317	17820	212	1844	6731
邳州市 Pizhou City	19222	13130	21464	61	1970	9383
常州市 Changzhou Municipality	**343032**	**165848**	**153820**	**12609**	**8042**	**36527**
市区 Urban District	195935	94498	71568	9962	1388	11233
溧阳市 Liyang City	28841	14759	20774	709	1462	6915
金坛市 Jintan City	24418	12860	16476	166	1069	5438
武进市 Wujin City	93838	43731	45002	1772	4123	12941
苏州市 Suzhou Municipality	**640757**	**324917**	**315448**	**14987**	**13863**	**69199**
市区 Urban District	191575	105361	101112	5546	3205	16555
常熟市 Changshu City	115312	55412	53210	7209	2046	10926
张家港市 Zhangjiagang City	95003	47054	47272	2104	2031	11098
昆山市 Kunshan City	60160	30191	32506	29	1120	8691

2—19 续表 1 Continued 1

市县名称 Municipality and County	财政收入 Total Financial Revenue	#地方财政收入 Local Revenue	地方财政支出 Local Financial Expenditure	#基本建设支出 Capital Construction	#支农支出及农村水利费支出 Farming and Rural Water Conservang Funds	#教育事业费支出 Educational Services Funds
吴江市 Wujiang City	57334	27814	24415	36	1504	7017
太仓市 Taicang City	43956	21964	20025	26	1039	5732
吴县市 Wuxie City	77417	37121	36908	37	2918	9180
南通市 Nantong Muncipatity	**307839**	**160108**	**201871**	**7183**	**9159**	**61591**
市区 Urban District	107676	54177	61319	6244	1866	8973
海安县 Haian County	26289	13925	20934	368	869	7396
如东县 Rudong County	29162	16650	23214	26	1121	8512
启东市 Qidong City	38467	21043	25872	264	1624	9535
如皋市 Rugao City	28011	14995	22262	9	1289	8512
通州市 Tongzhou City	43393	21142	25585	68	1340	10544
海门市 Haimen City	34841	18176	22685	204	1050	8119
连云港市 Lianyungang Municipality	**129515**	**84556**	**120244**	**7835**	**6148**	**30755**
市区 Urban District	72382	44801	58392	7071	1544	8314
赣榆县 Gaiyu County	18181	13429	17101	626	1319	5976
东海县 Donghai County	16620	12291	16946	111	1615	6168
灌云县 Guanyun County	14321	10386	16702	17	1054	6169
灌南县 Guannan County	8011	3649	11103	10	616	4128
淮阴市 Huaiyin Municipality	**128718**	**59690**	**108094**	**1238**	**7707**	**30003**
市区 Urban District	74765	27828	34884	973	2265	5272
淮阴县 Huaiyin County	9151	5122	12066	32	708	4481
涟水县 Lianshui County	9119	5104	15337	13	1121	5736
洪泽县 Hongze County	7571	4849	8471	20	877	2451
盱眙县 Xuyi County	7867	4743	11464	175	1020	3691
金湖县 Jinhu County	8501	4474	8399	3	728	2229
淮安市 Huaian City	11744	7570	17473	22	988	6143
盐城市 Yancheng Municipality	**188510**	**115199**	**185729**	**4215**	**7161**	**58296**
市区 Urban District	47761	28897	41139	3515	1815	6210
响水县 Xiangshui County	6898	4172	9146	48	428	3275
滨海县 Binhai County	10327	5965	18288	114	700	7386
阜宁县 Funing County	14076	8523	17595	155	860	7476

2—19 续表 2 Continued 2

市县名称 Municipality and County		财政收入 Total Financial Revenue	#地方财政收入 Local Revenue	地方财政支出 Local Financial Expenditure	#基本建设支出 Capital Construction	#支农支出及农村水利费支出 Farming and Rural Water Conservang Funds	#教育事业费支出 Educational Services Funds
射阳县	Sheyang County	18543	12472	20968	30	574	7822
建湖县	Jianhu County	17689	10269	19989	91	525	6582
盐都县	Yandou County	20002	12222	16617	79	404	5862
东台市	Dongtai City	29137	17853	23418	56	1216	7884
大丰市	Dafeng City	24077	14826	18569	127	639	5799
扬州市	**Yangzhou Mucipality**	**204067**	**99717**	**142919**	**5001**	**10743**	**34781**
市区	Urban District	61003	32247	51675	3633	3308	7993
宝应县	Baoying County	16221	8045	15588	85	1005	5572
邗江县	HanJiang County	20444	9252	14193	598	763	4376
仪征市	Yizheng City	48325	21645	22856	120	3049	4501
高邮市	Gaoyou City	17527	9119	16368	225	1308	5666
江都市	Jiangdu City	40547	19409	22239	340	1310	6673
镇江市	**ZhenJiang Municipality**	**178287**	**87458**	**107296**	**2442**	**9049**	**27788**
市区	Urban District	77036	37193	41947	904	3183	7035
丹徒县	Dantu County	17304	9721	13626	121	1790	4573
丹阳市	Danyang City	46843	21797	25111	1236	1546	8975
扬中市	Yangzhong City	20451	10088	13287	89	1202	3075
句容市	Jurong City	16653	8659	13325	92	1328	4130
泰州市	**Taizhou Municipality**	**207598**	**109894**	**146216**	**2384**	**5638**	**34066**
市区	Urban District	79857	44414	54405	1730	555	3177
兴化市	Xinghua City	22513	13264	21927	42	1300	8026
靖江市	JingJiang City	32672	17268	19265	110	1162	5476
泰兴市	Taixing City	42133	19235	27208	153	1328	10176
姜堰市	Jiangyan City	30423	15713	23411	349	1293	7211
宿迁市	**Suqian Municipality**	**76768**	**34224**	**80737**	**696**	**5235**	**26059**
市区	Urban District			5275	510	10	81
宿豫县	Suyu County	14745	9536	18203	162	1613	6488
沭阳县	Shuyang County	12065	8688	19022	7	949	7584
泗阳县	Siyang County	24535	7150	18665	11	1290	6720
泗洪县	sihong County	25423	8850	19572	6	1373	5186

2—20 金 融 主 要 指 标
MAJOR INDICATORS OF BANKING (1996)

单位:万元 (10000yuan)

市县名称 Municipality and County	年末金融机构存款余额 Yeat—end Deposits Balance of Banking Institutions	#银行存款 Deposits Balance of Bank	年末金融机构贷款余额 Year—end Loans Balance of Banking Institutions	#银行贷款 Loans Balance of Bank	城乡居民储蓄余额 Savings Deposit of Urban and Rural Residents	#城镇居民 Urban Residents
南京市 Nanjing Municipality	**8328407**	**7673563**	**5676672**	**5290792**	**3589993**	**3291438**
市区 Urban District	7437330	7032216	4765184	4535046	2996035	2852079
江宁县 Jiangning County	347357	237686	305238	237948	222980	148958
江浦县 Jiangpu County	118346	91667	134174	111707	71861	58768
六合县 Liuhe County	175820	132192	188329	163942	130161	103594
溧水县 Lishui County	133051	94324	149155	124780	87063	66055
高淳县 Gaochun County	116503	85478	134592	117369	81893	61984
无锡市 Wuxi Municipality	**5532623**	**3800296**	**4015055**	**2878161**	**2926110**	**2276542**
市区 Urban District	2724315	1855480	2090077	1579999	1258798	1081933
江阴市 Jiangyin City	1095485	732607	772486	519430	594694	435893
宜兴市 Yixing City	788517	559185	494934	350622	484988	361850
锡山市 Xishan City	924306	653024	657558	428110	587630	396866
徐州市 Xuzhou Municipality	**2950050**	**2141144**	**2388715**	**1901305**	**1828200**	**1423241**
市区 Urban District	1624215	1268792	1323614	1157848	811756	763162
丰县 Fengxian County	160051	110956	139456	102487	123305	82735
沛县 Peixian County	282481	195782	199805	136232	232008	155759
铜山县 Tongshan County	397126	230986	288921	167488	275204	144215
睢宁县 Shuining County	129704	74918	127800	102780	107658	78469
新沂市 Xinyi City	144377	106237	144036	115772	108385	76843
邳州市 Pizhou City	212096	153473	165083	118698	169884	122058
常州市 Changzhou Municipality	**3223611**	**2313854**	**2640750**	**1989131**	**1726519**	**1319672**
市区 Urban District	1709555	1279759	1470085	1190753	772196	679120
溧阳市 Liyang City	388504	278872	321352	240830	259967	185696
金坛市 Jintan City	226144	171646	214497	158142	142439	108568
武进市 Wujin City	899408	583577	634816	399406	551917	346288
苏州市 Suzhou Municipality	**7447982**	**5819282**	**5370165**	**4275544**	**4082648**	**3107614**
市区 Urban District	2304961	1981235	1739745	1588161	888649	807507
常熟市 Changshu City	1301154	855547	877708	554418	837401	550745
张家港市 Zhangjiagang City	1044547	830577	766552	612279	693995	533778
昆山市 Kunshan City	739210	575243	525857	396916	398843	299074

单位:万元　　2—20 续表1 Continued 1　　(10000yuan)

市县名称 Municipality and County		年末金融机构存款余额 Yeat—end Deposits Balance of Banking Institutions	#银行存款 Deposits Balance of Bank	年末金融机构贷款余额 Year—end Loans Balance of Banking Institutions	#银行贷款 Loans Balance of Bank	城乡居民储蓄余额 Savings Deposit of Urban and Rural Residents	#城镇居民 Urban Residents
吴江市	Wujiang City	657137	500151	523205	398643	343038	255002
太仓市	Taicang City	523096	390558	362082	277647	337449	229679
吴县市	Wuxie City	877877	685971	575016	447480	583273	431829
南通市	**Nantong Muncipatity**	**4562735**	**2924261**	**3017054**	**2079472**	**3218069**	**2259653**
市区	Urban District	1361135	1066069	1086378	859943	647024	597813
海安县	Haian County	465634	261342	260468	160642	377043	237969
如东县	Rudong County	433658	255247	329403	221478	358441	218449
启东市	Qidong City	652308	369101	371431	234456	539453	344495
如皋市	Rugao City	420957	248471	299067	195434	322262	223983
通州市	Tongzhou City	664952	355380	369994	208576	521626	322108
海门市	Haimen City	564091	368651	300313	198943	452220	314836
连云港市	**Lianyungang Municipality**	**1280764**	**1018886**	**1270659**	**1094098**	**773392**	**621672**
市区	Urban District	748686	638057	693534	615156	375526	341972
赣榆县	Gaiyu County	161892	111063	139811	106771	121439	83156
东海县	Donghai County	170605	120419	174516	141462	121701	82429
灌云县	Guanyun County	133598	96535	164442	141058	103137	73321
灌南县	Guannan County	65983	52812	98356	89651	51589	40794
淮阴市	**Huaiyin Municipality**	**1117811**	**899236**	**1260536**	**1126475**	**698254**	**584891**
市区	Urban District	466520	379352	523346	463123	204981	197948
淮阴县	Huaiyin County	90768	68632	97845	85862	68453	50147
涟水县	Lianshui County	99779	78522	132258	122859	79448	61609
洪泽县	Hongze County	87437	72178	100195	91804	65715	52551
盱眙县	Xuyi County	92281	70221	129261	116159	67092	49793
金湖县	Jinhu County	119696	96195	122859	108698	87111	69620
淮安市	Huaian City	161330	134136	154772	137970	125454	103223
盐城市	**Yancheng Municipality**	**2440212**	**1706640**	**2215659**	**1674407**	**1753668**	**1247049**
市区	Urban District	541223	387585	517777	401484	258524	210569
响水县	Xiangshui County	86199	62677	103236	90262	68099	50164
滨海县	Binhai County	151243	111972	137160	110933	123232	93425
阜宁县	Funing County	196597	143702	159341	117823	166603	121203

市县名称 Municipality and County	年末金融机构存款余额 Yeat—end Deposits Balance of Banking Institutions	#银行存款 Deposits Balance of Bank	年末金融机构贷款余额 Year—end Loans Balance of Banking Institutions	#银行贷款 Loans Balance of Bank	城乡居民储蓄余额 Savings Deposit of Urban and Rural Residents	#城镇居民 Urban Residents
射阳县 Sheyang County	260494	188696	294218	231179	197942	142158
建湖县 Jianhu County	213612	156980	198442	152609	168187	126126
盐都县 Yandou County	259771	165380	223558	154585	197360	132688
东台市 Dongtai City	424094	282425	293295	192917	342886	217594
大丰市 Dafeng City	306979	207223	288632	222615	230835	153122
扬州市 Yangzhou Mucipality	**2420954**	**1530767**	**2012994**	**1473125**	**1563311**	**1234185**
市区 Urban District	836648	505172	737550	520762	412087	389125
宝应县 Baoying County	210891	140384	213458	173755	163395	115251
邗江县 HanJiang County	229089	156872	181265	127011	156412	104827
仪征市 Yizheng City	307371	239510	230012	199018	187054	155825
高邮市 Gaoyou City	256919	158377	247307	174971	187114	133351
江都市 Jiangdu City	580036	330452	403402	277608	457249	335806
镇江市 ZhenJiang Municipality	**1834727**	**1478980**	**1552813**	**1238245**	**1151723**	**938650**
市区 Urban District	726836	619269	751955	634561	351102	331782
丹徒县 Dantu County	210409	164481	176322	131064	132308	98289
丹阳市 Danyang City	450665	349778	316464	238005	333392	256088
扬中市 Yangzhong City	260067	200925	158659	115247	193326	146781
句容市 Jurong City	186750	144527	149413	119368	141595	105710
泰州市 Taizhou Municipality	**2213975**	**1530648**	**1799569**	**1347773**	**1519494**	**1135227**
市区 Urban District	537274	451441	406023	344775	220853	202459
兴化市 Xinghua City	380515	205165	382274	277048	307932	186569
靖江市 JingJiang City	391065	258234	332035	243316	284779	225636
泰兴市 Taixing City	501497	367390	393476	290247	397106	294562
姜堰市 Jiangyan City	403624	248418	285761	192387	308824	226001
宿迁市 Suqian Municipality	**522479**	**365964**	**530021**	**460865**	**394439**	**304579**
市区 Urban District						
宿豫县 Suyu County	140480	98336	160060	137724	102228	79727
沭阳县 Shuyang County	128453	89917	145034	130444	104418	80384
泗阳县 Siyang County	118054	82867	113737	93342	90283	69544
泗洪县 sihong County	135492	94844	111190	99355	97510	74924

2—21 人　民　生　活
PEOPLE' S LIVELIHOOD (1996)

市县名称 Municipality and County	全部职工工资总额（万元） Goss Wage Bill of Total Staff and Workers	#国有经济 State-Owned Units	全部职工平均工资（元） Average Wage of Total Staff and Workers	#国有经济 State-Owned Units	农民人均纯收入（元） Per Capita Net Income of Persants
南京市 Nanjing Municipality	**1172621**	**901127**	**8013**	**8664**	**3128**
市区 Urban District	1057306	822900	8415	9020	
江宁县 Jiangning County	33818	22699	6028	6541	3255
江浦县 Jiangpu County	15456	10006	5481	5851	2865
六合县 Liuhe County	24685	17210	5208	5756	2937
溧水县 Lishui County	23121	14469	5545	5954	2970
高淳县 Gaochun County	18235	13843	5443	6350	2969
无锡市 Wuxi Municipality	**599231**	**365760**	**8059**	**8455**	**4610**
市区 Urban District	374849	221487	8403	8744	
江阴市 Jiangyin City	83118	45820	7834	8485	4909
宜兴市 Yixing City	69342	50599	6927	7344	4043
锡山市 Xishan City	71922	47854	7878	8485	4832
徐州市 Xuzhou Municipality	**584442**	**506673**	**6280**	**6933**	**2390**
市区 Urban District	402383	358696	7209	7878	3354
丰县 Fengxian County	23675	19331	4793	5239	2162
沛县 Peixian County	28358	23901	4410	4868	2362
铜山县 Tongshan County	39197	32588	5377	5840	2770
睢宁县 Shuining County	24565	21164	4418	4876	2121
新沂市 Xinyi City	29969	22876	5149	5762	2302
邳州市 Pizhou City	36295	28117	5034	5557	2360
常州市 Changzhou Municipality	**430388**	**260681**	**7983**	**8469**	**4172**
市区 Urban District	285095	168807	8595	8979	
溧阳市 Liyang City	45097	29372	6854	7474	3646
金坛市 Jintan City	32718	21285	6208	6888	3722
武进市 Wujin City	67478	41217	7590	8310	5046
苏州市 Suzhou Municipality	**735361**	**450781**	**7742**	**8340**	**5088**
市区 Urban District	320940	207730	8032	8573	
常熟市 Changshu City	100662	60894	7920	8674	5125
张家港市 Zhangjiagang City	80922	45444	7803	8072	5407
昆山市 Kunshan City	69966	35154	7924	8471	4827

2－21 续表 1 Continued 1

市县名称 Municipality and County	全部职工工资总额（万元）Goss Wage Bill of Total Staff and Workers	#国有经济 State-Owned Units	全部职工平均工资（元）Average Wage of Total Staff and Workers	#国有经济 State-Owned Units	农民人均纯收入（元）Per Capita Net Income of Persants
吴江市 Wujiang City	60966	36514	7008	8025	5153
太仓市 Taicang City	45474	30255	7566	7899	4874
吴县市 Wuxie City	56431	34790	6718	7498	4956
南通市 Nantong Muncipatity	**521924**	**294959**	**6232**	**6771**	**3168**
市区 Urban District	196568	113840	7294	7445	
海安县 Haian County	50273	24200	5248	6065	2964
如东县 Rudong County	54854	27588	5892	5984	3008
启东市 Qidong City	52822	31330	5902	6355	3880
如皋市 Rugao City	51575	27568	5142	6140	2271
通州市 Tongzhou City	66912	39837	6111	6857	3417
海门市 Haimen City	48920	30596	6130	6891	3789
连云港市 Lianyungang Municipality	**231570**	**182891**	**5175**	**5698**	**2396**
市区 Urban District	136167	108189	5832	6338	3343
赣榆县 Gaiyu County	22846	17814	4588	5046	2512
东海县 Donghai County	26409	20988	4716	4985	2545
灌云县 Guanyun County	31718	24792	4637	5343	2383
灌南县 Guannan County	14430	11108	3626	4192	1857
淮阴市 Huaiyin Municipality	**224669**	**178408**	**4647**	**5128**	**2276**
市区 Urban District	93963	78656	5928	6468	2770
淮阴县 Huaiyin County	18749	14762	4041	4254	2022
涟水县 Lianshui County	22591	16822	3734	3921	1923
洪泽县 Hongze County	15429	11618	4082	4520	2559
盱眙县 Xuyi County	22269	18589	4299	4556	2211
金湖县 Jinhu County	19637	14953	4743	5228	2622
淮安市 Huaian City	32032	23008	3678	4293	2548
盐城市 Yancheng Municipality	**359964**	**248603**	**4922**	**5621**	**2546**
市区 Urban District	100458	81710	6271	6809	2547
响水县 Xiangshui County	17047	11899	3780	4343	1866
滨海县 Binhai County	21761	16198	3720	4319	1998
阜宁县 Funing County	25493	18069	4380	4964	2257

2—21 续表 2 Continued 2

市县名称 Municipality and County		全部职工工资总额(万元) Goss Wage Bill of Total Staff and Workers	#国有经济 State—Owned Units	全部职工平均工资(元) Average Wage of Total Staff and Workers	#国有经济 State—Owned Units	农民人均纯收入(元) Per Capita Net Income of Persants
射阳县	Sheyang County	43696	28347	4683	5410	2861
建湖县	Jianhu County	33141	18390	4515	5123	2592
盐都县	Yandou County	29834	16541	4743	5645	2861
东台市	Dongtai City	46728	29226	4519	5127	3020
大丰市	Dafeng City	41806	28223	5479	6083	3225
扬州市	**Yangzhou Mucipality**	**396691**	**256223**	**6443**	**7119**	**2937**
市区	Urban District	175226	135368	7428	8082	
宝应县	Baoying County	35433	22401	4756	5572	2803
邗江县	HanJiang County	28575	13530	5761	6412	3129
仪征市	Yizheng City	68896	35382	7095	6701	2840
高邮市	Gaoyou City	37739	22033	5286	6070	2845
江都市	Jiangdu City	50822	27509	5828	6550	3090
镇江市	**ZhenJiang Municipality**	**296904**	**203480**	**6669**	**7249**	**3523**
市区	Urban District	165319	121157	7147	7582	
丹徒县	Dantu County	24803	15308	6035	6656	3161
丹阳市	Danyang City	54357	36263	6372	6920	3601
扬中市	Yangzhong City	25250	13097	6219	7157	4166
句容市	Jurong City	27175	17655	5794	6491	3134
泰州市	**Taizhou Municipality**	**266849**	**151334**	**5066**	**5809**	**2951**
市区	Urban District	60539	33789	5793	6143	3351
兴化市	Xinghua City	43352	30462	4433	5344	2585
靖江市	JingJiang City	51853	26590	4901	5922	3276
泰兴市	Taixing City	64780	39226	4934	5735	2890
姜堰市	Jiangyan City	46325	21267	5306	6042	2882
宿迁市	**Suqian Municipality**	**126593**	**101795**	**4325**	**4920**	**1993**
市区	Urban District	15213	9809	4168	4808	2010
宿豫县	Suyu County	19854	16402	4639	5378	2010
沭阳县	Shuyang County	28987	22051	3760	4341	2002
泗阳县	Siyang County	31125	26421	4281	4761	1920
泗洪县	sihong County	31414	27112	4939	5455	2028

2—22 文 教 卫 生 事 业
CULTURE EDUCATION AND HEALTH CARE SERVICES (1996)

市县名称 Municipality and County		高等学校在校学生(人) Student Enrollment in Institutions of High Education (person)	普通中学在校学生(万人) Student Enrollment in Primary Schools (10000 persons)	小学在校学生数(万人) Student Enrollment in Primary Schools (10000 persons)	卫生机构数(个) Health Care Institutions	医院床位数(张) Hospital Beds	医生数(人) Doctors (person)
南京市	**Nanjing Municipality**	**111956**	**22.90**	**44.33**	**1170**	**20383**	**15866**
市区	Urban District	111149	12.78	19.66	872	15904	13118
江宁县	Jiangning County		3.31	7.16	63	1174	801
江浦县	Jiangpu County	807	1.25	3.15	61	537	367
六合县	Liuhe County		2.45	7.33	74	1094	726
溧水县	Lishui County		1.59	3.62	39	617	422
高淳县	Gaochun County		1.52	3.41	61	1057	432
无锡市	**Wuxi Municipality**	**8808**	**20.93**	**39.52**	**1442**	**14034**	**9289**
市区	Urban District	8808	5.68	9.23	683	6458	4612
江阴市	Jiangyin City		5.17	11.67	254	2801	1673
宜兴市	Yixing City		4.91	9.50	333	2195	1507
锡山市	Xishan City		5.17	9.12	172	2580	1497
徐州市	**Xuzhou Municipality**	**18647**	**46.32**	**118.08**	**1052**	**15814**	**11525**
市区	Urban District	18647	7.99	15.99	519	8005	5619
丰县	Fengxian County		5.28	13.24	82	1027	761
沛县	Peixian County		7.05	15.94	109	1754	1457
铜山县	Tongshan County		8.18	16.51	123	1478	1030
睢宁县	Shuining County		5.66	17.50	69	1160	836
新沂市	Xinyi City		4.49	14.72	67	1174	936
邳州市	Pizhou City		7.67	24.18	83	1216	886
常州市	**Changzhou Municipality**	**12182**	**15.71**	**28.93**	**855**	**10839**	**7520**
市区	Urban District	12182	3.90	6.39	475	4791	3684
溧阳市	Liyang City		3.49	6.75	120	1751	1084
金坛市	Jintan City		2.55	5.20	92	1328	992
武进市	Wujin City		5.77	10.59	168	2969	1760
苏州市	**Suzhou Municipality**	**25749**	**26.01**	**45.59**	**1485**	**17401**	**12313**
市区	Urban District	21979	5.31	8.18	633	5546	4823
常熟市	Changshu City	2414	4.57	7.49	206	3125	1820
张家港市	Zhangjiagang City	1356	3.82	8.17	130	2273	1382
昆山市	Kunshan City		2.74	4.59	92	1551	1081

2—22 续表 1 Continued 1

市县名称 Municipality and County		高等学校在校学生(人) Student En-rollment in Institutions of High Education (person)	普通中学在校学生(万人) Student Enrollment in Primary Schools (10000 persons)	小学在校学生数(万人) Student Enrollment in Primary Schools (10000 persons)	卫生机构数(个) Health Care Institutions	医院床位数(张) Hospital Beds	医生数(人) Doctors (person)
吴江市	Wujiang City		3.19	5.84	72	1647	882
太仓市	Taicang City		1.71	3.07	155	1449	900
吴县市	Wuxie City		4.67	8.25	197	1810	1425
南通市	**Nantong Muncipatity**	**8359**	**31.26**	**61.24**	**1255**	**18810**	**12610**
市区	Urban District	8359	2.74	4.37	303	4438	3139
海安县	Haian County		4.39	8.05	126	1849	1337
如东县	Rudong County		3.87	8.49	173	2338	1685
启东市	Qidong City		4.68	9.27	123	2978	1733
如皋市	Rugao City		5.95	12.82	152	2502	1679
通州市	Tongzhou City		5.50	10.80	210	2624	1720
海门市	Haimen City		4.13	7.44	168	2081	1317
连云港市	**Lianyungang Municipality**	**6871**	**24.00**	**58.98**	**797**	**6603**	**5130**
市区	Urban District	6871	3.44	8.09	392	2703	2305
赣榆县	Gaiyu County		5.67	14.58	76	904	855
东海县	Donghai County		6.01	14.83	88	1097	678
灌云县	Guanyun County		5.43	12.59	143	1197	803
灌南县	Guannan County		3.45	8.89	98	780	489
淮阴市	**Huaiyin Municipality**	**5344**	**22.23**	**47.48**	**663**	**7860**	**5227**
市区	Urban District	5344	2.33	4.67	177	2512	1395
淮阴县	Huaiyin County		3.79	8.29	80	544	532
涟水县	Lianshui County		4.79	10.54	102	1121	779
洪泽县	Hongze County		1.77	2.64	63	613	428
盱眙县	Xuyi County		2.99	7.83	94	925	785
金湖县	Jinhu County		1.49	3.26	72	724	466
淮安市	Huaian City		5.07	10.25	75	1421	842
盐城市	**Yancheng Municipality**	**7150**	**39.98**	**85.90**	**907**	**12949**	**9845**
市区	Urban District	7150	2.76	5.37	126	1331	1281
响水县	Xiangshui County		2.54	8.23	52	919	603
滨海县	Binhai County		5.50	12.96	90	1028	1002
阜宁县	Funing County		6.32	12.67	80	1401	1152

2—22 续表 2 Continued 2

市县名称 Municipality and County		高等学校在校学生(人) Student Enrollment in Institutions of High Education (person)	普通中学在校学生(万人) Student Enrollment in Primary Schools (10000 persons)	小学在校学生数(万人) Student Enrollment in Primary Schools (10000 persons)	卫生机构数(个) Health Care Institutions	医院床位数(张) Hospital Beds	医生数(人) Doctors (person)
射阳县	Sheyang County		6.19	10.78	75	1646	1222
建湖县	Jianhu County		4.06	8.63	163	1408	969
盐都县	Yandou County		4.95	10.48	90	1445	937
东台市	Dongtai City		4.54	10.42	152	2524	1604
大丰市	Dafeng City		3.13	6.35	79	1607	1075
扬州市	**Yangzhou Mucipality**	**18930**	**18.18**	**34.86**	**789**	**10482**	**7552**
市区	Urban District	18930	2.37	3.83	274	3348	2503
宝应县	Baoying County		3.65	6.89	92	1224	883
邗江县	HanJiang County		2.44	4.75	75	838	685
仪征市	Yizheng City		2.46	4.76	111	1360	986
高邮市	Gaoyou City		2.94	6.23	98	1479	979
江都市	Jiangdu City		4.32	8.40	139	2233	1516
镇江市	**ZhenJiang Municipality**	**16433**	**12.29**	**22.73**	**731**	**7274**	**5318**
市区	Urban District	14583	2.39	4.09	402	3380	2515
丹徒县	Dantu County		2.17	3.55	75	695	433
丹阳市	Danyang City		3.75	7.19	129	1576	1133
扬中市	Yangzhong City		1.34	2.47	53	593	520
句容市	Jurong City	1850	2.64	5.43	72	1030	717
泰州市	**Taizhou Municipality**		**20.03**	**42.16**	**208**	**10351**	**6199**
市区	Urban District		1.26	2.11	17	1412	794
兴化市	Xinghua City		5.35	14.23	58	2252	1257
靖江市	JingJiang City		3.09	5.23	34	2053	1131
泰兴市	Taixing City		6.25	11.98	51	2774	1856
姜堰市	Jiangyan City		4.08	8.61	48	1860	1161
宿迁市	**Suqian Municipality**		**23.11**	**56.07**	**367**	**4766**	**3579**
市区	Urban District		2.16	2.41	86	135	85
宿豫县	Suyu County		4.19	8.84	28	840	585
沭阳县	Shuyang County		6.98	21.13	103	1372	1614
泗阳县	Siyang County		5.65	12.76	83	1235	686
泗洪县	sihong County		4.13	10.93	67	1184	609

县（市）社会经济序列指标 3

SOCIAL ECONOMIC INDICATORS OF COUNTY (CITY) BY RANK

3－1 年末总人口
YEAN END TOTAL POPULATION (1996)

位次 No.	县（市）名称 County (City)		指标值（万人）Value (10000 persons)	位次 No.	县（市）名称 County (City)		指标值（万人）Value (10000 persons)
1	沭阳县	Shuyang County	158.23	33	吴县市	Wuxie City	97.22
2	兴化市	Xinghua City	153.54	34	新沂市	Xinyi City	94.10
3	邳州市	Pizhou City	150.11	35	宝应县	Baoying County	90.61
4	通州市	Tongzhou City	145.57	36	宿豫县	Suyu County	89.51
5	如皋市	Rugao City	145.14	37	盐都县	Yandou County	87.00
6	泰兴市	Taixing City	142.86	38	张家港市	Zhangjiagang City	85.20
7	铜山县	Tongshan County	130.30	39	高邮市	Gaoyou City	83.18
8	武进市	Wujin City	122.96	40	丹阳市	Danyang City	80.96
9	睢宁县	Shuining County	122.12	41	淮阴县	Huaiyin County	80.57
10	淮安市	Huaian City	118.92	42	建湖县	Jianhu County	79.50
11	东台市	Dongtai City	117.37	43	吴江市	Wujiang City	77.65
12	启东市	Qidong City	116.66	44	溧阳市	Liyang City	77.64
13	江阴市	Jiangyin City	114.16	45	江宁县	Jiangning County	74.10
14	沛县	Peixian County	113.32	46	大丰市	Dafeng City	74.00
15	如东县	Rudong County	113.20	47	盱眙县	Xuyi County	70.95
16	泗阳县	Siyang County	110.85	48	灌南县	Guannan County	68.39
17	宜兴市	Yixing City	109.25	49	六合县	Liuhe County	68.32
18	阜宁县	Funing County	107.70	50	靖江市	JingJiang City	66.18
19	东海县	Donghai County	107.07	51	句容市	Jurong City	60.28
20	江都市	Jiangdu City	106.94	52	仪征市	Yizheng City	59.09
21	滨海县	Binhai County	106.68	53	昆山市	Kunshan City	58.34
22	姜堰市	Jiangyan City	106.33	54	邗江县	HanJiang County	55.19
23	常熟市	Changshu City	104.34	55	响水县	Xiangshui County	54.63
24	海门市	Haimen City	103.46	56	金坛市	Jintan City	54.15
25	射阳县	Sheyang County	102.31	57	太仓市	Taicang City	44.93
26	丰县	Fengxian County	102.14	58	高淳县	Gaochun County	43.10
27	赣榆县	Gaiyu County	100.89	59	丹徒县	Dantu County	41.58
28	涟水县	Lianshui County	99.10	60	溧水县	Lishui County	40.82
29	海安县	Haian County	99.00	61	洪泽县	Hongze County	36.68
30	锡山市	Xishan City	98.98	62	金湖县	Jinhu County	34.73
31	灌云县	Guanyun County	98.44	63	江浦县	Jiangpu County	29.71
32	泗洪县	Sihong County	97.53	64	扬中市	Yangzhong City	27.73

3—2 国内生产总值
GROSS DOMESTIC PRODUCT (1996)

位次 No.	县（市）名称 County (City)		指标值（万元）Value (10000yuan)	位次 No.	县（市）名称 County (City)		指标值（万元）Value (10000yuan)
1	锡山市	Xishan City	2317580	33	赣榆县	Gaiyu County	473348
2	张家港市	Zhangjiagang City	2300711	34	仪征市	Yizheng City	459919
3	江阴市	Jiangyin City	2220249	35	邗江县	HanJiang County	457513
4	武进市	Wujin City	1843389	36	扬中市	Yangzhong City	452658
5	常熟市	Changshu City	1802533	37	东海县	Donghai County	440034
6	宜兴市	Yixing City	1452390	38	丹徒县	Dantu County	430767
7	吴江市	Wujiang City	1425384	39	沛县	Peixian County	429850
8	吴县市	Wuxie City	1400295	40	高邮市	Gaoyou City	428834
9	昆山市	Kunshan City	1143808	41	宝应县	Baoying County	401001
10	丹阳市	Danyang City	1000029	42	建湖县	Jianhu County	365062
11	太仓市	Taicang City	951201	43	新沂市	Xinyi City	365004
12	通州市	Tongzhou City	905174	44	淮安市	Huaian City	364438
13	启东市	Qidong City	851191	45	灌云县	Guanyun County	361856
14	海门市	Haimen City	800092	46	睢宁县	Shuining County	325923
15	泰兴市	Taixing City	771996	47	阜宁县	Funing County	324106
16	溧阳市	Liyang City	720341	48	沭阳县	Shuyang County	320020
17	江都市	Jiangdu City	703614	49	泗洪县	Sihong County	305187
18	铜山县	Tongshan County	691963	50	六合县	Liuhe County	297426
19	江宁县	Jiangning County	660443	51	丰县	Fengxian County	296472
20	如东县	Rudong County	630091	52	溧水县	Lishui County	286322
21	东台市	Dongtai City	615000	53	滨海县	Binhai County	281313
22	如皋市	Rugao City	593511	54	泗阳县	Siyang County	269223
23	兴化市	Xinghua City	564199	55	宿豫县	Suyu County	258971
24	大丰市	Dafeng City	560982	56	高淳县	Gaochun County	237147
25	邳州市	Pizhou City	551857	57	盱眙县	Xuyi County	220494
26	靖江市	JingJiang City	531423	58	淮阴县	Huaiyin County	217565
27	姜堰市	Jiangyan City	526229	59	涟水县	Lianshui County	200877
28	盐都县	Yandou County	517772	60	金湖县	Jinhu County	186082
29	金坛市	Jintan City	513287	61	江浦县	Jiangpu County	157273
30	射阳县	Sheyang County	512612	62	响水县	Xiangshui County	157172
31	句容市	Jurong City	501397	63	灌南县	Guannan County	156136
32	海安县	Haian County	501108	64	洪泽县	Hongze County	133386

3－3 人均国内生产总值
PER CAPITA GROSS DOMESTIC PRODUCT (1996)

位次 No.	县（市）名称 County（City）		指标值（元）Value（yuan）	位次 No.	县（市）名称 County（City）		指标值（元）Value（yuan）
1	张家港市	Zhangjiagang City	27029	33	江浦县	Jiangpu County	5281
2	锡山市	Xishan City	23426	34	东台市	Dongtai City	5235
3	太仓市	Taicang City	21180	35	高邮市	Gaoyou City	5157
4	昆山市	Kunshan City	19656	36	海安县	Haian County	5062
5	江阴市	Jiangyin City	19486	37	射阳县	Sheyang County	5021
6	吴江市	Wujiang City	18349	38	姜堰市	Jiangyan City	4947
7	常熟市	Changshu City	17274	39	赣榆县	Gaiyu County	4715
8	扬中市	Yangzhong City	16341	40	建湖县	Jianhu County	4592
9	武进市	Wujin City	15079	41	宝应县	Baoying County	4415
10	吴县市	Wuxie City	14411	42	六合县	Liuhe County	4352
11	宜兴市	Yixing City	13301	43	东海县	Donghai County	4141
12	丹阳市	Danyang City	12367	44	如皋市	Rugao City	4089
13	丹徒县	Dantu County	10283	45	新沂市	Xinyi City	3941
14	金坛市	Jintan City	9486	46	沛县	Peixian County	3804
15	溧阳市	Liyang City	9292	47	灌云县	Guanyun County	3700
16	江宁县	Jiangning County	8919	48	邳州市	Pizhou City	3683
17	句容市	Jurong City	8326	49	兴化市	Xinghua City	3676
18	邗江县	HanJiang County	8252	50	洪泽县	Hongze County	3634
19	靖江市	JingJiang City	8040	51	泗洪县	Sihong County	3139
20	仪征市	Yizheng City	7806	52	盱眙县	Xuyi County	3117
21	海门市	Haimen City	7735	53	淮安市	Huaian City	3078
22	大丰市	Dafeng City	7584	54	阜宁县	Funing County	3005
23	启东市	Qidong City	7304	55	丰县	Fengxian County	2912
24	溧水县	Lishui County	7028	56	宿豫县	Suyu County	2894
25	江都市	Jiangdu City	6580	57	响水县	Xiangshui County	2885
26	通州市	Tongzhou City	6214	58	淮阴县	Huaiyin County	2712
27	盐都县	Yandou County	5905	59	睢宁县	Shuining County	2679
28	如东县	Rudong County	5560	60	滨海县	Binhai County	2641
29	高淳县	Gaochun County	5506	61	泗阳县	Siyang County	2441
30	泰兴市	Taixing City	5418	62	灌南县	Guannan County	2287
31	金湖县	Jinhu County	5366	63	涟水县	Lianshui County	2033
32	铜山县	Tongshan County	5319	64	沭阳县	Shuyang County	2031

3—4 工农业总产值
TOTAL OUTPUT VALUE OF INDUSTRY AND AGRICUTURE (1996)

位次 No.	县（市）名称	County (City)	指标值（万元） Value (10000yuan)	位次 No.	县（市）名称	County (City)	指标值（万元） Value (10000yuan)
1	锡山市	Xishan City	7659747	33	邗江县	HanJiang County	1237972
2	江阴市	Jiangyin City	6070665	34	丹徒县	Dantu County	1175566
3	张家港市	Zhangjiagang City	5195401	35	兴化市	Xinghua City	1170008
4	武进市	Wujin City	4720080	36	金坛市	Jintan City	1137087
5	吴县市	Wuxie City	4031844	37	扬中市	Yangzhong City	1089550
6	宜兴市	Yixing City	3983007	38	沛县	Peixian County	1065268
7	常熟市	Changshu City	3905243	39	高邮市	Gaoyou City	1065182
8	吴江市	Wujiang City	3149098	40	建湖县	Jianhu County	1007900
9	昆山市	Kunshan City	2481235	41	海安县	Haian County	992510
10	丹阳市	Danyang City	2426583	42	宝应县	Baoying County	942972
11	铜山县	Tongshan County	2238049	43	睢宁县	Shuining County	933498
12	江宁县	Jiangning County	2099400	44	新沂市	Xinyi City	915896
13	通州市	Tongzhou City	2048640	45	溧水县	Lishui County	912299
14	太仓市	Taicang City	2039801	46	阜宁县	Funing County	884397
15	启东市	Qidong City	1770897	47	淮安市	Huaian City	876581
16	句容市	Jurong City	1628962	48	灌云县	Guanyun County	782555
17	溧阳市	Liyang City	1606322	49	丰县	Fengxian County	768056
18	海门市	Haimen City	1603244	50	六合县	Liuhe County	750441
19	泰兴市	Taixing City	1595797	51	宿豫县	Suyu County	731742
20	东台市	Dongtai City	1578998	52	沭阳县	Shuyang County	638868
21	赣榆县	Gaiyu County	1499058	53	泗阳县	Siyang County	634386
22	江都市	Jiangdu City	1473888	54	泗洪县	Sihong County	605365
23	大丰市	Dafeng City	1424891	55	滨海县	Binhai County	573347
24	盐都县	Yandou County	1412250	56	高淳县	Gaochun County	565443
25	如皋市	Rugao City	1387135	57	淮阴县	Huaiyin County	528899
26	射阳县	Sheyang County	1357463	58	盱眙县	Xuyi County	435801
27	邳州市	Pizhou City	1342132	59	涟水县	Lianshui County	429842
28	如东县	Rudong County	1337026	60	江浦县	Jiangpu County	384952
29	仪征市	Yizheng City	1322810	61	洪泽县	Hongze County	383282
30	东海县	Donghai County	1306515	62	金湖县	Jinhu County	378619
31	姜堰市	Jiangyan City	1247477	63	灌南县	Guannan County	352420
32	靖江市	JingJiang City	1241990	64	响水县	Xiangshui County	334836

3—5 人均工农业总产值
PER CAPITA TOTAL OUTPUT VALUE OF INDUSTRY AND AGRICULTURE (1996)

位次 No.	县（市）名称 County (City)		指标值（元） Value (yuan)	位次 No.	县（市）名称 County (City)		指标值（元） Value (yuan)
1	锡山市	Xishan City	77426	33	江浦县	Jiangpu County	12927
2	张家港市	Zhangjiagang City	61036	34	高邮市	Gaoyou City	12809
3	江阴市	Jiangyin City	53279	35	建湖县	Jianhu County	12678
4	太仓市	Taicang City	45420	36	东海县	Donghai County	12297
5	昆山市	Kunshan City	42640	37	如东县	Rudong County	11798
6	吴县市	Wuxie City	41493	38	姜堰市	Jiangyan City	11728
7	吴江市	Wujiang City	40539	39	泰兴市	Taixing City	11199
8	扬中市	Yangzhong City	39334	40	六合县	Liuhe County	10981
9	武进市	Wujin City	38610	41	金湖县	Jinhu County	10918
10	常熟市	Changshu City	37424	42	洪泽县	Hongze County	10441
11	宜兴市	Yixing City	36478	43	宝应县	Baoying County	10383
12	丹阳市	Danyang City	30010	44	海安县	Haian County	10025
13	江宁县	Jiangning County	28351	45	新沂市	Xinyi City	9889
14	丹徒县	Dantu County	28063	46	如皋市	Rugao City	9556
15	句容市	Jurong City	27050	47	沛 县	Peixian County	9428
16	仪征市	Yizheng City	22451	48	邳州市	Pizhou City	8957
17	溧水县	Lishui County	22393	49	阜宁县	Funing County	8200
18	邗江县	HanJiang County	22330	50	宿豫县	Suyu County	8178
19	金坛市	Jintan City	21014	51	灌云县	Guanyun County	8002
20	溧阳市	Liyang City	20721	52	睢宁县	Shuining County	7672
21	大丰市	Dafeng City	19263	53	兴化市	Xinghua City	7623
22	靖江市	JingJiang City	18790	54	丰 县	Fengxian County	7543
23	铜山县	Tongshan County	17203	55	淮安市	Huaian City	7404
24	盐都县	Yandou County	16105	56	淮阴县	Huaiyin County	6593
25	海门市	Haimen City	15499	57	泗洪县	Sihong County	6227
26	启东市	Qidong City	15196	58	盱眙县	Xuyi County	6161
27	赣榆县	Gaiyu County	14932	59	响水县	Xiangshui County	6146
28	通州市	Tongzhou City	14064	60	泗阳县	Siyang County	5751
29	江都市	Jiangdu City	13784	61	滨海县	Binhai County	5383
30	东台市	Dongtai City	13441	62	灌南县	Guannan County	5162
31	射阳县	Sheyang County	13295	63	涟水县	Lianshui County	4349
32	高淳县	Gaochun County	13128	64	沭阳县	Shuyang County	4054

3—6 粮食产量
OUTPUT OF GRAIN (1996)

位次 No.	县（市）名称 County（City）	指标值（万吨） Value (10000tons)	位次 No.	县（市）名称 County（City）	指标值（万吨） Value (10000tons)
1	兴化市 Xinghua City	119.52	33	新沂市 Xinyi City	54.29
2	沭阳县 Shuyang County	102.81	34	丹阳市 Danyang City	53.69
3	东海县 Donghai County	90.65	35	丰县 Fengxian County	52.24
4	淮安市 Huaian City	83.35	36	常熟市 Changshu City	52.10
5	泗洪县 Sihong County	82.97	37	泗阳县 Siyang County	51.73
6	射阳县 Sheyang County	81.65	38	江宁县 Jiangning County	49.40
7	如东县 Rudong County	81.41	39	建湖县 Jianhu County	46.83
8	铜山县 Tongshan County	79.94	40	吴江市 Wujiang City	46.33
9	邳州市 Pizhou City	78.25	41	溧阳市 Liyang City	46.03
10	东台市 Dongtai City	75.08	42	江阴市 Jiangyin City	45.82
11	武进市 Wujin City	73.91	43	锡山市 Xishan City	45.50
12	泰兴市 Taixing City	73.66	44	昆山市 Kunshan City	45.49
13	睢宁县 Shuining County	69.75	45	六合县 Liuhe County	44.94
14	灌云县 Guanyun County	69.73	46	淮阴县 Huaiyin County	44.77
15	如皋市 Rugao City	68.76	47	灌南县 Guannan County	41.11
16	涟水县 Lianshui County	67.63	48	启东市 Qidong City	40.75
17	高邮市 Gaoyou City	66.33	49	句容市 Jurong City	37.37
18	盱眙县 Xuyi County	65.39	50	金坛市 Jintan City	36.61
19	通州市 Tongzhou City	63.14	51	张家港市 Zhangjiagang City	35.36
20	沛县 Peixian County	62.25	52	金湖县 Jinhu County	34.53
21	宜兴市 Yixing City	60.83	53	响水县 Xiangshui County	33.82
22	阜宁县 Funing County	60.56	54	仪征市 Yizheng City	33.81
23	滨海县 Binhai County	59.62	55	洪泽县 Hongze County	30.24
24	大丰市 Dafeng City	58.38	56	靖江市 JingJiang City	30.20
25	姜堰市 Jiangyan City	58.33	57	太仓市 Taicang City	30.03
26	海安县 Haian County	57.97	58	邗江县 HanJiang County	29.75
27	宿豫县 Suyu County	57.43	59	海门市 Haimen City	28.17
28	宝应县 Baoying County	57.24	60	丹徒县 Dantu County	27.94
29	赣榆县 Gaiyu County	56.91	61	高淳县 Gaochun County	27.78
30	盐都县 Yandou County	56.42	62	溧水县 Lishui County	26.69
31	吴县市 Wuxie City	55.74	63	江浦县 Jiangpu County	17.77
32	江都市 Jiangdu City	54.37	64	扬中市 Yangzhong City	12.77

3－7 油 料 产 量
OUTPUT OF OIL BEARING CROP (1996)

位次 No.	县（市）名称 County (City)		指标值（吨）Value (tons)	位次 No.	县（市）名称 County (City)		指标值（吨）Value (tons)
1	东海县	Donghai County	64051	33	海安县	Haian County	17707
2	东台市	Dongtai City	63718	34	阜宁县	Funing County	17554
3	海门市	Haimen City	60984	35	淮阴县	Huaiyin County	16119
4	赣榆县	Gaiyu County	57814	36	江都市	Jiangdu City	15808
5	盱眙县	Xuyi County	57360	37	金湖县	Jinhu County	15637
6	通州市	Tongzhou City	54459	38	太仓市	Taicang City	15613
7	启东市	Qidong City	51931	39	丹阳市	Danyang City	15402
8	吴江市	Wujiang City	44059	40	邗江县	HanJiang County	13838
9	溧阳市	Liyang City	38632	41	淮安市	Huaian City	13629
10	如东县	Rudong County	37220	42	泰兴市	Taixing City	13417
11	沭阳县	Shuyang County	35875	43	盐都县	Yandou County	13389
12	江宁县	Jiangning County	34639	44	丹徒县	Dantu County	13047
13	高淳县	Gaochun County	34216	45	泗阳县	Siyang County	12721
14	兴化市	Xinghua City	32967	46	张家港市	Zhangjiagang City	12145
15	大丰市	Dafeng City	31037	47	武进市	Wujin City	11591
16	句容市	Jurong City	30664	48	锡山市	Xishan City	11248
17	涟水县	Lianshui County	30479	49	江浦县	Jiangpu County	10685
18	昆山市	Kunshan City	30375	50	建湖县	Jianhu County	10585
19	泗洪县	Sihong County	28924	51	仪征市	Yizheng City	9771
20	新沂市	Xinyi City	27459	52	睢宁县	Shuining County	9626
21	如皋市	Rugao City	26949	53	响水县	Xiangshui County	8172
22	高邮市	Gaoyou City	25888	54	洪泽县	Hongze County	7631
23	溧水县	Lishui County	25822	55	邳州市	Pizhou City	7009
24	六合县	Liuhe County	25194	56	沛县	Peixian County	7000
25	宜兴市	Yixing City	22990	57	丰县	Fengxian County	6766
26	射阳县	Sheyang County	21267	58	宿豫县	Suyu County	6218
27	吴县市	Wuxie City	20276	59	靖江市	JingJiang City	4619
28	姜堰市	Jiangyan City	19368	60	江阴市	Jiangyin City	3809
29	金坛市	Jintan City	19101	61	铜山县	Tongshan County	3165
30	滨海县	Binhai County	18147	62	灌南县	Guannan County	3123
31	常熟市	Changshu City	18105	63	灌云县	Guanyun County	480
32	宝应县	Baoying County	17812	64	扬中市	Yangzhong City	77

3—8 猪 牛 羊 肉 产 量

OUTPUT OF PORK BEEF AND MUTTON (1996)

位次 No.	县(市)名称 County (City)		指标值(吨) Value (tons)	位次 No.	县(市)名称 County (City)		指标值(吨) Value (tons)
1	阜宁县	Funing County	92398	33	灌南县	Guannan County	31943
2	淮安市	Huaian City	77267	34	海安县	Haian County	29496
3	泰兴市	Taixing City	74152	35	盱眙县	Xuyi County	29423
4	沭阳县	Shuyang County	67690	36	宜兴市	Yixing City	28273
5	睢宁县	Shuining County	65363	37	响水县	Xiangshui County	27957
6	铜山县	Tongshan County	65290	38	锡山市	Xishan City	27896
7	东海县	Donghai County	64142	39	句容市	Jurong City	27107
8	邳州市	Pizhou City	61905	40	江都市	Jiangdu City	26141
9	丰县	Fengxian County	60499	41	溧阳市	Liyang City	25833
10	东台市	Dongtai City	57789	42	江阴市	Jiangyin City	25816
11	如皋市	Rugao City	53361	43	六合县	Liuhe County	25557
12	盐都县	Yandou County	51636	44	启东市	Qidong City	25427
13	涟水县	Lianshui County	50675	45	建湖县	Jianhu County	25065
14	沛县	Peixian County	50331	46	靖江市	JingJiang City	22459
15	宿豫县	Suyu County	48759	47	宝应县	Baoying County	22450
16	灌云县	Guanyun County	47575	48	邗江县	HanJiang County	20481
17	大丰市	Dafeng City	45502	49	仪征市	Yizheng City	19494
18	武进市	Wujin City	44433	50	丹徒县	Dantu County	19432
19	淮阴县	Huaiyin County	43795	51	吴县市	Wuxie City	19035
20	高邮市	Gaoyou City	41053	52	吴江市	Wujiang City	18075
21	滨海县	Binhai County	40572	53	洪泽县	Hongze County	17950
22	新沂市	Xinyi City	39870	54	常熟市	Changshu City	17720
23	射阳县	Sheyang County	38883	55	张家港市	Zhangjiagang City	15390
24	泗阳县	Siyang County	38748	56	金湖县	Jinhu County	15264
25	姜堰市	Jiangyan City	38259	57	金坛市	Jintan City	14534
26	赣榆县	Gaiyu County	37644	58	高淳县	Gaochun County	13854
27	江宁县	Jiangning County	36611	59	昆山市	Kunshan City	13819
28	兴化市	Xinghua City	36356	60	溧水县	Lishui County	13582
29	泗洪县	Sihong County	34660	61	海门市	Haimen City	13341
30	丹阳市	Danyang City	34212	62	太仓市	Taicang City	13329
31	通州市	Tongzhou City	33195	63	江浦县	Jiangpu County	11202
32	如东县	Rudong County	32258	64	扬中市	Yangzhong City	9361

3—9 全部独立核算工业利税总额
TOTAL PRETAX PROFITS OF ALL INDUSTRIAL ENFERPRISES WITH INDEPENDENT ACCOUNTING SYSTEM (1996)

位次 No.	县（市）名称 County (City)		指标值（万元）Value (10000yuan)
1	江阴市	Jiangyin City	291332
2	张家港市	Zhangjiagang City	211336
3	锡山市	Xishan City	195697
4	常熟市	Changshu City	115793
5	武进市	Wujin City	110101
6	昆山市	Kunshan City	103757
7	仪征市	Yizheng City	95913
8	吴县市	Wuxie City	87207
9	吴江市	Wujiang City	85373
10	宜兴市	Yixing City	80533
11	江宁县	Jiangning County	56689
12	铜山县	Tongshan County	54521
13	扬中市	Yangzhong City	52173
14	邗江县	HanJiang County	51944
15	泰兴市	Taixing City	49780
16	太仓市	Taicang City	49662
17	溧阳市	Liyang City	42963
18	丹阳市	Danyang City	42413
19	通州市	Tongzhou City	35821
20	丹徒县	Dantu County	33652
21	盐都县	Yandou County	33369
22	泗阳县	Siyang County	33089
23	启东市	Qidong City	32402
24	建湖县	Jianhu County	31909
25	泗洪县	Sihong County	31729
26	江都市	Jiangdu City	31641
27	句容市	Jurong City	28484
28	海门市	Haimen City	28265
29	射阳县	Sheyang County	26135
30	靖江市	JingJiang City	26101
31	大丰市	Dafeng City	22972
32	姜堰市	Jiangyan City	21116
33	邳州市	Pizhou City	19740
34	金坛市	Jintan City	18977
35	阜宁县	Funing County	18112
36	宝应县	Baoying County	16894
37	东台市	Dongtai City	16720
38	高邮市	Gaoyou City	14845
39	赣榆县	Gaiyu County	14710
40	如东县	Rudong County	14455
41	溧水县	Lishui County	13962
42	沛县	Peixian County	13885
43	淮安市	Huaian City	12674
44	淮阴县	Huaiyin County	12328
45	新沂市	Xinyi City	11742
46	丰县	Fengxian County	11377
47	东海县	Donghai County	11296
48	睢宁县	Shuining County	11171
49	灌云县	Guanyun County	9871
50	洪泽县	Hongze County	9820
51	高淳县	Gaochun County	9753
52	金湖县	Jinhu County	9496
53	盱眙县	Xuyi County	9320
54	江浦县	Jiangpu County	7711
55	滨海县	Binhai County	7630
56	灌南县	Guannan County	6149
57	六合县	Liuhe County	5298
58	海安县	Haian County	5255
59	宿豫县	Suyu County	5227
60	兴化市	Xinghua City	5011
61	如皋市	Rugao City	4518
62	沭阳县	Shuyang County	4203
63	响水县	Xiangshui County	2675
64	涟水县	Lianshui County	—692

3－10 社会消费品零售额
TOTAL RETAIL SALES OF CONSUMER GOODS (1996)

位次 No.	县（市）名称	County (City)	指标值（万元） Value (10000yuan)	位次 No.	县（市）名称	County (City)	指标值（万元） Value (10000yuan)
1	常熟市	Changshu City	604680	33	邳州市	Pizhou City	121083
2	江阴市	Jiangyin City	525785	34	沭阳县	Shuyang County	120974
3	宜兴市	Yixing City	467831	35	建湖县	Jianhu County	120046
4	锡山市	Xishan City	445136	36	句容市	Jurong City	118607
5	武进市	Wujin City	386970	37	高淳县	Gaochun County	115144
6	吴县市	Wuxie City	331887	38	铜山县	Tongshan County	113006
7	溧阳市	Liyang City	330375	39	宝应县	Baoying County	112523
8	张家港市	Zhangjiagang City	321754	40	东海县	Donghai County	111888
9	通州市	Tongzhou City	295748	41	盐都县	Yandou County	111641
10	启东市	Qidong City	282110	42	泗阳县	Siyang County	109736
11	海门市	Haimen City	275541	43	沛县	Peixian County	109634
12	昆山市	Kunshan City	259704	44	灌云县	Guanyun County	102772
13	江都市	Jiangdu City	245789	45	扬中市	Yangzhong City	99378
14	如皋市	Rugao City	240489	46	淮安市	Huaian City	95930
15	吴江市	Wujiang City	238811	47	阜宁县	Funing County	95144
16	泰兴市	Taixing City	238804	48	新沂市	Xinyi City	93889
17	丹阳市	Danyang City	235180	49	丹徒县	Dantu County	93220
18	金坛市	Jintan City	228973	50	丰县	Fengxian County	92494
19	如东县	Rudong County	227606	51	邗江县	HanJiang County	91470
20	靖江市	JingJiang City	223601	52	宿豫县	Suyu County	86709
21	姜堰市	Jiangyan City	206514	53	溧水县	Lishui County	84434
22	太仓市	Taicang City	188728	54	滨海县	Binhai County	77635
23	东台市	Dongtai City	188468	55	泗洪县	Sihong County	74047
24	仪征市	Yizheng City	183936	56	睢宁县	Shuining County	72674
25	海安县	Haian County	175189	57	金湖县	Jinhu County	65877
26	江宁县	Jiangning County	166903	58	涟水县	Lianshui County	65654
27	兴化市	Xinghua City	144297	59	江浦县	Jiangpu County	65449
28	大丰市	Dafeng City	140959	60	盱眙县	Xuyi County	65403
29	射阳县	Sheyang County	139899	61	洪泽县	Hongze County	50073
30	六合县	Liuhe County	133682	62	灌南县	Guannan County	49725
31	高邮市	Gaoyou City	122873	63	淮阴县	Huaiyin County	49568
32	赣榆县	Gaiyu County	122200	64	响水县	Xiangshui County	46099

3—11 财政收入
FINANCIAL REVENUE (1996)

位次 No.	县（市）名称 County (City)		指标值（万元）Value (10000yuan)	位次 No.	县（市）名称 County (City)		指标值（万元）Value (10000yuan)
1	锡山市	Xishan City	121281	33	扬中市	Yangzhong City	20451
2	常熟市	Changshu City	115312	34	邗江县	HanJiang County	20444
3	江阴市	Jiangyin City	104430	35	盐都县	Yandou County	20002
4	张家港市	Zhangjiagang City	95003	36	邳州市	Pizhou City	19222
5	武进市	Wujin City	93838	37	射阳县	Sheyang County	18543
6	吴县市	Wuxie City	77417	38	赣榆县	Gaiyu County	18181
7	宜兴市	Yixing City	65355	39	建湖县	Jianhu County	17689
8	昆山市	Kunshan City	60160	40	高邮市	Gaoyou City	17527
9	吴江市	Wujiang City	57334	41	丹徒县	Dantu County	17304
10	仪征市	Yizheng City	48325	42	句容市	Jurong City	16653
11	丹阳市	Danyang City	46843	43	东海县	Donghai County	16620
12	太仓市	Taicang City	43956	44	宝应县	Baoying County	16221
13	通州市	Tongzhou City	43393	45	溧水县	Lishui County	16010
14	泰兴市	Taixing City	42133	46	新沂市	Xinyi City	15125
15	江都市	Jiangdu City	40547	47	宿豫县	Suyu County	14745
16	启东市	Qidong City	38467	48	灌云县	Guanyun County	14321
17	海门市	Haimen City	34841	49	丰县	Fengxian County	14308
18	江宁县	Jiangning County	34058	50	阜宁县	Funing County	14076
19	靖江市	JingJiang City	32672	51	睢宁县	Shuining County	14002
20	姜堰市	Jiangyan City	30423	52	六合县	Liuhe County	13651
21	铜山县	Tongshan County	30026	53	江浦县	Jiangpu County	12717
22	如东县	Rudong County	29162	54	高淳县	Gaochun County	12218
23	东台市	Dongtai City	29137	55	沭阳县	Shuyang County	12065
24	溧阳市	Liyang City	28841	56	淮安市	Huaian City	11744
25	如皋市	Rugao City	28011	57	滨海县	Binhai County	10327
26	海安县	Haian County	26289	58	淮阴县	Huaiyin County	9151
27	泗洪县	Sihong County	25423	59	涟水县	Lianshui County	9119
28	泗阳县	Siyang County	24535	60	金湖县	Jinhu County	8501
29	金坛市	Jintan City	24418	61	灌南县	Guannan County	8011
30	大丰市	Dafeng City	24077	62	盱眙县	Xuyi County	7867
31	兴化市	Xinghua City	22513	63	洪泽县	Hongze County	7571
32	沛县	Peixian County	21534	64	响水县	Xiangshui County	6898

3—12 全部职工平均工资
AVERAGE WAGE OF TOTAL STAFF AND WORKERS (1996)

位次 No.	县(市)名称 County (City)		指标值(元) Value (yuan)	位次 No.	县(市)名称 County (City)		指标值(元) Value (yuan)
1	昆山市	Kunshan City	7924	33	六合县	Liuhe County	5208
2	常熟市	Changshu City	7920	34	新沂市	Xinyi City	5149
3	锡山市	Xishan City	7878	35	如皋市	Rugao City	5142
4	江阴市	Jiangyin City	7834	36	邳州市	Pizhou City	5034
5	张家港市	Zhangjiagang City	7803	37	泗洪县	Sihong County	4939
6	武进市	Wujin City	7590	38	泰兴市	Taixing City	4934
7	太仓市	Taicang City	7566	39	靖江市	JingJiang City	4901
8	仪征市	Yizheng City	7095	40	丰县	Fengxian County	4793
9	吴江市	Wujiang City	7008	41	宝应县	Baoying County	4756
10	宜兴市	Yixing City	6927	42	金湖县	Jinhu County	4743
11	溧阳市	Liyang City	6854	43	盐都县	Yandou County	4743
12	吴县市	Wuxie City	6718	44	东海县	Donghai County	4716
13	丹阳市	Danyang City	6372	45	射阳县	Sheyang County	4683
14	扬中市	Yangzhong City	6219	46	宿豫县	Suyu County	4639
15	金坛市	Jintan City	6208	47	灌云县	Guanyun County	4637
16	海门市	Haimen City	6130	48	赣榆县	Gaiyu County	4588
17	通州市	Tongzhou City	6111	49	东台市	Dongtai City	4519
18	丹徒县	Dantu County	6035	50	建湖县	Jianhu County	4515
19	江宁县	Jiangning County	6028	51	兴化市	Xinghua City	4433
20	启东市	Qidong City	5902	52	睢宁县	Shuining County	4418
21	如东县	Rudong County	5892	53	沛县	Peixian County	4410
22	江都市	Jiangdu City	5828	54	阜宁县	Funing County	4380
23	句容市	Jurong City	5794	55	盱眙县	Xuyi County	4299
24	邗江县	HanJiang County	5761	56	泗阳县	Siyang County	4281
25	溧水县	Lishui County	5545	57	洪泽县	Hongze County	4082
26	江浦县	Jiangpu County	5481	58	淮阴县	Huaiyin County	4041
27	大丰市	Dafeng City	5479	59	响水县	Xiangshui County	3780
28	高淳县	Gaochun County	5443	60	沭阳县	Shuyang County	3760
29	铜山县	Tongshan County	5377	61	涟水县	Lianshui County	3734
30	姜堰市	Jiangyan City	5306	62	滨海县	Binhai County	3720
31	高邮市	Gaoyou City	5286	63	淮安市	Huaian City	3678
32	海安县	Haian County	5248	64	灌南县	Guannan County	3626

3—13 农民人均纯收入
PER CAPITA NET INCOME OF PEASANTS (1996)

位次 No.	县（市）名称 County (City)		指标值 （元） Value (yuan)	位次 No.	县（市）名称 County (City)		指示值 （元） Value (yuan)
1	张家港市	Zhangjiagang City	5407	33	江浦县	Jiangpu County	2865
2	吴江市	Wujiang City	5153	34	射阳县	Sheyang County	2861
3	常熟市	Changshu City	5125	35	盐都县	Yandou County	2861
4	武进市	Wujin City	5046	36	高邮市	Gaoyou City	2845
5	吴县市	Wuxie City	4956	37	仪征市	Yizheng City	2840
6	江阴市	Jiangyin City	4909	38	宝应县	Baoying County	2803
7	太仓市	Taicang City	4874	39	铜山县	Tongshan County	2770
8	锡山市	Xishan City	4832	40	金湖县	Jinhu County	2622
9	昆山市	Kunshan City	4827	41	建湖县	Jianhu County	2592
10	扬中市	Yangzhong City	4166	42	兴化市	Xinghua City	2585
11	宜兴市	Yixing City	4043	43	洪泽县	Hongze County	2559
12	启东市	Qidong City	3880	44	淮安市	Huaian City	2548
13	海门市	Haimen City	3789	45	东海县	Donghai County	2545
14	金坛市	Jintan City	3722	46	赣榆县	Gaiyu County	2512
15	溧阳市	Liyang City	3646	47	灌云县	Guanyun County	2383
16	丹阳市	Danyang City	3601	48	沛县	Peixian County	2362
17	通州市	Tongzhou City	3417	49	邳州市	Pizhou City	2360
18	靖江市	JingJiang City	3276	50	新沂市	Xinyi City	2302
19	江宁县	Jiangning County	3255	51	如皋市	Rugao City	2271
20	大丰市	Dafeng City	3225	52	阜宁县	Funing County	2257
21	丹徒县	Dantu County	3161	53	盱眙县	Xuyi County	2211
22	句容市	Jurong City	3134	54	丰县	Fengxian County	2162
23	邗江县	HanJiang County	3129	55	睢宁县	Shuining County	2121
24	江都市	Jiangdu City	3090	56	泗洪县	Sihong County	2028
25	东台市	Dongtai City	3020	57	淮阴县	Huaiyin County	2022
26	如东县	Rudong County	3008	58	宿豫县	Suyu County	2010
27	溧水县	Lishui County	2970	59	沭阳县	Shuyang County	2002
28	高淳县	Gaochun County	2969	60	滨海县	Binhai County	1998
29	海安县	Haian County	2964	61	涟水县	Lianshui County	1923
30	六合县	Liuhe County	2937	62	泗阳县	Siyang County	1920
31	泰兴市	Taixing City	2890	63	响水县	Xiangshui County	1866
32	姜堰市	Jiangyan City	2882	64	灌南县	Guannan County	1857

3—14 城乡居民储蓄存款
SAVINGS DEPOSIT BALANCE OF URBAN AND RURAL RESIDENTS (1996)

位次 No.	县(市)名称 County (City)		指标值(万元) Value (10000yuan)	位次 No.	县(市)名称 County (City)		指标值(万元) Value (10000yuan)
1	常熟市	Changshu City	837401	33	仪征市	Yizheng City	187054
2	张家港市	Zhangjiagang City	693995	34	邳州市	Pizhou City	169884
3	江阴市	Jiangyin City	594694	35	建湖县	Jianhu County	168187
4	锡山市	Xishan City	587630	36	阜宁县	Funing County	166603
5	吴县市	Wuxie City	583273	37	宝应县	Baoying County	163395
6	武进市	Wujin City	551917	38	邗江县	HanJiang County	156412
7	启东市	Qidong City	539453	39	金坛市	Jintan City	142439
8	通州市	Tongzhou City	521626	40	句容市	Jurong City	141595
9	宜兴市	Yixing City	484988	41	丹徒县	Dantu County	132308
10	江都市	Jiangdu City	457249	42	六合县	Liuhe County	130161
11	海门市	Haimen City	452220	43	淮安市	Huaian City	125454
12	昆山市	Kunshan City	398843	44	丰县	Fengxian County	123305
13	泰兴市	Taixing City	397106	45	滨海县	Binhai County	123232
14	海安县	Haian County	377043	46	东海县	Donghai County	121701
15	如东县	Rudong County	358441	47	赣榆县	Gaiyu County	121439
16	吴江市	Wujiang City	343038	48	新沂市	Xinyi City	108385
17	东台市	Dongtai City	342886	49	睢宁县	Shuining County	107658
18	太仓市	Taicang City	337449	50	沭阳县	Shuyang County	104418
19	丹阳市	Danyang City	333392	51	灌云县	Guanyun County	103137
20	如皋市	Rugao City	322262	52	宿豫县	Suyu County	102228
21	姜堰市	Jiangyan City	308824	53	泗洪县	Sihong County	97510
22	兴化市	Xinghua City	307932	54	泗阳县	Siyang County	90283
23	靖江市	JingJiang City	284779	55	金湖县	Jinhu County	87111
24	铜山县	Tongshan County	275204	56	溧水县	Lishui County	87063
25	溧阳市	Liyang City	259967	57	高淳县	Gaochun County	81893
26	沛县	Peixian County	232008	58	涟水县	Lianshui County	79448
27	大丰市	Dafeng City	230835	59	江浦县	Jiangpu County	71861
28	江宁县	Jiangning County	222980	60	淮阴县	Huaiyin County	68453
29	射阳县	Sheyang County	197942	61	响水县	Xiangshui County	68099
30	盐都县	Yandou County	197360	62	盱眙县	Xuyi County	67092
31	扬中市	Yangzhong City	193326	63	洪泽县	Hongze County	65715
32	高邮市	Gaoyou City	187114	64	灌南县	Guannan County	51589

附录:主要统计指标解释

APPENDIX：EXPLANATORY NOTES ON MAIN STATISTICAL INDICATORS

主要统计指标解释
Explanatory Notes to Major Statistical Indicators

1. **经济类型** Economic Ownerships

国有经济单位　指生产资料归国家所有的各种企业、事业单位，以及各级国 家机关、人民团体等单位。

State-owned Economic Units refer to enterprises and institutions, as well as government administrative organizations at various levels and social organizations etc. with production means of state ownership.

集体经济单位　指生产资料归公民集体所有的各种企业、事业单位。包括农村各种经济组织经营的农、林、牧、副、渔业，乡、村经营的企业、事业单位；城市、县、镇以及街道举办的集体经济性质的企业、事业单位。

Collective-owned Economimc Units refer to various enterprises and institutions with of prduction means collective ownership, including various rural economic organizations engaged in agriculture, forestry, husbandtry, sideline production, and fishery; collective enterprises and institutions run by cities, counties, towns and street committees.

私营经济单位　指生产资料归公民私人所有的单位。包括私营独资企业、私营合伙企业和私营有限责任公司。

Private-owned Economic Units refer to units with production means owned by individuals, including individual-owned private enterprises, jointly-owned private enterprises, and private-owned companies of limited liabilities.

联营经济单位　指不同所有制性质的企业之间或者企业、事业单位之间共同投资组成新的经济实体。包括紧密型联营企业，半紧密型联营企业和松散型联营企业。

Joint-Ownership Economic Units refer to economic entities jointly invested by enterprises or different ownerships of by enterprises and institutions, the partnerships of whichcan be closetype, half closetype, or loosetype.

股份制经济单位　指全部注册资本由全体股东共同出资，并以股份形式投资举办企业。主要包括股份有限公司和有限责任公司。

Share-Holding Economic Units refer to enterprises invested in the form of share holding and registered with its investment by all the share holders, including limited companies and limited-liability companies.

外商投资经济单位　指外国投资者根据中华人民共和国有关涉外经济的法律、法规，以合资、合作或独资的形式在中国大陆境内开办企业。包括中外合资经营企业、中外合作经营企业和外资企业。

Foreign-Owned Economic Units refer to enterprises established by foreigners in the territory of the Chinese mainland according to related economic laws and regulartions of the People's Republic of China in the form joint venture, cooperative venture, or sole investment, including sino-foreign joint ventures, sino-foreign joint cooperation enterprises, and solely foreign-owned enterprises.

港、澳、台投资经济单位　指港、澳、台地区投资者参照中华人民共和国有关涉外经济的法律、法规，以合资、合作或独资的形式在大陆举办企业。包括合资经营企业、合作经营企业和独资企业。

Economic Units Owned by Business People from Hong Kong, Macao and Taiwan refer to enterprises established by investors from Hong Kong, Macao, Taiwan in the territory of the Chinese mainland according to related economic laws and regulations of the People's Republic of China in the form of joint venture, cooperative venture, and sole investment, including joint ventures, joint cooperation enterprises, and solely owned enterprises.

2. **各个计划时期** Various Planning Periods

表内所用各个"时期"代表的年份如下：恢复时期为1950年到1952年；第一个计划五年时期（简称一五时期）为1953年到1957年；第二个五年计划时期（简称二五时期）为1958年到1962年；第三个五年计划时期（简称三五时期）为1966年到1970年；第四个五年计划时期（简称四五时期）为1971年到1975年；第五个五年计划时期（简称五五时期）为1976年到1980年；第六个五年计划时期（简称六五时期）为1981年到1985年；第七年五年计划时期（简称七五时期）为1986年到1990年；第八年五年计划时期（简称八五时期）为1991年到1995年。

The conventional division of time period in this the tables yearbook is used as follows: Rehabilitation Period, 1950-1952; the First Five-Year Plan Period (cited as First-Five Period), 1953-1957; the Second Five-Year Plan Period (cited as Second-Five Period), 1958-1962; the Third Five-Year Plan Period (cited as Third-Five Period), 1966-1970; the Fourth Five-Year Plan Period (cited as Fourth-Five Period), 1971-1975; the Fifth Five-Year Plan Period (cited as Fifth-Five Period), 1976-1980; the Sixth Five-Year Plan Period (cited as Sixth-Five Period), 1981-1985; the Seventh Five-Year Plan Period (cited as Seventh-Five Period), 1986-1990; the Eighth Five-Year Plan Period (cited as Eighth-Five Period), 1991-1995.

3. **可比价格、不变价格** Comparable Prices and Constant Prices

可比价格　指在不同时期的价值指标对比时，扣除了价格变动的因素，以确切反映物量的变化。按可比价格计算有两种方法：一种是直接用产品产量乘某一年的不变价格计算；另一种是用价格指数换算。

Comparable Prices refer to prices compared with price fuctuations deducted in different time perids in order to reflect accurately the changes in real term. Two methods are used for calculating comparable prices: 1. output multiplied by constant price of certain year; 2. output in current prices divided by relevant price index.

不变价格　指用同类产品的年平均价格作为固定价格，来计算各年产品价值。按不变价格计算的产品价值消除了价格变动因素，不同时期对比可以反映生产的发展速度。新中国成立后，随着工农业产品价格水平的变化，国家统计局先后五次制定了全国统一的工业产品不变价格和农业产品不变价格，从1949年到1957年使用1952年工（农）业产品不变价格，从1957年到1971年使用1957年不变价格，从1971年到1981年使用1970年不变价格，从1981年到1990年使用1980年不变价格，从1990年开始使用1990年不变价格。

Constant Prices refer to the average prices of identical a produces given in a certain year, which is used as the fixed price to calculate the output value of products of each year. As the output value calculated according to constant prices excludes the factors of price changes, it reflects the production development of various periods. Since 1949 when New China was established, with the changes of the general price level, the State Statistics Bureau has issued for five times unified national constant prices for industrial and agricultural products. The 1952 constant prices were used in the 1949-1957 period; the 1957 constant prices were used for the 1957-1971 period; the 1970 constant prices were used in the 1971-1980 period; the 1980 constant prices were used in the 1981-1990 period; and the 1990 constant prices have been in use since 1990.

4. **指数** Index

指数　是一种表明社会经济现象动态的相对数。运用指数可以测定不能直接相加和直接对比的社会经济现象的总动态；可以分析社会经济现象总变动中各因素变动的影响程度；可以研究总平均指标变动中各组标志水平和总体结变动的作用。它是把各个年份的产值换算成可比价格的基础上，根据定基数等于相应各个环比指数的连乘积这个换算关系计算出来的。

Index refer to the relative figures indicating social and economic phenomenal and developments. Index is used to evaluate the overall development of social and economic phenomena which can not be determined by simple addition or direct comparision. It is also use to analyze the outcome of various changes in the general phenomenon movement of social and economic development, and to study the level of each sub-index in the changes of general average index and the role of the changes of the overall structure. It is calculated at the comparable prices conversed from the output value of each year, using the formula of index number with fixed base period equal to the continuous product of its relative chain index.

5. 平均每年增长速度 Average Annual Growth Rate

在我国计算平均增长速度有两种方法，一种是习惯上经常使用的"水平法"，又称几何平均法，是以间隔期最后一年的水平同基期水平对比来计算平均每年增长(或下降)速度。另一种是"累计法"，又称代数平均法或方程法，是以间隔期内各年水平的总和同基期水平对比来计算平均每年增长(或下降)速度。

在一般正常情况下，两种方法计算的平均每年增长速度比较接近，但在经济发展不平衡，出现大起大落时，两种方法计算的结果差别较大。

本《年鉴》内所列的平均每年增长速度，均用"水平法"计算。从某年到某年平均增长速度的年份，均不包括基期年在内。如建国四十六年的平均增长速度是以1949年为基期计算的，则写为1950—1995年平均增长速度，余类推。

There are two methods for calculating average annual growth rate in China. One is called "level approach" or geometry average, which is derived by comparing the growth rate for the last year of the interval with that of the beginning year; the other is called "accumulating approach" or algebraic average or equation method, which is calculated by comparing the total growth rate of each year for the interval with that of base year.

Usually the results cclculated by the two methods are fairly close, but they differ sharply when imbalance occurred in economic development with striking fluctuations in growth.

The Average Annuak Growth Rates listed in this statistical yearbook are calculated by "level approach" except for the growth rate of investment in fixed assets. The base years are not listed when the years are listed for average annual growth rates for instance, the average annual growth rate of 46 years since 1949 is listed as average annual growth rate of 1950-1995 without listing the base year 1949. And the analogy of this is also for the rest.

6. 国内生产总产值 Gross Domestic Product

国内生产总值　是按市场价格计算的国内生产总值的简称。它是一个国家(地区)所有常住单位在一定时期内生产活动的最终成果。国内生产总值有三种表现形态，即价值形态、收入形态和产品形态。从价值形态看，它是所有常住单位在一定时期内所生产的全部货物和服务价值超过同期投入的全部非固定资产货物和服务价值的差额，即所有常住单位的增加值之和；从收入形态看，它是所有常住单位在一定时期内所创造并分配给常住单位和非常住单位的初次分配收入之和；从产品形态看，它是最终使用的货物和服务减去进口货物和服务。在实际核算中，国内生产总值的三种表现形态表现为三种计算方法，即生产法、收入法和支出法。三种方法分别从不同的方面反映国内生产总值及其构成。

Gross Domestic Product refer to gross domestic product calculated at market price, which is all the final products of all resident units (enterprises and self-employed individuals) of a country (or region) during a certain period of time. Gross Domestic Product is precented in three different forms, i. e. value added, income, and products respectively. The form of value added refers to the total value of all products and services produced by all resident units during a certain period of time minus total value of inputs of non-fixed assets materials and services or the summation of the value added of all resident units; the form of income includes all the income items produced by all resident units and distributed primarily to all resident and non-resident units; the form of product refers to all final goods and services minus imports of goods and services. In the practice of national accounting, Gross Domestic Product is calculated by three approaches, i. e. product approach, income approach, and expenditure approach respectively to reflect Gross Domestic Product and its composition from different aspects.

7. 三次产业 Three Industries

根据社会生产活动历史发展的顺序对产业结构的划分，产品直接取自自然界的部门称为第一产业，对初级产品进行再加工的部门称为第二产业。为生产和消费提供各种服务的部门称为第三产业。它是世界上通用的产业结构分类，但各国的划分不尽一致。我国的三次产业划分是：

第一产业：农业(包括种植业、林业、牧业、副业和渔业)。

第二产业:工业(包括采掘工业、制造业、自来水、电力、蒸气、热水、煤气)和建筑业。

第三产业:除第一、第二产业以外的其他各业。由于第三产业包括的行业多、范围广,根据我国的实际情况,第三产业可分为两大部分:一是流通部门,二是服务部门。具体又可分为四个层次:

第一层次:流通部门,包括交通运输业、邮电通讯业、商业、饮食业、物资供销和仓储业。

第二层次:为生产和生活服务的部门,包括金融、保险业,地质普查业,房地产、公用事业,居民服务业,咨询服务业和综合技术服务业,农、林、牧、渔、水利服务业和水利业,公路、内河(湖)航道养护业等。

第三层次:为提高科学文化水平和居民素质服务的部门,包括教育、文化、广播电视,科学研究、卫生、体育和社会福利事业等。

第四层次:为社会公共需要服务的部门,包括国家机关、政党机关、社会团体,以及军队和警察等。

Three Industries Industry structure has been classified according to the historical sequence of development. Primary industry refer to extraction of natural resources; secondary industry involves processing of primary products; and tertiary industry provides services of various kinds for production and consumption. The above classification is universal although it varies to some extent form country to country. Industry in China comprises:

Primary industry: agriculture (including farming, forestry, husbandry, sideline production, and fishing).

Secondary industry: industry (including mining, manufacture, water suppply, electricity gerneration and supply, steam, hot water, gas) and construction.

Tertiary industry: all other industries not included in primary or secondary industry.

Due to the fact that tertiary industry involves in a large variety of industries in China, it is divided into two sectors: circulation sector and service sector and further into four levels:

The first level: circulation sector, including transportation, postal service and communication, commerce, catering, material supply and distribution, and storage.

The second level: service sector providing service for production and consumption, including banking, insurance, geological survey, real estates, public utilities, service for residents, consultancy service, and comprehensive technical services, and service for agriculture, forestry, husbandry, fishing, water conservancy, and maintenance of roads, internal water ways, etc.

The third level: service for improving education and cultural life of people, including education, culture, broadcasting, teleevision, research of science, health, sports, and social welfare. etc.

The fourth level: sector providing service for public needs, including government agencies, political and party institutions, social organizations, armes, and policemen.

8. 私营企业 Private-owned Enterprises

私营企业 指企业资产属于私人所有,雇工8人以上的营利性的经济组织。

Private-owned Enterprises refer to profit-making economic units with private ownership of capital and more than eight employees.

9. 人口 Population

人口 人口数为每年12月31日常住户口人数,不包括户口不在本省的临时户口人数。

Population refer to the population with permanent residence registered December 31 every year, excluding migrant population without registered residence in Jiangsu.

10. 出生率、死亡率、人口自然增长率 Birth Rate, Death Rate and Natural Growth Rate of Population

出生率(又称粗出生率) 指在一定时期内(通常为一年)平均每千人所出生的人数的比率,一般用千分率表示。计算公式:

$$出生率 = \frac{年出生人数}{年平均人数} \times 1000‰$$

出生人数是指活产婴儿，即胎儿脱离母体时（不管怀孕月数），有过呼吸或其他生命现象。
年平均人数是年初、年底人口数的平均数，也可用年中人口数代替。

Birth Rate (or **Crude Birth Rate**) refer to the ratio of number of births to the average population during a certain period of time (usually a year), which is often presented as ‰. The following formual is used:

$$Birth\ Rate = \frac{Number\ of\ Births}{Average\ Number\ of\ Population} \times 1000‰$$

Number of Births refers to live births, i. e. for births when babies had showed any vital phenomena regardless of the length of pregnancy.

Average Number of Population is the average of the number of population at the beginning of the year and the end of year and sometimes is substituted for with mid-year population.

死亡率（又称粗死亡率） 指在一定时期内（通常为一年）一定地区的死亡人数与同期平均人数（或期中人数）之比，一般用千分率表示。计算公式：

$$死亡率 = \frac{年死亡人数}{年平均人数} \times 1000‰$$

Death Rate (or **Crude Death Rate**) refers to the ratio of number of deaths to the average population (or mid-year population) during a certain period of time (usually a year), which is often presented as ‰. The following formula is used:

$$Death\ Rate = \frac{Number\ of\ Deaths}{Average\ Number\ of\ Population} \times 1000‰$$

人口自然增长率 指在一定时期内（通常为一年）人口自然增加数（出生人数减死亡人数）与该时期内平均人数（或期中人数）之比，一般用千分率表示。计算公式：

$$人口自然增长率 = \frac{本年出生人数 - 本年死亡人数}{年平均人数} \times 1000‰$$

$$人口自然增长率=人口出生率-人口死亡率$$

Natural Growth Rate of Population refers to the rato of natural increase in population (number of births minus number of deaths) in a certain period of time (usually a year) to the average population (or mid-year population) of the period, which is often presented as ‰. The following formula are applied:

$$Natural\ Growth\ of\ Population = \frac{Number\ of\ Births - Number\ of\ Deaths}{Average\ Number\ of\ Population} \times 1000‰$$

$$Natural\ Growth\ Rate\ of\ Population = Birth\ Rate - Death\ Rate$$

11. **人口预期寿命** Life Expectancy

人口预期寿命 指在一定年龄组死亡率水平下，对某一确定的年龄日后平均还能继续生存的年数（或该年龄组未来的平均寿命）。

Life Expectancy refers to average number of years a person of certain age would live if prevailing patterns of mortality of his age group were to stay the throughout his life.

12. 从业人员 Persons Employed

从业人员 指从事一定社会劳动并取得劳动报酬或经营收入的全部劳动力。包括：

(1)全部职工

(2)城镇私营企业从业人员

(3)城镇个体劳动者

(4)农村社会劳动者

(5)其他社会劳动者

这一指标反映了一定时期内全部劳动力资源的实际利用情况，是研究我国基本国情国力的重要指标。

各单位的从业人员是指在各级国家机关、政党机关、社会团体及企业、事业单位中工作，并取得劳动报酬的全部人员。包括职工、再就业的离退休人员、民办教师以及在各单位中工作的外方人员和港、澳、台方人员。

各单位的从业人员反映了各单位实际参加生产或工作的全部劳动力。

Persons Employed refers to total number of persons engaged in social labor which generates income, including:

(1)Total staff and workers

(2)Employees in urban private enterprises

(3)Urban individual laborers

(4)Rural laborers

(5)Other social laborers

This indicator reflects the actual utilization of total labor force during a certain period of time and is often used for the research of China's economic affairs and power.

Persons Employed in Various Units refers to total staff working for government agencies of various levels, political and party organizations, social organizations, and enterprises and institutions receiving income, including staff, reemployed retirees, non-government paid teachers, foreigners, and Chinese compatriots from Honf Kong, Macao, and Taiwan working in various units. This indicator reflects the total laborers actually engaged in production or other operations in various units.

13. 职工 Staff and Workers

职工 指在国有经济、城镇集体经济、联营经济、股份制经济、外商和港、澳、台投资经济、其他经济单位及其附属机构工作，并由其支付工资的各类人员。

Staff and Workers refers to those who work in (and receive income therefrom) enterprises and institutions by state ownership, colletive ownership, joint ownership, share holding, foreign ownership, and ownership by overseas Chinese from Hong Kong, Macao, and Taiwan, and otherownership and their affiliated units.

14. 城镇待业人员 Unemployment

城镇待业人员 指有非农业户口，在一定的劳动年龄内(16岁以上及男50岁以下、女45岁以下)，有劳动能力，无业而要求就业，并在当地就业服务机构进行待业登记的人员。

Unemployment refers to those non-agricultural population within working age (16-50 for male and 16-45 for female) who are able and willing to work but unemployed and registered in local employment service agencies.

15. 职工工资总额 Total Wage Bill of Workers and Staff

职工工资总额 指各单位在一定时期内直接支付给本单位全部职工的劳动报酬总额。

工资总额的计算原则应以直接支付给职工的全部劳动报酬为根据。各单位支付给职工的劳动报酬以及其他根据有关规定支付的工资，不论是计入成本的还是不计入成本的，不论是按国家规定列入计征奖金税项目的，还是未列入计征奖金税项目的，不论是以货币形式支付的还是以实物形式支付的，均包括在工资总额内。

Total Wage Bill of Workers and Staff refers to total remuneration payment to permanent workers and staff of various units during a certain period of time.

The calculation of total wages bill is based on the total remuneration payment and therefore, wage and salaries and other payments to workers and staff regardless of its resources, category, in kind or cash.

16. 职工平均工资 Average Wage of Workers and Staff

职工平均工资 指企业、事业、机关单位的职工在一定时期内平均每人所得的货币工资额。它表明一定时期职工工资收入的高低程度，是反映职工工资水平的主要指标。计算公式为：

$$\text{职工平均工资} = \frac{\text{报告期实际支付的全部职工工资总额}}{\text{报告期全部职工平均人数}}$$

Average Wage of Workers and Staff refers to the average wage in money terms per person during a certain period of time for workers and staff of enterprises, institutions, and government agencies, which reflects the general level of wage income during a certain period of time and is calculated as follows:

$$Average\ Wage\ of\ Workers\ and\ Staff = \frac{Total\ Wage\ Bill\ of\ Workers\ and\ Staff\ in\ Reference\ Period}{Average\ Number\ of\ Workers\ and\ Staff\ in\ Reference\ Period}$$

17. 劳保福利费用 Labor Insurance and Welfare Funds

劳保福利费用 指企业、事业、机关根据国家有关劳保福利规定，在工资以外实际支付给职工个人和用于集体的劳动保险和福利设施的费用。具体包括：(1)退职、退休、离休费等；(2)医疗卫生费；(3)职工生活困难补助费；(4)职工及供养直系亲属死亡丧葬费、抚恤费、救济费；(5)农业生产补贴；(6)文艺、体育、宣传费；(7)集体福利事业的补贴；(8)集体福利设施费用；(9)其他福利费用。

劳保福利费用不包括用于职工的劳动保护费用。劳动保护用品的支出是安全生产的需要，不属于福利费用范围。

Labor insurance and welfare funds refer to the real cost paid, in line with relative state labor insurance and welfare regulations, to workers and staff outside the wages and used by the collective as labor insurance and welfare ficilities funds. It mainly includes: (1)resignation pay, retirement pay and payment for retires with honours; (2)medical and health care fees; (3)subsidies for workers and staff with financial difficulties; (4)funeral expeneses for workers and staff and their direct relatives whom they support, pension for the disabled or for the family of the deceased, and relief payment; (5)agricultural production subsidies; (6)funds for cultrual, sports and propaganda activities; (7)subsidies for collective welfare works; (8)collective welfare facilities expeneses; (9)other welfare cost.

Labor protection cost is not included in the labor insurance and welfare funds. The need of appliances for labor protection is to ensure safety in production and can not be listed in the welfare funds.

18. 城镇居民家庭全部收入、生活费收入 Total Income and Income for Living Expenditure of Urban Households

城镇居民家庭全部收入 指被调查的城镇居民家庭全部的实际现金收入，包括经常或固定得到的收入和一次性收入。不包括周转性收入，如提取银行存款、向亲友借入款、收回借出款以及其他各种暂收款。

Total Income of Urban Households refers to the actual cash income of the sample households, including regular or fixed income and one-off income. Circulating income such as withdrawal from bank deposits, loans borrowed from relatives or friends, repayment of loans recieved and various temporary collection of money is excluded.

城镇居民家庭生活费收入 指被调查的城镇居民家庭全部收入中能用于安排家庭日常生活的实际收入。即城镇居民家庭的全部实际收入除"赡养支出"、"赠送支出"和缴纳的各种税款以及被调查户非本家庭人口的经济用饭人口所交的"搭伙费"。

Income for Living Expenditure of Urban Household refers to actual income which can be spent on daily life, i. e. total income minus supporting exlenses, gifts, various taxes payment, and food expeneses paid by non-family members.

19. 农村居民家庭纯收入 Net Income of Peasants' Households

农村居民家庭纯收入 指农村常住居民家庭总收入中，扣除从事生产和非生产经营费用支出、缴纳税款和上交承包集体任务金额以后剩余的，可直接用于进行生产性、非生产性建设投资、生活消费和积累的那一部分收入。它是反映农民家庭实际收入水平的综合性的主要指标。农民家庭纯收入，既包括从事生产性和非生产性的经营收入，又包括取自在外人口寄回带回和国家财政救济、各种补贴等非经营性收入；既包括货币收入，又包括自产自用的实物收入。但不包括向银行、信用社和向亲友借款等属于借贷性的收入。

Net Income of Peasants' Households refers to the total income of peasants' households during a year after the production of expeneses, which can be spent for investments for production and non-production construction and for improvement of daily life, while loan income borrowed from banks of friends and relative is not included. It is an indicator of peasants' actual income level.

20. 各种物价指数 Various Price Indices

目前，国家统计部门编制的物价指数主要有以下几种：居民消费价格指数、商品零售价格总指数、农业生产资料价格指数、农贸市场农产品成交价格指数、农产品收购价格指数、居民基本生活费用价格指数、工业品出厂价格指数、原材料、燃料、动力购进价格指数、固定资产投资价格指数、建筑安装工程价格指数、建筑业产值价格指数、主要建筑材料费用价格指数。

So far as the nationak statistical department have worked out the following main price indices: consmer peice index; retail price index; agriculture production means price index; farm products market price index; farm product pruchase price index; basic living price index; factory price index; raw materials, fuel and power purchse price index; fixed assets investment price index; architectural engineering price index; construction industry output value index; main construction materials price index.

21. 居民消费价格总指数 Consumer Price Index

居民消费价格总指数 是反映一定时期内城乡居民所购买的生活消费品价格和服务项目价格变动趋势和程度的相对数。是综合了城市居民消费价格指数和农民消费价格指数计算取得的。利用居民消费价格指数，可以观察和分析消费品的零售价格和服务价格变动对城乡居民实际生活费支出的影响程度。

1952年以前采用固定数量加权综合法（即总值法）计算，1953年到1956年采用加权算术平均公式计算，1957年以后根据消费品零售价格指数与服务项目价格指数汇编居民生活费用价格指数。

Consumer Price Index reflects the relative change in prices of consumer goods and services purchased by urban and rural residents, and is derived from urban consumer price index and rural consumer price index. Consumer price index can be to predict the impact of consumer price change on actual living cost expenditure of urban and rural residents.

Prior to 1952, consumer price index was calculated with a weighted mean price on a fixed quantity (total value method). The formula of weighted artimetic mean was used between 1953 and 1956. After 1957, consumer price index is based on urban retail prices index and service prices index, Commodities and services of 382 kinds were chosen for the calculation.

22. 零售价格指数 Retail Price Index

零售价格指数 是反映城乡商品零售价格变动趋势的一种经济指数。零售物价的调整变动直接影响到城乡居民的生活支出和国家的财政收入，影响居民购买力和市场供需平衡，影响消费与积累的比例。因此，计算零售价格指数，可以从一个侧面对上述经济活动进行观察和分析。

零售价格指数采用加权算术平均公式计算。每年根据住户调查资料调整一次权数。1992年全国有146个市、80个县城作为基层填报单位。城市指数所选商品352种左右，县城指数所选商品404种左右。每种商品的指数采用代表规格品的平均价格计算。

Retail Price Index reflects the general change in prices of retail commodities. The change and adjustment in retail prices directly affect living expenditure of urban and rural residents and government revenue, purchasing power of residents and equilibrium of market supply and demand, and the proportion of consumption and accumulation. Therefore, retail price index can predict to certain extent the changes of the above economic activities.

Retail price index are calculated by the formula of weighted artimetic mean. The weights used are adjusted annually based on data of household survey in cities. In 1992, more than 146 cities and 80 county towns are selected as the basic units for data collection; 352 items of commodities in the cities and 404 in the county towns are included in the calculation. The price of a standard commodity form each item of products is adopted in the calculation.

23. 农贸市场农产品成交价格指数 Farm Product Market Price Index

农贸市场农产品成交价格指数 是反映一定时期农贸市场农产品价格变动趋势和程度的相对数。编制农贸市场农产品成交价格指数，可以观察和分析农贸市场农产品价格变动及对农业生产和居民生活的影响程度。

Farm Products Market Price Index reflects the trend of price changes of farm products sold on farm product markets in a given period of time. Drawing up farm product market price index can study and analyze the price fluctuation of farm product markets and their impact on agricultural production and people's daily life.

24. 工业品出厂价格指数 Factory Price Index

工业品出厂价格指数 是反映全部工业产品出厂价格总水平的变动趋势和程度的相对数。其中除包括工业企业售给商业、外贸、物资部门的产品外，还包括售给工业和其他部门的生产资料以及直接售给居民的生活消费品。通过工业生产价格指数能观察出厂价格变动对工业总产值的影响。

Factory Price Index reflects the change in general factory price of all industrial products, including sales of industrial products to commercial enterprises, foreign trade sectors, materials supplying and disteibuting sectors as wel as sales of production means to industry and other sectors and sales of consumer goods to residents. It can be used to Predict the impact of factory prices on gross output value of industry.

25. 原材料、燃料、动力购进价格指数 Raw Materials, Fuel and Power Purchase Price Index

原材料、燃料、动力购进价格指数 是反映全部工业原材料、燃料、动力购进价格总水平的变动趋势和程度的相对数。用其可以观察和研究工业企业原材料价格变动对生产的影响，以及企业对原材料涨价的消化能力和承受能力，为制订价格政策提供依据。

Raw Materials, Fuel and Power Puechase Price Index reflects changes in the general purchase price of all industrial raw materials, fuel and power. The index can be used to study and analyze the impact of price changes of industrial raw materials on the production and enterprises capacity to bear and digest the price increase of raw materials, so as to provide basis for the government to formulate price policies.

26. 全社会固定资产投资 Total Investment in Fixed Assets

全社会固定资产投资 固定资产投资是社会固定资产再生产的主要手段。通过建造和购置固定资产的活动，国民经济不断采用先进技术装备，建立新兴部门，进一步调整经济结构和生产力的地区分布，增强经济实力，为改善人民物质文化生活创造物质条件，这对我国的社会主义现代化建设具有重要意义。

固定资产投资额是以货币表现的建造和购置固定资产活动的工作量，它是反映固定资产投资规模、速度、比例关系和使用方向的综合性指标。全社会固定资产投资包括国有经济单位投资、城乡集体经济单位投资、各种经济类型的单位投资和城乡居民个人投资。按照我国现行计划管理体制，国有经济单位固定资产投资总额分为基本建设、更新改造、商品房屋建设投资和其他固定资产投资四个部分；城乡集体经济单位投资包括城镇集体所有制单位投资和农村集体所有制单位投资；各种经济类型的单位投资包括联营经济、股份制经济、中外合资经营、中外合作经营、外资、与大陆合资经营、与大陆合作经营、港澳台独资及其他经济类型的单位投资。城镇居民个人投资包括城市、县城、镇、工矿区所辖范围内的个人建房和农村个人建房及购买生产性固定资产的投资。

Total Investment in Fixed Assets Investment in fixed assets is a major tool for social reproduction of fixed assets. In the Process of capital construction and technical updating and transformation, more advanced technologies and new equipments are adopted and new sectors are established, which promote the economic structure, production regional layout and productivity to improve people's livehood and speeded up the drive of four socialist modernization.

Value of investment in fixed assets refers to construction and purchase of fixed assets in money terms, which reflects the size, pace, structure, and utilization of investment in fixed assets. Total investment in fixed assets includes investment by state-owned units, urban and rural colletive units, and units of various other kinds of ownership and individual investment by urban abd rural residents. According to China's current planning and management system investment by state-owned units includes four parts, i. e. investment in capital construction, technical upgrading and transformation, construction of commercial building and residence, and others. Investment by units of various other kinds, of ownershio refers to investment by enterprises and institutions of joint ownership, share holding, foreign ownership, ownership by overseas Chinese from Hong Kong, Macao, and Taiwan and other ownership. Individual investment by urban and rural residents includes investment in personal house building and purchase of fixed assets for production purpose in areas under administration of city, county, town, and special mining zone and in rural areas.

27. 固定资产投资额的分组 Investment in Fixed Assets by Category

固定资产投资额按构成分 固定资产投资活动按其工作内容和实现方式分为建筑安装工程，设备、工具、器具购置，其他费用三个部分。

(1)建筑安装工程(建筑工作量) 指各种房屋、建筑物的建造工程和各种设备、装置的安装工程。包括各种房屋建造工程，各种用途设备基础和各种工业窑炉的砌筑工程；为施工而进行的各种准备工作和临时工程以及完工后的清理工作等；铁路、道路的铺设，矿井的开凿及石油管道的架设等；水利工程；防空地下建筑等特殊工程；以及各种机械设备的安装工程；为测定安装工程质量，对设备进行的试行工作。在安装工程中，不包括被安装设备本身的价值。

(2)设备、工具、器具购置 指购置或自制达到固定资产标准的设备、工具、器具的价值，固定资产的标准按财务部门规定。新建单位、扩建单位的新建车间按照设计和计划要求购置或自制的全部设备、工具、器具，不论是否达到固定资产标准均计入"设备、工具、器具购置"中。

(3)其他费用 指除建筑安装工程和设备、工具、器具购置以外的投资完成额。它包括两种性质的费用，一种是属于增加固定资产的费用，主要有：建设单位管理费，土地、青苗等补偿和安置补助费、勘察设计费、研究实验费、农林单位牲畜购置费、各种经济林木的营造费、办公和生活家具、器具购置费、引进技术和进口设备项目的其他费用、联合试运转费等；一种是属于不增加固定资产的费用，主要有：施工机械转移费、生产职工培训费、农业开荒费用及报废工程损失费等。

Investment in Fixed Assests by Structure refers three major parts of investment activities, i. e. construction and installation, purchase of equipments and instruments, and other expeneses.

(1)Construction and installation (work load of construction) refers to construction projects of various houses and buildings and installation of various equipments and instruments, including construction of various houses, equipment foundations and industrial kiln stoves, preparation works for project construction, and clearing up works post project construction pavement of railways and roads, drilling of mines and construction of oil popes, water conservancy, air defence underground constructions and other special projects, installation of various machinery equipment, testing operation for pretesting the quality of installation projects. The value of equipments installed in installation projects is not considered.

(2)Purchase of equipments and intruments refers to total value of equipments,tools, and vessels purchased or self-produced which come up to standards for fixed assets. Equipments, tools and vessels purchased or self-producced for new workshops by newly established or expanded units are categorized as "purchase of equipments and instruments" regardless of standards for fixed assets.

(3)Other expeneses refers to investment completed which are not included above. This category consists of two types of expeneses: one increases fixed assets, including administration expeneses of construction units, compensation for land and plants, compensation for moving, and expeneses on geological survey and designing, research and testing, purchase of animals by agricultural and forestry units, planting and operating of various cash forests, office and residence furniture, purchase of instruments and vessels, introduction of techpnology and imports of equipments, and joint pretesting of projects; the other does not increase fixed assets, including expenese on transportation of construction machineries, training for workers and staff, opening up agricultural land, and loss of discarded projects.

固定资产投资按建设性质分 建设项目的性质一般分为新建、扩建、改建、迁建、恢复。基本建设按建设项目划分建设性质、更新改造、国民经济单位其他固定资产投资及城镇集体投资按整个企业、事业单位的建设情况确定建设性质。目前基本建设和更新改造是根据我国现行的计划管理体制区分的,所以基本建设和更新改造都可以分别按新建、扩建等划分。

(1)新建 一般是指从无到有、"平地起家"新开始建设单位。有的单位原有的基础很小,经过建设后其新增加的固定资产价值超过原有固定资产价值(原值)三倍以上的也算新建。

(2)扩建 一般是指为扩大原有产品的生产能力,在厂内或其他地点增建主要生产车间(或主要工程)、独立的生产线或总厂之下的分厂的企业;事业单位和行政单位在原单位增建业务用房(如学校增建教学用房、医院增建门诊部或病床用房、行政机关增建办公楼等)也作为扩建。

(3)改建 一般是指现有企业、事业单位为了技术进步,提高产品质量,增加花色品种,促进产品升级换代,降低消耗和成本,加强资源综合利用和三废治理、劳保安全等,采用新技术、新工艺、新设备、新材料等对现有设施、工艺条件进行技术改造或更新(包括相应配套的辅助性生产、生活福利设施)。有的企业为充分发挥现有主产能力,进行填平补齐而增建不增加本单位主要产品生产能力的车间等,也属于改建。

Investment in Fixed Assets by Type of Construction in general can be divided into three categories as new construction, expansion, transformation, replacement. Capital construction projects are classified according to the purposes of construction and investment in technical updating and transformation and other fixed assets are identified by the general types of construction. The current distinction between capital construction and technical updating and transformation is determined by China's current planning and management systems, which are divided into new construction, expansion, etc. respectively.

(1)New construction in general refers to newly constructed units, In the case in which value of newly added fixed assets exceeds the original ones by three times expeansion construction is considered as new construction.

(2)Expansion refers to construction for increasing original product capacity of new major production workshops within factories or other locations, independent production line, or branch factory under major. Newly constructed business houses for institutions and administrative organizetions (such as school buildings, clinics or beds in hospitals, and office buildings, etc) are classified as expansion.

(3)Transformation refers to technical updating and transformation to existing equipments and technical conditions undertaken by enterprises and institutions for the purposes of technology advancement, improvement in product quality, enlarging variety of products, promoting new gerneration of products, reducing production consumption and cost, promoting comprehensive utilization of resources, strengthening streatment of wasted water, air, and solids, and safety in production, etc. through new technologies and techniques, and new materials (including accessory production and living and welfare facilities). Construction of new workshops for improving existing production capacity rether than increasing production capacity is considered as transformation.

固定资产投资按国民经济行业分 建设项目归哪个行业,按其建成投产后的主要产品或主要用途及社会经济活动性质来确定。基本建设按建设项目划分国民经济行业,更新改造、国有经济单位其他固定资产投资及城镇集体投资根据整个企业、事业单位所属的行业来划分。一般情况下,一个建设项目或一个企业、事业单位只能属于一种国民经济行业。为了更准确地反映国民经济各行业之间的比例关系,联合企业(总厂)所属分厂属于不同行业的,原则上按分厂划分行业。

Investment in Fixed Asssets by Branch of Industry Classifications of construction projects are determined by major products of those projects of the purpose of the projects, and the nature of their social economic activities. Investment in capital construction are classified by construction of projects, while investment in technical updating and transformation, other investment by state-owned units and urban collective units are calssified according to the branch of industry of enterprises or institutions which they belong to. In general, one project or one enterprises or institution can only belong to one branch of industry. In order to reflect more accurately the proportions of various industries, brancch factories which differ from their general factory in classification of industry are classified according to their economic activities.

28. 基本建设投资额 Capital Construction Investment

基本建设 是国有企业、事业单位以扩大生产能力或工程效益为主要目的的新建、扩建工程及有关工作。包括工厂、矿山、铁路、桥梁、港口、农田水利、商店、住宅、学校、医院等工程的建造和机器设备、车辆、船舶、飞机等的购置。

基本建设投资额是以货币表现的基本建设完成的工作量，是反映一定时期内基本建设规模和建设进度的综合性指标。它是根据工程的实际进度按预算价格(预算价格是编制施工图预算时所用的价格)计算的工作量，没有形成工程实体的建筑材料和没有开始安装的设备，都不计算投资完成额。

Capital Construction refers to in new projects or an addition to existion facilities for the purposes of enlarging production capacity or improving efficiency, which includes construction of plants, mines, railways, bridges, harbors, water conservation facilities, stores, residential ficilities, schools, hospitals, and purchase of machinery and equipment, vehicles, ships, and planes.

Value of Capital Construction Investment refers to completion of capital construction in money terms, which reflects the size and progress of capital construction during a certain period of time. It is calculated at budget prices according to the actual completion of the project and therefore, construction materials and equipment not put into operation are not included.

29. 更新改造投资额 Updating and Transformation Investment

更新改造 是指国有企业、事业单位对原有设施进行固定资产更新和技术改造，以及相应配套的工程和有关工作(不包括大修理和维护工程)。更新改造投资是以货币表现的更新改造完成的工作量。根据我国现行统计制度，基本建设和更新改造的划分是：(1)列入基本建设计划的项目作为基本建设投资，列入更新改造计划的项目作为更新改造投资；(2)更新改造计划与基本建设计划结合安排的项目及未列入计划的项目，根据工程性质分别作为基本建设投资或更新改造投资。属于对企业、事业单位原有设施进行技术改造或更新的项目和增建主要生产车间、分厂等。其新增生产能力或效益尚未达到大中型标准的项目，以及由于城市环境保护和安全生产的需要而进行的迁建工程，作为更新改造投资。

Updating and Transformation Investment refers to the investment in projects to renew, modernize or replace exisiting assets and related supplementary projects (excluding major repairs and maintenance projects), which is presented in money terms. According to China's current statistical system, the division between capital construction investment and technical updating and transformation is as follows: (1)projects which are listed in capital construction plan are identified as capital construction investment; projects which are listed in technical updating and transformation plan are identified as technicla updating and transformation investment; projects which are listed in technical updating and transformation plan are identifies as technical updating and transformation investment; (2)project which are involved in both capital construction and technical updating and transformation or not listed in specific plan are identified as either capital construction or technical updating and transformation according to the nature of the projects. Projects for the purpose of renewing or transforming exisiting assets of enterprises and institutions and construction of major workshops or accessory plant and projects for the purposes of environmental protection and safety in production are considered as technical updating and transformation if the capacity or profitability of those projects have not reached the standards of large or medium size.

30. 其他固定资产投资 Other Investment in Fixed Assets

其他固定资产投资 是指按照国家规定不纳入基本建设和更新计划管理，其总投资在五万元以上的固定资产投资。具体包括：国有经济单位用油田维护费和石油开发基金进行的油田维护和开发工程；煤炭、铁矿、森林工业等采掘采伐业用维检费进行的开拓延伸工程；交通部门用公路养路费对原有公路、桥梁进行改建的工程；商业部门用简易建筑费建造的仓库工程。

Other Investment in Fixed Assets refers to investment in fixed assets by state-owned units and valued above 50,000 yuan which are not included in capital construction and technical updating and transformation according to the state regulations, including oil-field development projects using special oil-field development funds-development and expansion projects of mining and forestry department using maintenance funds, road and bridge construction project using road tolls, warehouse construction of commerce department using simple construction funds, investment in fixed assets by urban collective units construction and purchase by units of joint ownership, share holding ownershiop, foreign ownership, and overseas Chinese from Hong Kong, Macao, and Taiwan and investment in real estate development and construction of commercial residential houses.

31. 固定资产投资的资金来源 Sources of Finance for Investment in Fixed Assets

固定资产投资的资金来源 根据固定资产投资的资金来源不同,分为上年末结余资金、本年资金来源小计和各项应付款。其中本年资金来源小计又分为国家预算内资金、国内贷款、股票、债券、利用外资、自筹资金和其他资金来源七种:

(1)国家预算内资金 指国家预算、地方财政、主要部门和国家专业投资公司拨给或委托银行贷给建设单位的基本建设拨款和中央基本建设基金,拨给企业单位的更新改造拨款,以及中央财政安排的专项拨款中用于基本建设的资金。

(2)国内贷款 指报告期企、事业单位向银行及非银行金融机构借入的用于固定资产投资的各种国内借款。国内贷款包括:银行利用自有资金及吸收的存款发放的贷款、上级主管部门拨入的国内贷款、国家专项贷款(包括煤代油贷款、劳改煤矿专项贷款等)、地方财政专项资金安排的贷款、国内储备贷款、周转贷款等。

(3)股票 是股份制企业通过发行股票筹集到的,用于固定资产投资的资金。

(4)债券 是企业(公司)或金融机构通过发行各种债券筹集到的用于固定资产投资的资金,包括由银行代理国家专业投资公司发行的重点企业债券和重点建设债券。

(5)利用外资 指报告期收到的用于固定资产投资的国外资金,包括统借统还、自借自还的国外贷款,中外合资项目中的外资,以及无偿捐赠等。其中,国家统借统还的外资,是指由我国政府出面同外国政府、团体或金融组织签订贷款协议,并负责偿还本息的国外贷款。

(6)自筹资金 指建设单位报告期收到的,用于进行固定资产投资的上级主管部门、地方和本单位自筹资金。

(7)其他资金来源 指报告期收到的除以上各种拨款、借款、自筹资金之外,其他用于固定资产投资的资金。

Sources of Finance for Investment in Fixed Assets are classified as funds unsettled from previous year, state appropriation, loans, and various payable funds. The state appropriation and loans are further divided into seven categories, i. e. state budgetary appropriation, domestic loans, stocks, bonds, foreign investment, self-raiesed funds, and others.

(1) State budgetary appropriation includes funds appropriated of entrusted to banks by state budget, local finance, responsible institutes to construction enterprises and appropriation by central government for the purpose of capital construction and technical updating and transformation, and special funds arranged by central government for capital construction.

(2) Domestic loan refers to funds borrowed by enterprises and institutions during reference period for the purpose of domestic investment in fixed assets. Domestic loan includs loans issued by banks from sources of self-owned funds and deposit funds, loans appropriated by responsible institutes, special loans by government (including loan for coal replacing oil, special loan for reform-through -labor mining enterprises), loans arranged by local government, domestic reserve loan, and working loan, etc.

(3) Stock refers to funds for investment in fixed assets raised by the share holding enterprises through issuing stocks.

(4) Bonds refers to funds for investment in fixed assets raised by enterprises (companies) or financial institutions through issuing various bonds, which includes Key Enterprises Bonds and Key Construction Program Bonds issued by the Bands on behalf of state-owned investment companies.

(5) Utilization of Foreign Capital refers to the foreign funds recieved during the reference period for investment in fixed assets, including foreign funds borrowed and managed by the government, by individual units, foreign fund in joint venture program, and grants and donations, etc, of which foreign funds borrowed and managed by the government refer to foreign loan borrowed by the government from foreign governments, organizations, or financail institutions under official agreements signed by both partes and the government is responsible for repayment of both the principle and interests of the foreign loans.

(6) Self-raised funds refers to funds recieved by construction enterprises from their responsible institutions, local governments, and within enterprises for the purpose of investment in fixed assets during reference period.

(7) Others refer to funds recieved during reference period which are not included above.

32. 基本建设项目按大中小型划分 Capitl Construction Projects by Size

基本建设划分大中小型项目 原则上应按照上级批准的设计任务书或初步设计所确定的总规模或总投资划分，没有正式批准设计任务书或初步设计的，按国家或省、自治区、直辖市年度基本建设投资计划中所列的总规模或总投资划分。上述两条均不具备的，按本年计划施工工程的建设总规模或总投资划分。生产单一产品的工业项目，按产品的设计能力划分；生产多种产品的工业项目，按其主要产品的设计能力划分。品种繁多，难以按生产能力划分的，按全部计划投资额划分。划分标准以国家颁发的《大中小型建设项目划分标准》为依据。国家曾在1958年、1962年、1977年和1979年先后五次修订《大中小型建设项目划分标准》，因此各历史时期的大中型项目数不完全可比。

Capital Construction Projects by Siza The division of size of capital construction projects should be determined according to approved construction plan by responsible institutes or tentative size of investment, otherwise according to current capital construction plan of the state, provinces, autonomous regions, and cities under central government. Industrial projects which produce unitary products are classified according to its planning capacity of products; projects which produce multi products are calsscified by total planned investment. Standards for Division of Sizes of Construction Projects issued by the government is the base for size division of construction projects, which was revised in 1958, 1962, 1977, and 1979 respectively and therefore, data on projects by sized are not comparable from year to year.

33. 新增生产能力 Newly Increased Production Capicity

新增生产能力 指通过固定资产投资活动而增加的设计能力或工程效益，它是用实物形态表示的固定资产投资的成果。新增生产能力的计算，是以能独立发挥生产能力或效益的单项工程（或项目）为对象。当单项工程（或项目）建成，经有关部门鉴定合格，正式移交投入生产，即可计算新增生产能力。

新增生产能力或工程效益有以下几种表现形式：

（1）以建设项目或单项工程建成后的年产能力表示。如煤炭开采、石油开采等。

（2）以建设项目或单项工程建成后处理原料的能力表示。如选矿工程的年处理矿石能力，洗煤厂年洗原煤能力等。

（3）以新增的主要设备数量或容量表示。发棉纺锭枚数、发电机组容量等。

（4）以建筑物容积、容量、面积或长度表示。如水库容量、铁路公路里程等。

新增生产能力的数量一般按设计能力计算。设计能力是指设计文件中规定的在正常情况下能够达到的生产能力，而不论投产后的实际产量如何。以设备数量、建筑物容积、面积、长度等表示的新增生产能力（或效益），则按建成的实际数量计算。

Newly Increased Production Capacity refers to increase of designed capacity and project efficiency through investment in fixed assets, which relects the accomplishment of investment in fixed assets in kind. The calculation of newly increased production capacity is based on individual projects which operate independently. When an individual project is completed and checked and accepted and put into production, it is counted as newly increased production capacity.

Several forms of presenting newly increased production capacity and project efficiency are often applilied as follows:

(1) Annual production capacity, such as extraction of coal and oil;

(2) Raw material processing capacity, such as ore prosseing capacity of ore dressing projects;

(3) Number or volume of major equipments increased, such as number of cotton spindles increased and capacity of electricity generating sets increased;

(4) Physical measures of construction as volume, capacity, area, and length, for instance, capacity of reservoirs, length of railways or roads.

Quantity of newly increased production capacity is calculated by designed capacity in general, which refers to the production capacity a project can come up to under normal conditions designed in construction documents regardless of actual output.

34. 新增固定资产 Newly Increased Fixed Assets

新增固定资产 指通过投资活动所形成的新的固定资产价值。包括已经建成投入生产或交付使用的工程价值和达到固定资产标准的设备、工具、器具的价值及有关应摊入的费用。它是以价值形式表示的固定资产投资成果的综合性指标，可以综合反映不同时期、不同部门、不同地区的固定资产投资成果。

Newly Increased Fixed Assets refers to increase in value of fixed assets through investment, including projects completed and put into production, and equipments, tools, and vessels considered as fixed assets, and relevant expenses as investment in fixed assets, which is a comprehensive indicator of investment in fixed assets, reflecting the accomplishment of investment in fixed assets in fixed assets in different periods, different sectors, and different regions.

35. 固定资产交付使用率 Rate of projects of Fixed Assets Completed and put into Operation

固定资产交付使用率 指一定时期新增固定资产与同期完成投资额的比率。它是反映各个时期固定资产动用速度，衡量建设过程中投资效果的一个综合性指标。

Rate of Projects of Fixed Assets Completed and Put into Operation refers to ratio of newly increased fixed assets to total investment completed in the same period, which is a comprehensive indicator, reflecting the employment of fixed assets investment and investment efficiency.

36. 城市基础设施 Urban Infrastructure Facilities

城市基础设施 包括第二产业中的电力、煤气及水的生产和供应业；第三产业中的水利业、铁路运输、公路运输、管道运输、航空运输、邮电通信、公共服务和环境保护投资等。

Urban infrastructure facilities include the production and supply of power, gas and tap water in the secondary industry and water conservancy, railway transportation, highway transportation, pipeline transportation, air transportation, post and telecommunications, public services, environmental protection investment in the tertiary industry.

海关进出口总额 Total Import and Export Through the Custuoms

海关进出口总额 指实际进出我国国境的货物总金额。包括对外贸易实际进出口货物，来料加工装配进出口货物，国家间、联合国及国际组织无偿援助物资和赠送品，华侨、港澳台同胞和外籍华人捐赠品，租赁期满归承租人所有的租赁货物，进料加工进出口货物，边境地方贸易及边境地区小额贸易进出口货物（边民互市贸易除外），中外合资经营企业、中外合作经营企业、外商独资经营企业进出口货物和公用物品，到、离岸价格在规定限额以上的进出口货样和广告品（无商业价值、无使用价值和免费提供出口的除外），从保税仓库提取在中国境内销售的进口货物，以及其他进出口货物。进出口总额用以观察一个国家在对外贸易方面的总规模。我国规定出口货物按离岸价格统计，进口货物按到岸价格统计。

Total import and export through the Customs refers to the actual total value of goods entering and exiting the Chinese territory, including the actual import and export of foreign trade; imported and exported materials for the processing and assembling trade; aid given gratis and gifts from foreign government, the United Nations and international organizations; donations from oveerseas Chinese, compatriots in Hongkong, Macao and Taiwan, and ethnic Chinese of foreign citizenship; leased goods which belong to the tenant after the leasing contract expires; imports and exports processed with imported materials; local border trade and small amount of imports and exports through the frontier areas (except barter trade among people living on the frontiers); imports and exports and common goods of Sino-foreign joint ventures, Sino-foreign cooperative ventures and solely foreign-invested ventures; samples of imports and exports and advertising materials with their cost, insurance, freight and FOB value higher than the quota (except goods without commercial and use value and free exports); bonded imports which are for sale in the Chinese territory; and other imported and exported goods. The total import and export through the Customs reflects an overall picture of a country's foreign trade. According to Chinese regulations, exports are calculated at free on board value while imports are calculated at cost, insurance and freight.

38. 利用外资 Utilization of Foreign Capital

利用外资 指我国各级政府、部门、企业和其他经济组织通过对外借款、吸收外商直接投资以及利用其他方式筹措的境外现汇、设备、技术等。

Utilization of Foreign Capital refers to credits, instruments and technology financed from abroad and Hongkong and Macao, by loans、direct foreign investment and other forms undertaken by Chinese government at all levels, by various departments, enterprises, and other economic units.

39. 协议总金额 Total Contracted Amount of Fund

协议总金额 是指合同(章程)规定的投资总额。即合作双方出资额及企业筹措的建设资金总和。

Total contracted amount of money refers to the total investment stipulated by the contract. It is the total sum of the investment from the both sides and the construction funds raied by the involved enterprises.

40. 实际利用外资 Actual Use of Foreign Investment

实际利用外资 是指利用外资协议(合同)的实际执行金额。包括现汇、实物和双方同意计价投资的劳务、技术等无形资本。

Actual use of foreign investment refers to actual usage of contracted foreign investment, including cash, investment in kind and incorporeal capital agreed by the both sides as part of the investment, such as services and technology.

41. 对外借款 Foreign Borrowings

对外借款 是我国利用外资的主要部分。包括我国通过外国政府贷款,国际金融组织贷款,外国银行商业贷款,出口信贷以及对外发行债券、股票等方式,从境外筹措的资金。

Foreign Borrowings constitute a major part of China's use of foreign capital, including funds borrowed from foreign countries and Hong Kong and Macao, loans by foreign governments, and international monetary organizations, commecial loans and export financed by foreign banks, and funds collected by Chinese bonds and shares issued in foreign countries.

42. 外商直接投资 Direct Investment by Foreign Business

外商直接投资 是指外国企业和经济组织或个人(包括华侨、港澳台胞以及我国在境外注册的企业)按我国有关政策、法规,用现汇、实物、技术等在我国境内开办外商独资企业、与我国境内的企业或经济组织共同举办中外合资经营企业、合作经营企业或合作开发资源的投资(包括外商投资收益的再投资)以及经政府有关部门批准的项目投资总额内,企业从境外借入的资金。

Direct Investment by Foreign Business refers to the investment inside China by foreign enterprises and economic organizations or individuals (including overseas Chinese, compatriots in Hong Kong and Macao, and Chinese enterprises registered abroad), following the relevant policies and laws of China, for the establishment of wholly foreign-owned enterprises, and the establishment of joint venture enterprises, contractual joint ventures or co-operative exploration of resources with enterprises or economic organizations in China (including re-investment of profits from foreign businessmen's enterprises), and the funds that enterprises borrow from aborad in the total investment of projects which are approved by the relevant department of the government.

43. 对外承包工程 Overseas Contracted Projects

对外承包工程 包括各对外承包公司以招标议标承包方式承揽的下列业务:(1)承包国外工程建设项目;(2)承包我国对外经援项目;(3)承包我国驻外机构的工程建设项目;(4)承包我国境内利用外资进行建设的工程项目;(5)与外国承包公司合营或联合承包工程项目时我国公司分包部分;(6)以服务成果向业主收费的技术服务项目(包括承担地形地貌测绘;地质资源勘探与普查;建设区域规划;提供设计文件、图纸、生产工艺技术资料和工程技术经济咨询;工程项目的可行性考察、研究和评估;进行技术指导和培训人员等);(7)对外承包兼营的房屋开发业务。对外承包工程的营业额是以货币表现的本期内完成的对外承包工程的工作量，包括以前年度签订的合同和本年度新签订的合同在报告期完成的工作量。

Overseas Contracted Projects refers to projects undertaken by Chniese Contractors (poject contracting companies) through bidding process. They include: (1) overseas civil engineering construction projects financed by foreign investors; (2) overseas projects financed by the Chinese government through its foreign-aid programs; (3) construction projects of Chinese diplomatic missions, trade offices and other institutions stationed abroad; (4) construction projects in China financed by foreign investment; (5) sub-contracted projects to be taken by Chinese contractors through a joint umbrella project with foreign contractor(s); (6) technical assistance projects in the form of service results and chargeable to the owners (such as topographic surveying, geological prospecting development zone programming, provision of documents, blueprint, materials on production process technical consultation, project feasibility studies and evaluation, personnel trainning, etc); and (7) housing development projects. The business turnover from international contracting is the work of contracted projects completed during the reporting period, expressed in monetary terms, including completed work on projects signed in previous years.

44. 对外劳务合作 Overseas Services

对外劳务合作 指以收取工资的形式向业主或承包商提供技术和劳动服务的活动。我国对外承包公司在境外开办的合营企业，中国公司同时又提供劳务的，其劳务部分也纳入劳务合作统计。劳务合作营业额按报告期内向雇主提交的结算数(包括工资、加班费和奖金等)统计。

Overseas Services refers to activities of providing technology and labor services to employers or contractors by collecting salaries and wages. Labor services provided by Chinese international contracting corperations to their overseas joint ventures shall be included into the statictics of overseas services. The business turnover of overseas services is the settlement price (including salaries, overtime pay and bonuses) submitted to the employers during the reporting period.

45. 旅游人数 Number of Tourists

旅游人数 指来我国参观、访问、旅行、探亲、访友、休养、考察、参加会议和从事经济、科技、文化、教育、体育、宗教等活动的外国人、华侨、港澳和台湾同胞的人数。不包括外国在我国的常住机构，如领使馆、通讯社、企业办事处的工作人员；来我国常驻的外国专家、留学生以及在岸逗留不过夜人员

Number of Tourists refers to the number of foreigners, overseas Chinese, and compatrios from Hong Kong, Macao and Taiwan coming to the Chinese mainland for sightseeing, visit, tours, family reunions, meeting friends, vacations, study tours attending meetings and other activities of an economic, scientific and technological, cultural, physical culture and religious nature. This does not include employees of foreign organizations stationed in China such as embassies, consulates, news agencies, representative offices of overseas firms and foreign exports and students residing in China and persons who entler, the country but without staying over.

46. 财政收入 Financial Revenue

财政收入 指中央和地方财政一年内从企业、事业、个体经营者、居民等部门取得的货币收入的总和，包括中央企业在本省收入。财政收入主要有下列来源：

(1)企业所得税：指国有企业所得税、集体企业所得税、私营企业所得税、股份制企业所得税、联营企业所得税等；

(2)税收收入：包括消费税、增值税、营业税、城市维护建设税、证券交易印花税、外商外国企业所得税、关税、盐税、农业税等；

(3)其他收入：包括能源基金、调节基金、排污费、各种附加收入等。

Financial Revenue is the total monetary income the central and local treasuries have collected from enterprises, institutions, individual operators, residents and other social sectors within a fiscal year, which includes the income reaped by the central government-run enterprises in Jangsu. The main sources of the financial revenue include:

(1) Enterprise income tax: such as the income taxes paid by the state enterprises, collective enterprises, private enterprises, share-holding enterprises and cooperative enterprises;

(2) Tax revenue: including consumption tax, value-added tax, business tax, urban maintenance and construction tax, security exchange stamp tax, income tax paid by foreign-funded enterprises, customs duties, salt tax and agricultural tax, etc.

(3) Other income: such as energy construction fund, regulatory fund, sewage discharging fee and other additional incomes.

47. 财政支出 Financial Expenditure

财政支出 指财政一年内各种支出的总和，主要包括下列内容：

(1)用于城市建设、发展生产，如基本建设拨款、更新改造拨款、科技三项费用拨款、支农支出、城市维护建设费等；

(2)用于行政事业部门的日常开支，如科教文卫事业费、行政经费等；

(3)用于改善人民生活的支出，如物价补贴、抚恤救济费等；

(4)用于其他方面，如民防事业费、战备费等。

Financial Expenditure refers to the total expenditures of the local treasury within a fiscal year, which include:

(1) Expenditure on urban construction and production development, such as allocations for construction, technical renovation and transformation, and scientific and technological projects; aid to agricultural production; and cost of urban maintenance and construction;

(2) Current expenses of administrative departments and institutions, including expenditures for scientific, educational, cultural and pulic health undertakings and spendings on administration and management;

(3) Expenses for improving the local peole's living standards, such as dearness allowances and pension and relief cost, and

(4) Spendings in other fields, such as costs of civil defence and preparations against war.

48. 储蓄存款 Savings Deposits

储蓄存款 指居民个人在金融机构的存款，包括各种形式的城镇居民储蓄和农村个人储蓄。

Savings Deposits refers to the deposits that individual residents have put into finacial institutions, including all kinds of urban residens' savings deposits and rural indivuals savings deposits.

49. 存款 Deposits

存款 企业、机关、团体或居民根据可以收回的原则，把货币资金存入银行或其他信用机构保管并取得一定利息的一种信用活动形式。根据存款对象的不同可划分为企业存款、财政存款、机关团体存款、基本建设存款、城镇储蓄存款、农村存款等科目。它是银行信贷资金的主要来源。

Deposits are a form of credit by which enterprises, institutions, organizations or residents can put money into banks and other credit institutions for safekeeping and earn intersts under the principle of free withdrawal. According to different depositors, deposits are divided into enterprises deposits, treasury deposits of government agencies and organizations, capital construction deposits, urban savings deposits, rural deposits and other deposits. Deposits contitute a major source of bank credit funds.

50. 贷款 Loans

贷款 银行或其他信用机构根据必须归还的原则，按一定利率，为企业、个人等提供资金的一种信用活动形式。我国银行贷款，分流动资金贷款、固定资产贷款、城乡个体工商户贷款以及农户贷款等科目。

Loans are a form of credit by which banks and other credit institutions provide funds with a prescribed interest to enterprises and individuals under the principle of unconditional repayment. Loans from Chinese banks include circulating capital loans, fixed assets loans and urban and rural individual industrial and commercial unit loans and farmer household loans.

51. **保险费** Premium

保险费 是保险人根据保险合同的有关规定，为被保险人取得因约定危险事故发生所造成的经济损失补偿(或给付)权利，付给保险人的代价。包括财产险和人身险储金收入。

Premium is the fee paid by the insurant based on a proportion of the benefit he may get from the the insurance plus the insurance value. It includes savings income from property and life insurance.

52. **保险赔款** Insurance Indemnity

保险赔款 指保险事故发生后，经查证确属保险责任范围以内的保险标准的损失，保险人根据保险合同的规定履行赔偿义务，给予被保险人的款项叫做赔款。赔款可分为已决赔款和未决赔款两种。

Insurance Indemnity is the compensation paid by the insurer for an accident happening to the insured property or the insurance value paid for an accident happening to a peerson who has insured his life. It is further divided into settled and unsettled reparation.

53. **年初实有耕地面积** The Actual Area of Plowland at the Beginning of a year

是指年初实有能够种植农作物，经常进行耕锄的田地。包括熟地，当年新开荒地，连续撩荒未满三年的耕地和当年的休闲地(轮歇地)。以种植农作物为主并附带种植桑树、茶树、果树和其他林木的土地以及沿海、沿湖地区已围垦利用的“海涂”、“湖田”等也应包括在内但不包括专业性的桑园、茶园、果园、果木苗圃、林地、芦苇地、天然草原等。

This refers to the real area of arable land and frequently-tended farmfields at the begingnning of a year. It includes cultivated land, the newly-reclaimed wasteland in the year, the farmland which has been laid idle for no more than three consecutive years, and land on fallow rotation that year. It shall also include farmland with mulberry, tea, fruit and other trees but used mainly for growing crops as well as the reclaimed "beachland" and "lakeland" along the sea coasts and the lake banks. However, it shall not include the land devoted especcially for muberry and the tea gardens, orchards, nurseries, woodlands, reed marches and natural grasslands.

54. **农业总产值** Gross Output Value of Agriculture

农业总产值 是以货币表现的农、林、牧、渔业全部产品的总量，它反映一定时期内农业生产的总规模和总成果。

农、林、牧、渔业的统计范围是：

(1)农业 包括农作物种植业和其他农业。

农作物种植业 包括谷物、豆类、薯类、棉、油料、糖料、麻类、烟叶、蔬菜、药材、瓜类和其他农作物的种植，以及茶园、桑园、果园的生产经营。

其他农业 包括采集野生植物的果实、纤维、树胶、树脂、油料以及柴草、野生药材、菌类等及农民家庭兼营的商品性工业。

(2)林业 包括林木的栽培(不包括茶园、桑园和果园的栽培、管理和收获等活动)、林产品的采集和村及村以下合作经济组织和农户的竹木采伐。

(3)牧业 包括除渔业养殖以外的一切动物饲养和放牧以及野生动物的捕猎和饲养。

(4)渔业 包括水生动物和海藻类植物的养殖和捕捞。

从所有制看，包括国有经济的各种专业农(农、林、牧、渔)场以及国家各级机关团体学校、科研机构、部队经营的农业；集体所有制的乡镇村各级办农场；农村各种经济组织经营的农、林、牧、渔业以及工矿企业家属集体经营的农业；农民家庭自营的农林牧渔业及兼营商品性工业等。

农业总产值的计算方法通常是按农林牧渔业产品及其副产品的产量分别乘以各自单位产品价格求得，少数生产周期较长，当年没有产品或产品产量不易统计的，则采用间接方法匡算其产值，然后将四业产品产值相加即为农业总产值。

1957年以前的农业总产值中包括了厩肥和农民自给性手工业(如农民自制衣服、鞋、袜,自己从事粮食初步加工等)。1958年及以后的农业总产值,林业中增加了村及村以下竹木采伐产值;牧业中取消了厩肥产值;副业中取消了农民自给性手工业产值,增加了村及村以下办的工业产值;渔业中增加了海洋捕捞水产品产值。1980年及以后的农业总产值,在副业中增加了农民家庭兼营工业商品部分的产值。从1984年起村及村以下办工业产值划归工业。从1993年起,取消副业,将野生动物的捕猎划入牧业,野生植物采集和农民家庭兼营商品性工业划归农业。

Gross Output Value of Agriculture refers to the total volume of products of farming, forestry, animal husbandry, and fishery expressed in the monetary terms. It reflects the overall scale and achievements of agricultural production during a given period of time.

The scope of statistics on farming, forestry, animal husbandry, and fishery is as follows:

(1) Farming includes cultivation of farm crops and other agricultural activities.

Cultivation of Farm Crops includes cultivation of grain crops, legume crops, tubercrops, cotton, oil-bearing crops, sugar crops, bastfiber plants, tobacco, vegetables, medicinal herbs, melon crops, and cultivation and management of tea plantations, mulberry fields and orchards.

Other Agricultural Activities includes harvesting wild fruits, fibers, tree gum, resin, oil-bearing plants, firewood, wild medical heerbs, fungus, and rural household commodity industries.

(2) Forestry refers to planting trees of various kinds (excluding tea plantations, mulberry fields and orchards), collection of forestry products and cutting and felling of bamboo and trees by villages and other cooperative organizations under villages.

(3) Animal husbandry refers to raising and grazing of all kinds of farm animals except fishing and aquatic cultivating, and hunting and raising of wild animals.

(4) Fishery refers to cultivation and catching of fish and other aquatic animals and cultivation and collection of seaweed and other aquatic plants.

In terms of ownership, China's agriculture includes specialized state farms (for farming, forestry, animal husbandtry, fishery), farms managed by various government agencies, organizations, schools, research institutions, and army, farms managed by rural collective organizations at level of the township, town, and village; farming, forestry, animal husbandry, fishery run by various rural collective organizations and farming run by collective family members' organizations of mining and industrial enterprises; farming, forestry, animal husbandry and fishery and some commodity industries run by individual farmers.

Gross output value of agriculture os obtained by first multiplying the output of products or by-products by their unit price. For a small number of products, annual output of which is not available or difficult to get due to the long production growing process involved, the output value will be estimated through an indirect approach. The aum of output value of all products of farming, forestry, animal husbandry and fishery will then equal to gross output value of agriculture.

Before 1957, China's gross agricultural output value included the value of barnyard manure and handicraft products for self-consumption (clothes, shoes, stocking, and initial grain processing undertaken by peasants). After 1958, the output value of cutting and felling of bamboo and trees by villages and other cooperative organizations under villages have been included in forestry; value of barnyard manure has been excluded from animal husbandry; the value of self-consumed handicrafts has been excluded from sideline occupations, while output value of industries run by villages and cooperative organizations under village has been included in sideline occupations and output value of fish catches by motor fishing boats has been added to fishery. Since 1980, the output value of handicraft products made for sale by farmer households has been added to sideline occupations. From 1984, industries run by villages and cooperative oranizations under villages have been included in the sector of industry. After 1993, the category of sideline occupations has been canceled and hunting of wild animals has been classfied into husbandry, and harvesting of wild vegetation and commodity industry run by rural households have been grouped into the category of agriculture.

55. **农业机械总动力** Total Power of Farm Machinery

农业机械总动力 指用于农、林、牧、渔业生产的各种动力机械的动力总和。动力机械包括耕作、排灌、种植、植物保护、收获、农产品加工、运输、畜牧、渔业、农田水利等各种机械。不包括专门用于乡办工业、基本建设、非农业运输、科学试验和教学等非农业生产方面的动力机械与作业机械的数量。

Total Power of Farm Machinery refers to total mechanical power of machinery used in farming, forestry, animal husbandry and fishery, including machines used for ploughing, irrigation and drainage, crcp growing, plant protection, Harvesting, farm product processing, transport, stock breeding, fishery and water conservancy. Mchinery employed for non-agricultural purposes such as township industry, capital construction, non-agricultural transport, scientific experiments and for teaching is excluded.

56. 乡镇企业 Township Enterprises

乡镇企业 即原来农村人民公社和生产大队两级集体经济举办的社队企业。在农村政社组织管理体制分设以后,除了乡、村合作经济组织办企业外,又出现了部分农民联营或其他形式的合作企业和个体企业。1984年3月确定将这类企业统称"乡镇企业"。

乡镇企业单位一般应拥有固定的组织、生产场所、生产设备和从业人员;有核算制度,承担经济责任和纳税义务;是一个比较稳定的经济实体。

Township Enterprises refer to enterprises originally run by the collective economies at the people's commune and the production brigade levels. After the rural administrative system reform, besides the enterprises run by townships and villages, farmers' cooperative or other types of cooperative enterprises and private enterprises had appeared in the rural areas. In march 1984, all the aforesaid enterprises were defined as the "township enterprises."

Towndhip enterprises usually have fixed organization, production sites, production equipment and employees. They also have accounting systems, undertake economic responsibilities and pay taxes. So, they are relatively stable economic entities.

57. 工业总产值 Gross Output Value of Industry

工业 指从事自然资源的开采,对采掘品和农产品进行加工和再加工的物质生产部门。具体包括:(1)对自然资源的开采,对采矿、晒盐、森林采伐等(但不包括禽兽捕猎和水产捕捞);(2)对农副产品的加工、再加工,如粮油加工、食品加工、轧花、缫丝、纺织、制革等;(3)对采掘品的加工、再加工,如炼铁、炼钢、化工生产、石油加工、机器制造、木材加工等,以及电力、自来水、煤气的生产和供应等;(4)对工业品的修理、翻新,如机器设备的修理、交通运输工具(包括小卧车)的修理等。

1984年以前农村的村及村以下办工业归属农业,1984年以后划归工业。

工业总产值 是以货币表现的工业企业在一定时期内生产的已出售或可供出售工业产品总量,它反映一定时间内工业生产的总规模和总水平。它包括:在本企业内不再进行加工,经检验、包装入库(规定了需包装的产品除外)的成品价值。工业性作业价值、自制半成品、在产品期末期初差额价值(生产周期较长的企业计算)。工业总产值采用"工厂法"计算,即以工业企业作为一个整体,按企业工业生产活动的最终成果来计算,企业内部不允许重复计算,不能把企业内部各个车间(分厂)生产的成果相加。但在企业之间、行业之间、地区之间存在着重复计算。

轻重工业总产值的划分也是按"工厂法"计算的,即一个工业企业在正常情况下生产的主要产品的性质属于轻工业,则按企业的全部总产值作为轻工业总产值;一个工业企业生产的主要产品的性质属于重工业,则该企业的全部总产值作为重工业总产值。

自1995年下半年起,为适应建立新国民经济核算体系的需要,工业总产值计算方法有所变化,称为工业总产值新规定。新规定与原规定的区别主要有三点:(1)全价与加工费的计算原则不同:新规定凡自备原材料,不论其生产繁简程度如何,一律按加工费计算总产值;原规定则对此有一些特殊规定,某些来料加工,允许按全价计算总产值,而某些自备原材料生产,只允许按加工费计算总产值;(2)自制半成品、在产品期末期初差额价值的计算原则不同,新规定要求,凡会计产品成本核算时计算了成本的差额价值,总产值中就应包括,否则,可不包括;原规定则区分了生产周期六个月的界限,凡生产周期六个月以上的企业,总产值计算中应包括这部分差额价值,否则可不包括;(3)计算价格不同:新规定按不含增殖税(销项税额)的价格计算;原规定按含增殖税(销项税额)的价格计算。本年鉴除有注明之外,工业总产值计算均为原规定。

Industry refers to material production sector which is engaged in extraction of natural resources and processing of natural resources and agricultural products and reprocessing, including: (1) extraction of natural recources, such as mining, extracting salt, felling trees (not including hunting and fishing); (2) processing of farm and sideline produces, such as rice husking, wheat milling, wine making, oil pressing, cotton ginning, silk reeling, animal slughtering, and medicinal herbs processing; (3) manufacture of industrial products, such as steel making, iron smelting, steel rolling, coke making, chemicals manufacturing, machine building, timber processing, spinning and weaving, printing and dyeing, dress making, and paper making; water and gas production and electricity generation and supply; (4) repairing of industrial products such as machinery and means of transport.

Prior to 1984, rural industry run by village and cooperative organizations under village was classified as agriculture and was grouped into industry after 1985.

Gross Output Value of Industry refers to the total valume, expressed in the monetary terms, of products turned out by industrial enterprises during a given period of time which are already sold or avaible for sale. It reflects the overall scale and level of the industrial production during a given period. It includes the value of finished products which are already examined, packed (excluding products whose packaging is required by set rules) and stored and which will not undergo further processing by their products; industrial operation value; and the differential value of initial and final self－made semi-finished products (calculated in enterprises with a relatively long production cycle). The gross output value of industry is calculated with the "factory act" method, which regards an industrial enterprise as a single unit and only takes the final production result of the unit into account thus avoiding double counting within an industrial enterprise or add-up of the production results of various workshops (branches) of the enterprise. However, doubling counting still exists among enterprises, trades and regions.

The gross output value of light and heavy industries is also calculated with the "factory act" method. Under normal conditions, if the major products of an enterprise belong to the light industry category, the gross output value of the enterprise shall be included totally into the gross output value of the light industry. The same rule applies to the gross output value of the heavy industry.

Since the second half of 1985, China has adopted new rules to calcute its total industrial output value, in an effort to build a new accounting system for the national economy. There are three major differences between the old and new rules.

(1) The definiton of full production cost and processing cost is different. The new rules stipulate that the output value of the production with self-supplied raw materials, whether its production procedure is simple or complicated, should be calculated according to the processing cost. According to the old rules, the output value of some processing production with raw materials supplied by customers can be calculated according to the full production cost, while some production with self-supplied raw materials can only be calculated according to the processing cost.

(2) For self-made semi-finished products, the principle of accounting diferential cost of the beginning and the end of the production is different. The new rules stipulate that if the differential cost is included in the production cost of the product, it should be included in the output value, too. Otherwise, the differential cost may not be included in the output value. The old rules set a limitation of six-month production period. An enterprise with a production period of more than six months should include the differential cost in calculating its total output value. Otherwise, the differential cost may not be included in the total output value.

(3) The accounting price is different. According to the new rules, the industrial output value will be calculated without value-added tax. The old rules calculate the industrial output value with value-added tax. Except those marked out, the industrial output value listed in this year-book is calculated according to the old rules.

轻工业 指主要提供生活消费品和制作手工业工具的工业。按其所使用的原料不同，可分为两大类：(1)以农产品为原料的轻工业，是指直接或间接以农产品为基本原料的轻工业。主要包括食品制造、饮料制造、烟草加工、纺织、缝纫、皮革和毛皮制作、造纸以及印刷等工业；(2)以非农产品为原料的轻工业，是指以工业品为原料的轻工业。主要包括文教体育用品、化学药品制造、合成纤维制造、日用化学制品、日用玻璃制品、日用金属制品、手工工具制造、医疗器械制造、文化和办公用机械制造等工业。

重工业 是指为国民经济各部门提供物质技术基础的主要生产资料的工业。按其生产性质和产品用途，可以分为下列三类：(1)采掘(伐)工业，指对自然资源的开采，包括石油开采、煤炭开采、金属矿开采、非金属矿开采和木材采伐等工业；(2)原材料工业，是指向国民经济各部门提供基本材料、动力和燃料的工业。包括金属冶炼及加工、炼焦及焦炭化学、化工原料、水泥、人造板以及电力、石油和煤炭加工等工业；(3)加工工业，是指对工业原材料进行再加工制造的工业。包括装备国民经济各部门的机械设备制造工业、金属结构、水泥制品等工业，以及为农业提供的生产资料如化肥、农药等工业。

根据上述划分原则，修理业中以重工业产品为修理作业对象的划为重工业，反之划为轻工业。

Light Industry refers to industry which produces consumer goods and hand tools. It consists of two categories, depending on the materials used:

(1) Industries using farm products as raw materials. These are branches of light industry which directly or indirectly use farm products as basic raw materials, including the manufacture of food and beverages, tobacco processing, textile, clothing, fur and leather manufacture, paper making, printing, etc.

(2) Industries using non-farm products as raw materials. These are branches of lihgt industry which use manufatured goods as raw materials, including the manufature of cultural and educational articles, crafts and art products, chemical instruments, and the manufature of cultural and office machinery.

Heavy Industry produces capital goods, which provides various sectors of the national economy with necessary materials and technical basis, and consists of the following three branches according to purpose of production or use of products:

(1) Mining and felling industry refers to industry that extracts natural resources, including extraction of petroleum, coal, metal and non-metal ores and timber felling.

(2) Raw materials industry provides various sectors of the national economy with raw materials, fuels and power. It includes smelting and processing of metals, coke making and coke chemistry, chemical materials and building materials such as cement, plywood, and power petroluem and coal processing.

(3) Manufaturing industry processes raw materials. It includes machine-building industry which equips sectors of the national economy, industry of metal structure and cement works, industry producing means of agricultural production, and industry of chemical fertilizers and pesticides.

58. 工业销售产值 Sales Output Value of Industry

工业销售产值 是以货币表现的工业企业在一定时期内销售的本企业生产的工业产品产量。包括已销售的成品、半成品价值,对外提供的工业性作业价值和对本单位基本建设部门、生活福利部门等提供的产品和工业性作业及自制设备的价值。已销售的成品、半成品不论是本期生产的,还是上期生产的,只要是本期销售出去的均包括在内。对外提供的工业性作业是指企业按合同对外提供的工业性劳务。企业为本单位基本建设部门、生活福利部门等提供的产品和工业性作业及自制设备也应视同销售,这部分也作为销售统计。

工业销售产值的计算范围、计算价格和计算方法与工业总产值一致,但两者计算的基础不同,工业销售产值计算的基础是产品销售总量,工业总产值计算的基础是工业产品生产总量。

Sales Output Value of Industry refers to total sale value of products produced by industrial enterprises during a given period, including sales of finished goods, value of semi-products, value of industrial services provided to other units, value of products provided for capital construction sector, welfare sector and value of industrial services provided and self-produced equipments within enterprises. Sales of finished goods and semi-products in current are taken into account regardless of their production period.

The coverage, pricing, and calculation method for sales output value of industry are the same as for gross output value of industry except that the former is based on sales of products and the later is based on output of products.

59. 独立核算工业企业、非独立核算工业生产单位 Independent Accounting Industrial Enterprises and Non-Independent Accounting Industrial Production Work Units

工业企业按其行政和财务是否独立,分为独立核算工业企业和非独立核算工业生产单位。

独立核算工业企业应同时具备下列三个条件:(1)行政上有独立的组织形式;(2)经济上独立核算、自负盈亏,编制独立的资金平衡表;(3)有权与其他单位签订合同,并在银行设有独立帐户。独立核算工业企业不论是单一性生产或联合性生产的企业,均以整个企业作为一个基层单位进行统计,而不按分厂、车间统计。

非独立核算工业生产单位是指不同时具备独立核算工业企业三个条件,附设于其他企业、事业、机关、团体、学校、科研机构、部队等单位的工业生产单位。非独立核算工业生产单位,必须同时具备下列三个条件,才能列入工业统计范围,即:(1)有固定的生产场所和生产设备;(2)有固定的生产工人和学徒在十人以上;(3)一般单位常年生产,季节性生产的单位全年开工时间在三个月以上。

Depending on whether they have independent administration and accounting, industrial enterprises can be divided into independent accounting industrial enterpeises and non-independent accounting industrial production work units.

An independent accounting industrial enterprise shall operate simulaneously under the following three conditions: (1)

having an independent organization in terms of administration; (2) economically having independent accounting, taking care of its own profits and losses, and filing independent balance sheets; and (3) enjoying the right to sign contracts with other work units and open independent bank accounts. An independent accounting industrial enterprise, no matter under a unitary management or cooperative operation, shall be counted as a single grassroots unit in statistics and its branch factories and workshops shall not be calculated separately.

A non-independent accounting industrial production work unit is an industrial production work unit which does not operate simulaneously under the aforementioned three conditions of independent accounting industrial enterprises and is attached to an enterprise, institution, government department, organization, school, scientific research institution, or army unit. A non-independent accounting industrial production work unit can be included into the industrial statistics only when it operates simultaneously under the following three conditions: (1) having fixed production sites and production equipment; (2) having more than 10 permanent workers and apprentices; and (3) operating all-year-round if it's a normal production work unit or operating more than three months a year if it's a seasonal production work unit.

60. **大、中、小型企业** Large, Medium and Small Enterprises

工业企业按其规模大小分成大型(特大型、大一型、大二型)、中型(中一型、中二型)、小型企业。

大、中、小型企业的划分标准有下列两类:

(1)按企业产品的年生产能力划分。凡产品比较单一的行业,如电力、原煤、石油、钢铁、有色金属、硫酸、烧碱、纯碱、合成氨、发电设备、汽车、拖拉机、木材采伐、水泥、平板玻璃、纺织、造纸、制糖、手表、缝纫、自行车等均以产品生产能力作为划分大、中、小型的标准(生产多种产品的企业,以其主要产品的生产能力来划分)。

(2)按企业拥有的固定资产原价划分。凡产品种类繁多,难以按生产能力划分的,则以企业拥有的固定资产原价作为划分大、中、小型的标准。

In light of their scales, industrial enterprises can be divided into large (extra large, large-Ⅰ, large-Ⅱ), medium (medium-Ⅰ, medium-Ⅱ) and smaal enterpeises.

The criteria for classifying large, medium and small enterpeises fall into the following two categories:

(1) Classification according to annual production capacity.

Enterprises with singular products, such as producers of power, raw coal, petroleum, iron and steel, non-ferrous metals, vitriol, caustic soda, soda ash, synthetic ammonia, power generation eqiupment, automobile, tractor, timber, cement, plate glass, textiles, paper, sugar, wrist watches, sewing machines, and bicycles, will be classified as large, medium and small enterprises in light of their production capacity (enterprises turning out a variety of products will be classified according to their production capacity of their major products).

(2) Classification according to the oringinal value of fixed assets. Enterprises which turn out a great variety of products and can handly be classified according to their production capacity shall be divided into large, medium and small enterprises according to the original value of their fixed assets.

61. **工业企业主要财务指标和经济效益指标**
The Main Financial Indexes and Economic Efficiency Indexed of Industrial Enterprises

(1)资本金合计:

资本金是企业在工商行政管理部门登记的注册资金。资本金合计包括国家资本金、法人资本金、个人资本金、外商资本金和集体资本金等。

国家资本金:是指有权代表国家投资的政府部门或者机构以国有资产投入企业形成的资本金。不论企业的资本金是哪个政府部门或机构投入,只要是以国家资金进行投资的,均作为国家资本金。

法人资本金是指其他法人单位以其依法可以支配的资产投入企业形成的资本金。

个人资本金是指以社会个人或者企业内部职工以个人合法财产投入企业形成的资本金。

外商资本金是指外国投资者以及香港、澳门、台湾地区投资者投入企业形成的资本金。

集体资本金是指集体所有制企业投入企业形成的资本金。

(2)资产总计:

资产是指企业拥有或者控制的能以货币计量的经济资源,包括各种财产、债权和其他权利。资产按其流动性(即资产的变现能力和支付能力）划分为：流动资产、长期投资、固定资产、无形资产、递延资产和其他资产。

流动资产合计是指可以在一年内或者超过一年的一个生产周期内变现或者耗用的资产合计。流动资产年平均余额是指一年内工业企业全部流动资产的平均余额。

固定资产合计，固定资产是指使用年限在一年以上，单位价值在规定标准以上，并在使用过程中保持原有物质形态的资产，包括房屋及建筑物、机器设备、运输设备、工具器具等。固定资产合计是指企业固定资产净值、固定资产清理、在建工程、待处理固定资产净损失所占用的资金合计，包括固定资产原价、固定资产净值、固定资产净值年平均余额。固定资产原价是指固定资产按取得时的实际成本计价。在固定资产尚未交付使用或者已投入使用但尚未办理竣工决算之前发生的固定资产的借款利息和有关费用，以及外币借款的汇兑差额，应当计入固定资产价值，之后的计入当期损益。接受捐赠的固定资产应按照同类资产的市场价格或有关凭据确定固定资产价值，接受捐赠固定资产时发生的各项费用，应当计入固定资产价值。融资租入的固定资产，按租赁协议确定的设备价款、运输费、途中保险费、安装调试费等支出计价，在原有固定资产基础上进行改建、扩建的固定资产，按原有固定资产帐面原价，减去改建、扩建过程中发生的变价收入，加上由于改建、扩建而增加的支出计价。盘盈的固定资产，按重置完全价值计价。固定资产净值是指固定资产原价减去累计折旧后的净额。

（3）负债合计：

负债合计是指企业所承担的能以货币计量，将以资产或劳务偿付的债务总计。负债一般按偿还期长短分为流动负债和长期负债。流动负债合计是指企业在一年内或超过一年的一个营业周期内偿还的债务；长期负债合计是指偿还期在一年以上或者超过一年的一个营业周期内偿还债务。

（4）产品销售收入：

产品销售收入是指企业销售成品、自制半成品、提供工业性劳务等取得的收入。

（5）利润总额：

利润总额是指企业在一定时期内实现的盈亏总额，是企业最终的财务成果，包括营业利润、补贴收入、投资收益、营业外净收入等。

（6）工业经济效益综合指数：

工业经济效益综合指数是综合衡量工业经济效益各方面在数量上总体水平的一种特殊相对数，是反映工业经济运行质量的总量指数，是以各项工业经济效益指数实际数值分别除以该项指标的全国标准值并乘以各自权数求得。计算公式：

$$\text{工业经济效益综合指数}(\%) = (\frac{\text{某项经济效益指标报告期数值}}{\text{该项指标全国标准值}} \times \text{权数}) \div \text{总权数}$$

计算工业经济效益综合指数时，各项经济效益指标分子、分母应按报告期止累计数（如产品销售收入为报告期上累计产品销售收入）或序时平均数（如平均流动资产为报告期止各月平均流动资产之和除以累计月数）计算。

全国的标准值：是根据"八五"期间全国乡及乡以上工业企业每项指标实际完成数值加权平均计算出来的。

权数：是根据上述各项工业经济效益指标在综合效益中的重要程度，由专家调查法确定的。

（7）工业企业主要经济效益指标的计算公式：

$$\text{工业产品销售率}(\%) = \frac{\text{工业销售产值}}{\text{工业总产值}} \times 100\%$$

$$\text{工业资金利税率}(\%) = \frac{\text{实现利税总额}}{\text{平均流动资产} + \text{固定资产净值平均余额}} \times 100\%$$

$$\text{工业增加值率}(\%) = \frac{\text{工业增加值}}{\text{工业总产值}} \times 100\%$$

$$\text{成本费用利润率}(\%) = \frac{\text{实现利润总额}}{\text{成本费用总额}} \times 100\%$$

$$\text{工业全员劳动生产率}(\text{元}/\text{人}) = \frac{\text{工业增加值}}{\text{全部职工平均人数}}$$

$$\text{流动资产周转次数}(\text{次}) = \frac{\text{产品销售收入}}{\text{流动资产平均余额}}$$

(8)流动比率：

流动比率是反映企业每百元流动负债中，有多少元流动资产作后盾。计算公式：

$$流动比率 = \frac{流动资产总额}{流动负债总额}$$

(9)速动比率：

速动比率是衡量企业流动资产中可以立即用于偿付流动负债的能力。计算公式：

$$速动比率 = \frac{速动资产}{流动负债}$$

(10)资产负债率：

资产负债率是反映在企业资产总额中有多少资产是通过借债而得的，也可以用于衡量企业利用债权人提供资金进行经营活动的能力以及企业在清算时保护债权人利益的程度。计算公式：

$$资产负债率 = \frac{负债总额}{资产总额}$$

(11)债务资本率：

债务资本率是反映企业长期偿债的能力。计算公式：

$$债务资本率 = \frac{负债总额}{所有者权益总额}$$

(1) Aggregate Capital in Cash

Capital in cash refers to an enterprise's capital registered with a local industrial and commercial administrative department. The aggregate capital in cash includes the capital in cash of the state, the legal persons, individuals, foreign investors and colletives.

State capital in cash means the capital in cash dervied from the state-owned assets invested into enterprises by government departments or organizations which have the right to invest on behalf of the state. No matter the capital in cash of an enterprises comes from which government department or organization, it shall be deemed as the state capital in cash if the investment comes from the state fund.

Legal person capital in cash refers to the capital in cash stemmed from the investment put into an enterprise by other firms using assets legitimately at their disposal.

Individual capital in cash is the capital in cash derived from investment put into an enterprise by individuals or the enterprise's employees using their legitimate personnal possessions.

Foreign investor's capital in cash is the capital in cash resulting from investment put into an enterprise by foreign investors or investrs from Hongkong, Macoa and Taiwan.

Collective capital in cash is the capital in cash derived form investment put into an enterprises by collective enterprises.

(2) Aggregate Assets

Assets mean economic resources owned or controlled by an enterprise which can be calculated in monetary terms. They included all types of properties, creditor's rights and other rights. In view of their liquidity (e. g. , cash-ability and paying capacity), assets can be divided into circulating assets, long-term investment, fixed assets, intangible assets, deterred assets and other assets.

The aggregate circulating assets refer to an enterprise's total cacheable or usable assets within a production cycle which can be either shorter or longer than a year. The average annual balance of circulating assets means the average balance of the total circulating assets of an enterprise within a year.

The aggregate fixed assets mean assets with a duration over one year, a unit price above the prescribed level and maintaining their original physical shape during the utilization period. They include houses, buildings, machines, equipment, transport facilities, tools and instruments. The aggregate assets are the add-up of the new value of the fixed assets, retirement fo fixe asets, projects under construction and the capital occupied for handling the net loss of the fixed assets of an enterprise. They include the original value, the net value and the aunnual net value balance of fixed assets. The original value of the fixed assets is the cost price of the assets at the time of their obtaining. The loan interest and other fees concerning the fixed assets before they are put into use or after they are put into use before the final settlement of account and the balance of exchange of the relevant foreign exchange loans shall be included into the value of the fixed assets, but they shall be grouped into the current period profits and lossed afterwards. The value of donated fixed assets shall be calculated according to the market price of the same type assets or relevant credentials and shall include all the fees related to accepting of the donating. The value of the fixed asets obtained through capital leasing shall include the equipment prices as prescribed in the leasing contracts, the transportation fee, the transportation insurance and the cost of installation and testing. The value of the renovated and expanded assets shall be equal to the original book value of the original assets minus the income from the current price occurred during the renovation and expansion process and plus the expenditure for the renovation and expansion. The value of the inventory profit-generated fixed assets shall be equal to the complete replacement price. The net value of the fixed assets is the result of deducting the accumulated depreciation from the original value of the fixef assets.

(3) Aggregate Liabilities

Aggregate liabilities refer to the total debts if an enterprise which can be calculated in monetary terms and will be repaid in the forms of assets or services. Usually, the debts are divided into liquid liability and long-term debt according to the lenth of the payback period. The liquid liability is the debt that an enterprise will pay back during an operation cycle which is either shorter or longer than a year. The long-term debt refers to a debt whose payback period is longer than a year or which will be repaid during an operation cycle which is longer than a year.

(4) Product Sales Income

Product sales income refers to the income obtained by an enterprise by selling its finished products, semi-finished products or by providing industrial services.

(5) Aggregate Profit

Aggregate profit is the total profits and losses realized by an enterprise during a given period of time and is its final financial result. It includes operating profit, subsidies, investment yield and non-operating income.

(6) Aggregative Index of Industrial Economic Efficiency

Aggregative index of industrial economic efficiency is a special relative figure which comprehensively appraises the overall levels in quantitative terms of the industrial economic efficiency in various respects. It is also a total quantity index reflecting the economic performance quality of the industry. It is the result of the real number of the industrial economic efficiency index in each field being divided by the national standard value in the same field and then multiplied by the respective weight number as shown below:

$$\textit{Aggregative index of industrial economic efficiency } (\%)$$
$$= (\frac{\textit{Reporting period figure of a certain economic efficiency index}}{\textit{National standard value in the same field}} \times \textit{weight}) \ (\textit{overall weight})$$

When calculating the aggregative index of industrial economic efficiency, the numerator and denominator of various industrial economic efficiency indexes shall be the accumulative figures by the end of the reporting period (for instance, the product sales income shall be the accumulative product sales income by the end of the reporting period) or the chronological average (for instance, the average circulating assets shall be the result of dividing the sum of average monthly figure by the number of months within the reporting period).

The national standard value is based on the weighted average of the real figure of each index of industrial enterprises at and above the township level in the country during the Eight Five-Year Plan period (1991-95).

Weight is determined by the expert investigation method in light of the degree of significace of each the aforementioned industrial economic efficiency indexes in the the aggregative industrial economic efficiency.

(7) Formulas for Calculating the Main Economic Efficiency Indexes of Industrial Enterprises

$$\textit{Industrial production-sales rate}(\%) = \frac{\textit{Industrial sales value}}{\textit{Total industrial output value}} \times 100\%$$

$$\textit{Industrial capital-profit-tax}(\%) = \frac{\textit{Total realized profits-taxes}}{\textit{Average circulating assets} + \textit{average balance of fixed assets net value}} \times 100\%$$

$$Industrial\ value\ increase\ rate(\%)=\frac{Industrial\ value\ increase}{Total\ industrial\ output\ value}\times 100\%$$

$$Cost\text{-}profit\ rate(\%)=\frac{Total\ realized\ profit}{Total\ cost}\times 100\%$$

$$Industrial\ all\text{-}personnel\ labour\ productivity\ (yuan/person)=\frac{Industrial\ value\ increase}{Average\ number\ of\ all\text{-}personnel\ labour}\times 100\%$$

$$Number\ of\ circulating\ assets\ turnover\ (time)=\frac{Product\ sales\ income}{Average\ balance\ of\ circulating\ assets}$$

(8) Current Rate

Current rate indicates how much (yuan) an enterprise has in its current assets to back up every 100 yuan of current liability. The formula is as follows:

$$Current\ rate=\frac{Total\ current\ asstes}{Total\ current\ liabilities}$$

(9) Quick Ratio

Quick ratio reflects the capability of an enterprise's circulating assets in immediately repaying the current liabilities. The equation ia as follows:

$$Quick\ ratio=\frac{Quick\ assets}{Current\ liabilities}$$

(10) Asset-Debt ratio

Asset-Debt ratio can not only revel what proprtion of an enterprise's total assets is obtained through loans, but also indicate the enterpeise's capability in utilizing the fund provided by creditors for operation and to what extent it can protect the interest of creditors at the time of liquidation. Calculation of the equity-debt ratio is shown below:

$$Asset\text{-}debt\ ratio=\frac{Total\ debt}{Total\ assets}$$

(11) Debt-Asset Ratio

Debt-Asset Ratio reflects an enterprise's long-term capability in repaying debt. The formula is as follows:

$$Debt\text{-}Asset\ Ratio=\frac{Total\ debt}{Total\ owner's\ equity}$$

62. 货(客)运量 Freight (Passenger) Traffic

货(客)运量 指在一定时期内,各运输部门实际运送的货物(旅客)数量。是反映运输业为国民经济和人民生活服务的数量指标,也是制定和检查运输生产计划,研究运输发展规模和速度的重要指标。货运按吨计算,客运按人计算。货物不论运输距离长短、货物类别,均按实际重量统计;旅客不论行程远近或票价多少,均按一人一次作为客运量统计。半价票、小孩票也按一人统计。

Freight (Passenger) Traffic refers to the physical volume of freight (passenger) transported. Freight transport is calculated by ton and passenger traffic by number of persons. Despite the type of freight and travelling distance, the freight transport is calculated by the actual weight; and despite the travelling distance and ticket price, the passenger traffic is calculated by one person per travel. The half-price and child tickets are also calculated on one-person ticket basis. The freight (passenger) traffic provides a quantitative measure to reflect how the transport industry serves the national economy and people, and an important indicator for planning the transport industry and for studying the development scale and speed of the industry.

63. 货物(旅客)周转量 Freight (Passenger) Traffic Volume

货物(旅客)周转量 指在一定时期内,由各种运输工具运送的货物(旅客)数量与其相应运输距离的乘积之和,是反映运输业生产总成果的重要指标,也是编制和检查运输生产计划、计算运输效益、劳动生产率以及核算运输单位成本的主要基础资料。通常以吨公里和人公里为计算单位。计算货物周转量通常按发出站与到达站之间的最短距离,也就是计费距离计算。

Freight (Passenger) Traffic Volume refers to the total of the product of the physical volume of transported cargo (passengers) by the transport distance, usually using ton/kilometre and person/kilometre as calculating units. Normally, the shortest distance between the departure point and the destination is the basis to calculate the freight traffic volume, that is to say, the payable distance. This is an important indicator to show the total results of the transport industry, to prepare and examine the transport plan and to measure the efficiency, the labour productivity and the unit cost of transport.

64. 邮电业务总量 Service Revenue of Posts and Telecommunications

邮电业务总量 指以货币表现的邮电部门用于传递信息和提供其他邮电服务的总数量。它综合反映了一定时期邮电工作的总成果,是研究邮电业务量构成和发展趋势的重要指标。根据邮电管理体制不同,分为中央国营业务总量和地方国营业务总量。它用各种邮电分类业务量,如函件件数、电报份数、长话张数、市内电话和农村电话的年均户数、订销报刊累计份数等,分别乘以相应的平均单价(不变价),加总后再加上出租电路和设备的收入、代用户维护电话交换机和线路等设备的收入、其他业务收入求得。

Service Revenue of Posts and Telecommunications refers to the total amount of the information delivered and other post and telecommunications services provided the post and telecommunications departments for the customers. It is arriived by first multiplying the business volume of different type, such as number of letters, telegrams, long distance calls, city and rural telephone subseribers and accumulted number of newspapers and journals subscribed and sold, etc. by their respective average unit price (fixed price) and then adding these products together: plus the income from maintenance of telephone switchboards and lines, and the income from other business operations. The service revenue of posts and telecommunications reflects the total achievement by the post and telecommunications department during a given perios of time in a comprehensive way, and is an important indicator to study the composition and development of the post and telecommunications business.

65. 社会消费品零售总额 Value of Retail Sales of Consumer Goods

社会消费品零售总额 指各种经济类型的批发零售贸易业、餐饮业、制造业和其他行业对城乡居民和社会集团的消费品零售额。这个指标反映通过各种商品流通渠道向居民和社会集团供应的生活消费品来满足他们生活需要,是研究人民生活、社会消费品购买力、货币流通等问题的重要指标。社会消费品零售额包括:(1)售给城乡居民作为生活用的商品和住房及修建房屋用的建筑材料;(2)售给机关、团体、学校、部队、企业、事业单位的职工食堂和旅店(招待所)附设专门供本店旅客食用,不对外营业的食堂的各种食品、燃料;企业、单位和国营农场直接售给本单位职工和职工食堂的自己生产的产品;(3)售给部队干部、战士生活用的粮食、副食品、衣着品、日用品、燃料;(4)售给来华的外国人、华侨、港澳台同胞的消费品;(5)居民自费购买的中、西药品、中药材及医疗用品;(6)报社、出版社直接售给居民和社会集团的报纸、图书、杂志、集邮公司出售的新、旧纪念邮票、特种邮票、首日封、集邮册、集邮工具等;(7)旧货寄售商店自购、自销部分的商品零售额;(8)煤气公司、液化石油气站售给居民和社会集团的煤气灶具和罐装液化石油气;(9)城市建设、房产管理部门、企业、事业单位售给居民的商品房;(10)农民售给非农业居民和社会集团的商品。不包括售给国民经济各部门企业、事业单位(包括国有经济的农场)生产经营用的各种原材料、燃料、设备、工具等和售给批发零售贸易业、餐饮业作为转卖用的商品、旧货寄售商店受托寄售卖出的商品、服务业的营业收入、邮局出售邮票的收入、自来水、电力、煤气生产(供应)单位的产品供应收入,也不包括农民之间的商品销售。

Value of Retail Sales of Consumer Goods refers to the sum of retail sales of consumer goods by wholesale retail, catering, manufacturing establishments and establishments in other industries of different type of ownership, to urban and rural households and institutions, as well as retail sales by farmers to non-agricultural households. Illustrating the supply of consumers goods through various channels to households and institutions to meet their demands, this is an important indicator for the study of issues on people's livelihood, on the purchasing power of consumer goods and on the circulation of money. The retail sales of consumer goods include: (1) commodities and housing (including building materials for the construction or repair of housing) sold to urban and rural households; (2) food and fuels sold to canteens of institutions, enterprises, schools, military units and to canteens of hotels and hostels that only serve their guests, and commodities producced by enterprises, institutions or state farms and sold directly to their employees or their canteens; (3) grain and non-staple food, clothing, daily articles and fuels sold to military pernnel; (4) consumer goods sold to foreigners, overseas Chinese, and Chinese compatricts in Taiwan, Hong Kong and Macao during their stay in the mainland of China; (5) Chinese and western medicines, herbs and medical facilities purchased by household; (6) newspapers, books magazines directly sold to households and institutions by publishers, new and old commemorative stamps, special stamps, first-day covers, stamp albums and other stamp-collection articles sold by stamp companies; (7) consumer goods purchased and then sold by second-hand shops; (8) stoves and other heating facilities and liquifies gas sold by gascompanies to households and institutions; (9) commodity housing buildings sold to households by ruban construction and real eatates management agencies, enterprises and institutions: (10) commodities sold by farmers to non-agricultural households and institutions. Excluded under this heading are: raw materials, fuels, equipment, tools sold to enterprises, institutions and state farms for production purpose: commodities sold to trade establishments for re-sellings, commissioned sales at secondhand shops; operational income of urban public utilities; stamps sold at post offices, income of water, power, gas production and supply establishments from the supply of their products; and sales of commodities among farmers.

66. 商品购进总额 Total Purchase of Commodities

商品购进总额 指从本企业(单位)以外的单位和个人购进(包括从国外直接进口)作为转卖或加工后转卖的商品。这个指标反映批发零售贸易业从国内、国外市场上购进商品的总量。商品购进总额包括:(1)从工农业生产者购进的商品;(2)从出版社、报社的出版发行部门购进的图书、杂志和报纸;(3)从各种经济类型的批发零售贸易企业(单位)购进的商品;(4)从其他单位购进的商品,如机关、团体、单位购进的剩余物资,从餐饮业、服务业购进的商品,从海关、市场管理部门购进的缉私和没收的商品,从居民收购的废旧商品等;(5)从国(境)外直接进口的商品。不包括企业(单位)为自身经营用,和未通过买卖行为而收入的商品以及销售退回、商品升溢等。

Total Purchase of Commdities refers to purchase of commodities from other establishments or individuals (including direct import from abroad) for the purpose of re-selling, either with or without further processing of the commodities purchased. reflecting the total value of purchases of commodities by wholesale and retail establishments from domestic and overseas markets, they include: (1) agricultural and industrial products purchased from products; (2) books, magazines and newspapers purchased from distribution departments of the publishers; (3) commodities purchased from wholesale and retail establishments; (4) commodities purchased from other units, such as surplus materials purchased from government agencies, enterprises or institutions, commodities purchased from catering and service establishments, confiscated goods purchased from customs authorities or market management agencies, second hand goods and waters purchased from households; (5) commodities directly imported from abroad. Excluded are coomodities purchased for own operation, commodities obtained without buying or selling procedures, rejected commodities, etc.

67. 商品销售总额 Total Sales of Commodities

商品销售总额 指对本企业(单位)以外的单位和个人出售(包括对国(境)外直接出口)的商品。这个指标反映批发零售贸易业在国内市场上销售商品以及出口商品的总量。商品销售总额包括:(1)售给城乡居民和社会集团消费用的商品;(2)售给工业、农业、建筑业、运输邮电业、批发零售贸易业、餐饮业、服务业等作为生产、经营使用的商品;(3)售给批发零售贸易业作为转卖或加工后转卖的商品;(4)对国(境)外直接出口的商品。不包括:出售本企业(单位)自用的废旧包装用品,未通过买卖行为付出的商品,经本单位介绍,由买卖双方直接结算,本单位只收取手续费的业务,购货退出的商品以及商品损耗和损失等。

Total Sales of Commodities refers to selling of commodities to other establishments and individuals (including direct export). Reflecting the total value of sales of commodities at domestic markets and export, this indicator includes: (1) commodities sold to urban and rural horsehholds and institutions for their consumption; (2) commodities sold to establishments in industry, agriculture, construction, transportation, post and telecommunications, wholesale and retail trade, catering and service trade and public utility for their production and operation; (3) commodities sold to wholesale and retail establishments for re-selling, with or without further processing; and (4) commodities for direct export to other countries. Excluded are selling of waste packaging materials for own use, commodities transferred without buying or selling procedures, commission income from brokerage in transactions whose settlement is directly handled by buyers and sellers, rejected commodities in the purchase, loss in commodities, etc.

68. 能源消费总量 Ttotal Domestic Energy Consumption

能源消费总量 指一定时期内全国(地区)物质生产部门、非物质生产部门和生活消费的各种能源的总和,是观察能源消费水平、构成和增长速度的总量指标,能源消费总量包括原煤和原油及其制品、天然气、电力。不包括低热值燃料、生物质能和太阳能等的利用。能源消费总量分为三部分,即终端能源消费量、能源加工转换损失量和损失量。

(1)终端能源消费量 指一定时期内全国(地区)物质生产部门、非物质生产部门和生活消费的各种能源在扣除了用于加工转换二次能源消费量和损失量以后的数量。

(2)能源加工转换损失量 指一定时期内全国(地区)投入加工转换的各种能源数量之和与产出各种能源产品之和的差额。它是观察能源在加工转换过程中损失量变化的指标。

(3)能源损失量 指一定时期内能源在输送、分配、储存过程中发生的损失和由客观原因造成的各种损失量。不包括各种气体能源放空、放散量。

Total Domestic Energy Consumption refers to the total energy consumption of various forms by material production departments, non-material production departments and households in the country (region)in a given period of time. It is a comprehensive indicator to observe the scale, composition and development of energy consumption. The total energy consumption includes raw coal, crude petroleum and their products, natural gas and electricity, but excludes fuel of low calorific value, bioenergy and solar energy. Total domestic energy consumption can be divided into three parts:

(1) Final Energy Consumption refers to the total energy consumption by material production department, non-material production departments and households in the country (region) in a given period of time, but excluded the secondary energy consumption and loss for the process of energy conversion.

(2) Loss During the Process of Energy Conversion refers to the total input of various forms for conversion, minus the total output of energy of various forms in the country in a given period of time. It is an indicator to observe the loss that occurs during the process of energy conversion.

(3) Loss refers to the total loss of energy due to mistakes or any objective reasons during the course of energy tranport, distribution and storage in a given period of time. The loss of various kinds of gas due to gas discharges and stocktaking is excluded.

69. 专业技术人员 Professional and Technical Personnel

专业技术人员 指事业、企业单位中已经聘任专业技术职务从事专业技术工作方面专业技术管理工作的人员,以及未聘任专业技术职务、现在专业技术岗位上工作的国家干部。

Professional and Technical Personnel refers to professional, technical and managerial staff members in institutions or enterprise who not only have professional and technical titles but also hold professional and technical posts. They also include state cadres who work on professional and technical posts but do not have professional and technical titles.

70. 发明、实用新型和外观设计 Invention, Utility Models and Exterior Designs

发明 专利法及其实施细则所称的发明是指对有关产品、方法或其改进所提出的新的技术方案。

实用新型 专利法及其实施细则所称的实用新型是指对产品的形状、构造或者其结合所提出的适于实用的新的技术方案。

外观设计 专利法及其实施细则所称的外观设计是指对产品的形状、图案、色彩或者其结合所作出的富有美感并适于工业上应用的新设计。

Inventions as specified by the patent law and its detailed rules and regulations for implementation refers to the new technical proposals to the products or methods or their modifications.

Utility Models as specified by the patent law and its detailed rules and regulations for implementation refers to the precticai and new technical proposals on the shape and structure of the product or the combination of both.

Exterior Designs as specified by the patent law and its detailed rules and regulation for implementation refers to the aesthetics and industry-applicable new designs for the shape, design and color of the product, or their combinations.

71. 独立研究与开发机构 Independent Research and Development Institutions

独立研究开发机构 指有明确的任务和研究方向，有一定学术水平的业务骨干和一定数量的研究人员，具有研究、开发、开展学术工作的基本条件，主要进行科学研究与技术开发活动，并且在行政上有独立的组织形式，财务上独立核算盈亏，有权与其他单位签订合同，在银行有单独户头的单位。包括国务院各部门、中国科学院、中国社会科学院和各省、自治区、直辖市以及在(市)以上〔含地(市)〕各部门所属的国有独立的科学研究与技术开发机构。

Independent Research and Development Institutions refers to the state-owned institutions which have direct mission and research purpopse, a certain research level and quantities of personnel, favorable conditions for R & D and engaging in scientific research and technological development. The institutions also have their own independent organization and finance, authority to sign contract with other units, with their own accounts in banks. Independent research and development institutions include the institutions attached to central government agencies and the institutions attached to local governments.

72. 普通高等学校 General Institution of Higher Learning

普通高等学校 指按照国家规定的设置标准和审批程序批准举办，通过国家统一招生考试，招收高中毕业生为主要培养对象，实施高等教育的全日制大学、独立设置的学院和高等专科学校、短期职业大学。

General Institutions of higher Learning refers to educational establishments set up according to government evaluation and approval procedures, enrolling graduates from high schools and providing higher education courses and training for senior professionals. They include full-time universities, colleges, high professional schools and short-term professional universities.

73. 成人高等学校 Institutions of Higher Learning for Adults

成人高等学校 指按照国家有关规定审批，招收通过全国成人高教统一招生考试的具有高中毕业或同等学历的在职从业人员利用脱产、半脱产、业余或函授等多种形式对其实施高等学历教育，培养高等教育专科或本科毕业水平的专门人才，修业年限、课程设置和总学时数均按高等学历教育要求付诸实施的学校。包括广播电视大学、职工高等学校、农民高等学校、管理干部学院、教育学院、独立设置的函授学院等。

Institutions of Higher Learning for Adults refers to educational establishments, set up in line with relevant rules approved by government, enrolling workers or staff with high school or equivalent education, and providing higher education courses in many forms of full-time, part-time, spare-time, or correspondence for adults. Professionals thus trained recieve a qualification equivalent to graduates studying regular courses at general colleges, universities and professional colleges. Institutions of higher learning for adult include Radio and TV universities, schols of high education for staff and workers and peasants, colleges for management cadres, pedagogical colleged, independent correnpondence colleges.

74. 文化事业机构 Cultural Instituions

文化事业机构 指从事专业文化工作和为专业文化工作服务的独立建制的单独核算的单位。不包括这些单位另外举办独立核算的其他机构和各部门的业余文化组织。

Cultural Institutions refers to units who have their own establishment and independent finance and specialize in or serve cultural development. Cultural Institutions exclude other establishments run by units under the cultural authorities and amateur cultural groups established by other departments.

75. 电影放映单位 Film Projection Units

电影放映单位 指具有放映机器设备、固定或不固定的放映场所与专职或兼职的放映技术人员，经有关部门登记批准，经常为一定的观众对象放映电影的机构。包括经批准对外开放进行营业，并与电影发行放映管理机构分帐的专用放映单位和军委系统租片单位。

Film Projection Units refers to units with film projection equipment, full or part-time projectionists, permanent or non-permanent places, approved by related administrative departments to show films regularly for certain groups of audience, including those film projection units which have been approved to give commercial shows and registered with film circulation and projection administrations as well as those film-rentign units of the military sytem.

76. 等级运动员人数 Number of Athletes in Proper Grades

等级运动员人数 指经考核正式批准授予等级运动员称号的人数。运动员等级分为国家级运动健将、运动健将、一级运动员、二级运动员、三级运动员、少年级运动员。

Number of Athletes in Proper Grades refers to the number of athletes who have been given titles through examination. The titles of graded athletes include international masters of sports, masters of sports, first-class, second-class and third-class athlethes and young athletes.

77. 等级裁判员人数 Number of Referees in Proper Grades

等级裁判员人数 指经考核正式批准授予等级裁判员称号的人数。裁判员等级分为国际裁判、国家级裁判、一级裁判、二级裁判、三级裁判。

Number of Referees in Proper Grades refers to the number of referees who have been given titles after examination. They are classified as international referees, national referees and referees of the first, second and third classes.

78. 卫生技术人员 Medical Technical Workers

卫生技术人员 指卫生事业机构支付工资的全部固定职工和合同制职工中现任职务为卫生技术工作的专业人员。包括中医师、西医师、中西医结合高级医师、护师、中药师、西药师、检验师、其他技师、中医士、西医士、护士、助产士、中药剂士、西药剂士、检验士、其他技士、其他中医、护理员、中药剂员、西药剂员、检验员，其他初级卫生技术人员。

Medical Technical Workers refers to all permanent medical workers employed by medical institutions, including doctors of Chinese and Western medicine, senior doctors of integrated Chinese Western medicine, head nurses, pharmacists of Chinese and Western medicine, laboratory specialist, other specialists, junior doctors of Chinese and Wstern medicine, nurses, midwives, druggists in Chinese and Western medicine, laboratory technicians, other technicians, other practitioners of Chinese medicine, nursing attendants, pharmacological workers of Chinese and Western medicine, laboatory workers, and other primary medical personnel.

79. 社会福利事业单位 Social Welfare Institutions

社会福利事业单位 指集中收养社会孤老、残、幼的机构。包括由民政部门管理的社会福利院、儿童福利院、精神病人福利院和城镇集体办的福利院，以及农村集体举办的敬老院。

Social Welfare Institutions refers to institutions taking care of old people without children, handicapped people and orphans. They include social welfare institutions run by civil affairs departments, children's welfare institutions, social welfare institutions for mental patients, and collectivelly-run old people's homes in rural areas.

·中国统计出版社最新统计资料书简目·